EMPIRES OF THE WORD

EMPIRES
OF THE
WORD

A Language History of the World

NICHOLAS OSTLER

HarperCollins*Publishers*

HarperCollins*Publishers*
77–85 Fulham Palace Road
Hammersmith, London, W6 8JB

www.harpercollins.co.uk

Published by HarperCollins*Publishers* 2005

2

A catalogue record for this book
is available from the British Library

ISBN 0-00-711870-8

Set in Times by Peter T. Daniels

Printed and bound in Great Britain by Clays Ltd, St Ives plc

To Jane
SINE QVA NON

CONTENTS

CONTENTS

CONTENTS

CONTENTS

CONTENTS

ACKNOWLEDGEMENTS

The first seed for this book came from John Coates of BRLSI, Bath's cultural society; he invited me to give a lecture on language, as part of a millennium series on 'Histories of the Future'. Only when I sat down to consider the histories of a few major languages, did I realise what a vast and important theme this opened up, yet one that was largely omitted from general knowledge.

Lola Bubbosh guided my first steps into the world of literary agents. There I was fortunate to find Natasha Fairweather, who could see how best to present my theme to publishers. Besides that, she pointed out other works which have enriched my own understanding of it. It is thanks to her, and my perceptive and conducive editors, Richard Johnson, Andrew Proctor and Terry Karten, that my first foray into publishing has been so straightforward. Colleagues of theirs have also amazed me in different ways—at A. P. Watt Linda Shaughnessy selling translation rights across the world before I had even written a word; and at HarperCollins Kate Hyde coping with unprecedented material coming from all sides, and the UK and US cover-designers Dominic Forbes and Roberto de Vicq. Others closer to home gave stern but helpful criticism on early drafts, my daughter Sophia, my father-in-law David Thesen, above all my wife, and prime literary consultant, Jane Dunn. The faults that they found were not—as they charitably thought—the result of my being too deep, but just of my being too opaque. At any rate, their efforts have made it much easier for others to see what I have been getting at all along.

As for intellectual debts while writing, I have been aided by scholars all over the world, who have given of their time and generously clarified details of languages in which they were far more learned than I: Ghil'ad Zuckermann, Geoffrey Khan (Akkadian and Aramaic); Rashad Ahmad Azami (Arabic); Hassan Ouzzate, Salem Mezhoud (Berber); Abdou Elimam (Punic); Christopher Child (Swahili); E. Bruce Brooks (Chinese); Harekrishna Satpathy, Radha Madhav Dash, Sanghamitra Mohanty, Prativa Manjari Ralt (Sanskrit), Ether Soselia (Georgian), María Stella González de Perez (Spanish and Portuguese), Frances Karttunen (Nahuatl), Aurolyn Luykx (Quechua), Emma Volodarskaya (Russian) and David Crystal (English). Andy Pawley and Darrell Tryon have sharpened my knowledge of languages in the

Pacific, and Otto Zwartjes, Even Hovdhaugen and Françoise Douay of language studies in Europe and the Middle East. Above all, Peter T. Daniels, after benefiting me with his profound expertise in Aramaic and Middle-Eastern languages, has gone on to improve the whole text in a variety of ways both as attentive reader and punctilious typesetter, even unto cuneiform. But needless to say, I am still responsible for mistakes that remain.

The intellectual journey to complete this book has incurred other debts. Most recently, my debts are to Tony McEnery, who conjured up my trips to India in 2001; and to Jane Simpson and David Nash, who—after twenty-five years of shared insights about languages and theories—made it possible for me in 2002 to visit Australia. That dawn-land of today's linguistics has access to the great feed-stocks of language data, and there I could present this material to audiences of the learned and enthusiastic in Perth, Sydney and Armidale. Among them I have John Henderson and Nick Reid to thank too, for invitations and memorable hospitality.

More distantly, but no less importantly, the background knowledge harvested here has come to me from a long and varied line of language teachers: I think particularly of Maurice Bickmore, Bella Thompson, Ken Batterby, James Howarth, Geoffrey Allibone, Jack Ind, Robert Ogilvie, Jasper Griffin, Peter Parsons, Oliver Gurney, Anna Morpurgo Davies, Wayne O'Neil, Paul Kiparsky, Ken Hale, Daniel Ingalls, Rama Nath Sharma, Susumu Kuno, Bart Matthias, Edwin Cranston, Rosalind Howard, Martin Prechtel, Damian McManus, Kim McCone and Stiofáin Ó Direáin.

These guides are like prophets. In our country language teaching is often misrepresented as misguided drudgery; and really to learn another language can often seem a nigh impossible task. There is no royal road to it, but gold glints in unexpected places all along the path. For me it has always been the surest route to new worlds that lie beyond my imagination. SIC ITVR AD ASTRA.

LIST OF MAPS, TABLES AND FIGURES

Maps

Tables

Figures

PREFACE

قوّة الإنسان فى عقله ولسانه.

qūwatu l-ʾinsāni fī ʿaqlihi wa lisānihi.

The strength of a person is in his intelligence and his tongue.

(Arabic proverb)

If language is what makes us human, it is languages that make us superhuman.

Human thought is unthinkable without the faculty of language, but language pure and undifferentiated is a fantasy of philosophers. Real language is always found in some local variant: English, Navajo, Chinese, Swahili, Burushaski or one of several thousand others. And every one of these links its speakers into a tradition that has survived for thousands of years. Once learnt in a human community, it will provide access to a vast array of knowledge and belief: assets that empower us, when we think, when we listen, when we speak, read or write, to stand on the shoulders of so much ancestral thought and feeling. Our language places us in a cultural continuum, linking us to the past, and showing our meanings also to future fellow-speakers.

This book is fundamental. It is about the history of those traditions, the languages. Far more than princes, states or economies, it is language-communities who are the real players in world history, persisting through the ages, clearly and consciously perceived by their speakers as symbols of identity, but nonetheless gradually changing, and perhaps splitting or even merging as the communities react to new realities. This interplay of languages is an aspect of history that has too long been neglected.

As well as being the banners and ensigns of human groups, languages guard our memories too. Even when they are unwritten, languages are the most powerful tools we have to conserve our past knowledge, transmitting it, ever and anon, to the next generation. Any human language binds together a human community, by giving it a network of communication; but it also dramatizes it, providing the means to tell, and to remember, its stories.

It is not possible, even in a book as big as this one, to tell all those stories.

Empires of the Word concentrates on the languages that, for one reason or another, grew out from their homes, and spread across the world. But even with such a stringent entry qualification, cutting the number of stories from many thousand to a couple of dozen, the remaining diversity is still overwhelming. In a way, there are so many tales to tell that the work is less a telling of a single story than a linguistic *Thousand and One Nights*.

We shall range over the amazing innovations, in education, culture and diplomacy, thought up by speakers of Sumerian and its successors in the Middle East, right up to the Arabic of the present day; the uncanny resilience of Chinese through twenty centuries of invasions; the charmed progress of Sanskrit from north India to Java and Japan; the engaging self-regard of Greek; the struggles that gave birth to the languages of modern Europe; and much later, the improbable details of how they were projected across the world.

Besides these epic achievements, language failures are no less interesting. The Western Roman Empire was thoroughly overrun by German-speakers in the fifth century. These conquests laid the basis for the countries of modern western Europe: so why did German get left behind? In Africa, Egyptian had been surviving foreign takeovers for over three millennia: why did it shrivel and disappear after the influx of Muḥammad's Arabic? And in the modern era, the Netherlands had ruled the East Indies for the same period that Britain ruled India: so why is Dutch unknown in modern Indonesia? Until such questions are answered, the global spread of English can never be understood.

On a cultural level, there is fascination too in the world-views that went with the advancing and receding languages. Ironies abound: Latin could make no headway with the sophisticates of the eastern Mediterranean, who spoke Greek and Aramaic, but it was quickly embraced by the illiterate peoples of Gaul and Spain. In the Americas, Catholic missionaries slowed for centuries the spread of Spanish, but in Asia, Evangelical Protestants turned out to be crucial to the take-up of English. We may as well admit at the outset that the mysteries of linguistic attraction and linguistic influence run deep: to tell the story is not always to understand it.

Nevertheless, I believe that the universal study of language history, of which this is a first attempt, is at least as enlightening and valid a focus for science as the more usual concerns of historical linguistics. It is as significant to compare the linguistic effects of the Roman and the Germanic conquests of Gaul as it is to compare the structures of the Latin and Germanic verb-systems—indeed just possibly one might throw some light on the other. Languages by their nature define communities, and so offer clearer units than most in social studies on which to base comparative analyses. Not enough attention has been paid to the growth, development and collapse of language communities through time, and the light these may shed on the kinds of society that spoke these languages. It is a received truth, for example, that in the Roman Empire the west was administered in Latin, the east in Greek, and the Greek administration lasted for many centuries more than the Latin: how surprising, but how revealing then, that when the time came for the defences to collapse and the Empire's provinces to be overrun, Latin survived—and has never been replaced—but Greek largely evaporated within a couple of generations.

The language history of the world can be eloquent of the real character of peoples, their past movements and changes. It also offers some broad hints for the future. Asked in 1898 to choose a single defining event in recent history, the German chancellor Bismarck replied, 'North America speaks English'. He was right, as the twentieth century showed. Twice the major powers of North America stepped in to determine the outcome of struggles that started in Europe, each time on the side of the English-speaking forces. Even more, the twentieth century's technological revolutions in communications, telephones, films, car ownership, television, computing and the Internet, were led overwhelmingly from English-speaking America, projecting its language across the world, to parts untouched even by the British Empire. It seems almost as if a world language revolution is following on, borne by the new media.

But though the spread of a language is seldom reversible, it is never secure. Even a language as broadly based as English is in the twenty-first century cannot be immune. It is still threatened by those old causes of language succession: changes in population growth, patterns of trade and cultural prestige. For all the recent technical mastery of English, nothing guarantees long-term pre-eminence in publishing, broadcasting or the World Wide Web. Technology, like the jungle, is neutral.

Language history does not, in itself, explain the past, or predict the future. There are thousands of language traditions, and their relative sizes are changing dynamically. Important innovations can arise in any one of them; in modern conditions especially, innovations may spread fast. Languages such as Egyptian and Akkadian, Sanskrit and Persian, Greek and Latin, in their day all seemed irresistible in their dominance and their prestige. But as they found to their cost, speaker populations can be unsentimental.

The language future, like the language past, is set to be full of surprises. But to find out what has happened in history overall, the true winners and losers among human groups, we cannot ignore the outcomes of the language struggle.

Little Solsbury Hill, 28 July 2004

PROLOGUE:
A CLASH OF LANGUAGES

On 8 November 1519 Hernán Cortés and a band of three hundred Spaniards met for the first time the supreme ruler of Mexico. The venue was the causeway across the lake leading to its capital city, Tenochtitlán. All around them was water. On the eastern horizon a volcano could be seen in eruption. Cortés was on horseback, bearded, in shining armour, belying his recent career as a small-town law officer and amateur gold prospector. Motecuhzoma,* born to sit on the royal mat of Mexico and already victorious in many wars, was carried on a litter, resplendent in a vast circular headdress with plumes of lustrous green quetzal, ornaments on his nose, ears and lower lip, behind him an escort of warriors wearing jaguar hides and eagle feathers.

After an exchange of gifts, the Spaniards were led into the city, and accommodated in a palace that had been the residence of Motecuhzoma's father. They were given a dinner of turkey, fruit and maize tamales. Then Motecuhzoma, whose official title was *tlatoani*, 'speaker', returned to greet his guests.

This was the first moment when the two leaders shared directly with each other their understanding of this epoch-making encounter: the ruler of the largest empire in the Americas, still at the height of his power, coming face to face with the self-appointed emissary of the king of Spain, who, though under guard in a well-kept and well-ordered city, larger than any to be seen in Europe, was yet strangely unawed. Their words set the tone for all that was to follow, above all the tragic diplomacy and incomprehension of the Aztecs, and the calculating, dissembling, but unremitting, aggression of the Spaniards. It was the first step towards the replacement of Nahuatl as the imperial language of Mexico, and the progress of Spanish towards its establishment as the language first of government and religion and then of everything else in the New World.[1]

Motecuhzoma opened with a flowery speech in Nahuatl, translated by the interpreters whom Cortés had brought with him: Malin-tzin, a Mexican noblewoman, rendered the Nahuatl into Yucatec Maya, and Fray Géronimo de

---

* Better known in the corrupted form *Montezuma*.

1

Aguilar, a Spanish priest, conveyed the sense of the Maya into Spanish. Cortés then replied in Spanish, and the process ran in reverse.

*Totēukyoe, ōtikmihiyōwiltih ōtikmoziyawiltih.**

Our Lord, how you must have suffered, how fatigued you must be.

This was a conventional greeting, although there would have been few whom the *tlatoani* of all Mexico would address as *tēukyoe*, 'Lordship'.

ō tlāltiteč tommahzītīko, ō īteč tommopāčiwiltīko in mātzin in motepētzin, Mešihko, ō īpan tommowetziko in mopetlatzin, in mokpaltzin, in ō ačitzinka nimitzonnopiyalīlih, in ōnimitzonnotlapiyalīlih ...

You have graciously come on earth, you have approached your water, your high place of Mexico, you have come down to your mat, your throne, which I have briefly kept for you, I who used to keep it for you.

This was already strange. Motecuhzoma was addressing Cortés as a steward to his sovereign. 'For they have gone, your governors, the kings, Itzcoatl, the old Motecuhzoma, Axayacatl, Tizoc, Ahuitzotl, who hitherto have come to be guardians of your domain, to govern the water, the high place of Mexico, they behind whom, following whom your subjects have advanced.'†

This was really bizarre. Motecuhzoma seemed to place Cortés as a long-lost, supreme king of this very land. 'Do they still haunt what they have left, what is behind them? If only one of them could see and admire what has happened to me today, what I now see in the absence of our lords, unbeknown to them. It is not just a fantasy, just a dream; I am not dreaming, not fantasising;

* In each chapter, a convenient form of romanised spelling has been adopted, to do justice to the pronunciation of fragments of an unfamiliar language, while not diverging too far from non-linguists' ideas of how the Roman alphabet is pronounced. In general, vowels are to be pronounced pure and simple, as in Spanish, consonants and clusters as in English, and any peculiarities are announced in the first footnote. Here, for Nahuatl, the traditional (Spanish-like) romanisation has not been followed: instead, č represents English ch, and š English sh; h is used for the glottal stop, like the unheard t in the English and Scots pronunciation of *Scotland*; z here is closer to English s than z. Long vowels are marked with a macron: ā, ē, etc.

† *Ka ōyahkeh motēčīuhkāhuān, in tlahtohkeh, in Itzkōhuātzin, in wēweh Motēukzoma, in Āšāyaka, in Tizōzik, in Āwitzōtl, in ō kuēl ačīk mitzommotlapiyalīlikoh, in ōkipačōkoh in ātl in tepetl in Mešihko, in īnkuitlapan, īntepotzko in ōwalyetiyā in momāzēwaltzin.*

for I have seen you, I have looked upon you.'* Now he was claiming to have had a vision of some kind. Cortés must already have been thinking that chance, or God, was delivering the Mexican leader into his power. 'For I have long (for five days, for ten days) been anxious to look far away to the mysterious place whence you are come, in the clouds, in the mists. So this is the fulfilment of what kings have said, that you would graciously return to your water, your high place, that you would return to sit upon your mat and your throne, that you would come.'† Too easy: Cortés was being recognised as a promised messiah, by none other than the leader of the country he hoped to conquer. 'And now that has come true, you have graciously arrived, you have known pain, you have known weariness, now come on earth, take your rest, enter into your palace, rest your limbs; may our lords come on earth.'§

Cortés was not slow to take advantage of this astounding appearance of fealty on the part of the Mexican ruler, but he did not simply accept the apparent submission to him personally, as perhaps he could have. What further behaviour, after all, might an Aztec expect of him, if he had claimed to be a returning god? And how would his own men react? Instead he reinforced Motecuhzoma's wonderment at the miraculous origin of his mission, and wove in a little flattery at how far the ruler's reputation must have travelled. But immediately Cortés appealed to his own duties to his own God and king as he saw them, imposing them heavily on his interlocutor. He even ended with a gesture at a sermon.

An eyewitness recounts:

Cortés replied through our interpreters [*lenguas*, 'tongues'], who were always with him, especially Doña Marina [Malin-tzin], and told him that he did not know with what to repay him, neither himself or any of us, for all the great favours received every day, and that certainly we came from where the sun rises, and we are vassals and servants of a

---

* *Kuix ok wāllamatih in īmonihka, in intepotzko? Mā zēmeh yehwāntin kitztiyānih, kimāwizzōtiānih in nehwātl in āxkān nopan ōmočīuh, in ye nikitta, in zā īmonihka īntepotzko totēukyōwān. Kamo zan nitēmiki, ahmo zan nikočitlēwa, ahmo zan nikkočitta, amo zan niktēmiki, ka yē ōnimitznottili, mīštzinko ōnitlačiš.*

† *Ka ōnnonēntlamattikaatka in ye mākuil, in ye mahtlāk, in ōmpa nonitztikah in kēnamihkān in ōtimokīštīko in mištitlan, in ayauhtitlan. Anka yehwātl in in ki tēnēuhtiwih in tlahtohkeh, in tik-momačitīkiuh in mātzin, in motepētzin, in īpan timowetzītīkiuh in mpetlazin, in mokpaltzin, in tiwāl-mowīkaz.*

§ *Auh in āškān ka ōneltik, ōtiwalmowīkak, ōtikmihiyōwilti, ōtikmoziyawiltih, mā tlāltiteč šimahšīti, mā šimozēwihtzino, mā šokommomačiti in motēkpankaltzin, mā xikmozēwili in monakayōtzin, mā tlāltiteč mahšītikan in totēukyōwān.*

great lord called the great emperor Don Carlos, who has subject to him many great princes, and that having news of Motecuhzoma and of what a great lord he is, he sent us here to see him and ask him that they should be Christians, as is our emperor and are we all, and that he and all his vassals would save their souls. He went on to say that presently he would declare to him more of how and in what manner it must be, and how we worship a single true God, and who he is, and many other good things he should hear, as he had told his ambassadors ...*

This exchange in Nahuatl and Spanish records a moment of destiny when the pattern was set for the irruption of one language community into another. It happens to be exceedingly well documented on both sides, but it is not unique. These pioneer moments of fatal impact have happened throughout human history: as when, on 11 July 1770, Captain James Cook of Great Britain's Royal Navy encountered Australian aboriginals speaking Guugu Yimidhirr in what is now the north of Queensland; or in the first century AD, when a South Indian named Kauṇḍinya came ashore at Bnam in Cambodia, and soon married its queen, called Soma (or *Liuye*, 'Willow-Leaf', in the Chinese report), so transplanting Sanskrit culture into South-East Asia.

This book traces the history of those languages which, in the part of human history that we now know, have spread most widely. Somehow, and for a variety of reasons, the communities that spoke them were able to persuade others to join them, and so they expanded. The motives for that persuasion can be very diverse—including military domination, hopes of prosperity, religious conversion, attendance at a boarding school, service in an army, and many others beside. But at root this persuasion is the only way that a language can spread, and it is no small thing, as anyone who has ever tried deliberately to learn another language knows.

---

* *Cortés le respondió con nuestras lenguas, que consigo siempre estaban, especial la doña Marina, y le dijo que no sabe con qué pagar él ni todos nosotros las grandes mercedes recibidas de cada día, y que ciertamente veníamos de donde sale el sol, y somos vasallos y criados de un gran señor que se dice el gran emperador don Carlos, que tiene sujetos a sí muchos y grandes príncipes, y que teniendo noticia de él y de cuán gran señor es, nos envió a estas partes a le ver a rogar que sean cristianos, como es nuestro emperador y todos nosotros, e que salvarán sus ánimas él y todos sus vasallos, e que adelante le declarará más cómo e de qué manera ha de ser, y como adoramos a un solo Dios verdadero, y quién es, y otras muchas cosas buenas que oirá, como les había dicho a sus embajadores Tendile e Pitalpitoque e Quintalvor cuando estábamos en los arenales.* (Díaz del Castillo, lxxxix)

4

PART I
THE NATURE OF
LANGUAGE HISTORY

…καὶ λέγειν ἐδίδου περὶ τῶν Ἑλληνικῶν ἃ βούλοιτο παρρησιαζόμενον. ὁ δὲ Θεμιστοκλῆς ἀπεκρίνατο, τὸν λόγον ἐοικέναι τοῦ ἀνθρώπου τοῖς ποικίλοις στρώμασιν· ὡς γὰρ ἐκεῖνα καὶ τοῦτον ἐκτεινονόμενον μὲν ἐπιδεικνύναι τὰ εἴδη, συστελλόμενον δὲ κρύπτειν καὶ διαφθείρειν· ὅθεν αὐτῷ χρόνου δεῖν. ἐπεὶ δ' ἠσθέντος τοῦ βασιλέως τῇ εἰκασίᾳ καὶ λαμβάνειν κελεύσαντος, ἐνιαυτὸν αἰτησάμενος καὶ τὴν Περσίδα γλῶτταν ἀποχρώντως ἐκμαθὼν ἐνετύγχανε βασιλεῖ δι' αὐτοῦ…

[King Xerxes] gave Themistocles leave to speak his mind freely on Greek affairs. Themistocles replied that the speech of man was like rich carpets, the patterns of which can only be shown by spreading them out; when the carpets are folded up, the patterns are obscured and lost; and therefore he asked for time. The king was pleased with the simile, and told him to take his time; and so he asked for a year. Then, having learnt the Persian language sufficiently, he spoke with the king on his own…

Plutarch, *Themistocles*, 29.5

1

Themistocles' Carpet

The language view of human history

From the language point of view, the present population of the world is not six billion, but something over six thousand.

There are between six and seven thousand communities in the world today identified by the first language that they speak. They are not of equal weight. They range in size from Mandarin Chinese with some 900 million speakers, alone accounting for one sixth of all the people in the world, followed by English and Spanish with approximately 300 million apiece, to a long tail of tiny communities: over half the languages in the world, for example, have fewer than five thousand speakers, and over a thousand languages have under a dozen. This is a parlous time for languages.

In considering human history, the language community is a very natural unit. Languages, by their nature as means of communication, divide humanity into groups: only through a common language can a group of people act in concert, and therefore have a common history. Moreover the language that a group shares is precisely the medium in which memories of their joint history can be shared. Languages make possible both the living of a common history, and also the telling of it.

And every language possesses another feature, which makes it the readiest medium for preserving a group's history. Every language is learnt by the young from the old, so that every living language is the embodiment of a tradition. That tradition is in principle immortal. Languages change, as they pass from the lips of one generation to the next, but there is nothing about this process of transmission which makes for decay or extinction. Like life itself, each new generation can receive the gift of its language afresh. And so it is that languages, unlike any of the people who speak them, need never grow infirm, or die.

Every language has a chance of immortality, but this is not to say that it will survive for ever. Genes too, and the species they encode, are immortal;

7

but extinctions are a commonplace of palaeontology. Likewise, the actual lifespans of language communities vary enormously. The annals of language history are full of languages that have died out, traditions that have come to an end, leaving no speakers at all.

The language point of view on history can be contrasted with the genetic approach to human history, which is currently revolutionising our view of our distant past. Like membership in a biological species and a matrilineal lineage, membership in a language community is based on a clear relation. An individual is a member of a species if it can have offspring with other members of the species, and of a matrilineal lineage if its mother is in that lineage. Likewise, at the most basic level, you are a member of a language community if you can use its language.

The advantage of this linguistically defined unit is that it necessarily defines a community that is important to us as human beings. The species unit is interesting, in defining our prehistoric relations with related groups such as *Homo erectus* and the Neanderthals, but after the rise of *Homo sapiens* its usefulness yields to the evident fact that, species-wise, we are all in this together. The lineage unit too has its points, clearly marked down the aeons as it is by mitochondrial DNA and Y-chromosomes, and can yield interesting evidence on the origin of populations if some lineage clearly present today in the population is missing in one of the candidate groups put forward as ancestors. So it has been inferred that Polynesians could not have come from South America, that most of the European population have parentage away from the Near Eastern sources of agriculture, and that the ancestry of most of the population of the English Midlands is from Friesland.[1] But knowing that many people's mothers, or fathers, are unaccounted for does not put a bound on a group as a whole in the way that language does.

Contrast a unit such as a race, whose boundaries are defined by nothing more than a chosen set of properties, whether as in the nineteenth and early twentieth centuries by superficial resemblances such as skin colour or cranial proportions, or more recently by blood and tissue groups and sequences of DNA. Likewise, there are insurmountable problems in defining its cultural analogue, the nation, which entail the further imponderables of a consciousness of shared history, and perhaps shared language too.[2] Given that so many of the properties get shuffled on to different individuals in different generations, it remains moot as to what to make of any set of characteristics for a race or a nation.* But use of a given language is an undeniable functioning

---

* The problem is not that the shared properties are always imaginary (as the Nazis' criteria for Jewishness may have been), or even objectively unimportant for survival (e.g. as the possession of genes

reality everywhere; above all, it is characteristic of every human group known, and persistent over generations. It provides a universal key for dividing human history into meaningful groups.

Admittedly, a language community is a more diffuse unit than a species or a lineage: a language changes much faster than a DNA sequence, and one cannot even be sure that it will always be transmitted from one generation to the next. Some children grow up speaking a language other than their parents'. As we shall soon see, language communities are not always easy to count, or to distinguish reliably. But they are undeniably real features of the human condition.

The task of this book is to chart some of the histories of the language traditions that have come to be most populous, ones that have spread themselves in the historic period over vast areas of the inhabited world. Our view will be restricted to language histories for which there is direct written evidence, and this means omitting some of the most ancient, such as the spread of Bantu across southern Africa, or of the Polynesian languages across the Pacific; but nevertheless the tale is almost always one that covers millennia. The history of humanity seen from its languages is a long view.

The state of nature

Languages have been the currency of human communities for hundreds of thousands of years, and naturally the typical language community has changed in that time. The presumption is that before the discovery and expansion of agriculture, human communities were small bands, just as the remaining groupings of hunter-gatherers are to this day. These groups all have languages, and ancient lore and stories which the old retail to the young. The density of the human population, wherever people were living, would have been far less than it is today. It is a commonplace of historical linguistics that related languages diverge when contact ceases between groups, so we can also presume that in this early period each self-sufficient

---

for sickle-cell anaemia and thalassaemia clearly predispose to inherited disease, while giving resistance to malaria). It stems from the logic of statistics: when picking out a population for study, a subset of properties always has to be chosen from a much larger set. But populations who share one subset may not share another—and who is to say (in advance of the study) which properties define the group with the interesting history? In practice, the properties chosen tend to bear out the preconceptions of the researchers, making (e.g.) the correspondence between genetic and traditional linguistic classification of the world's population groups less than astounding. This necessary arbitrariness in setting up the statistical models is a fundamental flaw in the credibility of the population-gradient prehistory associated with Luca Cavalli-Sforza (e.g. 2001) and his many followers.

community, of up to a few thousand people, would by and large have had its own language.

All this changed in communities that adopted a settled way of life, based on herding and agriculture. Now communities would have become both larger and more organised. In settled communities, one's neighbours in one year would remain one's neighbours for many years, indeed generations, to come. One might have dues to pay, and negotiate, with higher authorities. Festivals, and markets, would bring together people from a wide area. Militias would be raised to defend local communities, and to steal from others perceived to be weaker. There began to be a motive for communication among people over longer distances. Bilingualism would have increased in the population, and also languages would have grown in terms of the number of speakers; quite likely, too, the absolute number of languages would have fallen, smaller communities losing speakers through war, marriage or desertion, or simply a pragmatic tendency to use other people's languages.

From the very nature of the changing situation we could have inferred these processes. But in fact it has been possible to watch them. They have been observed in accelerated development in the last couple of generations in Papua New Guinea, as the old self-sufficient ways of life in villages and hamlets yield to a wider-ranging national way of life. A feature of this transition is the decline of many of the indigenous languages and their replacement through the expansion of neighbouring tongues, or more globally by languages associated with trade at the national level, or government: utility jargons or pidgins are quickly transformed into general-purpose creole languages, informally but effectively standardised across vast numbers of speakers.

Literacy and the beginning of language history

As long as there has been storytelling, and the dispensing of legal judgments and healing rituals, there have been linguistic records, retained verbally in the memories of learned members of the community. The minds of the old are a weighty resource, filled with songs and precedents, skills and maps, recipes and histories.

But there was always a subjective element in learning derived from recitation, as well as a practical limit on the amount that could be retained—unless perhaps complementary teams of record-keepers could be organised. Moreover, speaking now from the anachronistic point of view of the modern historian, there would always be a tendency to inauthenticity in ancient records held in memory. In use, there was always a pressure to update them little by little to meet the needs of the contemporary world: otherwise, as gradual changes accumulate in social institutions and in the language too, really ancient records would tend to become both irrelevant and incomprehensible. Even today, when oral traditions can be found intact, it is seldom possible to gain clear, unambiguous information about the past from the testimony of rememberers. Recall is an act of disciplined reimagination, and the remote past may be beyond anyone's ken.

All this is resolved through the miracle of writing. Writing traditions usually begin in some kind of process of accounting records—at least tallies and tokens are often the earliest clear predecessors of written documents to survive—the intent being to provide objective proof of the quantities involved in some transaction. But with practice it often became clear that the symbols were in principle capable of recording any message, and as facility in handling the symbols grew they became usable as a direct aide-mémoire even for fluent speech.

Once a culture has written documents, the first traces begin to be laid down which will later enable the history of the language to be written. If the writing system has a clear link to the language as spoken (and, despite the usual symbolic start in numbers and concepts, in practice it is impossible to develop a fully functional writing system without reference to words in spoken language), then the mute stones or clay tablets or preserved animal skins—whatever—begin to reveal to us something we might have thought quite evanescent—how the language was actually spoken, perhaps thousands of years ago.*

All the languages whose careers we shall consider have written histories that extend back over a thousand years, and sometimes two or three times this long. In almost every case, literacy is a skill that was learnt from visitors or neighbours, and then became part of a language's own tradition. As it happens, with the exception of Chinese, even the languages that originated writing, and so made the earliest use of it, have dropped their original system, and borrowed another.†

The past careers of languages are as diverse as the worlds that each language has created for its speakers. They have suffered very different fates: some (like Sanskrit or Aramaic) growing to have speaker populations distrib-

---

* A common problem, ironically, is that writers' conservatism has made their symbols refer to a version of the language already out of use. Memories of what was learnt in the scribal school can take precedence over what the scribe was actually hearing.

† Egyptian has dropped hieroglyphs, and (now known as Coptic) is written in an alphabet derived from Greek. Akkadian and Sumerian are no longer written at all; so cuneiform is a dead letter.

uted across vast tracts, but ultimately shrinking to insignificance; others (such as the languages of the Caucasus or Papua) twinkling steadily in inaccessible refuges; others still yielding up their speakers to quite different traditions (as in so many parts of North and South America, Africa and Australia). Some (such as Egyptian and Chinese) maintained their speakers and their traditions for thousands of years in a single territory, defying all invaders; others (such as Greek and Latin) spread by military invasion, but ultimately lost ground to new invaders.

Often enough, one tradition has piggybacked on another, ultimately supplanting it. One big language parasitises another, and in a *coup de main* takes over the channels built up over generations. This is a common trick as empires succeed one another, in every time and continent: Persia's Aramaic made good use of the networks established for Lydian in seventh-century Asia Minor; in the sixteenth century, Spanish usurped the languages of the Aztecs and Incas, using them to rule in Mexico and Peru; and in the early days of British India, English and Urdu gained access to power structures built in Persian. But the timescale on which these changing fortunes have been played out is astonishingly varied: a single decade may set the pattern for a thousand years to follow, as when Alexander took over the eastern Mediterranean from the Persians; or a particular trend may assert itself little by little, mile by mile, village by village, over thousands of years: just so did Chinese percolate in East Asia.

This means that, for all its bewildering variety, this history told through languages can give an insight into the long-term effects of sudden changes. This is true especially where what is changing is how nation shall speak unto nation, as it is today.

In fact, the complex effects on languages when cultures come into contact is the best record we have of real influence: contrast the more familiar analyses based on military conquest or commercial dominance, which may offer a quite spurious clarity. How thoroughgoing was the Germanic tribes' lightning conquest of the western Roman empire in the fifth century AD? Though it changed for good all the crowned heads, it left France, Spain and northern Italy still speaking variations of Latin, and they have gone on doing so to this day. What was really happening in Assyria in the seventh century BC? It was a period when the rulers' ascendancy was assured and new conquests were

---

Phoenician too is gone, although every alphabet in use from Ireland to Siam is derived from its original script. Mayan glyphs were discontinued at the time of the Spanish conquest, and now all these languages are written in Roman. Meanwhile Chinese continues to be written in the script first standardised by the man who ordered the burning of every book in the country. See Chapter 4, 'First Unity', p. 137.

being made: yet all the while its language was changing from Akkadian, the age-old language of its rulers, to Aramaic, the language of the nomads it was reputedly conquering.

The language history of the world shows more of the true impacts of past movements and changes of peoples, beyond the heraldic claims of their largely self-appointed leaders. They reveal a subtle interweave of cultural relations with power politics and economic expediency.

It also offers some broad hints for the future. It suggests rather strongly that no language spread is ultimately secure: even the largest languages in the twenty-first century will be subject either to the old determinants of language succession or some new ones that have arisen in the last five hundred years or the last fifty. Migrations, population growth, changing techniques of education and communication—all shift the balance of language identities across the world, while the focus of prestige and aspiration varies as the world's economies adjust to the rise of new centres of wealth. Future situations may well be unprecedented, with potential for languages to achieve truly global use, but they will still be human. And human beings seldom stay united for long.

An inward history too

But we can expect the language history of the world to be revealing in another way. A language community is not just a group marked out by its use of a particular language: it is an evolving communion in its own right, whose particular view of the world is informed by a common language tradition. A language brings with it a mass of perceptions, clichés, judgements and inspirations. In some sense, then, when one language replaces another, a people's view of the world must also be changing.

So as we survey the outward history of the large and influential language communities, in their expansions and retrenchments across the face of the earth, we shall also try to show some aspects of the inward sense of the communities who spoke the languages.

This is something that is very difficult to express, most difficult of all perhaps in the language itself. As Wittgenstein remarked, the limits of my language are the limits of my world; and these limits, he felt, could only be indicated indirectly, never stated explicitly. This book attempts in various indirect ways—and with copious use of translation—to show something of the temper of mind that was conditioned by a language, even as it gained or lost speakers.

It is a dangerous undertaking, but it is crucial if the succession of languages which have dominated human cultures is to have more meaning than the mere list of names and dates in a chronology. It is part of the contention of this book that there is an exchange of something far more subtle than an allegiance when one generation comes to speak a language other than its parents'.

We can get a first inkling of what that might be by comparing more for style than substance those speeches of Motecuhzoma and Cortés. Their languages, Nahuatl and Spanish, are quite distinct from one another, in ways that recall the traits of individual people. Most obviously, just as each person has a recognisable voice, each language has its own sound system or phonology. Consider the phrase 'your city of Mexico', in Nahuatl *in mātzin in motepētzin, Mešihko,* in Spanish *Su ciudad de México.* The phrase in Nahuatl uses a sound, tz (as in English *bits*), which is not used in Spanish, just as *ciudad* begins with a sound, θ (as in English *thin*), which is absent from Nahuatl. And even where Spanish was attempting to imitate Nahuatl directly, as in the name of *México* (pronounced MEH-shi-ko), it failed to capture the glottal stop, written with an h in *Mešihko,* which probably sounded more like a word that would be spelt in modern English as *Meshitko.*

But the rules of combination, to create longer words and sentences, are also radically different between the two languages. So the respect implicit in the Spanish use of *Su* for 'your' at the beginning is expressed in Nahuatl by adding *tzin* at the end of each of the words. In this same phrase, the Nahuatl word for 'city' is quite clearly a combination of *a-tl,* 'water', and *tepe-tl,* 'mountain', corresponding to nothing in Spanish, where the word *ciudad* has more connotations of civic status than geographical eminence. In general, Nahuatl words are mostly long sequences of short parts, often containing as much meaning as a whole sentence in Spanish: *ōtikmihiyōwiltih* is made up of *ō-ti-k-m-ihiyōwi-ltih* (past-you-it-yourself-suffer-cause), 'you have consented to suffer it', where the reflexive and causative bits (in fourth and final place) actually serve to show special respect, and to raise the formality of the utterance.

But phonology, vocabulary and grammar are just the beginning of what makes languages differ. Just as each person has a distinctive manner of speaking, quite apart from a recognisable voice, there is a characteristic style of expression which goes with each language. This difference may be minimised when languages are in close proximity, and very often translated one into another, as tends to be the case, say, among the languages of western Europe. But it is always there implicitly, and stands out very clearly in the encounter of Nahuatl with Spanish.

The most evident aspect of Nahuatl style is the constant doubling of near-synonyms: *ōtikmihiyōwiltih ōtikmoziyawiltih*, 'you have suffered, you are tired'; *in mopetlatzin, in mokpaltzin*, 'your mat, your throne'; *ahmo zan nikočitlēwa, ahmo zan nikkočitta, amo zan niktēmiki, ka yē ōnimitznottili, mīštzinko ōnitlačiš*, 'I am not dreaming, not fantasising; for I have seen you, I have looked upon you.' By contrast, the characteristic European style of reporting, where a whole speech is retailed curtly in the third person, as in the Spanish account of Cortés's words, is something quite alien to Nahuatl: not 'He said: "I do not know how to pay you..."' but 'He told him that he did not know how to pay him...', etc.

These are examples of the characteristic differences between languages in daily use. But then there is the area of language's past record, in the minds of its speakers as well as in writing.

Both Motecuhzoma and Cortés were in thrall to their verbal pasts. Cortés was soon engaged in giving an impromptu sermon, which would naturally have made little sense, since his audience lacked a knowledge of the Christian texts with which he had grown up in Catholic Spain. But the *tlatoani*'s speech, too, is a polished production, redolent of the *wewe-tlatolli*, 'the speech of the ancients', which was part of the curriculum at the *kalmékak*, the school for Mexican elite youth. This included, for example, a speech on duty, to be delivered to a recently appointed *tlatoani*: 'Our lord of greatest serenity and humanity, and our king of great generosity and valour, more precious than all precious stones, even than sapphire! Could it be a dream that we are seeing? Could we be drunk in seeing what our lord has done for us in giving us you for king and lord? And truly our lord God has set over us a new sun of great splendour and a light like the dawn's...'[3]

The same themes are here in this classic school text, of a new leader appearing as in a dream, and being like a light from the sky. But what was missing in Motecuhzoma's greetings to Cortés was anything like the speech that always preceded this one in the ceremonies of welcome to a new *tlatoani*, a speech in which he would be fully reminded of his duties, and the need not to let his new eminence go to his head. Would it have seemed strange to the Aztec audience that these friendly cautions were omitted in the greetings to Cortés?

A feature of Nahuatl style has always been the use of endearments as terms of honour: the *-tzin* we have seen used as an honorific is still used in modern Nahuatl as an affectionate suffix (*no-kokonē-tzin*, 'my dear child'), and it has been argued that this was in fact its original sense. Certainly, the polite use of Nahuatl involves some strange reversals from our point of view: a governor at a wedding feast may be spoken to as 'my dear child', while the retainers at a royal court would be addressed by their lord as 'our progenitors'. In Nahuatl etiquette, it seems that genuine respect was shown by adopting a rather daring familiarity, and perhaps the converse was also true. It has even been suggested[4] that the highly reverential tone and the absence of affectionate terms in Motecuhzoma's speech to Cortés actually show that he was demeaning the Spaniard, or at least trying to assert a distance between the two of them. If true, this was a singularly ill-judged approach. Cortés was himself a highly educated man—but he could hardly pick up on the courtly subtleties of such an alien rhetoric.

This brief analysis has already shown that the encounter between Spanish and Nahuatl in sixteenth-century Mexico pitted two developed cultures one against another. The switch to speaking Spanish that came about in the next few generations involved a change of heart as well as tongue. So much so that the social significance in Mexico of speaking Nahuatl (also called *Mexicano*) rather than Spanish has lasted up to the present day. Speakers make comments like these:

> There is no way that Nahuatl could disappear because it is the inheritance from our forefathers.

> Those of us who speak Mexicano, well, it's something that belongs to our grandparents. Let Mexicano never be lost. My grandfather and my grandmother always spoke in Nahuatl. They never used the Spanish language.

> It is important and at the same time nice to be able to speak Nahuatl because this is the authentic way of talking in Mexico. I consider it very important because we feel we are the authentic Mexicans, because Spanish was only brought here with the Conquest. From that time on people started to speak Spanish in our country. But before the Conquest our grandparents spoke Nahuatl. Obviously the Conquest brought a lot of changes. There was more civilization, and that's why I think it is important for us also to speak Spanish. But we haven't been able to stop speaking Nahuatl because our parents speak it and we follow them.[5]

Every language defines a community, the people who speak it and can understand one another. A language acts not just as a means of communication among them but a banner of their distinct identity, often to the despair of national governments trying to forge a single identity for all their different language communities. This can have quite perverse effects. It is no coincidence that Nahuatl, with many other ancestral languages of Mexico, largely disappeared from written use towards the end of the eighteenth century, just when political movements led by urban Spanish speakers were raising consciousness of Mexico as a separate country with a view to independence. The contrast between Spanish-speaking *mestizos* and 'Indians' speaking the ancient languages of Mexico was seen as a distraction from the emergence of the identity of the true Mexican. The older languages, seen as 'backward', had to go.

This book attempts to convey something of the characteristic viewpoint on the world of each language whose story it tells. Evidently, living in a particular language does not define a total philosophy of life: but some metaphors will come to mind more readily than others; and some states of mind, or attitudes to others, are easier to assume in one language than another. It cannot be a matter of indifference which language we speak, or which languages our ancestors spoke. Languages frame, analyse and colour our views of the world. 'I have three hearts,' claimed Ennius, an early master poet in Latin, on the strength of his fluency in Latin, Greek and Oscan.[6]

2

What It Takes to Be a World Language; or, You Never Can Tell

The historic forces of merger and acquisition which, over the last five hundred years, built up many of the European languages in the world's Top Twenty seemed to have spent themselves—or at least to be dammed up—by the end of the twentieth century.

Overt imperialism is no longer defended. The end is no longer openly willed, though the two surgical wars that led off the twenty-first century, to conquer Afghanistan and Iraq, show that the means are still accepted. Likewise, the flow of large-scale migration is for the time being halted. In the past two centuries, flows from European countries had created much of what are now the English-speaking and the Portuguese-speaking worlds, mostly in the Americas, but also in Africa, Australia and New Zealand. Then, in the second half of the twentieth century, there was a significant, but much smaller, flow from once colonised countries, which has created new language communities insulated in the heart of European lands.

The trends that will form the future are still obscure. At present, there is still a multitude of migration volunteers, found in a much wider range of countries, not just ex-colonies; the main brake on their movement and resettlement is the unwillingness of their desired host countries to take them in. While some pundits write of an impending 'clash of civilisations', pitting most immediately the Arabic- and English-speaking worlds against each other, the political fabric guaranteed by powerful nations seems firm.

But the world's language future is not a matter of current affairs, or even news analysis. Language spread is a long-term thing, measured at the very least in generations and more often in centuries and millennia. The fundamental question of this book is to ask how—in what circumstances and with what dynamics—language communities have come to flourish in the past, as well as how some of them have declined and even met their ends.

The most straightforward way in which a language can come to flourish could be called the Farmer's Approach. All the community needs to do is stay united, and grow its population. This is Organic Growth, which is the typical story of large languages in eastern and southern Asia, and not unknown even in Europe, especially towards the east.* It is not a strategy of active initiative, but it does raise a consequent question: how have languages that follow such a policy been able to defend themselves from foreign communities, which might be tempted to invade and disrupt their steady growth?

The disruption would come, by its nature, from language communities following a less placid path: they may be called the Merger and Acquisition languages (M&A), by analogy with the offensive players in the modern business world. If Organic Growth is the strategy of farmers, this alternative could rather be called the Hunter's Way.

Such change, resulting from direct contact between communities, is sometimes characterised as one of three types: Migration, where a language community moves bodily, bringing a new language with it; Diffusion, where speakers do not actually move in large numbers but where speakers of one community come to assimilate their language to that of another with whom they are in contact; and Infiltration, which is a mixture of the former two.[1] The progress of English into North America and Australia is a case of Migration; into India and Scandinavia, of Diffusion; and into South Africa, of Infiltration.† It is only, for example, through Diffusion or Infiltration that a language can become a lingua franca, a language of wider communication: for this, a language must have been taken up by people who did not speak it natively.

These M&A language communities are the ones whose role develops fast, often through deliberate actions. In practice, these will be the main languages whose careers we trace, because of course they are the most eventful.

Is there any common feature that makes a language community entice others to use its language, and so join it? A way of viewing this book's theme is as an inquiry into the roots of Language Prestige, defined as the propensity to attract new users. Under what conditions do languages have the power to grow in this way? And are there any properties of the relation between the new and the old language which make speakers willing and able to make the leap?

---

* As such it is prominent in forming the present-day Top Twenty language communities, to be considered close to the conclusion of this book (see p. 527).

† The widespread use of English in the European Union can be seen as Diffusion reinforced (after the UK's accession in 1973) by Infiltration.

There is a pernicious belief, widespread even among linguists, that there is a straightforward, heartless, answer to this question. J. R. Firth, a leading British linguist of the mid-twentieth century, makes a good simple statement of it:

> World powers make world languages...The Roman Empire made Latin, the British Empire English. Churches too, of course, are great powers...Men who have strong feelings directed towards the world and its affairs have done most. What the humble prophets of linguistic unity would have done without Hebrew, Arabic, Latin, Sanskrit and English, it is difficult to imagine. Statesmen, soldiers, sailors, and missionaries, men of action, men of strong feelings have made world languages. They are built on blood, money, sinews, and suffering in the pursuit of power.[2]

This is above all a resonant *cri de cœur* from 1937, the dying days of the British empire, muscular Christianity and male supremacism; and (in his defence) Firth seems mainly to have been concerned to contrast the effectiveness of lusty men of action with enervated scholars in building international languages.

Nevertheless it really does not stand up to criticism. As soon as the careers of languages are seriously studied—even the 'Hebrew, Arabic, Latin, Sanskrit and English' that Firth explicitly mentions as examples—it becomes clear that this self-indulgently tough-minded view is no guide at all to what really makes a language capable of spreading. It works neither as an account of where all world languages come from, nor what all world powers achieve.

The best case for it might be thought to come from the examples Firth cites, multinational military empires that lasted for centuries, such as the Roman and British efforts. But although Romance languages are still with us, their common name showing their common origin, they grew up in countries where Roman rule had been stably replaced by Germanic conquerors. The Franks, Burgundians, Vandals and Goths who set up the kingdoms of western Europe after the fall of the empire at most had an effect on the accent with which Latin was spoken and added a few words to its vocabulary; they nowhere succeeded in imposing their language on their new subjects. Yet at the other end of the Mediterranean, the Romans themselves had had no better success in spreading Latin: in 395, despite over five hundred years of direct Roman rule, Greeks, Syrians and Egyptians were still talking to each other in Greek. (Thereafter the empire was divided east from west, and Latin soon lost even a formal role in the east.)

Farther afield, in the north of China, repeated conquests by Turkish-, Mongol- and Tungus-speaking invaders, who ruled for some seven hundred years out of a thousand from the fourth century AD, had no effect on the survival of Chinese; finally, the Tungus-speaking Manchu conquered the whole country in 1644, and yet within a century their own language had died out. Back in the Middle East, the triumphs of the Arabic-speaking conquerors were only temporary: from the mid-seventh century, their civilisation monopolised Iran, along with its neighbours to west and east, but when the Seljuk Turks conquered the country from the other side in the eleventh century, it became clear that Arabic had never taken root, and the language of everything but religion reverted to Persian.

Evidently, total conquest, military and even spiritual, is not always enough to effect a language change. Yet at times an apparently weaker community can achieve just this. Consider Aramaic, the language of nomads, which swept through an Assyrian empire still at the height of its power in the eighth century BC, replacing the noble Akkadian, which went back to the very beginning of Mesopotamian civilisation. Or consider Sanskrit, taken up all over South-East Asia in the first millennium AD as the language of elite discourse, even though it came across the sea from India backed by not a single soldier. It even appears that Quechua, which became the language of the Inca empire in Peru in the fifteenth century, had actually been adopted as a dynastic compromise: the rulers gave up their own language in order to secure orderly acceptance of a vast extension of their power.

Economic power, often believed to lie at the root of the spread of English, whether under British or American sponsorship, seems even less coercive than the military. Phoenician shipping dominated the trade of the Mediterranean for most of the first millennium BC; for much of that time, it was backed up in the west by the dominance of the Phoenician colony of Carthage, which spoke the same language. But the Phoenician language seems to have remained unknown outside its own settlements: Greek was the lingua franca for international discourse, used even in the Carthaginian army. Farther east and later on, in the sixth to eighth centuries AD, the queen of the Silk Roads to China was the Iranian city of Samarkand: its language was Sogdian, but who has heard of it? Sogdian merchants, rich as they were, found it politic to use the customers' languages—Arabic, Chinese, Uighur-Turkic and Tibetan.[3]

In that muscular quote, Firth had emphasised the religious dimension of power, and this is often important: perhaps, indeed, we should be talking not of language prestige but language charisma. Sanskrit, besides being the sacred language of Hinduism, has owed much to disciples of the Buddha; and Hebrew would have been lost thousands of years ago without Judaism.

Arabic is more ambiguous: in the long term, Islam has proved the fundamental motive for its spread, but it was Arab-led armies which actually took the language into western Asia and northern Africa, creating new states in which proselytising would follow. Arabs were also famous as traders round the Indian Ocean, but the acceptance of Islam in this area has never given Arabic anything more than a role in liturgy. Curiously, the linguistic effects of spreading conversions turn out to be almost independent of the preachers' own priorities: Christians have been fairly indifferent to the language in which their faith is expressed, and their classic text, the New Testament, records the sayings of Jesus in translation; and yet Christianity itself has played a crucial role in the preservation of, and indeed the prestige of, many languages, including Aramaic, Greek, Latin and Gothic.

In fact, proselytising religion has been a factor in the careers of only a minority of world languages. It could be claimed that religion is just an example of the cultural dimension of language, which represents the ultimate source of language prestige. Culture, of course, is an extremely vague word, covering everything from the shaping of hand-axes to corporate mission statements, as well as the finer appreciation of the sonnets of Shakespeare and the paintings of Hokusai; so its relevance will need considerably closer attention.*

In the analysis of prehistoric movements of peoples, and the apparent ruthlessness with which one comes to replace another (as in the Bantu-speaking peoples' spread across the southern third of Africa, with consequent restriction of the domains of the San and Khoi; or the penetration of Austronesian sailors into South-East Asia and into contact with Melanesians), there is little reluctance to discuss the cultural factors presumed to have given the advantage. Finer arts and higher learning are not usually considered serious contenders. Cultural factors that enhance the ability to support larger populations (for example, by new forms of farming or husbandry) are deemed especially important. But simple innovations in military practice may also be effective.

Occasionally, brute biology takes over, and mere cultural differences are left on the sidelines, for a time irrelevant. If a population was vastly more liable to die from disease, as were the invaded inhabitants of the New World facing European interlopers in the sixteenth century, it hardly mattered that their weaponry and military tactics were also vastly inferior—or by contrast that the vegetables they cultivated (including potatoes and maize, tomatoes and chocolate) turned out to be world-beaters.

---

* It is also an inherently dangerous term, hard to separate from sweeping attempts to evaluate the achievements of whole peoples. (See, e.g., Macaulay's notorious verdict on Sanskrit- and Arabic-based cultures (see Chapter 12, 'Changing perspective—English in India', p. 496).

But the search for the causes of language prevalence is not usually so easily resolved. In the historic record of contacts between peoples, and contests between languages—when we have eyewitness testimony to keep us honest about what really went on—we often cannot point to cultural differences that were clearly crucial. Then we may have to look deeper: not just into the perceived associations of the different communities, how they looked to each other, the language communities' subjective reputations as well as their objective advantages, but even—and this is deeply unconventional, especially among linguists—to the properties of the languages themselves.

Bizarrely, linguists almost universally assume that the basic properties of languages which they study—the kinds of sounds a language uses, its basic word order, whether it works by stringing together short and independent words or by coordinating systems of prefixes or suffixes—are irrelevant to languages' prospects of survival. After all, they reckon, every language is by definition learnable by children: that's what makes it a human language. If a community has problems propagating its language, there must be a social cause, not a linguistic one.

But for us, viewing the language as distinctive of the community that speaks it, we can only wonder what all that linguistic structure is there for. Perhaps a language's type even has survival value, determining whether a new population that has long spoken another language can readily take it up or not. This is one of the innovations of this book: to suggest ways in which it might actually matter what type of a language a community speaks. (See Chapter 14, 'What makes a language learnable', p. 552.)

The plan of campaign for the book as a whole is to review, more or less in temporal order, the histories of languages that have loomed large in the world. It starts from the onset of literacy, because that is when we first have clear evidence of what languages people were speaking. Our policy at every point has been to require explicit evidence, in effect written traces, and so to pass over many events that are believed to have happened in a pre-literate past.* And the story continues until we confront the major languages of recent growth, what we have called 'M&A' languages.

As it turns out, the story falls into two major epochs, which divide at 1492.

---

* This has led to the total omission of two important known language spreads, and one conjectured one. The Polynesian islands gained their dozens of closely related languages over the four millennia from 3000 BC in perhaps the most intrepid sustained exploration ever. And the Bantu languages spread across southern Africa over much the same period, beginning in Cameroon and ending at the Cape. Both of these stories are crucial to understanding the full pattern of languages in today's world, but they are based purely on archaeology and linguistic comparisons. We have not a single word recorded from all the talk of those aeons. As for the geographical path of Indo-European, the ancestral

This is the beginning of the worldwide expansion of Europe and some of its languages. Before this point, languages almost always spread along land routes, and the results are regional: large languages are spoken across coherent, centred regions. After this point, the sea becomes the main thoroughfare of language advance, and spread can be global: a language can be spoken in distinct zones on many different continents, with its currency linked only by the sinews of trade and military governance that stretch across the oceans.

Besides this geographical difference, it is possible to see other gross patterns which distinguish the two epochs.

Before 1492, the key forces that spread languages are first literacy and civic culture, and later revealed religion. But when a community has these advantages its language is often spread at the point of a sword; without them, military victories or commercial development will achieve little. The general mode of spread is through infiltration: whole peoples do not move, but languages are transmitted by small communities and piecemeal colonies which do. But the foundation of English, which occurs in this period, appears to be an exception to all this.

After 1492, the forces of spread are at first much more elemental: disease devastates populations in the Americas and elsewhere, and the technological gap between conquerors and victims is everywhere much starker than it had been in the era of regional spread. But once the power balance moves back into equilibrium, with the stabilisation of the Europeans' global military empires, it becomes hard to distinguish military, commercial and linguistic dominance. At first, travel is difficult, and language spread is slow, still based on infiltration. However, with the spread of literacy and cheaper transport, the mode switches to migration, as large European populations seek to take advantage of the new opportunities. In the twentieth century, this too eases off; but new forms of communication arise, continually becoming faster, cheaper and more comprehensive: the result is that the dominant mode of language spread switches from migration to diffusion. English is once again exceptional, as it has been uniquely poised to take first advantage of the new technologies, but its prospects remain less clear as the other languages, both large and small, settle in behind it. It faces the uncertain future of any instant celebrity, and perhaps too the same inevitable ultimate outcome of such a future. This is not least because, for the world's leading lingua franca, the whole concept of a language community begins to break down.

language that is reconstructed to make sense of the evident systematic relationships among Hittite, Sanskrit, Russian, Armenian, Greek, Latin, Gaulish, Lithuanian and English, and many, many more, we can only speculate, and those speculations are the stuff of historical linguistics, not of language history.

But once informed with the varied stories of the world's largest languages, our inquiry can move on to ask some pertinent questions.

How new and unprecedented are modern forces of language diffusion? Do they share significant properties with language spread in the past?

How will the age-old characteristics of language communities assert themselves? In particular, can all languages still act as outward symbols of communities? And can they effectively weave together the tissues of associations which come from a shared experience? Can each language still create its own world? Will they want to, when science—and some revealed religions—claim universal validity?

These are the questions we shall want to ask. But first we must examine the vast materials of human language history.

PART II
LANGUAGES BY LAND

Two Italian opinions, separated by fifteen centuries, on the value of an imposed common language:

nec ignoro ingrati et segnis animi existimari posse merito si, obiter atque in transcursu ad hunc modum dicatur terra omnium terrarum alumna eadem et parens, numine deum electa quae caelum ipsum clarius faceret, sparsa congregaret imperia ritusque molliret et tot populorum discordes ferasque linguas sermonis commercio contraheret ad colloquia et humanitatem homini daret, breviterque una cunctarum gentium in toto orbe patria fieret.

I am aware that I may be quite rightly thought thankless and lazy if I touch so lightly on that land which is both the foster-child and parent of all lands, called by Providence to make the very sky brighter, to bring together its far-flung domains, to civilise their ways of life, to unite in conversation the wild, quarrelsome tongues of all their many peoples through common use of its language, to give culture to mankind, and in short to become the one fatherland of every nation in the world.

Pliny the Elder (AD 24–79), *Naturalis Historia*, iii.39

The yoke of arms is shaken off more readily by subject peoples than the yoke of language.

attributed to Lorenzo Valla, Italian humanist (1406–57),
in his *Elegantiarum Libri VI*

3

The Desert Blooms:
Language Innovation in the Middle East

ayu ṭêm ilī   qereb šamê ilammad
milik ša anzanunzî   iḥakkim mannu
ēkâma ilmada   alakti ili apâti
ša ina amšat ibluṭu   imūt uddeš
surriš uštādir   zamar uḫtabar
ina ṣibit appi   izammur elī la
in pīt purīdi   uṣarrap lallariš
kī petê u katāmi   ṭēnšina šitni
immuṣama   immâ šalamtíš
išebbâma   išannana ilšin
ina ṭābi itammâ   elâ šamā'i
ūtaššašama idabbuba   arād irkalla
ana annāta ušta-   qerebšina la altanda

29

Who can know the will of the gods in heaven?
Who can understand the plans of the underworld gods?
Where have humans learned the way of a god?
He who was alive yesterday is dead today.
One moment he is worried, the next he is boisterous.
One moment he is singing a joyful song,
A moment later he wails like a funeral mourner.
Their condition changes like opening and closing [the legs].
When starving they become like corpses,
When full they oppose their god.
In good times they speak of scaling heaven,
When they are troubled they talk of descent to hell.
I am perplexed at these things; I cannot tell what they mean.
from Ludlul Bēl Nēmeqi, 'I will Praise the Lord of Wisdom', Akkadian[1]

The names of civilisations that arose in the ancient Near East now ring with the note of remote antiquity. Three dozen and more are known that flourished in the three millennia from the start of records *c*.3300 BC until the invasion of Alexander in 330 BC, among them such powers as Babylon, Assyria, Phoenicia, Lydia and Persia. They bring to mind visions of oriental absolutism, breathtaking ruthlessness and gaudy magnificence. Despite their many pretensions, their cultural fertility and sometimes truly universal power, they have left no heirs. Something of this was foreseen by at least one of their own writers:

> *arad mitanguranni*
> > *annû bēlī annû*
> *umma usātu ana mātia luppuš kimi*
> > *epuš bēlī epuš*
> > *amēlu ša usātam ana mātišu ipuš*
> > *šakna usātu-šu in kippat ša marduk*
> *e arad anāku usātamma ana mātia ul epuš*
> > *la teppuš bēlī la teppuš*
> > *ilīma ina muḫḫi tillāni labīrūti itallak*
> > *amur gulgullē ša arkûti u pānûti*
> > *ayyu bēl lemuttima ayu bēl usāti*

Servant, listen to me.
> Yes, master, yes.
I will benefit my country.

So do, master, do.
The man who benefits his country
has his good deeds set down in the [record] of Marduk.
No, servant, I will not benefit my country.
Do not do it, master, do not.
Go up to the ancient ruin heaps and walk around;
look at the skulls of the lowly and the great.
Which belongs to one who did evil, and which to one who did good?

from 'The Dialogue of Pessimism', Akkadian[2]

But perhaps it is a little harsh to weigh up the persistence of political achieve-ments after a gap of two to four millennia. Some of their works really did defy the ages. It was here that writing was invented, and developed from a medium for taking notes into the basis for a full, explicit record of human life and thought; as a lucky complement to this, a plentiful and non-biodegradable material had been adopted to write on, patties of river clay, rolled out, in-scribed, and sometimes baked hard. As a result we can trace not just the broad outlines of events, but the personalities and even the diplomatic dialogue of royal families, the myths and rituals of the peoples' gods as well as their images, the laws under which they lived and the love songs they sang, and above all their multifarious languages.

This last gift is a particular godsend of the last two hundred years of ar-chaeology, since among the peoples of the area only the Hebrews on the western margin and the Iranians on the east have texts and cultural traditions that have survived to modern times. Yet their scriptures, the Old Testament and the Zend-Avesta, supplemented by the hearsay of bystanders such as the Greek Herodotus—all that was available to eighteenth-century scholars—give a very partial view, and that only of the latter stages of what was done, with no sense at all of what was said by those who did it.

Without nineteenth-century Europe's discovery that it could do historical research through digging, and the novel skills of decipherment and language reconstruction then heroically applied to what was unearthed, we should know nothing at all of the founding cities in Sumer and Elam, the steadily ex-panding might of Urartu from the Caucasus, or the pre-eminence of Hittites in what is now Turkey. Each of these groups spoke a language quite unrelated to that of its neighbours, hinting at radically different origins, and a wealth of unknown stories in their even more remote past. This fact of different lan-guages amazingly shines through the single script that so many of them used, based on patterns of wedge-shaped marks, even though it was originally de-signed to represent the meanings of words rather than how they sounded.

SUMERIAN:

kingia kan dugud šu | numundangigi en kulabake ime šu | binra inim dubgim bingub ubta inim | ima gubu nubtagala. The messenger's mouth was heavy, he could not repeat the message. The Lord of Kulab patted some clay, he put the words on it as on a tablet. Before that time, words put on clay had never existed.

Enmerkar and the Lord of Aratta (c.1800 BC)

AKKADIAN:

bulṭī ultu muḫḫi | adi ṣupri liqtī aḫûti tāḫizu nakla | azugall-ūt Ninurta u Gula mala bašmu | ina ṭuppāni ašṭur asniq abrema ana | tāmarti šitassīya qereb ekalli-ya ukīn.... remedies from the top of the head to the toenails, non-canonical selections, clever teachings, whatever pertains to the medical mastery of Ninurta and Gula, I wrote on tablets, checked and collated, and deposited within my palace for perusal and reading.

Colophon on medical text, library of Ashurbanipal (ruled Assyria 668–627 BC)

ELAMITE:

Daryamauš sunki na-n-ri | čaumin uramaštana u tuppime daae | ikki hutta harriyama. King Darius said: By the grace of Ahuramazda I made another inscription in Aryan.

Rock Inscription at Behistun, fifth century BC

Six languages written in cuneiform—
Sumerian, Akkadian, Elamite, Hurrian, Urartian, Hittite

HURRIAN:

𒀸𒈾𒄀 [cuneiform text]

keliašnnaan pašštxiiffuš | tive andi kuloža mannaan xilli | šenafšan nim-moriaš misrineveneš | evreš taže apli tanoža. And Kelia, my messenger, said this word: thus speaking, Your brother, Nimmoria, the lord of Egypt, made a great gift.

Letter of King Tushratta of Mitanni
to the King of Egypt, mid 14th century BC

URARTIAN:

[cuneiform text]

xaldiie evriie išpuiniše | sardurixiniše menuaše išpuinixiniše | xaldiei susi šidištuni. For lord Haldi, Ishpuni son of Sarduri, and Menua son of Ishpuini, built Haldi's shrine.

Haldi shrine inscription at Yeşilaliç, late 9th century BC

HITTITE:

[cuneiform text]

ABU.YAmakan INA KUR Mittanni | kuit anda ašanduléšket naškan | ašanduli anda ištantāit ŠA UTU | Arinnamakan GAŠAN.YA EZEN | šakuwandareškir. (Sumerian or Akkadian words used symbolically for Hittite words are in capitals.) But because my father remained camped in the land of Mitanni and delayed in the camp, the festivals of my Lady the sun goddess of Arinna went unobserved.

State annals of Mursilis II, Boğazköy, *c.*1353–1325 BC

Six languages written in cuneiform—
Sumerian, Akkadian, Elamite, Hurrian, Urartian, Hittite (continued)

This is a region of so many world firsts for linguistic innovation. Unlike Egypt, China or India, its cities and states had always been consciously multilingual, whether for communication with neighbours who spoke different languages, or because their histories had made them adopt a foreign language to dignify court, religion or commerce. This is the area where we find the first conscious use of a classical language; but also, by contrast, the first generalised use of a totally foreign language for convenience in communication, as a lingua franca, an early apparent triumph of diplomatic pragmatism over national sentiment.

This area contains the site of the earliest known writing, in the lower reaches of the Euphrates valley. But in its western zone, in the coastal cities of Syria, it was also the first to make the radical simplification from hieroglyphs that denoted words and syllables to a short alphabet that represented simple sounds. The political effects of this were massive. For the first time, literacy could spread beyond the aristocratic scribal class, the people who had leisure in childhood to learn the old, complicated, system; positions of power and influence throughout the Assyrian empire were then opened to a wider social range.

The area also contains the first known museums and libraries, often centralised, multilingual institutions of the state. But by an irony of fate which has favoured the memory of this clay-based society, its documents were best preserved by firing, most simply through conflagrations in the buildings in which they were held, a circumstance that was not uncommon in its tempestuous history. These catastrophes were miracles of conservation, archiving whole libraries *in situ*, on occasion with even their classification intact, and have materially helped the rapid reading of much unknown history in our era.

Not all the states of the area stayed focused within the Fertile Crescent, the zone of well-watered land that runs from the valleys of the Tigris and Euphrates up round the southern slopes of the Taurus mountains and down the Mediterranean coasts of Syria and Palestine. From the western coast of Palestine, the cities of Phoenicia sent trading expeditions far and wide, mostly within the Mediterranean. One result was the foundation of Carthage, and hence the world's first colonial empire, precursor of the kind of institution that has made English a global language. Others were the first circumnavigation of Africa (on behalf of the Egyptian pharaoh), and the discovery of navigable routes to Britain for tin, and the Baltic Sea for amber. On the way, the Phoenicians spread the practice of alphabetic writing throughout their network of trading emporia, providing perhaps the most important single key to unlock the progress of their great rivals, the Greeks and the Romans, who would ultimately supplant them as masters of the Mediterranean.

The best word for this Middle Eastern society is *cosmopolitan*, citizens of the world, but its world was never a sheltered one. Good communications and absence of natural borders made it difficult for any culture to hold power stably. We find a succession of kingdoms coming from every different direction, and (it turns out) many different language families, to seize control of the central area that is modern Iraq. After three thousand documented years of shifting power balances within the region, control was yielded to groups based far away, the Greeks and later the Romans from the west, then the Parthians from the north-eastern corner of Iran in the east. But these foreign powers were no more effective in achieving stability: Arabs, Mongols and Turks have succeeded one another through the centuries of the modern era, with the twentieth century from start to finish being a particularly bitterly contested period in its history.

Three sisters who span the history of 4500 years

The only stability this society has enjoyed has been in the substance of its ruling language. Akkadian, the language spoken by Sargon I, the first Assyrian king in 2300 BC, is a close relative of the Arabic spoken by his successor in this same land, Saddam Hussein, in AD 2000; another close relative, the Middle East's old lingua franca, Aramaic, bridges the gap between the decline of Akkadian around 600 BC and the onset of Arabic with the Muslims around AD 600. They are all sister languages within the very close Semitic family.*

They have many distinctive points in common. They have consonants pronounced with constriction of the throat (said to be glottalised or pharyngealised). Feminine words end in -*at*. There are only two or three cases in noun inflexion; there is an ending in -*ī* to make adjectives, and a prefix *m-* to make nouns; there is distinction in verbal forms between dynamic and stative tenses—dynamic have prefixes to mark the persons, but stative have suffixes. Above all, Semitic languages are highly inflected, using a distinctive system

---

* The family is named after Noah's second son, Shem, introduced in Genesis ix.18, and the linguistic use goes back to A. L. Schloezer, writing in 1781. He drew his inspiration from the fact that many of the peoples named as the descendants of Shem in Genesis x.21–31 spoke languages of this family, notably Hebrew (coming via Arphaxad), Asshur and Aram. But the term is not well chosen: Shem also had among his sons Elam and Lud, the patriarchs for Elamite and Lydian, which are quite unrelated languages; and Canaan (first of the Sidonians, as well as Amorites and Arwadites) and Nimrod (first of the Babylonians and Akkadians) are given as descendants of Ham, though their languages are in fact closely related to Hebrew, Assyrian and Aramaic.

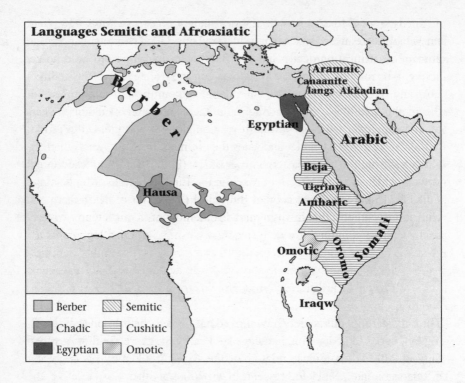

Languages Semitic and Afroasiatic

Berber | Semitic
Chadic | Cushitic
Egyptian | Omotic

in which the consonantal skeleton of the word has a meaning independent of the varying patterns of vowels and consonants that may come between them: to give the simplest of examples, in Akkadian, the root *k-š-d*, 'catch', can be discerned in *kašādu*, 'to attain, catch', *ikaššadu*, 'they were catching', *kišidtu*, 'booty', and *kuššudu*, 'captured', just as *š-p-r*, 'order', is reflected in *šapāru*, 'to send, rule, write', and *šipirtu*, 'mission, letter', and *š-l-m*, 'rest', in *šalāmu*, 'to be well', *šalimtu*, 'peace', and *šulmu*, 'peace, greeting, rest, sunset'.

Besides covering the major languages of the ancient and modern Middle East, the Semitic group also takes in some of the most populous languages of Ethiopia and Eritrea, including Amharic, Tigre, Tigrinya and the ancient language of the Ethiopian Church, Ge'ez.

These Semitic languages in fact share most of these properties with a larger group, called Afro-Asiatic or Hamito-Semitic, which includes Egyptian, Berber and some language families spoken farther south, Cushitic, Omotic and Chadic (including the now vast Hausa language). They are all spoken in northerly parts of Africa, and the usual assumption is that this is the primeval home of the Semitic languages too. There is in fact some indirect evidence of a mass movement of tribes at a prehistoric date, rather than simple diffusion of the languages among neighbours: in certain ways Akkadian and Ethiopic are more alike than their intervening Semitic cousins; and the rampant desertification of the Sahara *c*.3500 BC would have provided a fair motive to be moving out of North Africa.[3]

At any rate, by the time we first encounter them in their own historical record, about 2400 BC,* there are Semitic language speakers (and by the nature of the evidence, writers) in centres dotted along the northern edge of the Fertile Crescent, pretty much on the borders of modern Syria, from Ebla (60 kilometres south of Aleppo) through Nabada (Tell Beydar, 20 kilometres north of Al Hasake) and down to Mari on the Euphrates (near Abu Kamal) and Kish (15 kilometres due east of Babylon). (The names of the kings who ruled at Kish suggest that it was a mixed settlement of Semites with Sumerians.) All these communities were steadfastly using Sumerian logograms as the staple of their cuneiform script, but the language is discernibly Semitic, written with phonetic symbols to show the verb and noun endings and function words, and in a different word order from Sumerian. There are also bilingual school texts which specify how at least some of the Sumerian logograms should be pronounced. The language of Ebla does not seem to be written very consistently, and is in general difficult to differentiate from early forms of Akkadian, occurring in Kish and down in Sumer after the conquests of Sargon I in the twenty-fourth century.

These conquests are the first historical evidence of political unification, but mostly they unified people who were already speaking closely related Semitic dialects. The language history of the Middle East opens therefore with its leading player already on stage, Semitic written in Sumerian cuneiform. We do not know how the Semitic speakers had got there, how their remarkably unified dialects (or languages) had spread out to cover the whole Fertile Crescent. On the map, the deserts of Syria and Arabia look like good central points from which to start an expansion—but they seem inconceivable as areas in which to bring up the necessary large surplus populations.

As one result of Semitic language persistence, it can be shown that counting to ten has hardly changed here in over four thousand years, or two hundred generations:†

---

* The first Semitic names (in fact from Akkadian) appear even earlier, in Sumerian documents *c*.2800 BC (Caplice 1988: 3).

† Pronounce š as English 'sh', ḥ as the sound for blowing on glasses to mist them, θ as English 'th' in *thin*, ' as the clearing of a throat, ā as a long 'a' as in *father*, and ē as the long 'e' in *fête*.

Numeral	Akkadian 23rd–6th centuries BC	Aramaic 6th century BC – 6th century AD	Arabic 6th–21st centuries AD
1	ištēn	ḥad	wāḥid
2	šina	trēn	iθnāyn
3	šalaš	təlātā	θalāθa
4	erba	ʾarbaʿā	ʾarbaʿa
5	ḥamiš	ḥamišа	xamsa
6	šešš	šittā	sitta
7	sebe	šabʿā	sabʿa
8	samāne	təmāniyā	θamāniya
9	tiše	tišʿā	tisʿa
10	ešer	asrā	ʿašra

Counting 1–10 in Iraq from 2300 BC to AD 2000

The story in brief: Language leapfrog

אל תהחוי לערבי ימא ולצידני ברא כי עבידתהם פרישה

ʾal thaḥăwî laʿrabî yāmâ ūlṣîdōnî bārâ
kî ʿăbîdathem prîsâ

Do not show an Arab the sea nor a Sidonian the desert;
for their work is different.

Aramaic: Proverbs of Ahiqar, 110 [4]

The language history of the Near East—more objectively, of South-West Asia—does not need to be reconstructed: it is told in its own documents, from the late fourth millennium BC. It is brimming with interesting details, especially with linguistic and cultural firsts, but there are so many twists and turns in a narrative that takes in five thousand years that it is hard to keep one's bearings. We shall start with a very brief run-through of the major players, from Sumerian to Arabic, situating them around the central area of the Fertile Crescent from Iraq to Palestine; then we return to look in more detail at their particular contributions to our understanding of languages through time.

The overall focus of the story is on its pulsating centre at the mouth of the Euphrates on the Persian Gulf. As the centuries roll by, the centre's influence expands, first north, then westward, and neighbouring peoples come to take an interest, creating new, and often stronger, centres of their own, until the story becomes a struggle between the contending influence (and languages) of Mesopotamia, Anatolia, Iran and Syria; and the frame of reference has ex-

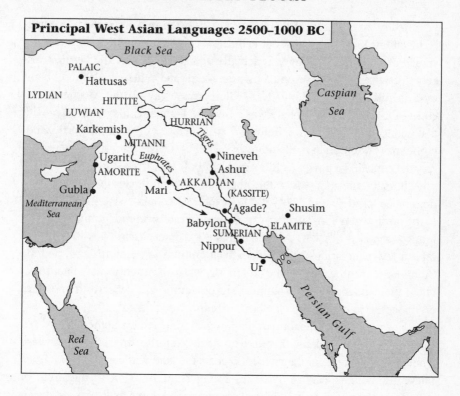

Principal West Asian Languages 2500–1000 BC

panded to the borders of Greece and Egypt in the west, and Afghanistan and India in the east. The finale comes not once but twice, in two sweeping conquests that lead to linguistic cataclysm, first by Greek from the north, and then by Arabic from the south.

When the story opens, there are two cultures with the skill of writing, next door to each other in the upper reaches of the Persian Gulf: Sumer, the Biblical 'land of Shinʿar' at the confluence of the Tigris and Euphrates rivers, and Elam, across the marshes to the east, between the Zagros mountains and the sea. Each was not so much a state as a gathering of towns and villages of people speaking a common language. The origins of Sumerian are quite unknown; Elamite, however, appears to be related to Dravidian, and so linked anciently with Brahui, still spoken by over 2 million in the west of Pakistan, and many more languages spoken in central and southern India.[5]

Both these cultures seem to have invented their writing systems independently, and approximately at the same time (around the thirty-first century BC). But Sumer was destined for a much more influential history than Elam. Elam did retain its language for over three thousand years (it was one of the three official media of the Persian empire in the late first millennium), yet already around 2400 Elamite is found written in Sumerian-style cuneiform, and its local script died out in the next couple of centuries. This cultural spread of Sumerian writing was actually occurring all over the Fertile Crescent: likewise by 2400 we find Sumerian words and cuneiform symbols common in inscriptions in Ebla, 1000 kilometres away on the Mediterranean coast of modern Syria. Eblaite was a Semitic language, like Akkadian, with a sound system and a morphological structure that, from a modern standpoint, makes Sumerian really quite awkward as a basis for writing: nevertheless the expressive power of Sumerian symbols was irresistible.

Politically, the boot was on the other foot. The Sumerians themselves were dominated a little later (2334–2200) by their Akkadian-speaking neighbours to the north when King Sargon—or more accurately *Šarrukîn*, 'the righteous king'—imposed himself. Although this Akkadian empire was overthrown after a few generations by invaders from Qutium in the north-east, and the Sumerians, spearheaded by the city of Ur, were able eighty years later to reclaim their independence, southern Mesopotamia was henceforth known to all under the joint name of 'the land of Sumer and Akkad'.*

When at the end of the third millennium Ur, the greatest Sumerian city, fell to more Semitic speakers, this time nomadic Amorites from the north-west, a new pattern set in: for the next 1500 years the land was periodically unified under Akkadian-speaking dynasties ruling from Babylon in the south or Assyria in the north, only to have their power disrupted every few centuries by power struggles between them, or invasions from the west or east. The invasions, although they might last a long time, notably four hundred years after the Kassites took control of Babylon in 1570 BC, never had any great linguistic effect. Like the various Turks who would conquer north China, or the Germans who were to topple Roman control of western Europe, these were all invaders who acquiesced in their victims' languages. From about 2000 BC, Akkadian had become the only language spoken throughout the region. But Sumerian was not forgotten. It moved upmarket, and kept its influence in the written language. Babylon and Assyria went on for a millennium and a half as the two powers within Mesopotamia, competing often with ruthless savagery, but speaking dialects of the same language.

While Akkadian held the central area until the middle of the first millennium BC, it was surrounded to the east, north and west by unrelated lan-

---

* The Greeks, on the scene too late to know any of these early origins, called the place Mesopotamia, 'Mid-River-land', emphasising the framing role of the rivers Euphrates and Tigris, Greek versions of the names *Purattu* and *Idiqlat*. But in this early period the Euphrates is much more central, flowing through Babylon and Ur, and watering the lands of both Akkad and Sumer. The Tigris, farther to the east, grows in importance with the rise of Assyria.

guages. Hurrian, replaced later by 'Urartian' (whose name lives on in Mount Ararat), was the major language of the north, spoken from modern Armenia as far south as Kirkuk in modern Iraq. (Its surviving relatives, tiny languages such as Avar and Lezgian in the East Caucasian family, are still spoken on the western shores of the Caspian.)

To the west of this, in the central plain of Anatolia, which is now Turkey, we see the first known Indo-Europeans, Hittites, with their close relatives who spoke Luwian and Palaic.* The Hittites, flourishing from the sixteenth to the thirteenth century BC, created a massively literate civilisation, and their royal library at Hattusas, discovered in modern Boğaz Köy, 150 kilometres west of Ankara, contains materials not only in Hittite and Akkadian, but also in Hurrian, Luwian and Palaic, interspersed here and there with phrases in Hattic, Sumerian and the Indo-Aryan language of the Mitannian aristocracy. The Hittites were often a threat to Sumer and Akkad, and it had been a swift Hittite invasion, not followed up, which had left Babylon open to the Kassite takeover already mentioned. In the event, the Hittite empire collapsed about the end of the thirteenth century, but related languages lived on for many centuries, particularly Luwian, and farther to the west Lydian.†

South of the Hittites but due west of Sumer and Akkad, in modern Syria, the languages were Semitic, close relatives of Akkadian. We have seen that it was from this direction that the Amorite invasion came (named after the region *Amurru*, Akkadian for 'the west', in northern Syria), which had delivered the *coup de grâce* to Sumerian independence, and hence Sumerian as a spoken language, around 2000 BC.

There seems, in fact, to have been some fraternity among these cities of Semitic speech, from Ugarit (on the coast near Lataqieh) through Iamhad (Aleppo), Karkemish and Qatna in northern Syria to Mari on the Euphrates. Mari and Ugarit both left massive libraries from the second millennium BC. But as to foreign influence in this period, there was a tendency here to look south towards the power centre in Egypt, rather than to their linguistic cousins in Mesopotamia. The Phoenician port city of Gubla (known to the Greeks later as Byblos) was growing rich on exporting timber, specifically the cedars of Lebanon, to the wood-starved Egyptians. The Amorite cities just mentioned all left quantities of royal vases, jewels and statues imported from

---

* The name Hittite (from the Hebrew *ḥittī*) comes from their power centre in the land of Hatti, where the natives spoke a quite unrelated language, Hattian. The Hittites in fact called their language Nesian (*nešili*), after their city of Nešaš (or Kanesh, modern Kültepe, in south-eastern Turkey) but the biblical misnomer 'Hittite' has stuck.

† Croesus, the proverbially rich last king of Lydia, fell to Cyrus the Persian in 547 BC. Linguistically, this was the ultimate death rattle of Hittite power.

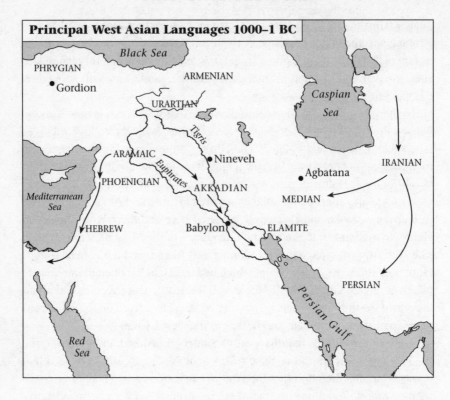

Egypt. Farther south, in Palestine, the general level of wealth and urbanisation was lower, and marauding Habiru (known to the Egyptians as *ʿapiru*) were a threat to more settled communities. Perhaps the ancestors of the nation later calling themselves *ʿibri* (Hebrews) were among them.

Throughout the second millennium BC, the land of Sumer and Akkad already enjoyed serious cultural prestige. This is clearly reflected in the spread of its cuneiform writing system to all its neighbours, including even Elam, which had independently developed its own alternative. Besides the script, its language, Akkadian, was in this period the lingua franca for diplomacy, even where the Babylonians or Assyrians were not a party to the matters under discussion.

But this favourable situation was ultimately upset by outside events: developments now occurred in the east, north and west which were to affect Mesopotamia, and its linguistic influence, profoundly.

At the end of the second millennium BC and the beginning of the first, new companies of Indo-Europeans were entering the northerly territory of Anatolia. They would have come from the Balkans, bringing speakers of Phrygian, and later Armenian, into the central and northern areas. They are known as

Muški on the one occasion (1115 BC) when they broke through to confront the Assyrian ruler Tiglath Pileser I,* but otherwise they had little direct impact on Mesopotamia, largely shielded as it was by the buffer kingdom of the Urartians in the east of Anatolia.

In the east, at about the same time, there came another large-scale invasion by people with an Indo-European language: for the first time Persian, or its direct ancestor (closely related to Vedic Sanskrit), was spoken on the plateaux of Iran. This language was a cousin of the Iranian speech of the people who remained widespread on the plains of the Ukraine and southern Siberia for at least another two thousand years, under the names Scythian or Śaka. Those who invaded Iran would become literate only after some centuries of contact with Mesopotamia, so the early evidence for their arrival is purely archaeological. Among the names of the tribes were two which (from the Akkadian records) seemed to settle close to the borders with Sumer and Akkad, the *Mādāi* in the north round Agbatana (modern Hamadan), and those who inhabited the *Parsūa* or 'borderlands' in the south (modern Fars province): these were to be the Medes and Persians, and they now hemmed in the land of Elam respectively from the north and the south. At first, they seemed just to be a rotation of the barbarians in the Zagros mountains on the eastern flank, successor to the Quti, Lulubi and Kassites who had been there from time immemorial; but from the seventh century they were to undermine, and then destroy, Mesopotamia as an independent centre of power.

Many now believe that the spread of all these Indo-European languages was achieved without massive change of people, but through wars that put a new elite in control of the old lands, with new languages spreading in the old populations through the prestige of the new social order. As to why these interlopers were able to force an entry, presumably it is no coincidence that this was also the era in which the use of iron became established.

But most immediately significant for the linguistic history of the Middle East is a third group, the Aramaeans, desert nomads from northern Syria speaking a Semitic language. They are first heard of as a particularly persistent enemy in an inscription of the same Tiglath Pileser I at the end of the twelfth century BC. Soon after we hear that Damascus was an Aramaean city. By the tenth century they had established themselves as a significant power, largely at the expense of the remaining Hittite–Luwian colonies. Then they

---

* This is his name in Hebrew. His real name was *Tukulti-apil-Esharra*, meaning 'my trust is in the son of Esharra', namely the Assyrian god Asshur. The Mushki are equated by Igor Diakonov with the Mysians, Thracian settlers in western Anatolia, and also the Armenians, named *Sa-mekhi* by the Georgians. The Bible also speaks of *Meshech* as a foreign people.

spread out towards the east, despite resistance from Assyrian monarchs, and by the end of the ninth century there were apparently settlements of them all over the land of Sumer and Akkad. The succession to the throne of Babylon was not routine in this period, and at least one dynasty, Bît Bazi in the early tenth century, appears to have been Aramaean. The Chaldaeans (*Kaldû*) were also an Aramaean tribe who settled in Sumer, and went on to found the last Babylonian dynasty in the seventh to sixth centuries, including Nabupolassar, Nebuchadrezzar II and Nabonidus. The Aramaeans had made themselves very much part of the establishment.

This must be part of the explanation for the way in which, beginning in the eighth century, their language came to replace Akkadian as the universal medium of Mesopotamia, and soon (as Assyria conquered Syria and Palestine) established itself as the lingua franca of the whole Fertile Crescent. This was not a culture-led expansion, since the Aramaeans are not associated with any distinctive style or civilisation of their own; nevertheless, they were the ones who brought simple alphabetic writing, the invention of their neighbours the Phoenicians, into the heart of the old empire, where for over two thousand years all culture and administration had been built on skill in the complicated cuneiform writing. They had thereby revolutionised its communications, and perhaps its social structure as well. Twenty-two simple signs could now do the work previously requiring over six hundred.

While this was going on in Asia, the Phoenicians themselves, strung out along the Mediterranean coast of what is now Lebanon, were expanding, or rather exploring and exploiting, in the opposite direction. In language, the Phoenicians (or Canaanites, as they called themselves) were very similar to their neighbours inland and to the south, the Hebrews; but they had a very different attitude to their homeland.

'Phoenicia' is a linguistic, and even more an economic, expression for the trading cities of coastal Lebanon.* There is no record of a political unit linking them even as a league, but from the middle of the second millennium BC this line of a dozen or so independent cities (Byblos, Sidon and Tyre the most famous among them) had established themselves as the preferred centres for the supply of copper and tin from Cyprus, timber from Lebanon and luxury goods, especially clothing and jewellery. Since either their suppliers or their customers (especially Egypt, for the timber) often lived overseas, this fostered the development of ships and the know-how for navigation. With these, uniquely in the Middle East, the cities had the wherewithal for exploration

---

* The *Phoinîkes*, especially the Sidonians, are renowned in the *Iliad* for fine weaving and metalwork, and in the *Odyssey* as travelling merchants.

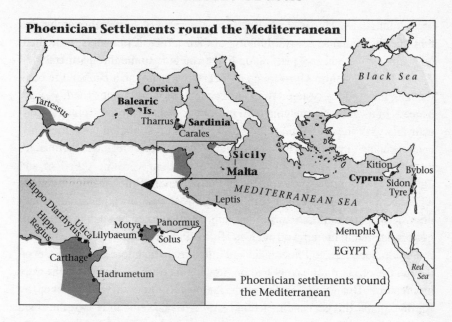

Phoenician Settlements round the Mediterranean

much farther afield. The original expeditions may have been earlier (ancient historians suggest the end of the twelfth century), but it is clear that by the eighth century there was a network of Phoenician settlements from one end of the Mediterranean to the other, with particular concentration on Sicily, Sardinia, the north-western shores of Africa and Cadiz (Phoenician *gader*, 'the fortress'). Mostly they were trading posts, and above all mining outlets, rather than cities, but in one case the settlement became much more than a commercial venture. This was Carthage, situated on a natural harbour in modern Tunisia, and soon developing not just a trade network but an empire of its own, in North Africa, Sicily and Sardinia.

By their presence, the Phoenician settlements will have spread far and wide a sense of what the cultivated and literate society of the Near East was like, as well as opening up a long-distance export trade in metals. The Phoenicians were the globalisers of Mesopotamian culture. Most concretely, they spread knowledge of their alphabetic writing system to the Greeks and Iberians, and just possibly also to the Etruscans and Romans; so they can claim to have given Europe its primary education.

Phoenician could be heard all round the Mediterranean, especially in its islands and on its southern rim, for most of the first millennium BC. Yet linguistically it had very little long-term impact on Europe. The Greeks and others accepted, quite explicitly, the Phoenicians' writing system as the basis of their own (using the term *phoinikéia grámmata*), but not a single element

45

of their language. This is partly perhaps a comment on how little of their culture the Phoenicians, always thinking of themselves as outsiders, only there on business, were in fact passing on to their new customers or partners.*

But further, it shows how much more abstract a tool an alphabet is than an ideographic writing system. With an alphabet, properly understood, you get a means of cleanly writing your own language, without further baggage. Contrast this with the knock-on effects when ideas of Sumerian cuneiform had been taken up. Two thousand years later, Babylonian scribes were still using bits of Sumerian as shorthand symbols for equivalent words in Akkadian, and indeed had still not worked out a way to express all the Akkadian sounds when they went beyond those in Sumerian. Nor was this a particular weakness on the part of Akkadian scribes: similar effects can be seen in other languages written in cuneiform, such as Hittite and Urartian.†

Paradoxically, then, Phoenician had little linguistic impact in Europe, even though the effect its speakers had on the languages they contacted was truly momentous. But Punic, as the same language is known when spoken by Carthaginians, did get established in North Africa. It evidently long survived the downfall of Carthage as a state in 146 BC, some 655 years after its foundation, and even the Latin-speaking Roman administration that followed for another five hundred years, since Augustine of Hippo is still quoting words of the language in the fifth century AD, remarking on its utility for a priest in a country parish in Numidia.[6] But tantalisingly and heartbreakingly, this language, once so widely used and the vehicle that had spread alphabetic literacy to Europe, could not ensure the survival of a single book from antiquity.

Back in western Asia, from the mid-seventh century the pace of change seemed to accelerate. In four decades to 627 BC Assyria expanded its power to its maximum, taking in Lydia in the north, Phoenicia in the west, the Nile delta of Egypt in the south, and Elam in the east. But just fifteen years later it collapsed. The Chaldaeans in Babylon had overthrown the Assyrians, enlisting the Medes to help them, and proceeded to rebuild their empire from their own perspective. This was the final incandescence of Mesopotamian power, under the last great emperor of Babylon, Nebuchadrezzar II. He died

---

* There are 6 million tons of ancient slag, covering ¾ of a square kilometre, at the silver mines of Rio Tinto, near Huelva (probably the site of Tartessos, believed to be the same as Tarshish in Hebrew). Despite this massive activity, extending over centuries, archaeological evidence tends to show that Phoenician settlements in Spain were commercial enclaves rather than towns (Markoe 2000: 182–6).

† Another ideographic system, invented at the other end of Asia, had similar effects. The Japanese, Korean and Vietnamese languages, all of which became literate through the use of Chinese characters, have sustained major linguistic (and cultural) borrowings from Chinese which are by and large still present today.

in 562 BC. Twenty-five years earlier, even as he had been conquering Jerusa-lem, and deporting its Jews, others were beginning a process of political con-solidation that would erase the greatness of Babylon. The Medes defeated the Urartians in the 580s and so established control of most of the north; but in 550 BC they themselves succumbed to a royal putsch executed by their south-western neighbour Persia, under its new king Cyrus. Cyrus went on to absorb first Lydia (thus grabbing the rest of Anatolia), then the eastern extremities of Iran, as far as modern Tajikistan, Afghanistan and Baluchistan. Finally he turned on the Babylonian empire itself, and took it with hardly a battle. His son Cambyses even conquered Egypt, though he died soon after. By 522 BC, there was a single overlord of all the land from Anatolia and Egypt to the borders of modern Turkestan and the Indus valley. If this had been a typical Mesopotamian achievement, a collapse would have been expected within a generation; but Persians used different methods, and the unitary empire they had created was to last for two hundred years.

The overlord's name was Darius, and he had administrative talents com-parable to Cyrus's genius for winning victories and retaining the loyalty of those conquered. Most interestingly from our point of view, he decreed that the administrative language of the empire should be not Persian or Lydian, but Aramaic. The result was the effective spread of the use of this Semitic language beyond all previous bounds—across to the coast of the Aegean, the Balkans and Egypt in the west, and out to the Hindu Kush and the banks of the Indus in the east.

This decision must have been purely pragmatic, for Aramaic was not the language that Persian royalty, the Achaemenid clan, actually spoke. Perhaps to remedy this problem, the same reign undertook to make Persian too a lit-erary language for the first time, devising a syllabary with which to write it (based on cuneiform symbols) and using it, together with Elamite and Akka-dian, on monumental inscriptions. (The Aramaic alphabet, which could just as easily have been used to write Persian, was evidently seen as too informal for imperial monuments.) But the script did not catch on, and had been aban-doned by 338 BC, even before the fall of the Persian empire to the Greeks. Nonetheless, the spoken language lived on, and indeed flourished, since it is the ancestor of the modern Persian language and related dialects, spoken in Iran up to the present day.

Although Aramaic did not live on as the language of western Asia, the unification of administrative language by Darius, essentially realised during the next two hundred years of Persian administration, had a number of impor-tant consequences.

It created a familiarity with administration conducted in a lingua franca, separate from the vernacular languages. So the structures were in place to allow the rapid spread of Greek, for the same purposes, after the fall of the empire to Alexander and his successors. Greek flowed through channels made for Aramaic for the next two hundred years. (See Chapter 6, 'Kings of Asia: Greek spread through war', p. 243.)

This superficial linguistic unity gave different long-term results in the various parts of the empire. In Anatolia, Greek seems to have gone deeper in its two centuries than Aramaic had: it replaced all the remaining indigenous languages. (These had largely been Lydian and its smaller relatives, but also Phrygian, the language of King Midas.) In the area of modern Iran and Afghanistan, where Iranian languages related to Persian were widely spoken, it supplanted Aramaic as lingua franca, but did not touch the vernaculars. The newly founded Greek colonies, however far flung, were of course exceptions to this.[7] In Mesopotamia, Syria, Palestine and Egypt, Greek made little headway with the general public against Aramaic; but certain local groups, such as long-distance merchants, and surprisingly the Jews resident in Alexandria in Egypt, seem to have taken it up.

The advent of the Romans in the west, and the Parthians in the east, in the middle of the second century BC, meant that Greek was challenged. It responded in different ways. To Latin, it yielded legal and military uses, but very little else, so that Syria, Palestine and Egypt found themselves now areas where three languages or more were in contention. But before Parthian, which was a close relative of Persian (and whose speakers shared allegiance to the Zoroastrian scriptures, the Avesta), Greek was effectively eliminated, while Aramaic had something of a resurgence at least as a written language. Its use went on to inspire all but one of the writing systems henceforth used for the Iranian languages, Parthian and Persian (Pahlavi) in the west, Khwarezmian, Sogdian and the Scythian languages Śaka and Ossetic in the east, as well as for the Avesta scriptures themselves.*

Aramaic was by now an official language nowhere, and a majority-community language only in the Fertile Crescent. Nevertheless, it remained the predominant language over this large area for almost a thousand years until the seventh century AD, when a completely new language overwhelmed it.

This was Arabic, brought with Islamic inspiration and a fervent will by the early converts of the prophet Muḥammad. The progress of this virtually un-

---

* The one exception is Bactrian, later to become the language of the Kushāna empire (first to second centuries AD), written in the Greek alphabet. This shows the lasting cultural influence of the independent Greek dynasties in the far east, whom the Kushāna supplanted.

known language over two generations, so as to cover the whole Near East to the borders of Iran, and the whole of North Africa to the Pillars of Hercules, is one of the most striking events in history. But its progress was not totally irresistible: and it will be interesting, when we describe it in greater detail below, to ponder the linguistic obstacles that proved unyielding.

This ends our exhaustingly rapid review of language leapfrog in West Asia, a linguistic zone which ultimately expanded to take in most of North Africa. We can now slow down a little, and look more closely at some of the individual languages: many were unique pioneers in the known language history of the world.

Sumerian—the first classical language: Life after death

Father Enki answers Ninshubur:
'What has happened to my daughter! I am troubled,
What has happened to Inanna! I am troubled,
What has happened to the queen of all the lands! I am troubled,
What has happened to the hierodule of heaven! I am troubled.'
From his fingernail he brought forth dirt, fashioned the *kurgarru*,
From his other fingernail he brought forth dirt, fashioned the *kalaturru*.
To the *kurgarru* he gave the food of life.
To the *kalaturru* he gave the water of life.
Father Enki says to the *kalaturru* and *kurgarru*: ...
'Sixty times the food of life, sixty times the water of life, sprinkle upon
    it,
Surely Inanna will arise.'[8]

Sumerian knows better than any the tantalising evanescence of life and fame for a language. All knowledge of this language had been lost for almost two thousand years when the royal library of the ancient Assyrian capital, Nineveh, was excavated in 1845, and it turned out that the earliest documents were written in a language older than Akkadian, and so different from it that the Assyrians of the seventh century BC had approached it armed with a student's panoply of bilingual dictionaries, grammars and parallel texts. Nothing in the Greek or biblical record of Mesopotamia had prepared the new researchers to expect such an alien foundation for this civilisation; the majority of the documents after all were written in a language reassuringly similar to Hebrew and Aramaic. Whatever had survived down the ages of the greatness of Nineveh and Babylon, the linguistic basis of their achievements had been totally effaced.

Sumerian, the original speech of *Šumer*, as they called the southernmost part of Mesopotamia, had in fact already been dead for another 1300 years when those documents from Sennacherib's library were written. But it turned out that the only way to understand Akkadian cuneiform writing was to see it as an attempt to reinterpret a sign system that had been designed for Sumerian use. The intricacy, and probably the prestige, of the early Sumerian writing had been such that any outsiders who wanted to adopt it for their own language had largely had to take the Sumerian language with it.

This was not too big a problem in cases where signs had a clear meaning: signs that stood for Sumerian words were just given new pronunciations, and read as the corresponding words in Akkadian. But Akkadian was a very different language from Sumerian, both in phonetics and in the structure of its words. Since no new signs were introduced for Akkadian, these differences largely had to be ignored: in effect, Akkadian speakers resigned themselves to writing their Akkadian as it might be produced by someone with a heavy Sumerian accent. Sumerian signs that were read phonetically went on being read as they were in Sumerian, but put together to approximate Akkadian words; and where Akkadian had sounds that were not used in Sumerian, they simply made do with whatever was closest.

So Sumerian survived its death as a living language in at least two ways. It lived on as a classical language, its great literary works canonised and quoted by every succeeding generation of cuneiform scribes. But it also lived on as an imposed constraint on the expression of Akkadian, and indeed any subsequent language that aspired to use the full cuneiform system of writing, as Elamite, Hurrian, Luwian, Hittite and Urartian were to do, over the next two millennia. It is as if modern western European languages were condemned to be written as closely as possible to Latin, with a smattering of phonetic annotations to show how the time-honoured Roman spellings should be pronounced to give a meaningful utterance in Dutch, Irish, French or English.*

The origin of Sumerian is obscure; only some Georgians claim that their language is related,[9] but the claim has not been widely accepted. Whatever their previous history, there was evidently a lively set of communities active in southern Mesopotamia from the fourth millennium BC, absorbing the gains from the then recent institutionalisation of agriculture, and establishing the first cities, which seem first of all to have been collectives each holding all

---

* And this is precisely what we do with our number symbols, whether Arabic or Roman.

their goods in the name of a presiding deity, with effective managerial power in the hands of the priesthood. The potter's wheel, the swing-plough and the sail all came into use, and a beginning was made in working gold, silver and bronze. Since pictograms, and their development into cuneiform writing, were invented in this period, this gives us our first direct testimony of the language history of the world. It seems that commercial uses came first: impressions of symbols on clay began as convenient substitutes for sets of clay tokens, used for inventories and contracts.[10]

The unprecedented riches and cultural brilliance of the city-states in third-millennium Sumer had soon attracted unwelcome attention from the north, resulting in a hostile takeover and political consolidation under the king of Akkad. The result of Sargon's invasion in the twenty-fourth century, and the five generations of Akkadian dominance that followed, must have been much greater contact between the Sumerian and Akkadian languages. Sumerian–Akkadian bilingualism would have become common in the elite, and one can see evidence of this at the highest level, since Sargon's daughter Enheduanna is supposed to have composed two cycles of Sumerian hymns, and the most famous (to Inanna) has been found in some fifty copies.[11]

This participation by women, especially princesses and priestesses, in Sumerian literature was not uncommon. They wrote funeral hymns, letters and especially love songs.

> Thy city lifts its hand like a cripple, O my lord Shu-Sin,
> It lies at thy feet like a lion-cub, O son of Shulgi.
> O my god, the wine-maid has sweet wine to give,
> Like her date-wine sweet is her vulva, sweet is her wine…[12]

There is also the occasional lullaby.

> *usa ŋanu usa ŋanu*
> *usa ŋanu ki dumuŋaše*
> *usa kulu ki dumuŋaše*
> *igi badbadani u kunib*
> *igi gunani šuzu ŋarbi*
> *u eme za malilikani*
> *za mallilil u nagule…*

> Come sleep, come sleep,
> Come to my son,
> Hurry sleep to my son,

Put to sleep his restless eyes,
Put your hand on his sparkling eyes,
And as for his babbling tongue
Let not the babbling hold back his sleep.

He will fill your lap with wheat.
I will make sweet for you the little cheeses,
Those little cheeses that are the healer of man...
My garden is lettuce well-watered...

May the wife be your support,
May the son be your lot,
May the winnowed barley be your bride,
May Ashnan the goddess of fruitfulness be your ally,
May you have an eloquent guardian angel,
May you achieve a reign of happy days...[13]

These works are usually written in *Emesal*, 'the fine tongue', a separate dialect of Sumerian, well documented in scribal dictionaries. In dialogue works this dialect is used for the speech of goddesses. It differs from standard Sumerian, *Emegir*, 'the princely tongue', both in vocabulary (including the names of many gods) and also in pronunciation (consonants by and large being articulated farther forward in the mouth); it differs not at all in its grammar. For example, when the goddess Inanna is affecting to repel the advances of an importunate suitor, she cries:

kuli Mulila šu bamu emeše daŋen
amaŋu lulaše ta munaben
amaŋu Gašangale lulaše ta munaben

Friend of Enlil, let me free! Let me go to my house!
What lie shall I tell my mother?
What lie shall I tell my mother Ningal?

Both Enlil and Ningal are, of course, gods. In Emegir this would have been (with the differences highlighted):

*kuli **Enlila** šu bamu **eŋuše gaŋen***
*amaŋu lulaše **ana** munaben*
*amaŋu **Ningale** lulaše **ana** munaben*[14]

So it seems that Sumerian, like many other languages all over the world, had a special dialect for women's speech. What marks out Sumerian is that this had gained a special, explicit, status, recorded in the grammar books: this could be taken as further evidence of the high status of women in Sumerian literature.

Returning to the question of Sumerian–Akkadian bilingualism, specialists agree that the balance of language spoken in Sumer shifted over the period 2400–1600 BC from total Sumerian to total Akkadian. Sumer began this period as a collection of independent city-states, suffered Akkadian domination in the twenty-third century, Amorite and (briefly) Elamite domination in the nineteenth, and the Babylonian rule of Hammurabi in the eighteenth. It ended with a restored independence, or rather anarchy, after the breakdown of this first Babylonian empire, but the language on the streets and in the homes was now Akkadian.

It was an interesting example of unstable bilingualism, since in many ways the situation is reminiscent of the relation between Greek and Latin in the Roman empire, one dominating cultural and the other political life. In that case, despite the political instability, and the generally shifty reputation of the Greeks, contrasting with the towering political prestige and steadiness of the Romans, Greek nowhere lost ground to Latin. Yet here in Mesopotamia, where the various Semitic peoples, for all their political dominance, were sources of disruption, where there was apparently no major movement of the Sumerian population, and where Sumerian culture's prestige was unchallenged, Sumerian steadily lost ground.

In some cases even Semitic rulers attempted to fight a rearguard action on behalf of Sumerian culture. In the kingdom of Isin, which held the three most important Sumerian cities of Nippur, Uruk and Eridu in the twentieth to nineteenth centuries BC, the ruling dynasty stemmed from Mari, in the Akkadian-speaking north of Mesopotamia; yet its king termed himself 'King of Ur, King of Sumer and Akkad', all its official inscriptions were in Sumerian, and there was flourishing production of new editions of the classics of Sumerian literature.

One factor working against the survival of Sumerian as a living language alongside Akkadian may have been the fact that the influential newcomers already spoke a Semitic language, and so found it easier just to get by in Akkadian. Only the Akkadians had lived in close proximity with Sumerian from time immemorial, and perhaps become bilingual. Others would be more impatient of the cultural complications they found down south. It is easy to imagine the average Amorite on the move saying: 'After all, they all speak Akkadian, don't they?' The whole Fertile Crescent was familiar with some

Semitic language or other, and by their nature they were all very similar, and to some extent mutually comprehensible. For all their cultural prestige (which clearly never diminished), the Sumerians found themselves having to compromise on language in their daily and business lives.

In a sense, though, Akkadian had already taken up the burden that the speakers of Sumerian were laying down. It remained unthinkable, as it always had been, to learn to write Akkadian in any way but as an extension of Sumerian, and this despite the fact that Sumerian and Akkadian were poles apart as languages, with all their basic vocabulary totally unrelated, and quite different sound systems. The system never provided the means to distinguish consistently between *b* and *p*, among *d*, *t* and *ṭ*, or among *g*, *k* and *q* in Akkadian. Akkadian appears to be rather lacking in many of the phonetic subtleties that are characteristic of many of its Semitic sisters, having only one *h* sound where they may have up to three, three *s* sounds where they have up to four. It is difficult to tell whether it is just the poverty of Sumerian spelling which causes this appearance.

The only innovations that Akkadian scribes appear to have permitted themselves were a new sign for the glottal stop, ʾ, and considerable licence with the Sumerian word symbols or logograms: they had always been available as punning devices, able to symbolise the same sound as the word they signified in Sumerian; now they could do the same trick for Akkadian as well. So, for example, the Sumerian sign ⬚, meaning 'hand', could now be read as *idu*, 'hand', in Akkadian; it could also represent the syllables *id*, *it*, *iṭ*, *ed*, *et* and *eṭ*.

Sumerian word symbols, and Sumerian literature, remained the basis of written Akkadian, even as the language swept all round the Fertile Crescent, and well beyond the domains of the Semitic-speaking peoples, as a lingua franca for international communication. The same educational system, based on the *edubba* 'tablet-house' schools, was maintained for at least two millennia, since sign lists to teach the symbols, in the same order, have been found in the Sumerian city of Uruk dating from the third millennium and Ashurbanipal's library in the Assyrian capital Nineveh from the mid-seventh century BC. Mastery of the classics of Sumerian literature, a canon of texts which was not extended after the mid-second millennium, remained the pinnacle of scholarly achievement, and the focus of later years spent at school. Even in mathematics, most of the terminology was in Sumerian, though the textbooks were written in Akkadian. It appears that Sumerian went on being spoken in the classroom: this has made the remaining exercises and textbooks less explicit on pronunciation than we should have liked.

It is the Akkadian culture's enthusiasm for all things Sumerian which has in fact saved Sumer's finer culture. Almost all the Sumerian literary texts that have been found were copied, often by schoolboys, in the first half of the second millennium, after the death of Sumerian as a living language; by contrast, most of what has come down from the pre-Akkadian days, when the cities of Sumer were proud and free (and still spoke Sumerian), is a mass of inscriptions and administrative documents.

But this six-hundred-year-long Sumerian heyday, after the death of the living language, at last came to an end, and showed that Akkadian could not support it indefinitely. After the fall of Babylon to the marauding Hittite King Mursilis in 1594 BC, and the takeover of Mesopotamia by the Kassite mountain tribes which followed, true appreciation of Sumerian culture never recovered. For the rest of the second and first millennia (indeed down to the Greek takeover under the Seleucid empire in 323 BC), no more Sumerian compositions were attempted, and in fact only two literary texts continued to be copied: *The Exploits of Ninurta* (which we have already sampled), and a companion piece, *Angim*, about Ninurta's return from the mountains to Nippur. Henceforth, the rest of the Sumerian classics would be known only in translation.

As a poet had remarked (on the earlier destruction of an Akkadian city that aspired to take the Sumerians under their control):

iribia gatuš bindugga kituš nummandadug
agadea ganu bindugga kinu nummandadug
agade hula inana zami.

He who said 'I would dwell in that city' found not a good dwelling place
    there.
He who said 'I would sleep in Agade' found not a good sleeping place
    there.
Agade is destroyed. Praise Inanna.[15]

Since Akkadian too was destined ultimately to be replaced—and when it happened, by a language whose literacy did not depend on the ancient tradition of cuneiform writing—Sumerian was ultimately to die out. Aside from the tablets waiting to be discovered in the tells of Iraq, it left no trace.

FIRST INTERLUDE: WHATEVER HAPPENED TO ELAMITE?

The clay tokens that had given rise to Sumerian script seem to have been widespread: not surprisingly, since they would have played a key role as bills of lading for long-distance trade. The development into groups of symbols on clay came independently in Sumer, and farther to the east in Shusim (known to the Greeks as Susa), the heartland of Elam. Elam's pictographic symbols never went far beyond their initial stage as a medium for inventories, although a proto-Elamite script, apparently a syllabary, was in use in the early third millennium. This line of development was aborted in the middle of the third millennium when the Sumerian system, which was by then a true writing system, even if one heavily adapted for the Sumerian language, was taken over.

In fact, Elam went farther than borrowing the writing system: for the nine hundred years from 2200 BC almost all the official inscriptions that have been found are in Akkadian. For much of this time it was under the direct political control of one of the powers to its west, Sumerian, Babylonian or Assyrian. Nevertheless, Elamite must have continued to be spoken in Elam, since in 1300 BC it springs back to life as the official language, replacing Akkadian for all written purposes, except curses.[16]

Elamite's subsequent career showed persistence for at least eight hundred years.

From 1300 BC Elam pursued a succession of wars, not always defensive, with its neighbours from across the Tigris marshes. Through the vagaries of these power struggles, which often resulted in periods of foreign control, Elam was able to retain its independence in the long term through retaining access to a large but defensible hinterland, Anshan, in the Zagros mountains to its south-east, never penetrated by Akkadian speakers.[17] The real disaster came only in the seventh century BC when the Elamites lost this stronghold: it was taken by the Persians, whose attack came, for the first time, from the south. Thereafter Anshan came to be called Parša. (The area is called Fars to this day.)

The Elamites had lost their safe redoubt for emergencies. Almost at once, in 646, the Assyrian Asshurbanipal sacked Susa. This calamity put an end to the last independent kingdom of Elam, if not to the Elamites or their language. But in the characteristic Assyrian way, Asshurbanipal deported many of the population, to Assyria on his own account, and according to the Book of Ezra (iv.9–10) as far away as Samaria in Palestine.

But events were now moving beyond the traditional pendulum swing of power shifts within Mesopotamia. The Elamites scarcely had the satisfaction of seeing Assyria itself fall to the Medes and Babylonians in 612 before they found themselves under Babylonian control, and then, within a generation, under Persian. This put Elam, for the first time, at the centre of world events. Two generations later, in 522 BC, Darius (*Dārayavauš*), the Persian heir to Anshan, took control of the whole Persian empire, which by now extended from Egypt and Anatolia to the borders of India. Despite two abortive Elamite rebellions shortly after his accession, he chose Elam as the hub of this empire, with Susa itself (known to him as *Šušan*) as the administrative capital, and *Parša*, i.e. Anshan, as the site for a new ceremonial capital, to be better known in the West by its Greek name of Persepolis.

The Persians had never prized literacy very highly. Famously, their leaders were educated in three things only: to ride a horse, to shoot a straight arrow, and to tell the truth. So their Elamite neighbours, with two thousand years of cuneiform education behind them, were well placed to be extremely useful in the more humdrum side of empire-building.

On the monumental inscriptions that Darius set up round his domains (most notably at Behistun, on the Silk Route), the legend was written not only in Persian and Akkadian but in Elamite. And although the official language of the empire was designated as Aramaic, it is clear that until about 460 the central administration was actually conducted in Elamite, since an archive of several thousand administrative documents on clay was discovered in Persepolis in the 1930s. They most likely owed their preservation to fire-raising by Alexander's conquering soldiers in 330 BC.

But these are the last Elamite documents to have survived anywhere.[18] Aramaic took over as the language of written administration, and Elamite, lacking any political focus to sustain the cuneiform tradition, apparently ceased to be written. Some time later, perhaps much later, the spoken language too must have simply died away. Arabs writing in the tenth century AD mention a language spoken in Khuzistan which was not Persian, Arabic or Hebrew: they do not record any words, so no one knows whether that was the last of Elamite.[19]

It has been speculated that Sumer and Akkad's struggles for control of the mountains behind Elam, with their raw material riches in stone, timber and metals, may be reflected somewhat abstractly in the surviving literature of the period.[20] In the poem *Lugale u melambi nirgal*, known in English as *The Exploits of Ninurta*, the god greets his mother, who has come to visit him in his mountain conquests:

Since you, Madam, have come to the rough lands,
Since you, Noble Lady, because of my fame, have come to the enemy land,
Since you feared not my terrifying battles,

I, the hero, the mound I had heaped up
Shall be called *hursag*, and you shall be its queen,
From now on *Ninhursag* is the name by which you shall be called—thus
it shall be.

...

The *hursag* shall provide you amply with the fragrance of the gods,
Shall provide you with gold and silver in abundance,
Shall mine for you copper and tin, shall carry them to you as tribute,
The rough places shall multiply cattle large and small for you,
The *hursag* shall bring forth for you the seed of all four-legged
creatures.[21]

In fact the king who had achieved the conquest of Elam and Anshan had been
Gudea of Lagash (2141–2122 BC): and he served the god Ningirsu, not
Ninurta. Still, Ninurta was the god of Nippur, which later became the cultural
centre of the Sumerian cities, and so the change of central god would have
given the piece a certain disinterested grandeur, which fitted it to be the literary classic it became.

Akkadian—world-beating technology: A model of literacy

Now all the earth had one language and words in common. And moving
east, people found a plain in Shinar and settled there. And they said to
each other: 'Come, let us make bricks and bake them thoroughly!' They
used brick instead of stone, and tar instead of mortar. Then they said:
'Come, let us build ourselves a city, with a tower that reaches to the
heavens, so that we may make a name for ourselves and not be scattered
over the face of the whole earth.' But Yahweh came down to see the city
that the sons of man were building. And Yahweh said: 'So this is what
they can do when all share one language! There will be no limit on what
they can accomplish if they have a mind for it. I shall go down and stu-
pefy their languages so that they may not understand one another.' So
Yahweh scattered them from there all over the earth. And they stopped
building the city. That is why it is called Babylon (*bābĕl*) because there
he mixed up (*bālăl*) the language of all the earth. And from there Yahweh scattered them all over the earth.

Hebrew scriptures, Genesis x

This Jewish myth, evidently inspired by the stupendous architecture on show
in the cosmopolitan city of Babylon, and the polyphony of languages to be

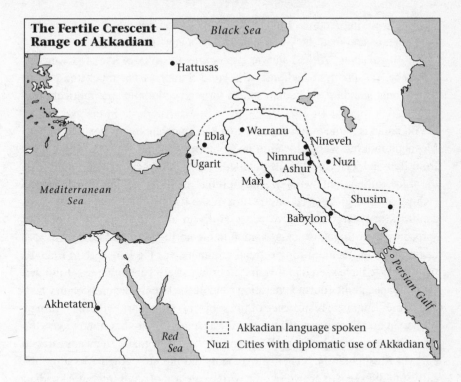

The Fertile Crescent – Range of Akkadian

Black Sea

Hattusas

Ebla   Warranu

Nineveh

Nimrud   Nuzi

Ugarit   Ashur

Mari

Mediterranean Sea

Shusim

Babylon

Persian Gulf

Akhetaten

Red Sea

Akkadian language spoken

Nuzi   Cities with diplomatic use of Akkadian

heard on its streets, is still deeply symbolic for European culture. But some-how the central mechanism of conflict between an arrogant superpower and a jealous god has been lost. It is now taken as a story of how a single language can give unity, the kind of unity that is necessary to bring off a magnificent enterprise: just confound their languages, and cooperation becomes impossi-ble. As such, it is bizarrely ill placed as a fable of Babylon, which was notable throughout its history for the leading role of a single language. For almost two thousand years this language was Akkadian, although in the last few cen-turies of its empire, as already seen, it yielded to Aramaic.

Perhaps the dream of Babylonians scattered and disorganised was a com-forting exercise in wish fulfilment for the sixth-century Jews who had been shattered and driven from their homeland by the Babylonian emperor Neb-uchadrezzar II. Perhaps it might even be taken as an ironic comment on how the Assyrian Asshurbanipal had been able to sack Babylon in the seventh century: many Babylonian traditionalists must after all have questioned the spreading influence of those rough-talking Aramaeans, and speculated that no good would come of it. But although Babylon was to lose its glory in time—indeed, very soon after Nebuchadrezzar—its decline cannot be blamed on language decadence, or some failure in communication. People went on speaking Aramaic, and studying Akkadian, for many centuries after the Persians, and then the Greeks, had taken away all their power.

Yet at its acme, Akkadian was pre-eminently a language of power and influence. If Sumerian had spread beyond Sumer as the touchstone of an educational standard, Akkadian spread through economic and political prestige.

Akkadian is named after Agade or Akkad, once the major city of southern Mesopotamia but whose location is now a mystery. (It was possibly not far from Babylon.) Records of the language begin in earnest with the middle of the third millennium, with an early climax in those conquests by Sargon (whose long reign centred on the turn of the twenty-fouth and twenty-third centuries BC). He campaigned successfully in all directions, thus not only spreading the official use of Akkadian in the north (Mari and Ebla), but also beginning a millennium-long official dominance of the language in Elam to the west. We have seen that this first fit of imperial exuberance was followed by a collapse in the fourth generation (end of the twenty-second century BC), and a brief linguistic resurgence of the subject populations, with the return of Sumerian and Elamite to official use for a century or so. Soon, however, the Amorites, Semitic-speaking 'Westerners', began to make their appearance all over Mesopotamia.* Their movements did not strengthen Akkad politically, but did seem to crowd out the wide-scale use of anything but Akkadian as a means of communication; and the written record (outside literature) from the beginning of the second millennium is exclusively in this language.

In the early days, there was some parity, and perhaps some specialisation of function, as between Akkadian and Sumerian: we have already noted that Sargon's own daughter had been an accomplished poetess in Sumerian. But the bilingualism proved unstable. While Akkadian was fortified as the major language of the Fertile Crescent by its everyday use for all literate purposes, and some degree of mutual intelligibility with the Semitic languages of the west, Sumerian was guaranteed only by its role in education and culture. The period of the rise of Babylon (2000–1600 BC) still fostered this, but when the power bases were shattered, and foreign rulers (the Kassites) took over, serious learning in Sumerian must have seemed an irrelevance. It was re-

---

* The Amorites did not have their own literate tradition, but their language can be partially reconstructed when their names are quoted in other languages, usually Sumerian. This provides a link with the later western Semitic languages, such as Ugaritic, Phoenician and Hebrew, which do not show up in the written record for another five hundred years or more. Since there was a tendency to assign names that are full sentences, they give a fuller picture of the language than might have been expected: *Aya-dadu*, 'Where is Daddu?', *Šūb-addu*, 'Return, Addu!', *Yašub-'ilu*, 'God returns', *Samsu-'ilu-na*, 'The Sun is our god.'

tained merely as an adjunct to Akkadian studies, in the same spirit as the list of Latin tags sometimes still found at the end of an English dictionary.

This 'Old Babylonian' period turned out to be as significant for Akkadian as it was for Sumerian, but in a different way. It was in this period that some fairly slight dialect differences are first noticeable between the south (Babylonian) and the north (Assyrian). Different dialects of Akkadian also become visible farther afield, in Mari, in Susa and to the east in the valley of the Diyala. Letters are extant from all periods, and provide the best evidence for spoken language.

At the same time, the dialect of Babylon (which even the Babylonians still called *Akkadū*) became established as the literary standard, the classic version of which would be used for official purposes throughout Mesopotamia. This privileged position endured for the rest of the language's history, essentially regardless of whether Babylon, Assyria or neither of them was the current centre of political power. The great model of classic Babylonian is the Laws of Hammurabi, compiled in the eighteenth century BC when this dialect was still the vernacular. But the best-known literary texts, such as the Epic of Gilgamesh and *Enuma eliš* ('When on high...', the Creation Epic), are also in this dialect, written down when it was no longer current.

In the north, the use of Akkadian was to die out about 600 BC, fully replaced by Aramaic. But use of the language persisted in Babylon till the beginning of the first century AD; it seems that by this stage most of the knowledge of the language was in the hands of professional scribes, who would read, write and translate even personal letters—but not without interference from the Aramaic in which they were actually thinking and talking.

Besides its use as a native language by most of the inhabitants of Mesopotamia, and its historic role as the first language of literacy for Semites anywhere, Akkadian also came to achieve a wider role as a lingua franca among utter foreigners. How was this possible? Ultimately, it was due to its association with the most sophisticated technology of its day, writing.

The first evidence of this cosmopolitan spread is the activity of Assyrian merchants in central Anatolia far to the north of the Taurus mountains, in a complex of market centres or *karum* set up between Nesas and Hattusas (Kültepe and Boğaz Köy on modern maps). This was in the first quarter of the second millennium, 1950–1750 BC. The merchants came from rich families of Asshur, and used donkey caravans for transport through the Taurus mountains. Their motive was trade in metals: they had found a source of silver, gold and copper. In the reverse direction, they brought tin, goat-hair felt, woven textiles and perfumes. The traders were apparently ready to pay duties to the local Hatti authorities. This is known from the trading correspondence (on clay tablets in clay envelopes) which they left behind, written in Old Assyrian, a dialect of Akkadian.

The trade seems to have been ended around 1750, perhaps by Hurrian incursions, perhaps by the first stirrings of Hittite expansion, the campaigns of the kings of Kussara. This, however, was already a distant memory by the time we find it described in the earliest chronicles of the Hittites themselves, written in the Nesas–Hattusas area about four hundred years later. And these, of course, are written in a cuneiform script, with copious use of Sumerian and Akkadian logograms, which itself derived from the Akkadian tradition.

The Hittites provide just one example of how Akkadian was taken up by the literate class in surrounding states. In the second millennium, Akkadian was being taught and used in every capital city that surrounded Mesopotamia, essentially regardless of the ambient language. Just going by the documents so far found which date from the middle of the second millennium, we can see that the same Sumerian *edubba* system was being practised in Susa for Elamite speakers, in Nuzi (modern Yorgan Tepe near Kirkuk) for Hurrians, in Hattusas for Hittites and Luwians, in Alalah and Ugarit near the Mediterranean coast for speakers of other Semitic languages as well as Hurrian, and in Akhetaten (briefly the Egyptian capital) for Egyptians.

The linguistic situations of the various nations were differently nuanced: in this period it seems that Elam, for example, had different segments of the population using predominantly either Akkadian (in the northern plain) or Elamite (in the mountainous south), while in Ugarit there was a much more general bilingualism, so that texts in Akkadian intended for home consumption may be tricked out with the odd explanatory gloss in Ugaritic.[22] But whatever the home situation, the general practice seemed to be that Akkadian was used for international correspondence, and often for treaties.

The classic demonstration of this is the Amarna correspondence, a cache of diplomatic letters from the fourteenth century BC, found on the site of the then Egyptian capital. There are 350 letters and attachments in this collection, and all but three are in Akkadian (two in Hittite and one in Hurrian).

It is interesting to reflect on how Akkadian had achieved this role as an international lingua franca. The middle of the second millennium was not a glorious period for the speakers of Semitic languages. In 1400 BC Babylon had been firmly under Kassite control for two centuries, and Assyria in vassalage to the Mitanni for a century. In northern Syria, established Mitanni control was being disputed by the Hittites. And the rest of Palestine was a collection of vassal states under Egyptian sovereignty.

It was not recent political influence, then, which made Akkadian the language of convenience at this time. The only explanation is a cultural one, and specifically the matter of literacy, and the culture of the scribal *edubba*.

With the exception of Egypt, and its trading partners in Phoenicia, every one of the powers had become literate in the course of the previous millennium through absorbing the cuneiform culture of Sumer and Akkad. As we have seen, this writing system was extremely committed to its original languages, shot through with phonetic symbols that only made sense in terms of puns in Sumerian and Akkadian, and taught in practice through large-scale copying of the classics of Sumerian and Akkadian literature. Although Babylonia and Assyria aspired to be world empires—and both would see themselves at least once more as mistress of the whole Fertile Crescent—their cultural dominance was almost wholly a matter of having been the leaders in a shared language technology.

The next, and last, great question in the history of Akkadian is why its dominance, and indeed its use, came to an end. One thing that the history of this language does teach is that the life and death of languages are in principle detached from the political fortunes of their associated states. For curiously, just as Akkadian had reached the height of its prestige and extension during a long eclipse of Assyro-Babylonian power, its decline began when the Assyrian empire was at its zenith.

The paradox deepens the more closely it is considered. Not only was Akkadian, the language replaced, at the height of its political influence: its replacement language, Aramaic, had until recently been spoken mainly by nomads. These people could claim no cultural advantage, and were highly unlikely to set up a rival civilisation. The expectation would have been that, like the Kassites eight hundred years before in Babylon, Aramaic speakers would have been culturally and linguistically assimilated to the great Mesopotamian tradition. Similar things, after all, were to happen to others who burst in upon great empires—the Germans invading the Roman empire, or the Mongols the Chinese.

But it was in the cultural sphere that the Aramaic speakers brought their greatest surprise. They did assimilate largely to Akkadian culture, certainly. But there was one crucial respect in which they did not, the epoch-making one of language technology. With Aramaic came a new tradition of writing, which used an alphabetic script. Along with this revolution in language representation came new writing materials: people wrote their notes, and increasingly their formal records and literary texts, on new media, sheets of papyrus or leather.

These changes went to the heart of Assyrian and Babylonian culture; so much so that the traditional view has been that it explains the triumph of

Aramaic as a language. So Georges Roux, for example, writes: 'Yet to these barbaric Aramaeans befell the privilege of imposing their language upon the entire Near East. They owed it partly to the sheer weight of their number and partly to the fact that they adopted, instead of the cumbersome cuneiform writing, the Phoenician alphabet slightly modified, and carried everywhere with them the simple, practical script of the future.'[23] And John Sawyer: 'The success of Aramaic was undoubtedly due in the main to the fact that it was written in a relatively easy alphabetical script.'[24]

This cannot be right. Writing systems, after all, exist to record what people say, not vice versa. There is no other case in history of a change in writing technology inducing a change in popular speech. And even if it were possible, it is particularly unlikely in a society like the Assyrian empire, where a vanishingly small portion of the population were literate. The real significance of the change in writing system that came with the Aramaic is to give an extra dimension to the Aramaic paradox: how could a mobile, and politically subservient, group such as the Aramaeans not only spread its language but also get its writing system accepted among its cultural and political masters, the Assyrians and Babylonians?

The answer lies in an unexpected effect of Assyrian military policy.

We have already noted the first hostile contacts between the Aramaean nomads and the Assyrians, at the end of the twelfth century. The Aramaeans, coming in from the wilderness of northern Syria, were able, presumably by force of arms, to settle all over the inhabited parts of that country. They did not limit themselves to the area of Damascus, but spread out north, south and, significantly, to the east. The whole area of the upper reaches of the Euphrates between the rivers Balikh and Khabur became known as *Aram Naharaim*, 'Aram of the Rivers'. Their progress southward towards Babylon was steady: they smashed the temple of Shamash in Sippar in the middle of the eleventh century, and by the early tenth century were sufficiently settled around Babylon to cut it off from its suburb Barsippa, and so prevent the proper celebration of New Year Festival, which required the idols of Marduk and Nabu to process to and from Babylon. Meanwhile, in the north, Assyrian resistance proved equally unable to stop their advance, and by the beginning of the ninth century they were on the banks of the Tigris itself.

The first successful resistance came from the Assyrian king Adad-nirâri (911–891 BC), who drove the Aramaeans out of the Tigris valley and the Kashiari mountains to the north. Thereafter, the Assyrian kings began a policy of annual campaigns against one or other of their neighbours, a policy of unrestrained aggression which lasted over 150 years, pausing only when the aggression turned inward, during the major civil wars of 827–811 and 754–

745. Within a hundred years the whole Fertile Crescent was under their control, together with southern Anatolia as far as Tarsus, and large swathes of Elam in the east. Farther afield, they undertook a punitive expedition deep into Urartu (eastern Anatolia) and even a brief, but unsustainable, invasion of Egypt.

Truly these were glory days for Assyria, but that seems to have been the sole point of these wars: after a victory, a ruinous demand for tribute was imposed on the defeated city or tribe. There is no evidence, in Assyrian business correspondence or the archaeological record, of any subsequent attempt to spread Assyrian culture thereafter, or even to establish the ruling caste on a wider basis. Wealth was transferred one way, and at the point of a sword. From Tiglath-Pileser III (744–727) to Sennacherib (704–681), a new tactic was added: vast numbers of the conquered populations were led off to some other distant part of the empire. Estimates attribute thirty-seven deportations to Tiglath-Pileser III (totalling 368,543 people), thirty-eight to Sargon II (totalling 217,635), twenty to Sennacherib (totalling 408,150). All in all, the Assyrians claimed to have displaced some 4.5 million persons over three centuries.[25]

A majority of these deportations would have involved Aramaic speakers, although the most famous, carried out by Sargon II against Samaria, capital of Israel, in 721 BC, probably involved speakers of Hebrew:

At the beginning of my rule, I took the town of the Samarians for the god…who let me achieve this triumph. I led away as prisoners 27,290 inhabitants of it and equipped from among them soldiers to man 50 chariots for my royal corps…The town I rebuilt better than it was before and settled therein people from countries which I myself had conquered. I placed an officer of mine as governor over them and imposed upon them tribute as for Assyrian citizens.[26]

The Hebrew scriptures (2 Kings xvii.6, 24) give more details of where the Israelite exiles were sent (including Aram Naharaim on the Khabur river, and the north-eastern extremity of the empire in Media), and of who were sent to replace them. (They included some Babylonians.)

Now and then, correspondence gives an insight into how these deportees were viewed when they arrived in Mesopotamia.[27] A letter to the king contrasts *qinnāte ša Ninua labīrūti*, 'old-time families of Nineveh', with *nasi ʾānni*, 'social upstarts', and *šaglūti*, 'deportees', itself perhaps a pun on *šaklūti*, 'ignorants'. But it is clear that people with western Semitic names were often entrusted with significant responsibility.

This scattering of Assyria's subject peoples could be seen as a shrewd policy to unify the diverse populations of the empire by cutting them off from their traditions—an imposed 'melting pot' solution.[28] All deportees, as the above inscription mentioned, are to be 'regarded as Assyrians'; as such they were deemed to have a duty to *palāḫ ili u šarri*, 'to fear God and King'.

Tending in the same direction was another new policy to buttress imperial unity, the recruitment of a royal guard, the *kisir šarruti*. This was drawn from non-Mesopotamian provinces, supplementing the more feudally organised Assyrian troops. In fact, bearers of western Semitic names crop up quite commonly as Assyrian army officers. Particularly famous was the force of *Itu'aia*, made up of Aramaeans of the *Itu'* tribe, which turns up at many of the hot spots, on duty to crush dissent within Babylonian provinces.[29]

The situation in the Fertile Crescent, then, over the period of the eleventh to the eighth century BC, was one of an extreme flux of populations. Aramaeans had settled themselves over the whole area in the earlier two centuries, and although they had been under more effective state control in the latter two, Assyrian policy had served not to push them back but to distribute them even more widely, either as forced migrants, or as members of the armed forces. Since the Aramaeans were the largest group being scattered in this way, when other western Semites, such as Israelites or Phoenicians, found themselves transplanted, they could tend to find themselves speaking more and more like their new neighbours.*

The Assyrians had therefore contrived to reinforce the spread of a new lingua franca across their domains, one that was not dependent on literacy or any shared educational tradition. Its effective usefulness would have increased as the Assyrian domain was spread yet wider, and its population of western Semitic speakers, predominantly Aramaic speakers, came to outnumber more and more the original population of Mesopotamia, who spoke Akkadian. The ruling class in the triad of capital cities, Asshur, Nineveh and Kalhu (Nimrud), maintained continuity, but elsewhere there was increasing social flux, and people had to make accommodations with the newcomers. In Babylon, particularly, this must have happened early on.

Nor were the newcomers handicapped by lack of the basic art of civilisation, literacy. Although the Aramaeans had appeared originally as nomads, presumed illiterate, they had even before the first millennium began taken over cities (most notably Damascus) and whole countries (the last Hittite

---

* This, after all, is exactly what happened to the various tribes of Angles, Saxons, Jutes and Danes who settled along with Frisians in Britain in the first millennium AD. Middle English, closest to Frisian, was the result.

kingdom, its capital at modern Zincirli, in the Turkish province still known as Hatay). Many of them would have come to know the value of writing, and since the cities they knew were of the west, the writing system they would have learnt was simple and alphabetic.

As they moved eastward, we can only presume that alphabetic literacy spread with at least some of the Aramaeans, since the new materials, ink and papyrus or leather, are biodegradable, and do not survive in the archaeological record. In fact, the earliest inscriptions in Aramaic, not clearly distinguishable from Canaanite languages at this time, are from the middle of the ninth century.[30] The short-term practical advantages of the new media (less bulk, greater capacity) must soon have made an impression. A new word for 'scribe' came into use in Akkadian, *sēpiru*, as opposed to the old *ṭupsarru*, 'tablet writer', which went right back to the Sumerian word *dubsar*. Pictures of scribes at work from the mid-eighth century show them in pairs, one with a stylus and a tablet, the other with a pen and a sheet of papyrus or parchment. As with the onset of computers, good bureaucrats must have ensured that the old and the new coexisted for a long time: the 'clay-free office' did not happen in Assyria till the destruction of the empire by the Medes in 610 BC.*

The net result seems to have been that spoken use of Akkadian receded before that of Aramaic with scarce a murmur of complaint. An officer in Ur does once ask permission to write to the king in Aramaic.[31] But no pedantic or puristic murmur has yet been found in any Akkadian tablet. The closest we have is an exchange of correspondence between a scribe and King Sargon (721–705):

SCRIBE: If it please my Lord, I will write an [Aramaic] document.
SARGON: Why do you not write Akkadian?[32]

Indeed, on the evidence of the pattern of words borrowed in Akkadian from Aramaic, as against those borrowed in the reverse direction, it has been claimed that Akkadian, by the time the changeover was taking place, was the less favoured language, with those who wrote it essentially thinking in Aramaic, while struggling (and failing) to put their Aramaic verbs out of their minds.[33]

The triumph of Aramaic over Akkadian must be ascribed as one of practical utility over ancient prestige, but the utility came primarily from the fact that so many people already spoke it. The fact that its associated writing system was quicker and easier was an added bonus; if anything, it just re-

* In Babylon some diehards were still writing Akkadian on clay six centuries later.

moved one argument that might have made sections of the Aramaic-speaking population want to learn Akkadian too. After all, what was the point? One would never be accepted as anything other than *šaglūti*; and even the royal court was taking up Aramaic.

As once had Sumerian, so now Akkadian fell victim to a new language brought by nomads and newcomers; unstable bilingualism followed, together with the death of the older language.

In such times, the only argument for an education in Akkadian was to maintain the link with the literature of the previous two thousand years, and the traditions of grandeur associated with the great cities of Mesopotamia. It lived on in Babylon as a classical language for six hundred years after its probable death: not only did the last dynasty of Babylon (625–539 BC) use it for chronicles of their rule, despite being of Chaldaean (i.e. Aramaic) extraction, but foreign conquerors, the Persians Cyrus (557–529 BC) and Xerxes (485–465 BC) and even the Greek Antiochus Soter (280–261 BC), all left inscriptions in the royal language glorifying their own reigns. There was certainly a new and, some would say, barbarous resonance when a Greek monarch could write: 'I am *An-ti- ʾu-ku-us* [Antiochus], the great king, the legitimate king, the king of the world, king of *E* [Babylon], king of all countries, the caretaker of the temples Esagila and Ezida, the first born of *Si-lu-uk-ku* [Seleucus], *Ma-ak-ka-du-na-a-a* [Macedonian], king of Babylon.'[34]

But there were few who could still understand them.*

Phoenician—commerce without culture: Canaan, and points west

מִי כְצוֹר כְּדֻמָה בְּתוֹךְ הַיָּם

mī ḵǝ-ṣōr kǝ-dumāh bǝṯōḵ hayyām

Who was ever silenced like Tyre, surrounded by the sea?†

Ezekiel xxvii.32

---

* As it happens, the last we hear about Akkadian is from a Syrian novelist writing in Greek in the second century AD: Iamblikhos (whose strange name is evidently Aramaic or Arabic, *ya-mlik*, 'may he rule') said he had learnt 'Babylonian' from his Babylonian tutor, a man 'learned in the wisdom of the barbarians'. (The third-hand source for this can be traced from Stephens and Winkler 1995: 181.)
† Hebrew and Phoenician include some of the complexities of their grammar in their spelling: most of the stop consonants are pronounced as fricatives in the middle of a word. In our romanisation, we

The Canaan sisters grew up together, but then set out on very different paths in life.

Phoenicia (not her real name, but one that recalls the lustrous colour for which she was famous*) chose the high life, and became associated with jewellery, fine clothing and every form of luxury. She travelled extensively, became known and admired in all the best social circles, and was widely imitated for her sophisticated skills in communication. She surrounded herself with all the most creative, intelligent and wealthy people of her era, and as a skilled hostess put them in contact with one another. She also had a daughter, Elissa, who was not perhaps as brilliant or as versatile as her mother, but who set up her own household, and went on to expand her mother's network, when Phoenicia's own energies were waning.

The other sister, Judith, had an obscure and perhaps disreputable youth, but then settled down to a quiet life at home. She never ventured outside her own neighbourhood, contenting herself with domestic duties. For all her homeliness, many thought she had far too high an opinion of herself, and she had considerable difficulties with local bullies: occasionally she was attacked in her own home and dragged off screaming; ultimately she lost her home altogether. All she could do was try to survive wherever she was led, in a dogged but non-assertive way, relying above all on her memories of her home as she had once kept it, and her unswerving religious devotion. She had no children of her own, but now and then she acted as a foster mother, undiscouraged though she received little gratitude or loyalty from her charges.

The world reversed the fortunes of these two sisters. Despite Phoenicia's glittering career, her enterprising nature and all her popularity, she quite suddenly disappeared, and among the people she had frequented, stimulated and dazzled for so long, she left no memory at all. Her daughter did perpetuate her memory, but in the end she did no better: she was mortally wounded by a rival, lost all her looks and wealth, and then wasted away to nothing.

---

represent this with an under- or overline: thus b̲, d̲, ḡ, k̲, p̄, t̲ are pronounced *v*, *th* (as in *then*), *gh* (a gargling sound), *ch* (as in *loch*), *f*, *th* (as in *thin*). Dots under s, t and d in Phoenician, Hebrew and Arabic mean that they are pronounced 'emphatically', giving them a somewhat dull, throaty quality.
* Agreement has never been reached on why the Greeks picked on *phoinīkes* as their word for these roaming Semitic traders. Literally it means 'date palms' (or indeed the mythical phoenix birds), but the association with *phoinos* or *phoinios*, 'gory, blood red', was always kept in mind, since the Phœnicians were the purveyors par excellence of purple-dyed fabrics, and farmed the dye's raw material, murex shellfish, on an industrial scale. The association of the colour with this part of the world goes beyond Greek: the Akkadian word for 'purple' was *kinaḫḫu*, derived from the place name *Kinaḫ(n)I*, 'Canaan' (Black et al. 2000: s.v.). Although the Hebrews lived in Canaan themselves, they used the word *kəna'aniy*, as Greeks did *phoinix*, to refer indifferently to a Phoenician or a merchant; and this seems to be what the Phoenicians called themselves.

Now it is as if Phoenicia and her daughter had never been. Yet Judith is still with us, often derided and dishonoured—especially by her foster children, who have been strangely resentful of her—but apparently as sturdy as ever. She has even, just recently, returned to her old home, and seems thereby to have gained a fresh lease of life.

This little parable points out the strange irony in the fates of the languages of the land of Canaan. Hebrew (often self-named as [yəhūdīth], 'she of Judah') and Phoenician are two of the languages of ancient Canaan, the others being Ammonite, Moabite and Edomite, spoken east of the River Jordan. There was also Ugaritic, spoken on the coast north of Phoenicia. All may have begun as the languages of nomadic tribes in this area, marauding Habiru. But some settled on the coast of Lebanon. During the first millennium BC, their trading activities developed mightily, and their language, Phoenician, became much the most widely spoken of the group. Hebrew and the others, by contrast, never became major languages, being restricted to the south-west of Canaan, and that only in the first part of that millennium. In the sixth century BC, Hebrew was weakened, and probably finished as a vernacular, by virtue of the enforced exile of the Jews to Babylon, coinciding with the spread of Aramaic all over the Babylonian empire.

Phoenician appears to have gone on being spoken on the coast of Lebanon until the first century BC (where it was replaced by Aramaic), and in North Africa until at least the fifth century AD. But although Hebrew had ceased to be spoken many centuries before this, its written and ritual use by Jews as the sacred language of Judaism had never lapsed. This underground existence was protected by a tradition of teaching in schools, and persistent reading, exposition and copying of the Jewish texts, of which the Bible's 'Old Testament' is quite a small part.*

The Canaanite languages are very much typical Semitic languages. One distinctive property they all have in common is a tendency to round their long A sound: hence Hebrew šəlōm for Arabic salām, 'peace'. In Phoenician (and Punic) this tendency goes farther, with even short A rounded to ō, and long A even more rounded to ū: so the Phoenician for eternity is ʿūlōm (versus Hebrew ʿōlām, Aramaic ʿāləm), and their chief magistrates hold the title sūfet, equivalent to Hebrew šōp̄eṭ, the word for 'judge' in the Old Testament. The

---

* This is known as the TaNaK (for Tôrāh Nəbi'îm wa-Kətûbîm, 'Law, Prophets and Scriptures'). But besides that there is the commentary on the Torah known as the Mishnah (200 BC–AD 200), the supplement known as Tosephta (AD 300), and a verse-by-verse commentary on the TaNaK, known as the Midrash (AD 200–600). These show that Hebrew continued to be written as well as read.

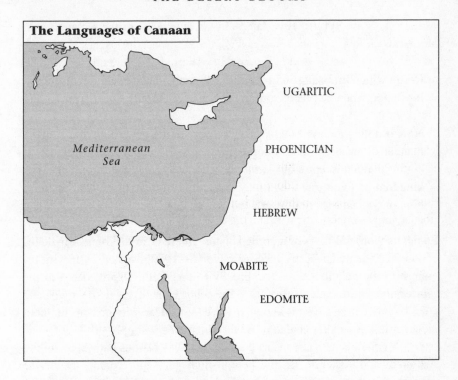

The Languages of Canaan

UGARITIC

Mediterranean Sea

PHOENICIAN

HEBREW

MOABITE

EDOMITE

evidence for Phoenician vowels is necessarily indirect, since their writing system marked consonants only.

Beyond its homeland in Lebanon, Phoenician inscriptions are found in Egypt, in southern Anatolia, in Cyprus, North Africa, Malta, Sicily, Sardinia and the south of Spain. These far-flung inscriptions tend to be in the dialect of Phoenician associated with the neighbouring cities of Tyre and Sidon, and Tyre is usually quoted as the mother city of Phoenician settlements abroad. In particular, it is the legendary original home of Elissa, or Dido, the Phoenician princess who is said to have founded Carthage (Phoenician *qart hadašt*, 'new city'). Many of the inscriptions are bilingual, showing active relations with Luwians, Greeks, Cypriots and ultimately Romans.

We also read of major Phoenician archives, the earliest being in an Egyptian tale of the eleventh century BC, where an Egyptian agent, Wen-Amun, goes to Byblos to order timber, and has to bargain aggressively with King Zakar-baal, who reads out the precedents from deals in earlier generations, written on rolls of papyrus. The city of Tyre also kept records, since Josephus records that the Greek historian Menander of Ephesus had compiled his history of Tyre from them.

As it happens, the earliest inscription in Phoenician is the epitaph of

Ahiram, king of Byblos. It is dated (by its language) to the eleventh century BC.

> Coffin which Ittobaal, son of Ahiram, king of Byblos, made for Ahiram his father, when he placed him in the house of eternity.

> Now if a king among kings or a governor among governors or a commander of an army should come up against Byblos and uncover this coffin, may the sceptre of his rule be torn away, may the throne of his kingdom be overturned, and may peace flee from Byblos! And as for him, may his inscription be effaced...

For all its thousand years of recorded history, there is no surviving artistic literature in Phoenician. However, a discovery in 1929 revealed an ancient literature in the neighbouring city directly to the north, Ugarit, dated to the fourteenth or thirteenth century BC.* The central characters in the myths and epics recorded here are gods known to have loomed large in the cults in Phoenician cities, especially Hadad or Baal (which means simply 'the Lord'), his father Dagon, a beautiful consort goddess who has various names, including Ashtoreth and Asherah, El, the benign high god, and Kothar, the divine craftsman and smith. Thirteen hundred years later, after Phoenician had largely died out as a language, one Philo of Byblos wrote in Greek a *Phoenician History*, claiming that it was derived from the work of Sanchuniathon of Beirut, who had himself read it on *ammouneis*, the pillars of Baal Ammon that stood in Phoenician temples. Since Philo, in typical ancient fashion, identifies many of the Phoenician gods by Greek names (of those of whom similar tales were told), his unsupported account of Phoenician mythology was received (for almost two thousand years) with some scepticism. But Philo does in fact mention El as the name of Kronos,† and makes Dagon his son. Dagon later fathers an unknown *Dēmarūs*, and after much action Demarus, *Astartē* (aka *Asteria*) and *Adōdos* end up as governors of the world, under El's direction. Khusor is the craftsman god, important in the creation of the world and the origin of inventions. Since Astarte and Asteria are plausible Greek transliterations of Ashtoreth and Asherah, and *Adōdos* without its

---

* It was written on clay tablets; this is why it survived. But it was incised in an alphabet based on cuneiform, so graphically too it throws an interesting light on the Phoenicians, until then reputed to have been the first to use an alphabet. The simpler shapes of the Phoenician letters are due to their usually being written with ink on papyrus, rather than stamped with an angled stylus on clay.

† El is simply the Semitic root for 'god', seen also in Hebrew *elohīm*, one of the two words for God in Genesis, and Arabic *Al-lah*, literally 'The God'.

Greek ending -os would (with its long O) be a natural Phoenician pronunciation of Hadad, the basic cast of Phoenician gods is in place.

The Ugaritic texts also give us a hint of how close Hebrew literature comes to the missing Phoenician works. Remember that Hebrew is a close relative of Ugaritic, but not as close as Phoenician. Now consider how the goddess Anath of Ugarit decks herself out to meet the emissaries of Baal:

> She draws some water and bathes;
> Sky-dew of the fatness of earth,
> Spray of the Rider of the Clouds;
> Dew that the heavens do shed
> Spray that is shed by the stars.[35]

The words for 'Sky-dew of the fatness of earth' are ṭl šmm šmn ʾrṣ. This is precisely what Isaac promises to Jacob (and denies to Esau) in the blessing scene in Genesis:

> wə yīten ləka ha ʾəlohīm m-ṭl ha-šāmīm ū-mišmanni hā-ʾāreṣ

> May God give you of dew of heaven and of fatness of earth[36]

(Traditionally, of course, Hebrew spelling too marked only consonants, as well as some long vowels.)

Hebrew and Ugaritic were close enough, then, to share some fixed phrases. Combining the dramatis personae of the Ugaritic epics with the phraseology of the Old Testament, and the narratives of Philo's *Phoenician History* of Sanchuniathon, we may be able to reconstruct something of the verbal culture of Byblos, Tyre and their sister cities.

There is a clear echo of what Tyrian poetry may have been like in a famous passage of Ezekiel. In the course of a series of prophecies of the downfall of Judah's various neighbours, the prophet digresses on the past glories of one city for which he foresees destruction:

> You say, O Tyre, 'I am perfect in beauty.'
> Your domain was on the high seas;
> your builders brought your beauty to perfection.
> They made all your timbers of pine trees from Senir;
> they took a cedar from Lebanon and made a mast for you.
> Of oaks from Bashan they made your oars;
> of cypress wood from the coasts of Cyprus

they made your deck, inlaid with ivory.
Fine embroidered linen from Egypt was your sail
and served as your banner;
your awnings were of blue and purple
with the coasts of Elishah.
Men of Sidon and Arwad were your oarsmen;
your skilled men, O Tyre, were aboard as your seamen.
Veteran craftsmen of Byblos were on board
as shipwrights to caulk your seams.
All the ships of the sea and their sailors
came alongside to trade for your wares.
Men of Persia, Lydia, and Put
served as soldiers in your army.
They hung their shields and helmets on your walls,
bringing you splendour.
Men of Arwad and Helech manned your walls on every side;
men of Gammad were in your towers.
They hung their shields around your walls;
they brought your beauty to perfection.
…*
The ships of Tarshish serve as carriers for your wares.
You are filled with heavy cargo
in the heart of the sea.
Your oarsmen will take you out to the high seas.
But the east wind will break you to pieces
in the heart of the sea.
…
As they wail and mourn over you
they will take up a lament concerning you:
'Who was ever silenced like Tyre,
surrounded by the sea?'[37]

The Carthaginians, like other Phoenicians, kept voluminous records. Those
that would have been kept on papyrus are lost, but there are several thousand

---

* The poem continues with listings of characteristic products for all the major client nations: Tarshish
(metals); Greece, Tubal, Meshech (slaves, bronze working); Beth Togarmah (equines); Rhodes
(ivory and ebony); Aram (turquoise, fine cloth, coral and rubies); Judah and Israel (wheat, honey,
oil and balm); Damascus (wine, wool); Danites, Greeks of Uzal (wrought iron, cassia, calamus);
Dedan (saddle blankets); Arabia, Kedah (sheep and goats); Sheba, Raamah (spices, gems, gold);
Haran, Canneh, Eden, Asshur, Kilmad (clothes, fabric, knotted rugs).

known inscriptions, assigning rights over sacrificial offerings, making dedications to the goddess Tanit or the god Baal Hammon, or commemorating ceremonies. It is also clear that Carthage had passed on the administrative use of its language to the neighbouring states to the west, Massylia and Massaesylia: their coins bear inscriptions in Punic letters, as do boundary stones.[38]

Indeed, there is evidence for a whole literature in Punic. St Augustine remarked famously that 'on the word of many scholars, there was a great deal of virtue and wisdom in the Punic books'.[39] This view was shared by the Roman Senate, which even as the city of Carthage was being finally destroyed in 146 BC gave orders for a new translation and edition of one especially admired treatise on agriculture. 'Our Senate presented the libraries of the city to African princes, with the sole exception of the 28 books of Mago, which they decreed should be translated into Latin ... The text was entrusted to scholars learned in Punic.'[40] Some forty fragments of it are quoted by later Latin authors, but the work as a whole is lost, even in Latin translation.

In fact, no Punic literary work has survived. The closest to it is a Greek translation, in about seven hundred words, of a Punic inscription engraved in the temple of Baal Hammon at Carthage, recording the voyage of exploration by a Carthaginian leader, Hanno, round the western coast of Africa (perhaps as far as Gabon). It ends:

> ... we came to the gulf named Horn of the South. In the corner was an island ... and in it a lake with an island full of savage people. By far the majority of them were female, hairy in body, called by the interpreters 'gorillas'. We could not catch the men because of their skill at climbing and defending themselves with stones, but we took three women, who fiercely resisted, biting and tearing. However, we killed them and skinned them, and brought the hides back to Carthage. We did not sail further since our supplies had given out.[41]

It is tantalising that this text, one of the few brief survivals from the wreck of Punic literature, should have recounted such a unique adventure.

How is the total loss of Phoenician, and its successor dialect Punic, to be explained, after such a widespread expansion across the Mediterranean world? We have here another unanswered, and as yet largely unasked, question.

After Alexander's sack of Tyre in 332 BC, Phoenician trade remained prosperous for many centuries, with no further disasters to threaten the traders' stability. The Punic language did not die out promptly, even in its overseas provinces, where all the administrative links to Carthage were cut by the end of the second century BC: in Sardinia, for example, several 'neo-Punic' inscriptions have been found, the latest, at Bithia in the extreme south, made as late as the end of the second century AD. And even if the life of Carthage as a city was brutally punctuated in 146 BC, it was refounded as a Roman town by Augustus a century later. It then enjoyed a flourishing later life till the end of the Roman empire in the west. We may surmise that its language survived in use in North Africa, until the fifth century AD: Augustine tells us that he had to quote his Punic proverbs in Latin since 'not everybody' would understand the original.[42]

Nevertheless, ever since Alexander's conquest of western Asia there had been a general cultural levelling in the Near East, with Greek and Aramaic spreading at the expense of all the minority languages. Although Aramaic was a language closely related to Phoenician or Hebrew, Greek had still been taken up by a large part of the Jewish community (especially those in Egypt) in this period. Greek had also become a basic subject in the education of Romans, who were by the second century BC clearly recognised as the rising power.

The cultural undertow was thus running strongly in favour of Greek. And in fact it is possible that, despite its users' commercial prowess, Phoenician or Punic had never been widely used as a lingua franca or even as a trade jargon outside Africa. The language of trade is, after all, perforce that of the customer, rather than that of the merchant.

The Roman comedian Plautus illustrates this in a scene from his play *Poenulus*, 'the Punic guy'—'Punk'?—which came out in the early second century BC, soon after the end of the Second Punic War.[43] A Carthaginian merchant tries talking to a couple of Romans in Punic, even though he knows Latin, but soon tires of their constant heavy puns and jokes on him and his language, to cloak the poor language skills of the one who claims to be a bit of Punic expert. (Hanno's Punic is in bold, and the Latin that echoes it is in bold italics.)

HANNO: **mechar bocca** MILPHIO: *Istuc tibi sit potius quam mihi.*
AGORASTOCLES: quid ait? MILPHIO: *miseram esse praedicat*
buccam sibi. fortasse medicos nos esse arbitrarier.
AGORASTOCLES: *si ita est nega esse; nolo ego errare hospitem.*
MILPHIO: *audin tu?* HANNO: **rufe ynny cho is sam**
AGORASTOCLES: *sic volo profecto vera cuncta huic expedirier.*

roga numquid opu' sit. MILPHIO: *tu qui sonam non habes,*
quid in hanc venistis urbem aut quid quaeritis?
HANNO: **muphursa** AGORASTOCLES: *quid ait?*
HANNO: **mi uulech ianna**
AGORASTOCLES: *quid venit?*
MILPHIO: *non audis?* **mures Africanos** *praedicat*
in pompam ludis dare se velle aedilibus.

HANNO: **Good morning to you.** MILPHIO: Better you than me.
AGORASTOCLES: What is he saying? MILPHIO: He says his jaw
hurts.
Perhaps he thinks we are doctors.
AGORASTOCLES: Then say we're not; as a stranger, I don't want him
misled.
MILPHIO: Are you listening? HANNO: **Doctor, no one is perfect.**
AGORASTOCLES: Yes, I certainly want all this explained to me.
Ask him if he needs anything. MILPHIO: You without a belt,
why have you people come to this city, or what are you after?
HANNO: **What do you mean?** AGORASTOCLES: What is he saying?
HANNO: **What is he on about to a stranger?**
AGORASTOCLES: Why has he come?
MILPHIO: Don't you hear? African mice [a joke for 'elephants'?] he
says he wants to present to the city wardens for the circus parade.[44]

Still, the fact that the Punic dialogue is in there at all suggests that a smattering of Punic was not strange to Romans at the time, and good for a laugh.

The Carthaginian army (largely made up of mercenaries from all over the
western Mediterranean) is said to have been commanded in Greek; certainly
the coins struck by the soldiers during the great mutiny in 241–238 BC, the
so-called 'Truceless War', were inscribed in Greek. And it is known that the
annalists who accompanied Hannibal on campaign in Italy, Silenos and Sosylos, wrote in Greek. When Hannibal put up a plaque recording his exploits
in a temple of Hera in Sicily, it was in Greek as well as Punic.[45]

The Phoenicians and Carthaginians, notorious as shrewd businessmen,
must have been pragmatists; like their modern analogues, they would have
focused on the practical utility of a means of communication, and chosen a
language accordingly. In the last couple of centuries BC, it was clear that the
most generally useful international language in the Mediterranean was
Greek.

In Carthage itself, and the North African provinces of Libya (to the east) and Numidia (to the west), Punic did continue to be used. But there is no evidence of Punic literary activity after the Roman conquest (146 BC). Literacy seems to have become restricted to the use of Latin and Greek. The Punic cultural traditions ceased to be fostered, and the physical record of this once highly literate society did not last much longer.

The universal medium for administrative and literary records had been papyrus, a material that survives long-term only in extremely dry conditions (such as those of the Egyptian desert). Texts that were not inscribed on a durable medium such as stone, ivory or clay would not survive unless they were repeatedly copied—a service that was maintained for seminal texts in Greek and Latin, and indeed Hebrew, throughout late antiquity and the Middle Ages, until the printing press made them safe. There was no tradition to preserve Phoenician or Punic texts, and so they perished with the papyrus on which they had been written.

As for the spoken dialects, they will most likely have survived until succeeded by larger-scale neighbouring languages. Interestingly, in both cases, these new languages were Semitic, closely related to Canaanite dialects and in fact rather similar to them. Phoenician in the Lebanon will have yielded to Aramaic in the first century BC; and the last remnants of Punic in North Africa probably succumbed to Arabic in the seventh or even eighth century AD.*

Aramaic—the desert song: Interlingua of western Asia

In the fourteenth year of King Hezekiah's reign, Sennacherib king of Assyria attacked all the fortified cities of Judah and captured them. Then he sent his field commander with a large army from Lachish to King Hezekiah at Jerusalem…The field commander said to [Eliakim, Shebna and Joah, Hezekiah's emissaries]:

---

* Elimam (1977) suggests that the Punic story had a happier ending, and that Punic is still alive today, as the ancestor of Maghrebi 'Arabic' (*maghreb* is Arabic for 'west'). It is certainly true that this Semitic language, usually characterised as a dialect of Arabic, diverges strongly from the classic language of the Koran; but this is true of all the Arab vernaculars. Where Punic did survive after the Roman period, it would very likely have made a significant contribution to Maghrebi. Unfortunately, the restricted evidence of what Punic was really like makes it hard to know to what extent this happened. Elimam himself suggests, on the basis of the longest Punic speech in Poenulus (ten lines, eighty-two words), that Punic has 62 per cent in common with Maghrebi, and a further 18 per cent has undergone some semantic evolution.

This is what the great king, the king of Assyria says: on what are you basing this confidence of yours? ... Yahweh himself told me to march against this country and destroy it.

Then Eliakim, Shebna and Joah said to the field commander,

Please speak to us in Aramaic [*'arāmīth*], sir, since we understand it. Don't speak to us in Hebrew [*yǝhūdīth*] in the hearing of the people on the wall.

But the commander replied:

Was it only to your master and you that my master sent me to say these things, and not to the men sitting on the wall—who like you will have to eat their own shit and drink their own piss?

Then the commander stood and called out in Hebrew:

Hear the words of the great king, the king of Assyria! This is what the king says: do not let Hezekiah deceive you. He cannot deliver you! ...

Isaiah xxxvi.1–14 (= 2 Kings xviii.17–29)

These events, which took place in 701 BC, show that at this stage Aramaic, although the lingua franca of senior officers in the Assyrian empire and the kingdom of Judah, was not the language of Judah's common soldier.

This was to change. The policy of internal deportation so thoroughly applied by the Assyrians was continued by their successors, and this time a notable victim was the Hebrew language, along with many of its speakers in the land of Judah.

When in 609 BC Assyria was at last subjugated by an alliance of Medes from the east and Babylonians from the south, there were no direct linguistic effects, except that Akkadian ceased to be written in Assyria. Aramaic continued as the standard spoken language of Mesopotamia, which was henceforth governed (if at all) from Babylon. But others had noticed the momentous political change. Egypt, in particular, saw an opportunity and invaded Palestine and Syria.

Babylon's crown prince Nebuchadrezzar (*Nabū-kudurri-uṣur*, 'Nabû, protect my offspring') responded effectively. Twenty years later, by the time this and perhaps two more Egyptian invasions had been repulsed, Jerusalem, which had twice sided with the Egyptians, was definitively in Babylonian hands. Most of its population went either as refugees to Egypt or as deportees to Babylon.

This is precisely the sort of treatment that kills off a language, as can be attested by the experience of so many indigenous people in the nineteenth and twentieth centuries, moved off their lands by colonists or social engineers, in regions as varied as North Carolina, Queensland, Ethiopia, Siberia and Tibet. There are Hebrew songs of lamentation, all too conscious of the danger:

> ʿal naharōṯ bābel šām yašbenō gam baḵînû
> bəzāḵrēnû ěṯ ṣîôn...

> By the rivers of Babylon we sat and wept
> when we remembered Zion.
> There on the poplars we hung our harps
> for there our captors asked us for songs,
> our tormentors asked for songs of joy;
> They said, 'Sing us one of the songs of Zion!'
> How can we sing the songs of Yahweh
> while in a foreign land?
> If I forget you, O Jerusalem,
> may my right hand forget its skill.
> May my tongue cleave to the roof of my mouth
> if I do not remember you...

Psalm cxxxvii.1–6

Yet they did forget, at least the speech of Jerusalem. Amid the crowds of Babylon, Aramaic, which had been the cosmopolitan language for the Jewish elite, became their vernacular, and Hebrew, the language of the people, became a tongue known only to the learned. It had already vanished from speech two generations later, when in 538 the Persian king Cyrus, in one of his first reforms after conquering Babylon, allowed the Jews to return.*

The Aramaic language was now inseparable from the Babylonian empire, and a new standard version of the language arose, usually known as Imperial Aramaic. It had developed in the eastern areas, where the Aramaean settlers had established themselves in Mesopotamia, and as such was more influenced by Akkadian than its more ancient, and some would say more authentic, version spoken in Aram and the rest of Syria. Yet this dialect was destined to become the standard not just for the Babylonian empire, but for the much greater Persian empire that replaced it, 'over 127 provinces stretch-

---

* The return is recorded at length in the books Ezra and Nehemiah of the Bible. They are in Hebrew, though much of the correspondence with the government is given in Aramaic (Ezra iv.8–vi.18 and vii.12–26). It is an amazing demonstration of the preservative power of a tradition consciously maintained that now, after an absence of two and a half thousand years, Hebrew is again the vernacular on the streets of Jerusalem.

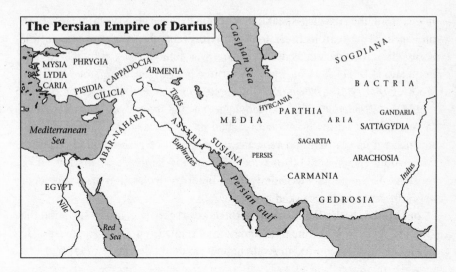

ing from *Hōdû* to *Kûš*', in the awed phrase of the Book of Esther, i.e. from Hindustan to the land of Kush, south of Egypt.

The distinctive traits of this dialect were fairly small things, such as plural *-îm* replaced by *-în*, plural *-ayyā* by *-ē*, and in some forms of the verb the dropping of initial h, to be replaced by a glottal stop ʾ (rather reminiscent of colloquial London English). In fact, the model for this standard seems to have been Babylonian Aramaic as spoken and written by educated Persians.[46] The fact of this colonial transplant becoming the effective standard is no more surprising than the current popularity of General American as a world standard for English. As 'Standard Literary Aramaic' it was to remain essentially unchanged for the next millennium.

More surprisingly, Aramaic was also used to an extent as a language for international communication. At Saqqara, near the site of the Egyptian capital Memphis, a late seventh-century papyrus from a Philistine king has been discovered, asking in Aramaic for the Egyptian pharaoh's help against the king of Babylon; soon afterwards, Jeremiah, an adviser to the kings of Judah just before Babylon sacked Jerusalem, breaks into Aramaic in the midst of a tirade in Hebrew. This is for a slogan to cast in the teeth of foreign idolaters:

ʾəlāhayyā ʾ dī šəmayyā ʾ wə ʾarəqā ʾ lā ʾ ʿaḇāḏû
yə ʾḇaḏû mə ʾarə ʿā ʾ ûmen təhôṯ šəmayyā ʾ ʾēlleh

These gods, who did not make the heavens and the earth,
will perish from the earth and from under the heavens.

Jeremiah x.11

81

In the event, the Aramaic-speaking believers in those gods were due to inherit the earth, at least from India to Kush. However, the language was usable across these vast distances not because it was actually spoken by the various populations, but because it acted as a written interlingua, understood by a network of literate translators and interpreters, the *sepīru*. A ruler or official would dictate a letter in his own language, and the *sepīru* would write it down in Aramaic; when the document reached its addressee—Persia was also renowned for its excellent postal service—it would be read by another *sepīru* who would speak it aloud in whatever was the language of his master or mistress. This process was called *paraš*, literally 'declaration' in Aramaic, or *uzvārišn*, 'explanation' in Persian.[47]

In Ezra iv.18, the Persian king Artaxerxes receives in oral translation the Aramaic letter of some local government officials from Trans-Euphrates. He begins his reply (reported in Aramaic, but no doubt dictated in Persian):

> *šəlām û-kə ʿet̲ :*
> *nišəttənwānā ʾ dī šəlaḥəttûn ʿaleynā ʾ məp̄āraš qərî qād̲āmāy :*

Greetings, and now:
the letter you sent us was translated and read in our presence...

The same practical system was in use internationally, though it must have been limited by the availability of bilingual *sēpiru* for languages beyond the Persian realm. In the Greeks' Peloponnesian War, a messenger from the Persian king to Sparta was intercepted in 428 by the Athenians: his letters then needed to be translated *ek tõn Assuríon grammáton*, 'from the Assyrian writing'. It is unlikely that its real addressees in Sparta would have been able to make any sense of them without the messenger's *paraš*.[48]

The convenience of this system must have acted as a strong motive for the spread of the language, and it gets into some amazing places, notably the Jewish scriptures. Besides the Aramaic letters in the book of Ezra, long passages in the book of Daniel (written in the second century BC) are written in Aramaic, appropriately so since it recounts the various adventures and visions of this Jewish counsellor at court in Babylon under a succession of Babylonian and then Persian kings. It begins with a Hebrew description of his training as a *sepīru*, after being recruited by the Babylonian king, a three-year course in *ṣēp̄ir ū-ləšôn kasdîm*, 'the writing and language of the Chaldaeans'.[49]

This discreet use of a lingua franca disguised by multilingual *paraš* (rather reminiscent of that naive sort of fiction where travellers can go anywhere and at once get into serious conversations with the local people, never noticing any language barrier) was quite compatible with continuing use of local languages in other official functions. One example is the legends on coined money: in fact, this means of payment with a government guarantee had only recently been invented (in Lydia, western Anatolia). It spread only slowly in the Persian empire, and most contemporary coins come from the western provinces. So there are Persian-era coins inscribed in Greek and pretty much every other language of southern Anatolia (Lydian, Sidetic, Carian and Lycian—all related to Hittite and Luwian); Aramaic is used in northern parts of Anatolia (where Phrygian was probably still in use), in Cilicia (which had been part of the Babylonian empire, and had had strong links with Phoenicia) and in Mesopotamia. In Egypt there were also coins struck in demotic Egyptian.[50]

Still the Egyptians became heavy users of Aramaic, despite the lateness of Egypt's annexation to the Persian empire. The language would have come in beforehand, along with a sizeable population of refugees and émigrés from Aram, Phoenicia, Edom, Judah and other countries threatened or dominated by Babylon, with a de facto common language in Aramaic. But many Egyptians were also drawn into this community, as the Egyptian names occurring in Aramaic texts show, and when the Persians were replaced by the Ptolemies Egyptians continued to use Aramaic for legal documents.[51]

Egypt, because of its dry climate, has provided almost all the surviving texts in Aramaic from this period, written on papyrus or leather, particularly the correspondence of a Persian governor (satrap) called Arsames, a packet of letters from a family distributed between Luxor and Syene (Aswan) up and down the Nile, and at Syene the archives of the Jewish military garrison, including a fair number of legal documents and business letters to Jerusalem. This also includes the proverbs of the sage Ahiqar, a legendary counsellor at the court of the Assyrian kings Sennacherib and Esarhaddon in the early seventh century BC, one of which appears as epigraph to the second section of this chapter. Having experience of life at court, he is particularly concerned about the power of leaks and malicious gossip:

My son,

Chatter not overmuch so that thou speak out every word that come to thy mind; for men's eyes and ears are everywhere trained upon thy mouth. Beware lest it be thy undoing. More than all watchfulness watch thy mouth, and over what thou hearest harden thy heart.

For a word is a bird: once released no man can recapture it. First count
the secrets of thy mouth: then bring out thy words by number. For the
instruction of a mouth is stronger than the instruction of war.

Treat not lightly the word of a king: let it be healing for thy flesh ...[52]

The letters reveal that some Jews, as Jeremiah had lamented, were indeed on
pretty familiar terms with alien gods. Consider this from a valet, written on a
piece of broken pottery: 'To my lord Micaiah, your servant Giddel. I send you
welfare and life. I bless you by Yaho [i.e. Yahweh] and Khnub [a local god].
Now send me the garment you are wearing and they will mend it. I send the
note for your welfare.'[53]

Away to the north in Anatolia, languages spoken must have been at least
as various as the coin legends; nevertheless, inscriptions in Greek, Lydian
and Lycian have been found accompanied by translation in Aramaic, especially for monumental inscriptions of laws.

The pervasiveness of Aramaic is also demonstrated at the opposite end of
the empire by three propaganda inscriptions of the Indian emperor Aśoka
(see Chapter 5, 'Sanskrit in Indian life', p. 187). These date from a later era,
the third century BC, when Aramaic had already been supplanted by Greek as
the official language of administration across Iran. Nevertheless, Aśoka still
saw fit to put up these permanent exhortations to virtue—with vegetarianism
specifically recommended—in Aramaic as well as Greek, three or four generations after the change.

...ΚΑΙ ΑΠΕΧΕΤΑΙ
ΒΑΣΙΛΕΥΣ ΤΩΝ ΕΜΨΥΧΩΝ ΚΑΙ ΟΙ ΛΟΙΠΟΙ ΔΕ
ΑΝΘΡΩΠΩΝ ΚΑΙ ΟΣΟΙ ΘΗΡΕΥΤΑΙ ΚΑΙ ΑΛΙΕΙΣ
ΒΑΣΙΛΕΩΣ ΠΕΠΑΥΝΤΑΙ ΘΗΡΕΥΟΝΤΕΣ...

... and abstains
the King from animals and the rest still
of men and all hunters and fishermen
of the King have ceased hunting ...

‏...ואף זי זנה במאכלא למראן מלכא זעיר‏
‏קטלן זנה למחזה כלהם אנשן אתהחסינן אזי נוניא אחדן‏
‏אלך אנשﬡﬡ פתיזבת...‏

...W ᵓP ZY ZNH BM ᵓKLᵓ LMR ᵓN MLKᵓ Z ᶜYR
QṬLN ZNH LMḤZH KLHM ᵓNSN ᵓTHḤṢYNN ᵓZY NWNYᵓ ᵓḤDN
ᵓLK ᵓNSN PTYZBT...

And besides, as regards food, for our lord the King few [animals]
are killed: seeing this, all men have ceased; even fish catchers,
those people are under a prohibition...[54]

There have been three Aramaic inscriptions discovered so far in this border
area, in Kandahar, in Laghman, east of Kabul (*Lampāka*),[55] and the academic
centre of Taxila (*Takṣaśila*), all of which would have been in the Persian
province claimed as Gandhara. In modern terms, they are on the borders of
Afghanistan, but on its far borders abutting Pakistan, demonstrating the penetration of Aramaic to the very limits of Persian control and perhaps even beyond, presumably with some cultural momentum of its own.*

When Aramaic came to the end of its glory, it was not through infiltration,
as Aramaic had ended the long reign of Akkadian. It was through outright and
sudden conquest.

Five generations after the Persian kings Darius and Xerxes had tried and
failed to end the independence of the Greek city-states across the Aegean (although they had quite easily tamed the Greek cities that bordered Anatolia),
another power succeeded where Persia failed. Philip of Macedon reduced all
of European Greece, claiming all the while to be a Greek himself. This claim,
made on grounds of language and culture, is surprisingly difficult to substan-
tiate, since hardly a word of the Macedonian language has survived.[56] But his
son Alexander, perhaps with an aggression that stemmed from insecurity,†
decided to demonstrate his belonging by undertaking to avenge the affront
that the Greeks had suffered when the Persians tried to invade. (Not that this
prevented him, after the reigning king of Persia had been assassinated by his
own people, from claiming to the Persians that he was the rightful successor.)

Within the ten years 333–323 BC he had succeeded totally. Although he
had not campaigned in every province, the vast Persian empire, including its
extremities in Egypt and Afghanistan, was now a possession of the royal
house of Macedon. Macedonians stayed in control of the Persian and Meso-

---

* This momentum was known anyway, since India's original scripts, Kharoshthi and Brahmi, are
both derived from Aramaic writing. Since Brahmi in turn is the origin of every other alphabet in
South and South-East Asia, the Persian king Darius was in effect setting the writing systems of most
of Asia for the next 2500 years when he chose Aramaic as the standard language for his empire.

† The French historian Fernand Braudel can hardly forgive him for missing his opportunity to go west
instead, and so take over the Mediterranean (Braudel 2001: 277–84, 'Alexander's mistake').

potamian part for almost two hundred years, yielding to Arsaces, first of the Parthians, only in 140 BC.

It is likely that in this 'Hellenistic' period the Middle East was in fact governed in a mixture of languages, the new masters' Greek competing with the old masters' Aramaic. (See Chapter 6, 'Kings of Asia: Greek spread through war', p. 243.) Aramaic clearly held its ground far better in Mesopotamia, Syria and Palestine, where it had at least five hundred more years of background than in Anatolia and Iran, where it had only been established as a language of government by the King of Kings' fiat, a bare two hundred years before. In addition, after Alexander's conquest, Greek settlement would have been much heavier in Anatolia, already surrounded as it was by Greek colonies on its coasts, than in Iran, far beyond the Taurus and Zagros mountains, even if Persia's Royal Road from Sardis in Lydia to Persepolis meant that the area already enjoyed better communications than anywhere else in the known world.

This led to rather different subsequent careers for Greek in these different parts of Alexander's empire. Greek remained as no more than a lingua franca in the centre and east. The Greek administration here was ended by the rise of the Parthians (from eastern Iran, and speaking a language close to Persian) in the second century BC, and this put an end to official status for Greek. It seems that there may have been a return to a language situation rather like the early years of the Persian empire, with Aramaic continuing for all practical purposes in Mesopotamia, but a form of Persian now in use farther east.

In the west, by contrast, Greek had fully replaced the previous languages (notably Lydian, Lycian and Aramaic). When the Romans took it over in the first century BC they kept Greek on as the de facto language of administration, insisting on Latin only in the courts and the army. (Educated Romans all knew Greek anyway.) This meant that Anatolia became almost monolingual in Greek, while in Syria and Palestine Greek was used to govern a public that still predominantly spoke Aramaic. In Egypt, the situation was complicated by the survival of the Egyptian language, as well as the extremely cosmopolitan society encouraged by the Ptolemies around their capital, Alexandria, where, for example, the Jewish community was largely Greek-speaking.

The advent of the single language Greek across the Persian empire, a domain supposedly already unified under Aramaic, thus had a remarkable effect in bringing the linguistic differences to the surface.

SECOND INTERLUDE: THE SHIELD OF FAITH

Jesus of Nazareth spoke Aramaic, though not of the best, by the standards of his own people. His native Galilee was generally reckoned to speak a substandard variety, a 'North Country' accent to the ears of the educated of Jerusalem and Judaea; famously, his disciple Peter's accent gave him away at a crucial moment, and even in the learned Talmud there is the occasional joke at the expense of Galilean pronunciation.*

The language of the group that formed after Jesus's death clearly was Aramaic; and Samaritan Christians (Samaria is just south of Galilee) have gone on speaking the language to the present day. But the new faith had cosmopolitan aspirations, and their first public event (recorded in Acts ii) was the pentecostal feast at which its apostles miraculously became able to preach in all manner of languages. This sudden gift for languages did not persist, and so a convenient medium had to be found to publish the scriptures. Given that they were in the Roman empire, centred on the Mediterranean, Greek was a reasonable choice. It was also free of the Jewish associations that hung about Aramaic, and might have tarnished Christianity's appeal to gentiles. Greek accordingly was the language in which the Christian scriptures, the so-called 'New Testament', were composed. It became the first language of the Church in the west.

Nevertheless, the world was bigger than Rome and the 'circle of lands' (*orbis terrārum*) that surrounded its sea. Significantly, the first foreigners mentioned as witnesses to the pentecostal miracle are Parthians, Medes, Elamites and dwellers in Mesopotamia, none of them at the time under Roman rule, and as we have seen by this time (seven generations after the fall of the Seleucid empire in the east) much more likely to understand Aramaic than Greek.

It took two hundred years to get established, but the early Christian Church did get a major wing oriented towards the east. It was based at Edessa (modern and ancient Urfa†), a city on the major route east from Antioch on the Mediterranean towards Nisibis (Nusaybin) in Aram Naharaim, and Agbatana (Hamadan) in Media. The language of Edessa and its believers was Aramaic, here known as Syriac. This is our first example of a radically new motive for language spread, the drive to win converts to a new religion. Although the originals were in Greek, the New Testament and most early Christian literature was translated into Syriac, and became the basis of a literature of its own, of hymns, sermons and wider disquisitions, continuing actively until the thirteenth century AD, despite the swirls of Islamic invasions that passed round and about it.§

---

* Matthew xxvii.74. Sawyer (1999: 84) quotes a lot of evidence for attitudes to Galilean.
† The name *Urfa* is probably derived from *Hurri* (cf. the Greek name of its surrounding province, *Orrhoēnē*), with a history going back to the Mitannian period.
§ The Muslims in themselves were never a physical threat to the Aramaic speakers, since they saw

As honey drips from a honeycomb,
and milk flows from a woman full of love for her children,
so is my hope upon you, my God.
As a fountain gushes forth its water,
so does my heart gush forth the praise of the Lord
and my lips pour out praise to him;
my tongue is sweet from converse with him,
my face exults in the jubilation he brings,
my spirit is jubilant at his love
and by him my soul is illumined.
He who holds the Lord in awe may have confidence,
for his salvation is assured;
he will gain immortal life,
and those who receive this are incorruptible. Hallelujah!

Odes of Solomon, no. 40[57]

The spread of a language has to be distinguished from the spread of the religion, of course. Edessa was the source, for example, of the Christianity that reached Armenia in 303. But the Armenians were not tempted to give up their own language, even if they were setting up the first national Christian Church in history, and even though without Aramaic script Bishop Mesrop Mashtotz would never have designed the Armenian alphabet, still in use today.

Still, the language did travel, at the very least in liturgical and written form, with the preachers. Christians of the Nestorian persuasion, judged heretical and exiled from Edessa by imperial order in 489, carried Syriac out to Persia, where as already seen Aramaic was still very much at home. Their next base was just up the road in Nisibis. But the Nestorians did not stop there. Their missionaries went on into India, where they established a bishopric in Kalyana (near Mumbai), and a cluster of monasteries farther south, especially in Kerala, joining forces with the St Thomas Christians, supposedly dating from the missionary activities of the apostle—another native speaker of Aramaic, naturally. When they were rediscovered by Europeans in the nineteenth century, they still had Bibles and religious manuscripts written in Syriac, though it seems the language was little used in worship.

them everywhere as *millet*, or distinct nationalities, separate but respected. But there was a tendency for Aramaic speakers everywhere to give up everyday use of the language in favour of Arabic.

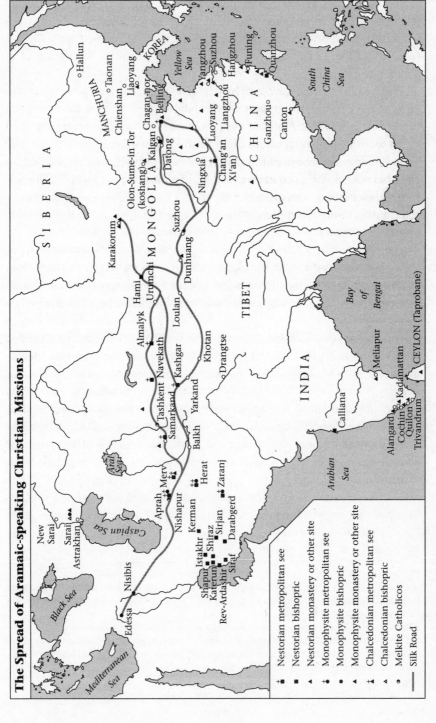

The Spread of Aramaic-speaking Christian Missions

Edessa
Nisibis
Black Sea
Mediterranean Sea
Caspian Sea
Aral Sea
New Sarai
Sarai
Astrakhan
SIBERIA
Aprah
Merv
Nishapur
Kerman
Istakhr
Shapur
Shiraz
Katerum
Sirjan
Rev-Ardashir
Siraf
Darabgerd
Herat
Zaranj
Balkh
Samarkand
Tashkent
Navekath
Almalyk
Kashgar
Yarkand
Khotan
Drangtse
Loulan
Urumchi
Hami
Karakorum
MONGOLIA
Olon-Sume-in Tor
(koshang)
Kalgan
Chagan-nor
Beijing
Datong
Ningxia
Chang'an
Xi'an
Suzhou
Dunhuang
TIBET
INDIA
Calliana
Alangard
Cochin
Kadamattan
Quilon
Trivandrum
Meliapur
CEYLON (Taprobane)
Arabian Sea
Bay of Bengal
MANCHURIA
Hallun
Taonan
Chienshan
Liaoyang
KOREA
Yellow Sea
Fanzhou
Suzhou
Funing
Hangzhou
Quanzhou
South China Sea
Luoyang
Liangzhou
CHINA
Ganzhou
Canton

Nestorian metropolitan see
Nestorian bishopric
Nestorian monastery or other site
Monophysite metropolitan see
Monophysite bishopric
Monophysite monastery or other site
Chalcedonian metropolitan see
Chalcedonian bishopric
Melkite Catholicos
Silk Road

The Nestorians also kept travelling east from Persia along the Silk Road into central Asia, at last reaching Karakorum in Mongolia, and the northern cities of China. The arrival of the monk Alopen in the Chinese capital Chang-an (Xian) in 635 is commemorated on a stele set up in 781, bilingual in Syriac and Chinese.[58]

Two centuries later they had largely disappeared from China; and remnants of the Church farther west were mostly exterminated in the fourteenth century by the warlord Timur-i-leng (Tamburlaine). But Nestorians survived closer to their founding areas, in Mesopotamia and farther north in Kurdistan. Their tradition, and the use of Syriac, survives in the Assyrian and Chaldaean churches. Other Syriac speakers, of the so-called Syrian Jacobite Church, who stayed more at home round Antioch and Edessa, and whose missionary activity was aimed more along caravan routes in Arabia, have also survived in small numbers.*

The net result of all this heroic proselytism has been modest: Aramaic or Syriac has survived in small pockets quite close to its original homes.† But the language has survived. It owes its survival to its speakers' determination to maintain their communities, and those communities have all been based on a religion.

This 'confessional' route to survival is at most two and a half thousand years old, and seems characteristic of the languages of the Near East, particularly Afro-Asiatic languages. The most notable language to survive by this strategy is Hebrew: we have already noted how it is the adherence to its own identity, marked out by a religious code, which explains its survival by contrast with the total oblivion suffered two thousand years ago by its sister language Phoenician. For the strategy to work, the religion of the language community must be significantly different from that of the population that surrounds it.

Another example is the Coptic language, the final survival of Egyptian. This had simply been Egypt's ancestral language,§ as distinct from the inter-

---

* Christians were not the only people to go on speaking Aramaic, though they have lasted longest. The Gnostic sect of southern Mesopotamia also spoke another dialect of Aramaic, known as Mandaic or Mandaean, at least until the eighth century. And for a few centuries AD, the Jews of Babylonia and Persia also continued, producing most notably the vast Babylonian Talmud. Both these communities were prolific in writing literature.

† There is a considerable modern diaspora too, to the major cities of Israel, Lebanon, Syria, Iraq, Iran and Turkey. Many are said to have emigrated to Armenia and Georgia after the Russo-Persian war of 1827; and a sizeable number have gathered in the USA. The use of the Internet in binding them together is examined in McClure (2001). She quotes estimates of worldwide numbers around 1–3 million.

§ Its name is derived from Arabic *qibt*, 'Egyptian', a shortening of the Greek *Aigyptios*.

Alopen stele in Chang-an

The bulk of the inscription in Chinese summarises the Christian creed (the shining doctrine from Dà Qín) and a history of the Church under imperial patronage in China. The Syriac part (at bottom left) is in vertical columns, like Chinese. It reads: 'In the year 1092 of the Greeks, my lord Yazedbouzid, priest and chorepiscopus of Kudan, royal city, son of the late Milis, priest from Balkh, city in Tahouristan, erected this monument, wherein it is written the law of Him, our saviour, the Preaching of our forefathers to the Rulers of the Chinese.' On the sides are lists of names in Chinese and Syriac.

loping Aramaic and Greek that had come in from the Near East, but after the Muslim conquest it became associated more and more with the Christian population of Egypt; for as in most parts of the empire, Christians had come to be the majority after the Roman emperor Constantine's public embrace of their faith in the early fourth century.

The Muslims' treatment of the Copts gradually soured. No one knows how fast the percentage of Christians in the population fell, but fall it did, especially in the north of the country, so that for some centuries Coptic was stronger in the south. Through the seventh to ninth centuries the Copts were guaranteed freedom of religion and civil autonomy, although like non-Muslims everywhere they were subject to special taxes. But in 829 the Copts revolted against tax collectors, and were severely put down. Thereafter conditions sporadically worsened and occasionally improved under a variety of Muslim dynasties, but the consistent trend was for the Coptic population—and use of the language outside the liturgy—to diminish. Theological works were still being written until 820, and new hymns went on being composed until early in the fourteenth century. The language community was in fact sufficiently lively for the Delta dialect, Bohairic, to supplant Sahidic, the dialect of Upper Egypt, as the standard: it was consecrated for use in liturgy by Patriarch Gabriel II in 1132–45. Although there were cultural revivals after the fourteenth century, the language did not come back into daily life. But it has persisted in liturgy to the present day, and there are signs of serious attempts to revive it.

Coptic, then, is another example of a language of the Near East which has been sustained through a period of growing adversity through its association with a distinctive faith. It can be contrasted with a survival a little farther south: Ge'ez, the language of the Ethiopian Church. This is a classical language (related to the ancient languages of South Arabia, and owes its position ultimately to a prehistoric invasion across the Red Sea). Although it survived, like Coptic, through its role in Christian liturgy, its fate is much more like that of Latin or Sanskrit than Coptic. Ethiopia continues to be a Christian country, and Ge'ez is surrounded by daughter and niece languages, Tigrinya, Tigre and Amharic. Ge'ez has been preserved by sentiment and linguistic conservatism, but the linguistic tradition it represents is alive and under no external threat, linguistic, social or religious.

By contrast, what we may call the 'Shield of Faith' strategy for language survival has indeed been used quite often in the last couple of hundred years, and far away from the Near East, or Afro-Asiatic languages. It is this, after all, which has preserved 'Pennsylvania Dutch', i.e. German, among the separate community of the Amish in New England.[59] And it is this which since

1865 has preserved Welsh in the Nonconformist chapel community of Argentina, on the wind-swept plains of Patagonia.[60] It could even be claimed that it is being reapplied, with a vengeance, to rebuild the Hebrew language in the new state of Israel.

But we must now turn, as the last part of our review of this area, to another language that has exploited its confessional associations mercilessly, not simply to survive but to expand, and to expand faster and more lastingly than any other language known.

Arabic—eloquence and equality: The triumph of 'submission'

احبُّوا العربَ لثلاثٍ: لأني عربيٌّ، والقرآنُ عربيٌّ، وكلامُ اهلِ الجنَّة عربيٌّ.

ʾaḥibbū alʿaraba liθalāθin: liʾanī ʿarabiyyun, wa al-qurʾānu ʿarabiyyun, wa kalāmu ʾahli al-jinnati ʿarabiyyun.

Love the Arabs for three reasons: because I am an Arab, because the Qurʾān is in Arabic and because the inhabitants of Paradise speak Arabic.

Saying attributed to Muḥammad[61]

Arabic is another Semitic language closely related to the Aramaic and Akkadian that preceded it in the Near East. Its records actually go back to North Arabian inscriptions of the fourth century BC. But its speakers, mainly desert Bedouin and pastoralists, had remained outside the effective control (and perhaps interest) of all the previous empires in the region.

When they showed their mettle, the results were truly astounding. Within twenty-five years of the prophet Muḥammad's death in 632, they had conquered all of the Fertile Crescent and Persia, and thrust into Armenia and Azerbaijan. Their lightning advance was even more penetrating towards the west: Egypt fell in 641 and the rest of North Africa as far as Tunisia in the next decade. Two generations later, by 712, the Arabic language had become the medium of worship and government in a continuous band of conquered territories from Toledo and Tangier in the west to Samarkand and Sind in the east. No one has ever explained clearly how or why the Arabs could do this.[62] An appeal is usually made to a power vacuum in the east (where the Roman/Byzantine empire and the Sassanian empire of Iran were just recovering from their exhausting war), and the absence of any power to organise resistance in the west.

Whatever caused the feebleness of the defences, a series of successful raids became harmonised into a wave of invasion that rolled on with the momentum of a tsunami. It originated in a small new state, based on the cities of Medina and Mecca in Arabia, which had recently been energised by divine revelation, embracing a new, and startlingly abstract, creed.

Lā ʾlāha ill' Allāhu, wa Muhammadun rasūlu ʾ llāhi

There is no god but God, and Muhammad is the apostle of God

This *šahādah*, the declaration of Muslim faith, and respected as the first of its 'pillars', was elemental in its power; it was a faith turned from shield into sword. Yet its name, *Islām*, is usually translated as 'submission' (to God); and its Semitic root **slm** (also seen in the agent form *muslim*) is also the basis of words for peace (as in Arabic's own greeting *salām ʿaleykum*, 'peace with you'). Doubly ironic, then, that this religion, whose name means peaceful acceptance, burst upon the world so mightily by storm.

But the importance of language in Islam went far beyond the production of a telling slogan. Eloquence, the sheer power of the word, as dictated by God and declaimed to all who would listen, played the first role in winning converts for Islam, leaving hearers no explanation for the beauty of Muhammad's words but divine inspiration. The classic example is 'Umar ibn al-Khattab, a contemporary of Muhammad and acknowledged authority on oral poetry, determined to oppose, perhaps even to assassinate, him. Exposed directly to the prophet's words, he could only cry out: 'How fine and noble is this speech!' And he was converted.

Language was used in a unique way in the spread of this religion too. The authentic utterances of the prophet, himself illiterate, were soon, in some undocumented way, reduced to writing. The text so arrived at was immediately holy and absolutely authoritative; it could not be changed, although it was permissible (as in the Hebrew scriptures) to annotate it with some dots and dashes to mark the vowel sounds, for the benefit of those whose Arabic was not native, and who consequently might need some help in reading the bare consonants.* It was known as the *Qur ʾān*, 'recitation', based on **qr'**, the

---

* This caused some philological problems, since Muhammad's dialect of Arabic was slightly non-standard: it lacked the glottal stop ', known as *hamza* (the stop heard in place of the tt of the London pronunciation of 'bitter'), had lost the -n ending of the nominative, and had turned the -t ending of feminine nouns into -h. The scholars wanted to retain the text exactly as written, but recite it according to the rules of standard Arabic. As a result, all these consonants of Arabic had to be inserted in the written text with special accent marks, as if they were vowels. These marks are all now standard in Arabic spelling.

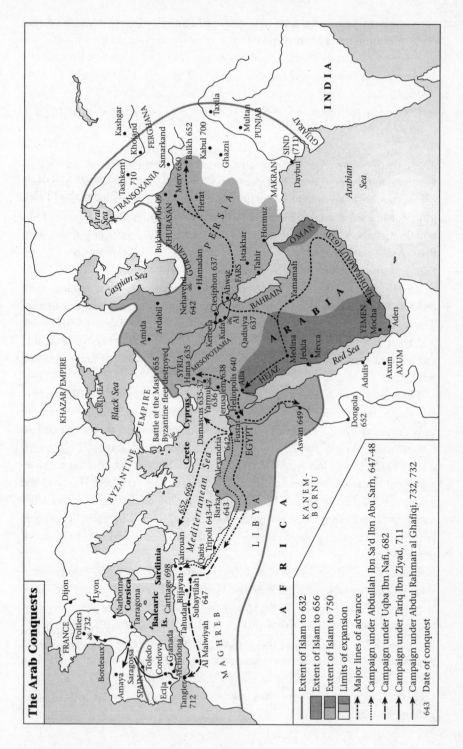

The Arab Conquests

INDIA

Kashgar

Khokand
Tashkent 710
FERGHANA
Samarkand
Balkh 652
Kabul 700
Taxila
PUNJAB
Multan
Ghazni
SIND
Daybul (711)

TRANSOXANIA
Merv 650
KHURASAN
Herat
Arabian
Sea

Aral
Sea
Bukhara 706-09
Hormuz
MAKRAN

Caspian Sea
P E R S I A
GURGAN
Nehavend 642
Hamadan
Ctesiphon 637
Istakhar
Tahir
FARS
OMAN

Ardabil
Ahwaz
HADRAMAUT 633

Amida
Al Qadisiya 637
Yamamah
A R A B I A

KHAZAR EMPIRE
Kerbela
Al Kufa
BAHRAIN

CRIMEA
Battle of the Masis 655
SYRIA
MESOPOTAMIA
Heliopolis 640
YEMEN
Mocha
Aden

Black Sea
Byzantine fleet destroyed
Hama 635
Yarmuk 636
Jerusalem 638
HEJAZ
Medina
Jedda
Mecca
Red Sea

E M P I R E
Damascus 635-37
Aila
Axum
AXUM

B Y Z A N T I N E
Cyprus
Crete
652, 669
Fustat 642
Alexandria 642
EGYPT
Aswan 649
Adulis

Dijon
Narbonne
Corsica
Sardinia
Balearic Is.
Carthage 698
Bijayah
Kairouan
Barka 643
Tripoli 643-47
Qabis
KANEM-
BORNU
Dongola 652

FRANCE
Poitiers 732
Lyon
Tarragona
Mediterranean Sea
Subaytilah 647

Bordeaux
Saragossa
Toledo
Cordova
Granada
Ecija
Arshidona
Tahudart
Al Malwiyah
A F R I C A
LIBYA

Amaya
SPAIN
Tangier 712
M A G H R E B

common Semitic root for reading aloud, and famously begun when the Angel Gabriel commanded Muḥammad:

iqra' bismi rabbika allaḏī xalaqa, xalaqa l'insāna min 'alaqin

Recite, in the name of your Lord who created, created man from embryo.[63]

These distinctive scriptures, a totally closed set, are the great treasure of Islam, constantly pondered and declaimed by the faithful. Their existence seems to have been taken by Muslims as the badge of properly revealed religion, for in their domains holders of other revealed monotheistic faiths, Jews with their TaNaK, Christians with their Testaments, Zoroastrians in Iran with their Avesta, were called likewise *ahl al-kitāb*, 'people of the book', and thereby exempt from forcible conversion.

The linguistic effects of the Arab blitzkrieg can only be compared with those of Greek's wild ride throughout Persia's domains nine centuries before. They were ultimately to be much more durable than the extension of Greek had been, but like the spread of Greek across the east, the take-up of Arabic did not quite measure up to the spread of temporal power that had caused its advance.

Politically, the Arab campaigns destroyed the hold of the Roman, now Byzantine, empire on the whole of the eastern Mediterranean—excepting only Anatolia. Despite their efforts to take Constantinople, this centre of Roman power survived, and lived on in Christian defiance for another eight centuries. Farther east, the Arabs overran Armenia but did not convert it. More significant was the Arabs' termination of Sassanian power in Iran and the mountains of Afghanistan. This was the beginning of the end for Zoroastrianism, gradually replaced in popular worship by Islam. Nowadays it survives only in the tiny minority of Parsees who were to flee to India three hundred years later.

Linguistically, the immediate effects were comparable to the political ones: Arabic established itself as the language of religion, wherever Islam was accepted, or imposed. In the sphere of the holy, there was never any contest, since Islam unlike Christianity did not look for vernacular understanding, or seek translation into other languages. The revelation was simple, and expressed only in Arabic. Furthermore, Islam was a religion that insisted on public rituals of prayer in the language, and where the muezzin's call of the faithful to prayer, in Arabic, has always punctuated everyone's day. *Allāh akbar*, 'God is greater.'

In 700, the caliph in Damascus, 'Abd el Malik, summoned his Greek adviser, Joannes Damascenus, to tell him that he had decided henceforth to ban the Greek language from all public administration. The adviser told his colleagues: 'You had better seek another profession to earn your living: your present employment has been withdrawn by God.' He then spent the rest of his long life (655–749) as a monk.[64]

This was the aspiration. In practice, for the first few generations administration lingered in the predecessor languages, Greek and Persian, to some extent Aramaic and Coptic, not least because the conquerors were unable to operate the elaborate bureaucratic systems they had seized, and because the methods of recruitment were mostly nepotistic. The same families continued to provide the scribal classes, but by the second century of the Muslim era they were reading and writing in Arabic. The process can be followed in the papyrus trail of Egypt. All documents remain in Greek for a good century after the Muslim conquest; then bilingualism sets in, but Arabic totally replaces Greek only in the late eighth century, after 150 years of Islam.[65]

But Arabic is now spoken only in an inner zone within the *Dār-al-islām*, 'House of Islam', as a whole. What happened to roll it back? In the long term there was a subtle linguistic limit on Arab success, or rather on the success of Arabic. Arabic progressed from the language of the mosque to establish itself permanently as the common vernacular of the people only in countries that had previously spoken some related language, one that belonged to the Afro-Asiatic (or Hamito-Semitic) family.*

This Afro-Asiatic zone included the Fertile Crescent, where Arabic replaced Aramaic; Egypt, where it overwhelmed Coptic; Libya and Tunisia, where it finally supplanted Berber and erased—or merged into—Punic; and the Maghreb (the north of modern Algeria and Morocco), where it also pushed Berber back into a set of smaller pockets. The tiny island of Malta, too, which had a Punic background from its origins in the Carthaginian empire, became Arabic-speaking after Arab conquest in 870 AD, belying its millennium of control from Rome since 218 BC. The area of permanent Arabic advance also included at the margin, and rather later, a more southerly zone

---

* Arabic script turned out to be much more universally attractive than its language, and has been taken up wherever Islam was accepted. This has happened despite its functional weaknesses, with no marking of vowels or tones, and a need for elaborate accents even to distinguish all the consonants. Nevertheless, compromises have been found, and it has been applied to languages as various and as unrelated as Persian, Turkish, Kashmiri, Berber, Uighur, Somali, Hausa, Swahili and Malay, as well as Spanish and Serbo-Croat. It must owe this success to the fact that literacy in Muslim countries finds its alpha and its omega in the sacred text of the Qur'ān in Arabic script; so any other writing system can only be an extra complication.

in Africa, Mauritania in the west, and Chad and Sudan in the east; here Arabic spread later through trade contacts, and would have replaced some Chadic and Cushitic languages.

In all these regions where Arabic became the dominant language, a characteristic state of what is called 'diglossia' has set in, with a single classical form of Arabic used as an elite dialect, but different local varieties, no more mutually understandable than the Romance languages of Europe, established in everyday speech. Classical Arabic is close to, but not quite identical with, the language of the Qur'ān.

The explanation for the limit on the spread of Arabic must be sociolinguistic rather than political, religious or cultural, since the situations in which it applied were extremely various.

Iran, for over a thousand years under Achaemenids, Macedonians, Parthians and Sassanians, had been the proud fortress of Zoroastrianism. Nevertheless, it was totally subdued militarily by the Arabs in twenty years from 634. Gradually thereafter, the faith of Islam spread within it, although religious-inspired revolts were still happening well into the ninth century. It then became a heartland of Islam, in fact the stronghold of its Shia tradition, and has remained Muslim ever since.

By the mid-eighth century the official language of the government all over Iran had become Arabic, replacing the Parthians' languages of Pahlavi in the west, and Sogdian in the far east.[66] In the early period, Arabic–Persian bilingualism was widespread even at the court of the caliph, notably in the days of Harūn al-Rashid (786–809), who was made into a figure of legend by his appearances in *The 1001 Nights*. Al-Jahiz, who died *c*.869, tells of one Persian sage who used to read out the Qur'ān, explaining it in Arabic to those on his right, and in Persian to those on his left. Poets from Persia, such as Abu Nawas and Basshar bin Burd, were key figures in Arabic literary history.[67] There were Persian colonies settled in Arabia and Syria, and the Arab geographer al-Muqaddasi claimed at the end of the ninth century that the purest Arabic of his time was spoken in Khurasan, in north-eastern Iran, because the Iranian scholars there made such efforts to learn it correctly.[68] At the elite level, Arabic must have achieved almost universal coverage within Iran.

Yet Arabic never penetrated any part of Iran as a language of daily life. In a sense, the insistence on the excellence of the Arabic spoken in Iran gives this away, for it implies that Arabic was not taking root, and taking on its own character as a local dialect, as it did everywhere in the Arabic-speaking world. Geographers describing the major towns of the west in the ninth century say they were Persian-speaking. Ibn Hauqal states that the entire population of Qum was Shiite, and mostly Arab; nevertheless they all spoke

Persian.[69] Ironically, the march of Islam seems to have supported the spread of Persian out to the east: the Arab conquests in what had been Buddhist central Asia in the eighth century spread Persian, at the expense of the local languages, especially Sogdian. Presumably most of the troops were from the east of Iran, where Persian was still the lingua franca.[70] That is why Tajikistan, and the north-western half of Afghanistan, is Persian-speaking to this day. And when five hundred years later an Islamic army penetrated into India beyond, and set up the Delhi Sultanate, it brought Persian rather than Arabic in its wake.

Some 6000 kilometres away at the other end of Islam's domains, in the Iberian peninsula, Islam had been spread at the point of a sword by an army made up mostly of converted Berbers. Under their leader, Tāriq bin Ziyād, they had crossed the Strait of Gibraltar (*Jibl al-Tāriq*, 'the mountain of Tariq') in 711, and after defeating the Visigothic king Roderik found themselves masters of the country. (They did attempt a major sortie north of the Pyrenees twenty years later, but were thrown back in 732, having got as far as Poitiers in central France.) Seven hundred and fifty years of Muslim presence in Spain and Portugal lay ahead; the country knew itself as *el-Andalūs*, its history was the story of different emirs contending for control, and the city of Cordoba especially became one of the cultural jewels of all Islam, especially as a home of Arabic poetry. Indeed, the emir 'Abd al-Rahman III considered himself strong and magnificent enough in 929 to declare himself *Amir al-mu'minîn*, 'Commander of the Faithful', and so a pretending caliph of all Islam. Nevertheless, later the area of Muslim control began very gradually to be rolled back, as Christian kings grew stronger in Leon and Navarre, and later Castile and Aragon. Toledo fell in 1085, causing a new incursion of Berbers, the Almoravids, called in to redress the balance between Christian and Muslim. But after a respite, the tide continued to run against Islam: Cordoba fell in 1236 and Seville in 1248. The '*reconquista*' culminated in the capture of Granada in 1492.

During this long period Iberia must have been a bilingual zone—probably trilingual as long as waves of invading Berbers retained their own language. Some have claimed that Spanish, or its Romance forebear, had almost died out in the Islamic region by the twelfth century, replaced not by classical but by *Andalusī* Arabic, its dialectal nature showing that the language had been taken up in earnest by the people. Certainly, more than a century after the return of Christian power to Toledo, there were still large numbers of documents being written and notarised in Andalusi.[71] Federico Corriente, an expert on Andalusi, has written: 'Bilingualism evolves rapidly into monolingualism, a process that was complete in the 13th century, which must not make us forget that in the 11th and 12th centuries, the pockets of bilingualism were already residual.'[72]

Executive and legislative action was taken by the new power to eliminate Arabic speech for at least three generations after 1492. In 1501 and 1511 laws were passed against the possession of most Arabic books, and in 1511 it was decreed (apparently without effect) that contracts in Arabic would no longer be valid. In 1526 it was still necessary for Charles V to order in council that only Castilian Spanish would be spoken, used for contracts and in the marketplace. Even in 1566 Philip II was decreeing that within three years all Moors ('*moriscos*') would be allowed to speak only Castilian and not Arabic.

In Persia, then, Arabic, despite its religious prestige, had been unable to overwhelm cultural inertia; in Spain, though much more successful at first, it had finally succumbed to political, military and religious suppression. In the intermediate zone of North Africa, the picture was rather simpler. Arabic established itself first in the towns, where its main immediate competitor in the early days was Latin—and to an extent, as we have seen, Punic. For the Berbers, who accepted Islam quite readily, Arabic was at first taken only as the language of the faith. This had quite an impact, given the role of Arabic in Muslim education, and more when members of the elite began to send their sons to the east to study theology and law. Berber kingdoms of the hinterland maintained their independence as best they could, but there is no evidence of any attempt to throw off Islam as such.

It seems that Arabic only really made progress in the tenth century, after the devastation of Berber society at the hands of the Banu Hilal, a savage band of nomads.[73] These seem to have been set on Maghreb society like so many wild dogs in the course of a dispute between emirates, the Fatimids in Egypt hoping that they would settle the hash of their erstwhile vassals the Zirids, a Berber clan who ruled from Tunis. Ibn Khaldūn, a historian of Berber stock (with roots in El Andalus), writing two hundred years later, in Arabic, likened them to 'a swarm of locusts': 'The very earth seems to have changed its nature. All the lands that the Arabs have conquered in the last few centuries, civilization and population have departed from them...'[74]

However, this put the Arabic-speaking cities in a position to provide form to this new world in North Africa: '...when there is an entire alteration of conditions, it is as if the whole creation had been changed and all the world transformed, as if there were a new creation, a rebirth, a world brought into existence anew'.[75]

The Berbers, once the dominant speech community all over North Africa, now became associated with distant regions, and a life unsettled. Their language lives on, though, strongest in the western area of the Maghreb, where the Banu Hilal never penetrated, and among the Tuareg nomads of the Sahara, although there are substantial pockets still along the Mediterranean.

Finally, consider the Turks, nomad forces who came into contact with Arabic, not through being conquered by its speakers, or proselytised by them, but through taking the initiative and conquering them. Coming from the north-east, they first dominated the eastern areas of Muslim power, moved to take the centre in Baghdad, and later expanded to be in effective control of the whole *Dār-al-islām*. Once they had conquered, there were none to match the Turks in their adherence to the Muslim faith. Nevertheless, they held on to their language even as they accepted the religion.

And they had one other linguistic effect: they also slackened the grip of Arabic on Persia as a whole. The Turks had first encountered the world of Islam through the Persian-speaking area of central Asia. In a sense, they saw it only through a veil of Persian gauze. And so, when the Turks began to exercise influence, Persian returned as official administrative language to Iran, with Arabic restricted more and more to religious functions.

The advent of full Turkish control under the Seljuks* in the eleventh century makes clear for the first time the emerging division of function between the spiritual responsibilities of the caliph and the temporal power of the sultan, his notional protector; the sultan relied on a Turkish army, but made full use of the Persian-speaking expertise of administrators.[76] Arabic was not going to spread across the expanse of Turkish-speaking peoples stretching out into the heart of Asia, even as they embraced Islam. They already had a lingua franca to use with their new subjects, and it was Persian. 'After all, they all speak Persian, don't they?' Arabic was needed only to address God.†

And this indeed was to be the pattern with all the further spreads of Islam that occurred in the second millennium, notably from North Africa south of the Sahara, from Egypt and Arabia down the coast to East Africa and Madagascar, from Baghdad and Bokhara into Siberia and central Asia, from Afghanistan into India, from India into South-East Asia: Arabic was accepted as a sacred language, but had no tendency to spread as a vernacular, or even as a lingua franca for contacts among the new Muslim populations. Except

---

* It may be worth noting that the j in this word is pronounced as in *judge*.

† But one is left wondering why the linguistic approach of the Germans, notably the Visigoths, had been so different, when in 410 they likewise took over control of the neighbouring higher civilisation, the Roman empire, only to cast themselves, almost immediately, as its protectors. But in the European case, there was no third language playing the role of Persian: Latin was still the only language of temporal power, as well as the language of the Roman Church.

for the Hausa speakers of West Africa, none of the converted communities spoke Afro-Asiatic languages; so this conforms to the linguistic constraint.*

Before leaving the subject of the spread of Arabic and its limits, it is right to consider one other way in which Arabic might have been expected to spread, but in fact did not. At least from the beginning of the first century AD to the advent of European adventurers in the fifteenth, it is known that Arab sailors, with perhaps some Persian competition, undertook most of the marine trade between the Near East and the coasts of Africa and India.

The first testimony dates from the first century AD, in the Greek guide for sailors *Períplous Thalássēs Eruthraías*, 'Voyage Round the Indian Ocean'.

(§16) Two days' sail beyond there lies the very last market-town of the continent of Azania [East Africa], which is called Rhapta; which has its name from the sewed boats [*rháptōn ploiaríōn*] already mentioned; in which there is ivory in great quantity, and tortoise-shell. Along this coast live men of piratical habits, very tall, and under separate chiefs for each place. The Mapharitic chief governs it under some ancient right that subjects it to the sovereignty of the state that is become first in Arabia. And the people of Muza now hold it under his authority, and send thither many large ships; using Arab captains and agents, who are familiar with the natives and intermarry with them, and who know the whole coast and understand the language...

(§21) Beyond these places in a bay at the foot of the left side of the gulf, there is a place by the shore called Muza, a market-town established by law, distant altogether from Berenice [*Ras Banas*] for those sailing southward, about 12,000 stadia. And the whole place is crowded with Arab shipowners and seafaring men, and is busy with affairs of commerce; for they carry on a trade with the far-side coast and with Barygaza [Broach, in western India], sending their own ships there.[77]

---

* Hausa, centred on Kano in northern Nigeria, is more of a problem for the constraint. It has certain features that are reminiscent of Arabic, e.g. two genders, masculine and feminine, the latter marked with *-a* (cf. Arabic *-ah*); and the absence of *p*—as in Arabic, it usually replaces *p* in loan-words with *f*. Moreover, its predominantly Muslim speakers have filled it with loan words from Arabic, including most of the numerals above ten, and the days of the week, and even some productive prefixes, such as *ma-*. ('School' is *makaranta*, formed from *karanta*, 'read', itself related to the word *Qur'ān*. In Arabic, 'school' is *maktab*, or *madrasa*, with the same prefix, but **ktb**, 'read', or **drs**, 'lesson', as the stem.) But it also has many features much more typical of its African neighbours, e.g. three contrasting tones, and explosive consonants. It may be that its own utility as a lingua franca, widely used in West Africa and not just among Muslims, has acted to maintain its independence.

Wherever Rhapta (Dar es Salaam?), Muza (al Mukha?) and Mapharitis (Maʿafir?) were, it is clear from this that Arab trade involvement with both sides of the Indian Ocean goes back for well over six hundred years before Muḥammad. It is also a known feature of Arab ships, up until 1500, that their hulls were stitched together, not nailed or pegged.[78] The *1001 Nights'* stories of Sindbad the Sailor (in fact, more a maritime merchant than a sailor) had a strong basis in Arab fact.*

This means that Arabic would have been heard in all the ports along the shores of the Indian Ocean from Mozambique to Malabar and Coromandel in southern India. Surely this might have had a linguistic effect, at least in the creation of a trade jargon? There is, after all, ample precedent, both, as we have seen, in the way that Phoenician was spread round the Mediterranean, and in more recent centuries as European powers have brought their languages to the parts of the world where they went to trade. Trade is usually accounted the first factor that set English on the road to becoming a world language.

In fact, the only vestige of such influence from Arabic is found in East Africa, where Swahili, the major Bantu language, shows heavy signs of Arabic influence. Its very name is derived from Arabic *sawāḥil*, 'coasts'. Counting up to ten, the numbers 6, 7 and 9 are all borrowed from Arabic: Swahili *sita*, *saba* and *tisa* versus Arabic *sitta*, *sabʿa* and *tisʿa*. Unlike almost every other Bantu language, it has no distinctive tones, but it uses certain sounds from Arabic which are unknown in other Bantu languages, notably distinguishing between r and l, and using the consonants th [θ], kh [x] and their voiced analogues dh [ð] and gh [ɣ].

Nevertheless, it remains in many ways characteristically Bantu, with lots of nasals before stops (-nd-, -ng-, -mb-, -nt-, -nk-, -mp-), a variety of special prefixes that show what type of concept is designated by a noun, and heavy agglutinative prefixing on its verbs, doing most of the work that would be done by pronouns, verb inflexions and auxiliaries in languages like English, or indeed Arabic: for example,

wa-zee   *ha-wa-ju-i*   *a-li-ko-kwenda*
people-oldster   not-they-know-not   he-past-there-go
The old men don't know where he has gone.

---

* They even plied, especially in the early centuries, to South-East Asia and China. *Abū Zayd* of *Sīrāf* wrote that sea traffic in 851 was regular because of a great exchange of merchants between Iraq and markets in India and China: in fact, he said, a trade colony of 120,000 Westerners (including Muslims, Jews, Christians and Zoroastrians) were massacred in Canton in 878 (Hourani 1995: 76–7).

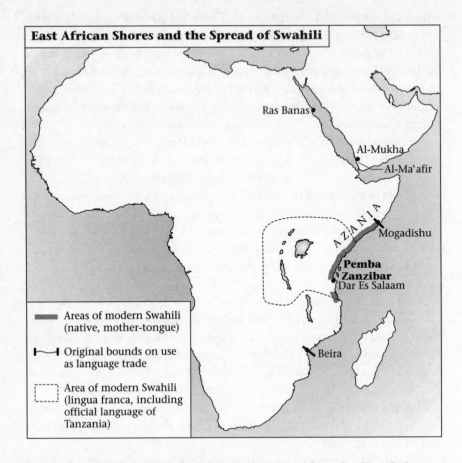

East African Shores and the Spread of Swahili

Ras Banas

Al-Mukha

Al-Ma'afir

AZANIA

Mogadishu

Pemba
Zanzibar
Dar Es Salaam

Beira

▬▬ Areas of modern Swahili
(native, mother-tongue)

⊢—⊣ Original bounds on use
as language trade

Area of modern Swahili
(lingua franca, including
official language of
Tanzania)

The reckoning is that the spread of Bantu languages from the Great Lakes region would have reached the Zanzibar* area early in this millennium, so that an early version of the language may well have been learnt by the Arab visitors mentioned in the *Períplous*. When Europeans first arrived on the scene (the Portuguese in 1498), Swahili was spoken in a thin strip all along the coast from Mogadishu in Somalia to Beira in Mozambique. The oldest surviving Arabic inscription in the region is from a mosque built in 1107, and it is clear that Arabic was much used as a trade language here, often in mixtures with other languages that have since died out. There may also have been influence in the opposite direction: it is said that some coastal dialects of Arabic in Arabia and Iraq show signs of Swahili influence.[79]

Be this as it may, Swahili is now the official language in the states of Tanzania and Kenya, and widely used in the neighbouring countries of Uganda,

---

* Zanzibar is in fact an Arabised form of Persian: *Zangi-bar*, 'blacks' land'.

Mozambique, Rwanda, Burundi, the Congos, Madagascar and the Comoros. Since the advent of European colonists, it has played a major role as a lingua franca of empires, as well as a less honourable one as the argot of slave-traders and their victims. Despite the vast numbers who use it (estimated at 40 million), Swahili is learnt as a native language only on the islands and coast close to Zanzibar. Perhaps as always, the vast majority of its speakers (some 90 per cent) pick it up later in life. Without Arab trade there would have been no Swahili as we know it, but Arabic influence on it ceased long ago.

THIRD INTERLUDE:
TURKIC AND PERSIAN, OUTRIDERS OF ISLAM

Kalkıp ta yerimden doğrulayım, derdim,
Yelesi-kara Kazılık atıma bineyim, derdim,
Kalabalık Oğuz içine gireyim, derdim,
Ala-gözlü gelin alayım, derdim,
Kara yere ak otaklar dikeyim, derdim,
Yürüyüp oğulu ak gerdeğe göçüreyim, derdim,
Muradına, maksuduna eriştireyim, derdim,
Murada erdirmedin beni!
Kara başım ilenci tutsun, Kazan, seni!*

I said to myself, let me get up from my seat and stand,
I said to myself, let me ride my black-maned Kazilik horse,
I said to myself, let me go among the throngs of Oghuz,
I said to myself, let me find a chestnut-eyed daughter-in-law,
I said to myself, let me pitch white tents on the black earth,
I said to myself, let me walk the boy to his bridal chamber,
I said to myself, let me bring him to his wish, to his desire,
You did not let me attain my wish,
May the dark head's curse seize you, Kazan!

> Dede Korkut, *The Lineage of Uzun the Prisoner, son of Kazan Bey*
> (A mother berates her husband for losing their son on a raid)

Two other major languages, Turkic (spoken in a variety of forms, but all fairly close to modern Turkish) and Persian, are now best known as the aux-

---

* In Turkish spelling (introduced by Atatürk in 1928–9), *c* is [dž] (j in *judge*), *ç* is [č] (ch in *church*), *ı* is i pronounced with the tongue root drawn back (as in Scots *kirk*), and *ğ* is either a gargling sound (like Greek gamma or Arabic ghain) or just a lengthening of the preceding vowel; *ö* and *ü* are as in German.

EMPIRES OF THE WORD

iliary languages of Islamic civilisation. We have had to give them walk-on roles in the history of Arabic, but unjustly: both have interesting histories which go back for a thousand years before their speakers' fateful conversions to Islam, and have contributed equally to their characters today and in the past.

The Turkic languages spread out over a vast area from western Mongolia to the Aegean Sea. As Xiongnu and Tabgatch, their speakers had harried and overrun the Chinese in the third and fourth centuries AD; in the fifth they were terrorising northern India as the Hūṇa, and eastern Europe as Hunni. In 451 they even briefly rode to France with Attila. Khazars ruled the south of Russia from the Black Sea to the Caspian from the sixth century to the eleventh. Turkic-speaking recruits made up the majority of the armies of Genghis Khan the Mongol in the early thirteenth century, and as members of the Golden Horde it was they who sacked Kiev in 1240, permanently shifting the centre of Russian power. (See Chapter 11, 'The origins of Russian', p. 426.) Other Turks, the Seljuks and later the Ottomans, brought down the Byzantine Greeks, and settled all over Anatolia, from the eleventh to the fifteenth centuries. In the sixteenth century, the Turkic-speaking Tatars in Kazan' and Astrakhan were still seen by the Russians as the major obstacle to their expansion, one that now needed to be dislodged; and in the eighteenth century it was the Tatars in the Crimea who were very much in the Russians' way.

In the eighth and ninth centuries, Turks were writing funeral inscriptions in the Orkhon valley in Outer Mongolia in a runic alphabet of their own devising. Then they took up Sogdian writing, converting it into the vertical Uighur script of central Asia. In the eleventh century they encountered the Persians, and adopted Arabic script from them, even writing a dictionary of their language and a long didactic poem, the *Kutadğū Bilig*, 'The Knowledge of Auspiciousness'. In fourteenth-century Persia and Samarkand, the form of Turkic known as Chagatay—after the second son of Genghis Khan—was the language of culture in courts of the Mongolian khans,[80] and when Babur, the first of the Mughals, swept down from Afghanistan to conquer India in 1505, this was the language he spoke to his men, even if he preferred to write in Persian.[81]

It would almost be fair to take Babur's approach as the spirit of Ottoman Turkish up to the twentieth century. Official Turkish was always heavily infused with literary Persian finery until Atatürk's attempts to reform it in the 1930s.[82]

* * *

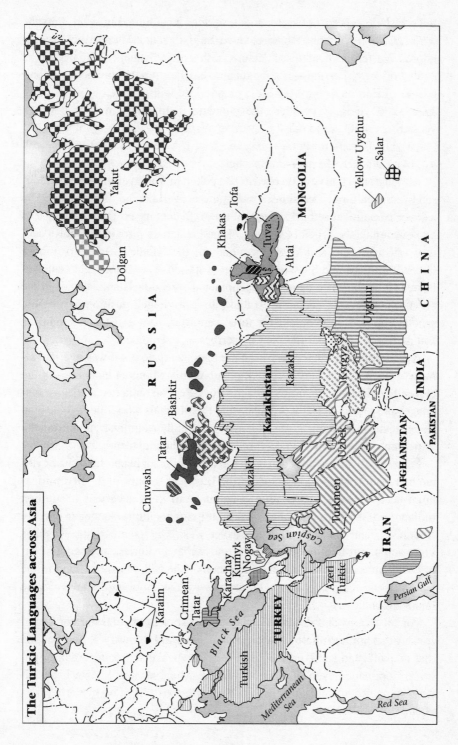

The Turkic Languages across Asia

If Turkish deserves its own treatment, so does its cultural big sister, Persian, or *Farsī*, a highly literate language since the sixth century BC. To this day, un-tutored Westerners tend to see Persia as rather an indistinct eastern part of the Arab world: yet Persian—as a language—has far more in common with languages of Europe or northern India than it does with Arabic or Turkish. Despite 1200 years of practice, the phonetic distinctions in Arabic which Westerners find hard to master, *s, z, t, d* versus *ṣ, ẓ, ṭ, ḍ*, and *ʾ* (alif) versus *ʿ* (ʿayn), are difficult for Persian speakers too. The Persian word for 'is' is still *ast*, like Latin *est*, German *ist*, Russian *yest*ʸ and Sanskrit *asti*.

Although it is has never ceased to be spoken in Iran over the last two thousand years, culturally it has been unfortunate, overlaid and disadvantaged by a series of political setbacks. First, in the sixth century BC Darius decided to make Aramaic the official language of the Persian empire; in the fourth century BC, when the empire was conquered, the Seleucids tried to impose Greek. Parthians and Sassanids reasserted its self-esteem for eight centuries from 140 BC, but then came the phenomenal spread of Islamic forces in the seventh century AD, elevating Arabic into a privileged position in religion, scholarship and government for three centuries. 'No assistance should be sought from pagans in office work,' scribes were enjoined.[83]

A resurgence of Persian began in the tenth century, but it was overlaid almost at once by the Turkic-speaking (nominally Mongol) incursions in the eleventh to fifteenth centuries. Nevertheless, Persian remained a prestige language; and thanks to Delhi Sultanate and the Mughals who followed, Persian also became the principal official language of Indian administration, from the thirteenth century until it yielded to English in the nineteenth.

Persian's relatives have also been highly significant in central Asia. Scythian had been spoken across most of the Eurasian steppes in the first millennium BC. (It survives as Ossetic, a language of the Caucasus.) In the first millennium AD, Śaka-Khotanese was an important cultural language of early Buddhism; and Bactrian, spoken farther west, was taken by the Kushāna kings across northern India in the first and second centuries AD. Sogdian, centred on Samarkand, was the lingua franca of the Silk Road to China in the eighth to the tenth centuries. (It survives as Yaghnobi, still spoken in the Pamir mountains.)

For all its ups and downs, Persian is still spoken beyond the borders of Iran in the northern half of Afghanistan (as *Darī*, 'courtly'), and beyond that in Tajikistan (as *Tajik*). And despite its speakers' frequent lack of political dominance even in their own lands, wherever it is known it has always remained a language of high cultural prestige, famed particularly for its poetry.

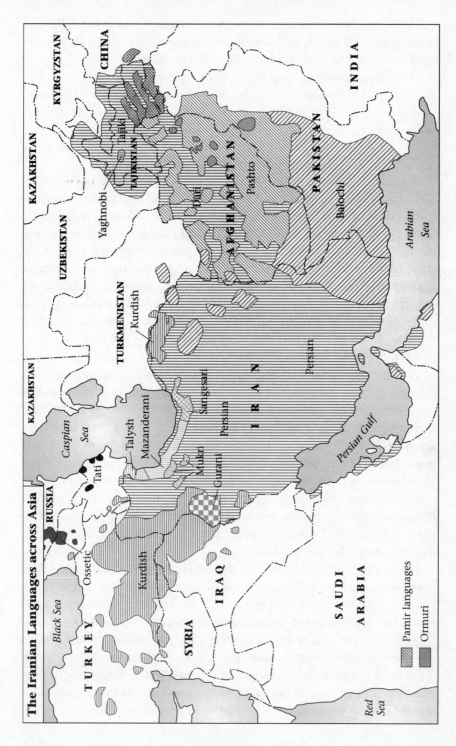

The Iranian Languages across Asia

Pamir languages
Ormuri

Three things have modelled themselves on three of yours –
Rose on cheek, grape on lip, beauty on face.
Three things each year are taken from three of mine –
Grief from heart, tears from cheek, fancy from eye.

Abul Qasim 'Unsuri (b. c.968 in Balkh, central Asia; d. c.1040 AD)

A Middle Eastern inheritance:
The glamour of the desert nomad

The present-day globalised world is full of Arabic. It is the language that would-be Islamist revolutionaries in Europe and the USA feel they have to learn to give authenticity to their struggle; and its ironic similarity to Hebrew, newly revived in the land of Canaan, is a standing reminder of how the bitterest conflicts set long-lost cousins at each other's throats: *salām* contends against *šəlōm*, but the common meaning, 'peace', continues to elude them. Meanwhile the classical language is still intoned every day in Muslim prayer, and broadcast to an audience of well over 200 million souls, all of whom think when they converse, in their very different ways, that they are talking Arabic, *ʿarabīya*.

The language tradition of large-scale, unitary Semitic languages to which they are all heirs goes back demonstrably for five thousand years. In that time, there has been opportunity for a lot of innovations; the world has seen in their tradition the first adoption of a foreign language as a classic model for literature, the first system of writing with multilingual application, the first lingua franca of international diplomacy, the first archival libraries, the first alphabetic scripts, the first spread of language through trading colonies, the first substitution of one language for another without breakdown of a single literate tradition, the first use of a language as the talisman of a minority religious sect, the first designation of the written record of a particular language as the unchangeable word of God.

That is a fair record of firsts for a single tradition, even if its dominant language has twice been replaced, or, to put it perhaps better, renewed. We shall consider elsewhere the significance of all these examples in the general pattern of the development of human language systems.

An appropriate final reflection here might be to consider whether there is any distinctive continuity of character in this ancient tradition. Is there something about Arabic which it shares with Aramaic and Akkadian? Or have so many innovations, on the way through remote antiquity and the Middle Ages into the modern world, in effect revised away any common core?

Fernand Braudel saw in the total success of Muslim advance, so sudden and apparently so inexplicable, the natural reassertion of the Near Eastern tradition, after a Greek and Roman interruption of a thousand years.[84] He did see the Arabic language as the surest proof that countries are truly part of Muslim civilisation,[85] yet the examples he gives of continuity in Near Eastern civilisation—dress, food, domestic architecture, even monotheistic faith—have nothing to do with language.[86]

At the most obvious level, the values promoted in Islam are the polar opposite of what their great imperialist predecessors the Assyrians embraced. The Muslims put forward their unique conception of God as a reason to accept their rule, emphasising all the while His infinite compassion. The Assyrian armies rolled over their neighbours to prove the greater might of their kings, and demonstrated their power through orgies of ruthlessness. Their gods followed, and if many chose to worship them, this was purely an acknowledgement of the greater power of all they stood for, an act of prudence and diplomacy, not the acceptance of a revelation or an act of sincere submission.

The Arabs going into battle for Islam can be seen in fact as an alloy of three very different preceding traditions among their fellow-speakers of Semitic languages: the abstract theology of the Jews, the embracing inclusiveness of the Aramaic Christians, and the military momentum of the Assyrians. Indeed, if one includes their propensity for long-distance navigation and speculative trading, they can also be ranged with the Phoenicians.

But there is one thing in the cultural background which does unite all the Semites, of whatever religion or desired level of opulence. However successful their cities, however developed their religions and philosophies, they never escaped the memory that they had all arisen from desert nomads. Arabic was the language of nomads, and Islam was founded by nomad aggression from Arabia. Aramaic penetrated the Assyrian and Babylonian empires, and so became established, through nomads spreading from Aram. The Hebrews and Phoenicians developed their cities and their cultures when Habiru nomads had finally settled down in the land of Canaan; explicitly, the Torah talks of the children of Israel wandering through the wilderness of Sinai for forty years. And the Akkadians might never have taken over from Sumer without the incursions of those little-known nomads of the west, the Amorites. Ultimately, surely, it must have been nomads who brought the Semitic languages in prehistoric times out of Africa and into the Fertile Crescent.

Nomads may be hard to find in the modern Semitic world. But aspects of nomadism are still central to the unsolved problems of the Arabs: the homelessness of the Palestinians, the moral queasiness about the unearned riches welling up from the desert wastes of Arabia, the wild men of al-Qaʻeda in self-imposed exile while they plan destruction for the iniquitous cities. In all this, speakers of Arabic are very true to their tradition. Indeed, the histories of Akkadian, Phoenician, Aramaic and Arabic are a five-thousand-year demonstration of the benefits of the desert—as a place to come in from.

4

Triumphs of Fertility: Egyptian and Chinese

jᵒw wār ʿar ptaḥ* For the very great one is Ptah,

sabaš ʿanḫ na nāt̯ᵘūraw nibuw who gave life to all the gods

kaʀuw-sin and their ka's

s nib m ḫāʀtj pᵒn through this heart

s nib m nis pᵒn through this tongue,

ḫāpir-na ḫōruw jᵒmf in which Horus has taken shape,

ḫāpir-na djᵒḥowtij jᵒmf in which Thoth has taken shape,

m ptaḥ as Ptah …

(Horus (*Ḫōruw*) personifies kingship. Thoth (*Djeḥowtij*), god of reason, is also the patron of scribes.)

māʀaʀ ījruwy Sight of the eyes,

---

* In the interests of readability and realism, Egyptian words are given according to the reconstruction of Loprieno 1995 for early Middle Egyptian, with the addition that vowels that he believes indiscernible are represented here by *ᵒ*. ʀ is the French (or Israeli) uvular r, and *j* is pronounced as in German, like English y in *yet*. ḥ is a deeper h, as when huffing on a pair of glasses; and ḫ is like ch in 'loch' or 'Bach'. ʿ is ayn, notorious from Semitic languages, the throat-clearing sound at the beginning of English 'ahem'. It should be remembered, however, that as written in hieroglyphs, Egyptian words are totally without vowels.

sādjim m°sdj°rwy   hearing of the ears,

s°s°n°w f°rdj   breathing of the nose –

sa ʿar-sin   they report

ḥar jib,   to the heart,

°ntaf   it

dadaj paraj   makes come forth

°rq°y°t nib   every understanding.

j°n nis j°m   As to the tongue,

kaʀat m ḥārtj   it says what is in the heart.

suw masjaw nātˢūraw nibuw   Thus all the gods were born

tam pisīdjat-°f   and his Ennead (Nine Gods) was
          completed.

s°k ḫāpir-na   For lo! there came about

j°s nātˢar maduww nib   every word of the god

m kaʀʀt hārtj   through what the heart devised

wadj nis   and the tongue commanded.

Memphite Theology ('The Shabaka Stone'), lines 53, 56
(Egyptian, mid-third millennium BC, recopied in 710 BC)[1]

子路曰：「衛君待子而為政，   zǐlù yuē:「wèi jūn dài zǐ ér wèi zhèng,
子將奚先？」   zǐ jiāng xī xiān?」
子曰：「必也正名乎！」   zǐ yuē:「bì yě zhèng míng hū!」
子路曰：「有是哉？子之迂   zǐlù yuē:「yǒu shì zāi? zǐ zhī yū
也！奚其正？」   yě! xī qí zhèng?」
子曰：「野哉，由也！君子   zǐ yuē:「yězāi, yóu yě! jūn zǐ

於其所不知，蓋闕如也。　　yú qí suǒ bù zhī, gài què rú yě.
名不正，則言不訓；　　　　míng bù zhèng, zé yán bù xùn;
言不訓，則事不成；　　　　yán bù xùn, zé shì bù chéng;
事不成，則禮樂不興；　　　shì bù chéng, zé lǐ lè bù xīng;
禮樂不興，則刑罰不中；　　lǐ lè bù xīng, zé xíng fá bù zhōng;
刑罰不中，　　　　　　　　xíng fá bù zhōng,
則民無所措手足。　　　　　zé mín wú suǒ cuò shǒu zú.
故君子名之必可言也，　　　gù jūn zǐ míng zhī bì kě yán yě,
言之必可行也。君　　　　　yán zhī bì kě xíng yě. jūn
子於其言，無所苟而已矣！」　zǐ yú qí yán, wú suǒgǒu ér yǐ yǐ!」*

Zi-lu said, 'If the Prince of Wei were awaiting you, Sir, to take control of his administration, what would be the Master's priority?'

'The one thing needed is the correction of names!' the Master replied.

'Are you as wide of the mark as that, Sir?' said Zi-lu. 'Why this correcting?'

'How uncultivated you are, Yu!' responded the Master. 'A wise man, in regard to what he does not understand, maintains an attitude of reserve. If names are not correct then statements do not accord with facts. And when statements and facts do not accord, then business cannot be properly executed. When business is not properly executed, order and harmony do not flourish. When order and harmony do not flourish, then justice becomes arbitrary. And when justice becomes arbitrary, people do not know how to move hand or foot. Hence whatever a wise man states he can always define, and what he so defines he can always carry into practice; for the wise man will on no account have anything remiss in his definitions.'

Confucius, Lúnyǔ† (Analects), xiii:3 (Chinese, early fifth century BC)[2]

---

* This Pinyin romanisation represents a modern Mandarin pronunciation of this text from the fifth century BC. As such it represents the words and the sentence structure, but not the sounds that Confucius would have used.

† In this book, Chinese is transcribed using the *pīnyīn zìmǔ* 'phonetic alphabet' system, usually known as Pinyin, officially promoted by the Chinese government since 1958. In it, the accents ($\bar{v}$, $\acute{v}$, $\check{v}$, $\grave{v}$) denote tone patterns, not different vowel sounds . Among consonants, c is English ts, j is English j, q English ch, and x English sh. You will also see zh, ch and sh: these are pronounced similarly to j, q and x, but with retroflex tongue, as if there were an r immediately following. Most Chinese outside the north-east area are in fact incapable of making the distinction. Pinyin has the virtue of being compact, accurate and consistent (without the irritating apostrophes of the older Western systems, Wade-Giles and Yale) but it can only claim to represent modern pronunciation. This can be misleading when it is applied to very old words and names.

Two ancient languages, widely distant in their lands and their eras, are yet strangely similar in their careers. In their attributes they are unmatched, except by each other.

Egyptian and Chinese are both vehicles of single cultural traditions of immense prestige. For each, the role as universal language was uncontested in their homeland. By the dawn of their recorded histories they were already established over the central zone of the lands where they were to be spoken. Each maintained this position of solitary and basically unchanging dominance for an awesome period of over three thousand years, or more than 120 generations. Yet, in each case, despite the fame and prestige of the culture among neighbours, who were often dominated politically by these powers, the languages never assumed any role as lingua franca beyond the territory that they considered their homeland.

Another parallel concerns their scripts. Each language originated its own unique system of writing, based on pictograms in a particular style; and each of these scripts early attained a form that would not change. Each was later taken up by another people, and simplified to yield the basis for a phonetic writing system: Egyptian hieroglyphs were the starting point for the Phoenicians' alphabet, and the Japanese drew their *kana* syllabary from Chinese characters. But in each case the original language culture disregarded the innovation, and maintained its ancient system essentially unchanged, despite the vast overhead this entailed in continuing lengthy scribal education.

Their careers are parallel. For us, their main interest lies in considering how a language can achieve steady state, a kind of homoeostasis where it appears to absorb any perturbation that might affect it. This steadiness is particularly interesting in the cases of Egypt and China, since the languages have not simply survived in isolation, but can be seen coping with human incursions for much of their history, and occupy spaces large enough to pose difficulties for a unitary government.

Another aspect of this puzzling unity, especially in the case of Chinese, is the strange coherence of the language itself. Certainly Chinese has dialects, and they are different enough often to be considered distinct languages. But this famous fact is less interesting than a less noted one: over 70 per cent of Chinese speakers speak a single variety, known as Mandarin or *Pŭtōnghuà*,*

---

* The word *Mandarin* is not Chinese at all, but a deformation of the Sanskrit word *māntrin*, 'counsellor', with some influence from the Portuguese verb *mandar*, 'command'. *Pŭtōnghuà* means 'common language', a term with an inclusive feel, which has largely replaced older terms such as *guānhuà*, 'official language' (the closest to a Chinese equivalent for *Mandarin*), or *guóyŭ*, 'national language', which referred to much the same thing. *Hànyŭ*, 'Han language', is another term used.

and this, the official language of the Chinese state, is spoken in more than 75 per cent of the country's area. It has some local accents but essentially no internal variation. Since both the Chinese population and surface area are vast, the degree of uniformity so achieved is unparalleled in any other known language. We need to consider how it could have come about.

The two also have some direct implications for the modern world.

Egyptian, after all, did ultimately succumb to the incursions of its neighbours, carried out with steadily increasing permanence by waves of Assyrians, Persians, Greeks, Romans and Arabs, and now survives, if at all, as Coptic, in the liturgy of what was a foreign religion, Christianity. There is evidence here of what it takes to obliterate a seemingly eternal tradition in the land of its birth. How is immortality undone?

By contrast, Chinese, for all the political reverses and atrocities its people have suffered at the hands of heartless foreigners in the last two centuries, has never been stronger than it is today. Its speakers make up one sixth of the world's population, and it has three native speakers for every one of English. Nevertheless, over 99 per cent of them live in China, so it cannot be considered a world language—unless China is your world. Those who speak it often call it *zhōng guǒ huà*, 'centre realm speech': in that at least Chinese ethnocentrism is undiminished. There is still time to consider those forces that have kept the Chinese realm so firmly, and compactly, centred on its traditional homeland: will they still prevail in the modern world?

Careers in parallel

The remarkable similarity of the careers of the Egyptian and Chinese languages can first be displayed in the form of two chronological charts. Foreign incursions and cultural influences are marked in boldface type.

Both Egyptian and Chinese history are made up of long periods of stable unitary government, interspersed with intervals of civil unrest, or at least disunity, when there were competing dynasties in different parts of the countries. Egypt has three such periods of stable self-government, the Archaic + Old, the Middle and the New Kingdoms, followed by a Late Period, when foreign rule was the norm rather than the exception. China also has three long periods of indigenous rule, the feudal age of the Shang and Zhou dynasties, the First Empire of the Qin and Han dynasties, and the Second Empire of the Sui, Tang and Song, which then were overlaid by a succession of partial or total alien invasions.

Both civilisations were formed originally along the valley of a single river,

China	Politics	Linguistic Events
? 2800?	Earliest settlements	First characters, on wine jars?
2100	*Xià dynasty* (5 centuries)	
1766	*Shāng dynasty* (7 centuries)	
c.1300		Characters on oracle bones
1027	*Zhōu dynasty* (3 centuries)	
721	*Disunity* (5 centuries)	
221	*Qín, Hàn dynasties* (4.5 centuries)	
210 BC		Standardisation of characters
AD 65		**First entry of Buddhism**
220	*Disunity* (3.5 centuries)	

Egypt	Politics	Linguistic Events
5000 3150	Earliest settlements	First hieroglyphs, on wall paintings
3000	Archaic period (3 centuries)	
2700	Old Kingdom (6 centuries)	
2100	*Disunity* (0.5 century)	
2050	Middle Kingdom (3 centuries)	
1750	*Disunity* (2 centuries)	

China	Politics	Linguistic Events
311		Hun (Xiongnu, Xian Bei) incursions of north
386		Tabgach (Wei) invades north
401		Kumarajiva sets up Buddhist translation in Chang-an
511		Liang Wudi invites Buddhist monks to Nanjing
589	*Súi, Táng* dynasties (3.3 centuries)	
610		Grand Canal links Chang-an to Hangzhou
635		Nestorian monk welcomed at Chang-an

Egypt	Politics	Linguistic Events
c.1639		Hyksōs kings in the Delta (1 century)
1550	New Kingdom (5 centuries)	
1180–74		Libyans (and Sea-peoples) repulsed
1050	*Disunity (3 centuries)*	

China	Politics	Linguistic Events
645		**Xuan-Zang welcomed home to Chang-an; Buddhism established at Tang court**
845		Wu Zong dissolves monasteries of Buddhism and Nestorian Christianity
907	*Disunity* *(0.5 century)*	
960	Sòng dynasty (3.2 centuries)	
916		**Khitan (Liáo) invade north**
1115		**Jurchen (Jin) invade north**

Egypt	Politics	Linguistic Events
945	**Libyan dynasty (2 centuries)**	
750	**Kushite dynasty (1 century)**	**Kushite invasion**
671–64		**Assyrian invasion**
664	Saite dynasty (1.4 centuries)	
525	**Persian rule (2 centuries, interspersed by Egyptian rule)**	**Persian invasion**
332	**Greek dynasty (3 centuries)**	**Greek invasion**

China	Politics	Linguistic Events
1200s		Plague (?) depopulates Sichuan
1211		Mongol invasion of North
1279		Mongol conquest of South
1271	*Yuán* dynasty (1 century)	Mongol conquest of Yunnan
1368	Míng dynasty (3 centuries)	
1644		Manchu invasion
1644	*Qīng* dynasty (2.5 centuries)	Repopulation of Sichuan
1911	*Disunity*	
1949	People's Republic	

Egypt	Politics	Linguistic Events
30 BC	Roman/Byzantine rule (7 centuries)	
AD 300	Spread of Christianity (3 centuries)	
394		Last use of hieroglyphs
641	Arab rule (6 centuries)	Arab invasion
1260	Mamelukes (2.6 centuries)	
1520	Ottoman rule (3.5 centuries)	
c.1550		Final loss of spoken Coptic; persistence in Christian liturgy

the Nile* and the Huang-he ('Yellow River') respectively, although China expanded to take in the next great river valley to the south, the Yangtze Kiang.† And both civilisations demonstrated that, although they were not capable of defending their borders indefinitely, successful invaders stood to be absorbed in the long term. The linguistic analogue of this was that no foreign invaders imposed their language on the population, nor indeed (until the Persians and then the Greeks took Egypt) managed to retain their own language for more than a generation after mastering the country.

These are both tales of solid growth and heroic maintenance, rather than massive spread. This chapter first sketches each language's history, particularly noting the encounters with languages spoken by foreign intruders: these often came to stay, but tended not to supplant their hosts. Armed with the facts, we can then consider what might be the secrets of such language stability.

Language along the Nile

Be a craftsman in speech, thou mayest be strong, the tongue is a sword to a man, and speech is more valorous than any fighting...

Instruction for King Merikare, line 32 (Egyptian, mid-twentieth century BC)[3]

The origin of the Egyptian language must be found close at hand, in the Afro-Asiatic or Hamito-Semitic family whose descendant languages cover most of North Africa and the neighbouring areas of the Fertile Crescent (from Palestine round to Iraq) and Arabia. Egyptian has no close relatives in this large family, but its family origins do account for some of its characteristic features, mundane things such as the fact that feminine nouns end in -t.§

---

* The origin of this name seems to be an early Greek attempt to represent late Egyptian n-irw-aʀ, 'the-rivers-great', referring to the Nile's many streams in the Delta area. This is related to jatruw, '(the) river', always its name in classical Egyptian (Luft 1992).

† The original name was Kiang alone, an Austro-Asiatic word, related to words for 'river' in Vietnamese sông (once pronounced 'krong') and Mon kruŋ, showing the kind of language spoken here before Chinese came in from the north (Norman 1988: 18).

§ Compare san, 'brother', with sānat, 'sister'. Most abstract nouns share this femininity, e.g. maʀ'at, 'righteousness' (always conceived as a goddess). See pp. 35ff. for a longer description of Semitic features.

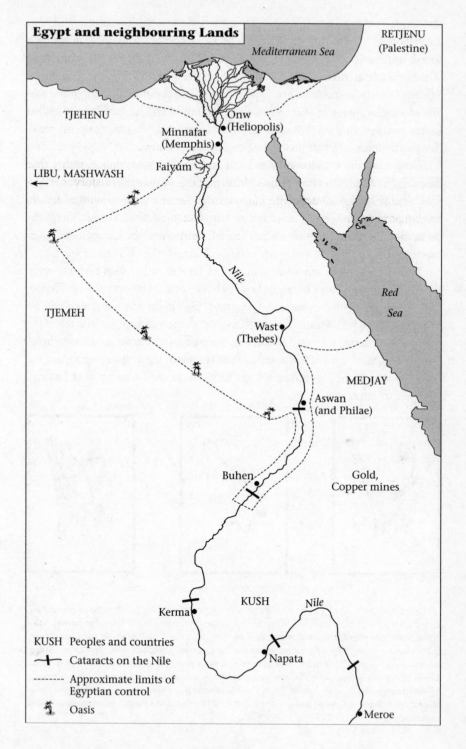

Egypt and neighbouring Lands

RETJENU
(Palestine)

Mediterranean Sea

TJEHENU

Onw
(Heliopolis)

Minnafar
(Memphis)

LIBU, MASHWASH

Faiyum

Nile

Red
Sea

TJEMEH

Wast
(Thebes)

MEDJAY

Aswan
(and Philae)

Buhen

Gold,
Copper mines

KUSH   Nile

Kerma

Napata

KUSH   Peoples and countries

━┼━   Cataracts on the Nile

┄┄┄   Approximate limits of
         Egyptian control

🌴   Oasis

Meroe

A stately progress

Archaeology shows that the Egyptian state was established first in the late fourth millennium BC, in the region surrounding the great salient of the Nile which was later dominated by the city of *Wast* (known to the Greeks as Thebes), hence in southern or 'Upper' Egypt. It is apparent that Egyptian was already the language spoken, since there are legible hieroglyphic captions on labels and pots in the royal cemetery in this area, at Abydos, from the early third millennium. In fact pre-dynastic sites, of this so-called Nagada culture, have been discovered along the whole length of the Nile from Aswan to the delta and including the Faiyum, showing that the whole area of ancient Egypt was already occupied. Since the surrounding desert remained uninhabitable, the kingdom of Egypt was always a ribbon development along the Nile. Traditionally, its history begins when King Menes unified the Upper and Lower lands, and set up his capital at *Min Nafər* (Memphis) in Lower Egypt.*

This achievement remained a matter of legend rather than history, since the king's name cannot be identified with any of the hieroglyphic evidence, and there is no written evidence of separate kings in the north and south. Nevertheless, there was a tradition of differently shaped and coloured crowns for the two kingdoms, unified formally in the historical crown of the pharaoh† (in a way reminiscent of the composite character of the Union Jack). And the name by which the Egyptians always knew their own country was *Tarwəj*, 'the pair of lands'.

The crowns of Egypt: Lower, Upper, and combined

---

* The name *Memphis* actually refers to King Pepi's pyramid there, built some seven hundred years later: 'stable in beauty'. *Egypt* is inexact as a name for the country. Reflecting the Greek word *Aiguptos*, it is in fact a title of Memphis: a slurring of *həyt kruw ptah*, 'temple of the Ka-energy of Ptah'. *kruw* was the sustenance to the life force *kar*, given by food and drink, and sacrificial offerings.

† This common word for the king of Egypt was established by its use in the Hebrew Bible. It represents the Egyptian ⌐◻ *pr-ʿr* (House-Great), and so is like using 'the Palace' to refer to the British monarch.

Thereafter, Egyptian has no history, in that it had achieved its historic domain, the Nile valley from the first cataract to the sea. Although Egyptian power would expand periodically and withdraw again, up the Nile into Nubia and north-eastward over Palestine and Syria, the language did not spread with it. For almost four thousand years its range stayed the same.

Nevertheless, spoken Egyptian did change phonetically and syntactically over this time. The classical language of Egyptian literature was refined and established in the third millennium. Known as 'Middle Egyptian', its use was maintained in writing as far as possible until the end of Egypt's civilisation, above all in formal and ritual texts. But evidently the language gradually changed on the lips of its speakers. Among a host of finer periods, linguists distinguish broadly an earlier era (3000–1300 BC) from a later one (1300 BC–AD 1500). From the middle of the second millennium, it is clear that the spoken language had moved on significantly.

On the simplest level, the sounds of the language change: *r* and the feminine ending *t* are lost at the end of words, and *t̠* (ch in *church*) and *d̠* (j in *judge*) are simplified away, replaced by simple *t* and *d*. But there are structural changes too. They are reminiscent of the way in which Italian came to differ from Latin, or Middle English from Anglo-Saxon. In the older period, Egyptian had been highly inflected, with a set of endings for number and gender; it had had no definite or indefinite article (corresponding to English *the* or *a*); and the characteristic word order had the verb first in the sentence, followed by subject and then object. In the later period the noun endings tend to be lost, but articles come into play, expressing the distinctions in a different way. The verb system becomes more dependent on auxiliaries, and so less highly inflected. Furthermore, the subject now tends to come first in the sentence (as it does in modern English).

Take a single example, the Egyptian for 'Hallowed be thy name'. This changed from

| *uw ʿobu* | *rin-k.* | to | *mare pe-k-ran* | *ouop.* |
| shall-be-purified | name-your | | let-do the-your-name | be-pure |

The pieces of classical Egyptian are still basically there, but now put together quite differently.

Charmingly, the first glimpse of this later language to appear in the record is the more popular style of writing seen under the religious reformer Pharaoh Akhenaten; this writing reform came along with official portraits that for the first time emphasised a pharaoh's home life, with his queen Nefertiti and their daughters, around 1330 BC.

Akhenaten with his wife and daughters

Although the state religion and the decorum of official iconography were restored after his reign, the antiquated style of written expression never fully came back. Religious texts (rituals, mythology and hymns) did continue to be written in the classical form of the language; indeed it persisted until the end of hieroglyphic writing in the fourth century AD; but popular literature, school texts and administrative documents show that a different variant of the language was now being used generally.

The language persisted in Egypt as the main medium of daily life for another two thousand years from the time of Akhenaten.

Against this underlying continuity, the main dramatic interest was provided by contact with other languages whose speakers came to live in Egypt. There were four such languages: Libyan, Kushite, Aramaic and Greek.

Immigrants from Libya and Kush

The Libyans first put pressure on Egypt in the thirteenth century BC, a generation after the fall of Akhenaten. We read of desert campaigns by the pharaohs Seti I and Ramses II, but there appears to have been a steady trickle of immigration. Companies of Libyan troops, notably the Qahaq, Shardana and Mashwash, were accepted into the Egyptian army as auxiliaries.[4] Ramses' successor Merneptah (1211–1202) reports a massive victory against would-be invading armies of Libyan peoples, Libu, Mashwash and Tjehenu. And

Ramses III, a generation later, tells of similar defensive actions c.1179 and 1176. Nevertheless, a steady infiltration into Egypt seems to have continued, and the Libyan presence became a fixture in the Delta area. Ramses III himself had a Libyan slave, Ynene, serving him at court.[5] Two hundred and seventy years later, the Libyan faction had established itself with sufficient stability to marry into the royal family. The XXII dynasty, ruling not from Memphis but from Tanis in the Delta, was founded by the Libyan parvenu Shoshenq, a Mashwash. It lasted 230 years, although it was riven by family feuding and was forced to accept a joint (equally Libyan-dominated) kingdom with a separate dynasty set up in another Delta town, Taremu (Leontopolis).

The incoming Libyans would have spoken a language related to modern Berber or Tamazight, still spoken in much of North Africa. But the linguistic effect of their arrival is imperceptible. An Egyptian pharaoh of the twenty-first century, Inyotef, had had a dog called ʿabaqero, which seems to be the Tuareg Berber name for a greyhound, abaikour.[6] And among the Egyptian numerals, the word for 'ten', mudjaw, is reminiscent of the Berber mraw.[7] This is not much.

To the Egyptian south was the land of Kush. In this direction aggression flowed in the opposite direction from that across the Libyan border. The Egyptian motive can be inferred from the transparent etymology of their name for Kush, Nubia—from nābaw (Coptic nūb), 'gold'—although the chief mines were inconveniently sited in the eastern deserts. But like Egypt, it could also be seen as an integral part of Kūmat, 'The Black Land', made up of fertile Nile silt, the kingdom that existed only as a ribbon development along the great river. Egypt had been operating south of the natural boundary at the first cataract throughout the Old Kingdom, mining gold and establishing a settlement at Buhen, by the second cataract. It gained full control of Nubia in the nineteenth century, lost it again in the eighteenth, re-established control in the sixteenth and then held it for five hundred years. The Egyptian viceroy was given the title zīr nasuwt kuš, 'King's Son of Kush', to emphasise his centrality in the government. Around 1087 the holder of this office abused his position to occupy the Egyptian capital, Thebes, and then withdrew south of the first cataract to declare effective independence for Nubia.

Nothing more is then heard of Nubia for 260 years, but around 728 the ruler of Kush, now based at Napata but investing himself with full pharaonic splendour, asserted a claim to celebrate the worship of the gods at Thebes, Memphis and Ōnw (Heliopolis). He was able to enforce his claim, and the next sixty years saw Kushites in (fairly loose) control of Egypt. The unity of the Black Land had come back to haunt its erstwhile masters.

This unity was ended, as it happened, by a full-scale Assyrian invasion, coming in from the opposite end of the country in 664 BC. In the aftermath, a new dynasty in Egypt restored indigenous control within its traditional borders,* while the Nubian kings returned to their own land and moved their capital from Napata to Meroe, 400 kilometres farther up the Nile. There they founded the Meroitic civilisation, which lasted until AD c.250, with an alphabetic script based on hieroglyphs. The language they wrote in this way is not related to Egyptian, and is not fully understood to this day.

Once again there was no known impact on Egyptian as used in Egypt itself, despite the long coexistence of Egypt with Nubia. The details of influence are difficult to judge since we have no direct evidence of the language spoken in Kush at the time. During the period of Egyptian control of Kush, Egyptian must have been used widely at elite levels in its northern regions, but use of Egyptian did not survive the withdrawal of links between the two countries, despite the evident enthusiasm for things Egyptian which persisted south of the border. The mutual imperial adventure had lasted, on and off, over two thousand years, but it had left both partners without any lasting linguistic link.

Another country where Egypt attempted conquest was the land of Canaan to its north-east. Since the earliest period there had been trade links with Palestine, and around the middle of the second millennium these became particularly strong with the Phoenician city of Byblos, which supplied cedar timber logged in Lebanon. Around 1830 BC, a pharaoh invaded the south of Palestine, but little is known of his motives or any consequences. Four centuries later, there was a sustained campaign to control the whole country as far north as the borders of Mitanni. This has been explained as an attempt to free Egypt once and for all from the threat of foreign domination, recently suffered under the so-called *Hyk-sōs* kings (a Greek rendering of *ḥqʀ ḫʀst*, 'ruler from abroad'). But there is no evidence, linguistic or other, that this dynasty, whoever they were, had come from the north-east.

Whatever the motive, Egypt did succeed in establishing Egyptian overlordship throughout Palestine and Syria as far as Ugarit in the north. This is confirmed by the Amarna diplomatic correspondence, which relates to the years from 1345 to 1330 BC, and is largely taken up with exchanges of letters between the pharaoh and many of his Canaanite vassals, notably Ribhadda, the ruler of Byblos. This part of the correspondence is exclusively in Akkadian. The letters from the Egyptian side are in quite good Akkadian, but the

---

* Based in *Saʀw* (Sais) in the Delta area, they are rumoured to have been of Libyan ancestry.

answers that came back are in a dialect heavily influenced by Canaanite languages.[8] Neither side was fully at ease in this lingua franca. But the point for us is that after a century of political domination Egypt had not transmitted effective knowledge of its language, not even to kings and officials who were professing themselves servants of an Egyptian master.* Instead they communicated in the language of the principal eastern power.

Competition from Aramaic and Greek

That power, first focused in Assyria, later in Babylon, finally in Persia, continued to grow in influence over the next thousand years. As Egypt lost its control of Palestine (its last hurrah was the campaign of the Libyan pharaoh Shoshenq through Palestine around 925), and then the eighth century BC saw Assyria advance its control in the same region, Egypt began to attract refugees and exiles. The language they spoke was Aramaic, which by this time had spread all over the Semitic-speaking Middle East, and had even replaced Akkadian throughout the Assyrian empire.

In the seventh century BC, Aramaic entered Egypt in earnest, borne by the Assyrian invasion force of 671–667 which sacked Thebes and installed a puppet pharaoh. But Assyrian domination turned out to be transient, and Psamtek, the son of the quisling pharaoh Neko, was able to reclaim Egypt's independence by 639. He soon began to reassert Egypt's role in Palestine, occupying the Philistine capital Ashdod in 630, and defeating and killing Josiah, king of Judah, in 610. His successors continued the policy for another sixty-five years, taking advantage of the eclipse of Assyria by Babylon, and turning Palestine and Syria as a whole into a buffer zone for all the hostilities between Egypt and Babylon. The sack of Jerusalem in 587, and the exile of the Jews to Babylon, was one of the prices that others paid for this policy.

Probably the net effect of this on language was to bring into Egypt not Aramaic, but Greek. An opportunistic alliance with Ionian and Carian pirates had enabled Psamtek to shake off Assyria. This set the tone for the dynasty's practice of acting in consort with Greeks, both militarily and commercially. An Egyptian fleet of Greek-built triremes patrolled the Red Sea and Mediterranean coasts, and there was a Greek mercenary contingent with the Egyptian forces sent up the Nile on a last mission against Nubia in the 590s. The Greek

---

* Yet, when the hero of the fictional *Tale of Sinuhe* reached Retjenu, in northern Palestine (the tale is set at the end of the twentieth century BC, with Retjenu ranged with Egypt's enemies), he was told: 'You will be happy here. You will hear the language of Egypt.' As Sinuhe recounts, there were already Egyptians with the ruler of Retjenu, who had spoken up for him (verse 30). The ruler's name was Ammulanasi, recognisably Amorite.

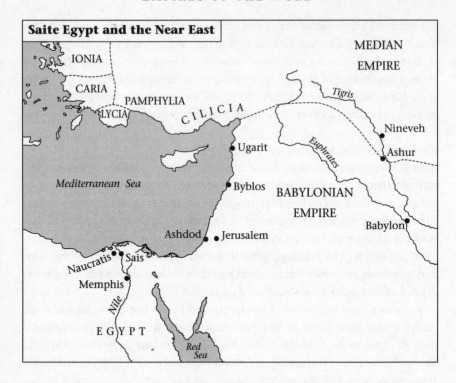

Saite Egypt and the Near East

IONIA

CARIA

PAMPHYLIA

LYCIA

CILICIA

MEDIAN EMPIRE

Tigris

Nineveh

Ashur

Ugarit

Euphrates

Mediterranean Sea

Byblos

BABYLONIAN EMPIRE

Babylon

Ashdod

Jerusalem

Naucratis

Sais

Memphis

Nile

EGYPT

Red Sea

trading colony of Naucratis was established close to Sais in the west of the Delta, as a treaty port very comparable to Shanghai in China in the nineteenth and twentieth centuries AD. There was a roaring trade, notably in Egyptian wheat and linen, paid for with Greek wine and silver. Greeks, when high on wine, says Bacchylides, a poet of the fifth century, would fantasise about ships from Egypt laden with wheat.[9]

This was the beginning of a rich, cosmopolitan atmosphere in the Delta that was to be fulfilled in the expansion of Alexandria as a Greek city three hundred years later. The sound of Greek would have become familiar in Egypt, even if few as yet would have been learning it.* But before Greek reached its acme, Egypt would undergo an involuntary infusion of Aramaic.

Aramaic, besides being the language of the Babylonians, was also adopted as the official language of the Persian empire, and it was this state which achieved the hitherto impossible task of subjecting Egypt durably to foreign rule. Egypt, drunk on Greek wine, was brought down to earth when the Per-

---

* Herodotus, ii.154, recounts that Psamtek put some Egyptian boys into the service of the Ionians and Carians, to be taught Greek, and thereby founded the Egyptian caste of interpreters. There is no reference to any Greeks studying Egyptian.

sians marched in in 522 BC, deposed and killed the pharaoh Psamtek III, and set up a standard Persian administration with Egypt reduced to a province under a satrap.

Persian rule lasted for two centuries, tempered by a resurgence of Egyptian independence in the fourth century that was later crushed. The Aramaic language established itself not just as a language of government and law, but also as a widespread medium of private communication. In fact, an accident of climate rather distorts the record. Because of its dry climate, Egypt provides the vast bulk of documents in Aramaic that have survived from this period, whether on papyrus, parchment, painted on stone or incised on metal.

Aramaic, then, was the first language in three millennia to make a significant inroad into Egypt. When Alexander took the country in 332 BC, initiating three centuries of Greek rule, he found an administration run in Aramaic; in some respects, for instance in the law courts, this language persisted under the Ptolemies,[10] but in general Aramaic was replaced in official use by Greek. Although the Ptolemies took their role as Greek successors to the pharaohs seriously, and Greek Egypt became an autonomous and prosperous country again, the Egyptian language was henceforth relegated to the extremes of sacred and profane: in the temples, and on the lips of the common people. Alexandria, which replaced Athens as the academic centre of the ancient world, was a Greek-speaking city. Famously, Queen Cleopatra, the last Ptolemy to rule (51–30 BC), was also the first to learn Egyptian—and that apparently only because she had a passion for languages.

> There was pleasure in the very sound of her voice. Like a many-stringed instrument, she turned her tongue easily to whatever dialect she would, and few indeed were the foreigners with whom she conversed through an interpreter, since she answered most of them in her own words, whether Ethiopian, Trogodyte, Hebrew, Arab, Syriac, Median or Parthian. The kings before her had not even had the patience to acquire Egyptian, and some had even been lacking in their Macedonian.*

---

* Plutarch, *Antony*, xxvii.4–5. All these languages must have been heard on the streets of Alexandria in Cleopatra's day. Ethiopian would be the language of Kush, and Syriac is a form of Aramaic. Trogodyte would have been spoken along the Red Sea coast, and is perhaps the ancestor of modern Beja. The *Medjay*, supposed to be the same, had been an eastern desert people employed in Egypt as police in the fifteenth to thirteenth centuries (Gardiner 1957: 183, n. 2). There is no mention here of Libyan—or of Latin, although Plutarch adds that Cleopatra is said to have spoken many other languages besides the ones he does mention. Most likely her amours with Caesar, and later Antony, were conducted in Greek.

Changes in writing

The Egyptian language went through more radical revolutions in its written form than it did orally. The elegant and exact pictorial symbols familiar from Egyptian monuments were called (by the Greeks) hieroglyphs, 'sacred carvings', translating the Egyptian term 𓀭, *maduww nātˁar*, 'words of god' (the phrase also used for Ptah's creative words in the text that heads this chapter). We have no indication as to how they arose, and they undergo essentially no modification in the 3400 or so years for which we see them in use, although in the last few centuries, when Egyptian religion was increasingly an antiquarian practice within a Hellenised and Christianised country, the scope the system gave for symbolism and imagery has increasing play. Vast numbers of new pictograms are invented, showing that the system is no longer bound by the constraint of being a practical script. The last inscription dates to AD 394, after which it was suppressed by the Christian authorities.*

They had, from the time of the first non-monumental documents (*c*.2600 BC) been paralleled by an equivalent but more cursive script, called hieratic—'priestly'. These two scripts made up what was essentially a single system, which could be rendered either in monumental glyphs or a cursive scrawl, with about 175 signs interpreted as consonants or sequences of consonants, and a few hundred signs used in conjunction with them to specify meanings.

From the seventh century BC, a new style of writing, known as demotic—'popular'—began to be used: it began as a radically simplified form of hieratic writing, but soon diverged from the traditional system when the link with the original hieroglyphs was forgotten.

After the Greek conquest at the end of the fourth century BC, Greek glosses begin to appear in demotic texts, to clarify a difficult reading here and there. Literacy in Greek was becoming widespread. Despite this, the indigenous system of writing still had a very long way to run. The last dated demotic text is from AD 452, 784 years after the Greek conquest, 482 years after the Ptolemies had been supplanted by Rome, and 310 years after the apostle St Mark is said to have first preached in the then Egyptian capital of Alexandria. Like the last hieroglyphs written fifty-eight years before, it was found on the last outpost of Egypt, the island of Philae.[12]

---

* The last inscription was made on the sacred island of Philae, just above the Nile's first cataract and symbolically the farthest outpost of the land of Egypt. The final desecration of the shrine, the last as well as the farthest in Egypt, was ratified by the Roman emperor Justinian (Johnson 1999: 229).

ϹⲈⲚⲀⲢⲒⲘⲈ ⲀⲚ Ⲙ̅ⲠⲈⲦⲘⲞⲞⲨⲦ Ⲛ̅ⲐⲈ Ⲙ̅ⲠⲈⲦⲞⲚⲆ̅ ϹⲈⲚⲀⲘⲈⲈⲨⲈ ⲘⲈⲚ ⲈⲢⲞϥ ⲆⲈ ⲞⲨⲢⲘ̅Ⲛ̅ⲔⲎⲘⲈ
ⲠⲈ ⲈⲦⲂⲈ ⲦⲈ ϥ ⲀϹⲠⲈ

Hieroglyph, Hieratic, Demotic, Coptic[11]

Final paradoxes

As we have seen, Christianity was to put an end to hieroglyphic writing and
with it the central stream of ancient Egyptian culture. But despite this it had
a last perverse effect, ensuring the long-term survival of the Egyptian language itself. By the third century AD Egyptian had long lost any role in government or elite life, which were now conducted exclusively in Greek. Yet at
this very point, the newly rising force of Christians saw the language as the
best means to advance the conversion of the Egyptian people. As such, they
made it the vehicle of a new sort of literature, in which the Greek alphabet
would be used to represent Egyptian. Since the Egyptian language is more
complex in its sound system than Greek, six new letters (borrowed from the
demotic script) were added: and so the Coptic alphabet was created. The new
tradition began with translations of the Bible, then expanded into original
compositions, narrating the lives of the Fathers of the Egyptian Desert, St
Pachomius and his followers. Coptic became a major channel for the development of the Christian doctrine, with homilies, letters and polemics all
widely read in the Egyptian Church.

Egyptian was written in this way for another thousand years. Ironically, it
was this late-acquired association with the Christian Church which saved it;
by contrast, the lightning spread of Islam and Arabic in the seventh century
soon blotted out the language of the previous masters, Greek.

Egyptian, now known as Coptic, had survived the first onslaught; but the threat from Arabic was always more insidious than that from Greek. Islam, after all, was an egalitarian religion; once Arabic was accepted, there were no other bars to social preferment under the new regime. Over the centuries, the fortunes of the Coptic language ebbed with its associated religion. The last great work written in Coptic is the Triadon, a long poem composed shortly after 1300. Even a hundred years later, Christians in Upper Egypt were said to speak little else,[13] but it seems that by the end of the sixteenth century Coptic conversation was gone, or almost gone. Its recitation, in the liturgy of the Coptic Church, has lasted to our day.

Language from Huang-he to Yangtze

The Master said:
Learning without thinking is useless. Thinking without learning is dangerous.

Confucius, *Lúnyŭ* (Analects), ii.15

The basic pattern of the history of the Chinese language is very similar to that of Egyptian, the maintenance of unity and linguistic stability despite repeated alien influxes.

Origins

The language's closest relatives are found in Tibet and Burma, but they are not close: Chinese is generally seen as a separate branch of the Sino-Tibetan language family, with no special link to any of the other major languages in it: these include Tibetan, Karen, Burmese, and even such languages of southern China as Yi, Lisu and Jingpo. In their basic structure, all these languages are very similar, as tone languages, with most of the words or word roots monosyllabic, and no inflexion of nouns, adjectives or verbs. But this is not enough to define the family: rather it defines the area, since other unrelated languages in the neighbourhood, such as Thai, Zhuang, Hmong and Mien, are also like this.

The Chinese language first turns up in the valley of the Yellow River or Huang-he. The earliest record is now a matter of controversy. In 2000, Chinese scholars recognised written characters in the markings on some 4800-year-old wine cups, found at Juxian in Shandong ('Mountain East')

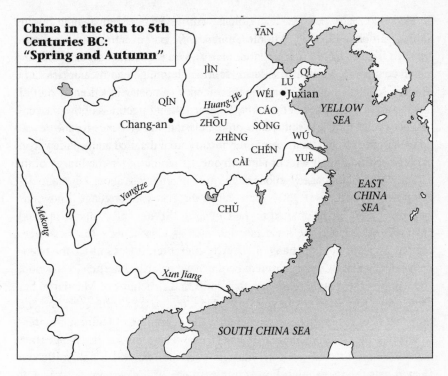

China in the 8th to 5th Centuries BC: "Spring and Autumn"

province, where the river meets the sea. Whether that analysis is correct or not, the next-oldest characters are still a good 3400 years old: they were found written on bronze vessels, and on tortoiseshells and ox shoulder blades (heated until they cracked—a means of telling fortunes), near Anyang in Hebei ('River North') province. Although the symbols are by origin pictographic, the system as a whole clearly represents the Chinese language. Visual puns are used to convey words with more abstract meanings (e.g. 來 , originally a symbol for *lái*, 'wheat', represents *lái*, 'come'), or more specific ones (e.g. *láng*, 'wolf', is shown as 狼 , a combination of 犬 *quǎn*, 'dog', and 良 *liáng*, 'good').*

The subsequent history of standard Chinese as spoken is conventionally

---

* Materials for writing changed over the millennia. For the early period our knowledge of what was current is of course reliant on its durability, hence the early prominence of bronze and bone. Later on (from the first millennium) the brush was used to write on strips of bamboo. More flexible materials, distinctive Chinese inventions, came later: rolls of silk from the second century BC, and paper from AD 105. Printing too was a Chinese contribution to world language technology: fixed blocks were cut to print whole pages from the end of the ninth century AD, and movable type was introduced from the eleventh. Naturally this last was harder work with a writing system that has always used several thousand symbols.

divided into many periods, Old Chinese (up to 500 BC, represented by the *Shījīng*, 'Book of Poetry'), Middle Chinese (500 BC–seventh century AD, represented by the *Qièyùn* rhyming dictionary), Old Mandarin (seventh to fourteenth centuries), Middle Mandarin (fourteenth to eighteenth centuries) and Modern Mandarin ever since. The prominence of poetry in the early part of this record is not a matter of aesthetics. Given the indirectness of the connection between Chinese script and its pronunciation, the evidence for the development of the spoken language comes mostly from detailed analysis of verse, particularly looking at which words rhyme.

The written language itself does not give much away about language development over the last 2500 years, since the classical language, known as *wényán* (文言), was defined in the *Chūnqiū*, 'Spring and Autumn', period (770–476 BC), when the great classics such as Confucius's Analects were written, and was kept unchanged virtually ever after. It was only in the twentieth century that *wényán* ceased to be the usual means of written expression, and a new written style, based on the words and structures of Mandarin, became universal. But *wényán* was formed in a region (the north-east) and at a time that is only a millennium or so after the beginning of Chinese progression across the country. As such, it gives a useful baseline for the changes that have affected different modern dialects over the two and a half millennia since it was the vernacular. For example, in one of the paradoxes typical of language history, it shows that the least-changed dialect of Chinese is the one spoken farthest away from the north-east: Cantonese, known to the Chinese by the name of the long-independent 'barbarian' kingdom of *Yuè*.

The gap between written evidence and spoken reality means that a fair amount of the detail of how influences have played out in the history of the language must remain conjectural. We can only infer, and we cannot fully document, the forces that we shall be describing, some of them operating piecemeal on Chinese to produce the variety of dialects heard, especially in the south, but others keeping the vast majority of speakers in close touch with each other even as the spoken standard gradually moved, all down the ages.

The degree of political unity in China, although its cyclical rise and fall is the usual tick-tock of Chinese history, is not particularly useful in recounting the spread and transformations of the Chinese language. Following the archaeological evidence, Chinese culture spread out from the middle Yellow River valley in all directions, but most significantly towards the south. In the Shang period (middle to late second millennium) we already find artefacts south of the Yangtze, and these spread out upstream into central China in the Zhou (early first millennium BC). But we know that a language different from

Chinese was still spoken in the kingdom of Chu (approximately modern Sichuan, north of the Yangtze) in the third century BC.*

Geographically, Chinese was moving from the cold, dry northern plains where wheat and millet were cultivated into the warmer, wetter uplands where the staple was rice. As well as a difference in climate, there was a difference in terrain, which made the going much tougher in the south: *nán chuán běi mǎ*, 'south boat, north horse', as the proverb has it. In practice waterways, defined by nature rather than human resource, are the only way to travel easily in the south. This was not a barrier to Chinese cultural and linguistic spread, but it did mean that uniformity, cultural or linguistic, was never so easily imposed there.

The motive behind the movement southward was no doubt the quest for more fertile soil, and its success must have been backed by the advantages in technology that the northerners were accumulating, symbolised by possession of a written language and large-scale organisation. The first reflection of this on politics comes in 221 BC, with the command of Shi Huang Di, the First Emperor, who unified most of central China, to half a million colonists to go and fill his newly conquered territories 'among the various Yue peoples'. By this time there was a political motive to add to the economic one: the despot of a united China desired to separate the traditional families from their ancestral power bases; and the political push was renewed from time to time over the next millennium.†

First Unity

Shi Huang Di ('First Emperor'), who had converted his rule of the Qin state§ into the first overlordship of all the known states of the Chinese world, was

---

* Mencius (*c*.250 BC according to Brooks 2002), 3.B.6: 'Suppose some great officer of Chu wanted his son to learn to speak Qi ...' Evidently, the ambitious were already setting themselves to learn Chinese. Qi was approximately modern Shandong, at the mouth of the Huang-he, and so at the centre of the spread of Chinese. Strangely, a text written only a decade or so later seems to pick Chu to contrast with an eastern barbarian language: 'Let a Chu man grow up among Rong, or a Rong man grow up in Chu, and the Chu man will speak Rong, while the Rong man will speak Chu' (*Lushi Chunqiu*, 4.E).
† These moves can be compared with the depopulations ordered by the kings of Assyria and Babylon after major military victories. (See Chapter 3, 'Akkadian—world-beating technology: A model of literacy', p. 64.) But since the Mesopotamian kings saw the greatest threat in foreigners, they ended up seeding their empire with a foreign language, Aramaic; the Chinese emperor, seeing threat in Chinese feudal lords, disseminated them (and therewith the Chinese language) to the farthest corners of his realm.
§ This is often proposed as the etymology for the name *China*, a name that seems to have reached the West through Persian and Italian. But the Chinese use rather the names of the Han or Tang dynasties as the name of their nation, and the form of the name suggests that it is derived from the Sanskrit name, *Cīna*. This applied mainly to the area of Tibet, though also on occasions included Assam and Burma (Sircar 1971: 104–5). China as a whole was known to the Indians as *Mahācīna*, 'Great

for many reasons a significant figure. He reigned over China for only eleven years (221–210 BC), after thirty-seven on the throne of Qin, but what years they were: besides completing the Great Wall (invaders from the north were already a problem), abolishing the power of feudal lords, carrying through an intellectual purge in a notorious rampage of book-burning, and installing the Terracotta Army in his tomb in the then capital, Chang-an, he is also famous for the standardisation of Chinese characters, as part of a general programme to introduce common laws, weights and measures. This meant imposing the local standard of his (far western) state of Qin, which happened to be one of the most conservative in use at that time. It existed in two versions, the heavily pictorial *zhuànshū*, 'seal script', still occasionally seen on ornate inscriptions and official seals, and the more cursive *lìshū*, 'clerical script'. This latter was taken up under the Han empire that followed, and codified in a dictionary of the time, the *Shuōwèn Jiězì* of *Xǔ Shèn*. This system has been the basis of Chinese writing, *kǎishū* (楷書 , 'standard script'), ever since.

Conscious of a common language in *wényán* and a common script in *kǎishū*, Chinese people took a millennium to begin to notice people diverging: early Tang literature (seventh century AD) talks of the south differing from the north in its *fāng-yán*, 'regional speech', the normal word for a dialect: this came to be a pretty strong term, also to be applied (much later[14]) to refer to foreign languages such as Korean, Japanese, Mongolian, Manchu and Vietnamese.

The languages spoken by China's equestrian neighbours to its north and west were quite unrelated to the family that includes Chinese, the Sino-Tibetan languages already mentioned. Furthermore—and in this they differed from the tongues of China's southern neighbours—they were not like Chinese typologically either. Like their modern descendants, the so-called Altaic languages* of central Asia, including the Turkic, the Mongol and the Tungus families, they are all highly polysyllabic; their words, at least the nouns and verbs, are built up systematically and agglutinatively out of strings of short elements. They are not tone languages, but they make extensive use of the principle of vowel harmony, so that the vowels in the suffixes echo the vowels of the word's root. Their word order places the verb at the end of the sentence. In all these respects, they are radically different from Chinese, a monosyllabic tone language with little or no word formation, and a basic order in which the verb comes second in the sentence.

China': this, for example, is where the Chinese pilgrim Xuan Zang told the Indians he was from, when he visited in 629. Si-Yu-Ki, v. 1 (in Beal 1884, part 1: 216).

* The Altai mountains of central Asia, the source of this name, are themselves named for their gold: cf. Turkish *altın*.

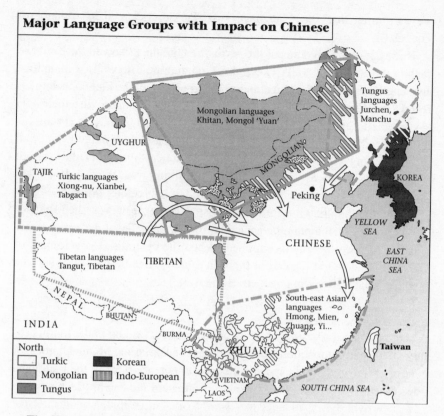

Major Language Groups with Impact on Chinese

Mongolian languages
Khitan, Mongol 'Yuan'

Tungus
languages
Jurchen,
Manchu

UYGHUR

TAJIK

Turkic languages
Xiong-nu, Xianbei,
Tabgach

MONGOLIAN

KOREA

Peking

CHINESE

YELLOW
SEA

EAST
CHINA
SEA

Tibetan languages
Tangut, Tibetan

TIBETAN

NEPAL

BHUTAN

INDIA

BURMA

South-east Asian
languages
Hmong, Mien,
Zhuang, Yi...

Taiwan

ZHUANG

North

Turkic	Korean
Mongolian	Indo-European
Tungus	

VIETNAM

LAOS

SOUTH CHINA SEA

The *Xiōngnú** were the principal steppe nomads of Mongolia and Turkestan in the third century BC. Despite their major role in Chinese history it is extremely difficult to find evidence of what their language was like. There is, however, a single quotation of ten Chinese characters, giving some advice of the Buddhist monk Fotudeng to a Xiongnu king. The characters would have been read in the fourth century AD as

syog tieg t'iei liəd kāng b'uok kuk g'iw t'uk tāng.

If we follow Louis Bazin in reading this as

süg tägti idqang, boqughigh tutqang

your army send-out, warlord hold

---

* This looks very much like a Chinese rendition of *Hunnu*, which would allow these people to be identified with those known to the Indians as *Hūṇa*, and to the Europeans as *Hunni*. But the phonetic resemblance unfortunately remains the only strong evidence. (See Sinor 1990: 177–9.)

we can infer that their language was Turkic, rather than Mongol or Tungus.[15]

Three Chinese kingdoms of the north, the Qin, the Zhao and the Yan, had each built sections of wall to keep the Xiongnu out. The walls were unified and lengthened when the Qin emperor incorporated all the kingdoms into his realm. The Chinese also learnt how to oppose the Xiongnu with their own cavalry tactics. Hostilities continued for five hundred years, and for all this time the Chinese were successful in keeping the barbarians out of China, and in maintaining a forward policy that kept control throughout the western regions now known as Gansu and Qinghai; in this way, the Silk Road was secured, as well as access to the far-away horse-breeding grounds of Ferghana by the Pamirs, vital for the Chinese defence. However, their defence also depended on maintaining an active frontier garrison, and it was a costly exercise to keep the guards supplied. When the centralised government of China broke down at the end of the Han dynasty, this failed, and it became possible for the Xiongnu to penetrate the wall.

Retreat to the south

A confused and increasingly bloody period ensued, leading in the fourth century AD to open competition among a number of Turkic and Mongol hordes for control of the north, and exposing the total impotence there of the traditional government. The effect was to displace southward the centre of Chinese. In 317 a new dynasty was founded in *Nánjīng*, 'Southern Capital', while different Turkic and Mongol hordes contested the north. Ultimately, the two centuries to 557 were dominated in the north by the Tabgach,* who at least proved effective in defending what they had won. These new lords were speakers of a Turkic language, but they soon endeavoured to take up local forms, adopting the Chinese name *Wèi*. This policy appears to have needed some enforcement, or at least encouragement: six generations later, in 500, their ruler, Xiaowen, outlawed by decree the Turkic language, costume and customs.

It was rather similar, politically and linguistically, to what was going on in the old Roman empire at the same time, with Germans taking over its heartland in western Europe, changing but not supplanting its language as they attempted to adopt it, and the successors of the old Roman power retrenching into what had historically been non-Roman lands in the eastern territories,

---

* Called in modern Chinese *Tùobá*, using characters 拓拔 that at the time would have been pronounced *Tak-B'uat*. The name has become the modern *Chuvash*: it still designates a Turkic-speaking people of whom there are 1.5 million scattered across Russia and Siberia (Clauson 2002 [1962]: 38; Dalby 1998: 134–5).

the Balkans, Greece and Anatolia. Yet the Chinese language faced no competition from a potential equal, as Latin faced Greek in the eastern Mediterranean. The land, in all its parts, was dominated by Chinese, even if increasingly spoken by people with some very strange accents.

Down in the south a unified Chinese dynasty continued; there large numbers of well-to-do Chinese immigrants were gradually spreading the range of Chinese. They had moved partly to escape the invaders, but also to occupy the more fertile land drained by the Yangtze. The languages of the native population there, whether of the Tai, Sino-Tibetan or Hmong-Mien families, were all of a type quite similar, though often unrelated, to Chinese. The result was a relatively smooth take-up of Chinese by learners in the south: some of the new Chinese dialects that arose, especially the southernmost (called Yue, or Cantonese), sound very much like the original.

Middle Chinese of the seventh century AD had syllables that could end in *m*, *n*, *ng*, *p*, *t*, *k* or a vowel, and so does Modern Cantonese, just like the (unrelated but neighbouring) southern language Zhuang; in Mandarin final *m* has become *n*, and final *p*, *t* and *k* have all been dropped. Again Middle Chinese is inferred to have had three tone contours, and a separate, so-called 'entering', pattern for words ending in *p*, *t* or *k*. These later split to eight tones, with a high and a low onset, depending on whether they started with a voiced or voiceless consonant (*b-d-g-z-j* versus *p-t-k-s-c*). This is the basis of the system in modern Cantonese, and also in Zhuang; Mandarin has taken a different route, splitting only one of the original tones, but when it dropped final *p*, *t* and *k* it assigned all the words affected to one of the other tones. It has ended up with four tones, while Cantonese (and Zhuang) have eight.[16]

In 589 it proved possible to reunite the country. A new Chinese golden age, of prosperity if not always peace, began under the Sui and then the Tang dynasties. Throughout this period, Chinese continued to spread southward.

The Tang dynasty lasted until the end of the ninth century, when it degenerated into a power struggle among regional warlords. Many foreign missions reached China in this period, including Buddhists from India, Nestorian Christians, Zoroastrians and Manichaeans, and Muslims. This would have spread the sounds of the Sanskrit, Aramaic, Persian and Arabic languages to the major centres, where they would have been used in worship; but the numbers actually speaking them must have remained tiny. In any case, by the end of the Tang all except the Buddhists and Muslims had been purged out of existence. During the eighth and ninth centuries there was an increasing threat of incursions from Tibet in the west, and stout resistance from the Nanzhao natives in *Yúnnán* ('South of the Clouds', in the south-west) but no long-term loss of territory. This period (from 847) also saw another Turkic-speaking group, the Uighurs,

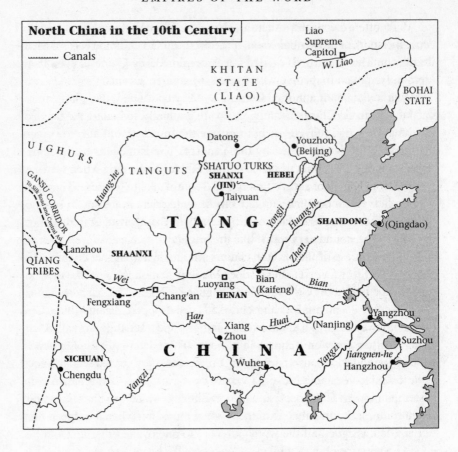

North China in the 10th Century

------- Canals

KHITAN
STATE
(LIAO)

Liao
Supreme
Capitol

W. Liao

BOHAI
STATE

UIGHURS

GANSU CORRIDOR
To Silk Road and Central Asia

TANGUTS

Datong

SHATUO TURKS
SHANXI   HEBEI
(JIN)

Youzhou
(Beijing)

Taiyuan

Huang-he

T A N G

Yongji

Huang-he

SHANDONG

(Qingdao)

Lanzhou   SHAANXI

QIANG
TRIBES

Wei

Zhan

Bian
(Kaifeng)

Bian

Fengxiang   Chang'an   HENAN

Luoyang

Han

Xiang
Zhou

Huai

(Nanjing)

Yangzhou

SICHUAN

C H I N A

Yangzi

Suzhou

Chengdu

Yangzi

Wuhen

Hangzhou

Jiangnen-he

settle in the northerly province of Gansu, and set up an independent kingdom,
friendly to the Chinese, in the far west (modern Xinjiang).

The breakdown of central government was repaired after half a century
(960) by the Song dynasty, but not before the extreme north, Manchuria and
the lands north of the Great Wall, had been taken by the Khitan, a Mongolian
tribe; Gansu too, in the north-west, was lost, invaded by the Tangut, who
spoke a language related to Tibetan. The Tangut held on to this area; but the
Khitan were in 1115 overwhelmed by another group from farther north—the
Jurchen, a Tungus-speaking people, whom the Chinese, ill-advisedly, assisted. Although the Jurchen adopted the Chinese name and style of *Jīn* (金 ,
'golden'), they almost immediately turned on their allies and, after invading
much of the south as well as the north, were left in control of the entire valley
of the Huang-he, the traditional Chinese heartland. This they held (like the
Tangut) until displaced by one greater, Genghis Khan himself, who led a
Mongolian invasion in 1211.

As so often, it proved much easier for the invaders to overrun the north than the south. For two generations the Song dynasty maintained a defence of the southern empire, based on Hangzhou, until in 1279 the Mongols were able to take them in the rear, having first conquered Yunnan (and indeed the north of Vietnam) in the south-west.

For the first time, a non-Chinese speaking dynasty (Mongols, now known as the *Yuán*, 元 , 'Original') controlled the full extent of China. Since the Mongols by this time also controlled most of the rest of Asia, it could be thought lucky for China that the Mongol Kublai Khan decided to move his capital from Kara Korum in Mongolia to *Běijīng* (北京 , 'Northern Capital'), since otherwise it might have suffered the fate of all colonies, to be disregarded by its ruler; but in any case, the unity of the Mongol empire was lost by 1295. The newly converted Muslim Khans of the west refused to accept the sovereignty of Kublai Khan's successor at Beijing, since he was a Buddhist.

Mongol control of China did not last much longer. Although Kublai was famous for his civility, his successors were less distinguished. It is worth mentioning the last of the dynasty, Togan Timur (1333–1369), since among much anti-Chinese legislation he passed laws forbidding Chinese to read or write Mongolian. It is evident that a strict racial policy was being followed. One would have expected, by comparison with the Manchu who were to follow much later—or the contemporary, but of course quite unknown, example of the English in Ireland*—that the elite would be passing laws to prevent their own members from taking up the language of the conquered people.

In 1369 Togan Timur and his Mongols ended up chased out by a popular Chinese warlord turned national hero, who established himself as the first Ming emperor. There was then for three centuries no interference by outsiders in the government of China.

Northern influences

Then the Tungus-speaking Jurchen people, now to be known as the Manchus, gained a second chance to dominate China. This invasion was the last permanent penetration of China by speakers of a foreign language.

In the early seventeenth century, the Manchus had been reorganised, under two able leaders, and advanced into the northern marches of Chinese territory to establish a capital at Mukden. Then, in 1644, they had the luck to be invited

---

* The Statute of Kilkenny was passed in 1366, requiring the English colonists (section III) 'to use the English language, and be called by an English name, leaving off entirely the manner of naming used by the Irish...'

China in the 17th Century

- ● Seat of main Lamaistic patriarch
- ★ Risings of non-Chinese peoples
- ◉ Sectarian risings of Chinese
- ▪ Official centre of foreign commerce
- → Military expeditions

—·— Border of China under the Qing dynasty, at its greatest extent c. 1760

Nerchinsk●
To China under Treaty of Nerchisk 1689
Irkutsk
Russian 1652
Kyakhta
MANCHURIA
Urga (Panchen Lama)●
★Rising 1765 ★Rising Olot 1750-57 Expeditions against the Dzungars 1758-59 OUTER MONGOLIA (KHALKHA) 1697 KHORCHIN 1629-30 Mukden
XINJIANG Ti-hua (Urumchi) Capital 1625-44
DZUNGARS Turfan Ha-mi (Kumul) INNER MONGOLIA (CHAHAR) 1635 KOREA Manchu invasions 1627, 1637-37
Kashgar Akso TARIM BASIN 1759-60 Incorporated in Gansu 1759 Beijing Eight Trigrams sect 1786-88
Major Muslim insurrection 1825-33 EASTERN TURKESTAN (Sinkiang) HEBEI 1644 Vassal status 1637
Yarkand Khotan Hui (Muslim) risings 1781-84 QINGHAI 1724 GANSU 1649 SHANXI 1644-45 SHANDONG 1645 Heavenly Principle sect 1811-14
Chinese invasion 1720-4 Tibetan tribal rising 1807 SHAANXI 1644-45 HENAN 1645-46 JIANGSU 1645
TIBET Protectorate established 1750, in final form 1751 White Lotus rebellion 1795-1804
Tashi-Ihunpo (Hutukhtu) Lhasa (Dalai Lama) Chin-ch'uan tribal risings 1746-49 order finally restored 1776 HUBEI 1645 ANHUI 1645
NEPAL BHUTAN SICHUAN 1646 ZHEJIANG 1646
Expeditions against Nepal 1788 HUNAN 1647-50 JIANGXI 1649-52

Manchu expansion
Phase I China
- ■ Manchu homeland
- ▦ Expansion before 1644
- ▨ Expansion 1644-59
- 1644 Date of incorporation

Tributary states
- ▨ Before 1644
- ■ After 1644

Phase II
New Territories
- 1724 Date of incorporation

BURMA Four abortive invasions 1766-69
YUNNAN 1659 GUIZHOU 1658 QINGHAI 1650-52 GUANGDONG 1650-55 Canton Macao Rising of aboriginal peoples 1787-88 FUJIAN 1646 TAIWAN
Dutch 1624-62 Ming loyalists 1662-83 Occupied by Qing 1683
Abortive Ch'ing invasion 1788 Vietnamese pirate raids 1800-09
TONKIN

into Beijing as a tactical move in a struggle between two generals contending to replace the Ming. The Manchus took the opportunity to install themselves, styling their new dynasty with the name *Qīng* (清 , 'Pure'), and by 1651 had put down all resistance in the rest of China. Although they came speaking their own language, and it remained an official written language of the Chinese state until the end of the dynasty in 1911, it had died out in speech even at court by the eighteenth century. The language did not survive even in Manchuria itself, a curious victim of its people's successful takeover of China and its way of life. Today it is only spoken, under the name of Xibo, by the descendants of a detachment of troops dispatched from the Manchurian capital Mukden to Xinjiang in 1764—a north-eastern language now spoken only in the Chinese north-west.

It was into the north that the invaders came, and the Chinese spoken in the north went on to become the standard language for the country. But although the northern dialect underwent significant changes, they can only partly be put down to the particular difficulties that Xiongnu, Tabgach, Jurchen, Mon-

gol or Manchu would have encountered as they tried to get by in Chinese.*
There is the interesting fact that Mandarin Chinese can distinguish *wŏmen*,
'we (excluding you)', from *zănmen*, 'we (including you)', just as Mongol
and Manchu do; this is an innovation since Middle Chinese. And perhaps one
can point to the absence of consonant clusters in modern Chinese, some of
which were allowed in Middle Chinese. For example, *sniwər*, 'appease', and
t'nwâr, 'secure', have become *sūi* and *tŭo*. Altaic languages cannot abide
more than one consonant at the beginning of a syllable.†

There are in fact a few written relics of the kind of Chinese that was spoken
in one of the intermediate periods before the invaders were absorbed. The
thirteenth-century Chinese translation of *The Secret History of the Mongols*
is full of Altaic patterns such as postpositions instead of prepositions, verbs
following the object, and existential verbs at the end of the sentence, all weird
in Chinese, whose basic word order is much more like English:

Da-fan   nyu-hai-er sheng liao lao zai   jia-li   de
Generally   daughter   born past always stay home-at particle

li   wu
reason is-not

There is no reason why a daughter, born to you, should always stay at
home.

And there is copious evidence for mixtures of Manchu and Mandarin in the
zĭ-dì-shū, 'Son's Books', which are a written record of the narrative entertainment the Manchu enjoyed in their early days in Beijing (1736–96),
though they are written more with Chinese word order scattered with Manchu
vocabulary.

---

* Briefly put, northern Chinese lost all its final consonants; and strings of previously free monosylla-
bles became congealed into longer words. No one knows why, but some explanations for the changes
have been proposed. Perhaps the semantic vagueness of Chinese morphemes, after losing so many
distinctive consonants, meant that reinforcing one word with another was necessary in order to communicate effectively. Perhaps the sheer phonetic weakness of the new shorter syllables meant that
doubling up had to occur to give the language an acceptable speech rhythm (Feng 1998). Perhaps the
advent of Buddhism, with chanting in Sanskrit and Pali which introduced longer words, and the complicated expressions that arose when they were translated into Chinese, inured people to polysyl-
labism. The various trends and possible influences are clearly discussed in Wilkinson (2000: 31–40).
† But this same trend can be seen in all Chinese dialects (and indeed farther south in the Yi and Vietnamese languages).

In northern dialects there is still a tendency for direct objects to occur rather often before the verb, and for *than*-phrases to occur before comparative adjectives, features that might be attributed to Altaic influence. But in general this mixed style of Chinese did not establish itself.[17] Later generations of invader families picked up Chinese naturally from their Chinese mothers, nurses and schoolmasters; probably the Altaic patterns were just too far opposed to Chinese for any compromise to develop. This is typical enough of Chinese linguistic relations: in general, there are not many loan words in Chinese borrowed from other languages in any direction, and certainly no structural influences; *dú*, 'calf', does seem to have come from Altaic, characteristically enough since its peoples lived by stockbreeding (cf. Mongol *tuyul*, Manchu *tukšan*, Evenki *tukučən*, all meaning 'calf'), but the many Mongol words that are found in the drama of the Yuan dynasty have since been lost again.[18]

Beyond the southern sea

Although Chinese has spent its three and a half millennia almost wholly confined to East Asia, it did put out some feelers across the sea to its south. In the last thousand years, this led to some permanent residence of Chinese abroad; in the last two hundred, partly as a reaction to—or exploitation of— European settlement, serious overseas communities have grown up, which may be significant in the future spread of the language.

The earliest inklings of Chinese in *Nán-yáng*, 'the Southern Ocean', as the Chinese called the shores of the South China Sea, are visits of merchants to Tongking (northern Vietnam) in the third century BC.[19] They were followed up in 111 BC by troops, and China annexed Tongking, along with Nan-yue* (modern Guangxi and Guangdong). China was to hold Tongking for over a thousand years, in fact until AD 938, despite sporadic and increasing resistance. China attempted to assimilate it culturally, with Chinese classics for the local elite, competitive examinations for administrators, and official use of *wényán*. There was Chinese immigration, and some married into Vietnam's princely families, providing many later leaders. Mahayana Buddhism, introduced under the Tang dynasty, became the majority religion.[20] Despite all this, the Chinese language did not spread permanently to this part of the world.

Somewhat later than the advance into Tongking, Chinese proceeded far-

---

* 'Southern Yue'. Mandarin *Nán-Yuè* 南越 and modern Vietnamese 越南 *Việt Nam* are just the same words, pronounced differently and reordered, so the name is still going strong two millennia on, its designation moved 750 kilometres to the south-west.

ther south, though apparently with instincts more scholarly than materialist. In the third century AD, two Chinese envoys, Kang Tai and Ju Ying, wrote a report on the foundation of Funan (in modern Cambodia).[21] There is little more to be said of it, or what the Chinese were doing there; but the route via Śri Vijaya (in Sumatra) to India became quite well travelled by China's Buddhist scholars a little later, in the fifth to eighth centuries. (See Chapter 5, 'Outsiders' views', p. 192.)

After the eighth century, trade comes to the fore as a motive, but the links seem to have been maintained by foreign merchants, Arabs, Persians and Indians, and it is only in the eleventh century that we find the first reports of capital-raising by Chinese merchants to finance their own expeditions. This was under the Song dynasty, which actively backed the traders. Thereafter government support for overseas expansion wavered, the Mongol Yuan staunchly in favour, even making a failed endeavour to invade Java in 1293, the Ming who succeeded in 1368 preferring isolation: private trade was banned, and all contacts had to be made through diplomatic channels. There was a brief resurgence during the famous global voyages of Admiral Zheng-He (in the period 1405–33); but after that episode resident Chinese merchants had, for a time, to go underground.

Most of the Chinese who had taken to this life came from Fujian, with a smaller contingent from Guangdong, a fact which is explicitly recorded in a fifteenth-century report, *Yíngyái Shènglǎn: The Overall Survey of the Ocean's Shores*, by Ma Huan, one of the sailors with Zheng-He. Ma writes, of two states in Java, 'Many people from Guangdong and Zhangzhou are staying there,' and he mentions many other exiles from Fujian elsewhere in the island.[22] The truth of this stands out very clearly in the predominance of Min, Hakka and Yue, south-eastern dialects, in the speech of overseas Chinese to this day.*

Dealing with foreign devils

From the sixteenth century until the present day, the Chinese government has increasingly come into contact with Japan and a series of European powers, culminating in the first approaches of the USA; these resulted in wars, and the

---

* In the Philippines, there are half a million Chinese, and in Thailand 1.8 million, almost all speaking Southern Min. Of Malaysia's 4.5 million Chinese speakers, half speak Southern or Eastern Min, a quarter speak Hakka, a sixth speak Yue, the rest (still half a million of them) speaking Mandarin. Chinese has largely died on the lips of Indonesia's 6 million ethnic Chinese, and only a third of them still speak some form of it in the home: but of those who do, over a third speak Min, a little less than a third Hakka, just under a tenth Yue. The remaining quarter speak Mandarin (Grimes 2000).

planting of foreign communities in trading colonies. For overseas Chinese communities, the effects were complex: they sometimes suffered from China's measures aimed at impoverishing and disarming foreigners; but they also profited from opportunities that were provided by the foreigners' enterprising new developments, especially those of Britain.

In the early sixteenth century, Japanese pirates were a persistent problem. China imposed an embargo on Japan. For good measure, in 1522 it also banned all commercial voyages to the Nan-yang, converting all overseas Chinese into smugglers or pirates. Meanwhile, European explorers were increasingly nosing about China's seas, looking for trading concessions. In 1557 the Portuguese were granted an enclave on the coast at Macao; this turned out to be sufficient to fob off their intrusions in the long term. But it added a further burden to the overseas Chinese, who seemed now to be at a disadvantage even as against the dastardly European *folangji*;* the ban on Chinese voyages to the Nan-yang was finally lifted in 1566.

Although the advent of the Spanish and Dutch, following the Portuguese, provided capacious new markets for the now long-resident Chinese traders of the East Indies, lack of clear support from China meant that Chinese traders were always at a disadvantage. In Luzon, in their newly Spanish colony of the Philippines, the Chinese population was massacred in 1602 and again in 1639, with utter impunity. Nevertheless, the trader community was beginning to be seen as a useful force: when the Ming dynasty was toppled by the Manchus in 1644, the last loyalist strongholds were found in the maritime communities of Zhejiang, Fujian and Guangdong, and later, until 1682, offshore in Vietnam and the Philippines. They suffered for their loyalty, of course, with the Manchus literally 'clearing the coasts' of all their inhabitants, moving them miles inland to prevent any support to mariners. Perhaps also—since the Manchu invaders through victory became the legitimate authority, the Qing dynasty—they laid the basis for a certain distrust felt ever since by China's central government towards its overseas community. This was the seed time for the Chinese Triads, and secret societies.

But there were new forces loose in the Nan-yang, and the Chinese were ready to profit from them. When Europeans were banned from Thailand in 1688, the Chinese became its principal traders and economic consultants through the eighteenth century. They were also well ensconced in the Malay kingdom of Johore. But in the same era, they found abundant opportunities for profit in collusion with the new Dutch VOC (East India Company); so

---

* This term, first applied to the Portuguese, derives from Arab-Persian *firengi*, ultimately from *Frank*.

much so that they suffered another major massacre at Dutch hands, in Java in 1740. And when the British started their own East Indian enterprise, on the empty Malayan island of Penang in 1785, it was the Chinese who volunteered to populate it. Likewise, they were in the forefront in Raffles' development of Singapore after 1819. As British power spread across Malaya and northern Borneo, and the Dutch interest farther south, into Sumatra, southern Borneo and Celebes, the Chinese interests accompanied them. They liked very well the British institution of free ports.

Pressure was now building up from trading interests in France and Britain on China itself. The French concern centred on Chinese possessions in Vietnam, but the British dealt more directly, and fiercely, with the Qing government, in defence of their opium trade out of Bengal: the result was the cession of Hong Kong (1842, enlarged in 1860 and 1898) and foreign access to five more treaty ports, including Shanghai (1842). Although the most prominent of these were not in Fujian, their classic recruiting area, the overseas Chinese now had guaranteed access to the mainland. Links grew, and for the first time since the seventeenth century direct involvement with the mainland became an important part of overseas Chinese trade. Nan-yang was coming home.

Whys and wherefores

Now that we have surveyed the full course of the histories of Egyptian and Chinese, we can consider what the major properties could be which might explain their unshakeable stability in the face of time and invasion.

Certain obvious possibilities can be eliminated at once, since in them Egyptian and Chinese are at opposite extremes.

In the most evident linguistic aspect, the structural type of their languages, Egyptian and Chinese were intrinsically always very different, and have developed in different directions over their recorded histories. And looking at them a little more abstractly, we can see too that they were also quite unlike in another aspect of their linguistic environments: their degree of similarity or difference to their neighbouring languages.

Egyptian remained throughout its history a highly inflected language with complex verbal morphology, and flexible word order, though it did develop somewhat over the millennia into a more analytic structure, with separable articles and personal pronouns becoming constituents of noun and verb phrases, and more rigid word order. Furthermore, the languages that might have been expected to influence or replace it, especially Libyan and Aramaic, were typologically similar to it—just as was its ultimate nemesis, Arabic.

There seems no reason in linguistic structure, absolute or relative, to explain its stability.

Old Chinese, by contrast, was an extreme example of an isolating language, its roots, monosyllabic and marked with significant tone patterns, largely functioning as independent words, and using word order as the most significant aspect of syntax. Again, there was some change visible over the millennia: but Chinese moved to become less analytic, with longer words developing on the basis of the previously detachable roots, and some of the roots changing into grammatical morphemes, marking such things as plurality, copular links between subject and predicate, or markers of relative and subordinate clauses. Unlike Egyptian, which was challenged by languages of its own type, the threat to Chinese came from the Altaic languages, which were, as we have seen, fundamentally different in type. In fact, where it was in contact with languages of similar type (in the south), Chinese was the incoming language, and tended to replace them.

Religious outlook is another important aspect of cultures, where we might look for a clue to their stability, which might then be reflected in language. We have seen (Chapter 3, 'Second interlude: The shield of faith', p. 86) that especially in the Middle East attachment to a religion could preserve a language against the odds. But here again, Egypt and China diverged.

Faith in an afterlife was important to Egyptians: they deliberately made their tombs the most permanent part of their built environment, and we find them in their literature very much concerned with what they could know about life after death, judgement and individual survival. Certainly they preserved their religion for most of the lifespan of their language, and they no more actively preached it abroad than they attempted to spread their language when they enlarged the boundaries of their power. But aspects of their faith did spread without the language none the less: their mother-goddess Isis became one of the most widely revered deities in the Roman empire, and has been seen as a root of the Christian cult of Mary as Mother of God. And paradoxically, when the Christians suppressed the Egyptian cult, Egyptian as a language took on a new life as the local language of Christianity. Egyptian religion was certainly favourable to the survival of the Egyptian language, but the two became detached long before the end.

The Chinese attitude to religion was very different, mostly characterised by down-to-earth practicality. There were two major traditions. One followed Confucius (Kung Fu-zi, 'Master Kung'), taking a highly socialised and worldly definition of virtue; the other followed the *Dào* (道 , 'way') of Lao-zi and Zhuang-zi, seeking to merge with the patterns discerned in nature. Aside from popular animist beliefs, no fulfilment of any Chinese yearnings for another world was available until Buddhism began to penetrate from India in the first millennium AD. (This, for the Chinese, was a Western religion.) It prospered in the troublous times of the third, fourth and fifth centuries, and then became the established faith of the Tang dynasty that returned strong universal government to China; the Pali and Sanskrit classics were translated in Chinese, and Buddhism became a naturalised Chinese faith.

Buddhism, with its emphasis on suffering, resignation and the ultimate unimportance of the daily round of life, was never a positive influence on kings who must preserve their realms against external aggression. No Buddhist king in its homeland of India, not even Aśoka, managed to found a dynasty that would endure more than a couple of generations; and the strange attraction of Buddhism to invading Altaic peoples, especially the Tabgach and Genghis Khan's Mongols, brought their soldierly virtues to an early end once they had settled in China. As Grousset remarks: 'These ferocious warriors, once touched by the grace of the bodhisattva, became so susceptible to the humanitarian precepts of the *śramanas* [i.e. Buddhist monks] as to forget not only their native belligerence but even neglect their self-defence.'[23]

But there was one aspect of Egyptian and Chinese religion which was similar, and is probably connected with the gross survivability of their languages *in situ* over many millennia. This is the attitude that each of them took to their emperor, and his relation to his land, his people and their gods.

Both these empires achieved early unity under a single ruler, Egypt under the legendary Menes, China under the historical Shi Huang Di. Although afterwards there were often divisions, and competition among the different kingdoms, the two civilisations never found such disunity tolerable: their histories, as we have seen, distinguished firmly between prosperous periods, when a single royal house controlled the whole country, and interregna, which may have been perfectly peaceable, but suffered from the cardinal flaw that the country was divided. These were very much centred countries, and the centre was not a place (each of them had many different imperial capitals—Thebes, Memphis, Tanis, Leontopolis, Sais in Egypt, Chang-an, Luoyang, Nanjing, Hangzhou, Beijing in China) but a royal court. In each case, the king's position* was sanctified by the national faith. The Egyptian pharaoh was seen as the incarnation (*Ḥam*) of kingship, maintaining a direct relation with the gods on behalf of all his people of the Two Lands. Likewise

---

* Both empires very occasionally permitted a woman to take up the office of king, notably Hatshepsut (1473–1458 BC) and Cleopatra (51–30 BC) of Egypt, and the empresses Wu (AD 690–705) and Ci Xi (AD 1895–1908) of China. Eerily, it was in the reign of a woman that both monarchies, after so many millennia, came to their end.

the Chinese emperor was Son of Heaven (*tiān zǐ*), guaranteeing order in the Central Kingdom.

Both rulers were absolute, deriving their sovereignty not from the people but the gods. Nevertheless each was subject to an explicit moral constraint. In Egypt, this was called *maʀ ʿat*, 'order', the moral and natural law. The pharaoh had a duty to put *maʀ ʿat* in place of *jazfat*, 'wrong', in his kingdom. The Chinese emperor had a duty to rule justly, and abstain from oppression; only so long as he did this, according to the influential doctrine of Mencius (Meng-zi), could he retain the Mandate of Heaven (*tiān mìng*), i.e. legitimacy: the oppressive ruler had forfeited his right to rule, and could be justly deposed by the people.

Both Egypt and China, therefore, had the same simple but sustaining political doctrine, which based the country's identity on the rule of a single emperor, and based the emperor's sovereignty on righteousness. The national philosophy therefore contained a built-in theodicy: the proof of a ruler's righteousness was his success in maintaining a ruling dynasty. The gods were ensuring that only righteous monarchs would be successful, and so, whether the king was failing or prospering, all was right with the world, and the Egyptian or Chinese citizen, whether recent interloper or long-standing resident, could give the system his loyalty.

This doctrine was extemely fitting for a stable long-term culture, with the linguistic consequences that we have seen. But it could be maintained that it was the result, rather than the cause, of the culture's stability. At least as revealing, from a more outward, objective point of view, is the gross fact of population density.

In absolute size, Egypt and China are very different. Although they are comparable in terms of their duration, their populations and areas are of quite different orders. Egypt's population in ancient times has been estimated at 2 million in the Old Kingdom, rising to 8 million over the three thousand years to the Roman conquest. The area inhabited, the Nile valley and the Fayyum, encompasses about 30,000 square kilometres. By contrast, Chinese census figures (first available in AD 2) show 57 million, rising to over 80 million in 1000, and over 1200 million at the recent turn of the millennium. The area of 'China inside the Wall' (excluding Inner Mongolia and Manchuria, and western areas such as Gansu and Qinghai, always very sparsely inhabited) amounts to some 4.5 million square kilometres.[24] The Chinese language, and Chinese history, has had fifty times more adherents than Egyptian, and 150 times the space in which to act.

This immediately leads, however, to another aspect that they do have in common—high density of population. From the figures quoted for Egypt, the population density would be 65 rising to 250 per square kilometre over the period. China is much more varied in its environments; however, the census figures make it possible to abstract a little from the situation in the country as a whole: in the Han period they show a density of 58 per square kilometre in the valley of the Huang-he, and 12 per square kilometre in the lower valley of the Yangtze. A millennium later, in 1250, canals linked the two river systems, and more importantly the north had sustained invasions from Xiongnu, Tabgach, Khitan, Jurchen and Mongol: in this period, the lower Huang-he population had declined by 45 per cent, whereas on the northern bank of the Yangtze it had increased by 176 per cent and twice that (337 per cent) on the southern bank. This puts the two regions of China much on a par, with 30–40 per square kilometre; each, however, less than half the density found on the Nile.[25] Compare this with the densities in the age of Constantine (fourth century AD)[26] estimated for Italy—20 per square kilometre—and for eastern Anatolia—19.*

By ancient standards, then, the density of population in Egypt and China was something truly exceptional. This too must have supported the long-term stability of their languages. The sheer numbers of speakers in their populated regions gave them immunity against swamping by incomers speaking foreign languages, even when they could not deny them entry. Strength in numbers reinforced languages already buttressed by their cultural prestige, and the robust institution of a monarchy endorsed by heaven.

The self-sufficient, resilient character of Egyptian and Chinese is revealed in many situations where they, or their speakers, had to interact with foreigners and their linguistic traditions. These dense, centralised societies were not always impervious to foreign influence, even in the representation and use of their own languages. But for millennia they had sufficient equipoise, or sufficient inertia, to keep the outsiders under their own cultural control.

In the remainder of this chapter, we shall consider three aspects of their cultures where foreigners were bound to have an impact: the history of writing, their knowledge of and attitudes to foreign powers, and their responses to invasion. In every case, the languages' steady continuity depended on a resolute refusal to see themselves, or conduct themselves, on others' terms.

---

* For comparison, the modern population density of the USA is 27 per square kilometre, of Italy 192 per square kilometre, of the United Kingdom 235, and of Japan 328.

Holding fast to a system of writing

Copy thy father and thy ancestors ... Behold their words remain in writing. Open, that thou mayest read and copy wisdom. The skilled man becomes learned.

Instruction for King Merikare, line 35 (Egyptian, mid-twentieth century BC)[27]

書不盡言言不盡意
Shū bùjìn yán yán bùjìn yì

Writing cannot express all words, words cannot encompass all ideas.

Yì Jīng (Classic of Changes), *Xì Cí* Appendix
(attrib. Confucius), i.12 (Chinese, pre-fifth century BC)

Egypt's writing system is strange in that it has no known precursors. The first hieroglyphic inscriptions, on seals, cosmetics palettes, epitaphs and monuments, though they may be short, are well formed in the system that was to persist for the next 3500 years. They use pictures phonetically, making an illustrated word's characteristic consonants do multiple duty, as if a picture of a knife were to stand in English not just for 'knife', but also for 'niffy', 'nephew' and 'enough'. Nevertheless, the characteristic style is prefigured in illustrations made by artists before the advent of writing, suggesting that the system was set up on an indigenous basis.[28]

The usual assumption is that the inspiration came from Mesopotamia, where writing had developed out of accounting tallies, using similar principles of phonetics, a few hundred years before. There were ancient trade routes along the Wadi Araba which connected the Nile valley with the Red Sea, and for all we know the origin may have been due to a genius like that of Sequoya, the illiterate Cherokee who in the nineteenth century AD took the fact of English literacy as a proof of concept, and proceeded then to develop a syllabary for his own language from first principles.

However it was, the system was immediately standardised in an Egyptian style of illustration. Although cursive forms of the hieroglyphs were developed for daily uses, a rigid pictorial exactitude was kept up for monumental inscriptions. This was maintained despite the fact that the materials used by the Egyptians, paint on walls or ink on papyrus laid on with a brush, would have permitted total freedom of style. The practice of fluid, stylish calligraphy never began in Egypt. In their steadfast approach, Egyptian scribes were very different from the masters of such systems as Chinese characters or Mayan glyphs.

Furthermore, although new hieroglyphs were added from time to time, the basic principle of the script, the punning use of the consonants in words pictured, clarified by the use of more pictures to determine the range of meaning and sound, did not change. We find experimental uses of the hieroglyphs to found an alphabet at quarry sites in the Sinai peninsula; and ultimately radically new uses were made of a small set of the symbols by their trading partners, the Phoenicians, to found their alphabet, the apparent progenitor of all the alphabets in the world today. But while some of these foreigners were taking perverse inspiration from them, the Egyptians themselves never modified the hieroglyphic system to write their own language.

This resistance to script reform, a trait shared by the Chinese, really shows no more than that these cultures had already—both very early by regional and global standards—achieved a stable incorporation of writing into their way of life. Asking for a replacement of the writing system in such a literate administration was no more practicable than the various attempts to introduce spelling reform into modern English. It could only become feasible if the systems of education and administration were so severely disrupted that the succession was broken, and a new start could be made. This never happened in Egypt until the country was taken over by cultures with rival administrative traditions, Persian, Greek and Roman. Then the use of Egyptian in administration was undermined, and replaced by Aramaic and Greek. But even so, it was only when Christianity provided a whole new use for literacy that Egyptian could make the leap to writing in a ready-made, alphabetic script. In China, the change to alphabetic writing has never happened at all, despite the 1905 abolition of the imperial examination system, which had indeed been the central educational and administrative institution, and despite all the radical speculation about the future of the character system in the first half of the twentieth century, which had even included the People's Republic's authorisation of a new system for romanisation, Pinyin (used throughout this book).

The Egyptian scribe, *zaḥraw*, represented from the earliest documented times the acme of ambition. This is amply confirmed by the kinds of texts that were copied in the scribal schools:

Behold there is no profession which is not governed;
It is only the learned man who rules himself.[29]

Set to work and become a scribe, for then thou shalt be a leader of men.
The profession of scribe is a princely profession; his writing materials
and his rolls of books bring pleasantness and riches.[30]

In the *Satire on Trades*, the scribe boasts:

> I have never seen a sculptor sent on an embassy,
> nor a bronze-founder leading a mission.

This complacency generated an extreme conservatism that may ultimately have been Egypt's undoing. Literacy in Egyptian remained the preserve of a small and highly educated caste long after the demise of the last independent Egyptian state, in fact until the Christians adapted the Greek alphabet for the language: this step was taken fully a thousand years after the rest of the Mediterranean, including the Assyrians and Babylonians, had adopted alphabetic writing.

But as if to show that there is no natural term to the life of a pictographic system in an alphabetic age, the Chinese system has survived even the turmoil of the twentieth century. It has persisted, essentially unchanged despite some simplification in penmanship, since Shi Huang Di's imposed standardisation in the third century BC of a system that was already over a millennium old. This system established a particular stylised picture, or a combination of phonetic pun plus determiner, in a notional square box, for each word or root in the language. Once established, it was less phonetically based than the Egyptian system, and so its practical use was even less affected by the phonetic changes in the language that have come about over the following two and a half millennia. Scholarly Chinese will have watched with amused unconcern the modifications, truncations and additions conceived by foreigners to produce the Japanese *kana*—two sets of forty-eight simplified outlines chosen to represent the full set of Japanese syllables—and the Korean *han-gŭl*—a true phonetic alphabet, but designed to harmonise on the page with Chinese characters. Each was an original solution to the poor match between Chinese characters and their own polysyllabic, agglutinative and nontonal languages—but this must have seemed no problem for Chinese itself.

In fact, in the last two and a half millennia the Chinese have become aware of a number of alphabetic scripts, conceived quite independently of their characters. The Buddhists brought the Siddha version of the Brahmi alphabet from India, and the Muslims who converted many of the Western peoples brought variants of the Aramaic scripts and Arabic. The Mongol emperor Kublai Khan even commissioned an alphabetic script for his empire, to be used officially for all its literate languages, Mongolian, Chinese, Turkic and Persian. Called 'Phagspa, it was based on the Tibetan version of Brahmi, and promulgated in 1269. It was a version of the Tibetan script converted to be written vertically (though unlike Chinese characters in columns from left to right), and in deference to Chinese taste in rather a squared-off form. However, it never caught on, and was discontinued, along with the Mongolian dynasty, just a century later.

The great advantage of the Chinese system is its masterly representation of the highest common factor of structure and meaning shared by all the Chinese dialects, many of which are not mutually comprehensible. All the modern dialects, and *wényán* as well, are built on a common set of meaningful syllables, which may be pronounced and strung together in different orders in the various dialects, but are still recognisable in graphic form. By and large, every one of these syllables is represented in writing by a single character, and so the meaning of a written Chinese text will be relatively clear to any literate speaker of any dialect. No alphabetic script, based perforce on the sounds of a language, could now be so conveniently neutral in terms of all the different Chinese dialects, unless perhaps it were designed on historical principles with a knowledge of all varieties of Chinese. Such a tour de force would have to be a miracle of subtlety and ambiguity. And so the traditional characters survive.

Despite the difficulty of learning the system, in China mere literacy did not remain the elite accomplishment it always was in Egypt. Different levels would have been attained according to the wealth and opportunities of the family, but poor families continued to throw out the occasional intellectual star. Literacy skills were still prized in China, but at a higher functional level. So the status of the scribe in Egypt corresponds in Chinese society more with that of graduates of the higher levels of the imperial competitive examinations. These were held by and large every third year from AD 622 to 1905.

The only possible Chinese adoption from foreigners in respect of writing concerns not writing itself, but the analysis of pronunciation. The traditional *fǎnqiè* system classifies a character's pronunciation in respect of its initial consonant and its rhyme plus tone, but the *déngyùn-xué* "study of graded rhymes" sub-classifies these constituent parts phonetically. This invention of Chinese scholars of the seventh and eighth centuries AD came about very much under the influence of the subtle phonetic analysis of the Sanskrit pronunciation, derived from the Buddhist tradition.[31] Even so, the analysis of the rhyme part of a character-syllable into its constituent semi-vowels, vowels and consonants had to await the more thoroughgoing approach of alphabetisation, and specifically romanisation, in the nineteenth and twentieth centuries.[32]

There was, then, a clear reluctance to continue the development of Egyptian and Chinese pictographic systems in the direction of reducing their complexity, despite awareness of simpler systems that foreigners were using. The civilisations were built around respect for tradition, and in particular the traditional difficulties in joining the literate class, who held the reins of government.

Foreign relations

Both Egypt and China mostly lacked an active posture towards their neighbours, and towards parts of the world farther away.

Egypt early relied on foreign trade for some of its staple goods, particularly timber. But it secured this through intermediaries, mainly Phoenicians in the third and second millennia, later Greeks. It had control of Palestine and Syria around the end of the second millennium and the beginning of the first, but as we have seen did not actively spread its language (or its culture) to build permanent links there. It never spread out along the Mediterranean coast to the west: population movement was all in the reverse direction, and the city of Cyrene, when it was established c.630 BC, was a Greek, not an Egyptian venture. It may have been more active southward, attempting to incorporate much of Kush (and its gold mines) permanently, and sending some of its own expeditions down the Red Sea to trade with the fabulous Land of Punt, perhaps in Somalia. Although there was seen to be cultural value in unifying the Black Lands, flooded by the Nile, and surrounded by desert wastes on either side, the net effect of these efforts was small. The populations in these harsh regions were just too scant. Politically, the most striking result was the reverse invasion of Egypt in the late eighth century—by Kushite enthusiasts for Egyptian culture.

China was in a very different position from Egypt, by an irony of fate having to defend an intrinsically open border in the north and west, but actively developing and colonising across a naturally occluded frontier in the south. The coasts to the east were seen more as another border, which left China open to pirate attack, rather than offering an opportunity for maritime expansion.

But beyond the encircling zones of barbarians, there was a sense that farther to the west, in India and the Persian and Roman empires, there were foreigners worthy of considerably more respect. In fact the Chinese court sent one or two emissaries to discover and report on these exotic civilisations; and Buddhism, Zoroastrianism, Nestorian Christianity and Islam all penetrated China under Tang rule, to the extent that the first three suffered official persecution in 845. (Only Buddhism and Islam survived it.) The Chinese emperor Yi Zong famously impressed the Muslim visitor Ibn Wahab in 872 with his knowledge of the principal facts of Judaism, Christianity and Islam. But the only material links with the countries that had produced them came through foreign traders visiting Chinese ports. Until the sixteenth century these were all from the Indian Ocean economies, Arabia, Persia and India.

The case of India was different. Once Buddhism had reached China (in the first century AD, through Indian initiative) and begun to establish itself, Chinese monks starting with Fa-Xian in the late fourth century were drawn to make the journey from China themselves, sometimes in stealthy disregard of the law. The most famous of them, Xuan-Zang, had to depart illegally and furtively in 627, but was able to return to an official welcome from the emperor Tai Zong in 644.* It became fashionable to fund large-scale centres for translation of Buddhist literature. There was also a series of expeditions by Chinese monks to study and gather literature in India—fifty-six are known before the tenth century, of whom thirty-four travelled by sea from Guangzhou (Canton) and twenty-two overland past the Taklamakan desert and the Hindu Kush.[33] All this must represent the greatest sustained initiative that China undertook before the modern period to make contact with outside civilisations.

There was a lasting effect on Chinese from the many thousands of new terms which the translations produced, usually building on existing simple Chinese words but combining them in new ways. Three characteristic examples are *guò-qu*, 'past', *xiàn-zài*, 'present', and *wèi-lái*, 'future', each built of two elements: *passing/go*, *appear/be-there*, *not-yet/come*. Each precisely reflects the metaphor of a corresponding Pali word: *atīta*, *paccuppanna*, *anāgata*.† Such words became central to active Chinese vocabulary.

There is an irony here, or rather a significant correspondence between grammar and government. Other countries and languages may simply have borrowed some mangled version of the Sanskrit or Pali words, and supplemented the language that way. This is what was happening all over South-East Asia, even though its languages were just as different from the Indian languages as was Chinese. (See Chapter 5, p. 183.) But the fact that new words were reconstructions in Chinese of the concepts derived from Sanskrit or Pali words is of a piece with China's general strategy in conducting its foreign relations: to attempt always to keep them under domestic control.

This attempt to maintain control was also a feature of China's management of its front and back doors, the 'Silk Roads' round the Taklamakan desert to

---

* Their views of India are considered at pp. 192ff. below.
† Sanskrit *atīta*, *pratyutpanna*, *anāgata*, 'past by', 'given in the presence', 'not come'.

Dunhuang and the ports along the eastern seaboard. Although China was prepared to defend the security of the Silk Roads against the neighbouring barbarians from Roman times onward, the importance of the route was gradually eclipsed by the growth of the maritime trade. The maritime route was actually closed to private trade during the three centuries of the Ming period from around 1368, but when allowed this trade was concentrated mostly at Guangzhou.(Canton), with some competition allowed from the more northerly port of Quanzhou in Fujian. From 1757 to 1842 and 1949 to 1979, Guangzhou enjoyed a monopoly, continuing the Chinese government preference for monitoring and easy taxation. This was forcibly broken open by European and American interests in the intervening century.

A strange exception to the general policy of the Chinese—which was to admit foreign trade on terms, but not to initiate it or to seek diplomatic contact with foreign powers—comes in the apparently unique case of Admiral Zheng-He, who undertook seven great voyages round the Indian Ocean between 1405 and 1433, reaching the Red Sea and Mogadishu.

In the Indian subcontinent Zheng-He's attention was mostly concentrated on Śri Lanka, where on his second voyage in 1411 he is known to have left a trilingual inscription on a stone tablet (prepared in advance in China) in Chinese, Tamil and Persian.

It conveys greetings from the Chinese Ming emperor, and in its three languages expresses respect to the Buddha, the god Tenavarai-Nenavar and Allah respectively, listing massive offerings in gold, silver, silk, etc. These expeditions were evidently not mere courtesy visits, and have a certain dramatic similarity to the notorious behaviour of Europeans abroad: faced with resistance, the Chinese abducted the Śri Lankan king and took him forcibly to the emperor in Nanjing, but then returned him, along with the most holy relic in the island, the Sacred Tooth of Buddha. This resulted in a Chinese claim of sovereignty over Śri Lanka, which was actually respected through payment of tribute by the Śri Lankans until 1459.

Despite their apparent success, such imperialist initiatives ceased abruptly after Zheng-He's final voyage, and were never renewed. No one really knows why. China's foreign policy returned to its characteristic inward-looking and defensive stance.

Nevertheless, as seen above ('Beyond the southern sea', p. 146), Chinese expatriates have given China, and the Chinese, a bridgehead into South-East Asia which its government never looked for—and indeed discouraged over many centuries. Now, in all the major countries of South-East Asia, Chinese-language communities are the principal source of investment capital.

Zheng-He tablet

In the Philippines, the overseas Chinese make up 1% of the country's population, but control over half of the stock market. In Indonesia the proportions are 4% and 75% respectively, in Malaysia 32% and 60%. In Thailand the overseas Chinese account for at least half of the wealth…According to one estimate, the 51 million overseas Chinese control an economy worth $700 billion—roughly the same size as the 1.2 billion mainlanders.[34]

Growing Chinese-dominated businesses will have the opportunity of communicating with one another in Chinese, whether Mandarin or Southern Min; and so for the first time the Chinese language has potential for expansion outside the mainland. China itself is no longer keeping its distance from its fellow-Chinese who have chosen to make their living abroad, and it is possible that this new, more diplomatic face of China will become openly influential, perhaps even hegemonic.

China's disciples

Although China was always reserved in accepting any influence from foreigners, its smaller neighbours who achieved some level of settled civilisation and independent statehood were nothing like so circumspect in their acceptance of influence from China. The states and peoples of Korea, Japan and Vietnam adopted this position. Each of them spoke a language unrelated to Chinese. Each of them had to resist sporadic Chinese attempts at conquest (though Japan suffered this only in the first flush of Mongol imperialism). But each first learnt to read and write not in their own languages but in classical Chinese. And each developed writing systems for their own languages by transforming or supplementing the use of Chinese characters.

Unlike Chinese with Sanskrit and Pali, they each adopted vocabulary from Chinese as it was, regardless of the fact that it did not fit well within the sound systems of their own languages. For them, after all, China represented the fountainhead of advanced civilisation.* As a result their languages became full of Chinese loan vocabulary, modified for their own pronunciation, and have remained so ever since. They soon had as clear an appreciation of the meanings of the syllables they borrowed, and the characters associated with them, as the Chinese had themselves—indeed, perhaps clearer, since they also used the same characters to represent words in their own languages, related only by meaning.

This faithful adoption and incorporation of Chinese language has provided a useful time capsule of a kind for modern comparative research on the history of Chinese. These three 'Sinoxenic' dialects, Sino-Korean, Sino-Japanese, Sino-Vietnamese, are made up of syllables and words borrowed

---

* So generally impressed were they with the way that their Chinese contemporaries did things that in the seventh century AD Korea and Japan even introduced the system of public examinations for entry into the government. (Vietnam, meanwhile, was spending the whole first millennium AD under direct Chinese rule.) But they did it as copycats, emphatically not because they appreciated the point of the system: the Japanese permitted only nobles to sit the examination; and in Korea, sons of higher-graded families were exempted.

from Chinese. They are so complete that it is possible to use them to read out whole texts in *wényán*. As such, they have preserved an echo of Chinese as it was pronounced when the words were borrowed. In fact, in the case of Japanese—complex as ever—there are three distinct echoes: *go-on*, *kan-on* and *tō-on*, depending on whether the word was borrowed in the sixth century, the eighth century or early in the second millennium. So the Mandarin word *nèi*, 'within', written 內 , is now *noi*, pronounced in the sixth tone in Vietnamese, *nae* in Korean and *dai* or *nai* in Japanese. These antiquated styles proved vital when in 1954 the Swedish scholar Bernhard Karlgren came up with a reconstruction of the sounds of seventh-century Chinese.[35]

This avid cultural discipleship of its neighbours could be considered a major secondary spread of the Chinese language. It is often compared to the role of Latin within English and other modern European languages, or Arabic within Persian and Turkish, but it is really more comparable with the fundamental role of Sumerian within Akkadian. Chinese was a language quite unrelated to its disciple languages, and totally unlike them structurally. Nevertheless, its writing system became the root of their literacy, its words became inescapable for any sort of educated discourse, and its literature was adopted as the foundation for their own education system.

With their neighbours so in awe of them, it must have been hard for the Chinese to see their superiority as anything but a universal, objective fact.

Coping with invasions: Egyptian undercut

Foreigners from the desert have become people everywhere … Indeed, the desert is spread throughout the land. The cultivated districts are destroyed. Barbarians from outside have come to Egypt … There are really no people anywhere …

Admonitions of Ipuwer, lines i.5, iii.1ff. (Egyptian, late third millennium BC)[36]

This is from a pessimistic analysis of Egyptian society, which became a literary classic. (The one surviving manuscript was copied out some thousand years after the text was written.) It shows that even early in its recorded history conservatives were bewailing barbarian influxes into Egypt, which as they saw it disrupted the social order: 'Serfs have become owners … She who looked at her face in the water is now the owner of a mirror …' The word for *barbarian* is *pīdjeti*, 'bowman', bringing his desert home (*ḥRswt*) with him, and pointedly contrasted with real people, proper Egyptians.

This text pre-dates any foreign incursions into Egypt that we know about, but evidently the immigrant, particularly unwelcome if he was a social success, was already a stock figure. Yet this ancient Egyptian insularity is telling us more about perennial attitudes than any actual crisis for patriots: the persistence of the Egyptian language shows that the country was able to absorb all the foreign immigration of the following two millennia without losing its central character and traditions.

It is an interesting feature of Egyptian history that, until the advent of the Muslims, they suffered no overwhelming nomadic invasions comparable to the coming of the Amorites and Aramaeans to Mesopotamia. Yet we know that Libyan immigration was significant over many centuries, and among Egyptian dynasties at least the Hyksos kings and the Kushites were foreigners who installed themselves by force. Why, then, so little effect on Egypt's language and culture? Part of the reason must have been the high density of the Egyptians on the ground (*pace* Ipuwer): there were so many of them, benefiting from the bounty of the Nile, that interlopers were doomed to merge.

And so despite the incursions, and the splits and discontinuities in the dynastic tradition, Egypt remained true to its religion, and the concept of a pharaoh ruling through *maʀ ʿat*.

But invasions ultimately did undo the Egyptian language in its homeland: after all, Egypt is today a predominantly Muslim country with a Christian minority, everyone speaking Arabic. How did Egyptian finally come to lose its grip on its speakers?

First of all, there must have been a progressive weakening and dilution of the Egyptian-speaking part of the population. It gradually became a highly multilingual society. Egypt, after all, underwent many invasions in its last five hundred years of independent existence, at the hands of Assyrians, Persians, Greeks and Romans. In the Hellenistic period (332–30 BC) there was also a major influx of Jews, whose major lingua franca was Greek. None of these brought a language that was to achieve full vernacular status in Egypt. But as we have seen, the Aramaic associated with the Assyrians and the Persians did spread within Egyptian society beyond the official sphere, and each of these succeeding powers brought in and fostered new communities that would have spoken something other than Egyptian.

Nevertheless, when Arabs in the first flush of Islam took possession of the country in the mid-seventh century AD, Egyptian was still the principal language spoken in its streets and fields.

The Arabs were not the first force of nomads to penetrate Egypt: the Libyans, and perhaps the Hyksos, had achieved this long before in the second millennium, and there may have been many other smaller incursions over the three poorly documented Intermediate Periods of Egyptian history. The Arabs were not the first power to use a foreign language for purposes of government: all of the Persians, Greeks and Romans had done this. The Arabs were not the first substantial power with a centre abroad to take possession of Egypt, and rule it as a colony: this had been done before for two centuries by the Persians, and for seven centuries by the Romans. The Arabs were not even the first to introduce a new religion: this had been successfully attempted by the Christians in the Roman period.

Why, then, was Arabic the first language successfully to replace Egyptian in its home country? The answer must lie in the combination of all these circumstances. Egyptian's strengths were subverted one by one.

First the Assyrian and Babylonian wars in Palestine created a large Aramaic-speaking émigré community in the Delta area. This would have been the end of Egyptian's language monopoly in the country, not very significant in itself. But then the country was penetrated by numerous business-minded Greeks, brought in by the Saite dynasty to buttress an alliance against Near Eastern powers, and granted their own, Greek-speaking, entrepôt in Naucratis in the Delta. Egypt was now very much a multilingual society, with foreigners' languages more and more associated with higher prestige. The Persian conquest, and a succession of foreign rulers from Persia and then (after Alexander) Greece, meant that now higher-level administration began to be conducted in a language foreign to Egypt: in Aramaic for two hundred years, and then in Greek for a millennium.*

Linguistically, not much would have changed when the Romans unseated the Greeks in 30 BC, other than a small influx of Latin speakers, principally soldiers. But this change of government was to prove the profoundest turning point for the fate of the language: Egypt was no longer to be governed by its own kings in its own interest, but by provincial governors as a useful bread basket for Rome, and (increasingly) a destination for rich tourists.

---

* Aside from Cleopatra's well-known bravura performance, Peremans (1964) finds little evidence of bilingualism in Ptolemaic Egypt, and much of Greeks and Egyptians (*egkhōrioi*, 'locals') sticking to their own languages. Some famous Egyptians, such as the high priest and Greek historian of Egypt, *Manĕthō*, did reach high rank in what remained to the end a Greek-speaking hierarchy. But so many public documents were bilingual (the most famous being the Rosetta Stone, but also judicial notices relating to private cases) that the population could not have been. He also quotes a touching letter: 'I was glad, both for you and for myself, to learn that you were learning Egyptian writing, because now you can come to the city and teach the children of Phalu…es the enema doctor, and have a means of support for your old age' (p. 57). Despite the mention of writing, the tutor was presumably to be employed to teach the middle-class Egyptian children Greek, not vice versa.

What all the invasions had in common was the fact that they were not no-madic movements: they were military affairs conducted by well-organised armies in pursuit of commanders' global political aims. The point in control-ling Egypt was to be associated with its ancient glory, and to appropriate its present agricultural wealth. Otherwise, Egypt was to be kept true to its traditions, and so the only population movements were movements of elites, and small groups such as the Jews. Egyptian civilisation had, however, be-come a hollow show. There was no longer any pharaoh to hold the country through *maʀ ʿat* and perform the sacrifices, unless the Roman emperor hap-pened to be visiting, and by the third century AD even this pretence had been abandoned.

The one elite activity retained by Egyptians was religion, and the language provided a link between its priests and the common people. Nevertheless, af-ter three centuries of Roman rule even this link was to weaken. The local Christian community had grown, first in the face of Roman persecution, and then with official support, adopting Egyptian rather than Greek as its lan-guage. In this way, it provided a new focus, of a spiritual kind, for Egyptian loyalty. But its growing strength was characteristically marked with intoler-ance, particularly towards the ancient religion. How were the Christians to know that in destroying it, they were also pruning away the deepest roots that anchored and sustained their separate identity? By the fourth century AD, Egypt had become a Christian country whose populace spoke Egyptian, but whose administration and cultural life were conducted in Greek. It was still true that Egyptian's one elite activity was religion, but now this was the local version of the Christian faith.

In 641, when political control moved to Arabic speakers, there was no space left for the elite activities in Greek. They soon withered, although some formal use of Greek continued for over a century. Religion was to yield much more slowly. But this was not just another political conquest: Islam, unlike Alexander and Augustus Caesar, aspired to win over all. When it did, the last motive for retaining Egyptian was removed: converts moved into a new con-fessional community, Arabic-speaking and cosmopolitan. Egyptian was left as the language of liturgy for those who were determined to hang on to their Christian faith, a gradually shrinking minority.

Even in hindsight, it is difficult to say whether Christianity was more of a blessing or a bane to Egyptian. It provided a strong ritual focus for the Egyptian-speaking community under Roman secular rule; but it was militant in cutting the links the language had had with its national pagan past. It pro-vided a new synthetic identity, that of 'Egyptian Christian' or Copt, to replace the ancient one, an identity that was to last for many centuries, and for a small minority even until the present day. But the theological motivation for a separate Egyptian sect of Christianity, promoted as a universal faith, was nil. Egyptian was correspondingly weaker when it faced the challenging embrace of the Arabic-speaking community: what ground was there to maintain their Egyptian identity when the gods and rituals of the land of Egypt had all been long forgotten?

Ultimately, Egyptian could not sustain itself when it ceased to be a majority language in its one and only environment, the land of Egypt. The language, like the pharaonic religion, had been a symbol of Egyptian identity. Egyptian could survive a government speaking a foreign language, as long as its religion was based in Egypt. It could not survive a foreign government and a truly cosmopolitan religion, for its speakers had nothing national left as a focus for their identity. They might as well become Arab Muslims, just like all the rest.

Coping with invasions: Chinese unsettled

羈縻	jīmí	'bridle and halter'
以夷攻夷	yǐyí gōngyí	'use barbarians to attack barbarians'
以夷制夷	yǐyí zhìyí	'use barbarians to control barbarians'
以夷變華	yǐyí biànhuá	'turn barbarians into Chinese'
和親	héqīn	'reconciliation and intimacy: marriage alliance'

Recognised Chinese strategies for border management[37]

The final decline of Egyptian can be understood as the long-term effect of losing the sense of its own centre.

After the Roman conquest, Egypt was at best a curiosity on the edge of Rome's Mediterranean world, no longer responsible for its own destiny, but looking hopefully to the west. Four centuries later, the change of focus from Rome to Byzantium had had little impact; Egypt's identity was sustained by its contributions to the new and growing faith of Christianity. Three centuries later still, the further shock of being incorporated into a quite different alien empire, one that was centred now to its east (in Damascus, then Baghdad), was more than its separate identity could stand. For the first and last time, Egyptian went into decline.

China has always viewed itself as being at the centre of its world, traditionally *Tiān Xià*, 'Heaven Below', encompassed on every side by lesser peoples, inferior in cultivation and morals. The modern word for the country, *Zhōng-*

gŭo, 'Central Realm', seems to say it all. But another way of referring to the whole country is *Sìhăi zhīněi*, 'Within the Four Seas', going back at least to Confucius. The Chinese conventionally saw themselves as living in Nine Continents within Four Seas. Each of those seas was seen as the haunt of a barbarian people, the so-called *Sìyí*, 'The Four Yi': *Dōng Yí Běi Dí Xī Róng Nán Mán*, 'east the Yi, north the Di, west the Rong, south the Man'. This idea of the steppes that surround China's heartland as seas, bizarre to anyone who looks at a modern map, had a certain reality when those steppes were populated by pastoral nomads, roaming the grassy plains to prey on the sedentary farmers who lived round the oases, the islands in this ocean. And beyond the *Sìyí* in the traditional world-view lay the *Bāhuāng*, 'the Eight Wastes', so it is understandable that the traditional Chinese was little tempted to explore farther abroad.*

Within this ring of hostiles, the Chinese saw themselves at its centre, with a shared conception of civilised values, and a persistent aspiration to bring willing neighbours into their fold.

There were three features of the Chinese situation that kept their vast community not only centred but also united, socially and linguistically. The first was a *fact* about their human environment, which quite literally came with the territory that they inhabited. The second was an *institution* invented quite distinctively by the Chinese, which turned out to be remarkably persistent. And the third was the *paradoxical result* of the barbarian conquests when they came.

The fact was the periodic influx of hostile marauding nomads, speaking languages radically different to Chinese, and preying on settled Chinese farmers. This had an objective effect on the language, and a subjective effect on Chinese consciousness. Linguistically, the periodic influxes kept the

---

* The Chinese have been unlike most other dominant language communities reviewed in this book in one way: they have not lumped all those speaking other languages under one unflattering name. The single term 'barbarian' is inescapable in English translation, but Chinese has many words, in principle all with different designations. Already in the third-century BC dictionary *Erya* ('Examples of Refined Usage'), the term *sìhăi* is defined: *jiŭyí bādí qīróng liŭmán*, 'the 9 Yi, the 8 Di, the 7 Rong and the 6 Man' (*Erya*, s.v. *Sidí*, cited in Wilkinson 2000: 710). Yet another term was 蕃 *Fān*, from the Chinese point of view divided into the 生 蕃 , *shēngfān*, and 熟蕃 , *shúfān*, 'raw' or 'cooked', depending on whether they had begun to settle to civilised Chinese ways. Not that this multiplicity betokened any particular discernment or respect for the lesser breeds. Although the different words were part of the language, they were often lumped together, e.g. *Róngdí*, *Yídí*, or used undiscriminatingly. In fact, the monosyllabic blanket terms are supplemented with more specific terms for particular tribes. These were often written out, as a kind of Chinese private joke, with insulting characters, e.g. 奴 *nú*, 'slave', in 匈奴 *Xiōngnú*, and 倭 *wō*, 'dwarf', in 倭國 *Wōgŭo*, 'dwarf-realm', i.e. Japan. With urbane malice, this chanced to be pronounced in Japanese identically with 和 *wa*, 'harmony', the term the Japanese preferred when referring to themselves.

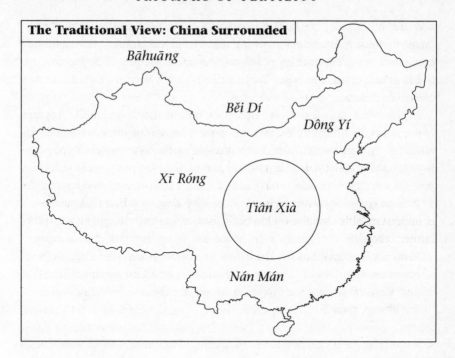

The Traditional View: China Surrounded

Bāhuāng

Běi Dí

Dông Yí

Xī Róng

Tiân Xià

Nán Mán

northern Chinese population on the move, preventing it from settling into distinct dialect areas. But even when, as in the golden ages of the Han and the Tang, the barbarian threat was effecively countered for centuries at a time, the consciousness of barbarians at the gate still remained, naturally causing a greater sense of unity in the population. The external threat of invasion kept the Chinese focused on what they had to lose; and recurrent partial failures of the centre's defences against it kept the north of China in flux, and so perversely maintained the cohesion of its spoken language.

The institution was the system of public examinations, persistent over thirteen centuries, where success was the key to a career in government. This meant that from a very early era China could boast a formally constituted civil service. When it was working, this had an effect on social order analogous to the influxes of invaders on the linguistic order. Both tended to reduce local groupings, and emphasise higher-level loyalties. The meritocratic civil service built loyalties to the state, and undercut the personal loyalties which, when the central government was weakening, tended to develop and split the country into the power bases of contending warlords. But it also had a further effect, bound up with the Chinese language.

The syllabus was almost entirely literary, including composition of classical poetry (introduced under the empress Wu at the end of the eighth century) and of the notorious 八股文 *bāgǔwén*, 'eight-legged essays', which rigorously elicited clear expression of the ideas from the classical texts and their application to contemporary problems. As such, it could only promote national standards for the major language in which it was conducted, *wényán*, classical Chinese.

In this sense it is fair to say that the Chinese state, outside the imperial court, was constituted as the political manifestation of the Chinese literary elite. Cai Xiang, himself a brilliant product of the system, remarked negatively in the middle of the eleventh century:

Nowadays in appointing people it can be observed that they are advanced in office mainly on the basis of their literary skills. The highest office-holders are literary men; those attending the throne are literary men; those managing fiscal matters are literary men; the chief commanders of the border defences are literary men; all the Regional Transport Commissioners are literary men; all the Prefects in the provinces are literary men.[38]

Accounts of the examination system are full of caveats about the distance between its meritocratic theory and its aristocratic and plutocratic reality. It could hardly have been otherwise in an institution that lasted for over two thousand years, every so often dropped or reconstituted. Nevertheless, however unsatisfactory it may often have been for the vast number of bright individuals whom it failed to favour (all women, for example, were excluded), it was never a dead letter: it always existed as a potential means which could be resurrected or reformed to bring new talent into power and influence, a built-in agitator of the sediments of the Chinese establishment, a perpetual grain of sand in the government oyster.

Just as invasion by Altaic hordes kept northern China's populace on the boil, so the examination system, and appointments based on it, kept the power structures open. It therefore promoted the cohesion of the body politic as a whole, with a common language whose standards were clearly defined by the examination syllabus.

The paradoxical result was the fact that although China was ultimately unable to stem the pressure from militarised pastoral nomads, and had to yield its throne to the Mongols and the Manchus, China remained Chinese. The struggle with the barbarians was, in the last analysis, lost—yet it did not matter for the future of the language, or of the culture that it conveyed. In a way, Chinese showed that it could transcend the most fundamental defeat.

Strategically, this may be characterised—in Chinese terms—as:

偷梁換柱 —*tōu liáng huàn zhù*

Steal the beams, change the pillars.[39]

This maxim from the Chinese '36 Strategems' refers to a technique whereby an opponent is gradually lulled into a false sense of confidence, thinking the structures he relies on are still sound, although in fact they have been undermined or suborned. Evidently to do this the strategist must be on close terms with the enemy's organisation, as he may well be, after suffering apparent total defeat and accepting surrender. In the case of the Mongols—who never, incidentally, accepted serious use of the examination system, and so were vulnerable to the growth of local lordships—it proved possible within a century to build up sufficient regional power bases to unseat the central government. With the Manchu, it was more difficult, since they themselves, conscious of their small numbers, made effective use of Chinese institutions such as the examinations to recruit loyal cadres. They also concentrated themselves in the military. Still, making up no more than 2 per cent of the population, it proved impossible for them to live with the Chinese and not be absorbed by them. In vain were they forbidden by law from intermarrying with Chinese or adopting Chinese customs, in vain compulsorily educated in Manchu, a language that continued in government papers until the fall of the dynasty in 1911: nevertheless, within 150 years of their successful conquest of China, all those of Manchu ancestry were speaking Chinese.[40]

It also leads us to the current Chinese response to the challenge from the Western world. Bizarrely, but revealingly, China is again adopting this traditional strategy.

After its traumatic experiences at the hands of Western powers in the nineteenth century, China abolished the examination system in 1905 and the imperial monarchy itself in 1911. A general air prevailed of bringing the country up to date, European-style. One suggestion considered was even to abolish the Chinese language itself in favour of Esperanto, an artificial but would-be international language fashioned by a Pole out of European roots in the late nineteenth century, and in particular vogue at the time. In the event, during the 1920s and 1930s the official form of Chinese was redefined: in place of *wényán*, which went back to the fifth century BC, came *báihuà*, 'white speech', the colloquial form of Mandarin as spoken in Beijing. Written in characters, it represents colloquial grammar and lexicon, but is of course neutral on actual pronunciation. This was not too much of a shock, since it had been current, and indeed used in popular literature,* since at least the middle of the first millennium AD, but had never previously had the feel of a language for serious business.†

China is now in a period of extremely rapid economic development, in which it has consciously adopted Western methods. In a sense this is the third Western-inspired revolution in a century, since the foundation of the republic in 1911, the communist revolution in 1949 and the initiation of capitalist reforms since Mao's death were all applications of Western ideas. All this in a country that had not internalised a major Western idea since the widespread take-up of Buddhism in the sixth and seventh centuries AD. If China succeeds in adopting and adapting these ideas in its own long-term interests, it will once again have turned the apparently conclusive victory of its adversary into a longer-scale triumph of its own. New beams and pillars indeed.

But if we take up again our comparison with the Egyptian case, the long-term future of the Chinese language may be hanging in the balance. The common feature we have found, which explains both Egyptian and Chinese persistence over so many millennia, is the maintenance of a distinct centre of identity and loyalty within the language community.

Gradually losing aspects of its historic centre, in the form first of its monarchy, then of its political independence, then of its own national religion, and finally of its national form of Christianity, Egyptian weakened steadily over the ages, and has now, as a language simply recited in formal liturgy, come close to disappearing altogether. If the analogy is valid, Chinese, despite its billion speakers, might consider that it too has now entered on a perilous path. To accommodate the challenge from the modern, European-inspired, world, it has already given up the link with its own monarchy, an ideal with which it had identified for over two millennia. It has not given up its political independence, but it has, at least officially, resigned its own religion: since the fall of the monarchy, it has no longer actively sustained the value of Confucian, much less Taoist, ideas.

---

* The famous Chinese novels of the sixteenth to eighteenth centuries, notably *Hongloumeng*, 'The Dream of the Red Chamber', by Cao Xueqin, *Sanguozhi Yanyo*, 'Romance of the Three Kingdoms', by Luo Guanzhong, and *Xiyouji*, 'Journey to the West', by Wu Cheng-en, were all written in this dialect of Chinese.

† There were also a number of attempts to replace Chinese characters with a romanised script, but with the acknowledged difficulty of finding a system that could be neutral in terms of the different dialects, none succeeded in becoming anything more than an aid to learners and foreigners. The Pinyin romanisation used in this book represents standard Mandarin, and is now close to being an international standard. It was developed in collaboration with Russian scholars, and published officially in 1957.

China's political independence may yet save its language from the downward slide of Egyptian. And even under foreign rule, Chinese has shown itself much more resilient, and indeed absorbent, than Egyptian ever was in its last two millennia. It has the advantage, which Egyptian never had, not just of high density but also of vast absolute population size. In its written mode, there is nothing yet in the history of Chinese to compare with Egyptian's loss of its indigenous writing system and adoption of the Greek script, though romanisation may yet come.

In sum, the cultural retreats that we identified as leading to Egyptian's demise all have their analogues in the recent history of Chinese, except for political conquest. The writing may already be on the wall for the language now spoken by one fifth of mankind.

5

Charming Like a Creeper:
The Cultured Career of Sanskrit

भाषा प्रशस्ता सुमनो लतेव
केषाम्न चेतांस्यावर्जयति।

bhāṣā praśastā sumano lateva
keṣām na cetāṃsy āvarjayati

Language, auspicious, charming, like a creeper,
whose minds does it not win over?*

(sūkta—traditional maxim)

The story in brief

There is a persistent image of Sanskrit as a creeping plant, luxuriant and full blossomed. Over two thousand years it spread itself round the centres of Asian population: from north to south of the Indian subcontinent, and thence to South-East Asia and the East Indies, to the Tibetan plateau and to the Far East.

The word *Sanskrit* (*saṃskṛta*) means 'composed' or 'synthesised'. It is a term for the language as formulated in the grammar books, contrasting it with its colloquial dialects, known as the *Prakrits* (*prākṛta*), the 'naturals'. It also

---

* In the romanised script for Sanskrit, c is pronounced as *ch* in *church*, j as in *judge*. A dot under t, d or n means that it must be sounded with tongue turned back, retroflex. A dot under an h means that it is followed by an echo of the previous vowel (e.g. *kaḥ*, 'who', as *kah*[a]). A dot under an r or an l means that it is pronounced as a separate syllable, as *bitter*, *little* in American English. A dot under an m means that is pronounced simply by nasalising the preceding vowel: *aham*, 'I', is like American 'uhuh?'. All the stop consonants (k, g, c, j, t, d, ṭ, ḍ, p, b) can be aspirated, and this is shown by a following h. There are three sibilants, ś, ṣ and s: the first two are close to English *sh*, the former as in *sheet*, the latter with the darker sound as in *push*.

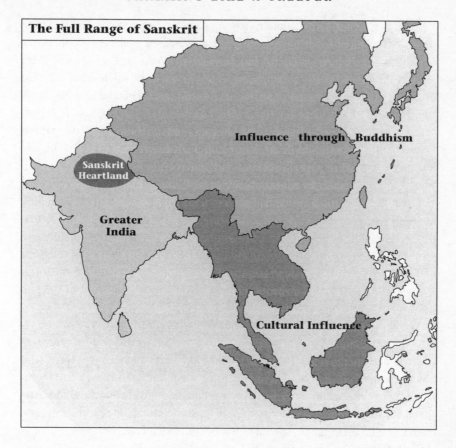

The Full Range of Sanskrit

Influence through Buddhism

Sanskrit
Heartland

Greater
India

Cultural Influence

distinguishes it from an older form, sometimes called Vedic, known from its use in the *Veda*, 'the knowledge': these are hymns to the gods which appear to go back to the earliest days of the language as spoken in India, in the last centuries of the second millennium BC, but which are still recited unchanged in Hindu rituals today. Most of the modern languages of northern and central India are descendants of Sanskrit, developed versions of the Prakrits, much as the Romance languages developed from forms of vulgar Latin. But outside the Indian subcontinent, Sanskrit was never taken up as a popular language; it remained purely a medium of learned communication and sacred expression, strongest where the dominant religion had come from India.

Although it is religious tradition which has proved the most reliable preserver of Sanskrit in many an *avatāra* ('descent', as of a divine being from heaven), and despite the heavy association, in the West today, of the language with transcendental spiritualism, Sanskrit was never just a liturgical language.

Even the Vedic corpus contains a joyous yet wry evocation of *māṇḍūkāḥ*,[1] 'frogs', doubly like the priestly caste of Brahmans: they take a vow of silence for a year (until the rainy season); and when they do pipe up 'one of them repeats the speech of the other, as the learner does of his teacher'. It also brings us the wry self-pity of a compulsive gambler,[2] enslaved to *babhravaḥ*, 'the browns', the nuts then used as dice: *rājā cid ebhyo nama it kṛṇoti*, 'even a king bows before them...' he excuses himself, going on: *tasmai kṛṇomi, 'na dhanā ruṇadhmi' daśāham prācīs, 'tad ṛtam vadāmi'*. 'I show him my empty palms: "I am not holding out on you—it's the truth, I tell you."'

Later on, Sanskrit becomes very wide ranging in its content, including among its most widely known works romantic comedy, theoretical linguistics, economics, sexology (notably the *Kāma Sūtra*), lyrical verse, history and moral fables, along with a continuing production of epic poetry and religious and philosophical tracts. It is a very self-conscious literary tradition, full of learned allusions, and above all the most elaborate development of the pun known anywhere on earth.

We begin with an outline of how Sanskrit was spread across Asia.

A dialect of Indo-Iranian, it is first heard of in the North-West Frontier area of Swat and the northern Panjab (now in Pakistan), spoken by peoples who have evidently come from farther north or west, and who like to call themselves *ārya* (later a common word for 'gentleman', and always the Buddhists' favourite word for sheer nobility of spirit). Somehow their descendants, and even more their language, spread down over the vast Indo-Gangetic plain, as well as up into the southern reaches of the *Himālaya* ('snow-abode') mountains, so that by the beginning of the fifth century BC the language was spoken in an area extending as far west as Bihar, and as far south, perhaps, as the Narmada. Sanskrit literature from the period, principally the epic poems *Mahābhārata* ('Great Bharata') and *Rāmāyaṇa* ('The Coming of Rama'), is full of military exploits and conquests.

The result was the present-day situation, a northern Indian heartland, stretching from sea to sea, of languages more or less closely related to Sanskrit. This centre is always known in India as *Āryāvarta* ('abode of the Aryas'). It also gained one offshoot in *Śrī Laṅkā* to the far south, creating the *Siṃhala* ('lion-y') community there: according to tradition, this group had come from Gujarat, on the north-western coast, in the fifth century BC. The advance of Aryan is continuing to this day in the northern regions of Assam and Nepal, where the official languages (Assamese, and Nepali or Gurkhali) are both Aryan, but have not yet become the vernaculars of large majorities of their populations.

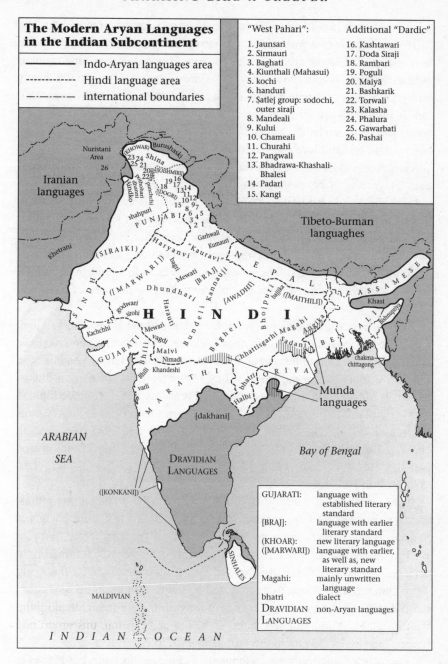

The Modern Aryan Languages in the Indian Subcontinent

——————— Indo-Aryan languages area

------------- Hindi language area

—·—·—·— international boundaries

"West Pahari":

1. Jaunsari
2. Sirmauri
3. Baghati
4. Kiunthali (Mahasui)
5. kochi
6. handuri
7. Ṣatlej group: sodochi, outer siraji
8. Mandeali
9. Kului
10. Chameali
11. Churahi
12. Pangwali
13. Bhadrawa-Khashali-Bhalesi
14. Padari
15. Kangi

Additional "Dardic"

16. Kashtawari
17. Doda Siraji
18. Rambari
19. Poguli
20. Maiyā
21. Bashkarik
22. Torwali
23. Kalasha
24. Phalura
25. Gawarbati
26. Pashai

GUJARATI: language with established literary standard

[BRAJ]: language with earlier literary standard

(KHOAR): new literary language

([MARWARI]): language with earlier, as well as, new literary standard

Magahi: mainly unwritten language

bhatri dialect

DRAVIDIAN LANGUAGES non-Aryan languages

Not all the spread of Sanskrit was through full take-up of the language as a vernacular. Even when pre-existing languages, such as Telugu, Kannada and Tamil, held their own, they were usually permeated with terminology from Sanskrit. It is quite possible for these borrowed words (called *tat-sama*, 'that-same') to be overwhelmingly numerous in a language whose grammar is non-Aryan. Conversely, in Urdu, or even Hindi, majority languages of northern India, Aryan roots may be almost invisible under the heavy influence of later borrowings from Persian and Arabic. (This widespread culturally induced borrowing has been the bane of Indian historical linguistics: nowhere has it been harder to sift the inherited part of languages from foreign borrowings, and so piece together their history.)

The process of Sanskritisation did not stop at the boundaries of the subcontinent. Over the course of the first millennium AD, Indian seafaring traders or missionaries made landfall, not only in Śri Lanka, but also in many places along the coasts of South-East Asia. Here, the language spread above all as a language of elite civilisation and religion (whether Hindu or Buddhist), but the influence, and evidently the study made of Sanskrit as a vehicle of high culture, was profound. The region is known as Indo-China, quite rightly, for it became a crucible for the competing cultural influences of India and China.

But when Sanskrit took its path northward, round the Himalayas to Tibet, China, Korea and Japan, it was above all the attractions of the Buddha's teachings which caused the spread of the language. The Buddha had lived in the fifth century BC, in the lower valley of the Ganges, speaking a Prakrit known as Magadhi. In the next two hundred years the faith he founded spread all over India and Śri Lanka, as well as into Burma, its scriptures largely written in a closely related Prakrit, Pali, but also, more and more over time, in classical Sanskrit. Besides the spread to South-East Asia, the most influential path that Buddhism took was to Kashmir, and back to the homeland of Sanskrit itself in Panjab and Swat.

Hence in the first century AD Buddhism, with its attendant scriptures, spread northward, perhaps here again trekking back up the historic route that Sanskrit speakers had used to enter India over a millennium before. But past Bactria, instead of turning left into the central Asian steppes, it turned right and, picking up the Silk Road, headed into China. Received by the rising Tang dynasty, and ultimately propagated by them, Buddhism became coextensive with Chinese culture. Thence it was ultimately transmitted, along with its Sanskrit and Pali scriptures, to Korea and Japan, its most easterly homes, arriving at the end of the sixth century.

Other, closer, areas took much longer to receive the doctrine, borne as ever by its vehicles Pali and Sanskrit. Nepal had been part of the early Indian spread of Buddhism under Aśoka, in the third century BC; but the first Indian monk invited into Tibet, *Śāntarakṣita*, came in the second half of the eighth century AD, a full 1200 years after the Buddha had lived just two hundred miles to the south (admittedly, over the Himalayas) in Magadha; and the religion was firmly established in Tibet only in the eleventh century.

The last area to be exposed to Buddhism (and hence sacred Sanskrit) on a large scale was Mongolia, its northernmost home. For many centuries there were strong links between the Tibetans and the Mongols, who from 1280 to 1368 achieved ascendancy over China. Kublai Khan, for example, the Mongol emperor of China well known in the West as the host of Marco Polo, was keen to spread Buddhism to the Mongol homeland in the early fourteenth century. But this aim was only achieved permanently by Chinese preachers rather later: in 1578 the Altan Khan of Mongolia accepted a version of the Tibetan Buddhist tradition, on behalf of his whole realm.

Sanskrit, then, has a far-flung history, and has been in contact with cultures conducted in other languages all over southern, eastern and central Asia. And an interesting generalisation emerges. Nowhere has this linguistic contact led to loss or replacement of other linguistic traditions, even though Sanskrit has always been central to new cultural developments wherever it has reached. This record makes a striking contrast with the impact, too often devastating, of languages of large-scale campaigning civilisations, such as Greek, Latin, Arabic, Spanish, French and English.

But in another way this widespread embrace of Indian culture is highly reminiscent of the enthusiasm for Americana that captured the whole world, and certainly the South-East Asian region, in the second half of the twentieth century. In that advance too the primary motives were the growth of profits through trade, and a sense that the globally connected and laissez-faire culture that came with the foreigners was going to raise the standard of life of all who adopted it. As with the ancient advance of Indianisation, there has been little or no use of the military to reinforce the advance of Microsoft, Michael Jackson or Mickey Mouse. There has been little sense that the advance is planned or coordinated by political powers in the centre of innovation, whether in India then, or in the USA today. And the linguistic effects are similar too: English, like Sanskrit, has advanced as a lingua franca for trade, international business and cultural promotion.

A major dissimilarity is the absence of any religious element in the American movement. There is nothing in it to set against the cult of Hindu deities, or the Buddha's Four Noble Truths and Noble Eightfold Path. This may be significant for the future of English, since we shall see that it was ultimately only religion, whether Hindu or Buddhist, which was to preserve any role for Sanskrit outside India. But with this one caveat, it seems more helpful than misleading to compare these two rising tides—of Indian culture in the early first millennium AD, and of American culture at the end of the second.

The rest of this chapter looks a little more deeply at what kind of language Sanskrit was, and how it came to be received so enthusiastically across southern and eastern Asia.

The character of Sanskrit

dūrīkṛtāḥ khalu guṇāir udyānalatā vanalatābhiḥ

Left far behind indeed in virtues are the garden-creepers by the forest-creepers.

Kālidāsa, Śākuntalā Recognised, i.17

Intrinsic qualities

Indian culture is unique in the world for its rigorous analysis of its own language, which it furthermore made the central discipline of its own culture. The Sanskrit word for grammar, *vyākaraṇa*, instead of being based, like the Greek *grammatikē*, on some word for *word* or *writing*, just means *analysis*: so language is the subject for analysis par excellence.

Patanjali, a noted grammarian of the second century BC, wrote at the beginning of his work the *Mahābhāṣya* ('great commentary') that there were five reasons for studying grammar: to preserve the Vedas, to be able to modify formulae from the Vedas to fit a new situation, to fulfil a religious commitment, to learn the language as easily as possible, and to resolve doubts in textual interpretation.[3] So it is clear that even at this stage, a good millennium after the composition of the Vedas, when the language had already changed quite considerably, enhancing the use of language for religious purposes was still felt to be the central point of grammar.

And religious uses have always loomed large in the figure that Sanskrit cuts in the world. Hindu liturgies have been intoned in the language over a continuous period of 3500 years, which is probably the age of the oldest hymns in the Rig Veda. The gods chosen to be the focus of worship have changed over the millennia, from Agni ('Fire'), Savitri ('Sun'), Varuna and Rudra in the Vedas, to Śiva , Krishna, Ganesha and Kali (and many others) today, but some gods are still with us (notably Vishnu), and the language has changed very little. In fact, in the Rig Veda there is one hymn that is an invocation of Vāc, speech itself. Here are two of its verses:

Ṛgveda X.71	[1]
bṛhaspate prathamaṃ vāco agre	When, O Lord of the World, the Wise established
yatprairata namadheyaṃ dadhānāḥ	Name-giving, the first principle of language,
yadeṣāṃ śreṣṭhaṃ yadaripramāsīt	That which was excellent in them, that which was pure,
preṇā tadeṣāṃ nihitaṃ guhāviḥ	Hidden deep within, through love was brought to light.
	[4]
uta tvaḥ paśyanna dadarśa vācaṃ	Many a man who sees does not see the Word
uta tvaḥ śṛnvanna śṛṇotyenāṃ	And many a man who hears does not hear it.
uto tvasmai tanvaṃ 'vi sasre jāyā	Yet for another it reveals itself like
iva patya uśati suvāsāḥ	A radiant bride yielding to her husband.

The last words show a blending of sexual and mystical imagery, often found in Sanskrit; but they also show that the skills of the linguist were early recognised. This is particularly interesting in that the discipline of grammar as it had been developed was an analysis not primarily of the religious language of the Vedas, but of a different, slightly simpler, and therefore presumably later, dialect. *Pāṇini*, the original fifth-century BC doyen of Sanskrit grammar, has to give extra rules to generate the forms used in the Vedas (called *chandas*) from a base in ordinary Sanskrit (designated as *bhāṣā*—'speech'). (Panini probably lived in the academic community of *Takṣaśilā*, known to the Greeks as Taxila, near modern Rawalpindi in the extreme north-east of the subcontinent, now part of Pakistan.)

Furthermore, the grammar that the tradition had defined was a vast system of abstract rules, made up of a set of pithy maxims (called *sūtras*, literally 'threads') written in an artificial jargon. These sutras are like nothing so much as the rules in a computational grammar of a modern language, such as might be used in a machine translation system: without any mystical or ritual element, they apply according to abstract formal principles.*

---

* This is not a metaphor, or anachronistic interpetation of Sanskrit grammar, but a straightforward description of the working of the sutras in Panini's system. Consider the application of a single sutra:

iko yaṇ aci

The three words that constitute the sutra are not words of Sanskrit itself, but of an artificial meta-language that refers tersely to other sutras of the grammar. Nevertheless, they are treated as if they are consonant-stem nouns, with the regular ending for genitive (*-as*), nominative (a bare ending) and locative (*-i*). (There is a slight complication, in that both a voiced segment, a final *-as*, is realised phonetically as *-o*. This is a regular principle of liaison in Sanskrit, itself a highly complicated part of the grammar.) The sutra could therefore be analysed functionally as

Formulation in sutras became the key feature of Sanskrit academic texts, but using maxims in regular Sanskrit and not this complex meta-language. Whereas Western didactic texts until the modern era were formulated in some Greek tradition as a set of axioms and theorems (after Euclid), or more often as didactic verse (after Hesiod), the preferred approach in the Sanskrit tradition has been to encapsulate treatises as a series of memorable aphorisms, usually phrased as verse couplets. So much so that there is even a sutra to define the qualities of a good sutra:

svalpākṣaram asandigdhaṃ sāravad viśvatomukham
astobham anavadyaṃ ca sūtraṃ sūtravido viduḥ

brief, unambiguous, pithy, universal,
non-superfluous and faultless the sutra known to the sutra-sages.

This approach was very much a part of another distinctive feature of Sanskrit linguistic culture, namely a strong ambivalence about the value of writing. Reliance on language in its written form was seen as crippling, and not giving true control over linguistic content. Hence this proverb:

$[ik]^{GEN} [yaṇ]^{NOM} [ac]^{LOC}$

In the context of a sutra, these cases have special interpretation, referring respectively to the input, the output and the right-hand context of a phonological rule. The sutra is therefore to be understood as:

$[ik] \rightarrow [yaṇ] / \_ [ac]$

But what is the reference of the strange words themselves? They are to be understood as applications of another set of sutras (known as the Śiva-sutras), which plays the role of a system for defining natural classes of sounds in Sanskrit. This begins:

a i u Ṇ; ṛ ḷ K; e o Ṇ; āi āu ā C; h y w r Ṭ; l Ṇ...

There is no distinction between upper or lower case in Sanskrit, nor any semicolons. But the use of this Roman typographical convenience is simply to show explicitly what a student of Paninian grammar learns by example, namely that the letters here written in upper case are functioning as control characters. Any term consisting of one of the lower-case letters a followed by one of the control characters b denotes the sequence of phones starting with a and ending just before b. So, for example, 'aC' denotes the set of vowels, 'haṬ' the set of semi-vowels excluding l. It can be seen then that the sutra being analysed is nothing less than a concise statement of the rule:

⟨i,u, ṛ ḷ⟩ → ⟨y, w, r, l⟩ before { a, i, u, ṛ, ḷ, e, o, āi, āu }

Terse, indeed, but it should be remembered that this level of concision is possible only because a number of controlling principles can be taken for granted—e.g. the interpretation implicit in the brackets: the first four phones map respectively on to the second four phones, but this occurs before any of the nine phones in the environment. Part of the task of the tradition of commentary which followed on from Panini was to make explicit the precise nature of the *paribhāṣā* (auxiliary principles) on which the correct interpretation of the sutras rests.

pustakasthā tu yā vidyā parahastagatam dhanam

Knowledge in a book—money in another's hand.[4]

In this ancient India was like many cultures as widely divided as the Druids of Gaul in the first century BC[5] and modern Guatemala (where Mayans remark that outsiders note things down not in order to remember them, but rather so as not to have to remember them).[6] Even Socrates recalled a story that when the the the god Thoth first offered the craft of writing to the king of Egypt, the king was not impressed: 'it will set forgetfulness in the minds of learners for lack of practice in memory'.[7] The doyens of Indian learning took this undeniable side effect of book learning very much to heart.

Even though the language had undergone a full phonological analysis by the fifth century BC, which was even incorporated into the official order of letters in the alphabet, reliance on written texts for important (especially spiritually important) documents was decried. Hence another saying:

vedavikrayiṇaścāiva vedānāṃcāiva dūṣakaḥ
vedānāṃ lekhakaścāiva tevāi nirayagāminaḥ

The sellers of the Vedas, the misreaders of the Vedas,
the writers of the Vedas, all go on the path to hell.[8]

By contrast the ideal was the rote learning of all the principal texts, through judicious use of mnemonic techniques. This learning then made possible true engagement with all aspects of them, including the composition of new texts and commentaries, which might indeed benefit from being written down.

The character of the language that received this attention has already been exhibited in the quotations. It was a typical ancient Indo-European language, with nouns, adjectives, pronouns and verbs all highly inflected in a system that, although susceptible to elegant analysis (as Panini and the grammatical tradition demonstrated), was rife with special exceptions. Words tended to be polysyllabic, and their length was often increased by the propensity of the language to tolerate compounds of almost unlimited length, a feature of Sanskrit that became more extreme (in all genres of literature) as the centuries and millennia wore on.

The vocabulary is vast: there are over ten thousand nominal (i.e. nonverbal) roots in the traditional thesaurus for poets (*Amarakoṣa*, 'the Immortal

Treasury', organised of course into sutras for memorisation) and, when verbs and compounds are allowed in, Monier Williams' 1899 dictionary runs to 180,000 entries.* This means that there are vast resources in near-synonyms: at an extreme, John Brough claims there are fifty synonyms for 'lotus', a favourite concept of Sanskrit poetry in both literal and metaphorical senses.[9] Words tend to have multiple senses anyway: the most straightforward word for lotus, *padma* has eleven extra senses in the neuter gender (*lotus-like ornament, form of a lotus, root of a lotus, coloured marks on the face and trunk of an elephant, an army formation, a trillion (10^{12}), lead, a tantric chakra, a mole on the body, a spot, part of a column*) and eight more in the masculine (*temple, quarter-elephant, species of serpent, Rama, a treasure of Kubera, a mode of sexual enjoyment, a posture in meditation, a treasure connected with magic*). These lexical resources are exploited to the full in Sanskrit poetry, which is gratuitously allusive and periphrastic, and addicted to *śleṣa* or punning.

But we have already noted that a special characteristic of Sanskrit is a complicated system of word *liaison*. This is known as *sandhi* ('putting together'). It means that word boundaries are often effaced, and a single stream of syllables, as pronounced or even written, becomes susceptible to multiple interpretations. The combined result of these two properties of Sanskrit is an opportunity for punning on an almost inconceivable scale. This opportunity was amply taken up in literary composition. The ultimate in this was achieved by the poet *Kavirāja* ('poet-king'), who in his *Rāghavapāḍavīya* (twelfth century AD), set himself the task of retelling simultaneously the stories of both the great epics of India, the *Rāmāyaṇa* and *Mahābhārata*, in ambiguous (and highly ornate) verses. In a way, this can be seen as a release of meaning from its expression in words, for it is difficult to conceive how the work could have been understood, in either of its senses, without active and detailed pre-knowledge by the audience of the tales being told. Author and audience share the stories, but are focused exclusively on the verbal details of their expression. This in practice forces not only the use of ambiguous terms, but an analogy to be set up between the narrative flow of the two epics. So, to quote one couplet (vi.8):

paracakraṃ parikrāmann aśokagahanaṃ gataḥ:
kṣanād iva kṛtārtho 'bhūn maheyīdarśanena saḥ.

---

* Compare the 215,000 or so entries in the latest *Chambers English Dictionary*, and over 500,000 in the latest *Oxford English Dictionary*.

Going round the enemy's **kingdom**/*forces*, he came to **a thicket of Aśoka trees**/*the reverse of grief*:
in an instant as it were, his task was accomplished, by his sight of **the daughter of the earth**/*the cows*.

Here the first of the variant translations (in bold) of phrases applies to Hanuman seeking Sita, and the second (italicised) to Arjuna on a cattle-rustling expedition behind enemy lines. But to maintain a coherent narrative, most of the phrases still have an unambiguous translation.

In every sense of the word, then, Sanskrit is a luxuriant language. Sir William Jones, Chief Justice of India and founder of the Royal Asiatic Society, memorably described it in 1786: 'The Sanskrit language, whatever may be its antiquity, is of a wonderful structure; more perfect than the Greek, more copious than the Latin, and more exquisitely refined than either.'

Sanskrit in Indian life

SOCIAL

The question of who or what provided the model for the best Sanskrit has been answered in various ways over its long life. It was far more fraught than the question of the standard for Greek or Latin, since those languages did not carry the heavy theological overtones that have remained with Sanskrit throughout.

Originally, as we have seen, the focus was purely religious, and the promoted aim was to pronounce and articulate the Vedas properly. What would now be seen as a matter of social and pious propriety was represented otherwise in ancient India. Intoning the Vedas, after all, was held to give supernatural power, and Patanjali gave an example of the potentially life-threatening nature of bad grammar: the demon Vritra performed a sacrifice to obtain a son who would be *indra-śatruḥ*, a killer of Indra, his sworn enemy among the gods. Unfortunately he accented it wrong, on the first rather than the last syllable, and so conjured up a son whom Indra would kill.[10]

Coming from Patanjali, this is an anecdote of the second century BC, showing that some features at least of the language defined by Panini's grammar had already ceased to be routine. Panini had lived in the fifth century in the extreme north-west of the Sanskrit- or Prakrit-speaking area. By Patanjali's time, this region had fallen under the control of *mleccha** peoples, non-Hindu

---

* This is the precise Sanskrit equivalent of the Greek *barbaros*, defined as someone who did not speak Sanskrit.

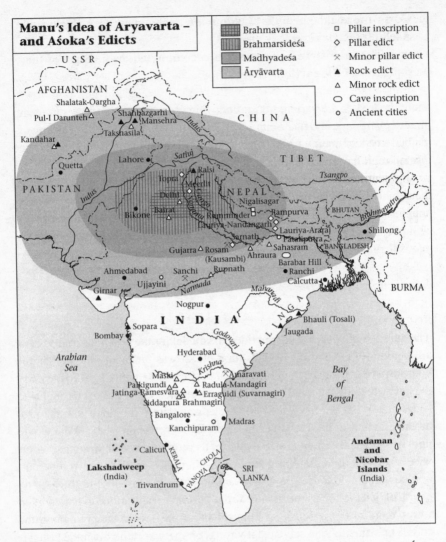

Manu's Idea of Aryavarta – and Aśoka's Edicts

Brahmavarta
Brahmarsideśa
Madhyadeśa
Āryāvarta

□ Pillar inscription
◇ Pillar edict
✗ Minor pillar edict
▲ Rock edict
△ Minor rock edict
○ Cave inscription
◇ Ancient cities

(and non-Sanskrit-speaking) foreigners, the *Yavana* (Greeks) and *Śaka* (Scythians speaking an Iranian language, comparable to Pashto) from the west and north.

The religious motives emphasised by Patanjali for ensuring one's Sanskrit was correct developed naturally, in India's hierarchical and theocratic society, into social markers, and indeed status symbols. Patanjali worries that there may be a circularity (*itara-itara-āśraya*) in his natural wish to identify the best educated (*śiṣṭa*) usage with what grammar prescribes: after all, how does the grammarian know what to prescribe? So he appeals to the usage of the *Āryāvarta*, defined geographically: this turns out to be northern India, bounded by the Himalayas in the north and the Vindhya mountains in the south, and the Panjab in the west and Allahabad in the east.[11] This was to remain the received view of the Aryan centre, although there are refinements to be found in the Manu Law Code, written perhaps seven hundred years later, about AD 500: *Madhyadeśa* ('Mid Land') is identified with this definition—effectively modern Haryana and Uttar Pradesh—while the *Āryāvarta* has expanded to encompass the whole of the north of the subcontinent; meanwhile, a small region round Delhi ('between the divine rivers *Sarasvatī* and *Dṛṣad-vatī*'), identified as the *Brahmāvarta*, has the supreme accolade: 'All men in the world should learn their proper behaviour from a Brahman born in that country.'[12]

POLITICAL

Patanjali conveniently places the limits of *Āryāvarta* more or less at the borders of the *Śunga* empire of which he was a citizen.[13] This would not have been so convenient a century earlier, when the political world revolved around the vastly larger, but less centrally located, empire of the Mauryas. Its centre was *Pāṭaliputra* (modern Patna), which is in eastern India beyond the confines of the then *Āryāvarta*. Furthermore, it extended as far to the east as the Brahmaputra, as far to the north and west as the southern part of Afghanistan, and to the south it reached modern Mysore and the Nilgiri hills. These bounds are marked by monumental inscriptions, set up on pillars or carved into the living rock, placed by the greatest Maurya emperor *Aśoka* ('grief-less'—or, as he preferred to called himself, *Piyadasi*, Sanskrit *Priya-darśin*, 'of friendly aspect'.)

The role of politics in the early spread of Sanskrit across India remains obscure. Very likely, the process of military conquest and dynastic subordination in the third century BC spread not Sanskrit as such but the Magadhi Prakrit, which was the language of the Maurya court; Sanskrit would have taken up its position thereafter, establishing itself here, and no doubt elsewhere, as the common language for educated discourse of all those who spoke some Indian Prakrit in day-to-day life. This has been its position in India ever since, although in the last millennium other languages, notably Persian (under the Mughals) and English (under the British), have entered the subcontinent and competed for this status as the prime language of education.

In fact, the kind of linguistic advance achieved by military conquest seems to have been particularly impermanent. There is a cluster of Aśoka's edicts round Raichur, on the borders of modern Karnataka and Andhra Pradesh; but this is now the very heart of the area where Kannada and Telugu are spoken—both Dravidian languages unrelated to Magadhi, or indeed to Sanskrit. Later, a series of Aryan-speaking empires based on the lower Ganges (such as Aśoka's) rose and fell: this happened in the second century BC, and the second and fifth centuries AD; after each fall Bihar, the area centred on the lower Ganges, relapsed into the (likewise unrelated) Munda language. It seems that the east and centre of India succumbed to the Aryan tendency only gradually, and fitfully: Bengal in the fourth century AD, Orissa in the seventh. Farther to the west, even in the fourteenth century, the official inscriptions of *Mahārāṣṭra* ('great kingdom') were still in Kannada; but it then became another totally Aryan-speaking area, with a language known as Marathi.* It appears that the social strata must have been speaking different languages for some time, with (in this case, at least) Aryan favoured much more by the lower orders.

Aśoka's inscriptions, the earliest in a decipherably Aryan language to survive, are not in Sanskrit but Magadhi Prakrit; and this absence of Sanskrit from inscriptions, or rather its presence only for literary decoration while the guts of the message are given in Prakrit, continues for several centuries. It is not until two hundred years later that the first inscriptions in Sanskrit are found, farther west, in Ayodhya and Mathura (south of Delhi). There is a clear division of function between Sanskrit and Prakrit visible in these inscriptions, which contain both: Sanskrit is used for the verse, Prakrit for the prose dedications. Ultimately, Sanskrit did come to predominate, and indeed to be the exclusive language of inscriptions. But this tradition did not get fully established for another 250 years, starting in AD 150 with the rock inscriptions of a fairly minor king, *Rudradāman*, at *Junāgaḍh* ('Greek fort') on the western coast, in Gujarat.

Something of the same division of function between Sanskrit for high and Prakrit for everyday use is also shown by the language conventions of Sanskrit drama. Every play was multilingual, or multi-dialectal. From the sixth century AD, noble males speak in Sanskrit; ladies speak in *Śaurasenī* (the Mathura Prakrit), but sing in *Mahārāṣṭrī*; meanwhile, low characters are scripted in Magadhi (ironically, the descendant of the dialect that had had royal overtones, nine hundred years before). We can only suppose that intervening political reversals (e.g. the rise of the *Sātavāhana* kings in the Maha-

---

* Bizarrely this only happened after Muslim incursions, which had brought in the completely alien Persian as the new elite language.

rashtra area over the first centuries BC and AD) had a more or less permanent effect on the perceived status of the dialects.*

Rājaśekhara, making recommendations *c*.AD 900 for the ideal poet, says that he should have servants fluent in *Apabhraṃśa* ('falling off', the quite generally used, but unflattering, term for later forms of Śauraseni Prakrit, on its way to becoming modern Hindi), maids in Magadhi and the like; but his wives should speak Sanskrit, or else 'Prakrit', which for him means Maharashtri, and his friends all languages.[14] The social imperative for Sanskrit had become inescapable, despite the poet's own personal enthusiasm for his local Prakrit. But to a large extent, the status of the dialects seemed to have become fully detached from awareness of their local origins, or their history.

RELIGIOUS

Interestingly, Magadhi had probably also been the dialect of Gautama, the founder of Buddhism, though about one millennium earlier. (His contemporary, *Mahāvīra*, the founder of Jainism, lived in the area too.) Magadha was also the area of the earliest Buddhist councils, which established the outlines of this faith for later generations. And Buddhism's most famous, and influential, early convert was King Aśoka himself, another resident of Magadha, in its chief city, *Pāṭaliputra* (modern Patna in the state of Bihar on the Ganges).

This geographical coincidence might have been expected to lead Buddhism to favour Magadhi. The Buddha had advised his monks to teach in their own language (*sakaya niruttiyā*). His view here seems to have involved not only a respect for the vernacular, but also a positive belief that his caste, the warrior *Kṣatriya*, was actually superior to the priestly *Brāhmaṇa* with its Sanskrit associations. This was part of his persuasive redefinition of the whole caste system and of what it was to be truly *ariya* (Aryan)—though this word is usually translated in Buddhist English as 'noble'—based on personal merit rather than birth.

But the monks did not in turn privilege the common speech of the Buddha himself and his region. Rather, they declared themselves in favour of any form of vernacular language. There are stories that this caused some unease among Brahman monks, who feared that the resulting slack grammar and

---

* Indeed, there is a famous story of the embarrassment caused when a king called Satavahana turned out to know less Sanskrit than a lady: in a water fight, one of his queens begged him to stop pelting her with water (*modakaih*, from *mā udakaih*, 'not with-waters'), but he responded by showering her with sweets (*modakaih*, 'with sweets'). He was so mortified when she pointed out his mistake that he took to his bed, and then embarked on a crash course in grammar (Somadeva, *Kathā-sarit-sāgaram*, 1.vi.108–22).

pronunciation would corrupt the sayings of the Buddha. However, in time a particular Prakrit did come to predominate: it was called *Pāli* ('canonical') and was a mixed Prakrit. Despite the claims of the Buddhist tradition (which also claimed that this language had been spoken by the Buddha and was, for good measure, the original language of all beings, *sabbasattānaṃ mūla-bhāsa*),* Pali was not predominantly Magadhi, but included many distinctively Western elements, reminiscent of Śauraseni: it must have arisen as a kind of Buddhist Aryan creole, by a process of compromise among monks speaking various Prakrits.

Later on, as the faith developed, and became more heavily institutionalised, it increasingly adopted a grander style of language, in form closer to classical Sanskrit, which is known as Buddhist Hybrid Sanskrit. This typically involves taking the grammatical structures of Prakrit, which are much simpler and more analytic than those of Sanskrit, and reclothing the words in case markings and verb endings that are reminiscent of classical Sanskrit, but quite often misapplied from the viewpoint of classical grammar.

Overall, throughout Indian linguistic history, Sanskrit's status has tended to rise, both in secular and sacred use; the Maurya kings', and the Buddhists' and Jains', early preference for the vernacular all ultimately yielded to the respect in which Sanskrit was held. It has been recognised throughout as an artificial (*saṃskṛta*) language; but if anything this has increased its status, and its use has come to be seen as a linguistic touchstone for the quality of a text.

Outsiders' views

It is interesting to compare briefly some external perceptions of Sanskrit, and of its role in society. There are two outsiders' traditions which have left records of their encounters: for the last three centuries BC, we have reports from the Greeks; and for the middle of the first millennium AD, from the Chinese to the north-east.

A glance at the map shows that, in an age of overland travel on foot, emissaries of both civilisations must have had to distinguish themselves in terms of determination even before they could reach the centres of Indian culture: Greece was over 5000 miles away (though Greek had been established as a lingua franca for most of that distance), while China, though closer as the crow flies, was in practice cut off not only by the Taklamakan desert but also by the mountains stretching from the Pamirs to the far Himalayas.

---

* One gets some idea of how much, and how little, Pali differs from Sanskrit by comparing the Sanskrit equivalent for this phrase: *sarvasatām mūlabhāṣā*.

THE GREEKS

The Greeks knew little about India until Alexander's campaigns brought them to its borders in 327 BC. Thereafter there were diplomatic exchanges between some of the great Indian rulers of the north and the Greek dynasts who controlled the east of what had been the Persian empire, the Seleucids. From 302 to 288 Megasthenes served as Seleucid ambassador to King Chandragupta Maurya in Pataliputra (Patna), which he introduced to the Greek world as Palibothra. He left a discursive study of Indian ways, the *Indiká*, which, taken together with some reports of Onesicritus and Nearchus, naval officers who had written memoirs of their service with Alexander, stood as the core of Greek knowledge of India until the end of the ancient world.

The *Indiká* has not survived, but can be reconstructed substantially from the extensive quotations that figure in other authors, such as Strabo and Pliny, writing (in Italy) two centuries later. It contains little or nothing on the political or literary aspects of Indian life, but does contain an analysis of the caste system, identifying no fewer than seven distinct 'tribes' or 'lineages', which can be fairly well mapped on to the time-honoured four-way division into Brahmans (priests and philosophers), Kshatriyas (kings and warriors), Vaiśyas (merchants) and Śudras (labourers). It also appears to note the prevalence of the cults of Śiva and Krishna, but the inference is indirect: in the usual Graeco-Roman way, it gives only the names of Greek gods which the author had identified with the Indian figures; so the Indians are said to have worshipped Heracles (since like Krishna he carried a club), and Dionysus (since like Śiva he was associated with thriving vegetable life and with Mount Meru, whereas Dionysus had been born from Zeus's thigh, in Greek *mērou*, and he was a pretty wild character, worshipped with music and dance).

Megasthenes does cope more explicitly with the more intellectual aspects of religions practised in the Maurya empire of his time, distinguishing Brahmans (*brak^hmanai* or *bragmanai*) and Śramans (*sarmanai*) as different kinds of philosophers. *Śramaṇa* is indeed a Sanskrit word sometimes used specifically for Buddhist monks, but there is no explicit mention of Buddhism, which would have been some two hundred years old at the time (having been founded in exactly the same region where Megasthenes was resident).

The commentary tends to be focused at a fairly superficial level, for example the presence of *gumnosophístai*, or naked sages, and the fact that male and female students were on a par as disciples to the Śramans. Megasthenes apparently never understood that the Brahmans are in fact one of the 'tribes', i.e. castes, that he had distinguished; nor that 'forest-dwellers' (what his hosts would have called *vanaprastha*) are not a species of Śraman, but rather those who have reached a certain period of life, whether Brahman or Śraman.

India remained the fabulous source of exotic products for the Greeks and beyond them the Romans. In fact, the truest elements of Sanskrit lore that they ever absorbed were the names of some of their favourite substances: canvas (Greek *karpasos*, 'cotton', from *karpāsa*), ginger (Greek *zingiber* from *śṛngavera*, named after a town on the Ganges), pepper (Greek *peperi* from *pippali*, 'berry'), sugar (Greek *sakkharon* from *śarkarā*, 'grit')— originally characterised by Alexander's admiral Nearchus as honey coming from reeds without the aid of bees.[15]

Megasthenes' work, which came to form Europe's knowledge of India up until the Renaissance, was in some ways lacking in understanding, and never offered any appreciation of philosophy, language or literature. In one case, a sage joked that since the conversation took place through three interpreters, they were as likely to get a clear idea of the philosophy being expounded as to purify water by running it through mud.[16]

But this did not mean that the Greeks who lived closer in were similarly lacking. One Greek king of the Panjab, Menander (second century BC), in fact became immortalised for his penetrating interest in Buddhism in the form of the Pali classic *Milinda-pañha*, or 'Questions of King Milinda': 'Many were the arts and sciences he knew—holy tradition and secular law; the *Sāṃkhya*, *Yoga*, *Nyāya* and *Vaiśeṣika* systems of philosophy; arithmetic, music; medicine; the four *Vedas*, the *Purānas* and the *Itihāsas*; astronomy, magic, causation and spells; the art of war; poetry; and property-conveyancing—in a word, the full nineteen.'[17]

And another Indo-Greek of the same period, announcing himself as Heliodorus, Greek ambassador (*yonadūta*) from King Antialkidas, left an inscription in perfect Prakrit on a column still standing at Besnagar in Madhya Pradesh. It ends with the spiritual precept:

> *trīni amutapādāni ... suanuṭhitāni*
> *neyaṃti svagam dame cāga apramāda*

> Three steps to immortality, when correctly followed,
> lead to heaven: control, generosity, attention.

THE CHINESE

By contrast with Greek writers, who were in India largely as traders, conquerors or representatives of power, the Chinese came as serious students of India's culture, and particularly Buddhism: some evidently learnt Sanskrit (with Pali and Magadhi Prakrit) in depth during their stay. Their descriptions, therefore, have an authority and penetration that far exceed the Greek testimony; in many cases, they provide the best evidence we have for the details of Indian life at this time, the Indians themselves having always been remarkably unconcerned to set down straightforward descriptions of their own daily life.

The Chinese testimony comes from four pilgrims in search of authentic Buddhist scripures, most of whom struggled past the Taklamakan desert and across the Hindu Kush to enter India through this northern route. They came at intervals of about a century. Each of them, besides bringing home quantities of Buddhist manuscripts which they then set about translating, went on to write a memoir after their return to China.

Fa-Xian (法顯), the first whose tale has survived, travelled to India via the Hindu Kush from AD 400 to 414, returning by sea. For three of these years he was at Pataliputra, 'learning to read the books in Sanskrit* and to converse in that language, and in copying the precepts'.[18] (His comrade Do-Zhing was so impressed with the holy life of the Indian *śramanas* that he decided not to go home.) Fa-Xian then moved down the Ganges to another major city, Champa (near modern Bhagalpur), where he spent two more years, principally seeking to acquire Buddhist texts,[19] before an extremely eventful voyage home via 'Ye-po-ti' or *Yava-dvīpa* (Java). He says he had resided in central India for six years in all.[20]

In 518 Song-Yun (宗雲) came. He penetrated no farther than *Nagarahāra* (Jalalabad) and *Puruṣapūra* (Peshawar), at either end of the Khyber pass, which now links Afghanistan and Pakistan; and returned to China by the same route after three years.

Then, in 629, the most famous of them all, Xuan-Zang (玄奘), reached India by stealth (the Chinese border being closed at the time), and after a three-year journey stayed for ten years, mostly as a student at *Nālandā* university outside Pataliputra, but also undertaking a journey around most of the south of the subcontinent.

Xuan-Zang was followed, a generation later, in 671, by a pilgrim called Yi-Jing (義淨). Yi-Jing travelled by sea from Canton, but he stopped at the Indianised kingdom of Śrī Vijaya (Palembang) in southern Sumatra for two years of Sanskrit study. (He wrote: 'if a Chinese priest wishes to go to the west to understand and read there, he would be wise to spend a year or two in Fo-Shi [Vijaya], and practise the proper rules there; he might then go on to central India.') He himself then proceeded to the university of Nalanda, where he studied for ten years. Afterwards, he returned by sea to Śrī Vijaya,

---

* He called it *Fan*, probably a Chinese reduction of the word *Brahmana*.

where he spent most of his time until 695, organising the translation of Buddhist texts from Sanskrit into Chinese, and writing two memoirs: *On eminent monks who sought the law in the West*, and *On the spiritual law, sent from the Southern Seas*.[21]

India for them was the home of Buddhist enlightenment. But it was also a fascinating country in its own right. Their accounts of their time there are very largely taken up with travelogue, but Xuan-Zang is particularly detailed about the intellectual life he encountered, and to which he contributed, during his stay. He wrote:

> The letters of their alphabet were arranged by *Brahmādeva*, and their forms have been handed down from the first till now. They are forty-seven in number, and are combined so as to form words according to the object, and according to the circumstances [viz. tenses, and local cases]: there are other forms [viz. inflexions] used. This alphabet has spread in different directions and formed diverse branches, according to the circumstances; therefore there have been slight modifications in the sounds of the words [viz. spoken language]; but in its great features there has been no change. Middle India preserves the original character of the language in its integrity. Here the pronunciation is soft and agreeable, and like the language of the Devas [viz. the gods*]. The pronunciation of the words is clear and pure, and fit as a model for all men. The people of the frontiers have contracted several erroneous modes of pronunciation; for according to the licentious habits of the people, so will be the corrupt nature of their language.[22]

Strictly speaking, Manu's contemporary conception of *Madhyadeśa* ('midland') would, as we have seen, have excluded Magadha and the region of the lower Ganges as too far to the east. But in practice we can infer from Xuan-Zang that in his day the speech of 'Middle India' included the language of Pataliputra, ancient capital of several Indian empires, and of Nalanda, even then the pre-eminent university in the land.

---

* The most widely used alphabet in this area of India is still known as *deva-nāgarī*, 'the gods' urban [script]'.

The spread of Sanskrit

Sanskrit in India

Sanskrit first appears to us, as do most of its Indo-European sister languages, as the speech of conquering warriors, well capable of using horses and wheeled vehicles to establish domination over their neighbours, and turn them into serfs and subjects. The way of life is familiar from heroic poetry of Indo-European peoples in every direction: men who fight from chariots, speak forthrightly, and care for their own personal honour more than life itself. When, in the Sanskrit epic *Mahābhārata*, Krishna advises Arjuna on his duty that day, he could be speaking to the Greek Achilles attacking Troy (a thousand years earlier), or the Irishman Cúchulainn standing against the hosts of Connacht (in a thousand years to come).

> *svadharmam api cāvekṣya na vikampitum arhasi:*
> *dharmyāddhi yuddhācchreyo 'nyat kṣatriyasya na vidyate.*
> *yadṛcchyā copapannam svargadvāram apāvṛtam*
> *sukhinaḥ kṣatriyāḥ pārtha labhante yuddham īdṛśam.*
> *atha cet tvam imaṃ dharmyaṃ sangrāmaṃ na kariṣyasi*
> *tataḥ svadharmam kīrtim ca hitvā pāpam avāpsyasi.*
> *akīrtim cāpi bhūtāni kathayiṣyanti te' vyayām*
> *sambhāvitasya cākīrtir maraṇād atiricyate.*

> Looking to your own duty too, you must not flinch;
> for there is nothing better for a Kshatriya than a righteous fight.
> Blest are the Kshatriyas who gain such a fight,
> offered unsought, O Partha, as an open door to heaven.
> But if you choose not to carry on this righteous conflict,
> then discarding personal duty and glory, you will fall into sin.
> Beings will tell of your eternal dishonour
> and, for a respectable man, dishonour is worse than death.
>
> *Bhāgavad Gītā*, ii.31–4

Being a Hindu god, Krishna does go on to ground this exposition of the heroic code within a theology of reincarnation and a theory of knowledge that reduces the world of action to a shadow-play of appearances; but the basic ethic of nobility expressed through courage and military prowess is clear.

It is usually presumed that it was this attitude to life, together with the dominating technologies of warhorses, wheeled vehicles and metal weapons, which spread Aryan lordship and language across northern India, and then kept the various kingdoms in an almost constant roil of mutual warfare over this period. (This model of language spread is, after all, well attested in many parts of the world in the historical period, as when the Normans brought Norman French to England, or the *conquistadores* brought Spanish to Central and South America.)

But besides the battles recounted in Sanskrit epics there is very little evidence, from archaeology, inscriptions or indeed from indigenous tradition, that the language was spread with fire and sword. Particularly in India, there is an ingrained belief that Hinduism and Sanskrit are not the result of alien invasions, but developed rather wholly within the subcontinent. There has even been a recent attempt to give this story a full quasi-mythological backing, developing the theory that, if there are linguistic and genetic links with the rest of the Indo-European language family, this is due to the spread of the Aryans round Europe before their return to their true home of India.[23]

Whatever the truth of the Aryans' prehistoric wanderings, there is a lot that shows that horses were important to them from the beginning. In the Hittite libraries of central Anatolia (2500 miles to the west of the Indus) we find a manual on horsemanship and chariotry, written by Kikkuli the Mitannian in the mid-second millennium BC: he gives his profession as *assussanni-*, which can be equated with the Vedic Sanskrit *aśvasani* 'gaining or procuring horses', and his text is full of loan words which are evidently Indo-Aryan: courses can be *aikawartanna, terawartanna, panzawartanna, sattawartanna, nawartanna*, '1-, 3-, 5-, 7- or 9-turns', which is just Sanskrit *eka-, tri-, pañca-, sapta-* and *nava-vartana*. Most Mitannians spoke a completely unrelated language, Hurrian, but in another text written in this language at much the same time (from the city of Nuzi—Yorgan Tepe—in northern Iraq) horse colours are given in something close to Sanskrit: *babru* (*babhru*), 'chestnut', *parita* (*palita*), 'grey', *pinkara* (*pingala*), 'roan'.

Here the Aryan elite culture of the horseman had been superimposed on a populace that spoke another language. The evidence stems from long before and far away; but the situation of the early days of Aryan language in India was probably very similar. This can be seen even within the structure of Sanskrit itself.

Sanskrit and its related Indo-Aryan languages are different from all their relatives to the north and west, in Iran, Russia and Europe, in possessing an extra series of consonants, known to Sanskrit grammarians as the *mūrdhanya* ('in the head') sounds, or to Westerners as the retroflex stops, after the position of the tongue: *ṭ, ḍ, ṭh, ḍh* and *ṇ* with the tongue curled backward against the roof of the mouth, as against *t, d, th, dh* and *n*, where the tongue touches the back of the front teeth. So *paṭati*, 'splits', is a different word from *patati*, 'falls', and *maṇḍaḥ*, 'foam, cream', from *mandaḥ*, 'dull'. These sounds are also characteristic of the Dravidian languages now spoken to the south of the Aryan languages in India, as well as other neighbours, such as the Munda languages dotted around the north-east of India. Whereas no other Indo-European language has them (making them unlikely as a feature of whatever language they all originate from), they are so systematic in Dravidian that they are probably as old as the family. It would appear, then, that they have established themselves in Sanskrit and Aryan as a 'substrate', a residual feature of the languages that the earliest adopters of Sanskrit were speaking, and could not lose when they learned the new language.

There is also some cultural evidence in the Rig Veda which suggests how the invading Aryans felt they differed from the peoples, the *dāsa* and *dasyu*,* their language came to dominate, for they saw them as having darker skins, 'of black origin', *kṛṣṇayonīḥ*.[24] This fits with the Sanskrit word used traditionally for the four-fold division into social castes, Brahman~Kshatriya~Vaiśya~Śudra, namely *varṇa*, 'colour'. They are represented in the epic *Mahabharata* as the two younger sons of Pandu ('the Pale'), Nakula and Sahadeva, born to his second wife Madri, who is said to be black eyed and dusky complexioned. Throughout the epic, they act as faithful, but unimaginative, supporters of their apparently nobler Aryan elder half-brothers, Yuddhishthira ('Firm in Fight'), Bhīma ('terrible') and Arjuna ('Resplendent').

We have seen that the process of assimilation with various local groups continued well into the second millennium AD, and seems to have involved a kaleidoscopic succession of languages in some parts of north and central India. One of the most memorable moments, at least politically, in this long series of shifting patterns occurred about 260 BC, when Aśoka conquered the eastern kingdom of Kalinga (approximately the area of modern Orissa). This conquest was a high-water mark for imperial unity in India, one not to be exceeded for two thousand years. Aśoka wrote this of the experience all over the rest of his empire (in Magadhi, Aramaic and Greek): 'In the eighth year of his reign, Piyadasi conquered Kalinga. 150,000 people were captured there and deported, 100,000 others were killed and almost as many perished. Since that time, pity and compassion gripped him, and he was overwhelmed by that...'

This compassion put an end to his wars of conquest, and made him turn

---

* These two terms came to mean 'slave' and 'demon, robber, bandit' respectively. Compare the development of the English word *slave* from *Slav*, and the apparently opposite route taken by Serb from Latin *servus*. The feminine of *dāsa*, *dāsī*, came to mean 'whore' (*devadāsī*, 'a god's slave-girl', was a temple prostitute), and one of the most routine Sanskrit insults is *dāsyaḥ putraḥ*, equivalent to 'whoreson' or 'son of a bitch'.

instead to the propagation of *dhamma* (Sanskrit *dharma*), variously translated as 'virtue', 'duty' or 'the Law'. It is said that he stood on the hill at Dhauli, and saw the Daya river flow red with blood. Writing specifically to the Kalinga population on a rock inscription at that spot, he says, instead of re-counting the campaign: 'All men are my children. Just as, in regard to my own children, I desire that they may be provided with all kinds of welfare and happiness in this world and in the next, the same I desire also in regard to all men. But you do not understand how far my intention goes in this respect. A few among you perchance understand it but even such of you understand it partly and not fully...'

In fact, it remains obscure what, if any, linguistic effect Aśoka's conquest had on Kalinga. It is just too long ago, and too much has happened since.

Orissa is now a mainly Aryan-speaking area (with a strong sprinkling of unrelated *ādivāsi*, i.e. 'aboriginal', languages): the earliest inscriptions in its language date from the tenth century AD. The language is Oriya, closely re-lated to the Bengali spoken farther north; but little is known of its earlier his-tory, and it has been suggested that Orissa was still non-Aryan even in the seventh century AD.[25] Xuan-Zang recognised at least three distinct countries in this region: *Uḍra* (the origin of the name Orissa), which he said had 'words and language different from Central India', *Kōnyōdha*, 'with the same written characters as those of mid-India, but language and mode of pronunciation quite different', and *Kalinga*, where 'the language is light and tripping, and their pronunciation is distinct and correct. But in both particulars, that is, as to words and sounds, they are very different from mid-India.'[26] This kind of evidence is just one example of what makes it so difficult to depict in any detail the language map of India in past centuries.

Sanskrit influence permeated farther south, with the cultural spread of Hinduism, eventually saturating with borrowed words three of the major non-Aryan languages, Telugu, Kannada and Malayalam. Tamil, in the extreme south-east, was less affected linguistically, although its society was ulti-mately no less Hindu. And besides this gradual export of words, there had also been, in the middle of the first millennium BC, a major transplant of a whole community, with its Aryan language, to the extreme south. This accounts for the presence of Sinhala in Śri Lanka. The history of the move-ment of people that brought this language is not documented, but it may be reflected through legend in the epic *Ramayana*, which climaxes in a mili-tary expedition to this island.* About two hundred years later, in the late

---

* The purpose was to rescue Rama's kidnapped wife Sita—rather similar to Homer's motivation for the Trojan War, where a Greek fleet set out to rescue Menelaus's wife Helen.

third century BC, the links between Śri Lanka and the Aryan north were reinforced when Aśoka sent his son Mahinda to the island as a Buddhist missionary, so founding the Theravada school of Buddhism which has endured to
this day.

Sanskrit in South-East Asia

The move to Śri Lanka may be seen as the beginning of Sanskrit's spread beyond the shores of India. This seaborne expansion makes its significance far
greater to the global story, for Sanskrit is the first example in history of a language travelling over a maritime network, through the establishment of trade
and cultural links with peoples on the other side. In this, it can be seen as a
precursor of the spread of the western European languages in the last five
hundred years.

By the middle of the first millennium AD, Sanskrit was established as the
hallmark of Indianised civilisation, all over South-East Asia, including the
main islands of modern Malaysia and Indonesia. There is no clear record of
how this came about. But one feature of the spread of Sanskrit is clear: it was
not a military expansion. There was never a warlike move by Indians into
Asia, even of the typical short-term Indian empires, which even in north India
never seemed to last more than a very few generations.

But if we leave aside military ambition, the motives that have been suggested for the Indian successes exhaust every other possibility: refuge from
imperial wars from the Mauryas and Aśoka onward, piratical raids, a spirit of
adventure, the peaceful pursuit of trade, or a desire to spread sacred learning,
of Buddhism certainly, and perhaps earlier even of Hinduism.*

Each of these has something to recommend it, and they are not mutually
exclusive. It must mean something, for example, that the name for India
current among Malays and Cambodians was 'Kling', that is Kalinga, the
coastal realm in eastern India bloodily conquered by Aśoka. There, and especially in its northern region *Tāmralipta* ('copper-smeared', modern Tamluk
in West Bengal), there was a tradition of producing *sārthavāhāḥ* or
sādhavaḥ, 'merchants', who were easily confused with *sāhasikāḥ*, 'pirates,
buccaneers', proverbial in Sanskrit for their bravery, as well as violence. In
the treasury of practical wisdom from the sixth century AD, *Pañcatantra*, it is
remarked:

---

* In a total reversal, Hinduism was later to renounce even the possibility of foreign voyages. It was
held to bring unassuageable impurity upon higher castes, e.g. in the late-thirteenth-century law digest
by *Hemādri* (iii.2: 667).

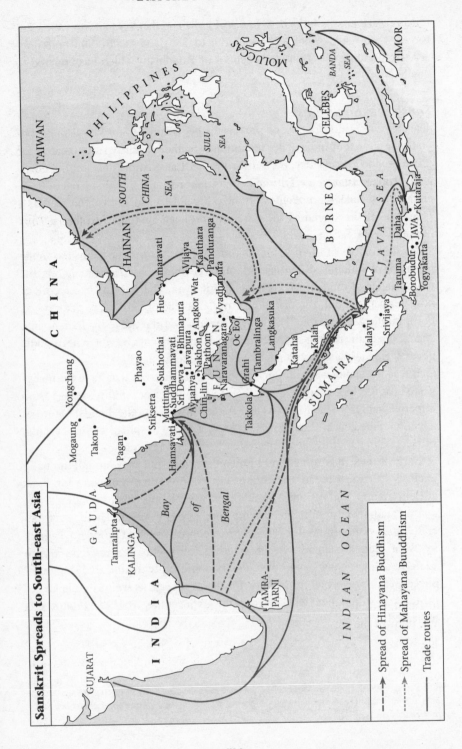

Sanskrit Spreads to South-east Asia

TAIWAN

PHILIPPINES

MOLUCCAS

BANDA

CELEBES

TIMOR

SULU SEA

SOUTH CHINA SEA

BANDA SEA

JAVA SEA

C H I N A

HAINAN

BORNEO

Daha

Taruma · Kutaraja
JAVA
Borobudur
Yogyakarta

Amaravati

Hue

Vijaya

Kauthara

Panduranga

Angkor Wat

Bhimapura

Vyadhapura

Lavapura

Nakhon

Pathom

Srivijaya

Malayu

Oc Eo

Tambralinga

Langkasuka

Grahi

Katoha

Kalah

Naravaranagara

Ayuthya

Chin-lin

F U N A N

Takkola

Yongchang

Phayao

Sukhothai

Suddhammavati

Sri Deva

Muttima

Sriksetra

Takon ·

Pagan

Mogaung

Hamsavati

SUMATRA

G A U D A

Tamralipta

KALINGA

Bay

of

Bengal

I N D I A

GUJARAT

TAMRA-
PARNI

INDIAN OCEAN

Spread of Hinayana Buddhism

Spread of Mahayana Buuddhism

Trade routes

CHARMING LIKE A CREEPER

bhayam atulam gurulokāt tṛṇam iva tulayanti sādhu sāhasikāḥ

Merchant-buccaneers reckon light as straw the fear instilled by the
weighty.[27]

The popular *Jātaka* tales of previous lives of the Buddha, composed around
this time, are also full of merchants who seek wealth in *Suvarṇabhūmi*.

The motive for the trade is also hinted at by the Sanskrit names that the Indians gave to parts of this eastern world. Śri Lanka was known as *Tāmrad-
vīpa*, 'copper island', or *Tāmraparṇī*, 'copper-leafed'; the land beyond the
eastern ocean as *Suvarṇadvīpa*, *Suvarṇabhūmi*, 'the isle, or the land, of gold'.
These names survived to be taken up, or translated, by Greek explorers, *Tap-
robanē* for Śri Lanka, and *Khrysē Khersonēsos*, 'Golden Peninsula', for
South-East Asia. There is little in these countries' known geology to suggest
that the names were well founded. But the quest for precious metals was
clearly part of the legend of such ancient navigation. One of the most evoca-
tive tales in the Sanskrit equivalent of the *1001 Nights*, Somadeva's
Kathāsaritsāgaram ('Ocean of the Streams of Story'), recounts the quest of
a Brahman, setting out for his lost loves in *Kanakapurī*, 'The City of Gold',
located somewhere beyond 'The Islands'. One of the merchants he meets on
his way has a father who returns rich from a long voyage to a far island, his
ship loaded specifically with gold.

More realistically, there was scope for immense profit either in entrepôt
business, exchanging Indian aromatic resins (including frankincense (*kun-
dura*) and myrrh (*vola*)) for Chinese silk, or in obtaining local products such
as camphor (*karpūra*) from Sumatra, sandalwood (*candana*) from Timor or
cloves (*lavanga*) from the Moluccas.[28]

Indians set out for this Land of Gold from all round the subcontinent. Evidently, the shortest journey was from *Gauḍa* (modern Bengal) and Kalinga:
we know that Fa-Xian and Yi-Jing took ship from Tamralipti. But the prevailing wind across the Bay of Bengal from June to November is south-west-
erly, so the most direct sailing was to be had from the southern shores, and
this is the area of all the ports noted by the Greeks.[29] A handful of inscriptions
in Tamil, turning up in Sumatra and the Malay peninsula, confirm this route.
The ports of the western coast also had their share of departures for the east:
an old Gujarati proverb mentions the wealth of sailors back from Java.[30]

More interesting for us than the motivation of the Indian *sādhavaḥ* is how
they would have appeared to the receiving populations, known to the Indians
as *dvīpāntaraḥ*, 'islanders'. These people, Burmese in the east, Austro-
Asiatic in the south (Mon, Khmer, or Cham), Malay in the islands, already

BURMESE: ပါဠိအရေးအသားသည် မြန်မာစာအရေးအသားကို အတော်
ပင် လွှမ်းမိုးခဲ့ဟန်တူသည်॥

palí- ˀɔjè ˀɔθàði mjãmasa ˀɔjè ˀɔθàgo ɔtɔbī hlũmmògéhãtuði Pali writing
seems to have had considerable influence on Burmese (Myanmar) writing.

THAI: คำภาษาไทยให้เขียนตามหลักเกณฑ์นิรุกติศาสตร์

kham pha:sǎ: thay hây khǐan ta:m làk ke:n nirúktisà:t Words in the Thai
language should be written on the basis of principles of etymology.

LAO: ຄຳພາສາລາວໃຫ້ຂຽນຕາມສຽງເວົ້າ

khám pha:sǎ: law hây khǐan ta:m sǐaŋ vàw Words in the Lao language
should be written according to pronunciation.

KHMER: ពេលនោះគាត់រុកបានត្រីរស់មួយហើយនិងបានទន្សាយលោងទឹកមួយ

pe:l nuh koɔt rut ɓa:n trɔi rɔh muɔy haɔj nɔŋ ɓa:n toɔnsa:j loɔŋ tɨk muɔj
At that time, he fished out a trei-rah (kind of fish) and then got a rabbit
which was drowning in the water.

South-East Asian scripts of Indian origin

used bronze, irrigated rice, domesticated cattle and buffalo, and had ships and
boats of their own. They would not have been able to read or write. The Indians would have presented themselves to the local chiefs as visiting digni-
taries, probably claiming royal connections back across the ocean, and
offering gifts, and perhaps medicines and charms. Winning favour with local
elites, some went on to take their daughters in marriage, and thus sow the
seeds of new dynasties.

What the Indians brought with them was literacy, and an ancient culture
with a vast array of rules (the sutras of the Hindu *Dharmaśāstras*, or the suttas
of the Buddhist *Tipiṭaka*) for every occasion. There was the whole mythology
of Hinduism, making Agastya, Krishna, Rama and the Pandava brothers into
household names, as they have been ever since in South-East Asia. There was
the distinctive idea of the complementary roles of king and priest, admittedly
at sixes and sevens over which was ultimately the higher, but clearly in a relationship of mutual support. This relationship could underwrite, and make
permanent, the legitimacy of rulers. And so the rulers that the Indians met
were happy to become their friends, business partners and fathers-in-law. The
new generation that sprang from the mixed marriages would have been the
first to receive a full Sanskrit education.

One characteristic of Indian civilisation that they brought with them was a
tendency to modify and customise the alphabet. Just as there are now at least

South-East Asian temple architecture

ten major scripts* derived in India from the Brahmi characters (diffused all over the subcontinent in Aśoka's time), there are another nine that developed in South-East Asia, Indonesia and the Philippines,† all derived from Indian scripts, many through the Pallava script of the south. The origin of this diversity lies in the variety of writing materials available in different places, but the different styles evidently came to be national icons. In the Cambodian pillars that carry rules for monasteries, Sanskrit in Khmer script on one side is paralleled by Sanskrit in a North Indian script on the other: perhaps there were North Indian devotees as well as Khmers resident here.[31]

This is just one of many signs that there was heavy cultural traffic in both directions between India and Indo-China during this period. Another example is given by the life of Atīśa, a monk born in Bengal in 982, who went on to become one of the founders of Buddhism in Tibet in his sixties. He had spent his student days in Śri Vijaya, in Sumatra.

In a way, the culture as the Indians brought it will always be a mystery to us. The splendours of Shwe Dagon in Burma, Borobodur in Java, Angkor

---

* Devanagari, Gujarati, Panjabi, Bengali, Oriya in the north; Telugu, Kannada, Tamil, Malayalam and Sinhalese in the south. There is another related alphabet, used farther north for Tibetan.

† Burmese, Lao, Thai, Khmer (Cambodian) on the mainland; in the islands, Javanese, Balinese, Tagalog (in the Philippines), Batak (in Sumatra) and Bugis (in Sulawesi).

Wat in Cambodia, as well as less well-known magnificences in Pagan, Champa, Laos, Bali and Sumatra, built over a millennium from about AD 500, all stemmed from the seminal ideas of the Indians, but at least in terms of architecture there is nothing now quite like them back in India. We can only speculate that styles executed in stone at Borobodur and Angkor Wat may echo the architecture of wooden buildings long vanished from southern India.

Nevertheless, this roll-call of states and civilisations that took their beginnings from India reminds us how vast, how varied and how long lasting this influence was, all the more remarkable because no military force seems to have been applied anywhere to bring in the new, more organised, Indian society. This contrasts sharply with the record of incursions from the other developed civilisation to the north. Ever since the first century AD, China had been putting constant pressure on the Annamite kingdom of northern Vietnam, periodically invading it, and insisting on recognition of China's emperor as its overlord.

The earliest documented Indianised kingdom—the documentation is Chinese—was set on the lower Mekong, in modern Cambodia and southern Vietnam, probably in the first century AD. It is usually known as Funan, which is a Chinese version of its name. It was really called, in Khmer, *Bnam*, 'the mountain',* and its king as *kurung bnam*, a translation of *Parvatabhū-pala* or *Śailarāja*: bearing this title of 'King of the Mountain', he would have established a cult of the god Śiva in a high place, so reconciling his legitimacy as an Indian king with the native spirits of the land.[32]

Funan's foundation myth, read from a Sanskrit inscription in Champa,[33] confirms this. A Brahman named Kauṇḍinya (derived from *Kuṇḍin*, one of Śiva's titles) received a javelin from another Brahman, a hero from the *Mahabharata* named *Aśvattāman*, and threw it to find the right site for the city. He married a local princess named Soma, daughter of the king of the *Nāgas*, the many-headed water cobras worshipped as protectors of Khmer riches.

Thereafter, major Sanskrit-speaking states were set up all over South-East Asia, Sumatra and Java.† Their names are themselves in Sanskrit, and show

---

* The same word is now pronounced Phnom, as in Phnom Penh.

† Java, Sumatra and Malaya are derived from *Yava-dvīpa*, 'barley island'; *samudra*, 'sea', and *Malaya*, actually from a Dravidian word, *malai*, 'a hill', in south India near Malabar. Cambodia (*Kamboja*) evokes *Kambuja*, a kingdom in the Khyber pass area; but had a competing etymology as *Kambu-ja*, i.e. born of *Kambu Svāyambhūva*, a hermit who united with the celestial nymph Mera to found the race of Khmers (Coedès 1968: 66). Champa shares its name with the kingdom of the lower Ganges, but is probably the local ethnonym Cham in Sanskrit form. The River Irrawaddy in Burma is named for the *Irāvatī*, 'having drinking water', the old name of the Ravi river in Panjab.

either a sentimental link with other Indian holy places far away, or an attempt to Indianise local names. It is often difficult now to locate them exactly. In Malaya, *Lankasuka*, controlling one much-used overland route from the Bay of Bengal to the Gulf of Siam, beside *Tāmbralinga* (Ligor), *Takkola* (Takuapa) and *Kāṭaha* (Kedah); in Cham, the south of modern Vietnam, *Amarāvatī* (Dong-duong), *Vijaya* (Binh-dinh), *Kauṭhara* (Nha-trang), *Pāṇḍuranga* (Phanrang); in Java, *Tārumā* (round Jakarta) and *Kuṭarāja* in the east; in Sumatra, *Malāyu* (Jambi), *Śrī Vijaya* (Palembang); in Burma, *Sudhammavatī* (Thaton), *Śrīkṣetra* (Prome or Thayekhettaya), *Haṃsavatī* (Pegu), *Śrī Deva* (Si Thep); and in the region of modern Thailand *Dvāravatī*, north of Bangkok.

Names of rulers too are typically Sanskritic. Good examples are the more than thirty Cambodian kings whose names end in -*varman*, 'bastion', from *Jayavarman*, who died in AD 514, to *Śrīndrajayavarman*, 1307–27, and the Majapahit kings of Indonesia from *Rājasa* in 1222–7 to *Suhitā*, 1429–47.* These led to many more Sanskrit place names, since it was customary to name a city after the king that founded it. To give one example among many dozens, *Śreṣṭhapura* (literally 'best of cities'), capital of Cambodia, was named after its founder, King *Śreṣṭhavarman* ('best bastion'). It is likely also that *Śri Vijaya*, the dominant kingdom in southern Sumatra, was named after a king named *Vijaya*, 'Victorious'.

This is just a sample of some of the better known; as could be expected, the history of the relations of all these cities and kings over a thousand years is a vast and labyrinthine subject, and not one to be broached here.

It is easy to overlook what a major change the introduction of Sanskrit must have been for the local peoples. Sanskrit, as a type of language, was fearsomely different from the local languages, now classified as Burman, Austro-Asiatic and Austronesian. Sanskrit is polysyllabic, and highly inflected, with a complicated consonant system that is not averse to long clusters. Word order is free. This language was being taken up by speakers of other languages where words were short, often distinguished by tone, and made up of simple syllables with single consonants at beginning and end. Inflections were simple or absent, but word order was rigid. It was at least as radical a change as it would be to bring Japanese in as an elite language where previously everyone had known only English or Dutch. What a wrench it was can be seen in the mangled remains of some of the Sanskrit names: *Śrikṣetra* came out as Thayekhettaya, *Śrī Deva* as Si Thep.

---

* To an extent, this still continues: so Megawati Sukarnoputri, at the time of writing president of Indonesia, has a name that translates as 'Cloudy, Beneficent's Daughter'.

Nevertheless, the quality of written Sanskrit that the natives acquired in this part of the world deviated hardly at all from that of India. We do not see strong 'substrate influence' in the texts written here. Talking of Cambodia, R. C. Majumdar remarks that its inscriptions, known from AD 475 to 1327, are generally 'composed in beautiful and almost flawless *kāvya*—i.e. poetic—style, and some of them run to great lengths... Almost all the Sanskrit metres have been successfully used in these verses, and they exhibit a thorough acquaintance with the most developed rules and conventions of Sanskrit rhetoric and prosody.'[34] The inscriptions are also full of learned, even witty, allusions to the Vedas and all the different branches of Indian learning, especially grammar.

Particularly accomplished was Queen Indradevi, consort of Jayavarman VII (who ruled in Cambodia 1181–*c*.1218): she was a pious Buddhist and taught the Buddhist nuns of three convents. She has left an inscription, in praise of her younger sister, another scholar, who had sadly died young: it runs to 102 verses in several different metres.[35]

Some of the literature written in Indo-China joined the canon of Sanskrit classics. Vararuci's *Sārasamuccaya* ('collection of essences') could be hard hitting: to show how views can differ, he evokes a woman's breast—seen by her child, and by her husband; and then her dead body, seen first by an ascetic, then by her lover, and then by a dog. Later on, he prefigures Pascal's wager in his advice to the atheist (*nāstika*—literally the 'isn't-ist'): if there is no world after death, there is nothing to fear either way; but if there is, it will be the atheists who stand to suffer.[36]

Sanskrit texts apparently played an important role in the foundation of new Hindu cults, which might be founded to buttress newly independent states: so when Jayavarman freed Cambodia from Javanese control in the twelfth century, he invited a Brahman named *Hiraṇyadāma* ('Golden Cord') to perform Tantric rites to guarantee this freedom, under its own ruler. The resulting cult of *Devarāja* ('god-king') lasted for 250 years, explicitly based on four named *śāstra* texts. It could not have been done without Sanskrit, and the access to ancient wisdom that it implied.

The sense of numinous power infusing Sanskrit led on occasions to a sort of spiritual nostalgia. One king of Champa, Gangaraja, is said to have abdicated his throne so as to have the chance to give up the ghost on the banks of the Ganges. And, more public-spiritedly, there is evidence from an inscription put up at Vat Luong Kau in Laos that a king called *Śrī Devanīka* planned to set up a new *Kurukṣetra* at home as a substitute for the sheer holiness of the real *Kurukṣetra* north of Delhi. As the site of the *Mahabharata*'s great battle, it was peerless among shrines, but sadly inaccessible. He quotes the epic:

Pṛthivyāṃ Naimiṣam puṇyam antarīkṣe tu Puṣkaram
Trāyānām api lokānām Kurukṣetram viśiṣyate.

On the earth the blessed Naimisha, in the ether Pushkara,
But in the three worlds, Kurukshetra holds the crown.[37]

The long years of Indian influence came to an end only after a full millennium. A major jolt had already come in the thirteenth century, when the Mongols sacked Pagan and other Burmese kingdoms in the north. But it has been suggested by one of the leading scholars, not without nostalgia, that Indian civilisation was the victim of its own increasing popularity: 'The underlying causes of this decline were the adoption of Indian civilization by an increasingly large number of natives who incorporated into it more and more of their original customs, and the gradual disappearance of a refined aristocracy, the guardian of Sanskrit culture.'[38]

In any event, in the fifteenth century Vietnam expanded its influence into Champa, annexing permanently the south of Indo-China; and about the same time groups of mountain peoples, the Shan in Burma, and the Thai in Siam, established new kingdoms that thrust aside the old powers of Pagan and Angkor. Nonetheless, when founding their new capital, the Thai could not help calling it Ayutthaya, in direct tribute to the Hindu hero Rama's residence, Ayodhya.

Sanskrit carried by Buddhism: Central and eastern Asia

So far we have largely spoken of Sanskrit as a vehicle of Hinduism. And it seems that for the most part this is what it conveyed at first in South-East Asia. Fa-Xian, returning to China via Ye-po-ti (*Yava-dvīpa*) in the East Indies in the early fifth century AD, remarked: 'in this country heretics and Brahmans flourish, but the law of Buddha is not much known'.[39]

To this day, Hinduism survives on the island of Bali, east of Java. However, elsewhere in South-East Asia the picture is now very different, Hinduism long ago replaced by Buddhism. This is the result of a long and complex, though not especially bloody, history of doctrinal contests between the two faiths. Hindu cults' close associations with ruling dynasties ultimately worked against them, when those dynasties fell. But there was also competition among strains of Buddhism, *Tantra*, originally 'the loom' or 'the framework', *Mahāyāna*, 'the great vehicle' and *Theravāda*, 'the docrine of the elders'. Theravada, buttressed by links with the Sinhala in Śri Lanka, ultimately triumphed in South-East Asia. Nevertheless, all these struggles took place against an unchallenged background of Indian learning.

Buddhist missionaries actually came very soon after the first Indian buccaneers and traders, if not along with them. Ceylonese chronicles tell of Aśoka sending two monks, *Soṇa* and *Uttara*, to *Suvaṇṇabhūmi* in the third century BC,[40] although the first archaeological records of Buddhist activity in South-East Asia (in the areas of modern Burma and Thailand) are from the fifth century AD. Hinduism was always a religion likely to appeal to kings and a ruling elite, but not voluntarily to the lower orders, the Śudras and outcastes, who are singularly downtrodden in the Hindu caste system; by contrast, Buddhism, with its egalitarian emphasis on personal quest for enlightenment, could in principle appeal much more widely. It seems likely that in the early days of Indian advance into the region both religions were represented; their complementary charms may even have served to back each other up, while promoting Indian culture among outsiders.

The religious distinction always had some linguistic implications, the Hindus favouring classical Sanskrit, while the Buddhists preferred the closely related but somewhat simpler Pali. As time wore on, there was also a tendency for Pali to be reclothed in archaic Sanskrit forms, giving rise to the particular style of Buddhist Hybrid Sanskrit. Real learning, and creativity, in classical Sanskrit tended to be at its best in the Hindu areas, such as Champa, Cambodia, Java and Bali.

Despite the Buddha's original urgings to his disciples to leave behind strict linguistic codes and work in any vernacular (*sakayā niruttiyā*) in order to get the message across, the Buddhist scriptures remained in Pali in South-East Asia, where—in contrast with China and Tibet—there was no major effort to translate them into local languages. Pali became an esoteric liturgical language, unknown to the general population, but apparently without adverse effects on the spread of Buddhism.

Nor was there any converse tendency to have Pali, or some form of Sanskrit, taken up as a language of general communication outside Buddhist liturgy and debate. There is no secular literature in Pali, even if the *Jātaka* tales, which nominally recount the past lives of the Buddha, are rather like such other story books as Aesop's Fables, or its Indian equivalent, the *Pañcatantra*. And in South-East Asia, where Pali survives as a liturgical language, the local vernacular has nothing to do with it: Burmese, Thai, Khmer, Acehnese, Malay and Javanese are all unrelated to Pali, heavy as they are with loans from the Indian languages.

Buddhism has proved a faith of remarkable attractiveness from India outward to the north and east, and so Pali and Sanskrit are extremely well known in these vast areas. But they have remained no more than liturgical languages. As a result, Buddhism's linguistic effects have been far weaker than those of Christianity or Islam. After all, Latin, the language of Western Christianity, provided the foundation for the growth of a common language in the monasteries and then the universities of Europe in this same period (AD 500–1500). Islam propagated Arabic all round North Africa, Arabia, Palestine and Mesopotamia, persisting up to the present day, both in unchanged form as an international lingua franca for the educated and, with local variations, as the basis of many vernaculars. There is no comparable linguistic union of Buddhists, in their daily languages.

As for how the language was used in this part of Sanskrit's story, there is little to say. In Hinduism, the virtue implicit in the very sound of the Vedas had long since been separated from any need to understand their meaning. Now once again for the Buddhists, with the language no longer widely understood, but still widely heard in chants and ceremonial, its substance and sound began to be given a mystic value of their own. Sanskrit became for many a language of *mantra*, 'incantation' and *maṇḍala*, 'circle, sacred diagram'. In medieval Japan, repeating *namu amida butsu*, a version of *nama Amitabha Buddha*, 'Bowing to you, O Resplendent Enlightened One', was the infallible means of reaching the Pure Land after death. And to this day millions of Tibetans chant *om maṇi padme hum*, 'Hail the jewel in the lotus', a mystical phrase from Tantric Buddhism, its original sexual imagery now quite forgotten.

More pragmatically, the technology and systems associated with writing and analysing Sanskrit provided the basis for literacy in other languages. In this way, sacred languages, unavailable for direct communication among people, could still go on inspiring developments in the local vernaculars.

The advent of Sanskrit, known as 梵文 *fànwén*, 'Brahman writing', in China, 梵語 *bongo*, 'Brahman talk', in Japan, had only a small effect on the character-based system of writing in use in East Asia, since this had already been well established in China for over a millennium: rather, Chinese characters are often used (though only phonetically) to represent Sanskrit itself in the Buddhist practice of these countries.

One effect it did have was on Chinese phonetics. Chinese scholars of the Tang period (seventh to eighth centuries), knowing the Sanskrit alphabetic tradition could identify the initial consonants of characters, called them 字母 *zìmǔ*, 'word mothers', apparently after the Sanskrit term *mātṛkā*, 'maternal', which is also a letter of the alphabet. These were used to systematise the traditional practice for indicating pronunciation in dictionaries: Chinese dictionaries have always done this by what is called *fànqiĕ*, linking a character with two others, one with the same initial consonant, and the other with the same tone and rhyme. Putting this into a systematic chart was a very modest step in linguistic understanding, since no further analysis of the rhyme part (for example, into vowels and consonants) was undertaken.[41]

There is also an interesting curiosity in one of the other writing systems used in this vast area of Asia.* Japan owes the order of symbols in its syllabary, the so-called *kana*, or *go-jū-on*, 'fifty sounds', to the order of letters in Indian alphabets. The order of Sanskrit letters is conventionally

```
a ā i ī u ū ṛ ṝ ḷ
e āi o āu
ḥ ṃ
k kh g gh ŋ
c ch j jh ñ
ṭ ṭh ḍ ḍh ṇ
t th d dh n
p ph b bh m
y r l v
ś ṣ s h
```

This is not an arbitrary order like our ABCD...† Rather it appeals to various purely phonetic properties of the sounds represented. So, for example, all the consonants are placed in an order where tongue contact gradually advances from the back to the front of the mouth cavity. And the nasal consonants (*m*, *n*, etc.) always come immediately after the other consonants formed at the same place of articulation. The strange order of the vowels is partly conditioned by the fact that most instances of *e* and *o* in Sanskrit actually derive from the diphthongs *ai* and *au*, and so are well classified next to their long equivalents *āi* and *āu*.

Now the Japanese *kana* represent syllables, rather than individual consonants. Their pronunciation has definitely changed over the last millennium, but using the most ancient pronunciation reconstructible, we can state the conventional order as:

---

* A variant called *Siddha-mātṛka*, 'settled alphabet', or simply Siddha, is the version of the script most generally used in the East Asian (i.e. Mahayana) Buddhist traditions.
† The motivation for this is purely historic. It ultimately goes back to an equally arbitrary 'aleph beth gimel daleth...' specified by the Phoenicians.

a	i	u	e	o
ka	ki	ku	ke	ko
sa	si	su	se	so
ta	ti	tu	te	to
na	ni	nu	ne	no
fa	fi	fu	fe	fo
ma	mi	mu	me	mo
ya	(yi)	yu	(ye)	yo
ra	ri	ru	re	ro
wa	wi	(wu)	we	wo*

Immediately we note that the arbitrary order of the vowels (a i u e o) is precisely as in Sanskrit, although this has no motivation in Japanese grammar. Furthermore, although there are many fewer consonants in Japanese than in Sanskrit, they occur in almost exactly the same order as in the Sanskrit alphabet. In fact, there is only one apparent exception, s, which occurs where c or ṭ should be, not at the end like the Sanskrit sibilants. In fact there is reason to believe that the pronunciation of this phoneme was actually [š] (English 'sh') or [tˢ], when the conventional order was set up, which means it would be closest to Sanskrit *c* (English 'ch', [tš]).

This thoroughgoing intellectual borrowing at the root of the writing system demonstrates that not just the sound of the Buddhist chants but also elements of the traditional analysis of the language had spread to Japan with Sanskrit.

Another example of Sanskrit intellectual influence on the technology of writing is the Tibetan script, which we first see in use in the eighth century AD, derived directly from the Siddha script. The earliest-known use of it is on a stone pillar at Žol near Lhasa, dated to 764.[42]

It is not quite clear if Tibet owes its literacy to Buddhism, or to attempts to modernise administration. The era of the first surviving inscriptions is precisely the time when Buddhism first came to Tibet, with the monk *Śāntarakṣita*. But there is no mention of Buddhism on the Žol pillar inscription, which is a record of a royal minister's achievements.[43]

Whatever the motivation, it is clear that the Tibetan alphabet was inspired by an Indian model, and one that was used for the writing of Sanskrit or

---

* The items in parentheses do not exist separately, in the spelling or the language, for phonetic reasons.

Prakrit.* And Tibetan writing, once established, was very largely taken up with the translation of Buddhist classics from Sanskrit or Pali. This became such an industry that there was a Tibetan royal commission in the early ninth century to establish precise rules for equivalences (comparable to the 'controlled language' used in some industrial translation today). The result was a lowering of the literary skill displayed in translation, but such punctilious work was done that it is often possible to reconstruct lost Sanskrit originals simply on the basis of their Tibetan versions.

These religious foundations of Tibet's Sanskrit culture were surmounted by a superstructure of wider-ranging classical literature in the thirteenth century, for then Muslim invaders devastated all the centres of higher learning in northern India, and many scholars fled northward into Tibet with their books. Nine Sanskrit pundits accompanied the *Khatšhe pantšhen Šākyaśrībhadra* to Tibet in 1206, and fifty years later there was collaboration on Sanskrit drama, poetry and poetics between the Indian pundit *Lakṣmīkara* and the Tibetan scholar *Šoñ-ston Rdo-rdže rgyal msthan.*[44]

It is somehow reassuring to think that eight hundred years ago Tibet was a refuge for Buddhists fleeing from marauding infidels in northern India—the precise opposite of what we have known in the latter part of the twentieth century.

Sanskrit supplanted

Muslim invasions had started from Ghazni in Afghanistan in the late tenth century. It took three hundred years for the Muslims' 'Delhi Sultanate' to take control of the whole plain from Indus to Ganges, and another century to grasp most of the rest of the subcontinent. Their unity was not sustained, but their presence in India continued to count, especially after 1505, when Babur, leading yet another army down from Afghanistan, founded the Mughal empire.

The incomers were known to the Indians as *Turuṣka* ('Turks'). They brought in a new self-confident civilisation that conversed in a form of eastern Turkic (Chagatay), prayed in Arabic, but was literate above all in Persian.

---

* Nevertheless, the script had been modified deftly to represent more effectively features of Tibetan which are alien to the Aryan languages for which Brahmi and all its successors had been designed. Notably, it can distinguish initial vowels that have glottal stops in front of them and those that do not. (In Sanskrit, as in English, a glottal jerk is inserted automatically when a vowel begins an utterance.) The script was later (in the thirteenth century) borrowed by the Chinese at the court of Kublai Khan, to create the 'Phagspa script for Mongolian, this even being declared the official script of the empire in 1269. It was also used to write Chinese. (See Chapter 4, 'Holding fast to a system of writing', p. 156.)

Their cultural self-confidence, their totally alien concepts of decorous behaviour and the point of life, and above all their developed systems of administration conducted in Persian, meant that they had far, far more linguistic effect than the previous, non-doctrinal, incursions from the same direction of the Śaka, Kushāna and Hūṇa. Now for the first time Sanskrit was supplanted as the elite language of India.

Ironically, the Muslims' success in invading the continent was largely a result of their skill with cavalry, and the fine Afghan-bred horses that they brought with them. The distant descendants of the Aryan horse-borne invaders of the second millennium BC had at last been beaten at what had once been their own game.

At about the same time, some of the civilisations of South-East Asia that had been Sanskrit-speaking were taking up the same new religion, but apparently for quite different motives.

There was no military conquest here, nor social revolution in favour of lower castes. Nevertheless, some ports in northern Sumatra became Muslim in the late thirteenth and early fourteenth centuries, and Melaka (Malacca), the most important trading centre, situated on the Malay peninsula, embraced Islam some time in the early fifteenth.* The religion spread widely among its trading partners, notably to Java, south Sulawesi, the Moluccas and Mindanao. It is presumed that the influence came from Muslim traders out of India, perhaps in a kind of commercial domino effect, with kingdom after kingdom reckoning that they stood to maintain their Indian links only if they took up the faith—or perhaps responding to a desperate Islamic rush to proselytise before the arrival of the Portuguese.[45] Whatever the linkage, the new religion created a new social climate, and put an end to Sanskrit's reign as the representative language of culture here.

---

* Malacca's role as an entrepôt firmly established Malay, *Bahasa Mělayu*, as the lingua franca of the region, and this has lasted up to the present day. (See Chapter 11, 'Dutch interlopers', p. 400.) Malacca was itself a colony of Śrī Vijaya (Palembang) on Sumatra, also a major trade centre, and that is where the earliest (seventh century) inscriptions in Malay have been found, one of them upriver from the city of Jambi, previously known as Malayu (Hall 1981: 47–8). Ironically enough, '*Bahasa*' is none other than the Sanskrit word *bhāṣā*, 'language'.

The charm of Sanskrit

The roots of Sanskrit's charm

keyūrā na vibhūṣayanti puruṣaṃ hārā na candrojjvalā
na snānaṃ na vilepanaṃ na kusumaṃ nālaṃkṛtā mūrdhanaḥ
bhāṣāikā samalaṃkaroti puruṣam yā saṃskṛtā dhāryate
kṣīyante khalu bhūṣaṇāni satataṃ vāgbhūṣaṇaṃ bhūṣaṇam

Bracelets do not embellish man, nor necklaces bright as the moon;
bathing, cosmetics, garland, head-dress, none can add a whit.
Man's one true embellishment is language kept perfected:
finery must perish, but eternal the refinement of fine language.

Bhartṛhari, ii.17–20

A language that began as an Indo-European offshoot settled in a decidedly quiet corner of the world, the foothills of the Hindu Kush, spread as a vernacular all over the Indo-Gangetic plain, and as an elite language, borne by Hindu religion, to the rest of the Indian subcontinent. From there it spread eastward across the sea through trade, and became for a thousand years the cultural inspiration to a whole new subcontinent and archipelago. This was the autonomous growth of Sanskrit.

But one of the religions that had started in Sanskrit's first millennium continued to grow through its second and third: Buddhism spread first with Sanskrit and the Prakrits across India and Indo-China. Then the religion showed that it could transcend its native state, its home in Indian culture. Moving northward and finally eastward, it won converts and flourished in Chinese, Korean, Japanese, Tibetan and Mongolian societies. Although the religion metamorphosed as it progressed across the world, Sanskrit and Pali travelled with it without significant change, as adjuncts to Buddhist higher learning wherever it took them. This was Sanskrit's free ride, its vehicle Buddhism in all its many forms.

It is now time to consider what it was about Sanskrit which made it grow, and whether Buddhism itself may have owed something to this consummately charming form of human expression.

Sanskrit had many advantages. It was the language of a self-conscious elite, the Brahmans and Kshatriyas, who considered themselves entitled to dominate other peoples with whom they came into contact, and had the technical means to do so. Furthermore, their language was at the very centre of their own picture of their culture, since grammar was the queen of their sciences. Facility in Sanskrit was seen as the hallmark of civilised existence, of one's place in the world as an *ārya*, but it was also something that was teachable, and was taught.

Beliefs about the true value of this knowledge gradually changed over the centuries, from the need to guarantee the cult of the gods, to maintenance of the social order, and then to enhancement of the patina of cultural appreciation.

Although some social forces promoted less elite forms of the language, both at a secular level (for example, in the practice of kings such as Aśoka) and in the spiritual world (for example, in the attitudes of the Buddha), they gradually lost out to the cultivated, self-conscious charm of the self-styled Perfected Language, *saṃskṛtā bhāṣā*: because of its elaborated descriptions and analyses of itself, it could always demonstrate what was best and why it was best. It thereby made itself irresistibly attractive to upwardly mobile institutions: Hindu kingdoms (such as that of Rudradaman) seeking wider recognition in India, Indo-Chinese dynasties (such as the *Śailendra* of Bnam) seeking to demonstrate their legitimacy, Buddhist schools wanting to endow their devotional texts with prestige.

The natural conservatism of institutions meant that their symbols would tend to ossify—witness the fate of the Pali language among the Buddhists, starting as an attempt at an unstuffy people's lingua franca but ending up as just another classical language. India, with its caste system, was nothing if not a home of conservative institutions. Such conservatism always played into the hands of Sanskrit: it was defended through its own sutras as the unchanging linguistic standard, from which any change would mean decline and degradation.

Being concretely defined in the grammar books, Sanskrit was eminently learnable: indeed, it could be held that since the standard was so explicit, if complex and abstruse, it encouraged explicit displays of lawyer-like intelligence, though always in a strangely impractical realm divorced from the usual imperatives of penalties, property and military force. There were no wars based on the results of its debates, hotly disputed though they often were (and are). *Vyākāraṇa*, grammatical analysis, provided a natural forum for intellectual exercise and argument, simply concerned with the establishment of what was right in the world of language, or how it should best be formalised. As the saying had it:

ardhamātrālāghavena putrotsavam iva manyante vāiyākāraṇāḥ

The grammarians rejoice at the saving of half a measure as at the birth of a son.

One result was that Brahmanical skills could never decline into mere rote learning and stipulation, since they were based in a rigorously articulated intellectual structure.

As in linguistics, so in the gamut of Indian sciences. In its continual appeal to abstract principle, rather than its own specific cultural tradition, Sanskrit-based civilisation is different from those of Greece and Rome to its west. Indian culture does not revolve around its epics and its literary classics, treasured though these are. Nor does its philosophy emphasise socially useful theories, such as politics, ethics or the art of persuasion. Rather it theorises about states of being and modes of perception. There is a certain sense in which Sanskrit theory fails to connect with the practical world. As Basham points out:

> ...the geographical knowledge of the learned was of the vaguest description. Even within India distances and directions, as given in texts, are usually very vague and inaccurate. The conquerors who led their armies thousands of miles on their campaigns, the merchants who carried their wares from one end of India to the other, and the pilgrims who visited sacred places from the Himalayas to Cape Comorin must have had a sound practical knowledge of Indian geography, while that of the seamen who sailed the ocean from Socotra to Canton must have been even wider; but there are few echoes of this knowledge in the literature of the time.[46]

Ethereal in its interests, above local loyalties and personal detail, Sanskrit achieved, and still enjoys, a status within Indian civilisation as a quasi-universal language, even if there are now persistent voices in parts of India who would disown it, and emphasise its origins as a local language of the north. Pali, its younger sister, has enjoyed something of the same status, though only among Buddhists, and mostly outside India itself. One sign of these two languages' pan-Indian, almost pan-Asian, status is the fact that, unlike all the other languages of India and Indo-China, they are written indifferently in all the different scripts that have descended from Brahmi: they are thus 'globally local' in the Indic context, at home as a holy language whatever the vernacular.

But for classical languages, they have always been strangely indifferent to a written existence, in whatever script. We have noted the characteristic distrust of writing in Indian culture. This in fact applies not just to these Aryan languages, but more generally: in fact, the first sacred written text anywhere in India is the Sikhs' *Guru Granth Sahib*, produced in the seventeenth century. (And Sikhism explicitly takes Islam, with its adoration of the written text of the Koran, as a major inspiration.)

This greater esteem for texts preserved and transmitted orally has probably kept Sanskrit accessible to a wide public, a language of prayers and devotion, as well as a language of ancient works of literature. To pick one example, a popular local hymn, *vande utkalā janani*, 'I salute, O mother Orissa', is in fact expressed in Sanskrit, although those who sing it hardly notice.

Meanwhile the fact that it was preserved by two media, straightforwardly written down in a manuscript tradition, as well as distinctively through the oral tradition of the Sanskrit grammarians, may have prevented the pronunciation of Sanskrit from changing markedly over the three thousand and more years of its liturgical life.*

One side of this story is like the survival of Hebrew: a holy tradition, built on recitation of texts in a language that no one spoke any longer, has preserved the language more or less intact. But the other side is like nothing else on earth: it is as if the Hebrew tradition of *gematria*, which assigned numerical values to letters and by so adding them gave mystically significant numbers to phrases,† had defined, in a set of equations, an alternative means of representing the whole Hebrew language, so preserving its grammar and pronunciation quite independently of what was written in the Torah and Talmud.

For all this, the attractiveness to outsiders of Sanskrit and the Indian culture it expressed remains elusive. I have questioned Indian friends about it, pointing out the apparently unreasonable readiness of Mon, Munda or Mongolian to accept Aryan culture, language and religion when presented to them without coercion. They point out how little was asked of converts, either to take up as new observance or to cast aside from their old ways. Offerings are made to deities, but explicit duties as an adherent of Hinduism or Buddhism are few. Hinduism can apparently find a place within it for all other faiths: old allegiances can simply be incorporated, as in the foundation myth of Funan. Mahayana Buddhism was as accommodating as Hinduism, with an eternity of universes and gods in its purview. Other forms of Buddhism were oriented in a completely different direction, giving guidance on ethics and personal enlightenment, but leaving old beliefs and allegiances undisturbed.

But this is purely the absence of an obstacle: it does not explain why in so many different contexts people have chosen to follow the Indian example rather than stick with their old ways. The decision to adopt the new culture transmitted in Sanskrit was no doubt often made by members of an elite, then

---

* Although we know that some features, e.g. the tonal accent, and the pronunciation of over-long (*pluti*) vowels, have been lost along the way.

† Most famously NRWN KSR ('Nero Emperor') added up to 666, the number of the Beast in the Book of Revelation.

enforced or induced in a wider population. The decision to adopt Buddhism may more often have been for individuals to make. But at whatever level the decision was made, the decision-makers must have felt they were taking a step towards a wider, more open world—opening links to the surmised wealth of India and the Western world, and to its ancient and elaborate wisdom.

The decision will not have been taken once and for all, nor with any pre-science of the fundamental changes in Indo-China, China and the East that it would bring about. But by and large the decision, wherever taken, stuck. And the absence of any military inducement, either at the outset, or in the later years or centuries when both Indians and the converts were well aware each of the other, argues that the cultural assimilation was recognised somehow as good value, and well worth pursuing and developing.

Limiting weaknesses

And yet the human world of Sanskrit was not, and is not, without its disadvantages.

Militarily, it never created a strong defensible centre, tending to rely rather on natural barriers, which were periodically breached by invaders from the north-west. Socially, it remained conservative and stratified, preferring to theorise about why it was best for society to be closed and rigid, rather than to use its talents to innovate, militarily, politically or economically. In religion, Hinduism and Buddhism tended to create an other-worldly system of values, so undercutting practical concerns for loyalty and social cohesion, and compounding the fundamental weaknesses in defence and flexibility.

All these problems were implicit in the Sanskrit community. The creeper spread charmingly, but in time it tended to harden into an extremely intricate, and fairly unyielding, tangle of branches. In time, it would be pruned by un-sympathetic hands.

We begin with the domains of war, diplomacy and government.

We have seen (from the record of inscriptions) that Sanskrit, at first a sa-cred language, established itself as the outward language for political state-ments only in the middle of the second century AD, 650 years after the grammarian Panini had established its canon. Previously, it appears that the language of government was the common speech of the ruling city, notably the Magadhi Prakrit of Pataliputra: 250 years after Panini, when Aśoka had set monuments all over north and central India, they were written in this Ma-gadhi Prakrit. Nevertheless, there is some evidence that Sanskrit had already penetrated to the highest levels in the state: the great handbook of Indian statecraft, the *Arthaśāstra* of Kautilya, is written in Sanskrit, not Magadhi. This is traditionally attributed to the chief minister of Candragupta ('Moon-secret') Maurya, Aśoka's grandfather, who had established his northern Indian empire shortly after Alexander's brief foray along the Indus, but it could have been written at any time in the five centuries to AD 150. By then, certainly, the primacy of Sanskrit in political records was assured.[47]

Regardless of the cultural unity signalled by Sanskrit, India was not nearly as successful as Rome and Persia to the west, or China to the east, in establishing a large-scale political unit that could defend its borders and secure orderly succession beyond a half-dozen generations at most. From the fifth century BC to the fifth century AD, indigenous dynasties such as the Nandas, Mauryas, Shungas, Satavahanas and Guptas rose and fell with a persistent rhythm, their capital often at Pataliputra, but with no sense of direct succession: usually these larger empires collapsed into a couple of generations of decentralised feudal mêlée, before the next would-be *cakravārtin*, 'wheel-turner', i.e. universal monarch, emerged. Sometimes major incursions from the north-west would get as far as Pataliputra, for example when the Yavana kings (such as Menander—Buddhism's Milinda) swooped down from Swat, or when Kanishka, a Bactrian-speaking Iranian, founded the Kushāna empire, in the first to second centuries AD. But they never lasted any longer.*

All the invaders in this period—they also included Scythians (*Śaka*) speaking Iranian, and Xiongnu (*Hūṇa*) speaking Turkic—conformed to the pattern of Mongols in China or Germanic tribes in western Europe. They did not establish their own cultures, but after a first period of rapine simply adopted the existing culture and settled down as the new aristocracy, with no lasting linguistic effects. Sanskrit, and the Prakrits, were thus transmitted to new generations and new peoples. The tradition was not politically unified, though the *Arthaśāstra* shows that it was highly organised and self-conscious, legally and economically.

There was no apparent technical or military innovation in this period, and communications must have remained difficult, two reasons which explain why the various cities and regions retained so much independence, with the centralised power of the *cakravārtin* largely an unrealised dream.

The *Arthaśāstra* has an elaborate theory of foreign policy, implying a large number of smallish states. Most of the states were monarchies, but there were in fact also republics, ruled by councils of men of substance. The Licchavi, living in *Vaiśalī* north of the Ganges, are said to have had 7,707 *rājās* or 'kings', all in the tribal assembly. The Buddha himself had grown up in one

---

* Ironically, the most lasting contribution of Kanishka's rule was 'Shaka' era, a dating system still in use in India. It runs from AD 78, and is even used in many of the Sanskrit inscriptions of South-East Asia.

such community, not far away among the *Śākya* of the Himalayan foothills. This tradition is said to have inspired the noticeably democratic practice of the *sangha*, the full community of Buddhist monks.

As for the social limitations of Indian society, it must be seen as overwhelmingly stratified, with one's caste, and hence status, determined by birth. Sanskrit-speaking theorists, usually referring back to the Vedas, had no difficulty in justifying and rationalising flagrant inequalities—even if, from time to time, natural leaders who happened to be low-caste made themselves into kings without too much scruple over Hinduism's taboos. The status of women was also not a matter for discussion, with the Sanskrit word *satī*, originally just the feminine of the adjective meaning 'true, correct, good', coming to be understood as best applied to a wife willingly burnt on her husband's funeral pyre.

The real contribution of indigenous thought to subverting the rigidities of the caste system was Buddhism. This was true in both the variants that developed in this period. The earlier *Hīnayāna* tradition encouraged anyone to seek their own enlightenment, though they would have to give up the world as monks or nuns in order to do it. Early on, it also gave women equal, or at least comparable, status in pursuing a contemplative life. The later *Mahāyāna* was less austere, more a religion for everyday life. It allowed believers to develop a personal relationship with the holy figures of bodhisattvas, and its much stronger social ethic, of general compassion and altruism, was also attractive.

There does not seem to have been much religious intolerance or violence as between the different faiths. Where people felt aversion, it seems to have been more fastidious or superstitious than based on piety. In the Sanskrit dramas and romances being written at the time, a chance meeting with a monk may be viewed as a sign of bad luck to come. In this same period, the Buddhists were building up a formidable reputation for intellectual rigour as well as high-mindedness.

The Great Monastery of Nalanda (*Nālandā Mahāvihāra*), a couple of days' walk south of Pataliputra, was the supreme monument to Buddhist learning. Aśoka founded the core monastery on the site of a favourite haunt of the Buddha in the third century BC, and all the major dynasties that flourished during its lifespan re-endowed and rebuilt it as a seat of learning: the Guptas in the fifth century, King Harsha in the seventh, the *Pālas* in the ninth. Besides the scriptures of the Mahayana, and the eighteen sects of the Hinayana, subjects taught included *śabdavidyā* (Sanskrit grammar), *hetuvidyā* (logic and metaphysics), *cikitsavidyā* (medicine), *śilpasthānavidyā* (literally 'technology', including mechanics, yin and yang, and the calendar), apparently also the Vedas, and 'miscellaneous studies', generally understood as secular literature. Xuan-Zang, who was enrolled as a student and later a teacher there in the seventh century, describes the institution in terms very reminiscent of a modern elite university:

> The priests to the number of several thousands are men of the highest ability and talent. Their distinction is very great at the present time, and there are many hundreds whose fame has rapidly spread through distant regions...
>
> From morning till night they engage in discussion; the old and the young mutually help one another. Those who cannot discuss questions out of the *Tripiṭaka* are little esteemed, and are obliged to hide themselves for shame. Learned men from different cities, on this account, who desire to acquire quickly a renown in discussion, come here in multitudes to settle their doubts, and then the streams of their wisdom spread far and wide. For this reason some persons usurp the name of Nalanda students, and in going to and fro receive honour in consequence. If men of other quarters desire to enter and take part in the discussions, the keeper of the gate proposes some hard questions; many are unable to answer and retire. One must have studied deeply both old and new books before getting admission. Those students, therefore, who come here as strangers, have to show their ability by hard discussion; those who fail compared with those who succeed are as 7 or 8 to 10.[48]

Although there was continuous production of new works, or at least commentaries on old ones, such large-scale concentrations of intellectual fire-power (like their contemporaries in Europe and the Islamic world) were profoundly conservative: they aimed at sustaining the religious and philosophical status quo, although they might defend it with new arguments.*

The *mahāvihāra*s did not in the end sustain Buddhism in India. Buddhism was already losing adherents in the time of Xuan-Zang. From the tenth century it was gradually absorbed by Hinduism, as if it were just another sect, the Buddha having been imaginatively recast as an earthly manifestation of Vishnu, on a par with Hindu heroes Rama and Krishna. This closed the loophole in the caste system, and left the lower castes and untouchables con-

---

* The three fabled libraries of Nalanda, *Ratnodadhi* ('sea of jewels'), *Ratnasāgara* ('ocean of jewels') and *Ratnarañjaka* ('jewel-adorned'), were all to be burnt down. Perhaps it is significant that, according to Tibetan Buddhist accounts of their end, the fires resulted from spells cast by visitors affronted by the rudeness they received from the scholars of Nalanda.

demned again to inferiority. Many of them would have provided eager listeners when Muslims began to invade, bringing news of a world where all were equal before God.

The *mahāvihāra*s were not spared when these invaders finally overran northern India and sacked its treasures at the end of the twelfth century. Sanskrit retained its charms, but like many with this virtue it was unable to defend itself bodily against those unable to appreciate them.

> *agrāhyā mūrdhajeṣv etā striyo guṇasamanvitāḥ*
> *na latāḥ pallavacchedam arhanty upavanodbhuvāḥ*

Ladies like these, who are accomplished, should not be seized by the hair;
for creepers growing in orchards deserve not to have their foliage lopped off.

Śūdraka, The Little Clay Cart, 8.21

Sanskrit no longer alone

After the Muslim invasions, India became a very different place.

It is hard now to conceive what opposite and harshly conflicting extremes, both of daily life and of values deeply held, had to be reconciled to create the India now familiar to us.

Indians had perceived themselves as being firmly at the centre of their world, their gods running it, their social order complex but immutable, because ordained at the highest level. Even as austere an analyst as the Buddha had called the highest path the Arya way. Intellectually, they knew that they were not alone in the world, but the only role in which they had seen foreigners was as outsiders whose best hope was to partake in the blessings that India could provide, whether by trade or by adoption. They dressed scantily, as was comfortable in their climate, but adorned themselves as gaudily as their incomes and caste allowed. Their relations with their gods were largely a matter of personal devotion, except at festival time. They built their monuments with loving attention to intricate detail, and lavish illustration and decoration. Their religions were frank in acceptance of all aspects of life and nature, with destruction on a par with creation, and sexuality openly acknowledged as central to all.

Their rulers were now foreigners with an alien, and uncompromising, vision. They were firm believers that there was but one god, of universal dominion, and that idol-worshippers were fit only for conversion or death. They believed that all men were spiritually equal before God, and that they should worship him, publicly and en masse. Their style of dress was to cover the body fully, and they believed that modesty required this. Their buildings were austere, and they believed that any graphic or sculptural illustration was tantamount to blasphemy. Their idea of the workings of the world was austere and abstract: sex had no part in creation, and females (and the delights associated with them) should be kept decently out of sight in purdah.

Somehow, around the middle of the second millennium, a compromise, or at least a modus vivendi, was reached between these polar opposites.

Linguistically, the effects of this are visible in the largest and most widespread single language now spoken in India, especially in its northern regions. It goes under two names, Hindi and Urdu, because it is felt to be two different languages. Hindi is written in Devanagari, the characteristic 'washing on the line' script derived from the Brahmi tradition, and likes to borrow words from Sanskrit. Urdu is written in Persian (by origin Arabic) script, and draws on Persian and Arabic. Urdu is the official language of the state of Pakistan, while both Hindi and Urdu are dignified as official languages in the Indian constitution.

But neither can really run true to its cultural ideal in sourcing its vocabulary, and when they are spoken Hindi and Urdu are in practice one language.* This maintenance of a distinction without a difference speaks eloquently for Indian civilisation after the Muslim invasions, each side believing it maintains its own standard, but in fact conforming to a common, wider, norm, which unites them in a common society.

Despite their determined maintenance of Islamic ideals—along with educated use of Persian, which lasted until the British imperialists had fully taken over from the Mughals, well into the nineteenth century—the invading *Turuṣka* have ultimately fallen into the old pattern of invading conquerors adopting the speech of the conquered. For if the names Hindi and Urdu come from the Persian side of the language's heritage, its substance turns out to be pretty much pure Aryan, with the basic vocabulary, and the endings on verbs, adjectives and nouns, all traceable to something like Sanskrit, though radically simplified. Historically, it is evidently the continuation of the Prakrit

* The name Urdu is short for *zabān e urdū e muallā*, Persian for 'language of the camp exalted', where the first and last words are originally Arabic, the middle one Turkic, and the linking *e*'s pure Persian. Hindi is a shortening of Hindui or Hindvi, the word for 'Indian talk' originally used by Muslims, since the word Hind itself is a Persian version of the name of the Sindhu river, known to the Greeks (and Europeans) as the Indus.

spoken round Delhi, known successively as *Śauraseni* ('language of Śura-sena', the region to the south of the city), *Apabhramśa* ('falling off') and *Khaṛi Boli* ('standing speech').

In a quite different and unexpected way, the fall of Sanskrit into a world where it was no longer seen as the sole standard of linguistic excellence came to enrich the whole world's understanding of language. The new Muslim masters, despite their independent knowledge of Arabic, Persian and Turkish, did not distinguish themselves for their linguistic scholarship. But when the British succeeded in the eighteenth century, a new and equally confident alien civilisation became acquainted with Indian culture, and through it with San-skrit. They approached it from the new perspective of knowledge of the clas-sical languages of Europe, Greek and Latin, and were soon struck by its remarkable similarity to both of them. Sir William Jones, Chief Justice in In-dia, ventured in 1786 the wild surmise that they were all three 'sprung from some common source, which, perhaps, no longer exists'.

This was the origin of historical comparative linguistics. Applying it to languages all over the world was one of the great intellectual adventures of the nineteenth and twentieth centuries; and as a direct result we now know much of the flow of human languages, and so of human history, well before the start of the written documents. To give just three examples, this is how we know that the Hungarians came from northern Siberia, that Madagascar was colonised from Borneo, and that the European Gypsies originated as far away as India.

For all the self-generated excellence of Sanskrit's own tradition in lin-guistics, it could never have gone off in this new direction on its own: what was needed was confrontation with other languages, far beyond the Indian ken, but also the ability to view these languages as somehow on a par with Sanskrit, something else that the tradition would have found simply inconceivable.

Sanskrit's subsequent history is one of survival, rather than new triumphs. In India it is still the language of a traditional elite, but now it is denied its ancient and medieval role as the principal vehicle of intellectual discourse in India. That is conducted either in the principal vernacular languages, or much more in English. Sanskrit's culture was always based on a disarming view of its own importance, which held India to be the only significant part of the world; it has not adapted to a world where even in India itself this view is dis-missed. The world touched by Indians, the whole of East and South Asia, once took India at its own valuation, but not any more.

Perhaps it could still have achieved the revolution in viewpoint needed to incorporate Western learning. Until the early nineteenth century the English

East India Company, like the Mughals before them, had patronised Indian learning as they found it, both Arabic/Persian and Sanskrit. When a Committee of Public Instruction was formed in 1823 to spend an annual sum of 100,000 rupees on 'the revival and improvement of literature and the encouragement of the Natives of India and for the introduction and promotion of a knowledge of the sciences among the inhabitants of the British Territories in India' they were split for a decade on whether this should go towards the traditional learning or on modern studies conducted in English. The decision ultimately came down in favour of English, a cultural clean break: and no serious attempt was made afterwards to bridge the gap between India's tradition and the swiftly developing sciences, ideologies and technologies that created the modern world in the Victorian age. Sanskrit became more and more a symbol of certain religions, certain cultures, certain philosophies—of interest to humanists, but somehow offering no contest in the world of the scientists.*

It continues to enjoy an enviable status for a language that was codified 2500 years ago, and has admitted no significant change except new words since. In 1947, it was adopted as one of India's official languages, and 200,000 people still claimed to speak it in the Indian census of 1971—though out of a then population of 400 million.

In a final irony, it assumed a new symbolic value in the last decade of the twentieth century, adopted by the *Bhāratiyā Janatā*, 'Indian Community' Party (BJP), which was often in government, as a totem of Hindu identity. So, for example, 1999 was declared a Sanskrit Year in India, and a government-funded 'World Sanskrit Conference' held in New Delhi. There is something decidedly bizarre in this. Outside its use for prayers and mantras in the temple, as we have seen, the study of Sanskrit has always been an elite pursuit; and Hinduism's strict hierarchies, denying status to lower castes, have long encouraged them to desert it for the totally egalitarian Islam. Now this badge of Brahman intellectuals is paraded as the banner for a popular mass movement that demolishes mosques as a crass and simple assertion of Hindu power.

Sanskrit's career is not over, although the exclusively Indian world-view that has underlain its distinctive character over the past 3500 years probably is. Nonetheless, it coexists in India with a large family of modern daughter languages, and carries on in its own right as the sacred language of two world religions, Hinduism and Buddhism.

---

* For the view from the English side, see Chapter 12, 'Changing perspective—English in India', p. 501.

It is a language of paradox. Perhaps it is technically extinct, since there can be few if any infants who pick it up as their first language. Yet it continues to be transmitted to the next generation by an artificial system of rote learning and grammatical analysis that has somehow proved as robust as the natural way—and far less liable to introduce change.

Sanskrit has always been very much a garden variety of language, but in the tropical climate where it has flourished the gardeners have always chosen to encourage its luxuriant side.

adharaḥ kisalayarāgaḥ komalaviṭapānukāriṇāu bāhu
kusumam iva lobhanīyaṃ yauvanam angeṣu saṃnaddham

Truly her lower lip glows like a tender leaf, her arms resemble flexible stalks.
And youth, bewitching like a blossom, shines in all her lineaments.

Kālidāsa, Śākuntalā Recognized, i.21

6

Three Thousand Years of Solipsism:
The Adventures of Greek

Spartans to Athenians (urging an alliance to resist the Persians, 480 BC):

... βαρβάροισί ἐστι οὔτε πιστὸν οὔτε ἀληθὲς οὐδέν.

...barbároisí esti oúte pistòn oúte alēthès oudén.

Barbarians have nothing trustworthy or true.

Athenians to Spartans (in reply):

... οὔτε χρυσός ἐστι γῆς οὐδαμόθι τοσοῦτος οὔτε χώρη κάλλει καὶ ἀρετῇ μέγα ὑπερφέρουσα, τὰ ἡμεῖς δεξάμενοι ἐθέλοιμεν ἂν μηδίσαντες καταδουλῶσαι τὴν Ἑλλάδα. πολλά τε γὰρ καὶ μεγάλα ἐστὶ τὰ διακωλύοντα ταῦτα μὴ ποιέειν μηδ' ἢν ἐθέλωμεν, ... αὖτις δὲ τὸ Ἑλληνικόν ἐὸν ὅμαιμόν τε καὶ ὁμόγλωσσον, καὶ θεῶν ἱδρύματά τε κοινὰ καὶ θυσίαι ἤθεά τε ὁμότροπα, τῶν προδότας γενέσθαι Ἀθηναίους οὐκ ἂν εὖ ἔχοι.

...oúte chrusós esti gē̃s oudamóthi tosoũtos oúte chórē kállei kaì aretē̃i méga huperphérousa, tà hēmeĩs dexámenoi ethéloimen àn mēdísantes katadoulō̃sai tèn Helláda. pollá te gàr kaì megála estì tà diakōlúonta taũta mè poiéein mēd' èn ethélōmen,...aũtis dè tò Hellēnikòn eòn hómaimón te kaì homóglōsson kaì theō̃n hidrúmatá te koinà kaì thusíai étheá te homótropa, tō̃n prodótas genésthai Athēnaíous ouk àn eũ ékhoi.

There is nowhere so much gold or a country so outstanding in beauty and merit that we should be willing to take it as a reward for going over

227

to the Medes and so enslaving Greece. In fact there are many important things stopping us from doing that even if we wanted to... and then again there is Greekness, being of the same blood and language, and having shared shrines and rituals of the gods, and similar customs, which it would not be right for the Athenians to betray.

Herodotus* viii.142–4

Καὶ τώρα τί θὰ γένουμε χωρὶς βαρβάρους; Οἱ ἄνθρωποι αὐτοὶ ἦσαν μιὰ κάποια λύσις.

ke tóra ti tha yénume xorís varvárus? i ánthropi aftí ísan mya kápya lísis.

And now what will become of us without barbarians? These people were some sort of a solution.

Constantine Kavafis, *Waiting for the Barbarians*, 1949, ll.35–6

After the stately self-possession of Chinese and Egyptian, the sensuous prolixity of Sanskrit, and the innovative absolutisms of the Near Eastern languages, Greek makes a much more familiar, not to say modern, impression. This is the language of the people who brought wine, olive oil and literacy to the Mediterranean world, who invented logic, tragic drama and elective government, famed as much for competitive games as for figurative arts of striking realism. All of Europe became directly or indirectly their students. The dictionaries of European languages are all full of words borrowed from Greek to express Greek concepts and artefacts, and their grammars too, when they came to be written down, were organised on Greek principles.

Yet the history of the Greek language itself is far more complex and beguiling than its net influence would suggest. It was played out as much in the Near East as in the Mediterranean, in areas that are today all but purged of any trace of Greek. Like English, it was spread through a variety of means—speculative commerce, naked imperialism, cultural allure; and the means were very different in the long-term durability of what they achieved.

---

* In this chapter, Greek names in the text are given in the conventional Latinised form: hence not *Hēródotos, Akhaiós* but *Herodotus, Achaeus*. In the romanised transcription, h has much the same force as in English, but is often used to aspirate a consonant: kh, ph, th could more accurately have been written k^h, p^h, t^h, in fact as in English 'Can Pete take it?' Except in diphthongs, *au, eu*, the Greek *u* was pronounced in Attic much as it is today in French, phonetically [y]; *ou* was a long ū, as in English *rune*. The accents in Greek up to the early centuries AD give some image of the pattern of tone, not stress; thereafter they just mark the stressed syllable.

Above all, Greek stands as an example of a classical language that ran its course, fostered with a self-regarding arrogance that for over a thousand years its neighbours were happy to endorse, giving it their military support as they accepted the benefits of its more advanced culture and technology. These powerful, but impressed, neighbours included the Roman empire and the Christian Church. Greek's influence was eclipsed only when it ran out of new alliances, and was forced to face alone an unsympathetic enemy which drew its cultural support elsewhere. It is an instructive example of what can happen to a prestige language when its community ceases to innovate, and the rest of the world catches up.

Greek at its acme

The high point of Greek expansion came for a century or so approaching the close of the first millennium BC. Then the language could be heard on the lips of merchants, diplomats and soldiers from Emporiai (modern Ampurias), a trading post in the north-east corner of modern Spain, to Palibothras (*Pāṭaliputra*, modern Patna) in India, a distance of 40,000 *stadia*, or 8,000 kilometres, approaching a quarter of the circumference of the globe. Within this range, and over 80 per cent of its extent, there was a continuous band of lands under Greek-speaking administration, all to the east of the Greek home-land in the south Balkans, and extending as far as what is now Pakistan. This total expanse of Greater Greece, the Hellenised world, had been built up over about seven hundred years, without the benefit of any technology but the ship, the shoe, the wheel, the road, the horse, and writing.

This de facto world language had a currency that ranged over half a dozen distinct empires and kingdoms of the time. Known as *hē koinḗ diálektos*— 'the common talk'—or simply the *koinē*, Attic Greek, the particular dialect of the city of Athens, had become current all over the eastern Mediterranean. In Greece too it was gradually replacing all the twenty dialects that had flourished up until the fourth century BC. Probably this levelling began through the commercial prestige of Athens itself, with Piraeus, its port, giving an Attic linguistic tinge to the hub of intra-Greek trade. Pericles, who had presided over Athens' glory days in the mid-fifth century BC, had already boasted to his fellow-Athenians of a prosperity that allowed them to benefit from the produce of the whole earth. As more outsiders felt the need to learn Greek, and Greeks themselves began to have an outlook wider than their own city, Attic Greek spread.

And despite the different means of achieving its spread, it was already elic-

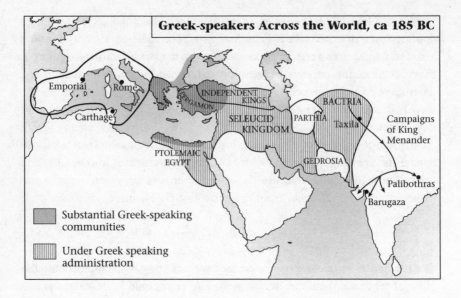

Greek-speakers Across the World, ca 185 BC

iting some of the same attitudes that English evokes today. A political pamphlet of the fifth century had claimed that while Greeks in general used each their own dialect, Athenians spoke a mixture of all of them, and all barbarian languages too.[1] In a comedy of the second century, written by the Macedonian Posidippus, a Thessalian (from the north of Greece) reproaches the Athenians for seeing all Greek as Attic. Athenians had some of the same problems in taking the rest of Greece seriously that Greeks in general had with the rest of the world. If they failed to speak proper Greek, they were, after all, no better than barbarians.*

Who is a Greek?

Tí dè tis? Tí d' ou tis? Skiãs ónar ánthrōpos.

What is someone? What is no one? A shadow's dream is man.

Pindar, Pythian Odes, viii.95–6

---

* As it happens, this pre-eminence of Attic was the result of cultural and commercial, not military, dominance. Athens, as we have seen, was early a major trading centre. But until the fifth century Greek literature had been the joint product of many different dialects.

Until their independence in AD 1821, the Greeks had only ever been united politically in the aftermath of joint conquest by some outsider. This happened for the first time in the fourth century BC, when the outsider was Philip, the king of Macedon on their northern border. Nevertheless, over the previous thousand years other civilisations encountering the Greeks appear always to have seen them as members of a single ethnic group.

In a way, this was strange, since outsiders always knew them simply by the tribal name of the group they happened to encounter. The Greeks' shared name for themselves, *Héllēnes*, never caught on outside Greece.* The Persians knew them as *Yauna*, for their encounter was with the Ionian Greeks, who are called *Iáwones* in Homer, the earliest Greek attested.† At the opposite end of the Greek world, the Romans got to know the Greeks as *Graii*. They were meeting Greek colonists from Euboea and Boeotia, who were setting up a new city of Cyme in Italy (later known by the Romans as Cumae). In fact, *Graii* seems to memorialise a small town in southern Boeotia called Graia.§ The word *Greek* comes through the Latin *Graecus*, a straightforward adjective formed from this name (from *Grai-icus*), and came to take over from the original *Graii*.¶

---

* It was the name for some of Achilles' people in Homer's *Iliad* (ii.684), and since he was the greatest Greek hero in that greatest of Greek poems, this may have been sufficient to name the whole race by association.

† w, written as ϝ in some Greek alphabets, dropped out of pronunciation (and hence spelling) in most dialects. Hence the w in this Homeric word is, strictly speaking, conjectural. *Iōnes* is the same word, with a common contraction of a+o into ō. Later the Indians came to call the Greeks *yavana* too—although their first major encounter was with a warlike force led by Macedonians.

§ Near Oropus, which is on the coast facing Eretria, according to Strabo, ix.2.10.

¶ Two other ethnonyms for *Greek*, seemingly much older, are *Danaoi* and *Akhaioi*. They are the words used by their ethnic poet Homer, writing some time in the early first millennium BC. The name *Danaoi* has associations with the city of Argos, a major city at the time when Homer represents Greece. Danaos is a legendary king of that city. *Akhaioi*, when it is used specifically, refers either to the people of an area in the north of the Peloponnese, with no particular claim to representative status, or to the people of Phthiotis, which is also notable in Homer as another part of the kingdom of Achilles (*Iliad*, ii.684). Its Latin form, *Achîvî*, shows that it originally had a W at the end of the stem (hence really '*Akhaiwoi*'). But in this form, with an inversion of the A and I, as *Ahhiyawa*, it does seem to figure as a term for a major kingdom in other documents, namely the royal correspondence (in cuneiform on baked clay tablets) of the Hittites who dominated Anatolia in the second millennium BC. So it seems that, early on, the Greeks were known abroad by yet another name.

Both these terms may have been used by the Egyptians. There is an inscription *c*.1370 BC (on a statue base in a funerary temple of Amenophis III) which mentions the TNY along with a variety of other names locatable in Crete. Egyptian hieroglyphics usually omit vowels, and i or y between vowels is often lost in Greek, so this could be an explicit reference to the *Danaioi*. In another inscription *c*.1186 BC, the DNYN are mentioned as one of the Sea-Peoples attacking Egypt. But in an earlier inscription *c*.1218 BC, the IKWS, which could just possibly be the *Akhaiwoi* or *Ahhiyawa*, are mentioned as allies in the resistance against the Sea-Peoples (Strange 1980; Muhly et al. 1982).

What, then, was a Greek, by any of these appellations? Although the main criterion was language, there was a general feeling that Greeks had much more in common than that. In a famous passage of Herodotus, the Athenians are made to explain why they will never betray Greece.[2] They advert to *tò Hellēnikón*, 'Greekness', which is defined as having the same blood and the same language, common shrines of deities, common rituals and similar customs. Common blood, of course, was not something that could be proved or ascertained objectively, though there would have been a feeling for facial features and no doubt skin colour. Common language was evident through mutual intelligibility of all the Greek dialects. As for common service to common gods, the Olympian pantheon was validated in the narrative of the Homeric epics and other hymns, even if the actual practice of cults in different places could be quite unique. Respect for common oracles where prophetic insight could be sought, the most notable being Apollo's oracle at Delphi, and attendance at the quadrennial Olympic games (whose records of victors extend back to 776 BC) were two other major institutions that bound the Greeks together.*

In fact, the Greeks always felt that there was a rational basis that set them apart from the *bárbaroi*, the rest of humanity, whose varying speech could just be thought of as an elaboration of 'bar-bar', hardly worth distinguishing from the noises made by animals.† Anything foreign was felt somehow to be ridiculous.

So the historian Herodotus describes the language of the Ethiopian Trogodytes (*sic*) as sounding like screeching bats,[3] and in the midst of a serious tragedy[4] Queen Clytaemnestra—admittedly a picture of condescending arrogance—conjectures that Cassandra, the Trojan princess, may speak an unknown language like that of swallows. Even Strabo himself, cosmopolitan geographer of the Mediterranean world in the time of Julius Caesar, writes in the midst of his gazeteer of the peoples of Spain (3.3.7): 'I am loath to go on about the names, conscious of the unpleasantness of them written down, unless someone could actually enjoy hearing of the Pleutauroi, the Bardyetai or the Allotriges, or other names even fouler and more meaningless.'

---

* These were not the only pan-Hellenic games: two others were the Pythian games in Delphi, and the Isthmian games, organised by Corinth.

† The only known case where early Greeks took a less ethnocentric view of their language was in Egypt: there is a graffito from 591 BC, written by a Greek mercenary on the leg of a statue at Abu Simbel. He refers to the Greeks among his party as *alloglōssous*, 'of another language', i.e. than the Egyptians. And Herodotus too uses this term of Greeks in Egypt (2.154). Contrast the more typical attitude of Strabo (vi.1.2), viewing Romans in Italy as still barbarians by contrast with the Greeks there.

There are many classic texts where Greeks have set out their ideals. Outstanding among them is Thucydides' account of Pericles' Speech for the War Dead made in 431 BC.[5] Pericles was the leader of Athens who built the Parthenon and led the city into its great war against Sparta. This speech is an attempt to summarise Athens' contribution to civilisation, not claiming that the city was like others, but rather setting them an example (*parádeigma*). He talks of a free approach to politics which is open to all, however poor, of tolerance in private life, of the enjoyment of public entertainments. He glories in the city's military accomplishments, but no less in the fact that they do not (unlike their main enemy, Sparta) make a fetish of military preparedness. All lies in striking the right balance; in a very Greek phrase, he says:

philokaloũmen met' euteleías kaì philosophoũmen áneu malakías

we are beauty-lovers with a sense of economy, and wisdom-lovers without softness.

Overall, he said, the whole city of Athens was an education to Greece.[6] Art, value for money, wisdom and physical prowess: that is what Athens liked to think it stood for. (And as for love of wisdom, Greek does not easily distinguish between philosophy and appreciation of cleverness.)

Evidently, these reflected an optimistic statement of Athenian ideals. Beautiful and wise deeds were not conspicuous in the conduct of the war that followed, and which indeed Athens went on to lose. Nevertheless, Pericles had been right to see Athens as an education to Greece: although it gradually lost political importance in the century that followed his speech, it never lost its status as the focus of Greek culture. It remained a city where serious students would come to study for the next thousand years, always in Greek, even though they might come from anywhere in the Roman empire, or beyond.

In fact Athens' intellectual leadership lasted until Christianity came to resent its continuing self-confidence and fidelity to its pre-Christian open-mindedness. The Roman emperor Justinian closed the school at Athens in AD 529. But the pre-eminence of its language remained, throughout the eastern Mediterranean, for another thousand years.

What kind of a language?

Andròs kharaktèr ek lógou gnōrízetai

A man's type is recognised from his words.

Menander[7]

ēthos anthrṓpōi daímōn

Character for man is fate.

Heraclitus[8]

The language that so united the known (Western) world, especially its educated members, over all those centuries was a complex organism that made few concessions, if any, to foreign learners. Its words were polysyllabic, with complex clusters of consonants (*p^{h}t^{h}árthai*, 'to be destroyed', *tlēmonéstatos*, 'most wretched', *stlengís*, 'scraper' (used with oil at bath-time), *sp^{h}rāgídion*, 'signet ring', *glisk^{h}rós*, 'sticky').

Speakers needed to tell long vowels from short, plain consonants from breathy ones, and be able to manage elaborate systems of prefixes and suffixes, where an ordinary noun would have nine different forms, and an adjective nineteen, and a verb well over two hundred. There were, of course, regularities in the system, but they fought a losing battle: there were ten major patterns for nouns, ten more for adjectives, and besides ten different patterns for verbs, there were well over 350 individual verbs that were irregular somewhere. These complex inflexions, taken together with the tendency to compound terms (as seen in Pericles' remarks quoted), meant that words could become very long, a characteristic that sometimes amused the Greeks themselves: the longest on record, a term for a gastronomical masterpiece, comes in a fifth-century BC comedy:[9]

lopadotemakhoselakhogaleokranioleipsanodrimhypotrimmatosilphiok
arabomelitokatakekhumenokikhlepikossuphophattoperisteralektruono
ptokephalliokinklopeleiolagōiosiraiobaphētraganopterúgōn.

But words ten letters long and more occur in almost every sentence of every text. And proper names, which are themselves very often clearly analysable as compound nouns, are particularly heavyweight.

Together with complexity of individual words went the flexibility of

Greek style: within a clause, word order was almost totally free, and so it was largely the endings of the nouns, adjectives and verbs, marking gender, case, number and person, which made clear the relationships between the meanings of words: who did what to whom, what in effect was being said. Here art began to take over from nature: the elaboration of Greek prose style by the *sophistaí* ('wise-guys', as professional pundits were known) meant that sentences, especially in fine speaking, tended to become ever longer and more ramified, with artfully balanced clauses, in the so-called *léxis katestramménē*, 'constrained style', so widely admired by Greek audiences.

The language in those centuries BC would have sounded very different from Greek as spoken today. The main reason for this was the fact that it was tonal, each word given a distinctive melody of high and low tones, in a way that is most closely paralleled today by accent in Japanese. The system gradually broke down in the first few centuries AD, but was transmuted rather than disappeared: nowadays Greeks stress the same syllable that used to have high tone.

Overall, it seems to have been the complexities in sound structure, rather than grammar, which pressed hardest on language-learners. Most of the mistakes we find in correspondence from around the turn of the millennium (usually on sheets of papyrus preserved in Egypt) concern spelling: above all, they were already finding it difficult to keep many of the various high vowels and diphthongs apart (*i, ei, ē, oi, u*). Sure enough, all these distinct sounds have merged as *i* in the modern language. The noun and verb systems held up remarkably well: they have been simplified to an extent, but to this day the typical Greek noun still has five or six forms, and the verb twenty.*

One feature of the language community up until the second century BC was its disunity. In the second and early first millennia BC, Greek had developed in small communities all over the south of the Balkans and the Aegean islands and coastline; many of these communities were isolated by sea and mountain, and until they began to develop specialised economies, their size must have remained small. The result was a tendency for individual dialects to develop and go off in their own directions, a pattern that was further complicated when a large-scale migration brought the Doric Greeks out of the north and into the centre of the Peloponnese. Greeks remained able to intercommunicate throughout, but until the events of the fifth century BC, individual communities, *póleis*, as they were called, remained independent; local

---

* Compare the figures for modern spoken English: two forms for most nouns (*word, words*), four for most verbs (*talk, talks, talked, talking*).

pride flowered, and with it a self-conscious use of local dialects. Before there was a common external threat, or any power with a military superiority sufficient to submerge their independence, ties among Greeks remained on the level of a sense of shared ancestry and religion. Shared festivals, and a shared literature, reminded them of a common heritage: but the initiative remained with the individual cities, each with their own hinterland of farms, pastures and fisheries.

Typically, when the Greeks of the ancient world looked for knowledge about their own history, they turned to poetry, and particularly to Homer, whose *Iliad* and *Odyssey*, together with a host of hymns addressed to particular gods, largely defined their conception of the past. More such literature is attributed to Hesiod, who is a less shadowy figure from around 700 BC; but there was great dispute in the ancient world about which was the earlier. Hellēn, the eponymous forefather of the Greeks, was said to have had three sons, Aeolus, Xuthus and Dorus. Hesiod wrote:[10]

Héllēnos d' egénonto philoptolemou basilēos | Dǒrós te Xoūthós te kai Aíolos hippiokhármēs

And of war-loving king Hellēn were born | Dōrus and Xuthus and Aeolus the chariot-fighter.

Xuthus then had two sons of his own, Ion and Achaeus. This neatly accounted for the origin of the four major dialect groups recognised in antiquity, namely Aeolic, Doric, Ionic and Achaean. These major groupings were felt to define the highest level of kinship among the Greeks as a whole, and they have something in common with the dialect relationships recognised when Greek inscriptions began to be studied objectively in modern times: at least Ionic, Aeolic and Doric are major groups. The main supplement needed is to recognise an Arcado-Cyprian group, since the dialects of Arcadia in the central Peloponnese and Cyprus are almost identical, and very different from the neighbouring Dorian dialects in Sparta and Crete. Theories about how the different groups came to occupy their various parts of Greece remain purely speculative.

One of the important features of Greek culture was a tendency to formalise its linguistic productions, thereby creating styles and genres in which writers could go on to compose consciously. So heroic lays were pulled together and integrated, producing the epic style consummated by Homer. Travellers' tales were organised and then presented as the first works of geography and history. Choral songs sung for inspiration at public gatherings, such as ath-

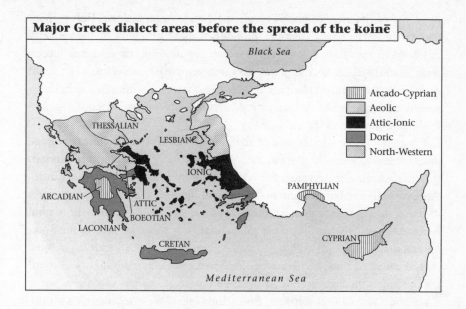

Major Greek dialect areas before the spread of the koinē

letic games, were preserved as lyric poetry. Religious liturgy, which had been performed regularly to expound and enact the myths of particular gods, was transformed into drama; the celebrants would now be seen as actors, their words not rituals but examinations of the situations set up in the ancient stories. This gave rise to the first tragedy. Above all, the public discussions of city policy, and examinations of those suspected of crimes, became regularised into the practice of public speaking: training was given by those who were particularly interested in it, and the field of rhetoric was born, probably the most influential intellectual discipline in ancient Western history. Other conversations, on more general themes, when written up became the foundation of philosophy.*

A striking characteristic of most of these early products of Greek literature (all well established by the end of the fourth century BC) is their 'public' character: they arise from language used in a public context, and they are

---

* The fact that Greek speech was so dialectally riven at the time had an interesting impact on these styles and genres: for the first few centuries after written literature began, each became associated with a particular dialect, typically that of its first practitioners, even though the literature was largely shared. So epic poetry had to be written in Homer's mixture of Ionic and Aeolic, lyric poetry in Doric, history at first in Ionic, tragedy in Attic. This played some role in perpetuating knowledge of the dialects, even after the increasing unity of the Greek world was pushing them out of actual use in conversation. It is a particularly good example of how so much of a language's flavour comes purely by association.

largely about matters of public concern.* This is of a piece with the political context of early Greek history: although the constitutions of the different *poleis* were very varied, and very few were egalitarian democracies, a common property of the societies was openness. Open assemblies were frequent, and the expectation was that all citizens (excluding women, children, slaves and foreigners) would take an active part—if only as a member of a mob—in the political life of the community. Greek, therefore, began its spread as a language for the public-spirited. And in much the same way as one sees in the political media in modern democracies, the pursuit of public affairs becomes the stuff of mass entertainment: on one famous occasion, an orator in the Athenian assembly accused his public of being *theataì mèn tõn lógōn, akroataì dè tõn érgōn*, 'spectators of speeches, listeners to events', i.e. paying more attention to what they were told, and how it was said, than to their own common sense.[11]

The outward-looking nature of the Greek-speaking community is worth contrasting with that of another prestige language, which was spreading at much the same time—Sanskrit. Both languages developed significant theories of language use. But Sanskrit's theory, as we have seen, was aimed at preservation of the details of religious texts; as such, it was focused on the minutiae of the language's grammar and pronunciation, with little to offer to improve communication with other people. Greek linguistic theory (until the school requirements of the Roman empire take over†) is focused above all on the effective use of language to persuade others: native command of the grammatical details tends to be assumed (despite their complexity), and the theorists talk rather about the construction of a case at law, or (if philosophically inclined) about the form of a valid argument. One could say that whereas Indian linguistic theory is an exercise in disinterested analysis, the Greek theories are always close to practical application.

---

* This early Greek range is very different from the genres of medieval and modern European literature. There is no novel, no essay, no fantasy literature. Neither is there any literature devoted to religious devotion. As it happens, the first three of these were all Greek inventions too, but from a much later period, in the first centuries AD, when Greece was an enforced part of the Roman empire, and there was no serious expectation of a public career or public responsibilities. Affluent individuals were then free to explore more personal concerns, to write romances, and descriptions of personal adventures. Likewise, explorations of individual religious experience were alien to the Greek spirit in these earlier days, although they were later to become central after the spread of Christianity. The religious outpourings of the earlier period take the form of hymns to the Olympian gods, with an emphasis on recounting their myths.

† Greek analysis of grammar was essentially complete when Dionysius the Thracian, working in Alexandria, the intellectual centre of Greece at the time, published his compilation of Stoic and Alexandrian work as *Tékhnē Grammatiké* at the beginning of the first century BC.

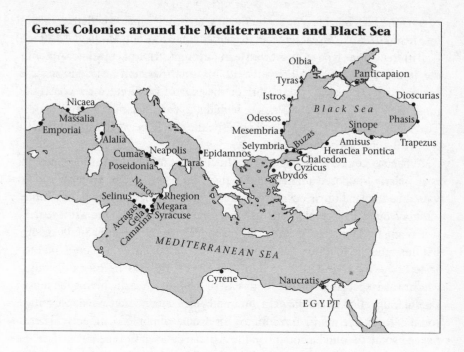

Greek Colonies around the Mediterranean and Black Sea

Homes from home: Greek spread through settlement

The Greek language was spread from its historic home, the southern Balkan peninsula and Aegean islands, through two processes, one piecemeal, long lasting and diffuse in its direction, the other organised, sudden and breathtakingly coherent. One is usually known as the Greek colonisation movement; the other is Alexander's conquest of the Persian empire.

The first process, the colonisation of the Mediterranean and Black Sea coasts by Greek cities, lasted from the middle of the eighth to the early fifth century BC. The question why, of all the inhabitants of these shores, only the Greeks and the Phoenicians set up independent centres in this way has never been answered. The foundations clearly served a variety of purposes, as political safety valves, as trading posts for raw materials, and as opportunities to apply Greek agriculture to more abundant and less heavily populated soil, but it is noteworthy that they are exclusively coastal, never moving inland except on the island of Sicily. The Greek expansion came after the period of Phoenician settlements (eleventh to eighth centuries), so it may be that the most important factor was who had effective control of the sea. Although by the end of the period almost all available Mediterranean coasts had been populated, it was the western end which loomed largest in the Greek conception of what had been achieved: southern Italy and Sicily, par excellence, made up *Megálē Héllas*, 'Great Greece', usually named in Latin *Magna Graecia*.

Different cities tended to specialise in different strips of coastline. Among the Ionians, Chalcis and Eretria went for south-western Italy and north-eastern Sicily; Phocaea (itself a city on the edge of Lydia) took the coasts of modern Spain, Corsica and France, including *Massalia* (now Marseilles).* The south Aegean city of Miletus covered the whole perimeter of the Black Sea, with nineteen colonies.

Achaeans largely took over the south-eastern coast of Italy. This country is popularly supposed to have been given its name by the Greeks: *Italia* would be the land of *(w)italoí*, 'yearling cattle', a dialectal variant of *etaloí*, later borrowed in fact into Latin as *vituli*, and still with us in the word *veal*.

Among the Dorians, Corinth, Megara and Rhodes all targeted Sicily again, but this time the south-east and south. Sparta placed one colony only, on the instep of Italy (*Táras*, the modern Taranto).† Besides its role in Sicily, Megara also specialised in the south-east of the Black Sea, including the most fateful foundation of all, *Búzas*, a thousand years later chosen as a new capital for the Roman empire, Byzantium§ or Constantinople. Uniquely, Thera headed south to found a colony on the African coast at Cyrene.¶

Although colonies (*apoikíai*—literally 'homes-from-home') were generally led by a 'home-builder', *oikistés*, from the 'mother city' or *mētrópolis*—with whom there would be a historic and emotional, though not political or military, bond—their founding populations might be recruited from a number of cities, so the new foundations could be quite mixed in population, although less so in dialect. The inscriptions suggest that the language spoken was almost always close to that of the metropolis.[12] One could compare the

---

* It also had one colony on the Black Sea coast of Anatolia, Amisūs, modern Samsun.

† Although not prohibited by Carthaginian or Phoenician influence, the Adriatic received rather little attention from Greek colonists, and was not identified with a particular metropolis. However, it was de facto a Dorian area. Three major cities here were Epidamnos, later Dyrrhachium (now Durrazzë in Albania), founded by Corinth and the neighbouring island of Corcyra *c.*625 BC; Atria, in the Po delta, founded in late sixth century BC by Aegina (a Dorian city later cleared and repopulated by Athens); and Ancona, an Umbrian city later refounded by Greek refugees from Syracuse in 387 BC. (The promise of the Venetian lagoon was not exploited in antiquity.)

§ For all its stately sound, this name (*Buzántion*) is just the diminutive of *Búzas*, as if *Hongkers* had become the official name of Hong Kong.

¶ Cyrene, founded *c.*630, specialised in the growth and export of *sílphion*, a medicinal plant. But Greek was also to be heard farther east on the African shore, where a rather different kind of enterprise was established. Naucratis, 'Sea-Queen', was a pan-Hellenic emporium in the Nile delta, a centre for trade with the Egyptian market, in a trading concession allowed by the pharaoh. The initiative here had come from Ionian Greeks, from Miletus and Samos, conveniently sited just to the north. (See Chapter 4.)

continued dominance of English in North America, even though English colonists were outnumbered by speakers of other languages in the nineteenth century (see p. 492).

The immediate effects of this movement were arguably more cultural than linguistic. The areas were not uninhabited before the newcomers arrived, and the local populations (among them Gauls, Etruscans, Romans, Scyths and Armenians) did not fade away over time.* Although the Greeks dominated their coastal regions, and many colonies put out offshoots to create new colonies in the same region, they never became the focus for states on a larger scale. (Contrast this with the powerful self-aggrandisement, over this period and later, of Carthage, once a Phoenician colony.) The colonies, especially in Sicily and southern Italy, were famed for their wealth, and their scientific culture: Parmenides, Zeno, Pythagoras, Xenophanes, Empedocles and Archimedes were all Greeks of the west. Political innovation was not a particular forte.†

The colonies in fact became bridgeheads for Greek culture into the western Mediterranean and Black Sea; and this separate scattered Greek presence continued for close on a thousand years. Strabo, at the end of the first century BC, wrote: 'But now except for Taras and Rhegion and Neapolis [Taranto, Reggio and Naples], all [of Magna Graecia] has been "barbarised out",§ and some parts are taken by Lucanians and Bruttians, and others by Campanians. But that is just in name; in fact by Romans—for that is what they have become.'[13] The three cities mentioned are supposed to have retained their Greekness for another couple of centuries. And Greek is spoken to this day in the extreme toe and heel of Italy in two tiny enclaves: Bovesia in Calabria (south-east of Reggio), and the villages Calimera and Martano south of Lecce in Puglia.

The colonies played a cardinal role in introducing neighbouring peoples of Gaul and Italy to writing: from Massalia on the French Riviera, Gauls learnt to write their own language in Greek characters; Pithecusae (Ischia) and

---

* An exception to this tendency for indigenous populations to survive Greek settlement was Sicily, where the Greek presence must have been particularly dense. They had at least thirteen separate colonies there, and the western end of the island was in the hands of another foreign incomer, Carthage, with three more. Nevertheless, the pre-existing Sicans, Elymians and Sicels had been very much a factor when land was originally sought for the new cities.

† Such political fame as they acquired was associated with experiments in tyrannous megalomania, notably those of Dionysius of Syracuse (430–367 BC) and Agathocles of Acragas (361–284 BC), both of whom organised Greek wars against Carthage with zero net effect.

§ *ekbebarbarōsthai*: it had been two hundred years since Rome had conquered Greece, and begun its attempt to assimilate its culture; yet a Greek—and one educated at Rome at that—still classed Romans as barbarians.

Cumae on the south-western coast taught the Etruscans first of Campania, and hence of the whole centre and north of Italy; a little farther south, Paestum (Poseidonia) could pass literacy on to the Oscans in Lucania, and over in the heel, Taras to the Messapians in Calabria. Most significant of all was one indirect path of such education: as well as many others in north Italy (for example, the Insubrian Gauls in the foothills of the Alps), the Etruscans went on to teach their great adversaries the Romans to read and write. Through an elaborate cascade of successful conquests and commercial infiltrations over the next twenty-seven centuries, the Roman alphabet has become the most widely used in the world at large.

The alphabets that were passed on in this way were not today's Greek alphabet, which was to be effectively standardised in Athens in 403–402 BC,* and then adopted throughout Greece in the next generation.† At this earlier time in Greek history (from the eighth century BC), there were still competing variants favoured by different dialects, and most of the cities with colonies in Italy favoured the so-called Western alphabet, in which H was used to represent the aspirate consonant 'aitch', X not Ξ was used to represent [ks], the letters Θ Ξ Φ Ψ Ω were dropped, but F and Q were retained.§ This was the alphabet taken up by the Italians, though, as usual in an age before mass-produced writing, in various local versions. (Lepontic, Etruscan, Oscan, Umbrian, Faliscan and Messapian all had alphabets distinct from Latin's.)

Another cultural, and economic, boon of the Greek expansion was wine, now passed on to a very welcoming western Mediterranean—probably along with another luxury liquid, olive oil. Justin (43.4) represents the Phocaeans who founded Massalia as teaching the surrounding Gauls not just civic and urban life, but also how to tend vines.¶ Here again, it may be that indirect influence was more powerful than direct, for it is known that the Romans,

---

* This was a significant year for Athens, the first year of restored democracy after its conclusive defeat by Sparta in the Peloponnesian War.

† Athens adopted the Ionic alphabet as used in Miletus, in preference to their own 'Attic' style, which had not distinguished long E (H—eta) and long O (Ω—omega) from their short versions.

§ Q (*qoppa*) was originally a back [k] used before back vowels [o] and [u]. Early inscriptions use FH to represent [f], since F was originally a sign for [w] or [v]. Most of the Ionic dialects (including those at Miletus and Athens) had lost this sound, hence its disappearance from the offical Greek alphabet. But there is a bizarre twist here. Chalcis and Eretria, which founded Pithecusae and Cumae, actually spoke Ionic dialects, and so might have been expected to drop F in writing too.

¶ In principle, it is possible that this distinctive product of the eastern Mediterranean was brought to the west by the other great colonial civilisation, the Phoenicians, but the countries that became (and have remained to this day) pre-eminent in wine-making happen to be in the Greek sphere of influence, Italy and Gaul/France, rather than North Africa and Spain.

who had learnt of the vine from the Greeks, were extremely active in promoting it when they moved into Gaul, superseding the Greeks by taking it far beyond the Mediterranean coast.

At the other end of the then Greek world, the colonies round the Black Sea appear to have played a more integrated role in mainland Greek life, since they came to supply it both with wheat (grown on the vast fields of Scythia/Ukraine) and the all-consuming *opsa*, relishes made of dried fish, the most sought-after spices for the Hellenes.

The Greeks came to have a sneaking respect for the nomadic Scythians: like them they would see off an attempted Persian invasion. In general, they were quite impervious to Greek ways: but Herodotus recalls two who had a taste for things Greek, Anacharsis (who became a legendary sage) and Scyles. In both cases, ultimately it was the forbidden charms of Greek religious ceremonies to which they yielded: the Greeks were not then seen in their modern light, as the arch-rationalists of the ancient world.

Kings of Asia: Greek spread through war

Hoi huméteroi prógonoi elthóntes eis Makedonían kaì eis tèn állēn Helláda kakōs epoíēsan hēmãs oudèn proēdikēménoi; egō dè tòn Hellēnōn hēgemòn katastatheìs kaì timōrḗsasthai boulómenos Pérsas diébēn es tèn Asían, huparksántōn humõn...Kaì toũ loipoũ hótan pémpēis par' éme, hōs pròs basiléa tẽs Asías pémpe, mēdè ex ísou epístelle, all' hōs kuríōi ónti pántōn tõn sõn phráze eí tou déēi...

Your ancestors entering Macedonia and the rest of Greece wronged us without previous grievance; but I, constituted as leader of the Greeks and wishing to take vengeance on the Persians, have crossed into Asia, something that you people started...And in future when you send to me, send to me as King of Asia, and do not correspond on equal terms, but as to the lord of all that is yours, tell me if you need anything...

Alexander to Darius, king of Persia, 332 BC: Arrian, ii.14

About a quarter of the way through the three thousand years of Greek's recorded history came the single decade that changed everything.

Over the period 334–325 BC a Greek army under Alexander III of Macedon eliminated the Persian empire, over almost the whole area of the modern states of Turkey, Syria, Israel, Egypt, Jordan, Iraq, Kuwait, Armenia, Iran, Afghanistan and Pakistan. Alexander's declared motive was to take revenge

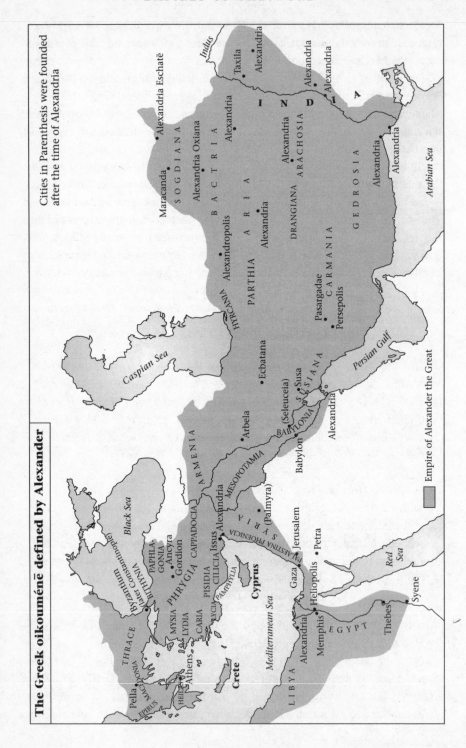

The Greek oikouménē defined by Alexander

Cities in Parenthesis were founded after the time of Alexandria

Empire of Alexander the Great

for Persian aggression in the Persian Wars, still very present in Greek minds, although they had been an experience of their great-great-grandparents, a century and a half before, and Greece at least was now under very different management. On the same timescale Britain should now be preparing for Russia's serious retaliation for the Crimean War.

The result of this lightning advance, the wholesale takeover by Greek military administrators of a multi-ethnic empire that had existed for over two hundred years, was an instant trebling of the area where the Greek language might be heard, and Greek cultural traditions known and appreciated. Unlike the colonial advance around the Mediterranean and Black Sea, this advance did not hug the coastline, but assumed supreme control over all the major established urban centres. Although the unitary control by a single ruler did not last (Alexander died two years after his momentous campaign, and his empire fell apart into the domains of his different marshals), Greek overlordship did survive. It lasted for a century in central Persia, until another Iranian-speaking power, this time the Parthians from south-east of the Caspian, reasserted control. But it was to be three hundred years before it relaxed its grasp on Egypt, Syria or Babylonia. And although Alexander's claim on the west bank of the Indus was almost immediately annulled by the advance of the equally magnificent Indian emperor Chandragupta ruling from Patna, Greek kings based in Bactria (Afghanistan) continued an independent dominion for about as long as those in Syria. They moved south into Gandhara (Swat) and the Panjab (in what is now Pakistan); though they lost hold of Bactria itself, for a time they even reached as far to the east as Patna on the Ganges.* In fact, Greek kingdoms lasted longer here than in Greece itself, where Macedonian kings yielded sovereignty to Rome after two centuries in 146 BC.

The process of Hellenisation in the realms conquered by Alexander created the heartland of a vast Greek-speaking community that would dominate the eastern Mediterranean for over a thousand years. It had already existed for half this time when it was recognised officially, in AD 286, on the formal division of the Roman empire into east and west. The eastern Roman empire then transmuted gradually into a consciously Greek empire: appropriately,

---

* This event is immortalised (along with other evidence, Greek and Indian) in two example sentences of the second-century Sanskrit grammarian Patañjali (3.2.111): *aruṇad yavanaḥ sāketam*, 'The Greek has besieged Saketa' (a city close to Faizabad on the Gaghra); *aruṇad yavanaḥ mādhyamikām*, 'The Greek has besieged Madhyamika' (a city close to Chittaurgarh, south of the Rajasthan desert). In each case, the sentence needs to be veridical in order to illustrate the point, that this tense (LaN, the imperfect) is used 'of a recent public occurrence not actually witnessed by the speaker but potentially so'. Since of these two only Saketa is actually on the way to Patna from the Panjab, it appears that the Greeks also campaigned farther south and west, in Rajasthan.

the word it used to describe itself, *rōmaîos*, 'Roman', has become a popular word that now means 'Greek'.*

Although Greeks were, for a long time, politically pre-eminent—never as democrats—all over this vast dominion, the actual spread of their language was probably much more patchy. For two hundred years, Aramaic, originally the lingua franca of Babylon and Canaan, had been the convenient standard for the whole Persian empire. As we have seen, its take-up had not been uniform. But Alexander's new subjects must have expected a separate, common, language, for imperial administration. Effective conversion from one such language to another, if it happened at all, cannot have been instant.

Reviewing the evidence from east to west, we can begin with Greek spoken in India. In the mid-third century BC, when the emperor Aśoka was setting up edicts urging the importance of *dhamma*, virtue, all over north and central India in the local vernacular, he chose at Kandahar to write the inscription in Aramaic and Greek. Kandahar was better known to Greeks as Alexandria of the Arachosians, founded by Alexander in 329, and Aśoka's rock edict is not the only Greek inscription to have been found there.[14] This would have been on, or beyond, the edge of his domain. Coin evidence is copious for the Greek monarchies of India, and this alleges some form of bilingualism, since the coins have Greek on one side, and an Indian Prakrit, written in Kharoṣthi script (another derivate of Aramaic script), on the other. In fact, Greek legends on coins continued for a century after the death of the last Greek king and queen, Hermaios and Calliope, who had ruled little more than Peshawar and the Khyber pass, and died about 30 BC. Since the government was by then in the hands of Śaka/Scythians, Pallava/Parthians and Kushāna, whose own (Iranian) languages stemmed from north of the Hindu Kush, this might argue for a persisting public of Greek speakers; but the Kharoṣthi Indian inscriptions on the coins continue too, so it might simply be an attempt to put the weight of tradition and continuity behind the currency, even as the real power moved into the hands of illiterate rulers.

Overall, the general picture is of a Greek-speaking government having relatively little impact on a populace persistently speaking Indian languages. Although both sides were literate, there is no record of bilingual grammars or dictionaries; and no account is given of what language was used when the most famous Greek king, Menander (Milinda to the Indians), engaged the sage Nagasena in a debate about Buddhism, recorded in the *Milindapañha*. Perhaps Prakrit-speaking Greeks were no great exception by then. Not long

---

* It is also the origin of the romantic boy's name *Romeo*.

afterwards a pillar was erected (at Besnagar in modern Madhya Pradesh) by Heliodorus, an ambassador from King Antialkidas in Taxila. It is all in Prakrit.[15] One hundred and fifty years earlier, Megasthenes had served as a Greek ambassador (sent by King Seleucus) at the court of Chandragupta in Patna from 302 BC, and he had been followed by Deimakhos from the next king (Antiochus I), and Dionysius, from the competing Greek domain of Egypt; all had written books about their experiences which became current in Alexandria on the Nile, now the fast-emerging centre of Greek learning.

Back in the kingdom of the Seleucid successors to Alexander (Persia, the Fertile Crescent and Anatolia), there is evidence that Greek became ingrained more widely and deeply than in India, though the picture is not uniform. For instance, although in the eastern area of Iran Greek power yielded within a century (c.230 BC) to the rising Parthians, the new rulers continued to issue their coins in Greek (occasionally too in Aramaic), only going over to Parthian (Pahlavi) legends in the first and second centuries AD, when the remaining Greek legends were becoming increasingly garbled. There are official documents written in Greek up until the fourth century.[16] But farther south, on the Persian Gulf, the small kingdom of Persis (in existence from 280 BC to AD 224) always issued its coins in Aramaic.

In the Fertile Crescent, Babylonia, Mesopotamia, Syria and Palestine, the Aramaic-speaking lands at the core of the old Assyrian empire, which became the actual centre of gravity of the new Seleucid government, the penetration of Greek was likewise significant, but seems to have led to a situation of more or less stable diglossia, people using different languages in different communities and for different purposes. Babylon, despite its strategic importance to the Seleucids, probably never had more than a small Greek community, and they and their language are unlikely to have flourished after the city was yielded to Parthia in AD 126. Edessa, modern Urfa, which came to be on the border with Parthia, maintained a strong Aramaic (Syriac) literary tradition throughout the Greek and Roman periods.

However, round northern Syria, Seleucus I made a serious attempt at establishing Greek colonies, which have by and large survived to the present day: Antioch (Antakya), Apamea (Hamah), Seleuceia (Silifke), and Laodiceia (Latakia). Antioch on the Mediterranean coast, which went on to a glorious career as capital of Roman Syria, started with a core of 5300 Athenians and Macedonians transplanted from a nearby Greek colony. Nevertheless, they always had a large Aramaic-speaking, as well as a Jewish, community. Nearby Palmyra seems to owe its Greek speakers (and its name—it was previously Tadmor) to the advent of Roman control (AD 17–19); and there is a famous Greek–Aramaic inscription on tariffs (AD 137) found there, to show that both languages had status. But nine hundred years later, when Greek control was ended by the Arab conquest, it appears that Greek had never spread outside these few cities.[17]

In Jerusalem, there was major trouble beginning in 168, led by Judas Maccabaeus,* involving resistance to the Seleucid government's perceived measures to Hellenise the Jews, although unsurprisingly the religious cult rather than the language aspect was to the fore. It led to the setting up of the Hasmonaean kingdom, which ruled Judaea from 142 to 63 BC, minimising Greek influence. Aramaic remained the dominant language in Palestine, with Hebrew restricted to liturgical use, and Greek interestingly assigned a role in the more cosmopolitan aspect of Jewry, and such spin-offs as the Christians. But as Acts of the Apostles, chapter 2, graphically recounts, every language still spoken in the Roman empire could be heard in the streets of Jerusalem at the time of the Passover festival.†

Greek texts of the Hebrew scriptures were in fact commissioned by Ptolemy II,§ the second in the Greek dynasty that ruled Egypt after Alexander's death. (He ruled 308–246 BC.) The process by which this was achieved is detailed, with some legendary accretions, in the Alexandrian 'Letter of Aristeas'. Whatever the true details, the Greek Septuagint (named—in Latin—for the seventy-two scholars supposedly summoned from Jerusalem to work on it) became an authoritative text of the Bible, and was widely used by Jews outside Palestine, as well as the later Christian movement. Greek therefore became the vehicle for a major culture outside its own traditions, freed from associations with Athenian *eleuthería* (or by now Macedonian magnificence), and in a sense thereby secularised as a language. On pragmatic grounds, it became able, when in later centuries the need was felt for new Christian scriptures to transmit to the wider world, to assume equivalent, and then superior, status to Aramaic.

In Egypt as a whole, although the Ptolemies, like all the Hellenistic Diadochi (*diádokhoi*—heirs of Alexander), relied on their armies to guarantee their authority, there was a major cultural project started to validate it. A Museum (*Mouseîon*—temple of the Muses) was established as a government-funded research institute, and the eternally famous Library, both close to the

---

* He would have hated the irony that he is generally known by this Latinised Greek version of his name. He was Judah the Hammer, *yəhūdāh maqqābā*.

† Visitors from Parthia, Media, Elam, Mesopotamia, Judaea, Cappadocia, Pontus, Asia Minor, Phrygia, Pamphylia, Egypt, and Libya around Cyrene, together with Romans, foreign Jews, Cretans and Arabs, are explicitly distinguished (Acts ii.9–10).

§ Known as *Philádelphos*, 'Lover of His Sister': indeed he married her, in an amazing Greek adoption of Egyptian pharaonic tradition.

royal palace in Alexandria, the newly founded capital city. These attracted Greek-speaking scholars from all over the *oikouménē*, the inhabited world. Coinage was issued in Greek, from a single mint, also at Alexandria. Greek was gradually introduced as a new language of administration, in this country with the longest tradition of central administration in the world.

Greek seems to have remained a language for the ruling elite in Egypt. Although the literature that came out of Alexandria (which is copious) developed new genres for talking in prose and verse about picturesque features of everyday life, the everyday life talked about always seems to be somewhere else, more traditionally Greek, such as in the Aegean islands or perhaps in Syracuse. The last of the Ptolemies, Cleopatra, who ruled from 51 to 30 BC, is said to have been the first of them to learn Egyptian.[18] So it was still worth learning; the popular language, even after three hundred years of Greek government, was still Egyptian.

Documentation of actual ancient correspondence is more copious here than anywhere else in the ancient world, because of the general use of papyrus, and the preservative power of the dry soils away from the Nile valley. These give occasional glimpses of how the use of Greek was perceived from outside the charmed circle of the immigrant Hellenes. So in the mid-third century BC, a couple of generations after the conquest, a letter to Zenon, the Carian manager of a farm in the Fayûm, complains (in Greek) that he is despised because he cannot speak Greek, or literally 'Hellenise' (*hellēnízein*).

In a way, the area least changed immediately by the new dispensation was Anatolia. But its conversion was to be the most long-lasting among Alexander's new provinces. We know from inscriptions and coins that the penetration of Aramaic had been variable here: strongest in Cilicia (the south-eastern region bordering its homeland in Syria), weakest on the south-western coasts, Lydia and Phrygia, and with some presence in bilingualism with Greek on the Black Sea. (See Chapter 3, 'Aramaic—the desert song: Interlingua of western Asia', p. 78.) The Greeks had been an influential presence on the periphery for at least a thousand years. They were now installed throughout, in what D. Musti calls a 'military monarchy', but allowing 'a privileged relationship for cities (*póleis*) and a much-trumpeted respect for their freedom and democracy (*eleuthería kaì dēmokratía*).'[19]

Although the Greek administration of the Seleucids was not to last more than two hundred years before yielding to the Romans, the language situation was much more consistent. For the next thousand years, Greek spread relentlessly, supplanting the local languages of the south coast and the interior. One example: although we still find inscriptions in Phrygian until the third century AD, local peasants' votive tablets to Zeus (available even to poor people because of the availability of marble offcuts from the quarry at Dokimeion) are from the second century AD all in Greek.[20]

And there was a hidden symmetry in this sudden spread of Greek into the east, for the Aramaic that remained Greek's principal competitor throughout the old Persian empire was a close relative of the Phoenician or, in Latin, Punic language, Greek's main competitor in the colonial world of the Mediterranean's western shores. Indeed, the two Semitic sisters had originated within a hundred miles of each other, their foci at Tyre and Damascus, in the west and centre of northern Syria. It was as if the entire region from Cadiz beyond the Pillars of Heracles to the banks of the Indus was now the field for a simple two-sided competition, between the Greek *koinē* and an alliance of Semitic twin sisters.

As one might expect from the self-centred Greeks, they never noticed.*

A Roman welcome: Greek spread through culture

Graecia capta ferum victorem cepit et artes | Induit agresti Latio ...

Greece, once captured, captured its wild conqueror, and instilled arts into boorish Rome ...   Horace, Letters, ii.1.156

In these two major spreads of Greek by migration and infiltration, the colonisation of Mediterranean coasts, and the results of Alexander's lightning conquest of the east, the prestige of the language and its culture played little, if any, role. Greeks had explored and settled; Greeks had conquered and settled. But the new populations who first heard Greek in consequence had little choice in the matter. A vast expansion of the world where Greek was spoken had come about in this way; but outside Anatolia, Syria and Egypt there is little evidence for its everyday use having spread much beyond the community of Greek émigrés.

Greek was poised, however, for a major surge of spread by diffusion. All round the Mediterranean, above all among the elite of the rising power of Rome, Greek culture was about to become the centre of the educational curriculum.

---

* Libanius, a Greek resident of Antioch in Syria in the fourth century AD, wrote sixty-four speeches which range over municipal, educational and cultural matters, as well as an autobiography and an encomium of the city. He mentions the existence of Aramaic just once, although it was spoken in the country all around (Mango 1980: ch. 1).

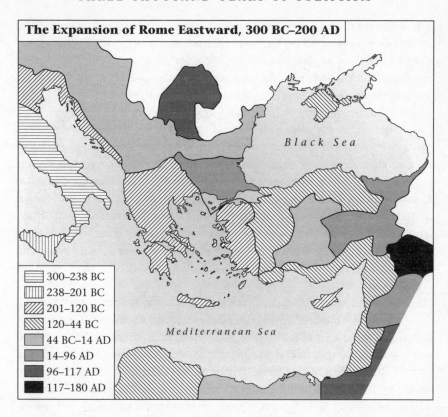

The Expansion of Rome Eastward, 300 BC–200 AD

Legend:
- 300–238 BC
- 238–201 BC
- 201–120 BC
- 120–44 BC
- 44 BC–14 AD
- 14–96 AD
- 96–117 AD
- 117–180 AD

Black Sea

Mediterranean Sea

Inevitably, the Greeks began with a cultural advantage on Mediterranean coasts, having brought the alphabet, and some display of what a literate society was like, Greek-style, with formal education and a curriculum based on a corpus of poetical classics (notably Homer) and active training in skills of public speaking. Then, in the third century BC, a number of political events brought the Greek-speaking eastern Mediterranean into active contact with the west. In 280 BC Pyrrhus (coming from Epirus, in western Greece) had tried to invade Italy and Sicily: his initial victories were proverbially pyrrhic, and within five years he was effectively seen off by dogged Roman resistance, but Roman garrisons were then placed in all the Greek cities of southern Italy. In 273 BC King Ptolemy II of Egypt entered into a treaty with Rome, sealing their new status as a coming power in the Mediterranean.

Bilingual authors began building a bridge between Greek and Roman literature. Greek plays were performed (in Latin translation) at Rome from 240 BC. Others, such as Livius Andronicus, tried adapting Greek master works such as the *Odyssey* for Roman audiences, but using traditional Roman language and patterns of verse. Late in the century came the tense days of the war with Hannibal: victory was followed by a vogue for Greek culture. (The victorious general, Publius Cornelius Scipio, was a notorious enthusiast for things Greek.) A leading figure was the poet Ennius, who had grown up speaking Greek in southern Italy, but learnt Latin during his army service: he brought Greek works and literary values into the heart of Latin education, beginning the refashioning of Latin literature on completely Greek lines.

Foreign policy reinforced the cultural interest, since Rome intervened decisively in Greece in the next century, famously taking advantage of one of the pan-Hellenic athletic meetings. In 196 BC the Roman general Flamininus announced to an incredulous crowd gathered for the Isthmian Games at Corinth that all the Greek cities were henceforth free, courtesy of the Roman Senate and people. There followed a complicated series of wars in which Rome was involved ever more deeply in Greek affairs, and which led to the downfall of the successors of Alexander in both Greece and Asia. By the end of the century, the whole of Greece and the west of Anatolia were under direct Roman rule.

The outcome was a total penetration of Greek into Roman culture, so that for the next five hundred years, essentially until the Greek east was split off from the Roman west of the empire, well-educated Romans could be counted on to be bilingual in Greek. Romans came to be educated basically on a Greek pattern, but with a strong emphasis on poetry and the practice of public speaking: the musical and gymnastic sides were rather neglected. The tutors and schoolmasters were typically bilinguals of Greek extraction; and one effect was a permanent demand for personable educated Greeks, who could find employment as educators all over the Mediterranean. Overall, the situation was comparable to the prospects for graduates from English-speaking countries in rich non-English speaking countries today. Educated Greeks often found that their language was their fortune.

As one example, in the first century BC Gaulish notables were sending their children to be educated in Greek in Massalia (Marseilles). Strabo says that 'sophists were employed, both privately and at the city's expense, just like medical doctors'.[21] Meanwhile it became usual for elite Romans of rich families to send their young people to Athens or Rhodes to finish their education. But this does not mean that knowledge of Greek was found only among the upper classes. Plautus, writing comedies in the early second century BC, puts most of his Greek loan words and slang into the mouths of slaves and low types: *graphicus servus*—the picture-perfect slave.[22]

Polybius, writing a generation later, could remark, perhaps making the best of things: 'our men of action in Greece have been released from the pressures of political or military ambition, and so have plenty of opportunities to pursue inquiries or research'.[23]

A century later, the implicit compact was stated more explicitly, from the Roman point of view, by Vergil:[24]

> others will hammer out more finely bronze that breathes
> (I do not doubt), will draw from marble faces live,
> will plead court cases better, and use rod to measure out
> the wanderings of the sky and constellations' rise;
> you, Roman, mind to rule peoples at your command
> (these arts will be yours), to impose the way of peace,
> to spare the conquered, and to battle down the proud.

The world of the arts and sciences was the Greek province, par excellence. But the world of power and order belonged to Rome. The civilisation of the Mediterranean world became a stable Graeco-Roman mix.*

It is worth spending a moment to consider what was the real attraction of Greek, and its associated culture, its character or ethos (both Greek words). The Romans certainly did not believe that they had much to learn about traditional virtues, as shown in war, law and politics, from these voluble and innovative foreigners.† Greek art, which had become familiar through the army's campaigns in southern Italy and Greece, was attractive in itself; but the Greeks also seemed to have an advantage in the pursuit of pleasure more generally: haute cuisine, wine, music, frolics with either sex. The Greeks were the masters of luxury, and it took little higher discernment to want more of this. The Latin word *pergraecārī*, 'to Greek off', meant devotion not to high thinking but to high living, feasting and drinking.[25]

At the same time, the sheer knowledge possessed by the Greeks impressed the Romans: Greeks knew their own history, as well as that of their neighbours, they could theorise on any topic, and provide quotations from poetry centuries old. Above all, they were fluent and convincing speakers: they had been trained in how to hold an audience, and get people to do what they wanted. This explicit skill in rhetoric was highly in demand in the civic society that the Romans had created, where people were constantly running for

---

* It is interesting from a modern standpoint—and indeed from a classical Indian one, concerned to distinguish the complementary roles of *Brahman*/scholar, *Kshatriya*/warrior-king and *Vaiśya*/trader—that the question of who the leaders in business were never seems to have occurred to the Greeks or Romans. Fortunes were certainly being made, but this was seen as an occasion more for indulgence than glory.

† Two fields where the Romans never used Greek were law and the military. This was true even in Greek's heartland in the eastern Mediterranean, where Latin otherwise made little headway.

office at every level from village council to the republic itself, and measures were presented orally for approval by assemblies.

Above all, we can see the Romans (and hence the whole Mediterranean world) attracted by the sheer sense of savoir-faire generated by a large-scale and highly elaborated culture, self-confident to the point of solipsism. Much the same thing was to happen when Sanskrit and the wonders of classical India washed up on the shores of South-East Asia (see Chapter 5, 'The spread of Sanskrit', p. 201); or when French became the language of refinement throughout Europe, and especially in Russia, between the seventeenth and nineteenth centuries (see Chapter 11, 'La francophonie', p. 410). Something of the same charm of brash, large-scale self-confidence can be seen today powering the worldwide taste for Americana, and with it the English language. And as these examples show, the prestige behind it is something other than association with a successful army, or a successful economy.

Mid-life crisis: Attempt at a new beginning

eukharisteîn oudeìs tôn dokímōn eîpen, allà khárin eidénai.

None of the classics said '*eukharisteîn*' (meaning 'thank') but '*khárin eidénai*'.

Phrynichus Arabius, v.6 (second century AD)

eukharistô tôi théôi pántote perì humôn, epì têi kháriti toū theoū dotheísēi humîn en Khristôi Iēsoū.

I thank (*eukharistô*) God always for you, for the grace of God given to you in Jesus Christ.

St Paul, First Letter to the Corinthians, i.4 (first century AD)

Greek speakers have always held particularly strongly to their literary heritage, and this is one reason why their language has remained unitary over so many centuries, despite once being so widely spread around the world. But they have always interpreted it extremely narrowly, not so much as a living tradition, but as an unchanging (and unattainable) canon of classic authors, the main Athenian ('Attic') writers of the fifth and fourth centuries BC.*

---

* The authors are in fact extremely few, and are still recognisable as the core of a traditional, classical education in western Europe. The dramatists Aeschylus, Sophocles, Euripides and Aristophanes; the

This provided a clear basis for education, and a model for writing and formal speech. But it meant that really good style was unattainable (and increasingly unintelligible) once the language had begun to change, as of course it immediately did. So, from the third century BC, correct diction was never distinguishable from archaising pedantry. To some extent, this can be seen as a meritocratic policy in a language that was being used all round the Mediterranean and Near East: native speakers and second-language learners were more on a par when nobody was a natural speaker of the best Greek. But more importantly, it implied that nobody without an extensive literary background would ever be accepted as cultured. Greek has always fostered a disputatious culture, and the cult of 'Atticism' has been queried, criticised, parodied and reviled throughout the last 2500 years—but all to no avail.

As we have seen, it was not as if there was no other standard, of a more de facto, indeed demotic, nature: Attic Greek had almost immediately given rise to the more accessible *koinē*, close to Attic in its forms, defined in usage, and intelligible wherever Greek was spoken. But for all its utility, it had no class. And in the pre-modern world where status was bound up with literacy—and without mass education literacy would always be for the few—this mattered.

Occasionally, though, a kind of inverted snobbery prevailed. The Greek language had spread round the Roman empire to others than the educated elite. The Jewish community in Rome spoke Greek until the fourth century AD.[26] In the early centuries of the first millennium AD, a number of mystery religions were spreading from the eastern provinces, Egypt, Syria and Asia, most famously the cults of Isis, Mithras and Jesus Christ. All adopted Greek as their ritual language.[27] They were attracting converts first among the poor and downtrodden of the empire. And for all of them, the authority of the Greek classics, whose gods, if any, were the imagined residents of Mount Olympus, was no authority at all.

Yet, for Christianity at least, this did not mean that they rejected the authority of written literature. With its origins in the Jewish tradition, the Christian faith soon began writing and recognising its own scriptures, primarily in Greek, although later there were vernacular texts written in Aramaic in Syria, Coptic in Egypt and Ge'ez in Ethiopia—and of course Latin. Language for the early Christians seems universally to have been chosen to maximise access, without thought for the privileged status of any particular code. But this meant that there was the beginning of a new canon for Greek lit-

historian Thucydides; the philosopher Plato; and a handful of orators culminating in Demosthenes, who inveighed against the threat of Philip of Macedon. Greek traditional attitudes dating back to the Roman empire effectively still defined the British school syllabus that I studied in the 1960s.

erature, and one based—for the first time in four centuries—on popular usage.*

We have already remarked on the 'Shield of Faith' phenomenon, the way in which religions, particularly those of west Asian origin, have contributed to the survival of the languages that were their vehicles. Greek hardly needed any help from Christianity in these early years, but many must have taken up Greek as a second language in order to get better access to its literature. And Christianity did effect some extensions to the range of Greek literature, transforming rhetoric into the art of the homily or sermon,† and philosophy into theology.

These extensions in fact tended to undo the change to Greek linguistic sense that was at first brought about by the new informal literature. Here Christianity was a victim of its own success. In the time of its growth, the struggle to maintain the empire's vast edifice of a single administration for western Europe and the whole Mediterranean was becoming harder and harder. Rulers looked for a new means of securing loyalty over the vast domains. The major insight of the emperor Constantine was that this could be found in Christianity. In 330 he reorganised an increasingly regionalised empire around a new capital at Byzantium, henceforth Constantinople (*Kōnstantinoúpolis*), and he made it a Christian foundation.

This set the crown on the social advancement of Christianity. For over a century it had begun to attract converts of a new kind. Clement of Alexandria (born in AD 150), for example, had used his extensive classical education to write a *Protreptikós*, or 'Encourager', attempting to *argue* Greeks out of paganism and into Christianity, and then went on to build a logical system on top of the Christian *lógos*. Origen (185–255) had been a textual critic of the Bible, and Eusebius (260–339) the first historian of the Church. Such characteristically Greek academics had been well able to write in the classical style. But now the Church would also attract the general ranks of those seeking preferment in the temporal world, or indeed simply seeking to assert their due as members of distinguished families. The result was a full-blooded return to the old Atticising tendency. Ecclesiastical Greek was firmly reinstated in the classical tradition, and was never again tempted to deviate from it. The

---

* Another feature of the writings besides their style was innovative. Christians were important in popularising the new format for books, the 'codex', with separate two-sided pages attached to a spine, as against the traditional scroll. This set the format for at least the next two thousand years. The conjecture is that this made books much easier to access when bookmarking, and quoting, important passages (Harris 1989: 296).

† Both Greek *homilía* and Latin *sermō* originally meant an informal conversation, a chat.

empire's increasing tendency to proscribe paganism, defined to include all pre-Christian philosophy, culminated in Justinian's closure of the School of Athens in 529. But the survival of Attic style was never in doubt.

This conviction of Greeks that, in writing, the very old ways were the best ways turned out to be as deeply rooted as the empire itself. People were still attempting to write in some tolerable version of classical Attic when in 1453 the city of Constantinople fell to the Turks, over a thousand years later.

Intimations of decline

The story of Greek for the next thousand years is one of infrequent, but sudden and massive, retrenchments, as the vast extent built up in the late first millennium BC was pushed back at the edges. In the western Mediterranean, where Greek's empire had never been a temporal one, this loss of parts of the Greek language community came about simply because the focus of culture shifted: an education in Greek ceased to be part of western European education, and contacts with the east became much rarer. But elsewhere these withdrawals were caused quite directly by military defeats.

In the West Roman Empire, where Latin was dominant, the military defeats that diminished and soon extinguished the empire politically were to have only very limited effects on language. (See Chapter 7, 'Einfall: Germanic and Slavic advances', p. 304.) But in the east, the effect of the defeats was much simpler. Hostile forces took charge, and after a decent interval—often of many generations—Greek was no longer to be heard or seen.

Bactria, Persia, Mesopotamia

The first area to go was over to the far east: Iran and Afghanistan, down to the Indus valley. Seleucid control here was not long secure, but for the first century after the death of Alexander (323 BC) the competition came mainly from other Macedonian and Greek kings, who would not dispute the spread of Greek. By 260 BC the Indo-Greeks in Bactria, first led by Diodotus, had declared themselves independent. At just about the same time (and possibly caused by this rebellion) the Iranian-speaking Parthians thrust south from the eastern shores of the Caspian into the plateau of Iran. A century later, in 146 BC, Mithradata I of Parthia completed the job, and drove the Seleucids out of the rest of Iran, taking Mesopotamia for good measure. Ten years later, as it happened, the Indo-Greek kings of Bactria were overwhelmed by a Scythian (Śaka) invasion from the north, shortly followed by the Kushāna (also known as Tocharians or Yuezhi) from the north-east.

Extinction of Greek over this vast area was not immediate. In the east, there is the fact that Bactrian, the official language of the Kushāna empire, which lasted from the middle of the first to the end of the second century AD, came to be written in Greek script. This is unique among Iranian languages, and it shows that the Kushāna had a longish period of cultural interaction with the Greeks. In AD 44, 190 years after the fall of the Indo-Greek kings, the sage Apollonius of Tyana is said to have had no difficulty communicating in Greek on a tour that took him all the way across the Hindu Kush to Taxila, where he was entertained (in Greek) by a Parthian king, who expatiated on his own Greek-style education.[28] We know from official inscriptions that in the western regions Greek-speaking communities continued for several generations within the Parthian empire. There are Greek inscriptions at Susa, which had been the Greek capital as 'Seleuceia on the Eulaeus', one of them from AD 21; and farther west in Mesopotamia, in Seleuceia on the Tigris, there is a bilingual inscription in Greek and Parthian explicitly dated as late as AD 151, recording a Parthian victory over a (presumably) Greek-speaking Mesene, on the Persian Gulf, near modern Basra. (It is tellingly inscribed on the loins of a statue of Hercules, one language on each thigh.[29]) Mesene was also home to Isidorus of Charax, a Greek who around the time of Christ wrote a book, *The Parthian Stations*, describing the route across Parthia from south-west to north-east.

The Parthians' own language policy was to reverse history. They reinstated Aramaic as the lingua franca of their empire, leaving numerous inscriptions in it, and also using its writing system for their own (Iranian) language. The fact that this was possible shows that Greek had never fully replaced it during the two centuries of Seleucid rule.

But the Parthians were not anxious to efface the heritage of Greek rule in Iran. Their coins all bear a legend in Greek:

*BASILEŌS BASILEŌN ARSAKOU EUERGETOU DIKAIOU
EPIPHANOUS PHILELLĒNOS*

Of the King of Kings, Arsaces, Beneficent, Just, Outstanding, Greek-loving.

And Plutarch recounts the story that when in 53 BC the Parthian king Orodes received the gruesome evidence of the Roman general Crassus's defeat, his severed head, he was actually attending a performance of Euripides' *Bacchae*.*

Perhaps because Greek remained the language of the neighbouring super-power, the Roman empire, its prestige lasted in Parthia long after its use must have actually died out. The Parthian kingdom in Iran lasted for five centuries. In AD 224 the last Parthian yielded to Ardashir, the first king of the next dynasty, the Sassanids, who spoke Persian. And yet when his son Shapur came to have his own achievements inscribed on rock at Naqsh-i Rustam, facing the tombs of the Persian kings at Persepolis, he wrote them up in three languages: Persian, Parthian and Greek.[30]

Syria, Palestine, Egypt

Iran was never part of the Roman empire, and Mesopotamia only in very small part.† So they never acquired the sense of permanent Greek possessions that came to characterise Syria, Palestine and Egypt. They had been incorporated into the empire of Alexander, hence 'Hellenised', in 332 BC; in 64 BC the Roman general Pompey had incorporated Syria and Palestine as a directly governed province of the empire; and in 30 BC Augustus had added Egypt, deposing Cleopatra, last of the Ptolemies. These Roman conquests, as we have seen, had no linguistic effect, except to introduce some use of Latin in the army and the courts. But they did serve to underline the sense that this part of the world, the far south-east of the Mediterranean, was to be permanently, and as far as possible stably, under western control. Greek remained widely spoken there by foreign elites, and in some special cities such as Palmyra, Gaza and Alexandria by many more.

A sense of the language situation in a centre of international pilgrimage in the region is given by Egeria, who visited Jerusalem around AD 400:

> Seeing that in that country part of the people know both Greek and Syriac, another part only Greek and yet another part only Syriac, given also that the bishop, although he knows Syriac, always speaks in Greek and never in Syriac, there is always by his side a priest who, while the bishop is speaking in Greek, translates his comments into Syriac so that everyone may understand them. Similarly for the lessons that are read in church: since these must be read in Greek, there is always somebody

---

* His host, Artavazdes, the king of Armenia, was also a Greek scholar, apparently, to the extent of having written his own plays in the language (Plutarch, *Crassus*, fin.).

† Over the three years AD 114–17, the whole area was taken and lost again by the emperor Trajan. But the north-western portion, Osroëne, was incorporated for two centuries after a Roman campaign in 164.

there to translate them into Syriac for the benefit of the people, that they may receive instruction. As for the Latins who are there, i.e. those who know neither Syriac nor Greek, to them also is an interpretation given lest they be displeased; for there are some brethren and sisters, proficient in both Greek and Latin, who give explanations in Latin.[31]

We have already considered (see Chapter 3, 'Arabic – eloquence and equality: The triumph of 'submission'', p. 93) the series of lightning campaigns by the newly declared Muslims which reversed this state of affairs, and so created the linguistic situation that has lasted to the present day. A single decade from the death of Muḥammad in 632 sufficed to draw a thin, but indelible, line under 950 years of Greek control and Greek language, and to turn the page, opening what is so far 1300 years of Arabic sway in these same lands. A shock for all concerned, but particularly so since it came a couple of years after the emperor Heraclius had reasserted the imperial defences, and in four years of campaigning rolled back a Sassanid invasion of these same territories which had denied them to the Greeks since the beginning of the century.

This was a devastating blow to the empire politically and economically: the losses included Egypt, still after 650 years the major supplier of grain to the empire's capital. And the best estimates* suggest that the Arab conquests deprived the empire of over half its population. But it could have been worse. The Arabs failed in repeated attempts to take Constantinople itself, and also failed to detach Anatolia, despite raiding it virtually every year for the next two centuries.[32] The region had been reorganised by Heraclius, effectively combining civil and military administration, and imposing martial law. The clear perception that the enemy was at the gate imposed this new discipline, and kept the empire effectively mobilised for defence.

There is an interesting pattern to the Byzantine losses in the mid-seventh century. The places that held firm were precisely those where Greek was the majority language, spoken by the people at large and not just elites. This had an effect on the linguistic self-image of the Roman empire (for they still considered themselves Roman). Latin had been dropping out of use for some time, losing even its last redoubt in the law: since the time of Justinian, a century before, most legislation had been drafted in Greek; and the emperor's second-in-command, the praetorian prefect, was now often a man who knew

---

* Mango (1980: ch. 1) puts the population of the eastern Mediterranean provinces in the mid-sixth century at 30 million, with 8 million in Egypt, 9 million in Syria-Palestine-Mesopotamia, 10 million in Anatolia and 3–4 million in the Balkans. Note also how Anatolia had twice the population of Greece and the European provinces.

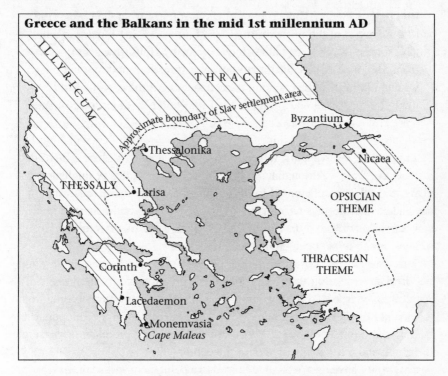

Greece and the Balkans in the mid 1st millennium AD

ILLYRICUM

THRACE

Approximate boundary of Slav settlement area

Byzantium

Thessalonika

Nicaea

THESSALY

Larisa

OPSICIAN
THEME

Corinth

THRACESIAN
THEME

Lacedaemon

Monemvasia
Cape Maleas

no Latin. The empire still held much of southern Italy, and would hang on to parts of it for another four hundred years, until the middle of the eleventh century. But now for the first time Greek, not Latin, was seen as the unifying language of the whole community. Confusingly for moderns, they called Greek *rōmaíika*, 'Romanish', contrasting it with *latiniká*. But looking back from the mid-tenth century, the emperor Constantine VII Porphyrogenitus remarked that it had been in the time of Heraclius that the Romans 'had been Hellenized and discarded the language of their fathers, the Roman tongue'.[33]

Greece

Although the unsettling bellows motion of the imperial frontiers did not stop, the attrition of Greek-language areas effectively now did, for the next four hundred years. This would not have been clear at the time, for while the southeastern lands of the Levant were being lost, the north too was in turmoil.

It was touch and go whether Greek would survive in its own heartland. After invasions from Germanic-speaking Goths in 378, Turkic-speaking Huns in 441–7, Germanic Ostrogoths in 479–82, and Turkic-speaking Bulgars in 493, the mayhem continued in the sixth century. Fifty years after the crisis, the Byzantine historian Procopius recounted:

Illyricum and all of Thrace, i.e. the whole country from the Ionian Gulf [the Adriatic] to the outskirts of Byzantium, including Greece and the Chersonese, was overrun almost every year by Huns, Slavs and Antae, from the time when Justinian became Roman emperor, and they wrought untold damage among the inhabitants of those parts. For I believe that in each invasion more than two hundred thousand Romans were killed or captured...[34]

Then, in 581, as John of Ephesus records: 'an accursed people, called Slavonians, overran the whole of Greece, and the country of the Thessalonians, and all Thrace, and captured the cities, and took numerous forts, and devastated and burnt, and reduced the people to slavery, and made themselves masters of the whole country, and settled in it by main force, and dwelt in it as though it had been their own'.[35]

This was not a temporary phenomenon, and it led to large-scale emigration by Greeks. According to the Chronicle of Monemvasia, by the year 587/8 scarcely any part of Greece was immune to the Slavic scourge, this time from the Avars (another Turkic group): 'Only the eastern part of the Peloponnese, from Corinth to Cape Maleas, was untouched by the Slavonians because of the rough and inaccessible nature of the country.'

This might have been expected to lead to a permanent spread of Slavic languages, as indeed it did in Serbia and Bulgaria farther north (see Chapter 7, 'Slavonic dawn in the Balkans', p. 309). But somehow the preponderance of Greek over Slavic speakers was restored in the south. In the seventh, eighth and ninth centuries the empire organised a series of resettlement programmes and missionary campaigns, moving Slavs into northern Anatolia, and bringing others into southern Greece. We hear that in 805 Nicephorus I 'built *de novo* the town of Lacedaemon and settled in it a mixed population, namely Kafirs, Thracēsians, Armenians and others, gathered from different places and towns, and made it into a bishopric'.[36]

Likewise, in the 860s, Basil I was hard at work to convert the Serbs in the north: 'having greeked them [*graikōsas*], he subjected them to governors according to Roman custom, honoured them with baptism, and delivered them from the oppression of their own rulers'.[37]

The details are impossible to clarify, if the aim is to explain why some communities became Greek-speaking, as well as Christian; certainly the religious liturgies they learnt would have been in Greek. Later, service in the army would also have served to bring many Slavs into the Greek-speaking world. But the net effect is clear. Greek remained, or was re-established as, the dominant language of its traditional homeland.

Anatolia

Greek dominance in Anatolia lasted until 1071: in that year the empire lost the battle of Manzikert (modern Malazgirt, north of Lake Van) to a new power dominating the Muslim world, the sultanate of the Seljuk Turks.* Even so, it could still have avoided the loss of its whole heartland that resulted: the Seljuk sultan, Alp Arslan, with other wars to fight, had attempted to reinstate the defeated emperor, Romanus Diogenes, on terms that would have established an alliance between the two powers, and given the Turks access to the Mediterranean through Edessa, Hierapolis and Antioch in northern Syria. But Romanus, and the proffered terms, were rejected: the consequence was the Seljuks' swift advance through most of Anatolia, a territory that was thenceforth to be dominated by speakers of Turkish, and known—in curious reminiscence of the old empire's origins in Italy—as the Sultanate of Rum.

This spread of Turkish hordes, who rapidly converted into Turkish settlers, within a hundred years had deprived the Greek language community of the heart of its major territory. The population of Greek speakers worldwide was therefore set to fall rapidly, whether by emigration, or simple loss of later generations of learners. Some whole communities of Greek speakers would depart en masse; many individuals would leave their homes to find better opportunities elsewhere; and the children of some Greek families, assimilating to the new environment, would grow up speaking Turkish.

This was a direct blow to the survival of Greek as a major language. Five generations later, it suffered a political blow that shattered its remaining prestige. In 1204 the Fourth Crusade, made up of knights from western Europe, turned aside from its appointed mission of attacking the Muslim powers that held Palestine, and captured Constantinople, as well as parts of Greece and the coast of Anatolia. It then proceeded to hold its gains as a 'Latin Empire', masterminded by the Venetians, which lingered on pointlessly for a couple of centuries before being absorbed by the Turks. The Fourth Crusade had reduced the East Roman Empire to a set of five separate statelets: although one of these did manage to retake Constantinople in 1261, and reconstitute itself as a rump of empire, no Greek state was ever again more than a minor constraint on the growing power of the Turks. The empire was finally extinguished by the Turks in 1453, and the last Greek statelet, Trebizond, in 1471. It had taken the Turks just over 380 years to advance from Manzikert to

---

* The writing was on the wall for the Byzantines in that year of 1071: news also arrived that the Normans had taken Bari, ending 535 years of their empire in Italy.

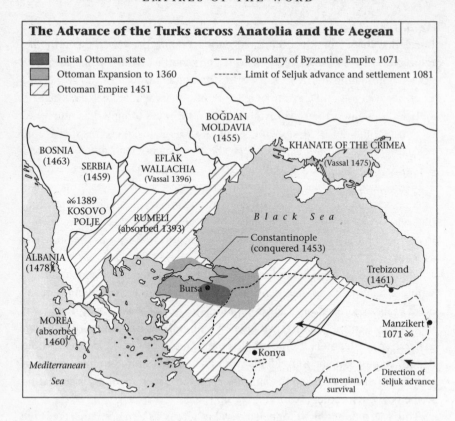

Constantinople—the same interval of time that Greece was subsequently to spend under *Tourkokratía*, as they called the domination of the Turks.

From being the language of a universal empire, so catholic in its aspirations that it scarcely noticed whether its language was Hellenic or Roman, Greek had now become the tongue of a conquered people, the Orthodox Christians, just one of the *milletler* ('nations'—really, religious groupings) that had a place in the cosmopolitan empire of the Ottoman Turks. Humbled at last, the Greeks now did notice what language they were speaking: it was inseparable from their Orthodox faith, and became an important token of their identity for the long centuries in which they lacked their freedom.

Given that Anatolia had been, in the late first millennium BC, no less Greek-speaking than the Balkan peninsula that culminates in the Peloponnese, the place that we now think of as the farthest natural extent of Greece, it is almost an accident that the Greek-speaking community ended up concentrated in the same place from which it spread two and a half thousand years before. Looking back, we can see that this only reflects the fact that the Muslim powers that threatened from the east, the Arabs and above all the

Turks, were better organised, and more coherent in the long term, than the threats that came from the north, the Goths, Avars and Slavs. Slavs could be assimilated; Turks could not.

Consolations in age

ksipnó ke vlépō efθís áno na méni
i ídia Aθiná me parrisían
ky étsi apo psilá mú sindiχéni:
'Tis Eládos tin brín din evδoksían
χrónos tinás poté δen din maréni,
yat' amárandos íne i sofía.'

I awake and see at once above me
The same Athena is waiting candidly,
And with these words from on high she talks to me:
'The renown of Greece of old
No time will ever efface:
For wisdom is imperishable.'

Andreas Myiares (*c*.1708)

Greek had been undone: it was no more the language of a community with universal aspirations. When the Renaissance took hold in western Europe, it did enjoy a resuscitation as a source of scholarly wisdom. Ability to read the language, and a familiarity with its classics (focused on the fifth and fourth centuries BC, as ever—though with more attention now to Aristotle), became a useful touchstone of authenticity for scholars, but it never rose to the level of a lingua franca among them: that position was held by its old colleague, Latin.

But Greek itself, as a living language, was now the property of a number of small communities, with no right or power actively to influence others. And their sense of unity one with another was diminished by the breakdown of any link with traditional Greek literary education, a development that had begun in the thirteenth century, a century and a half before the Turkish triumph, when the Latin powers had first taken control of so many of the empire's old domains.

In these home communities, it did not die out. Its transmission was shielded by its role in Orthodox liturgy: but in fact, even as the language of a subject people, it was under no threat. There was no pressure for Christians to convert to Islam. Although the Seljuk advance had favoured the spread of Turkish-speaking settlers across Anatolia in the eleventh and twelfth centuries, the political advance of the Ottoman Turks, begun in the late thirteenth century, served mainly a military purpose, reorganising resident Turks into devastating campaigners. Although the Ottoman empire then took the Near and Middle East by storm, historically it had no tendency to favour the spread of any language whatever. Rather it seemed totally laid back—indeed, never systematically organised for any purpose beyond military conquest—and allowed ample self-governance to its constituent *milletler*.*

Nevertheless, Greek effectively ceases to be a world language at this point. For all the gratifying interest in its tradition out in the west of Europe, now that it was no longer master in its own house the Greek-speaking community could no longer see itself as the autonomous centre of its own world. The Greeks began to think of themselves as a small people, able to act only through negotiation with others far stronger than them. Their solipsism was at an end. We shall not trace its history further, although there is much to tell. The new centre of gravity in the language community, for the first time a rural one, with no duty to maintain an ancient past or a wider sense of Greek's place in the world, led to the composition of popular lays and romances, untrammelled by earlier classical hang-ups. There was a new sense of Greek, based on the spirit of the *kléftis*, the outlaw who accepted no foreign oppression. But when the western powers, in sympathy with the Romantic movement, guaranteed Greece's liberation from the Ottomans in 1821, there was renewed discussion as to what true standard to set for the Greek language— and once again the Greek elite gave its judgement in favour of a policy of conscious archaism.

Yet now, for the first time in over two thousand years, the policy would not stick. Something had changed, perhaps because of the break in urban dominance, and hence classical education, during the *Tourkokratía*. A popular— in Greek, 'Demotic'—style of written language had established itself, and its role could now be asserted. The nineteenth and twentieth centuries witnessed further struggles: but since the fall of the colonels' regime (1967–74) and the Education Act of 1976, there is now acceptance of a new written standard based on something close to ordinary spoken Greek.

---

* The Greek Orthodox patriarchate indeed gained from the Turkish conquest, since the Sultan Mehmet rationalised his Orthodox subjects after taking Constantinople, incorporating the Bulgarian and Serbian patriarchates under the authority of Constantinople. Linguistically, of course, they remained separate.

Retrospect: The life cycle of a classic

Aièn aristeúein kaì hupeírokhon émmenai allōn
mēdè génos patérōn aiskhúnemen, hoì még' áristoi…

Always to be the best, and to be superior to others,
And not to shame the race of fathers who much the best…

Homer, Iliad, vi.208 (a father's parting advice to a Homeric hero)

This survey of the expansion and contraction of the Greek language community over three millennia only makes more urgent a fundamental question. What was it about Greek speakers which had commended them over their contemporaries, Phoenicians, Egyptians, Persians, Etruscans, Gauls, Carthaginians or whatever? What was it about them that made them think their group, and their way of life, more civilised than all these others, and furthermore by and large persuaded these miscellaneous 'barbarians' to take the Greek view of the matter? Most importantly, given the flow of power relations through the ancient world, why did the Romans become philhellenes, rather than admirers of Etruscan, Punic or indeed Egyptian ways?

Western Europe likes to think itself an indirect heir of the Greeks; but the countless modern accounts of what the Greeks were like never ask, much less answer, this question. Rather, they simply trace the processes by which the Greeks produced so many pioneering contributions to Western civilisation, in mythology, politics, literature, the arts, architecture, philosophy and science. Part of the answer is thus given implicitly: for none of their contemporaries has laid by as vast a record of their cultural product as the Greeks— unless one counts the Romans, who chose to build on the Greek work, rather than replace it. Literacy could be seen as the Greeks' secret weapon.

But this can't be the whole answer. After all, literacy was a gift to them from the Phoenicians, who themselves were just the lately travelling sales representatives of a vast Middle Eastern range of literate societies, from Egypt at one end to Babylon and Elam at the other. But unlike the Phoenicians, the Greeks had chosen to use their literacy to record their culture: the ability to read Greek brought a vast range of original works in its wake. The result was that the Greeks had access to 'the arts of civilisation' in a way that could only impress others when they came into contact with them. Civilisation, after all, when combined with such delights as olive oil and wine, is apt to be attractive.

The question can be thrown one stage farther back: why was it that the Greeks, living on the lands that adjoined the Aegean Sea at the end of the

Mediterranean, were able to develop and propagate arts of civilisation in this way? Any answer to this one becomes extremely speculative: but it is notable that the Greeks were the only language community around the Mediterranean where the groupings were large enough to form cities, but which, though literate, had no tendency to be agglomerated into larger states, and hence ultimately to be united into an empire. This may have been a result of the mountainous and island-studded environment in which they lived, making small communities easier to feed and defend than large ones: but it did mean that Greece became a vast competitive playground for cultural developments— developments that could spread to other Greeks if successful or attractive (as, for example, was Attic literature), but which which would not tend to crowd each other out. In this sense, the early history of Greece can be seen as comparable to that of Europe after the Renaissance—a fertile marriage of competitive independence and good communications.

It is often, somewhat romantically, claimed that Greece's greatest contribution to subsequent civilisation was the invention of democracy, the highest mechanism invented to realise *eleuthería*, 'freedom', always a virtue that the Greeks claimed to care for. This is certainly false: false as a theory of what appealed in Greek to outsiders confronted by it, and false as an account of what made Greek capable of spreading so far to the east and west of its homeland. It has already been pointed out that most Greek city-states were never democratic; and the larger states with Greek as their official language, established all over Egypt and much of Asia after conquests by Alexander, were without exception monarchies. They were bureaucratic states, where civic control by concerned citizens was not possible, nor even an ideal. They were also much bigger than any city-states had ever been. When the Greek language spread, it did not carry with it the properties that had possibly been crucial in the original creation of its attendant culture.

Indeed, a major property of Greek culture, throughout its long continuous history since the third century BC, has been a wish to hark back to the classics, aping their linguistic form as well (as far as possible) as their style and content, but never the excitement of innovation and originality that must have attended their actual writing in the fifth and fourth centuries. Whatever has proved enduring in the Greek language tradition—and leaving aside the question of whether its classics really are the best things ever written—it has far more to do with rigid conservatism than openness to exciting new ideas. If nothing else, the history of the Greek language community shows that conservatism too can be attractive, if something attractive is being conserved.

We can see that what Greek had to offer was highly attractive in the context of the ancient world. Even those whose careers were dedicated to limiting and diminishing Greek influence nevertheless took as much as they could from it: the Kushāna kings of Afghanistan, who went on using Greek on their coinage after unseating Greek kings; the Parthian and Armenian courtiers entertaining themselves with Greek tragedies, even as their armies were besting the Greeks' Roman students; the Carthaginian generals who used Greek to communicate with their own forces of mercenaries. The Greeks were undoubtedly the Great Communicators of the Mediterranean world.

But the agents who spread this undoubtedly attractive commodity round the *oikouménē*, the inhabited world, were seldom actually Greek. The spread of the Greek language is, rather, an object lesson in the effectiveness of hitching a ride. Macedon was beyond the pale of the Greek language community; yet its king planted Greek-speaking colonies all the way to the boundaries of India. Aramaic was the language of Greece's greatest foe, the Persian empire; yet the two-hundred-year-old use of it as a chancery language across the empire meant that there was a clear model for Greeks to follow in seeding a Greek-based communications network round their newly won domains. Two hundred years later Rome, and with it Latin, was taking the whole Mediterranean rim by storm; yet Greek, the language of colonies in southern Italy, was accepted into a kind of equality with Latin, and went on to become the true cultural milieu of the Roman empire—in the sense that no cultivated inhabitant of the empire could be without it. Two hundred years later still, the new brooms sweeping the empire were mystery religions, especially Christianity; yet although none of them originated in Greece, their language of preference was Greek, and so Greek built an indissoluble link with the greatest movement of the late Roman empire, the Christian Church. By a final stroke of good fortune, this same movement, now specialised as Christian Orthodoxy, turned out to be the key to preserving Greek through four centuries of Turkish domination, after the dissolution of the Roman empire in the east. Greek thus owes its remarkable career to help from its friends, at every crucial turning point of the last 2300 years.

Yet curiously, for all its close relationship with other cultural powers (military, administrative and spiritual), Greek has been highly resistant to influence from others with which it has been in contact. We have already seen that out in the farthest eastern reaches Greek was prepared to take on loan words for interesting new substances from India;* but the influence of its bedfellow language Aramaic was negligible. In the west, its five centuries of cohabitation with Latin as a principal language of the Roman empire led to a

---

* e.g. *zingiberi*, 'ginger', *sakkharon*, 'sugar' (see Chapter 5, 'The character of Sanskrit', p. 192).

crop of borrowings to designate official and military matters, administration and finance (for example, names of months, coins, ranks, military ranks, taxes) but hardly any day-to-day words.* Many words where one might have expected borrowings, such as *consul*, *senātus*, *Augustus*, *imperātor*, are in fact usually translated: *húpatos* (literally 'topmost'), *gerousía* ('gathering of old men'), *Sebastós* ('reverend'), *autokrátōr* ('self-controller'). Likewise, the Christian and other mystery religions' adoption of Greek left it surprisingly untouched, if one discounts the names of people and places, and interjections such as *amḗn* and *hōsanná*.†

Things changed after the Greeks were disempowered by the Fourth Crusade. Latin elements came into the language and stuck: *bánio*, 'bath', *bastarðo*, 'bastard', *bíra*, 'beer'. After this, within a Turkish-run world, Greek did behave more like a colonised language, and absorbed a whole host of Turkish words, not just for new concepts such as *tzamí*, 'mosque', *χatzís*, 'Mecca pilgrim', *oðalíski*, 'concubine' (from Turkish *oda-lık*, 'roomer', combined with a Greek diminutive), but for such mundane and apparently gratuitous things as *boyatzís*, 'painter', *tembélis*, 'lazy', *yakás*, 'collar', *bólikos*, 'abundant' and *sokáki*, 'street'. A lot of such vocabulary has since dropped out, or been suppressed by language planning policies since independence. But the new tolerance of borrowed words since the collapse of the empire is evidence in itself that we were right to see Greek's self-image as changing around that time: relieved of responsibilities to keep order in its historic dominions, and indeed to stand as the bulwark of Christian Orthodoxy, the language was no longer maintained in such conscious isolation from its neighbours.

Having developed autonomously as a cultural area, linked primarily by a common language, a common set of gods and a general sense of kinship, Greek effectively had global reach pressed upon it: this was its reward for impressing so mightily the imperial powers of Macedon and Rome. Over the centuries, those powers ebbed away, leaving large-scale political units in their wake, and Greek speakers as the de facto guardians of a political dispensation not of their making. They reacted by holding to the core of their own

---

* Close to the full list seems to be *spíti*, 'house' (from Latin *hospitium*, 'inn'), *skamnío*, 'bench' (*scamnum*), *pórta*, 'door', *kámara*, 'room', *vérga*, 'rod', and possibly *áspros*, 'white' (from Latin *asper*, 'rough'). Compare the vastly longer list of borrowings by Welsh (which was in close contact with Latin for half the time). (See Chapter 7, 'Consilium: The rationale of Roman imperium', p. 303.)

† It has been suggested that the favourite choice of the Christian word for 'love', *agápē*, is influenced by Hebrew *'āhēb*, 'love' (which happens to have much stronger sexual overtones than the Greek), and Greek *skḗnē*, 'tent', by Hebrew *šeken*, 'dwelling' (Moule 1959: 186).

traditions, which in the last analysis turned out not to be political, or even intellectual, but linguistic. Their distinctive, civic, approach to government fell away when confronted with units larger than city-states; their rationalist, or polytheistic, philosophies yielded to Christianity; but they never lost faith in the rhetoric of Lysias or Demosthenes, the poetry of Aeschylus or Euripides, or the prose of Plato and Xenophon. It was a curious faith, confronted with a multinational, multilinguistic empire. But it served.

Greek's solipsism in effect came to an end with the downfall of its associated empire. After two millennia of steadfast concentration, it was no longer constrained to preserve its unity by holding the line that the unchanging standard of excellence, linguistic if not spiritual, was the language of one Greek city in the fifth and fourth centuries BC. From our perspective in the twenty-first century, and especially in a language community, such as English, which has cut itself free from adoration of classics, whether in its own language or anyone else's, it is hard to see real value in this central myth. But the Greek achievement stands as an interesting monument of one way to keep a language tradition, even one of vast extent, self-consciously united. The absence of serious division in the Greek language is quite striking to this day. While Latin is succeeded by a handful of separate national language traditions, all of which have moved on from their common roots in the Latin of Rome in, say, the second century BC, Greek—even as spoken on the Turkish shores of the Black Sea, and in villages in the remote south of Italy—knows what is its common centre. The adulation of Attic did actually work, in the grand programme of making sure that Greek remained the language of a single community.

7

Contesting Europe:
Celt, Roman, German and Slav

κατὰ δὲ ταῖς ὁμιλίαις βραχύλογοι καὶ αἰνιγματίαι καὶ τὰ πολλὰ αἰνιττό-
μενοι συνεκδοχικῶς.

[The Gauls are] in their conversation terse and enigmatic, often speaking in allusive riddles.

Diodorus Siculus, v.31

*Trí húaithaid ata ferr sochaidi: úathad dagbríathar, úathad bó hi feór,
úathad carat im chuirm.*

Three scarcities that are better than plenty: a scarcity of fine words, a
scarcity of cows in a meadow, a scarcity of friends at beer.

The Triads of Ireland, ed. Kuno Meyer, 93

οὐδὲ τῷ Ῥωμαίων πολιτεύματι ἐπεοικὸς ἦν; μίσει τε εἴπερ τινας ἄλλους,
τοῦ τυραννικοῦ γένους τε καὶ ὀνόματος κατεχόμενους.

nor was it fitting for the government of the Romans ... given that they
were possessed more than anyone by a hatred of the very nature and
name of absolute power ('tyranny').

Arrian, *Alexander's Campaign*, vii.15.6

hoc vero regnum est, et ferri nullo pacto potest.

But this is kingship, and can in no wise be tolerated.

Cicero, *Letter to Atticus*, ii.12.1

...et ingrata genti quies et facilius inter ancipitia clarescunt magnum-
que comitatum non nisi vi belloque tueare.

Peace is disliked by the [German] nation; they distinguish themselves
more easily in a crisis and you will not see them in large numbers except
in wartime.

Tacitus, *Germania*, 14.2

Want her dô ar arme wuntane baugâ, cheisuringu gitân, sô imo se der
chuning gap,
Huneô truhtîn: 'dat ih dir it nû bi huldî gibu.' Hadubrant gimahalta
Hiltibrandes sunu
'Mit gêru scal man geba infâhan, ort widar orte.'

He took from his arm twisted torcs worked with specie gold, given him
by the king, lord of the Huns: 'This I now give you in friendship.'
Rejoined Hadubrand, son of Hildebrand:
'With spears are gifts to be taken, point against point.'

Hildebrandslied, 33–8

Reversals of fortune

The history of Europe, over the three thousand years for which we have evidence, is dominated by the changing fortunes of four closely related families
of languages: Celtic, Italic, Germanic and Slavonic. In every age, their advances across the continent have been warlike: there is a depressing brutality
about the heroics in which they all gloried. But like the languages themselves,
the cultures they fostered characterise different peoples, each with rather different values.

This chapter focuses on the crucial part of that history, which witnessed a
major shift in ambient language, all over western Europe, from Celtic to
Latin. This linguistic shift was unambiguously due to military conquest, and
the sheer clarity of it lives on to this day in Europe's everyday conception of
what changes languages: control, backed by military and economic strength.
And yet, as if to provide an object lesson in the inadequacy of that simple
view, this conquest was itself overwhelmed. After half a millennium of stability, the military balance was overturned in a wide-ranging military catastrophe from which there was no recovery: indeed, it set the pattern of political
and national boundaries that has lasted to the present day. Yet while the lin-

273

The Language Distribution in Europe 500 BC

guistic effect of all this in most of the West was nil, in Britain, and in the Balkans, it proved decisive.

Looked at as a whole, the history of these crucial thousand years, approximately from 500 BC to AD 500, has a certain symmetry. It begins and ends with the triumph of mobile military societies organised round kinship relations, the Celts at the outset, the Germans and Slavs at the close. In between, we see the triumph of a civic society, which unified Europe, organised its defences and provided good communications throughout, through well-kept roads and well-patrolled sea routes.

For the first 250 years, Gaulish raiders (backed by the best weapons technology available, in iron) dominate the continent, then settle down. They may have participated then in large-scale trade up and down the Atlantic coast, which also spread their language. Then, over a period of 250 years, they are gradually but systematically overwhelmed, by a better-organised and strategically self-conscious foe, the Romans. Ironically, it is only when the raiders begin to unify and organise themselves jointly for defence (under Vercingetorix) that they can be undone with finality. Four hundred years of stability ensue, while the Roman empire effectively resists continuing pres-

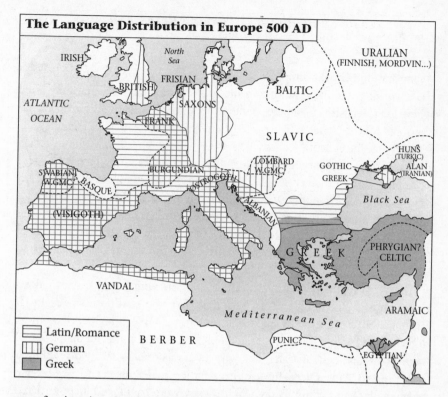

The Language Distribution in Europe 500 AD

IRISH

North Sea

URALIAN
(FINNISH, MORDVIN...)

BRITISH FRISIAN

BALTIC

ATLANTIC OCEAN

SAXONS

FRANK

SLAVIC

HUNS
(TURKIC)

LOMBARD W.GMC

GOTHIC

ALAN
(IRANIAN)

SWABIAN W.GMC

BURGUNDIAN

BASQUE

OSTROGOTH

GREEK

Black Sea

(VISIGOTH)

ALBANIAN

G R E E K

PHRYGIAN?
CELTIC

VANDAL

Mediterranean Sea

ARAMAIC

☐ Latin/Romance
▥ German
▦ Greek

B E R B E R

PUNIC?

EGYPTIAN

sure for immigration from Germany. Under greater stress (originating in north and east Asia), the resistance fails, first sporadically, then totally; and the last hundred years are spent watching the effects of allowing new sets of raiders to pass as they will through the old imperial domains.

All in all, the major changes of language in this period, the spread of Latin across Italy, and into Gaul and Iberia, the spread of English in Britain, and the spread of Slavic in the Balkans, are the best markers of serious cultural change. The cases where serious language change failed to follow on from conquests expose the hollowness of much military glory—the conquests in western Europe by Franks, Vandals and Visigoths, even the conquests in Britain by Romans and Normans.

We now turn to look at this tale in more detail. It costs some effort to forget the well-known recent centuries, and see these languages as they appeared at the beginning. Perhaps the best way to begin is to consider how they appeared to those ever curious, but in this case uninvolved, bystanders, the Greeks.

The contenders: Greek and Roman views

The Celts

At the start the Greeks simply saw the Celts as one of the framing nations of their world: Herodotus, writing in the fifth century BC, says that they lived where the river Istros (Danube) came from, farthest west of all European nations, but for the Cynetes.[1] He places them beyond the Pillars of Hercules, effectively on the Atlantic coast where Portugal is today, just as the historian Ephorus[2] does a century later, Celts in the west, Scythians in the north. There was something of conventional legend in this story, reminiscent of the Chinese world image which saw the familiar, civilised, world surrounded on all sides by unknown barbarians (see Chapter 4, 'Foreign relations', p. 158). But if so, the cliché had been a lucky guess. On modern evidence there were at the time Celtic speakers all the way across from the source of the Danube to the north of Iberia.

Their first real appearance is in the tale of the young prince Alexander's reception of Celtic ambassadors from the coast of the Adriatic in 335 BC. It was apparently reported by his friend Ptolemy, who as it happened went on to be king of Egypt.[3] They were big men, he says, in stature and in opinion of themselves, and demonstrated this with a famous remark. They offered their friendship to Alexander—his empire-building had then yet to begin—but when challenged by him to say whether they were frightened, they declared that there was only one thing which filled them with dread, and that was the thought that the sky might one day crash down on them. This remained a by-word for Celtic grandiloquence, but it seems to have been a misunderstanding of a Celtic oath formula. A thousand years later, Irishmen were still binding themselves 'unless the firmament with its showers of stars fall upon the earth, or unless the blue-bordered fish-abounding sea come over the face of the world, or unless the earth quake...'[4]

Subsequently the Celts (also known as Gauls: *Galatai* in Greek, *Galli* in Latin—Caesar comments that *Celtae* is the Gauls' own word[5]) did gain a certain reputation. It is set out at length by the historian Diodorus Siculus, writing in the late first century BC, and probably following the personal researches of the Greek polymath Posidonius.[6] Physically, they were supposed to be tall, lithe and fair, often with their hair artificially bleached with lime, the nobles sporting moustaches that covered their mouths and served as de facto wine-strainers. (This particular joke is over two thousand years old.) Their language sounded deep and altogether harsh. They were not without flair or subtlety, but did lack fixity of purpose, delighting to talk tersely in aphorisms and riddles. Nevertheless, they grew wordy when the time came to build themselves up, or belittle an opponent, in the lead-up to a fight. They dressed in bright colours, with cloaks often in check patterns, and—distinctively in the ancient world—the men wore trousers, called *bracae*.*

The Germans

As for the Germans, the Greeks tended to confuse them with the Celts: after all, they all lived somewhere to the north-west, and no one had yet thought to look for significant differences among such impenetrably barbarous tongues.† For the ancients, clear distinguishing features could only be cultural; linguistically, the best that could be done was to note that one tribe had difficulty understanding another.

Even writing in the first century AD, after Caesar had subdued Gaul up to the Rhine, the Greek Strabo could not give much of a description of the Germans.[7] Living to the east of the Rhine, they were wilder, bigger and fairer than the Celts, but otherwise very similar. In fact, so quintessentially similar did they appear to Strabo that he etymologised their name *Germani*, as the Latin for 'out and out [Celts]'. Caesar seems to have been responsible for setting the Rhine as a divider, but there is precious little evidence, archaeological or inscriptional, to back up his distinction, and he probably took the river as a convenient natural boundary to his conquests. Nevertheless, this did soon become the permanent boundary of the Roman empire, which meant that henceforth Gauls and Germans would be politically, if not ethnically, divided along this line.

Caesar's view was that German society was simpler than that of the Gauls, without agriculture but more polarised around military prowess, and less capable of forming large-scale communities. In this he may have uncovered the secret of the Germans' long-term success in fending off Roman conquest.

A century and a half later, the basic separation between Gaul and German at the Rhine was reiterated by Tacitus in his treatise *Germania*, although he noted that there were a few German tribes who had crossed over. He also provided the classic treatment of the character of German society, as Posidonius and Caesar had done for Gaul. He saw them as a society of small isolated families, feeling crowded if they could see their neighbours' chimney smoke even in the distance, and coming together only for the ennobling purpose of

---

* In fact, this word is borrowed from Germanic. Besides *breeks* or *britches*, it underlies the Celtic word for footwear, *brogues*.

† Such differences would in fact not be sought until 1599, when Joseph Justus Scaliger classified Latin, Greek, Germanic and Slavonic languages through their different words for God.

glory in war. He rather admired their egalitarian upbringing, physical fitness in harsh conditions, and simple morality.

We now know, on the basis of contemporary Gaulish inscriptions, and the subsequent development of the languages into the distinct families of Celtic and Germanic, that there were substantive linguistic divisions between Celt and German. There are monumental inscriptions in discernibly Celtic languages (in Iberian, Greek, Etruscan and Roman scripts) from the first centuries BC and AD from all over northern Iberia, Gaul, northern Italy and even (though only of Celtic names) in southern Germany, at Manching on the Danube. Likewise, discernibly Germanic inscriptions (written in the runic alphabet) have been found on small portable items such as weapons and safety pins (*fibulae*), from Slovenia in the first century BC to Denmark two hundred years later. From the extremely sketchy evidence we have, it seems that Caesar's Gallic/Germanic distinction was real, but that there was a major overlap of the languages' spheres in the area that today comprises western Germany and Austria.

The Romans

More interesting than the Greeks' failure to distinguish the essence of the Gaul and the German was their evolving attitude to the Romans, the third contender for linguistic spread over western Europe.

There is nothing to pre-figure the destiny of Rome in classical Greek literature. The first surviving mention of the city is from the fourth century BC, in a fragment of Aristotle.[8] He also mentions their neighbours the Oscans ('*Opikoí*, also called *Aúsones*') in a global discussion of the origins of communal dining, quoting chroniclers of the Greek colonists. But he does not mention the radically new constitution that the Romans had adopted in the past century, abolishing kings and instituting a republic under the balanced equality of two elected consuls.

Evidently, the first Greeks to encounter Latin speakers would have been colonists: they probably saw them as a bit of local colour among the Etruscans who controlled the landward side of the Greek settlements at Pithecusae (Ischia) and Kyme (Cumae). It would have been Greek colonists then who, over five hundred years, witnessed the gradual emergence of Rome, chief city of the region of Latium, from domination by Etruscans to independence and then commanding influence among the indigenous nations of Italy. There is a story[9] that in 323 BC the Romans sent one of the many deputations that went to Babylon to congratulate Alexander, the new master of the Persian empire. If true, it probably shows that they had heard rumours that he next planned to turn his conquering attentions to the west. This was 150 years before the Romans had any serious interests in the eastern Mediterranean.

Greeks were fascinated by Rome's winning ways in global politics, and characteristically began to theorise some sort of explanation. Polybius had made the best of his deportation from Greece to Italy in 167 BC (his father had been a prominent Achaean politician) by getting to know the Roman elite: he then devoted much of his life to writing an account of 'how and by what kind of government almost the whole inhabited world was brought under Roman rule…'[10] In the event, although he knew many of the Roman protagonists or their children and grandchildren, and reconstructed a meticulous narrative of events and motives since 220 BC, he offers no simple answer to his question. But he does stress the moral impression made by the Romans: 'Italians in general have a natural advantage over Phoenicians and Africans both in physical strength and personal courage, but at the same time their institutions contribute very powerfully towards fostering a spirit of bravery in their young men.'[11] He also cites the Roman fear of divine retribution after death, superstition though it may be, as fostering honesty: 'At any rate, the result is that among the Greeks, apart from anything else, men who hold public office cannot be trusted with the safekeeping of so much as a single talent, even if they have ten accountants and as many seals and twice as many witnesses, whereas among the Romans their magistrates handle large sums of money and scrupulously perform their duty because they have given their word on oath.'[12] Less cultivated the Romans might be; but there was something about them that impressed the Greeks.

Two hundred years later, Egypt, Syria, Asia Minor and Gaul had been added to Roman domains, and Roman dominance must have come to seem a fact of nature. Nevertheless, even then Greeks did not think of the Romans as quite on a par with themselves. Strabo, in the midst of a review of the geography of the whole world, still sees southern Italy outside the remaining Greek enclaves of Tarentum, Naples and Rhegium as barbarian territory, explicitly because it has been taken over by Romans.[13]

Ironically, this southern region was the area of Italy that had retained its own language until the first century BC, a language known as Oscan to the Romans, Opic to the Greeks. This language, related to Latin but as different from it as German is from English, had once been spoken far more widely than Latin; it had been the language, for example, of the Romans' early rivals, the Sabines (whose women the Romans had famously stolen) and the Samnites.

In fact, when they wanted to put them down, the Greeks liked to refer to their Roman masters as *Opikoí*. 'They keep calling us barbarians and insult us more foully than others with the name of *opics*,' the proverbially stiff Marcus Cato complained.[14] The point of this slur seems to have been lack of education, since the word was being borrowed back into Latin as a byword for illiteracy. Juvenal talks about a pedantic lady telling off her 'opic' girl-friend for using the wrong word.[15] 'Opic' was malapropic. This was another cruel irony. Had they forgotten that the first poet to adapt Greek metrics for use in Roman poetry had himself been an Oscan speaker, Quintus Ennius? Ennius had liked to boast that his three languages gave him three hearts.[16] His mother tongue had been Oscan, as he grew up in Calabria, in the heel of Italy; he knew Greek, because his local big city was Tarentum; and he had learnt Latin serving in the Roman army in the war against Hannibal. Two hundred and fifty years later, the last faint echoes of Oscan could still be heard, in the annual mime shows at Rome.[17]

The Slavs

In a way, trying to get a Greek view of the Romans to compare with their view of the Celts or Germans is unrewarding. The Celts and Germans may have been entertaining strangers, but after the second century BC the relation-ship between the Greeks and the Romans became more like a marriage (see Chapter 6, 'A Roman welcome: Greek spread through culture', p. 250). The Slavs, on the other hand, became a factor in the language map of Europe only when they forcibly made their presence felt on the Greeks. Understandably, there is little sympathetic insight in the early Greek descriptions, which were in any case written much later, when they were bearing down on the Balkans and Greece itself (see Chapter 6, 'Intimations of decline', p. 262). Prior to this, though, Tacitus (in his *Germania*, AD 98) has some remarks to make on their ancestors, the Veneti (latterly known as the Wends, or Sorbs) and Fenni (whose name was later given to the Finns, but who may have been Slavs).

> The tribes of Peucini, Venethi and Fenni, I hesitate whether to classify as Germans or Sarmatians...[18] The Venethi have brought many customs from them [the Sarmatians]: they prey on the whole range of woods and mountains between the Peucini [in the south] and the Fenni [in the north]. But they are more like Germans, since they build houses, use shields, and like to move on foot and fast: this is all very different from the Sarmatians who live in wagons and on horseback. The Fenni's sav-agery is amazing, their poverty appalling: they have no arms, no horses, no homes: they live on grass, dress in skins, sleep on the ground; their only resource is arrows, sharpened with bone for lack of iron. The same hunting sustains both men and women: they accompany each other everywhere, and claim their share of the prey. The children have no shelter from beasts or showers beyond the covering woven from

branches, and this is where youths return, and old people take refuge. But they think this is happier than groaning in fields, working in houses, and trying their and others' fortunes in hope and fear; they have no care for people, no care for gods, but have achieved something of outstanding difficulty, not even to need to wish for anything.[19]

The Veneti also appear in the pages of Ptolemy, mid-second century AD, as the *Ouenédai*, a 'very large nation occupying Sarmatia along the whole Venetic Gulf'. Apparently then they were living along the Baltic shore.[20]

Rún: The impulsive pre-eminence of the Celts

Rún: (a) something hidden or occult, a mystery; hidden meaning; (b) a secret; (c) secret thoughts or wishes, intention, purpose; (d) full consciousness, knowledge; (e) darling, love.

Royal Irish Academy, *Dictionary of the Irish Language*

Celtic origins are obscure, but when first heard of this culture was already seated at the heart of western Europe.

Archaeologically, they are identified with the culture, or rather succession of cultures, typified first by the Hallstatt site in Austria (dated thirteenth to sixth centuries BC), and then by the La Tène site on Lake Neufchâtel in Switzerland (from the sixth to the first century BC). Together with comparable sites, these defined the Iron Age way of life as experienced in central Europe. Their material goods, well preserved by salt and by marshland respectively in the two sites, include weapons, bronze and ceramic vessels, jewellery, clothing, wooden tools, pins, buckles, razors and wheeled vehicles. The decorative style with elaborate swirls and spirals, which we still see as Celtic, is very much in evidence.

This, then, defined the home life of our Celts. What of their linguistic existence?

Traces of Celtic languages

The longest-lasting, and most widely broadcast, evidence of the spread of Celtic languages is given by their place names: Celtic place names have a certain feel to them. Towns set up by Celts would often have suffixes such as *-dūnum*, 'fort', *-brīga*, 'hill', *-magus*, 'plain', *-brīva*, 'crossing', *-bona*, 'settlement' or 'spring'. There is also a recognisably Celtic tendency to self-congratulation: *sego-*, 'powerful', *uxello-*, 'high'. Such names can be found from the north of Britain (Uxellodunum to Segedunum at either end of Hadrian's Wall) to the very south of Iberia (Caetobriga—Setúbal, just south of Lisbon), and from the English Channel (Rotomagus—Rouen) to the Danube (Vindobona—Vienna, Singidunum—Belgrade). The snag is that such etymologising is so easy it may even have led to some towns being given a Celtic name for purely sentimental reasons. It is noticeable that many of them were created under Roman rule: Iuliobona, Augustodurum, Caesaromagus in Gaul, Flaviobriga, Augustobriga, Iuliobriga in Spain. A single place name is hardly evidence that the language from which it is drawn was spoken when the name was given.

It is also possible just to take the testimony of people, usually Greeks or Romans, who met or knew of Celts in different parts of Europe. Strabo records that three tribes of Gauls, the Boii,* Taurisci and Scordisci, were mixed up with the Thracians, which would place them towards the Balkans. He also says that the Scordisci lived near where the Noaros, the river swelled by the Kolapis, flows into the Danube.[21] Now a look at the map shows that the river swelled by the Ku(l)pa is in fact the Sava, and it flows into the Danube at Singidunum, modern Belgrade. Strabo is quite careful to distinguish Gauls from other races, for example noting that the Bastarnae may be considered Germans (vii.3.17), and that the Dacians and Getai speak the same language (vii.3.13). Although he makes no explicit reference to the language of these Gauls, it would seem that in the first century AD some form of Gaulish would have been spoken not just in southern Germany, but down into what is now Croatia and Serbia.†

Finally, there is the evidence of what languages are spoken where today. The Celtic languages spoken in the British Isles up to the present day are the direct descendants of the indigenous tongues that the Romans heard about them over the four hundred years when Britain was occupied, and Ireland was visited occasionally. There is also a continuing Celtic-language tradition

---

* The Boii were well known as a far-flung tribe of Gauls, having connections with Bohemia (etymologically 'Boii-home', though in Germanic not Celtic) and having a major settlement in north-eastern Italy (around such modern cities as Bologna, Parma and Modena). Somehow they also showed up as allies of the Helvetii in southern Gaul, and were defeated by Caesar at Bibracte in 58 BC. The name means 'hitters', according to Lambert (1997: 44).

† How they were related to the Celts in western Europe is quite unclear. Yugoslavia and Hungary are in fact the heart of the so-called Urnfield culture, dated by archaeologists to the first half of the first millennium BC, and so preceding the high points of Hallstatt and La Tène. The Urnfield culture had been on the path of the spread of Iron Age civilisation from the Aegean; and so it is quite possible that Celts had been in this area even longer than in western Europe. But as historians of Celtic-language speakers, we can only be agnostic about the link to these prehistoric material cultures.

in the Breton corner in the north-east of France, even if it remains unclear whether this has been strictly unbroken; i.e. whether Breton is a continuation of Gaulish, or a reimport of the language from Cornwall in the first millennium AD. Perhaps it is both, remixed.

Whatever the travels that took them there by the third century BC, we therefore have evidence of a variety of peoples most likely speaking Celtic, predominating in western Europe and its islands but extending right round the Alps north and south, and on into Dalmatia. They were predominantly settled populations, living in farming villages with roads linking them. Latin has shown up one characteristic of contemporary Gaul by (quite consciously, it seems) borrowing from Gaulish so many words for wheeled vehicles: *benna*, 'buggy', *carrus*, 'hand-cart', *cisium*, 'cabriolet', *carpentum*, 'carriage', *essedum*, 'war chariot', *raeda*, 'coach'. Indeed, magnificent four-wheeled carriages are significant grave-goods in many of the La Tène graves. So although basically settled, Gaulish society could also be very mobile when it chose.

But for linguists, the hardest evidence of where and when the language was used comes from writing. Since none of the Celts had a written literary tradition until fifth-century AD Ireland, this means that we are largely reliant on inscriptions. These come from many different places. Celts appear to have been literate only where they had neighbours who could teach them. And the places where this happened are far flung indeed, though naturally they tend to be on the margins of Celtic-speaking areas. Sadly, but unsurprisingly, they do not include sites equated with the Hallstatt or La Tène cultures.

How to recognise Celtic

Recognising an inscription as Celtic means knowing something about the properties of ancient Celtic languages. It turns out that an important characteristic of Celtic was the loss of the sound [p]. Such Latin basic words as *pater, piscis, plenus, super, pro* (translated by their English relatives *father, fish, full, over, before*) turn up still in modern Irish Gaelic as *athair, iasc, lán, for, roimh*. The same phenomenon can be seen in some of the remaining vestiges of Gaulish or British: *Cambo-ritum*, the British name of Lackford in Suffolk, seems to mean 'Crooked Ford', the last element, like *rhyd* in Welsh, meaning 'ford' (cf. Greek *poros*, Latin *portus*). And it is conjectured that the source for the name of the notorious 'Hercynian forest' mentioned by Caesar and Tacitus (now the Black Forest, but extending all the way across the German highlands to modern Leipzig) must have been a Celtic speaker who dropped his Ps: if its real name were *Perkun* this would make it the same as some Germanic words for mountain (Gothic *faírguni*, Old English *firgen*), but also allow a nice tie-up with the origin of the old Latin word *quercus*, 'oak'. It is natural to derive this from **perquus* (cf. known parallels such as *quinque*, 'five', from **penque*, *coquo*, 'cook', from **pequo*). And then it looks very like the name of the Lithuanian god *Perkūnas*, known for his association with oak trees!*

In other ways, Celtic languages of the period are remarkably like Latin. The system of inflexion for Gaulish nouns was just a little more complex than the Latin one, with seven cases to Latin's six, but tantalisingly close to it. So, for example, the noun *EQVOS*, 'horse', has the genitive *EQVI*, 'horse's'—the very same words in Latin and Gaulish. 'He has given to the mothers of Nîmes' comes out as *DEDE MATREBO NAMAUSIKABO*; in Latin it could be **DEDIT MATRIBUS NEMAUSICABUS*. An everyday piece of authentic Gaulish could be very close to its Latin equivalent: take for examples two typically frisky inscriptions on spindle whorls: *MONI GNATHA GABI BVθθVTON IMON* and *NATA VIMPI CURMI DA* would translate to *MEA NATA, CAPE MENTVLAM MEAM* and *NATA BELLA, CERVISIAM DA*: 'my girl, take my todger' and 'pretty girl, give some ale'.[22]

On a modern estimate, these divergences would represent something like one and a half millennia of separate development, or sixty generations. Although both were speaking variants of what had once been the same language, this was enough time for very different traditions to have developed in each variant.

Celtic literacy

The earliest known Celtic inscriptions (from *c*.575 to 1 BC) are found in the southern foothills of the Alps near Lakes Como and Maggiore. This was the home of the Lepontii. Their language is hence known as Lepontic, and is written in a script, the 'Lugano' alphabet, evidently borrowed from the

---

* (These asterisks show forms that have been reconstructed by linguists, but are not actually found in some text.) This absence of P is not as strange as it might seem. It also seems to have afflicted the indigenous language of Iberia, and even early Basque, and is typical too of modern Arabic. But Celtic did not remain a totally P-less language for long. At least some of its variants, including most dialects of Gaulish, and also British (leading to modern Welsh, Cornish and Breton), later started to pronounce the sound qu- as p. Hence its presence in the words for four and five (*pedwar* and *pimp* in modern Welsh, probably **petuar* and **pinpe* in Gaulish, on the evidence of some kiln records, mentioned in note 22 on p. 566). As a result, where initial qu- had been the mark of question words in the original language (cf. Latin's conservative *quis*, *quid*, *quando*, 'who, what, when'), initial p- has this role in this variety of Celtic language (cf. Welsh *pwy*, *pa*, *pam*, 'who, which, why', and presumably much the same in Gaulish). The other Celtic languages also changed the qu-, but just simplified it to a k- sound. Hence Irish *ceithir*, *cóic* ('four, five'), and *cé*, *cad*, *cá* ('who, what, where'). What evidence there is for Celtiberian suggests it was more like Irish than Gaulish in this respect.

Insubrian inscription at Briona

Etruscans, who were the dominant literate people in northern Italy.* The texts are usually only two or three words long, which can make interpretation difficult, and it is likely that most of the words are proper names.

No classical author characterised the Lepontii as Celts (despite vague rumours of a very early Gallic settlement of this region in Polybius and Livy).[23] Nevertheless, there are grounds for viewing Lepontic as a form of Celtic. It seems to have lost P, having *uer-* and *latu-* in place of Indo-European *uper-*, 'over', and *platu-*, 'flat'; it also has some proper names very reminiscent of Gauls, for example *alKouinos*, like Alkovindos, which would contain the root *windo-*, 'white', seen also in *Winchester* (once more clearly called *Vindobona*) and *Guinevere*.

Over four hundred years later, from about 150 BC, the same Lugano alphabet was used in mirror image (now left to right), a little farther south round Novara, to record a more clearly Gaulish language. This would be the written footprint of the Insubrians, who had invaded the north of Italy in the historic period. Livy (v.34) remarks that the city of Mediolanum (Milan—Gaulish

---

* The earliest known Etruscan inscriptions date from about a century earlier, *c.*700 BC. The Etruscans had themselves learnt how to write from the Greeks, though probably through contacts much farther south, round Cumae in the Bay of Naples.

for 'mid-plain') was founded by Gaulish incomers, pleased to find that the name Insubrian (familiar to them as a cantonal name in their homeland across the Alps) was already established in the neighbourhood.

This typical inscription reads:

TANOTALIKNOI	Dannotalos-son
KUITOS	Quintos
LEKATOS	the legate
ANOKOPOKIOS	Andocombogios
SETUPOKIOS	Setubogios
ESANEKOTI	(sons) of Essandecotos
ANAREUIZEOS	Andareuiseos
TANOTALOS	Dannotalos
KARNITUS	built the tumulus

with a vertical note at the side:

TAKOS TOUTAS   decision of the tribe

But Caesar notes that the most familiar script to the Gauls was Greek writing, and sure enough, Gaulish inscriptions written in Greek are found dating from 300 BC to AD 50. What is now the French Riviera was then very much a Greek coast, with notable colonies such as Nicaea (Nice) and Antipolis (Antibes), all focused on the metropolis of Massilia (Marseilles), which had been founded *c*.600 BC. There are about seventy such inscriptions on stone discovered so far, mostly gravestones and dedications, and there are also another 220 pieces of broken pottery with writing on them: this ancient equivalent of scrap paper and old bottles and cans is often gratifyingly durable.

σεγομαρος ουιλλονεος τοουτιους ναμαυσατις ειωρου βηλη σαμι σοσιν νεμητον

segomaros uilloneos tooutious namausatis íorou belesami sosin nemeton

'Segomaros son of Uillu, citizen of Nemausus, dedicated to Belesama this shrine'

These Greek-lettered inscriptions are found along the coast, and all the way up the River Rhône, with a few more in the centre of France, on the upper

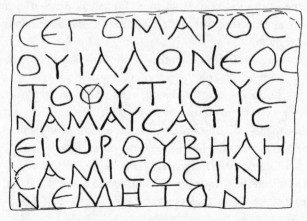

Gallo-Greek inscription found at Vaison, near Arausio (Orange)

reaches of the Loire and Seine. Caesar refers to Helvetian records written in Greek, and kept on wooden tablets. But this brings us well into the period of Rome's conquest of Gaul (completed in 51 BC). Thereafter we do find Gaulish written in Roman letters, but only for a century, and never actually replacing the use of Greek script: there have only been sixteen such Gallo-Roman inscriptions discovered to date. The most magnificent remnant of this period yet discovered is a fragmentary Druidical calendar engraved on bronze found at Coligny, not far from the Roman administrative centre of Lugdunum (Lyon).

North of the Seine, the only inscriptions that have turned up are on potters' stamps, which probably came from farther south. Advertising could also use 'eye candy' in a way decidedly reminiscent of the twentieth century: The inscription reads:

rextugenos sullias avvot   Rextugenos (son) of Sulla made (this pot).

Potter's stamp, found at Caudebec-en-Caux, near Rotomagus (Rouen)

Otherwise, the only evidence of written Gaulish is a few Celtic personal names on pots at Manching in southern Germany, and on a sword at Port in western Switzerland.

But there is hard evidence of another Celtic language, known as Celtiberian, being written in the north-east of central Spain. There are in fact eighty-five inscriptions, and fifty legends on coins, from the last two centuries BC. There is not much in these that incontrovertibly proves them Celtic,* rather than some other related strain of Indo-European, though the suitably grandiloquent name Divorix does appear: 'Divine-King', comparable with Julius Caesar's early adversary Dumnorix, 'World-King'. But they are in the right time and place to be Celtiberians, and it was an accepted truth in the ancient world that these people were Celts: Martial, a first-century AD poet born in the local capital of Bilbilis, liked to claim ancestry from Celts and Iberians.[24]

However, by AD 50 Gaulish, and indeed Insubrian and Celtiberian, appear largely to have lost their literate status, even in their heartland areas.

How Gaulish spread

How, then, did these languages reach the far parts of Europe where they were spoken? The spread of Celtic across Europe, phenomenal as it was, happened before recorded history. The forces that drove it are a matter for speculation and intuition, rather than for observation and inference. But if we take the culture at its own evaluation, Gaulish owed its success, or rather the success of the lineages that spoke it, to their distinctive equipment, notably wheeled vehicles drawn by horses, and to the magnificent products of their smiths, especially ironwork for warriors' swords, helmets and ring-mail armour.

A linguistic note confirms this. The words for 'iron' in Greek (*sidēron*), Latin (*ferrum*) and Celtic (*isarno-*)† have separate origins, but the Germanic word (e.g. Gothic *eisarn*, Old English *īsern*, *īren*) appears to have been borrowed from Celtic.[25] This is unsurprising, since the Celts were evidently the middlemen for the transmission of ironworking to the north of Europe. (Tacitus even mentions (*Germania*, xliii) that the Cotini, a Gaulish tribe, paid tribute to the German Quadi in iron ore. He adds typically, '*quo magis*

---

* Contrast Lusitanian, spoken farther south: we know hardly more than two words of this language, but those two words are enough to disqualify it as Celtic: *porcom tavrom*, 'pig bull'. The first has a P; the second has its V and R in the wrong order: compare Gaulish *tarvos*, Old Irish *tarb*, Middle Welsh *tarw*.

† Recorded in the Gaulish name of an old village in the French Jura, *Isarnodori, ferrei ostii*, 'iron door'. Grimm (1876, vol. I, ch. 4: 5).

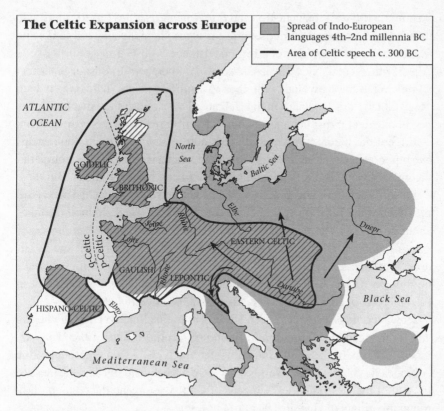

The Celtic Expansion across Europe

Spread of Indo-European languages 4th–2nd millennia BC

Area of Celtic speech c. 300 BC

ATLANTIC OCEAN

North Sea

Baltic Sea

GOIDELIC

BRITHONIC

Seine

Rhine

Elbe

EASTERN CELTIC

Dnepr

q-Celtic
p-Celtic

Loire

GAULISH

Rhône

LEPONTIC

Danube

Black Sea

HISPANO-CELTIC

Ebro

Mediterranean Sea

pudeat—the more shame to them': they should have been able to use the iron to turn the tables.)*

Although the technical level was high, then, its military application tended to emphasise individual leaders' prowess, sustained by these prestige products, rather than the development of overwhelming large-scale organisation. Their communities remained small, without even a feudal structure of overlords and kings. Literacy was unnecessary, and largely avoided. Perhaps, as some of their descendants would do two thousand years later on the other side of the world, they had been able to rely on their superior weapons, and prevail against vast odds without troubling to outwit their opponents.

Although Celtic warriors and their villages became widespread, they did not eliminate or submerge the communities in their path. (In this, they con-

---

* By contrast, Germanic has the same underlying root for 'bronze' as Latin: Gothic *aiz*, Old English *ār*, Old High German *ēr* versus Latin *aes*, suggesting that this technology was already an established acquisition before the common ancestors of the Italic- and Germanic-speaking tribes went their separate ways.

trast markedly with the spread of the *Pax Romana*, and of Latin with it.) To mention only the ancient communities of whose language we can find some trace, Celtic speakers are found in coexistence with Germans north of the Alps, with Veneti and Etruscans south of them, with Basque speakers (*Aquitani*) in southern Gaul, with Iberians and Tartessians in Spain, and with Macedonians and Thracians in the Balkans. This was a culture that harried its neighbours and thrust them aside, but did not subjugate or incorporate them.

But besides the raid, and military conquest of new land, there was perhaps one other channel through which the Celtic languages spread, and indeed developed into new and separate languages. This was navigation.

It was an accepted tradition of medieval Europe that Ireland had been populated from the coast of Spain. The usual grounds quoted are twin mistakes about geography and etymology. The reconstructed *Tabula Peutingeriana* shows Ireland as an island offshore from Brigantia (La Coruña), and St Isidore's influential sixth-century *Etymologiae* states: 'Hibernia…extends north from Africa. Its forward parts face (H)iberia and the Cantabric Ocean [viz. the Bay of Biscay]. Whence too it is called Hibernia.'[26]

However, there may have been a lot more to this link. Avienus, gathering coastal navigation information in the fourth century, says, of the 'Holy Island': 'the race of the Hierni inhabits it far and wide. Again the island of the Albiones lies near, and the Tartessians were accustomed to carry business to the end of the Oestrymnides. Citizens of Carthage too and the common folk round the Pillars of Hercules went to these seas.'[27]

Now *Iernē* was the common Greek term for Ireland, and the Oestrymnides are probably the Scillies, or Cornwall, since he also notes that these islands are 'rich in mine of tin and lead'.[28] The whole passage is evidence for a link between the British Isles and the southern Iberian region of Tartessus, known to be a focus of Carthage's trade empire.

This link is amply confirmed by archaeological evidence. Impressed by the apparent profusion of exchange relations among the different Atlantic-facing sectors of the European coast, including Ireland, Wales, Cornwall, Brittany, Galicia and Portugal in the late Bronze Age, 1200–200 BC, Barry Cunliffe has suggested that 'Atlantic Celtic' may have grown up as a lingua franca, or perhaps an elite language, among the various communities on the eastern seaboard.[29]

This hypothesis, though archaeologically inspired, has a certain attraction from the linguistic and cultural point of view. It gives a medium for the spread of Celtic across to the southern side of the Pyrenees, when there is no tradition of invasion from the north, and most of the intervening territory between southern Gaul and central Spain was in fact always held by Basques. It gives a basis in history to a persistent theme of old Irish literature, the *im-*

The Domain of "Atlantic Celtic"

- Main Phoenician colonies
- - - → Shipping routes
- Bronze cauldrons found
IRISH Language with Celtic-Hamito-Semitic perculiarities

mrama, tales of magical voyages, such as that of St Brendan. And it provides an explanation for a niggling fact of Celtic historical linguistics: the dialectal similarity between Celtiberian and the Goidelic languages of Ireland and western Scotland.

While Lepontic, Gaulish and Brythonic (P-Celtic) all usually convert old k^w to p, Celtiberian and Goidelic (Q-Celtic) retain the k element. It would be possible, then, to see Q-Celtic as the original form, spread to the shores of Gaul by effective users of iron, and then, through the establishment of exchange relationships and trade, beyond to the south and north across the sea. Subsequently, the Celts in Gaul and the Alps innovated in converting k^w to p, followed by their close associates in Britain, while the peripheral ones, Celtiberian and Goidelic, retained the k^w, those in the north, *Iernē*, later simplifying it to k. *

* In fact, few linguists today take this P/Q criterion as a very strong discriminant. The change could happen anywhere: indeed it has, in modern Romanian, and quite independently in the Italic dialects

In fact, some strange changes came over Celtic in the British Isles, as no-where else: verb–subject–object as basic word order, mutation of initial con-sonants, conjugated prepositions, strange locutions to express status and activity ('I am in my student', 'I am at reading of my book'), and much else. There are those who believe that these strangenesses are really inherited from the lost previous languages of the old inhabitants, perhaps spoken by the civilisations that raised megalithic monuments. Failing to learn the incoming language fully, they simply continued with many features of their old lan-guages. This is the *substrate* hypothesis; interesting, but it explains little since we know nothing of the languages of the British Isles prior to Celtic.

Another hypothesis is language mixing, or *creolisation*. It too can be brought into the theory of Celtic spread by navigation along the Atlantic coast, by noting that major partners in this network, for most of the first mil-lennium BC, were the Phoenicians, many of them (specifically the Carthagin-ians) based in North Africa, and quite capable of maintaining links along the whole Mediterranean. Now it so happens that in the North African language families, Egyptian, Semitic and Berber, there are direct parallels for at least seventeen of these curious characteristics of British and Irish Celtic, charac-teristics that are quite unparalleled in any Indo-European language, let alone their Celtic cousins, and which are indeed extremely rare globally.[30] If Celtic was indeed spread as a coastal lingua franca, these North Africans, in trade and exchange, would have been among its speakers, and effective in mould-ing it.

But there is no direct linguistic evidence for any of this at the moment: as to the spread of Gaulish across most of Europe, and the origins of Celtiberian, and the Celtic languages of the British Isles, we are in the realm of specula-tion and reconstruction. By contrast, we have direct testimony on the advent of Celtic speakers in Italy and the eastern Mediterranean.

The Gauls' advances in the historic record
It is clear that the ideal of the raid, whereby parties of young men would seek to cover themselves with glory and booty, never ceased to be current in Celtic societies that remained independent. Successful raids, especially if perpe-trated by younger sons without prospects at home, could turn into de facto in-vasions. And we also encounter examples of deliberate decisions by Celtic

(e.g. Oscan changed to P, Latin didn't). And even in the centre of the P-dialects, not all Qs changed to P: on the Coligny calendar in the Rhône valley we find EQVOS, EQVI, 'horse' (even though the usual Gaulish name for the horse goddess is Epona), and the 'Sequani', living on the river 'Sequana' (Seine) in northern Gaul, seem unaffected. But P-Celtic and Q-Celtic are such a chestnut in the tra-dition that it seems deceptive to leave it out of the discussion.

tribes to seek new land in a mass migration: a famous one is the tribe of the Helvetii, whose intent to move from the Alps into southern Gaul was frustrated by Julius Caesar at the beginning of his Gallic Wars.

These kinds of movement twice led to major incursions by parties of Gauls into the centres of Graeco-Roman civilisation. The first was the sack of Rome by Brennus in 390 BC, followed almost immediately by a withdrawal with massive booty and extorted payments. Polybius describes the characteristics of the Gauls who moved into the valley of the Po around this time:

> They lived in unwalled villages and had no knowledge of the refinements of civilization. As they slept on straw and leaves, ate meat and practised no other pursuits but war and agriculture, their lives were very simple and they were completely unacquainted with any art or science. Their possessions consisted of cattle and gold, since these were the only objects that they could easily take with them whatever their circumstance and transport wherever they chose. It was of the greatest importance to them to have a following, and the man who was believed to have the greatest number of dependants and companions about him was the most feared and powerful member of the tribe.[31]

The second was the pillage of Delphi, the Greek religious centre, in 279 BC, carried out by another Brennus, but soon beaten off by the rallying Greeks. Remnants remained as roving mercenaries in Macedonia. But one party (numbering twenty thousand, half of them women and children—so not just a war band) was invited next year to cross the Sea of Marmara into Anatolia, to fight on behalf of Nicomedes, king of Bithynia, against the Seleucid king Antiochus. They gave good service, but afterwards became a liability, until they were settled more permanently in the region around Ancyra. This became the capital of this new settled community, henceforth known either as the Galatians or Gallo-Greeks. Their wars with neighbours, especially the city of Pergamum, and their service as mercenaries (as far afield as Egypt), continued for another century.

Both in northern Italy and in Anatolia it was the Romans who finally settled the hash of restless Gaulish marauders.

A series of Roman pre-emptive aggressions on the Adriatic coast, and the founding of military colonies in the area, between 330 and 270 BC, gained them considerable respect. The first Punic war then intervened (264–41), but after the Romans had seen off the Carthaginians, they returned to the fray, and from 232 to 218 BC pressed farther into the heart of northern Italy with pitched battles and new colonies of their own citizens and allies (hence permanent pockets of Latin speakers) at Placentia (Piacenza) and Cremona. Once again the Carthaginians interrupted, this time with an invasion right through the heart of northern Italy (Hannibal and his elephants, in 217 BC); amazingly, this had no effect against the strengthening Roman hold on the area. When Hannibal had been eliminated—an ordeal that itself took sixteen years—the Romans proceeded once again to battle, with a victory over the Insubrians at Como in 196, and more colonies in the valley of the Po at Bologna, Modena and Parma, effectively staking out the area where the Gauls had previously been able to organise raids. The Boii, the principal warlike tribe, were defeated and stripped of half their territory. Writing fifty years later of a visit to the valley of the Po, Polybius observed that 'Gallia Cisalpina' was now just a name: the place had become a part of Italy.[32]

In Anatolia, the Romans started to try to bridle the independent Galatians just after they had finished the job on their kinsmen in Italy. In 189 BC a Roman general, as part of a campaign in support of Pergamum (still suffering from Galatian mercenaries), defeated all three constituent tribes, the Tolistobogii, Trocmi and Tectosages, and sold forty thousand of them into slavery. (The previous century had evidently been good to them, and their population had grown massively.) But Galatian provocation continued, not only with Pergamum, but also with other neighbours, Cappadocia to the east, Pontus in the north. A century later, under King Deiotarus, they were allied with Rome, on the strength of a common enmity with the ambitious king of Pontus, Mithradates VI; in a signal feat of political juggling he managed to remain in favour throughout the civil war that followed Caesar's assassination, and to die in his bed in 40 BC. Thereafter little more is heard of the Galatians' irrepressible ways, but in 25 BC Augustus made Galatia part of a much larger unit including all the provinces directly to its south, diluting any remaining Celtic identity.

The Gallo-Greeks never left a trace of written Gaulish, although they provided the inspiration for some of the finest artistic evocations of the Gauls (in statuary at Pergamum); and the evidence of their names is pretty authentic (*Tectosages*, 'home-seekers', *Deiotarus*, 'holy bull'.*) Nevertheless, a memory of their linguistic identity lingered: at the end of the fourth century AD, St Jerome, famous for his Latin translation of the Bible, which became the Vulgate, was declaring that he could communicate with Ancyra's Galatians in much the same language as he had heard spoken in his youth near Trier, on

---

* Perhaps this is a glimpse of Gaulish with a Greek accent: the natural Gaulish for this would be *Deiwo-tarwos*, but Greek had dropped all [w].

the Rhine. But four hundred years is an awfully long time for a language without a written tradition to survive in the midst of Hellenised Asia Minor: perhaps he was just alluding to something he had read.

This venture into Asia Minor, with its linguistic impact on the central highlands round Ancyra, is instructive about the way in which a language like Gaulish could be spread, and the conditions for its survival. It was the language of a lineage. When its speakers moved, its domain would move with them, and if the community grew, so would the number of its speakers. If the community lost its identity, or its distinguishing customs, the language would disappear.

Consilium: The rationale of Roman imperium

Consilium: (a) deliberation, consultation, a considering together, counsel; (b) a conclusion made with consideration, determination, resolution, measure, plan, purpose, intention; (c) the persons who deliberate, a council.

Lewis and Short, *A Latin Dictionary*

The Celtic speakers in Britain proved surprisingly impervious to Latin in the long term, even if it was the country's language of officialdom and literacy for four hundred years. Latin never became the language of the common people in Britain. So it was that Britain's derisory reputation with the Romans was ultimately fulfilled: 'neither brave in battle nor faithful in peace'.[33] We must ask how this spread of the conqueror's language could fail to occur.

Mōs Māiōrum—the Roman way

It is no secret that the basis for the spread of Latin was the political and military spread of the Roman imperium (a word originally meaning *command*, but later carrying all the connotations of its French rendering, *empire*.) In this it was unlike Celtic, but rather like English in its early modern career. But like the speakers of English too (and again unlike the Celts), the Romans were seldom nakedly aggressive or belligerent in motivating their campaigns. There was also, among both sets of empire-builders, an unwillingness to talk openly about the commercial and material benefits of what was achieved—again unlike the Celts with their emphasis on the joys of booty. What really drew Rome out to conquer every country round the Mediterranean?

We have seen that very early on (the second century BC) it was a matter of curiosity to Greeks such as Polybius to figure out what made the Romans so

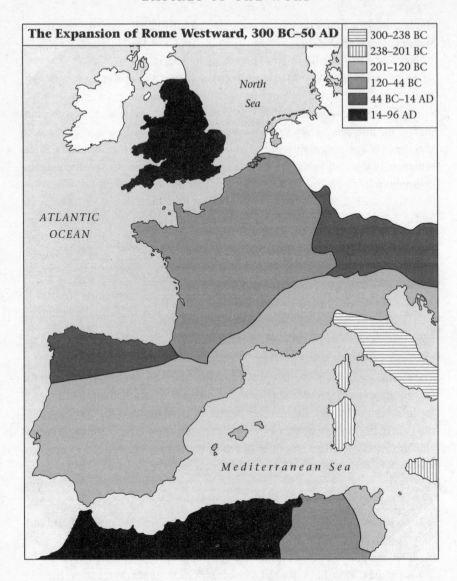

The Expansion of Rome Westward, 300 BC–50 AD

300–238 BC
238–201 BC
201–120 BC
120–44 BC
44 BC–14 AD
14–96 AD

speedily victorious, apparently against all comers. Although he made some trenchant remarks about the Roman character (see 'The contenders: Greek and Roman views', p. 279), he did not settle for any easy or simple answer. And even with the benefit of two thousand years' hindsight, it smacks of special pleading (or *ex post facto* rationalisation) to detect reasons why it had to be just this village halfway down the Mediterranean's central peninsula which was bound to take over the whole circuit of its coasts. Nevertheless, it is possible to see differences between the Romans' way and that of their neighbours, especially those in western Europe, which are our special interest in this chapter.

The Romans were an intensely civic society, with an overriding and persistent aversion to long-term dominion by a single man. Their system of government took checks and balances to heights unequalled before or since. From 510 BC, the traditional date of the foundation of their *Rēs Publica* (this Latin term for their constitution, the basis for our word *republic*, means simply 'the people's property'), they had organised annual elections for the main offices of state, and each holder was matched with one or more colleagues with whom he must share his power. The two holders of the supreme executive office, called consuls, were each in effect joint king for the year; but their power was only absolute when on campaign outside the city; otherwise every decision, like those of all the office-holders, was subject to *prōvocātio* ('challenge'), i.e. appeal to the Roman people. (The joint nature of consulship even led to their assuming the post of commander-in-chief on alternate days, which could cause military chaos at times of crisis.) The only persistent executive institution was the *Senātus*, the council of 'elders', usually about three hundred strong, made up mostly of men who had previously held office. They were responsible for setting the level of taxes. The Senate was always dominated by the old families that had taken responsibility for government since the beginning. Nevertheless, there was room for the occasional *novus homō* ('new man') of talent (and the necessary means*) to break into the ranks from time to time.

Holders of the top two offices, consuls and praetors, might expect an overseas governorship, to exercise authority *prō cōnsule*, 'on behalf of the consul', or *prō praetōre*, 'on behalf of the praetor', for a period of years after their term of office ended. These officers undertook many of Rome's foreign wars. In time of national emergency, the consular system could be suspended for six months at a time, and a (single) dictator appointed. Although there were persistent problems from the later second century BC onwards, with over-mighty generals unwilling to accept the limits the system placed on them, these institutions were all more or less functioning during the acquisition of Rome's foreign empire, which was largely complete by 44 BC, when Julius Caesar was made dictator for life, and then assassinated, leading to the downfall of the Republic. All the institutions continued to exist for another

---

* Senators needed to be at least of equestrian rank, for which the qualification (in landed property) was set at 400,000 sestertii. Taking the 1879 valuation in Lewis and Short's *Latin Dictionary*, and applying inflation rates since, this would equate to a present (2003) value of £186,000 or $315,000.

five hundred years, but henceforth they were always dominated by a *Princēps*, 'top man', as the emperor was called, who ruled for life (though this was often cruelly, or mercifully, brief). The term *rēx*, 'king', was still avoided, a taboo surviving from 510 BC, but Rome had in fact returned to being a monarchy, however skilled it might be at dissembling.

This was evidently a very elaborate system, which could only work because of an ingrained respect for tradition and law. It provided a framework in which an expanding city-state could govern itself in an orderly fashion, while keeping the control of organised force, the army, in the hands of the established classes. The Romans preferred predictable principle to charismatic leadership, and as their influence increased (for in fact their disciplined military organisation seemed to give them the edge in most conflicts) they exported this pattern of government into the cities they conquered and then enlisted. Little by little, the benefits of Roman citizenship were extended throughout the expanding empire, giving the new subjects (some of them) a strong motivation for loyalty. In effect, the Roman empire in its day stood for the benefits of globalisation: good communications, access to all that the world could provide, and freedom (usually) from arbitrary government and oppression. To adopt a favourite Roman phrase: *ōtium cum dignitāte*—peace with honour, or (equivalently) leisure with good value.

But this respect for tradition did not extend to a particular respect for the older remnants of their language, Latin. Although the Romans' most ancient code of laws, the famous Twelve Tables, was written in Latin, somehow no authoritative version of them survived until the end of the Republic. The Romans were unsentimental about their own language; even their closest equivalent to Holy Writ, the Sibylline Books, consulted for guidance in time of trouble, were not written in Latin, but Greek hexameter verse.

Latin was simply the language that they had grown up with; when dealing with foreigners, it was practical to use it, since the solid base of the Roman Republic meant that in negotiations foreigners were almost always in the suppliant position. The Greek language created an exception to this preference, since, as the Romans expanded their knowledge of Italy and the world beyond its shores, they discovered Greek colonies everywhere, doing business, and generally projecting a self-confident attitude, derived from an aggressively literate culture, and links with their *mētropóleis* ('mother cities') back in the eastern Mediterranean. And as the Romans discovered the undreamt-of heights to which Greek culture had been developed, they were happy (at first) to use the Greek language for their own intellectual work rather than undertake the onerous task of trying to build up Latin to compete with it. The first known literary production by a Roman, Fabius Pictor's history of Rome (late third century BC), was in Greek. Although there was an attempt early on to establish a literary tradition that was more traditionally Roman, with Livius Andronicus and Naevius writing their Latin epics in Saturnian metre, they failed to carry the day. Henceforth almost all Latin works were closely modelled on Greek originals.

One aspect of Greek culture found an immediate resonance in Rome. This was the respect for rhetoric, what the Romans called *ars ōrātōria*, the skills of persuasion, which were just as important as those of fighting and military command in these city-states (both Greek and Roman), where decisions were almost always taken by assemblies, not individuals. Training in oratory became the core of Roman higher education, students working up debates (*contrōversiae*) and policy speeches (*suāsōriae*) in the way in which nowadays they turn out essays; and the effect on Latin style was pervasive, lasting long after the decline of free institutions. Even love poetry can sound rather hectoring in Latin, a favourite trick being to turn to an imaginary audience. And poems and speeches were seen as very much the same game: in the second century AD Marcus Aper ('Mark Hogg'), a noted advocate from Gaul, was pointing out how much harder it was to get a name for oneself through poetry than through oratory, especially in the provinces.[34]

Latin was spread round the empire not least by the army, originally made up of citizens but into which increasingly men were enlisted from all over, and also by the common Roman policy of granting soldiers land on which to settle after their discharge. (We have already noted the role played by the army in Latinising one of their earliest poets, Ennius, originally an Oscan speaker; and how strategically placed colonies ultimately converted Cisalpine Gaul into just another part of Italy.) This never had a major effect in the eastern Mediterranean, where the lingua franca, Greek, was just too well established ever to be shaken. But in Gaul and Iberia the Roman colonies seem to have led to the eventual decline and replacement of their Celtic languages by Latin.

The desertion of Gaulish

Inscriptions in Gaulish had all died out a hundred years after the Roman conquest, although there are scattered anecdotes indicating some survival of the spoken language for a couple of hundred more years. In the second century St Irenaeus, who came west from Asia Minor to take up a bishopric in Lugdunum (Lyons), reports having to learn 'a barbarous tongue' when he arrived there.[35] In the third century, the great lawyer Ulpian stated that certain sworn statements could be made in Gaulish.[36] Then, towards the end of that century, the historian Lampridius mentions that a Druidess had used Gaulish to foretell the death of Alexander Severus (who reigned 222–35). And in a dialogue of Sulpicius Severus (363–425), a Gaul who does not speak Latin well is told: 'speak to us in Celtic, or if you prefer, in Gaulish'. And even in the fifth century, Sidonius Apollinaris[37] declares that the nobility of the Arverni, a tribe in central southern Gaul, had just recently learnt Latin and cast off the 'rough scales of Gaulish speech' (*sermōnis Gallicī squāmam*).

But from the evidence of the languages' progeny (the sorry fact that they had none), it is clear that Gaulish and Celtiberian were effectively finished by the Roman takeover, and its introduction of Latin. Despite the Gaulish respect for eloquence noted by Lucian, Classical culture had nothing positive to say about the value of the Celtic language traditions, and they were allowed to lapse.

This total loss is surprising, since five hundred and more years later so many myths were written down in Irish and Welsh, retelling the adventures of gods such as Nuada of the Silver Hand (Gaulish *Nodens*), Lugh of the Long Arm—or Lleu Skilful Hand—(*Lugus*), Brigid the High (*Brigindona* or *Brigantia*), Goibhniu or Gofannon the Smith (*Gobannio*), Morrígan or Rhiannon the Great Queen (*Rigantona*), and not forgetting Ogma (*Ogmios*) himself; and surviving iconography (for example, on the magnificent cauldron found at Gundestrup) shows that other gods, such as the horned Cernunnos, had complicated myths. This demonstrates that there must have been a wealth of fascinating and unfamiliar subject matter that the Gauls could have retold if they had had the will.

The loss was not inevitable, for the transformation that Latin had undergone to incorporate prestigious Greek shows that it was quite possible for one ancient language to take on board another's culture without being capsized; * and the survival of Greek in the east itself shows that even Latin was not invincible, in the face of a self-confident tradition. But neither Gauls nor Celtiberians made any attempt that we know of to recast Roman culture in their own Celtic terms. Rather, they seem to have adopted the new Roman, and Latin-speaking, ways with alacrity, since it is precisely the areas of western Europe that spoke Celtic in the ancient world which now have Latin-derived languages: French, Occitan, Spanish, Catalan, Portuguese, as well as a few other smaller languages derived from Latin. This is doubly surprising when we contrast the nature of Roman society with what the Gauls and Celtiberians had previously known. A civic, centralised, urban society replaced the more

---

* And just about the same time, Armenian was doing much the same thing with an infusion of Persian.

scattered, and sometimes more mobile, village life of the past. Evidently, for the Celts, it felt like progress. The Romans must have won the loyalty of the rising generation, for Vercingetorix, the organiser of Gaul's last struggle for independence, was never invoked as a heroic inspiration (until Napoleon III took him up 1900 years later), and there were only a couple of revolts, fairly easily put down, in the generation following the Roman conquest of Gaul. Gaul had fallen to Caesar in a blitzkrieg taking just eight years. By contrast, it had taken Rome almost two centuries to completely establish its control of Spain (from the expulsion of the Carthaginians in 206 to Augustus's Cantabrian Wars ending in 19 BC). Nevertheless, Spain too quietened down about the same time, and at last accepted as its fate the *Pāx Romāna*.

Latin among the Basques and the Britons

Surrender, then, or perhaps even enthusiastic take-up, was the majority option when the inhabitants of ancient western Europe were brought into the Roman empire. But it is worthwhile sparing a moment to consider two cases where this option was not taken.

One was Basque, presumably the language of the Aquitanians of southwest Gaul* (and the Vascones in Iberia) in Caesar's time, which survived the influx of Latin to replace its Gaulish and Celtiberian neighbours, as it has survived everything else that history has thrown at it in the last two thousand years. It is the special case, par excellence, of European language history, since it pre-dates all the Indo-European languages. There are records of Basques serving in the Roman army (indeed, a group of them travelling with the over-mighty general Marius allowed him to mount a brief reign of terror in Rome in 86 BC;[38] others are known to have served on Hadrian's Wall in Britain), but their identity proved equal to the challenge of Roman rule. They borrowed the words for 'olive' and 'oil' (*oliva, olio*), and 'statue' (*estatu*), showing the acceptance of certain aspects of Roman life that had been new to them, but otherwise show no effect from five hundred years of presence in the Roman empire.

The more complicated case is that of language survival in Britain. We have already seen from the evidence of place names that a language either very like Gaulish, or a dialect of it, was spoken here at the time of the Roman invasions. Personal names tell the same story: among the names of noted kings

---

* Names mentioned in Aquitanian inscriptions appear to have Basque roots, e.g. Cison, Andere, Nescato and Bihoxvs beside Basque *gizon*, 'man', *andere*, 'lady', *neskato*, 'girl', and *bihotz*, 'heart' (Gorrochategui 1995: 38).

and queens among the Britons we have *Cassi-vellaunos* ('oak-dominator'), *Tascio-vanos* ('badger-slayer'), *Cuno-belinos* ('dog of the god Belinos'— Shakepeare's Cymbeline), *Caratacos* ('beloved'), *Boudicca* ('Victoria'— cf. Irish *búadach*, 'triumphant').

After the conquest of AD 43, which led to full-scale permanent occupation, the Romans made a conscious effort to spread Latin, and indeed Roman education, among the British elite. Tacitus comments cynically on the education plans of Agricola (governor of Britain from 77 to 84 and, as it happened, his father-in-law):

> he instructed the sons of the chiefs in liberal arts, and expressed a preference for the native wit of the British over the studies of the Gauls, so as to plant a desire for eloquence in people who had previously rejected the Roman language altogether. So they took to our dress, and wearing the toga. Gradually they were drawn off into decadence, with colonnades and baths and *chic* parties. That was called a civilized life [*humānitās*] by these innocents, whereas it was really part of their enslavement.[39]

In a bitter irony, these studies were initiated in the winter after Agricola had finally obliterated, with much carnage, the centre of Druidical learning on the Isle of Anglesey.

Although they had started from the same language, we can detect, from the odd remark made by Romans, that the British were bracketed with, but not quite up to, the continental Gauls in their adoption of Latin. In a satire on the way the world had gone mad, Juvenal (a contemporary of Tacitus in the second century AD) wrote:

> Today the whole world has its Greek and Roman Athens;
> the eloquent Gauls have taught the British to be advocates,
> and Thule is talking of hiring an oratory teacher.[40]

The mention of Thule here, which as far as the Romans were concerned might have been the North Pole, shows that Juvenal is thinking in terms of extremes. This is the condescension of the Roman establishment, showing much in common between old and more recent imperialisms: the conquerors might well tell subject minorities that their only hope lay in civilising themselves, but would never take them seriously when they tried to make good on this aspiration.

There is direct evidence that Latin did spread beyond formal and government uses. Odd tiles with scribbled Latin graffiti have turned up on sites, most amusingly at Newgate in London: AVSTALIS DIBVS XIII VAGA-TUR SIB COTIDIM, 'Gus has been wandering off every day for thirteen days', an example of ancient whistle-blowing. The waters at the health resort and holiday centre that the Romans developed at Bath have yielded over a hundred ritual curses and oath tokens, written in rough Latin (sometimes backwards): DOCIMEDIS PERDIDIT MANICILIA DVA QVI ILLAS IN-VOLAVI VT MENTES SVA PERDET OCVLOS SVS IN FANO VBI DES-TINA, 'Docimedes has lost a pair of gloves. May whoever has made off with them lose his wits and his eyes in the temple where [the goddess] decides.'

And Welsh, that modern descendant of the British language which was being spoken in and among this colloquial Latin, has preserved over six hundred words borrowed from it, including such household terms as *mur*, *ffenestr*, *gwydr*, *cegin*, *cyllell*, *ffwrn*, *seban*, *ysbwng* (wall, window, glass, kitchen, knife, oven, soap, sponge) and *ceirios*, *castan*, *lili*, *rhos*, *fioled* (cherry, chestnut, lily, rose, violet). There are many more words in more intellectual domains such as law and Christianity.

In the modern era it has been argued, from some phonetic properties of these borrowings, that Latin as spoken in Britain was more conservative than in other parts of the Roman empire.[41] Conceivably, this could suggest that it was less well established in ordinary currency, remaining instead a stiff and formal means of expression. St Patrick, who grew up on the Scottish borders in the early fifth century, complained that his Latin was always weak, because having been captured by Irish raiders when he was sixteen, he had missed out on the crucial years of education. Evidently Latin was not an everyday means of expression even in his well-to-do family.

But whatever the glimmer of truth that may have been detected here, our reliance on written records distorts our sense of the role that must have gone on being played by British. This absence of written British is quite surprising, and has not been explained. Gaulish was often written down on the Continent, but British was evidently not: in Britain, only two inscriptions from the Roman period in a language other than Latin have ever been discovered. They are two of the inscriptions on tin/lead sheet from the waters of Bath, and seem to be in something like Celtic, but are not decipherable at all.[42]

Latin persisted after the Roman conquest as the language of learning: in Britain, as elsewhere, essentially unchallenged until the Renaissance and the Enlightenment of the sixteenth to eighteenth centuries gradually made the use of European vernaculars acceptable for serious factual writing. But somehow, some time in the fifth century, between the Roman withdrawal from Britain and the Saxon conquest of England, it got lost as a language of the British people.

There is no point in contenting ourselves, as some have, with non-explanations, such as a general retreat, visible in the period, from the cities, something that is evidenced by a run-down in developed services such as aqueducts, and part of the decline of the empire as a whole before the incursions from the east. This may indeed have happened, and may have weakened the areas in Britain where Latin was most likely to be used. But it does not discriminate between the situation in Gaul and that in Britain: we would still need to explain why only in Britain did Latin remain a language of the cities, leaving British strong in the country, whereas Latin spread to every corner of the land in most of Gaul.

We shall return to this when we consider what became of British itself, over most of what is now England. But however weak British turned out to be in competition with English, it must be remembered that British had outlived Latin in this island, even if it had never been seen as a language worth writing down. There is no trace of any Romance language assuming a life of its own in Britain after the departure of the last Roman garrisons from Britain to defend Italy in the early 400s.

Einfall: Germanic and Slavic advances

einfallen: (a) to collapse, to cave in; (b) *in ein Land* ~ to invade (a country); (c) (night) to fall, (winter) to set in; (d) (beams of light) to be incident; (e) (game birds) to come in, settle; (f) to join in, come in (on a piece of music), break in (to a conversation); (g) (thought) occur to somebody...

Collins German Dictionary

einfallen: ... loan translation of Latin *incidere*.

Reklams Etymologisches Wörterbuch von Lutz Mackensen

The Germanic invasions—irresistible and ineffectual

The end to the Roman occupation of Britain, when it came, was determinate and sudden. Alaric, leader of the Visigoths, was threatening to invade Italy. In 401 Stilicho, himself a Vandal but the empire's commander-in-chief, withdrew the garrison from Britain to reinforce the empire's heartland. This left Britain itself defenceless against the steadily increasing incursions of Germani along its 'Saxon shore', the coast facing Europe. In 410 the Britons sent an appeal to the emperor for reinforcement: his reply was to order them to

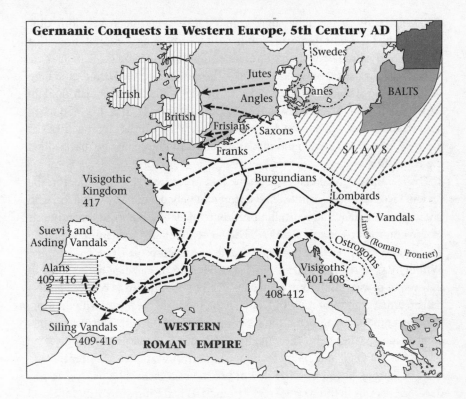

Germanic Conquests in Western Europe, 5th Century AD

Swedes

Jutes

Irish   Danes   BALTS

Angles

British

Frisians   Saxons

Franks   S L A V S

Visigothic
Kingdom
417   Burgundians   Lombards

Vandals

Suevi and
Asding Vandals   Ostrogoths   *Limes (Roman Frontier)*

Alans
409-416   Visigoths
401-408

408-412

Siling Vandals
409-416   **WESTERN
ROMAN EMPIRE**

look to their own defence; somewhat surreally he added that the raising of
local forces would not be taken as hostility to Rome. That was the last they
heard. Within a generation, there was no British province to defend. The
Saxons had come to stay.

The end of the Roman empire in the west was soon to follow. On 31 December 406 there had been a mass crossing of the frozen Rhine: Suebi from
the east side of the Rhine, together with Vandals originally from farther east,
and Alans (not German speakers at all, but Iranians, driven out of the Pontic
steppes by the Huns), then cut a swath across Gaul and entered Spain. The
Vandals kept going, crossed the Strait of Gibraltar (then still known as the
Pillars of Hercules), and by 439 were established at Carthage in North Africa
(where they built a navy and became the new power in the Mediterranean).

Alaric had succeeded in entering Rome in 410 (although the centre of government had moved to Ravenna), and committed the ultimate horror of sack-
ing it, but died shortly after. The Visigoths then continued an advance that
took them across southern France and into Iberia, constricting into its corners
the preceding Suebi, Alans and Vandals. There they founded a new kingdom

that lasted 250 years, ruling first from Toulouse, and later Toledo.* Ultimately, in 711, their reign was terminated by something completely new for Europe, a Muslim (Arabic-speaking) invasion from the south.

But back in the east, the generation following Alaric had seen Attila, king of the Turkic-speaking Huns from 435 to 453, bring the Hunnish domain west to include all of Germany.† He was held off from Gaul in 451, and when he died soon after, his empire disintegrated into a mosaic of German tribes in the west, and a Slav area in the east, with the Huns dominant only back round the Black Sea.

By 476 the political centre of Rome had fallen, and the last emperor, the juvenile Romulus Augustulus, had been humanely deposed by Odoacer, who had once been a German-speaking follower of Attila, but most recently one of the empire's own commanders. Different tribes of Germani then spread and settled with bewildering speed across the corpse of the old empire. Within fifty years, the Franks (who for two hundred years had been settled in the area of modern Belgium, even employed by the empire as border patrols) had assumed control of most of Gaul, spreading from the north, with the Burgundians holding a large, but diminishing, area in the south. The Ostrogoths, soon to be displaced by the equally Germanic Lombards, held Italy, the south-west of Gaul and Dalmatia on the eastern Adriatic coast. After this the west of Europe began to settle down; but the east of Europe had yet to undergo incursions in turn from Avars (from 550) and Bulgars swiftly followed by Khazars (from 650) and Magyars (from 750).§

Amazingly, the linguistic effects of this political and demographic turmoil, which lasted 150 years in the west of Europe, were slight. Certainly a polyphony of new languages must have been heard, if briefly, west of the Urals between 400 and 850. But west of the Elbe there can have been precious little change from the state of affairs essentially brought about by Caesar's con-

---

* Their ascendancy was notable for unending struggle against the Basques: each king making the proud, but apparently empty, boast in his annals 'domuit Vascones—he tamed the Basques'.
† Strangely, Attila is really his nickname in Gothic, and means 'Dad'.
§ Of these, only the language spoken by the Magyars is clear: it was Hungarian, related to the Uralian languages of northern Siberia. As for the others, Avar was probably a Mongol and Bulgar and Khazar Turkic languages. Old Avar does not seem to have been the same as what is now known as Avar, which is a language of the north-east Caucasus, spoken in Daghestan and Azerbaijan, and quite unrelated to Turkic. Bulgar may survive in scattered pockets across Siberia to this day, known as Chuvash. (This name is identical with Tabgach, the name of a people famous for their fourth-century conquest of northern China.) (See Chapter 4, 'Language from Huang-he to Yangtze', p. 140.) The Khazars ruled from the Caspian Sea to Kiev for a century (c.650–750), and are chiefly famous for their choice of mass conversion to Judaism in 861. Today's Karaim are their descendants. Another Turkic group, the Tatars of the Golden Horde, moved across in the thirteenth century.

quest of Gaul around 50 BC, other than the vanishing echoes of Germanic languages, Saxon, German and Gothic, as they passed rapidly across the central plains of Gaul and out of hearing in the farther reaches to the south and west .

When the dust from galloping hoofs had cleared, the creak of covered wagons had died away, and the gilt had dried on the palaces of the newly self-appointed royal families of medieval Europe, language boundaries were eerily familiar. The edge of Germanic had possibly slipped a little to the west during the long period when the empire's borders had still been defended, not least because neighbouring Germans had increasingly been invited across it, as *foederati*, 'treaty people', or *laeti*, 'joyous ones', to serve in the army, or on the land, for the benefit of Roman society. But the line between Germanic and Romance was still drawn from the western end of the mouths of the Rhine in a south-eastward direction. And the repeated falling of parts of Gaul under German domination, and ultimately being firmly settled under the Franks, did not serve to translate it or rotate it further.

The failure of Frankish domination to replace the language of Gaul was paralleled in the other new German kingdoms. In Italy under the Ostrogoths and Lombards, in Iberia under a succession of Vandals, Suebi, Alans and Visigoths, in coastal North Africa under the Vandals, the language established under the Roman empire persisted.* Despite the fact that the Visigoths ruled Spain for 250 years, one cannot even detect a significant number of Gothic words borrowed into Spanish from this period. Menéndez Pidal, the Spanish historical linguist, writes:

> It appears that the Germanic elements in Spanish do not proceed, in general, from the Visigoth domination of the peninsula, as might have been expected: the number of invaders was relatively slight to have much influence; moreover, the Visigoths, before reaching Spain had lived for two centuries in intimate contact with the Romans, now as allies now as enemies, in Dacia, Moesia, in Italy itself and in Gaul, and were very much permeated with Roman culture.[43]

---

* Latin bore a charmed life in North Africa, for a century (428–533) under the Vandals, and then controlled by the Roman empire resurgent from Constantinople until 696. The career of the most famous resident, St Augustine (354–430), bishop of Hippo, would have been unthinkable outside a Latin-speaking milieu. Remarks he makes in some of his sermons provide evidence that bilingualism with Punic, the old language of Carthage, may have persisted until the fourth century (Sznycer 1996). Evidently the common people continued to speak Berber (as they do to this day). But the Arab takeover in the eighth century, backed up by the conversion to Islam of the Berber-speaking hinterland, would be much more quickly influential in changing the region's working language than the Vandals had been (or perhaps even the Romans, in the 750 years since the destruction of the independent Carthage).

Our explanations have to be *post hoc*. No doubt the majority of advancing Germans would have been fighting men, and no doubt they would have taken brides from the populations among whom they eventually settled. The language in the new homes, so far from Germany, would have been set by the local mother and her family. But the same could have been said about the Roman invaders of Gaul five hundred years before, or indeed Mexico and Peru after the Spanish conquests a millennium later. Yet there, the conquerors' language, spreading no doubt through the opportunities it gave to be part of the new economic order, soon began to win out. Here, apparently, the conquerors had no wish other than to put the old order under new management. But after beating its defenders, they ultimately depended on their victims to provide the life they sought. It is a tale more familiar in China than anything in the history of the West.*

Spoken Latin is from this point on called Romance, signalling that the emerging dialects of Vulgar Latin were now free to develop independently of one another (although the first vernacular document that survives in a precursor of French dates only from 842).† The German and Alan invasions marked the final, total failure of the empire's civil defence. One of the effects of the social dislocation that came in its train would have been a breakdown in the availability of education. In fact, there is evidence that illiteracy had been growing everywhere since the instability of the preceding century. Numbers of preserved inscriptions decline in the mid-third century, severely in Italy, drastically in a border region such as Upper Moesia (modern Bosnia), dying out everywhere around 400.[44] Augustine, writing in North Africa in the early fifth century, recounts as a miracle the story of a slave who could read.[45] In the middle of the sixth century, Caesarius of Arelate (Arles, near Marseilles) recognises that not only *rūsticī* but even *negōtiātōres* (merchants and businessmen) may be unable to read.[46] Without widespread education, consciousness of the norms of classical Latin would no longer act as a brake on oral transmission.

Besides the weakening of scholarly tradition and memory, two other forces will have fostered the break-up of Latin as a single language. One is that, all over its range, Latin had speakers who were in positions of influence

---

* Just the latest example is the Manchu, who ruled China from 1644 to 1911, but were totally absorbed by their subject population. Their language is now on the edge of extinction. (See Chapter 4, 'Language from Huang-he to Yangtze', p. 143.)

† The 'Strasburg Oaths', a treaty between Ludwig the German and Charles the Bald. Ironically, it comes only after the restoration of a single government across most of France, German and Italy. (See Chapter 8, p. 317.)

but whose parents had grown up speaking something else, most often a Germanic language. The other stemmed from the breakdown of the centralised systematic administration, and the rise of feudal society: individuals and families were organised much more into personal hierarchies, from the king and his baronial supporters down to the smallholder and his serfs, each link bound by personal loyalties of homage. This meant that localities became more inward: increasingly, people stayed put, in contact only with their neighbours; and the result was a faster separation of Roman speech into local dialects and languages.

Slavonic dawn in the Balkans

But if, from the language point of view, the net effect of the Germans' westward *Völkerwanderung* was nil, their fellow victims of incursion from the east, the Slavs (Tacitus's *Veneti*), had far better luck. In the mid-fifth century, the Huns surged through and past them, then withdrew to the Black Sea, leaving the Veneti and their kin to move permanently into the eastern plains ($pol^y e$) of Poland vacated by the Vandals and Lombards, among others. The following surges of Avars and Bulgars were more or less successfully resisted by the eastern Roman empire. But they served not only to flush the remaining Germans (Gepids, Ostrogoths and Lombards) out of the more southerly areas, the Carpathians and the Balkans; they also served to cover the Slavs' push southward. In the sixth century, the Slavs took possession of the arterial route from Aquileia on the Adriatic to Constantinople, a road that had kept this part of the empire, alone in the east, strongly linked to Latin-speaking Italy. In this way they finally moved into the Balkan territories of the Roman empire, including—as we have seen (see Chapter 6, 'Intimations of decline', p. 261)—Greece itself. In that traditional centre of the civilised world they were to be diffused and assimilated by the residents; but farther north, their relative numbers were far more overwhelming. By the seventh century the Slavs had been left in linguistic possession of most of eastern Europe, where they are to this day.*

The question naturally arises: why did the Slavic conquerors' language establish itself, while that of the Germans largely disappeared? But there is no evident answer. Latin survived as Romanian at least; and this might suggest that, as in western Europe, the Slavic invaders had abandoned their language in an area where they were confronted with a more organised culture. But the

---

* They made a late exception to admit the Magyars in the tenth century, creating the Hungarian pocket in the midst of Slavic central Europe.

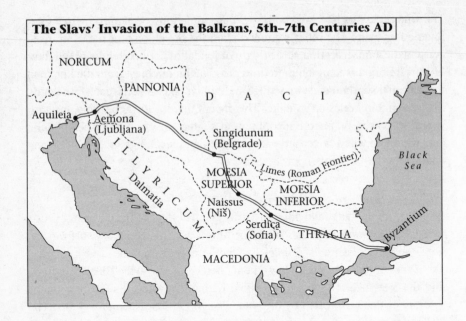

The Slavs' Invasion of the Balkans, 5th–7th Centuries AD

geography hardly fits. It was Dalmatia and Moesia (former Yugoslavia, and Bulgaria) that were long-term Roman provinces, unchallenged since Trajan had conquered the whole area of the Balkans in AD 106–7; Dacia (modern Romania) had been abandoned for strategic reasons in 271, when Germanic-speaking Gepids and Visigoths had taken over. It is true that Dacia had at first been heavily settled with colonists by Trajan.[47] And there were surviving Romance speakers (known to the Greeks as *Rhōmânoi*) up and down the Dalmatian coast until the beginning of the twentieth century. But the explanation seems to be that the Latin-speaking population drifted northward from Moesia into Dacia over the next few centuries; *Bláxoi hodîtai*, 'Vlach nomads', were a feature of the scenery on the northern marches of the empire up until the eleventh century.[48]

Whatever the intervening history, the Roman culture of the Balkan area, always something of an outpost, does not seem to have been strong enough ever to revive under the new Slavic masters.

Against the odds: The advent of English

Perhaps something similar happened at the opposite end of the Roman dominions, for Britain too lost its Latin in the face of invasions in this period. It also lost its British. This event of language replacement, which is also the origin of the English language, was unparalleled in its age—the one and only time that Germanic conquerors were able to hold on to their own language.

310

Prima facie, the fate of Britain should have been just like that of Gaul or Iberia, or indeed Italy. Germanic invaders, in this case from the north-western coast of Europe, entered a reeling province of the Roman empire in the fifth century AD, and never went home. In light of the experience of western Europe, this should have resulted in a few centuries of turmoil before the establishment of a more or less stable kingdom or (failing unification) an array of states, which would have ended up speaking some new variant of Latin. In fact what happened was a gradual advance and settlement of the invaders (whom we may term oversimply 'Saxons'*), from the south-east towards the north-west, a process arguably never completed but at least covering the lowland areas up to the Pennines and Dartmoor by the end of the sixth century, and most of modern England and south-eastern Scotland by the end of the seventh. Gradually, over the same period, the number of regional kingdoms reduced to three, Northumbria, Mercia and Wessex .

Linguistically, the intermediate stages are obscure, but the triumph of Latin as a popular language, analogously to what always happened on the Continent, never even looked possible. There is never any sense of a takeover of British society by Saxons; it is more the classic story of alien invaders gradually establishing a bridgehead, then spreading out, and building a new order on their own terms, like European imperialists in the Americas. There are no records in British of the period, but the records left in Latin (notably Gildas's *De Excidio Britonum*, 'The Ruin of the British', *c*.540, and Nennius's compilation of *Excerpta* up to *c*.800) paint a hostile picture of the Saxons as destroyers. West Saxons were literate from the ninth century in their own language (itself a curiosity for Germanic invaders), the Norsemen from a little later. Neither pay much heed to their British predecessors.

How could this be? The Britons, after all, were heirs to four hundred years of Roman civilisation, just like the Gauls, and were if anything notorious for their military prowess; indeed, potentates from Britain (Maximus in 388, Constantine in 407) had twice led successful forces on to the Continent in the

---

* There is actually an implicit dispute in the sources on who these invaders were. Evidently they were speakers of a Low German dialect, but Gildas (a Celt, writing before 550) calls them Saxons (or more exactly *Saxones ferocissimi illi nefandi nominis Saxones deo hominibusque invisi*, 'those ferocious Saxons of unspeakable name hateful to God and men', xxiii.1), while Procopius (a Greek—less personally involved—writing also before 550, and probably using information from Angles on a Frankish mission to Byzantium) says they were Angles and Frisians (*Gothic War*, iv.20). It is the Venerable Bede, in his history published in 731, who calls them Angles, Saxons and Jutes (i.15). The Saxons and Franks (named for their favourite weapons, the *seax* or knife and the *franca* or javelin) were not among the tribes known to Tacitus, but would have lived where he places the Chauci and the Tungri, at the mouths of the Weser and Rhine respectively.

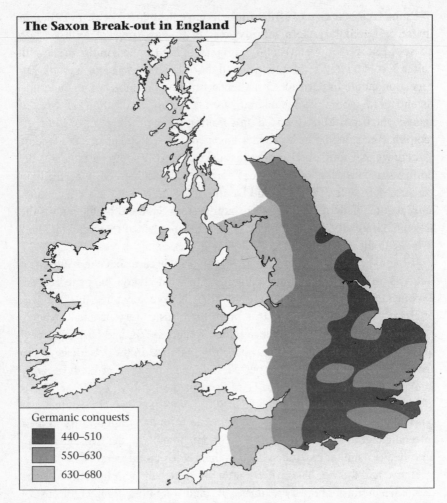

The Saxon Break-out in England

Germanic conquests

440–510

550–630

630–680

previous fifty years. Granted that the major forces had already been withdrawn to Italy, allowing the Saxons to make their bridgehead, in the generations that followed the Britons should still have had expertise in depth to
regroup in the 90 per cent of the country they still controlled, and either drive
back, or force a compromise with, the incomers.

Instead we see a steady fall-back, and the unmixed spread across the country of English, a mixture of Angle, Saxon, Frisian and perhaps Jutish varieties
of Low German. The only parallel, in fact, to this spread of a Germanic language is what happened when the Germanic invaders encountered virgin territory, in the islands of the North Sea and in Iceland. There of course the
Vikings' language, Old Norse, spread, because it had no competition. Could
the Britons of the urbanised lowlands somehow have just melted away?

Nothing less is needed to explain the complete walkover within Britain of those Germanic languages, and above all of English.

A recent theory, from David Keys, says that they may have.[49] The mid-sixth century (close to 550) was the time when bubonic plague entered Britain, along trade routes from the Mediterranean. Significantly, it would have been Britain (the west and centre of the island) which it hit, rather than England (the south-east), because only Britain maintained trade links with the empire. And it would be less likely to spread to the Saxons since they did not consort with Britons and, living outside the established Roman towns and cities, may have lived at a lower density. It would have been virtually simultaneous with the *mortālitās magna* that hit Ireland, according to the *Annals of Ulster*, devastating the aristocracy (and no doubt every other class). Maelgwn, king of Gwynedd in Wales, also died of plague in 547 or 549, according to the *Annales Cambriae*. A folk memory of this dreadful disease, and the depopulation it caused, would remain in the Arthurian legend of the Waste Land, combining famine with military defeat, and a mysterious wound (to the king) in the groin area—one of the characteristics of bubonic plague.

There is even a little genetic evidence that strikingly bears this out. Comparing the pattern of Y-chromosome DNA from samples in a line across from Anglesey to Friesland, a recent study found that the Welshmen were to this day clearly distinct from those in central England, but that the English and Frisian samples were so similar that they pointed to a common origin of 50–100 per cent of the (male) population; this could have resulted from a mass migration from Friesland.[50] On the usual assumption that the Roman-period population of the island had reached 3 to 4 million, it seems hardly possible that anything other than an epidemic could have so eliminated the Britons from the ancestry of central England.

So English supervened. It did not long have the eastern and central regions of the island to itself: in the late eighth century a new force entered the system, a new set of Germanic invaders, the Norsemen or Vikings, from Scandinavia. They progressed from coastal raids to settlement in the west of Scotland and the east of Northumbria to a partition of the island with the Saxons by treaty (*c*.886), and finally in 1013 to outright conquest of the whole kingdom. This was by Sveinn Forkbeard, succeeded by his son Knútr, better known as Canute.

Unlike the British–English divide, relations between Anglo-Saxon and Viking, if initially hostile, proved fairly permeable in the longer term. One way of understanding this is to see the Vikings as classic Germanic invaders, military raiders who won most of the battles but lost the peace, in that they settled down—perhaps with English wives—and largely picked up their sub-jects' or victims' language. Nevertheless, since the language into which they were settling was a close-ish relative (though with a good twenty generations of separate development behind it), there was easy scope for bilingualism and a degree of mutual understanding. The result was an abundant infusion of Norse loan words into English, and quite a lot of impact on the grammar too. In modern English, some 7 per cent of the basic vocabulary is of dis-tinctly Norse origin (including such words as *take*, *get*, *keep*, *leg*, *sky*, *skin* and *skirt*);[51] and it is this mix of the two languages which gave rise to the bi-zarrely unrelated set of third-person pronouns *he*, *it*, *she* and *they*.*

The early era of western European conquests thus closed with a kaleido-scopic shifting of Germans westward, and of Slavs southward. The Germans were able to retain their language only when they conquered territory that was largely, or totally, empty—Britain devastated by plague, and Iceland previously uninhabited. Their conquests in the western heartlands of the Ro-man empire had essentially no linguistic impact. Latin remained strong in the west and south of the continent; there, the linguistic effects of Roman con-quest were never undone. The Slavs, perhaps because they were invading less civilised—and hence less highly populated—regions had much greater effect where they settled in the Balkans; but they too were absorbed or eliminated in the areas of ancient civilisation that they overran, parts of Greece and Anatolia.

The long-term effect was a linguistic partition of Europe that has been fa-miliar ever since: Romance in the south and west, Germanic in the north and centre, Slavic in most of the east, and Greek in the extreme south-east. The main event in the fifth century was in fact the switch of Britain in the north-west from the Romance (or perhaps still Celtic) to the Germanic zone. There was considerably more change to come in this island: the further spread of Germanic into the last redoubts of Celtic over the next thousand years, com-pounded by a late attempt at a reassertion of Romance over Germanic, and the Norman conquest of England. But the tale of these events must wait until we turn to the growth of English itself.

---

* Compare these pronouns in Old English (*hē*, *hit*, *hēo*, *hīe*) with Old Norse (*hann*, *that*, *hon*, *their/thau/thær*—using English th for the Norse ð). Mix-ups between rather different systems of endings, well preserved in both Old English and Norse, may also have caused the breakdown of case marking for nouns.

8

The First Death of Latin

Philosophantem rhetorem intellegunt pauci, loquentem rusticum multi.

The rhetorician philosophising is understood by few, but the plain man speaking by many.

Gregory of Tours, Preface to *Historia Francorum* (*c*.AD 575)[1]

The history of western Europe after the German invasions is the tale of how the kingdoms established by the conquering tribes went on to become distinct nations. Dialectal differences in the Latin that people spoke widened, and wide-ranging travel became less common, as the road system decayed and public order became unenforceable far from cities. No longer was there a Roman army with a common tradition, and troops that might expect to be transferred anywhere. Where literacy survived, principally in the Church, so did written Latin. But this was not enough to maintain any spoken standard. The gap between spoken and written language widened, but without people having any sense of what was really happening, namely that the spoken language was changing. Little by little Latin spelling came to seem more and more irregular and perverse: but this obscurity was acceptable, even desirable, as reading and writing were the preserve of a small elite, mostly clerics and lawyers.

This period, the second half of the first millennium AD, gives us our main evidence of what happens to a universal language in the western European, Christian, tradition, when it begins to lose currency, when people, although still speaking it, begin to lose sight of its vast scope, and live above all in their local communities. Three hundred years after the Goths and Germans had divided up the territories of the empire, it had become extremely difficult for the people of Spain, France and Italy, when they did meet, to understand one another's speech. The learned, the only ones who would be conscious of the problem, came to call anyone's ordinary speech an *idioma*, to be contrasted

315

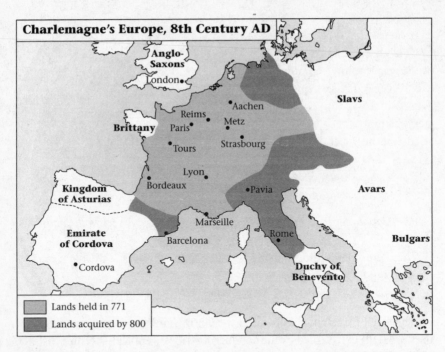

Charlemagne's Europe, 8th Century AD

Lands held in 771

Lands acquired by 800

with the universality of *grammatica*, which was the normal word for Latin in the Middle Ages.*

From the early fifth to the mid-eighth centuries, the powers in western Europe shifted from generation to generation, allowing the idea to establish itself that universal kingdoms or citizenships could never be of this world. But then, from the late eighth century, the power of the Frankish king grew, in alliance with the papacy, and for a century the areas of France, western Germany and most of Italy were united. The Frankish king who presided over the height of this glory was Charlemagne, who reigned from 768 to 814. His aspirations were cultural as well as political. In 781 he invited Alcuin, the head of the cathedral school at York, to become head of a new academy of scholars at Aachen, his capital. The fruit of this congregation has become known as the Carolingian Renaissance. In the course of it, and along with many other reforms in education, Alcuin established new standards for the spelling† and pronunciation of Latin.

---

* The word *idioma* was a borrowing into Latin from Greek *idíōma*, 'peculiarity', while *grammatica* was of course the name of the school subject in which everyone learnt their Latin.

† It was Alcuin who instituted the systematic difference between capital and lower-case letters, which has lasted in Roman scripts (such as the English used in this book) to this day.

Alcuin, as a speaker of North-Country English, approached Latin as a foreign language, to be learnt *ab initio* from books; in this he would have been at one with perhaps the majority of the scholars at Aachen, many of whom would have come from the German-speaking east of Charlemagne's empire. He succeeded in establishing a common pronunciation for Latin, close to what we now think of as 'the modern pronunciation', which was an intelligent attempt to reconstruct the sound of the language on an authentic ancient model; as he entitled his work:

Mē legat antīquās vult qui prōferre loquēlas;
Mē quī nōn sequitur vult sine lēge loquī.

Let him read me who wishes to carry on the ancient modes of speech;
He who does not follow me wishes to speak without law.[2]

This involved a practical shift which was greatest for the Romance-speaking scholars. When reading out a text, they now had consciously to deviate from their traditional, vernacular pronunciation of the language: for example, *viridiārium*, 'orchard', could no longer come out as *verger*, as it would when they were speaking naturally.[3] The practical shift ultimately led to a conceptual one. Gradually, they began to see this written style differently: *grammatica* was not just the natural, indeed the only correct, way to write for speakers of a Romance *idioma*; once given a distinct style of pronunciation, it was a separate language, just as it was for their German-speaking fellow-citizens (and the English- and Irish-speaking scholars across the seas).

Once written Latin had become established as a distinct, if not yet foreign, language, occasions began to arise when there was a need to write down something that would explicitly record the sounds of a vernacular. The earliest known example of this is the so-called Strasburg Oaths of 842, when two brothers, Ludwig the German and Charles the Bald, grandsons of Charlemagne, had to swear to support each other in the hearing of their respective followers, but in a situation complicated by the fact that their audiences spoke different languages, German and Romance. Their words have been recorded for us verbatim by Nithard, yet another grandson of Charlemagne,[4] and the Romance version provides the first surviving text in Romance rather than Latin. It seems that the texts had been set down before they were uttered. It was highly unusual for anything other than proper Latin to be written down, and to explain it, it is assumed that the purpose was to offer each of the two brothers a crib sheet.[5] Any Romance speaker could of course read out a Latin text to the common people in a pronunciation that they might understand: he would just come out with the vernacular words suggested by the Latin text. But it was a very different matter if a German speaker were to be asked to do this. And so Ludwig was offered the ninth-century equivalent of a tele-prompter.

The first few phrases will show that speaking Romance was no longer just a matter of changing a few details of regular Latin:

> *Pro Deo amur et pro christian poblo et nostro commun salvament, d' ist di in avant, in quant Deus savir et podir me dunat, si salvarai eo cist meon fradre Karlo et in ajudha et in cadhuna cosa, si cum om per dreit son fradra salvar dift...**

In proper Latin, one cannot get much closer to this than:

> *Pro Dei amore et pro christiano populo et nostro communi salvamento, de hoc die in posterum, in quanto Deus sapientiam et potentiam mihi donabit, sic servabo ego hunc meum fratrem Carolum et in adiumento et in re quaque, ut quis iure suum fratrem servare debet...*

This need for transition between written and spoken language was the major problem left unsolved by Alcuin's reforms. He had provided a common spoken and written form of Latin that would unite the literate across western Christendom, from Donegal to Dalmatia. But the cost was that now ordinary Romance parishioners could not understand their own priests during church services; and in this era, to ensure orthodoxy, not only liturgy but even the sermons tended to be recited or read from a written Latin text, rather than delivered extempore. As a result, at the Council of Tours in central France in 813, as at the Council of Mainz in Germany in 847, an explicit exception is made, to guarantee the continued understanding of the people: '...And that each should work to transfer the same homilies into plain Romance or German language [*rusticam Romanam linguam aut Thiotiscam*], so that all can more easily understand what is said.'[6]

Preservation of documents for a thousand years tends not to happen without serious intent, and so not surprisingly there is little record of the vernacular languages when all the serious records were still being kept in Latin.

---

* For God's love and the Christian people and our common salvation, from this day forward, insofar as God gives me knowledge and power, I shall so keep this my brother Charles both in aid and in every thing as when a man in right his brother should keep...

There is a cheese-larder list from a Spanish monastery datable to the late tenth century, preserved because it had been scribbled on the back of a document of donation.[7] But in the ninth, tenth and eleventh centuries, phonetic transcriptions of vernacular languages are usually found as little snippets in Latin documents. There are verbatim statements in Italian, recorded as sworn, to validate ownership for lands belonging to Montecassino monasteries. There is a vivid caption to a fresco on the wall of St Clement's church in Rome from the late eleventh century, illustrating a famous but futile attempt at persecution of St Clement, when his attackers were miraculously deluded into mistaking him for a column. Their leader shouts to his men:

Fili delle pute, traite. Gosmari, Albertel, traite. Fàlite dereto colo palo, Carvoncelle

Sons of whores, pull! Gosmario, Albertello, pull! Push back with the stick, Carvoncello!

while the saint comments in (ungrammatical) Latin:

Duritiam cordis vestris saxa traere meruistis

Hardness of heart yours rocks to pull you have deserved.

Only when serious works of literature started to appear in the vernacular, invading the traditional ground held by the written language, did the real status of the 'rustic' languages begin to become clear. And this happened first at the other end of the Romance-speaking world, in Normandy and England, where the Normans started writing down ballads and lays of the kind that they heard the minstrels sing. The *Chanson de Roland*, from the late eleventh century, is the oldest and best of these works, telling the tale of a heroic rearguard action fought against the Moors in the time of Charlemagne. It is signed in its last line:

Ci falt la geste que Turoldus declinet

Here ends the adventure that Turoldus retold

and there seems no reason not to identify this Turold with a specially named character who appears in the Bayeux Tapestry, delivering a message to William the Conqueror.

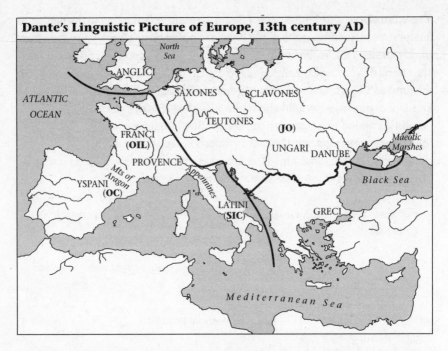

Dante's Linguistic Picture of Europe, 13th century AD

In the twelfth and thirteenth centuries, poetry in the Romance languages begins to be written down all over western Europe, in Provence, in northern France, in Galicia, Castile and Catalonia, and in Italy. The breakthrough came in areas that Latin had never strongly represented, in the celebration of courtly love—the modern sense of the word 'romance' is no coincidence— and in heroic tales of chivalry and war. Latin was increasingly hived off as a learned language for monasteries, schools and universities.

The first theorist of these new linguistic developments is none other than the leading Italian poet, Dante Alighieri, who lived from 1265 to 1321. In his *De vulgari eloquentia* he recognised that Latin, *grammatica*, was in essence the preserved older form of the Romance languages.*

He seems to have had as much difficulty in convincing his audience that

* Dante (*De vulgari eloquentia*, viii.1) distinguishes Greek from the Germanic languages, and also from the Romance. His criterion (the word for 'yes'—*jo* in Germanic) would tend to split up the Romance languages into at least three groups (*oc, oil, sì*), but he notes that they have a large amount of basic vocabulary in common: '*quia multa per eadem vocabula nominare videntur, ut Deum, caelum, amorem, mare, terram, est, vivit, moritur, amat, alia fere omnia*'; 'because they seem to name many things with the same words: *God, sky, love, sea, earth, is, lives, dies, loves*, and almost everything else.'

Surprisingly, Dante sees *oc* as marking Spanish Romance, not the Provençal of southern France (known anyway as Langue d'oc). Perhaps he was affected by Provençal's similarity to Catalan.

these ancestral differences were the predictable result of gradual change as Darwin was to find, with a different subject matter and timescale, five centuries later.

> Nor should what we say appear any more strange than to see a young person grown up, whom we do not see grow up: for what moves gradually is not at all recognized by us, and the longer something needs for its change to be recognized the more stable we think it is. So we are not surprised if the opinion of men, who are little distant from brutes, is that a given city has existed always with the same language, since the change in language in a city happens gradually only over a very long succession of time, and the life of men is also, by its very nature, very short. Therefore if over one people the language changes, as has been said, successively over time, and can in no way stand still, it is necessary that it should vary in various ways quite separately from what remains constant, just as customs and dress vary in various ways, which are confirmed neither by nature or society, but arise at human pleasure and to local taste. This was the motive of the inventors of the faculty of *grammatica*: for *grammatica* is nothing but the identity of speech unalterable for diverse times and places.[8]

Besides this work in Latin, Dante wrote another one, the *Convivio* or 'Banquet', in Italian—not a poem, but a prose work aimed at explaining some of his earlier poems, but at the same time educating people who could not read Latin: 'I was motivated by the fear of infamy, and I was motivated by the desire to give teaching such as others truly cannot.'[9]

This was the beginning of the end of Latin's monopoly on learned information. Henceforth, there would be no field of discourse or function of speech reserved for it. Latin, the language of the grammar books, once felt to be eternal but now recognised as artificial, faced ever increasing competition from spoken languages being committed to writing. It began to die.

PART III
LANGUAGES BY SEA

And who, in time, knows whither we may vent
The treasure of our tongue, to what strange shores
This gain of our best glory shall be sent,
To enrich unknowing nations with our stores?
What worlds in the yet unformèd Occident
May come refined with accents that are ours?

from Samuel Daniel, Musophilus (1599)

DAVID: What newes? haue you heard nothing of the coming of any ship?

ABRAHAM: I heard the thundering of Ordnance, which is a signe of ships coming.

D.: And I heard that a shippe was come from Guiserat.

A.: And what Marchandizes doth she bring?

D.: She is laden with rice, almonds and raysons, she bringeth also many cloathes of all sortes, and very much bombace.

A.: Is this so? surely this news is very much desired.

D.: I heard it so affirmed for a truth.

DAOEDT: *Appa ach gabar? tieda ga-barbarou derribarang cappal?*

EBRAHIM: *Souda beta denga'r boenij bedil, iang itoe alamat derri cappal dagang.*

D.: *Lagihamba deng'ar catta iang satoe cappal derri Guiserat souda datan.*

E.: *Appa peruiniága debaua dia?*

D.: *Ini ber'isi, ken bras, ken gorma, zebibt; lagi bauadia bania káyin alus derri samoe' aieni: lagicapas bania.*

E.: *Begitou? itoe gabar bania baick.*

D.: *Ia beta deng'ar catta sach begitoe.*

Augustine Spaulding,
Dialogues in the English and Malaiane Languages, 1614, pp. 1–2 [1]

9

The Second Death of Latin

The discovery by the western Europeans that their ships could cross oceans, and bring them directly to distant lands, whether for trade or outright conquest and exploitation, opens a new era in the global history of language spread. All too often, the language communities at the destinations of European shipping proved unable to mount effective military, or political, resistance to the adventuring invaders. When this happened, the victims were frequently decimated, and always forced to submit to a new elite. The spread of languages through the dominance of the new elites was far more pervasive than anything that had been seen before. The results are evident today in the presence of six colonising languages in the list of the world's top ten languages by population.*

The Romance half of these colonising languages, as we have just seen, owed their very existence to the changes that came over the Roman empire after its western regions were dissolved by the Germanic conquests; the decline in mutual intelligibility, and the redefinition of Latin or *grammatica*, to be no longer just their written form but a language separate from them, had led to their development as vehicles of a different sort of community. This community was less intellectual, but often as rich culturally as the Church, which continued to rely on Latin, spoken and written.

Yet before these languages began their accelerated progress round the world, there came an epoch-making development, which emphasised and reinforced the spread of literacy in western Europe. It widened the range of competition between Latin and the vernacular languages, including the Romance ones, and massively raised the stakes in the contest. The result was the dethronement of Latin as the lingua franca of western Christendom: in effect its death, after two millennia, as a language of any real communication and innovation.

* See Chapter 13. The six are English, Spanish, Russian, Portuguese, German and French. There was a seventh, Dutch, which holds position 21 in the population league. Their imperial careers are reviewed in Chapters 10, 11 and 12.

The event was the rise of a mass market in printed books. Like the information revolution reorganising the world in our own time, it was in essence the economic effect of the spread of a new technology. Johannes Gutenberg published his edition of the Bible in Mainz in 1450. Very soon, publishing houses sprang up all over Europe, and by 1475 most of the classic works in Latin were available in print.[2] By 1500, 20 million printed volumes had been produced, estimated to correspond to one book for every five people in western Europe.[3]

Almost at once comes the Reformation, and the rise of Protestant churches opposed to the established Christianity of the Pope in Rome. This, of course, was no coincidence, but a sign that the new book-publishing revolution had broken open the previously well-guarded access to media of communication. Martin Luther's works, starting theatrically with his ninety-five theses nailed to the church door in Wittenberg in 1517, were printed and distributed in German translation. His translation of the whole Bible soon followed. The output of German-language publishing houses over the 1520s and 1530s was three times the total of the previous twenty years; Luther's works accounted for 33 per cent of all German-language publications between 1517 and 1525.[4]

The tide of new, unfiltered, information was too much for some. In France in 1535, King François I—briefly, and without effect—declared the printing of any books at all a capital offence. The Vatican, more circumspectly, set up the *Index Librorum Prohibitorum*, first so named in 1559. But the flow was not stemmed. The important effect was that the channels of long-distance and high-level discourse were switching from oral diffusion at court and university, mediated through manuscript messages, to written distribution of mass-produced texts. Latin had retained its domination as the vehicle of the old-style communications, but under the weight of sheer volume it now yielded to the new. Books might be printed in Latin as well as any other language, and those that were might be expected to enjoy a wider circulation for being written in an international language; but the economics of the book trade remaindered them, clearing its shelves for books in vernacular languages, which would sell in large quantities nearer to the point of production.[5]

What was happening was one facet of the growing power of the nation-state in western Europe: the replacement of an international intellectual elite, which provided a common background for different kings' governments, by a much more vocal and influential bourgeoisie, taking control of their local monarchies and making them serve their more worldly purposes. One linguistic effect of this was to replace Latin with national vernaculars, not just for local purposes but even at the level of the latest research.

Latin remained, in theory, a superior vehicle for high-level intellectual dis-

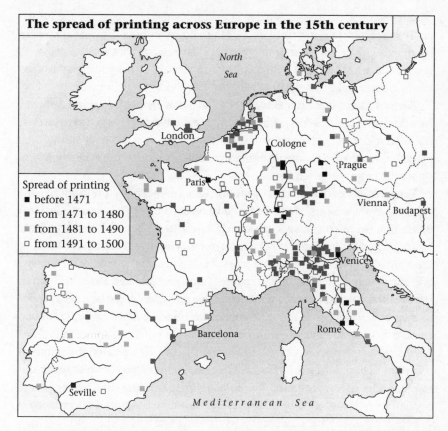

The spread of printing across Europe in the 15th century

Spread of printing
- before 1471
- from 1471 to 1480
- from 1481 to 1490
- from 1491 to 1500

course: as a language, it had the vocabulary, built up over more than a thousand years of thought and disputation; and as a community, it had the reach, since scholars from all over the west of Europe were accustomed to talking, thinking and writing in it. Each vernacular, by contrast, had to build up equivalent strengths little by little from a much smaller base.

But wherever there was a riot, or a market, the vernaculars had the force of numbers on their side; and the religious controversies and wars of the sixteenth and seventeenth centuries showed that intellectual issues were as apt to generate sales booms, riots and civil wars as disputations or dynastic conflicts. It was not until the twentieth century that communications media could penetrate deeply enough for an international language to compete effectively with vernaculars on the street. Modern English has found in broadcasting the answer to the threat that book publishing posed for medieval Latin.

Intellectual life conducted in Latin gradually fell away. It took about a century to go. Francis Bacon, publishing his *Advancement of Learning* in English in 1605, wanted to have it translated into Latin 'to ring a bell to call

327

other wits together...and have that bell heard as far as can be'. It did not actually come out in Latin until 1623, when he remarked: 'For these modern languages will at one time or another play the bank-rowtes [bankrupts] with books; and since I have lost much time with this age, I would be glad as God shall give me leave to recover it with posterity.'

The last major intellectual work in England to be published in Latin was Newton's *Principia* in 1687. Since then, science has in general had to be conducted less conveniently, in a variety of languages. It is the price the modern world has paid to keep scientists and intellectuals more closely in touch with society at large.*

This second death was more profound than Latin's first. It was not like the vernacular movements of five hundred years before, when Latin had just lost its use as a written disguise for Romance languages. They had moved on from Latin, and apart, in phonetics and structure; trying to access in written form through a Latin overlay was hard work, and increasingly pointless. But even as it made way for vernacular literature, Latin had retained a significant use: it was still the vehicle for the intellectual discourse that went beyond the popular themes being produced (and appreciated) in Romance. Now, Latin was ceasing to be used in any new thinking at all.

It is revealing to compare the final stages in the life of Latin with those of its fellow classic languages, Greek, Chinese and Sanskrit. Each of these languages, after all, represented the unitary linguistic ideals of an area large enough to split into a number of popular varieties. But only Latin ended up largely replaced by the set of its daughter languages.

Greek never put down deep roots in the regions to which it spread; and when these regions were conquered by others, so that Greeks ceased to be their governing elite, Greek was essentially lost in them. The result was that Greek ended up confined to a relatively small region, mostly under a single, authoritarian government. When the government was reduced in power and then ceased to exist, after the Latin and especially the Turkish conquests, the classical norms that had kept the language united were weakened; but when unitary government was returned, it proved possible, gradually, to move to a new, single, standard for the whole language.

Chinese has retained its role as the high-level focus, political and intellectual, for all the communities that speak related dialects (or daughter languages). Unlike Greek, it has lost linguistic unity, all over its south-eastern

---

* Contrast Alcuin, propagating his new standard for Latin in the ninth century, and working in quite the opposite direction: for the important mission then was to put the intellectual world back in touch with itself, and its own ancient traditions.

provinces; but political unity by and large has held firm. The phonetic inexplicitness of its writing system has, to an extent, allowed it to ignore emergent differences between its standard core and those dialects. This same ambiguity has enabled it, in the last century, to switch its linguistic norm from classical *wényán* to Beijing *báihuà* without losing the allegiance of the whole set of Chinese-speaking communities. The logographic writing system, then, has enabled Chinese to escape the 'first death', without preventing numbers of its daughter languages from diverging.

Sanskrit, like Latin, has given rise to (or been closely associated with) a number of daughter languages; this marks the major common feature of its history and Latin's, namely the breakdown of political unity over its speech area for a long time. As such Sanskrit shared what we have called the 'first death' of Latin. As in the case of Latin, this led to the daughter languages establishing themselves as independent literary languages for popular themes. But it long retained its role as high-level intellectual centre, and hence in some sense linguistic ideal, for these independent languages. Despite the impact of English from overseas, eliminating its high-level secular role, it has never been replaced as the focal religious vehicle for the majority of Indians.

The next tale in this history is the phenomenal spread of Latin's daughter languages; to this we shall very soon pass. This, after all, is the real, continuing, story of the Latin speech community. And yet, in a way, Latin as a living language did find a new disguise.

In the thirteenth to fifteenth centuries, western Europe had been enlightened by a new and more direct knowledge of ancient Greek and Latin, aided by the influx of Byzantine scholars after the fall of Constantinople and its empire. Westerners began for the first time in a thousand years to have a reading knowledge of Greek, and eagerly lapped up the associated stylistic doctrines of Atticism (see Chapter 6, 'Mid-life crisis: Attempt at a new beginning', p. 254). Perhaps by contact, perhaps because of the nature of self-consciously classical studies, many began to develop a corresponding linguistic snobbery about their Latin, wanting to go back to the most ancient sources. Only Cicero's work would do. Not all humanists caught this bug: in particular Erasmus, a witty Dutch classicist writing in the early sixteenth century, wrote a *Dialogus Ciceronianus* to satirise the aspiration, envisioning a character called Nosoponus ('labouring under a disease') exerting himself to work out which inflected forms of each verb were actually found in Cicero's work, and which (more importantly) were not. For such a man, even his dreams were restricted to Cicero (*'Nec aliud simulachrum in somnis occurrit praeterquam Ciceronis…'*); the naive witness Hypologus comments that he looks more like a ghost than a man (*'Larvae similior videtur quam homini'*).

When this kind of devotion to the details of expression established itself as respectable, it became possible to see the style of expression as far more important than the content, and the knowledge of what had been said as far superior to the ability to innovate and strive for progress. So just as the highest aspiration for Greek scholars in the West was to read the texts (and perhaps write a pastiche—but only in classical style), now people came to think they were preserving the value of Latin if they became experts in the language and its extant early literature, for their own sake alone. The primary uses of a language, to think and feel, to express ideas and to communicate them, became purely subordinate to this 'classicism'.*

It would have been better if Latinists had accepted the resigned verdict of one of their favourite poets:

Soles occidere et redire possunt:
Nobis cum semel occidit brevis lux
Nox est perpetua una dormienda.

Suns can set and can come back again:
For us when once the short light has set
There is one night perpetual to be slept.

Catullus

---

* This backward-looking spirit is still familiar to me from an education in the classical stream of an English public school in the 1960s. It is expressed in a thousand prefaces to school textbooks. Consider this from Ainger and Wintle (1890, 17th impression 1963: iii): 'Latin verse composition...is the proof and the flower of that scholarship which loves the old writers with an unselfish love, and delights to clothe modern thoughts and modern expressions in the dress of ancient metre and rhythm.' Or Pym and Silver (1952), who state that a chapter 'illustrates the continuing vitality of the Latin language in England during the last two hundred years' when all it contains is epitaphs, a couple of parliamentary speeches (in English) which allude to Latin literature, a section of a papal encyclical, a poem (admittedly witty) on the fuel crisis of 1947, and a number of jokey prize compositions from schools and the University of Oxford. The book's very title, *Alive on Men's Lips*, is a highly ironic lie, since it is simply a translation of a phrase from the epitaph of Ennius, '*vivu' per ora virûm*', dead in the second century BC.

10

Usurpers of Greatness:
Spanish in the New World

Quando bien comigo pienso mui esclarecida Reina: i pongo delãte los
ojos el antiguedad de todas las cosas: que para nuestra recordacion &
memoria quedaron escriptas: una cosa hállo & sáco por conclusion
mui cierta: que siempre la lengua fue compañera del imperio: & de tal
manera lo siguió: que junta mente començarõ. crecieron. & flore-
cieron. & despues jũta fue la caida de entrambos.

When I consider well, most illustrious Queen, and set before my eyes
the antiquity of all the things which remain written down for our record
and memory, one thing I find and draw as a most certain conclusion, that
always language was the companion of empire, and followed it in such
a way that jointly they began, grew, flourished; and afterwards joint was
the fall of both.

Antonio de Nebrija, opening words of the preface to his
Gramatica de la lengua castellana, 1492

Portrait of a conquistador

The beginnings of the global spread of European languages came just as
printing presses and publishers were asserting the existence of vernaculars,
Spanish, Portuguese, French and Italian, English, Dutch and German, over
the body of a Latin that was gradually being drained of life. The languages
that spread were those of the successor states of the western Roman empire;
and so their educated elites were no strangers to the ideal, and indeed the romance, of vast, multinational empires. They had been brought up on the histories of Rome and Alexander; and they were filling their imaginations with
tales of chivalry, conquest and adventure in strange lands, of Amadís de
Gaula (hero of a popular romance of the fifteenth century, published in

Zaragoza in 1508), his son Esplandián (1510), and many, many others.* History was about to make their dreams come true.

The country that would play the leading role in the conquest and colonisation of the New World already felt itself entering a golden age. A century of uncertain intrigue had been resolved in the peaceful union of Spain's competing kingdoms, Castile in the north and centre, and Aragon in the east: Castile had come to Isabella in 1474, and Aragon to Fernando in 1479; princes already joined in marriage, they were so acceptable to the Pope that they went on to be granted the title of '*Reyes Católicos*'. They were to reign together for another twenty-five years, during which they completed the Christian conquest of Spain. The last Moorish kingdom, Granada, fell on the second day of 1492, but the ten-year war had stretched the Spanish treasury to its limit.

Linguistically, Spain was an alliance of three major Romance languages, Galician (*gallego*) in the west, Castilian (*castellano*) in the centre, and Catalan (*català*) in the east.† Catalan is much more similar, as a language, to Occitan or Provençal, as spoken in southern France. It is possible to see the origins of the Spanish three in the different Germanic groups who took control of Iberia in the fifth century, the Suevi in the north-west, Visigoths in the centre and south, Alans in the east. (The name *Catalan* is etymologised as a version of 'Goth-Alan'.)§ At any rate, Castile established itself as the most powerful state in the region, having absorbed the western kingdom (ruled from León) in 1230. Aragon, in parallel, had come to dominate the west, uniting in a fairly equal partnership with Catalonia in 1140.

The linguistic effect of the union of Castile and Aragon, with Aragon as the junior partner, was to make Castilian the *de jure* standard for the whole of Spain, just before the flowering of literature in the early seventeenth century. And as Christians went on to replace Moors in the southern reaches of Andalusia, they recolonised the south of Spain with speakers of this Castilian. Henceforth, although Galician and Catalan retained their independence and still have their own literary traditions, *Castilian* became a synonym for 'the Spanish language', as it is to this day.

---

* These fantasies were a mannered outgrowth of the heroic lays of early Romance three centuries earlier, such as *Chanson de Roland*, in Norman French, and *Poema de Mio Cid*, in Castilian Spanish. Many of the recent titles are listed in ch. 6 of Cervantes' *Don Quixote de la Mancha* (first half published 1605), where most of them are scheduled for burning. Enthusiasm for King Arthur and the Knights of the Round Table is part of the same European phenomenon. Sir Thomas Malory's *Le Morte d'Arthur* was published by William Caxton at Westminster in 1485.

† Linguistically, Galician was (and is) much the same as Portuguese, divided from it by the course of the River Minho, and the political fact that Portugal became independent of Castile in 1143.

§ The Vandals left their name in Andalusia, but passed on to Tunisia, and were largely erased by the subsequent Muslim conquest.

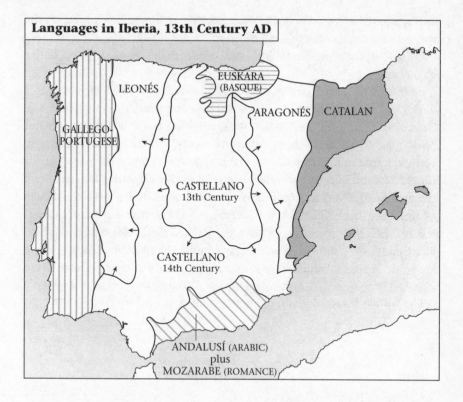

The Spanish approach to Christianity emphasised high-level authority as a guarantee of orthodoxy, and led all Christendom in the fifteenth and sixteenth centuries in vigorously prosecuting this belief. The Inquisition had been founded in 1480, and in 1492 the extraordinary measure was taken of expelling all Jews from the kingdom. Then, in 1502, all practice of Islamic faith was abruptly banned, although it had been explicitly guaranteed in the terms of the Muslims' surrender of Granada ten years before. There was a sense in the ruling circles of Spain that the truth was only to be found in inherited tradition; likewise the political ideal was for total unity of purpose between Pope and King, Church and State.

This was to have some strange effects on language policy in the Americas. Free thinking was seen as pernicious and indeed contagious; and a consequence of this was the preference, when Spain became responsible for education in South America, that native students should learn Latin, rather than Castilian; vernacular literature could never be guaranteed free of deceptive influences. But in spreading Spanish civilisation among foreign-language speakers, it would also become clear that the linguistic priorities of the secular and the sacred diverged: nothing matched the symbolic power of the Spanish language to signify empire—but it was easier, quicker and more reliable to spread understanding, and hence faith, in one of the native languages.

Faith and righteous government might be one thing: but the getting of wealth was another. Here there was scope for innovation. Indeed, the new departure that Castile authorised was so far reaching in its consequences that it transcended even the wildest fifteenth-century romance. The Portuguese were exploring south and eastward in this period, finding a route round Africa to India and the spice islands; they had rounded the Cape in 1488, and were to reach the fabled orient on follow-up expeditions, India in 1499, Melaka (Malacca) in 1511, Guangzhou (Canton) in 1514. But in that same cardinal year of 1492, the Spanish were offered, by the Genoese adventurer Christopher Columbus, a more speculative path to the same destination, travelling due west. Queen Isabella backed him, and the result was quite different from what had been hoped: not an economic back door to the Orient, but a whole new set of worlds to conquer, ultimately a far richer prize.

An unprecedented empire

Caliban to Prospero:

You taught me language; and my profit on't
Is, I know how to curse: the red plague rid you,
For learning me your language!

Shakespeare, The Tempest (1611), i.2.1, l.321

It is of note that the Indians of Peru, before we Christians had come to them, had certain and particular modes of swearing, distinct from ours. They had no assertive oaths, such as 'by God' or 'by heaven' but only execration or curses ... e.g. 'if I am not telling the truth, may the sun kill me' they said *mana checcanta ñiptiy, indi guañuchiuancmancha ...* Once when I asked a chieftain in a certain province if he was a Christian, he said 'I am not yet quite one, but I am making a beginning.' I asked him what he knew of being Christian, and he said: 'I know how to swear to God, and play cards a bit, and I am beginning to steal.'

Fray Domingo Santo Tomás,
Arte de la Lengua General ... del Perú (1560), ch. xxiii

The spread of Spanish into the Americas was the first linguistic effect of a totally new development in recorded human history. The Spanish and the Portuguese discovered, in the late fifteenth century, that a new technology, the ocean-going ship, powered by sail, and guided by the magnetic compass and an evolving knowledge of prevailing winds, could give them direct access to distant parts of the world. Although this came as a surprise to these navigating nations, the shock was much greater to the peoples already living in the parts of the world on to which they burst. The Arabs of the Indian Ocean instantly lost their monopoly of trade with India and China; the Indians, the Chinese and all between them faced a new military threat from rapacious Europeans. But for the inhabitants of the Americas, without a seafaring tradition of their own, and so isolated for millennia from the hazards of long-distance contact, it was a shock that was usually fatal.

The surprise of the Spanish irruption into the New World was registered in many ways. Spanish incomprehension can be seen in the permanent misnomer of their new subjects, called 'Indians' (*indios*) by Christopher Columbus.* It is also seen in Columbus's assumption, followed by many later chroniclers, that hostile Caribbean islanders were clearly *cannibals* (a term that as a result became synonymous with 'eaters of human flesh').† Never substantiated, this may have been a hangover from the traditions of European travellers' tales about the ends of the earth; Herodotus said that beyond the Scythians lived the flesh-eating Androphagi; and Strabo had retailed the same story about the Scythians themselves, and even the Irish.[1] But the European mariners may have been misinterpreting—to fit with more conventional horror—the first evidence they were finding of the true, but for then still truly inconceivable, indigenous practices of human sacrifice.

Most directly for our purposes, the Spanish incomprehension can be seen in the linguists that Columbus had chosen to bring in the hope of easing communication: Luis de Torres, who knew Hebrew, Aramaic ('Chaldaean') and some Arabic, and Rodrigo de Jérez, who had perhaps visited some of the Portuguese colonies in Guinea. Although he may rationally have believed he

---

* '... they reached an islet of the Lucayas, which was called Guanahani in the language of the Indians.' Columbus, *Diario de a bordo*, Friday, 12 October 1492, quoted by De las Casas (1957 [*c*.1530]). Columbus had at first thought he was within the domain of the Chinese Great Khan, and then (12 November) amid 'the islands of India'. He no longer called the people he met *indios* after mid-December of that year, but the name had stuck (Sale 1990: 109).

† '... These islands are inhabited by *Canabilli*, a wild, unconquered race which feeds on human flesh. I would be right to call them anthropophagi. They wage unceasing wars against gentle and timid Indians to supply flesh...' Letter of Guillermo Coma, *De insulis meridiani...nuper inventis*, on Columbus's second voyage, for Sunday, 3 November 1493.

could run into Arab traders when he reached China, his choice is eloquent of the sheer ignorance of what the rest of the world was like linguistically, when the only alien that even an educated Spaniard was likely to meet was a Moor or a Jew.* And indeed Spaniards went on calling the spiritual centres of the Americas 'mosques': for example, in a letter to his king in 1520, Cortés wrote, of a city in Mexico that had never seen a Muslim: 'And I assure your Majesty that I counted from a mosque some 430 towers in the said city, all of them belonging to mosques.'[2]

The incomprehension of the extent of the new horizons now opening up was of course not confined to the Spaniards. Seeing themselves quite explicitly as emissaries of Christendom in these new realms, they turned to the Pope—Alexander VI, conveniently a Spaniard—to validate their title to the territories. It was a situation familiar to us from the modern rush for patents in the uncharted areas of information technology and genetics. In 1493 the Pope, after granting Spain sovereignty over Columbus's discoveries on his first voyage, went on to award it title to all territories more than a hundred leagues west of the Azores and Cape Verde Islands, approximately longitude 30°W, explicitly all the way to India. If it had become established, this would have given Spain rights to all the Americas. But no one could know this, a year after Columbus's first voyage. The Portuguese were at this stage the only major competitors and were duly concerned about the Pope's dispensation, above all in order to guarantee their routes through the Atlantic to Africa and beyond. They succeeded in negotiating with the Spaniards to have the north–south demarcation line moved 270 leagues farther west, effectively to longitude 45°, and this notional limit was agreed in the Treaty of Tordesillas in 1494. It was never clearly identified in practice, and corresponds to no modern boundary—Brazil, for example, extends inland all the way to longitude 74°W, and even on the coast as far as 50°—but it did serve as a convenient rule of thumb, giving Portugal a prior claim to Brazil, whose south-eastern coast was first visited by both Spanish and Portuguese ships in 1500, but inhibiting its interest in the Amazon until 1637.

On the American side, the shock of incomprehension was registered more brutally, by a devastating loss of population. It is impossible to estimate safely the numbers living in the Americas before European contact. Estimates vary between 13 million and 180 million. But everywhere there is ev-

---

* Columbus's world-view was informed by copious reading. We have seven of his books with his personal annotations, preserved to this day in the Biblioteca Colombina in Seville. They include works of Marco Polo and Pliny the Elder's *Natural History*, and others more fanciful. His son Fernando also gave an account of his father's reading, in chs 6 and 7 of his biography (Sale 1990: 15).

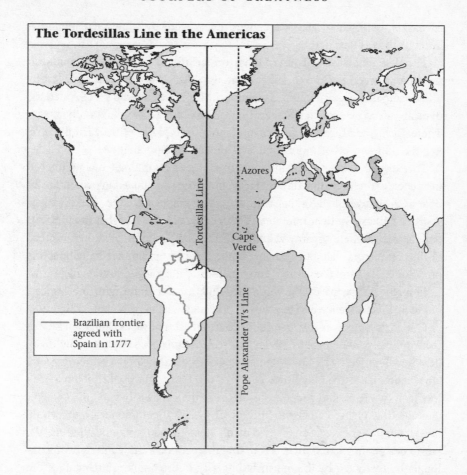

The Tordesillas Line in the Americas

Tordesillas Line

Pope Alexander VI's Line

Azores

Cape
Verde

—— Brazilian frontier
agreed with
Spain in 1777

idence of a massive fall in the early years after the Europeans arrived. First of all, the Spaniards complained of depopulation in the first islands they colonised, Cuba and Hispaniola, and the figures bear them out: a census of Hispaniola in 1496 gave a figure of 1.1 million, but just eighteen years later the *repartimiento* of 1514 listed 22,000. Mexico witnessed a series of epidemics, beginning with the Spanish visit to their capital Tenochtitlán, which carried off most of the native population, and spread southward into Guatemala. Of the whole Caribbean, Joseph de Acosta was writing in the 1580s: 'the habitation of which coasts is ... so wasted and condemned that of thirty parts of the people that inhabit it there wants twenty-nine; and it is likely that the rest of the Indians will in short time decay'.[3]

Hernando de Soto led an expedition through Florida and the North American south-east in the mid-sixteenth century, finding a thick population of Indians, clustered in small cities, on the Mississippi river near modern

Memphis. In 1682, when the area was next visited by white men (this time French), it was deserted.

The diseases travelled faster than the spearheads of Spanish conquest: smallpox arrived in Peru in 1525, Francisco Pizarro in 1532. It had already killed Huayna Capac, the Inca, and many of his relations, and precipitated the dynastic struggle that the Spaniards were to turn to their own advantage. Thereafter, as everywhere, further epidemics, of typhus, influenza, diphtheria and measles as well as more smallpox, ravaged the population.

The Spanish were not notably humane conquerors, but they had no interest in genocide. From the first days in Hispaniola, they had hoped to exploit the labour of the natives, and for this alone they were dismayed at the sudden and disastrous collapse in their numbers. Yet everywhere, the fact that the previous population was melting away would have materially aided the long-term spread of the conquerors' language, changing the balance in numbers by subtracting predominantly from the speaker communities of the indigenous languages.

From the perspective of the world, with full benefit of hindsight, three aspects of the Spanish advance into the New World stand out as quite new to history.

One is that this was the first direct confrontation of races of human beings from quite separate lineages, divided by tens of thousands of years of independent development. The last common ancestor of Christopher Columbus and Guacanagarí, the first king he encountered on Hispaniola, could not have lived less than two thousand generations before, a period over twenty times longer than the time elapsed since the birth of Christ. That common ancestor would have lived in Africa, and so the two men's lineages had to extend all round the world before they could meet. From that moment onward, contacts would no longer be restricted by this intrinsic linearity in the human settlement of the world: nation would speak unto nation, from anywhere to anywhere.

This aspect was fundamental to the special catastrophe that, as we have seen, hit the American population. It turned out that the long millennia of development that had culminated in America and Spain had given the European lineage an attribute that acted like a secret weapon: resistance to a variety of diseases which, since they were endemic, were likely to spread to any other population with which they were in contact. This, far more than the technical superiority in arms which meant they could win battles against overwhelming numbers, eliminated swathes of the native population before they had any chance to adapt culturally, or rally in the long term. It is this biological factor, above all, which explains why the majority population in the Hispanic countries of America nowadays is everywhere *mestizo*.

The second unprecedented aspect of the Spanish advance is that this was the first conquest of a foreign continent by seaborne invasion. Maritime empires had certainly been a feature of the ancient and medieval Mediterranean (Athens, Carthage and Venice stand out), and in the first millennium AD Indians had projected their civilisation across the Bay of Bengal, though without apparent military intent. Only eighty years before the Spanish founded their empire, China's Admiral Zheng-He had cruised the Indian Ocean, exacting tribute from Śri Lanka, and demonstrating that China was capable of reaching the eastern coasts of Africa, if it so chose. But no previous empire had been gained or maintained through the control of oceanic seaways. Now for the first time a subject territory could be a continent away from its government, the link maintained through the projection of power by a navy across oceans.

Third, the conquest of the New World was the first major invasion to be undertaken in a number of independent initiatives, often by free enterprise, even if the *adelantados*—'advance men', as the pioneer captains-general were known, their title previously reserved for the governors of frontier provinces facing the Muslims—all claimed to be acting on behalf of the king of Spain. The invasion forces tended to be so small (607 with Cortés in Mexico, 160 with Pizarro in Peru) that the defending leaders were misled as to the nature of the threat, and delayed fatally in their defences by attempting to negotiate with, or at least to observe, their unwanted Spanish visitors. The New World was conquered through a patchwork of campaigns of soldier adventurers: Columbus in the Caribbean (1490s), Cortés in Mexico, Alvarado in Guatemala, García in Bolivia, Pizarro in Peru (1520s), Quesada in New Granada (the future Colombia), Mendoza in Argentina (1530s), de Soto in Florida, Coronado in Texas, Cabrillo in California, Valdivia in Chile (1540s), to mention only the most famous or successful. Each campaign was aimed primarily at enriching its participants, even while the formal justification was to demand wider loyalty to the king, and to save souls by gaining converts to the True Church.

These three aspects of the event usher in a radically new age, and were to become commonplace features of the major language contacts to come, as maritime nations of Europe sent fleets to every temperate and tropical part of the world that possessed a coastline, and attempted to claim them as colonies, and their people as customers, subjects and converts. This sequence of conquests marked the crucial transition in the development of the fully global world of today, where practically anywhere on the planet is within twenty-four hours' travel of anywhere else.*

Almost as an afterthought, the conquest of the Americas did eventually

* Although the contacts over the first few centuries always involved the projection of the mariners' languages on to the peoples who received their landfalls, more recently we have seen that the new

serve the purpose with which Columbus had set out, a link with Asia. In 1565, on the instructions of King Philip II, an expedition from Mexico crossed the Pacific to the islands of Cebu and Luzon, and established the beginnings of Spanish dominion in what was to be the Philippines. Other smaller Spanish colonies in the Pacific included the Marianas and Guam. Spanish control, and the attempt to spread the Spanish language here, was to last until the USA took over in 1898, after winning the Spanish-American War.

Since these Pacific colonies were gained at much the same time as the Americas, but were very much part of the Old World of the spice islands, on the edge of India's and China's zones of influence, they provide a useful contrast to highlight the special features of the progress of Spanish in the New World. Spanish never made widespread or deep-seated progress in the Philippines, and despite over three centuries of presence was soon displaced by English in the early twentieth century. It will be interesting to ponder the roots of the difference with Spanish in the Americas, where despite US economic dominance Spanish is still growing at the expense of English.

One can state at the outset that the conquest of the Philippines did not share in all the unprecedented properties of the conquest of the Americas. It was, admittedly, a seaborne invasion, and its point of origin was, like many expeditions of exploration into North America, in Mexico. But the land targeted was part of the Old World, not the New, and hence did not suffer from the disastrous lack of immunity to European diseases which devastated America: the advent of the Spanish was not followed in the Pacific by any collapse in the native population. Furthermore, the settlement of the Philippines did not proceed by individual groups spreading out to explore and exploit in their own interest. It was a Spanish government foundation, set up first at Cebu, and then, more permanently, in Manila. Thereafter, expansion of Spanish presence, and hence the Spanish language, came through the (more or less) disinterested activities of missionaries. The Philippines lacked the precious metals found in the Americas, and were much harder to reach from Spain, since the only barely practical route lay through Mexico: the colony offered little practical incentive for a Spanish-speaking community to grow and expand.

---

links can work in both directions, as immigrant communities from colonised countries gather in the homelands of once colonial powers, bringing their own languages with them.

First chinks in the language barrier:
Interpreters, bilinguals, grammarians

General de Quesada tried to find out what people were arrayed against him. There was an Indian whom they had captured with two cakes of salt and who had led them to where they were in this realm, and who through conversation already spoke a few words of Spanish. The General had him ask some Indians of the country whom he had captured to serve as interpreters. They replied in their language with the words *musca puenunga*, which is the phrase for 'many people'. The Spaniards who heard it said: 'they say they are like flies [*moscas*]' ... [Quesada] gave them a blast from the arquebuses. Then when the Indians saw that without coming up to them the Spaniards were killing them, without waiting a moment they took flight; our men gave chase and attacked them, until the great host came apart and disappeared. In the pursuit they say that the Spanish said: 'There were more of these than flies; but they have taken flight like flies'; with which the name [Mosca] was fixed for them; and this assault finished off the whole war.

Juan Rodriguez Freyle, *Conquest and discovery of the New Kingdom of Granada*, ch. vi (written in 1636, describing events in the region of Bogotá in 1536)

Perhaps disappointed by the inadequate, because misguided, linguistic support he had brought on his first voyage, Columbus had kidnapped a handful of the people in his ships as he sailed onward around the islands he was exploring, and then taken them back to Spain. 'It appeared to him that he should take to Castile, from this Isle of Cuba or the mainland as he was already reckoning it to be, some Indians so that they might learn the tongue of Castile and to know from them the secrets of the land, and in order to instruct them in the matters of the faith.'[4]

Several of them were presented at court, and received baptism, with royal godparents, no less. Most of them either died in Spain or took flight as soon as they returned to the Indies, and only one of them, now (after baptism) known as Diego Colón, did service as an interpreter. Columbus had at first been under the impression that all the 'Indians' he met spoke the same language; but the limited usefulness of Diego as he toured even the rest of the Caribbean islands gave him, first of the Europeans, an inkling of how diverse the language stock of these lands really was.

This kind of attempt to capture likely lads and train them up as interpreters was never a great success, although persisted with for thirty years or so. It caused resentment when candidates were taken by force—the native populations of Taino Indians already had bitter experience in their own culture of raids by neighbours for enslavement and human sacrifice—and far too often the apprentices died in the unnatural setting of life in Europe.

More effective was the natural process whereby an isolated Spaniard, shipwrecked or on the run from his own people, would take up life in an Indian village, and so get to know their language, before returning to act as interpreter. There are a good dozen such cases on record.[5] One of these turned out to be crucial for the first Spanish advance into the interior of America, when in 1519 Cortés penetrated to the heart of the Mexican empire. He communicated through a relay of two interpreters, one of them Jerónimo de Aguilar, a Spaniard who had spent eight years in a Mayan village after a shipwreck on the coast of Yucatán, the other the famous Malin-tzin, a Nahuatl-speaking woman from Coatzacoalcos who had been traded to a nearby Mayan community, Xicalango, in childhood.

As interpreters of Spanish, many native trainees remained rather inadequate, lacking the background to understand the Spaniards' real interests, even if they were as self-motivated as the Peruvian Felipillo, who had 'learnt the [Spanish] language without anyone teaching him ... [and] was the first interpreter that Peru had'.[6]

He was the main interpreter during the conquest of Peru, and mediated the first, crucial, conversation with Atahuallpa, the Inca emperor, just before the decisive battle of Cajamarca. Felipillo was called on to translate a harsh and pithy address by the Dominican friar, Fray Vicente Valverde, which ran through the basic doctrines of Christianity, the apparent duty of the Pope and the Spanish emperor Charles to convert the world, and the consequent need for Atahuallpa to submit to them without further ado.

Atahuallpa's reply is transmitted by Inca Garcilaso, himself a *mestizo* bilingual in Spanish and the Inca language Quechua, but also a highly educated student of Ciceronian rhetoric, writing more than a lifetime after the event. By his account, the poverty of the translation seems to have vitiated any chance that understanding, or at least courtesy, could be maintained. Atahuallpa is supposed to have replied at length, starting with a comment on the poor quality of the interpreting:

> It would have caused me great satisfaction, since you deny everything else I have requested of your messengers, that you should at least have granted me one request, that of addressing me through a skilled and faithful translator. For the urbanity and social life of men is more readily understood through speech than by customs, since even though you may be endowed with great virtues, if you do not manifest them by

words, I shall not easily be able to perceive them by observation and experience. And if this is needful among all peoples and nations, it is much more so between those who come from such widely different regions as we; if we seek to deal and talk through interpreters and messengers who are ignorant of both languages it will be as though we were conversing through the mouths of beasts of burden.[7]

A speech of this level of elaboration was evidently going to floor such a simple interpreter as Felipillo, but it is most likely a fiction of Garcilaso's, in accord with the best traditions of classical history-writing. Nevertheless, Garcilaso does claim that the Spaniards 'who were unable to brook the length of the discourse, had left their places and fallen on the Indians'. So intolerance of long-windedness in an unknown language perhaps played a role in the action that did develop.

After the conquests were achieved and Spaniards installed in positions of power, there was little in the new economic order that was established, with native inhabitants of a region assigned to work on the land or in mines, that would have encouraged widespread diffusion of the Spanish language. Repetitive duties among static populations would minimise the need for communication between master and subject. There was nothing analogous to military service in the Roman empire, or the spread of monasteries and universities in medieval Europe, which would diffuse the language of the Spanish masters around their domains. There was, in any case, a constant flow of Spanish speakers emigrating from Spain itself to boost the speaker population. Yet a substantial number of bilinguals would have been needed to organise the work of the natives. They would have arisen naturally as the Spanish immigrants, overwhelmingly male, took Indian wives or mistresses (*mancebas*) and began to raise families with them. Their children, known as *mestizos*, would learn both languages from their parents. 'As early as 1503, the Court recommends to the governor of Hispaniola that some Christians should marry some Indian women, so that they may communicate with and teach one another.'[8]

Such enthusiasm for the *Nueva Raza*, the 'new race' generated by these interracial unions, is one feature that strongly distinguishes Spanish imperialism from the attitudes of later Anglo-Saxon empire-builders. Among the famous *conquistadores*, almost every one had *mestizo* children, often with several different women, and they were fully recognised as heirs to their fathers. Cortés, Pizarro, Benalcázar and Alvarado all conform to this tradition; indeed, Pope Clement VII officially legitimised three sons of Cortés in a bull of 1529, although he did temporise a little: 'the virtues' beauty purges in the sons the stain of the birth, and with the purity of customs the shame of origin is effaced'.

So common was interracial matrimony (soon complicated by the import of black slaves from Africa) that a taxonomy of the terms for mixed-race children was devised, and famously illustrated.[9] Modern Hispanic commentators tend to idealise this state of affairs, referring, for example, to the mixed racial background of the Spanish in Europe, but the facts that the attempt was made to keep everyone classified, and that the power and status of the nominally pure Spanish families (*criollos*) remained high until the end of the empire—exceeded indeed only by that of immigrants from Spain—suggest that the society was not so free of race-based oppression as is sometimes claimed. However, whatever the level of acceptance and encouragement of the various types of union that were solemnised (or not), there is very little documentary evidence of language usage in these families.

What evidence there is comes from the unchallengeable fact of literary distinction in many early *mestizos*. They were not only interpreters, but also literary translators and authors, in Spanish and in Latin too.* Fernando de Alva Ixtilxóchitl, from the line of the kings of Tezcoco, Cortés' allies, was known as the 'Livy of Anáhuac', author of the *Historia Chichimeca*. And his son Bartolomé adapted into Nahuatl two contemporary Spanish plays by Lope de Vega, and another by Calderón. They were not alone; chronicles of the conquest of all parts of the empires of the New World were soon being written up, in Spanish, by the very people produced by that conquest.[10]

The most distinguished of the literary mestizos was probably the Inca Garcilaso de la Vega (1539–1616), born in Cuzco, the Inca capital, seven years after the conquest, his father being the Spanish nobleman Captain Sebastián Garcilaso de la Vega y Vargas, and his mother Palla Chimpu Ocllo, second cousin of the two last Incas, Huayna Capac and Atahuallpa. He emigrated to Spain in his early twenties, and lived there until his death, so his career says little directly about the relative strength of languages in Peru. But he was a man familiar with the sense of different languages: having learnt Quechua and Spanish as a child, and Latin in his youth, he had then learnt sufficient Italian to translate a book entitled *Dialogues of Love*. He went on to write two lengthy historical works of his own, *The Florida of the Inca*, about de Soto's campaign through Florida, and a two-part history called *Royal Commentaries of the Incas* and *General History of Peru*. In this last work, he has a lot to say

---

* The word '*ladino*', indeed, carried over from its application to Moors in Spain, was a term often used of non-Spaniards who knew Spanish, first applied to Indians but later also to African slaves.

about the relative roles of the Quechua and Spanish languages, often quoting the views of another famous literary *mestizo*, Father Blas Valera (who had written a history of Peru in Latin).

It was Garcilaso and Blas Valera's view that the advent of Spanish power to Peru, with the civil wars and social disruption that it brought in its train, had disrupted the convenient linguistic unity that the Incas had succeeded in imposing over their empire, and which should have been exploited in the propagation of the Christian faith.

> Whence it has come about that many provinces, where when the Spaniards entered Cajamarca the rest of the Indians knew this common language, have now forgotten it altogether, because with the end of the world and Empire of the Incas, there was no-one to remember something so convenient and necessary for the preaching of the Holy Gospel, because of the widespread oblivion caused by the wars which arose among the Spaniards, and after that for other causes which the evil Satan has sown to prevent such an advantageous regime from being put into operation... There are some to whom it appears sensible to oblige all the Indians to learn the Spanish language, so that the priests should not waste their efforts on learning the Indian one. This opinion can leave no-one who hears it in any doubt that it arose from failure of endeavour rather than stupid thinking...[11]

It has been claimed[12] that Garcilaso's underlying point was that the Incas understood better than their conquerors the fundamental point of Nebrija, whose ground-breaking grammar of Spanish—as we have seen—had begun with the thesis 'that always language was the companion of empire'. Garcilaso certainly held the view, still widely held today though not among knowledgeable linguists, that a shared language makes for common understanding and good mutual relations: 'because the likeness and conformity of words almost always tend to reconcile people and bring them to true union and friendship'.[13]

Whatever the truth on this point of ideology, the existence of Antonio Nebrija's works, grammars both of Latin (*Introductiones Latinae*) and contemporary Spanish (*Gramatica de la lengua castellana*), demonstrated that it was possible to capture the 'art' of a language explicitly on the page. And the missionaries soon flocking to the New World made use of this demonstration to found the world's first tradition of descriptive linguistics.

Entering Mexico, this new virgin territory for the Church, where bilinguals hardly existed at any level of society, the Franciscan, Dominican and

Augustinian friars immediately realised that they would have to work through the people's own languages if they were to make serious progress in spreading the faith.* This meant the languages would have to be learnt. The population to be contacted was vast: many million to set against the 802 friars present in Mexico in 1557.[14] Clearly, this was work for many generations. And since there would necessarily be a circulation of missionaries, with old ones retiring and fresh recruits coming out from Spain—i.e. the tradition had to be carried on without the natural transmission of languages through raising children—the languages would have to be taught afresh, over and over, to each new generation of adult learners. For the first time in the world's history, there was a clear demand for language-learning textbooks, specifically grammars ('*Artes*') and dictionaries, as well as native-language versions of the prayer books and confessionals that were the tools of the Catholic missionary's trade.†

And conveniently enough, there were now the technical means to satisfy the demand: printing presses were installed in Mexico City in 1535; their first known product, the *Breve y más compendiosa doctrina christiana*, which came out in 1539, was for ecclesiastical use, and despite its title was written in Nahuatl. In 1546 it was followed by Fray Alonso de Molina's *Doctrina christiana breve traduzida en lengua Mexicana*, and in 1547 by *Arte de la lengua mexicana* by Father Andres de Olmos, and an accompanying volume, *Vocabulario de la lengua mexicana*.§ Volumes in others of the country's languages followed, beginning with expositions of Christian doctrines in Huastec in 1548 and Mixtec in 1550. Peru could not wait for the press, and the first *Arte* of the Quechua language, *Grammatica, o arte de la lengua general de los Indios de los Reynos del Peru*, was actually printed in Spain, in Valladolid, in 1560. But when printing started in Lima (Peru) in 1583, among its first products were *Catecismo en Lengua Española y Quichua*, *Catecismo en Lengua Española y Aymara* (both 1583), and *Doctrina christiana...traduzido en las dos lenguas generales de este Reyno, Quichua y Aymara* (1584).[15]

This was just scratching the surface of the unknown continent's languages.

---

* The people in Hispaniola, Cuba and the rest of the Caribbean islands, discovered in the previous generation, and immediately pressed into servitude by self-appointed Spanish masters, had spoken too many languages with too few speakers, and by and large died off too quickly, for a missionary effort to become established.

† On the uniqueness of this, see Ostler (2004). Almost all the dictionaries are from Spanish into the alien language, not the reverse. The aim is to teach, rather than to learn: to encode a Spaniard's thought, and so pass it to the Indians, rather than to try to decode anything novel that they might have to say.

§ *Lengua mexicana* refers to the Nahuatl language, the principal lingua franca of the Aztec (Mexica) empire, and at first also of its successor empire, New Spain.

The ultimate harvest of linguistic knowledge that was gained in the Americas, primarily to serve missionary activity, was vast. In 1892 the Count of Viñaza listed 493 distinct languages identified by Spanish linguists in the Americas over three and a half centuries of research, and the titles of significant documents describing some aspect of 369 of them. In that period 667 separate authors had produced 1,188 works.[16]

Looking back on this immense multilingualism of the Americas revealed by the penetration of the Spanish empire, we almost quail at the enormity of what the Spaniards took on. For the spread of Spanish as the first or second language of people from so many different traditions was by no means inevitable.

The situation of Spanish in its empire in the sixteenth century, and even in the seventeenth and eighteenth centuries, was very different from that of English in the nineteenth or twentieth. Although the empire was an open institution for the Spaniards, who continued to emigrate to the colonies until these achieved independence in the early nineteenth century, it was something else for the indigenous rural population, the speakers of those 493 or so alien languages. For most of them, often living in the collective settlements called *reducciones*, there was little mobility, physical, economic or social, except perhaps through the Church hierarchy. They might be looked after by priests who spoke their languages, but otherwise they were quite segregated from contact with the Spanish masters. The Indians were offered a ticket to salvation in the next world, but not to any sort of advancement in this one. It was a situation more like that of medieval Europe than that of the Reformation. Hence there could be no rapid, or automatic, shift towards Spanish, outside the *mestizo* communities and the towns.

One can even speculate that if some political force had undercut, or superseded, Spanish control of the continent in that period, Spanish would have faded away very fast. After all, we can recall what happened to Sanskrit in South-East Asia at the end of the first millennium, or to Greek in the Near East when the Parthians and then Muslims advanced: both these were in similar situations to Spanish, top-level languages that remained the preserve of a small elite. There is even a comparative experiment to prove our point, since the Spaniards were indeed expelled from their Pacific colonies at the end of the nineteenth century.

But before we consider how Spanish came to consolidate its hold on the American population, we need to consider the varied backgrounds of some of the American languages that, in the sixteenth and seventeenth centuries, were still widely spoken and hardly losing ground.

Past struggles: How American languages had spread

Early on, as we have seen, Columbus was dispirited by the vast numbers of languages, with no mutual understanding among their speakers, which he encountered on his voyages. First running along the coast of the American mainland, *Tierra Firme*, he noted to his disappointment that 'they no more understand one another than we do the Arabs'.[17] The peoples he met as he cruised down the coasts of what are now Honduras, Nicaragua and Panama must have spoken Paya, Miskitu, Guaimí and Kuna.

There was no relief from this apparently boundless babel when the Spaniards, from a base in Santiago de Cuba, began to explore the coastline farther north. Hernández de Córdoba, who in 1517 ran along the north and east of the Yucatán, could have encountered only (Yucatec) Maya in his two landfalls: a single language to be sure, but distinct from any the Spanish had previously encountered—and there is no sign that any attempt was made to identify or learn anything of the language.* Then in 1518 Juan de Grijalva undertook a longer coastal exploration, with more stops in the Yucatán, and one at Xicallanco, where he would have encountered a different Maya language, called by the Spanish Chontal de Tabasco—though its own speakers now call it Yokot'an—and then further stops at Potonchan, where the language would have been Zapotec, followed by two more in the region of modern Vera Cruz, where the language was Totonac. Sign language remained the best means of communication for the time being.

This was not an encouraging beginning, if the Spaniards were hoping to establish widespread communications with the Indians; but it was not unrepresentative: at least two thousand distinct languages were being spoken in the Americas at the time, 350 of them in the central regions of Mexico and the isthmus which the Spanish explored first.[18]

Nevertheless, when the Spaniards succeeded first in contacting, and then conquering, the few great multinational states that America had already produced, they found that Nebrija's dictum, indeed predictive theory, 'that always language was the companion of empire' was amply borne out in the New World. The two great ancient empires of the Americas, the Aztecs and the Incas, had spread use of their languages throughout their realms, covering

---

* Other than to misidentify some phrases in it, and apply them permanently to the lands he was 'discovering' (and of course claiming in the name of the Spanish Crown). *Ekab kotoč*, 'we are from Ekab', became Cabo (cape) Cotoche, its name to this day. And, if we follow Diego de Landa (*Relación de las Cosas de Yucatán*, ch. ii, written *c*.1566), *ciuyetel ceh than*, 'They call it land of turkeys and deer', ended up as 'Yucatán'.

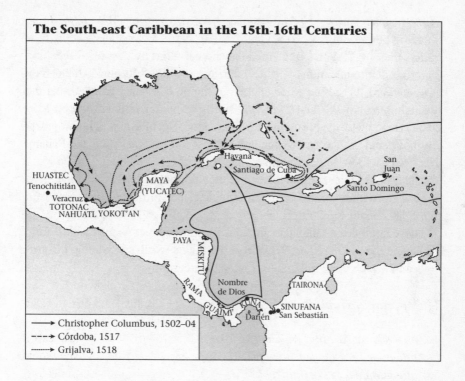

The South-east Caribbean in the 15th-16th Centuries

→ Christopher Columbus, 1502–04
---→ Córdoba, 1517
......→ Grijalva, 1518

most of central Mexico and the central and southern Andes down to the Pacific Ocean. Less spectacular in terms of political and social development, but still highly gratifying to Spaniards in quest of gold, the Chibchan settlements in the northern Andes (at the centre of what is now Colombia) were characterised by a widespread common language, known as Muisca. And when Spain reached the southern region of the Río de la Plata and the Gran Chaco, it found a vast area where everyone spoke Tupinambá or Guaraní,* two closely related and mutually intelligible languages. Farther south still, in the chilly and mountainous land of Araucania, the Mapuche, so warlike that they were successfully to resist Spanish takeover until the mid-nineteenth century, were also united by a common language, called Mapudungun.

These languages of wide extent were very much the exception, understood over less than 10 per cent of the territory of central and south America; but this territory was very highly populated, with perhaps as much as 40 per cent

---

* Guaraní is so called for historical reasons, because the first people whom Europeans (with Sebastian Cabot in 1526–9) met who spoke this language were the Guaraní of the islands in the Río de la Plata and lower reaches of the Paraná. Its own preferred name is *avañe'e*, 'language of the men of the plain'.

of the people. The widespread languages were to prove highly useful to an invading power, since when standardised as auxiliary languages in the new empire they could short-circuit the long and laborious process of establishing effective communications. By an amazing stroke of fortune, all but one (Tupinambá) turned out to be spoken in the parts of the continent that the Spanish were to make their own. This jumbo set of linguistic advantages may be one reason why the economic development of Spain's empire in the Americas began at least a century sooner than those of Portugal, France or Britain. The vast support systems underlying the large-scale mining of gold in Zacatecas in Mexico, and of silver in Potosí in the Andes, would have been impossible without some common language, but the language was not in those days Spanish.

These large-scale languages had not always been so widespread. Before looking at the use the Spanish made of them, it is worth considering the processes by which these indigenous linguistic areas arose.

The spread of Nahuatl

Zan yuhki nonyaz in oompoliwi šočitl ah?
Antle notleyo yez in kenmanian?
Antle nitauhka yez in tlaltikpak?
Ma nel šočitl, ma nel kuikatl!
Ken končiwaz noyollo, yewaya?
On nen tonkizako in tlaltikpak.

Shall I just go like the flowers which were fading?
Will my glory be nothing one day?
Will my fame be nothing in the earth?
At least flowers, at least songs!
Alas, what will my heart do?
In vain do we pass this way across the earth!

Nahuatl lyric (*Cantares Mexicanos*, folio 10 recto, ll. 23ff.)

First in terms of magnificence, and also in population, was the realm where Nahuatl was spoken.* This language was usually known in the Spanish pe-

---

* The name is a nominalisation of the verb *nawati*, 'to speak up'. We shall stick to the conventional spelling of this name, which is based on Spanish, and so pronounced *nawatl*. There are dialects, often called Nawat and Nawa, which (as their names show) differ in the pronunciation of this final consonant.

riod as *lengua mexicana*, since the Aztecs, as we have seen (see Prologue), referred to themselves as Mexica, and their land as Mexico.* But this language had never been exclusive to the Aztec community. Specifically, when Cortés arrived in the valley of Mexico in 1519, Nahuatl was spoken by their neighbours in Tlaxcallan to the east also, outside the circle of the Aztecs' vassal states, neighbours who, as it turned out, were ready to ally themselves with the Spanish against their fellow-speakers of Nahuatl. But this was just one of the last traces of a distribution of Nahuatl that pre-dated the Aztecs. In fact, there is evidence that the language's presence in the general area of central Mexico goes back at least to the seventh century AD, when the monumental city of Teotihuacán was destroyed by fire: at that time the Pipil community are supposed to have moved south, through some interaction with the then dominant Toltec civilisation. The Toltecs left little concrete trace except a memory hallowed among the Aztecs who assumed control of central Mexico after them: but of the Pipil descendants who are left today, living far to the south in El Salvador, twenty or so still speak a form of Nahuatl. The straightforward assumption is that Nahuatl was the language of almost all the people living in the Valley of Mexico around the turn of the first millennium AD, encircling what was then a vast lake: the Tepanecs of Atzcapotzalco on the north-western shore, the states of Tezcoco and Culhuacán, apparently successors of the Toltecs, on the eastern. There were also areas of Nahuatl farther afield, westward in Jalisco on the Pacific coast, and eastward in the isthmus of Tehuantepec, perhaps remnants of an earlier empire, centred on the Toltecs or even Teotihuacán.

Comparative studies in the late nineteenth and early twentieth centuries have shown Nahuatl as almost the southernmost member of a family, known as Uto-Aztecan or Yuta-Nawan, which extends in a wide swath as far north as the Shoshone and Paiute peoples in modern Oregon. This reconstructed linguistic geography fits with the Aztecs' foundation legend, by which they claimed to have come from Aztlán ('heron place'), an island somewhere unknown in the north-west. So they may have learnt their Nahuatl before they came to the Valley of Mexico in 1256, initially as vagrants and scavengers and eaters of snakes.† Yet they always represented themselves as a branch of the Chichimeca people, renowned hunter-gatherer nomads of the north. If

---

* The x is authentically pronounced as English *sh*, and the stress falls on the i, followed by a glottal stop: *Mešíhko*.

† The dates quoted are actually specified with equivalent accuracy in the original text of the *Crónica Mexicayotl*. The many different peoples of central America shared an elaborate system of interlocking calendar cycles which tolerated no vagueness.

Languages of Mexico in the 16th Century

this story is true, they must have learnt their Nahuatl fairly late; for the Chichimeca or Pame language is related to Otomí, also spoken north and west of the Valley of Mexico, but quite unlike Nahuatl. The Aztecs may have been like the Normans in France, settling and learning a new language before projecting it through conquest.

First squatting in the western region of Chapultepec, then chased out and enlisting as mercenaries with Culhuacán (another people who claimed descent from the Chichimeca), they accepted a very lowly billet on the lava beds of Tizaapan.

'Good,' Coxcoxtli [king of Culhuacan] said. 'They are monstrous, they
    are evil.
Perhaps they will meet their end there, devoured by snakes,
for it is the dwelling-place of many snakes.'
But the Mexicans were overjoyed when they saw the snakes.
They cooked them, they roasted them and they ate them...

After twenty-five years of this, they brought matters to a head, requesting a Culhuacán princess, presumably as a bride, but then committing a characteristic atrocity on her.

> Then they slew the princess and they flayed her,
> and after they flayed her, they dressed a priest in her skin.
> Huitzilopochtli [Humming-bird on the Left, the Aztecs' tribal god] then
>   said:
> 'O my chiefs, go and summon Achitometl [the princess's father].'
> The Mexicans went off, they went to summon him.
> They said, 'O our lord, O my grandson, O lord, O king...
> your grandfathers, the Mexicans beseech you, they say,
> 'May he come to see, may he come to greet the goddess.
> We invite him.' ...
> And when Achitometl arrived in Tizaapan, the Mexicans said in
>   welcome:
> 'You have wearied yourself, O my grandson, O lord, O king.
> We, your grandfathers, we, your vassals, shall cause you to become ill.
> May you see, may you greet your goddess.'*
> 'Very good, O my grandfathers,' he said.
> He took the rubber, the copal, the flowers, the tobacco and the food
>   offering,
> and he offered them to her,
> he set them down before the false goddess whom they had flayed.
> Then Achitometl tore off the heads of the quail before his goddess:
> he still did not see the person before whom he was decapitating the
>   quail.
> Then he made the offering of incense and the incense-burner blazed up,
> and Achitometl saw a man in his daughter's skin.
> He was horror-struck.
> He cried out, he shouted to his lords and vassals,
> He said, 'Who are they, eh, O Culhuacans?
> Have you not seen? They have flayed my daughter!
> They shall not remain here, the fiends!
> We shall slay them, we shall massacre them!
> The evil ones shall be annihilated here!'

> Fernando Alvarado Tezozomoc, *Crónica Mexicayotl*, trans. Thelma D. Sullivan

---

* The phraseology is very similar to Motecuhzoma's formal greetings to Cortés. See Prologue and Chapter 1, 'An inward history too', p. 15. Note also that, in accord with the conceits of Aztec etiquette discussed there, the junior party, the Aztecs, represent themselves as the grandfathers.

The Aztecs were then driven into the lake, but they made improvised rafts out of their arrows and shields, and when they emerged on the other side, they were inspired. It was prophesied that they must settle 'where the eagle screeches, where he spreads his wings, where the eagle feeds, where the fish fly, where the serpent is torn apart'. In the distance, on a prickly-pear cactus, they saw this vision, of an eagle eating a snake. A voice cried out: 'O Mexicans, it shall be here!' But no one could see who spoke. They knew that the reedy, but defensible, islands in the middle of the lake should be their home, Tenochtitlán, 'place of the prickly-pear'. It was the year *ome calli*, '2 House', 1325.

This was the origin of the vast and miraculous lake city, which so entranced the invading Spaniards when they reached it in November 1519. The Aztecs had regrouped and prospered in their lakeland home for a hundred years, and then begun to expand their domains through a series of aggressive wars. First, under Itzcoatl ('Obsidian-Snake'), 1427–40, they achieved control of the Valley of Mexico as a whole, then under Motecuhzoma I Ilhuicamina ('Heaven-Shooter') they outflanked the territory of their resistant neighbours to the west, Huetxotzingo and Tlaxcala, to reach the Caribbean coast and the central highlands to the south. Two more long-reigning *tlatoani* added to the empire, and by the beginning of the sixteenth century the Aztecs had conquered about 100,000 square kilometres of territory in the centre of modern Mexico, from the Caribbean to the Pacific, including the curious enclave of Xoconochco, down the coast on the Pacific border of Guatemala.

A single minister, Tlacaelel, presided over the first five decades of this bloody expansion. With an eye to the future, his policy was to burn all the books of conquered peoples to erase memories of a pre-Aztec past. Even though Huetxotzingo and Tlaxcala had been bypassed in the Aztec advance, he imposed on them a curious agreement to conduct continual, but formally regulated, warfare, the *šoči-yaoyotl* or 'flower-war', a regular engagement to do battle in order to capture prisoners for sacrifice. The word *šočitl*, 'flower', has a positive, ethereal value in Nahuatl imagery (for example, *in šočitl in cuitatl*, 'the flower the song', meaning 'poetry', used in the verse that begins this section), but it is never free of association with the role of flowers in sacrificial offerings, just like human blood.

Familiarity with Nahuatl was spread all over central Mexico by this successful aggression of the Aztecs, but it does not seem to have happened at the expense of the languages of tributary peoples. Rather the Aztecs planted officials, especially tribute overseers, in all the major cities, and ensured that the subject peoples provided a corps of *nauatlato*, 'interpreters', to ensure effective transmission of the rulers' wishes. Two Nahuatl speakers were among the officials from the subject Totonac territory who met Cortés when he first landed. And Nahuatl had clearly been spread by other, unknown, population movements prior to this: Cortés's interpreter Malin-tzin, for instance, was a native speaker of the language, but she had acquired it in Coatzacoalcos, on the Caribbean coast 50 kilometres south of the border of the Aztec empire.

Before the Spanish conquest, Nahuatl should thus be seen as at best an effective lingua franca of a multinational and multilingual empire: the empire included areas where the indigenous population to this day speak Zapotec, Mixtec, Tarascan, Otomí, Huastec and Totonac languages, none of them related to one another or to Nahuatl. But in the fifteenth century, contact between the subject lands and the centre in Tenochtitlán must have been intense, at the level of tribute-gathering, and also through the network of *pochteca*, 'merchants', who also functioned as ambassadors and spies, and were so highly placed in the Aztec hierarchy that they could offer their slaves for sacrifice to Huitzilopochtli along with the war captives offered by great warriors.

The spread of Quechua

K' akichanpi millmacháyuj,
nina ráuraj puka runa,
mana ñuqaqa atinichu
watuyta chay simiykita.
Imatachus ñiwankipas
*manapuni yachanichu.**

Red man who blazes like fire
and on the chin raises thick wool,
it is quite impossible for me
to understand your weird language.

---

* Quechua is basically spelt and pronounced like Spanish, but w and k are common. Hence ñ is *ny* as in *canyon*, and j is *ch* in as in *loch*. An apostrophe after a consonant marks a glottal catch in the voice. A major exception to Spanish convention is that q is pronounced with the uvula at the back of the mouth, as in Arabic; and immediately before or after it i is pronounced more like [e], and u as [o]. This is the fundamental reason why the language's name is given sometimes as 'Quechua', and sometimes as 'Quichua'. The first u is in any case just a reminiscence of Spanish spelling: the pronunciation is more like [qečwa].

I do not know what you are saying to me,
I cannot know in any way.

> (An Inca addresses Pizarro, before the battle of Cajamarca)
> *Atau Wallpaj p'uchakakuynninpa wankan*
> The Tragedy of the End of Atawallpa[19]

Language spread had been a far more complex process in the growth of the other great pre-Columbian empire, the Inca realm known as *Tawantin-suyu*, 'Four Portions'. When the Spanish reached Peru, its empire—and its language—covered the whole altiplano to the west of the Andes, from Quito in the north to Talca in the south, linked by a royal road that stretched some 4,000 kilometres, and uniting under one government the Andean and Pacific strips of modern Ecuador, Peru, Bolivia and northern Chile. The language is known by its speakers as *runa simi*, 'human speech', but there was no accepted term for it when the Spanish arrived: Inca Garcilaso, a well-connected bilingual writing at the end of the sixteenth century, refers to it always as *la lengua cortesana de Cuzco*, 'the courtly language of Cuzco'. The first published grammar, by Domingo de Santo Tomás, in 1560, names it, however, *la lengua general del Perú, llamada, Quichua*, following a tradition that had been attested for at least twenty years,[20] and this has stuck. The term *qhišwa* actually refers to 'temperate zone' or 'valley', intermediate between the coast and the highlands. The general view at the time was that the temperate zone round Andahuaylas in Apurímac province, south of the city of Cuzco (*Qusqu*, 'navel'—the Inca capital), had been the heartland of the language.[21]

In fact, this seems to have been a later rationalisation.[22] Quechua was by origin the language of a coastal region round Lima, with an oracle located at Pachakamaj ('earth-ruler'), the base of a seaborne trading community called the Chincha, who spread their language primarily as a trade jargon out towards the north, particularly up into the northern highlands round Cajamarca and into Ecuador, the area that was to be designated the *Chincha-suyu*, the most northerly portion of the Inca empire. This all happened in the first millennium AD, long before the Incas were a force to be reckoned with. The grafting of the language on to the growing Inca empire would in fact come almost as an afterthought, by a process rather similar to the adoption of Aramaic by the politic Persian emperor Darius (see Chapter 3, 'The story in brief: Language leapfrog', p. 47).

The Inca story began far to the south, on the southern shores of Lake Titicaca, where a group speaking the Puquina [*pukína*] language had established a major centre now known as Tiahuanaco. It seems that in the first millennium, in concert with speakers of Jaqi [*háki*], another language to the north (the ancestor of modern Aymara, still spoken in Bolivia), they developed an inland trading zone to the north and west; this trade would have spread knowledge of the Aymara language, and its sisters Kawki and Jaqaru (which still survive vestigially south-east of Lima), over much of the area of southern Peru. It is visible in the archaeological record in a distinctive style of pottery, depicting a face surrounded by rays or serpents, which could be the creator god Viracocha. It is, in fact, still possible to find place names that stem from this period, for example Cajamarca itself (Jaqi *q'aja marka*, 'town in the valley').

The Tiahuanaco rulers, apparently finding their old home threatened by mud slides, then moved across or round Lake Titicaca, to set up a new base of command in Cuzco: this began the ascent of the Inca, immortalised in their mythology as the career of their first king, Manco Capac, who emerged from the lake, bearing a golden sceptre that would show where they should settle. (Only at Cuzco could it be plunged straight into the ground.) He came with his wife Mama Ocllo, and together (but respectively) they taught men and women the arts of civilisation. At this point, the Incas accepted Aymara de facto as the language of their kingdom, preserving Puquina as an elite language for court use. (Of course, it continued to be used by their 'poor relations', left behind south of Lake Titicaca.) Cuzco must have been a bilingual city. This situation did not change for some nine generations (from the Incas Manco Capac to Pachacutec), as the realm of the Incas was expanded east, south and finally northward.

Then, in the time of Inca Pachacutec, serious aggression began. Expansion northward brought the Inca domains into conflict with the Chincha: but the solution found was peaceable and extremely positive. Pachacutec (already married to his own sister) offered his son, the formidable Tupac Yupanqui, in marrage to a Chincha princess, and the result was a merging of the Inca and Chincha domains. This led to a switch of imperial language, from Aymara to Quechua, presumably reflecting a judgement on which was more widespread and useful in the combined Inca and Chincha domains. For a time, Cuzco became a trilingual city. This would have been much less than a hundred years before the Spanish conquest in 1528. Cuzco Quechua, for all its political importance, was still seen as a substandard variety, which interpreters from the north liked to look down on. The new language was then projected with the sudden, and extremely warlike, advances of the empire which, under Tupac Yupanqui, took it northward to Quito, incorporating the significant Chimú state on the way, and southward into Chile.

Father Blas Valera insists on the explicit language acculturation policies pursued by the Incas within their domains.

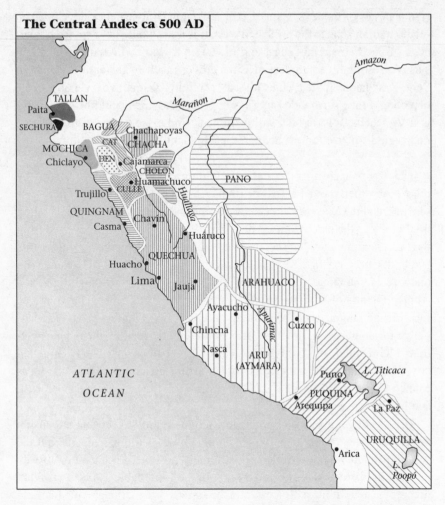

It remains to say something of the *lengua general* of the natives of Peru, which although it is true that each province has its own language different from the others, there is one universal one that they call Cuzco, which in the time of the Inca kings was used from Quito to the kingdom of Chile and the kingdom of Tucuman, and now the chieftains use it and the Indians who the Spaniards hold as servants and to administer business. The Inca kings, from antiquity, as soon as they subjected any kingdom or province, would...order their vassals to learn the courtly language of Cuzco and to teach it to their children. And to make sure that this command was not vain, they would give them Indians native to Cuzco to teach them the language and the customs of the court. To whom, in such provinces and villages, they would give houses, lands

The Central Andes ca 1400 AD

COLOMBIA

QUITO
ECUADOR

Cuenca

Napo

Tigre

Amazon

Iquitos

Marañón

Chachapoyas

Lamas

Chiclayo

Ucayali

BRAZIL

Trujillo

Huaraz

Lima

Huancayo

Ayacucho

PERU

Ica

Cuzco

BOLIVIA

Puno

Lake Titicaca

Arequipa

LA PAZ

Cochabamba

Oruro

PACIFIC

Sucra

OCEAN

Potosi

CHILE

ARGENTINA

Santiago del Estero

All languages marked are
varieties of Quechua

Waywash

Limay

Chinchay

and estates so that, naturalizing themselves there, they should become perpetual teachers and their children after them. And the Inca governors preferred in the offices of the state, in peace as in war, those who best spoke the *lengua general*. On these terms, the Incas ruled and governed their whole empire in peace and quiet, and the vassals of various nations were like brothers, because all of them spoke one language...[23]

And Inca Garcilaso adds:

Those kings also sent the heirs of the lords of the vassals to be educated at the court and reside there until they came into their inheritance, to have them well taught and to accustom themselves to the condition and customs of the Incas, treating them kindly, so that afterwards, on the strength of their past communion and familiarity they should love them and serve them with affection: they called them *mítmac*, because they were newcomers... This injunction made it easier for the *lengua general* to be learnt with more enjoyment and less effort and grief... Whenever they returned to their lands they took something they had learnt of the courtly language, and spoke it with such pride among their own people, as the language of people they felt to be divine, that they caused such envy that the rest would desire and strive to learn it... In this manner, with sweetness and ease, without the particular effort of schoolmasters, they learnt and spoke the *lengua general* of Cuzco in the domain of little less than 1,300 leagues' [4,000 kilometres] extent which those kings had won.[24]

To these apparently benign methods, the Incas had added the harsher one of repopulating some areas with colonies of Quechua-speaking immigrant families, also known as *mitmaj*, 'transplants'. These were sent with the aim of diluting and pacifying the original population. There were ten to twelve thousand of them, settled with some finesse:[25] 'They were passed to other villages or provinces of the temper and manner of those from which they issued; because if they were from a cold country they were taken to a cold country, and from hot, to hot... They were given estates in the fields and lands for their labours and a place to make their houses.'[26]

The spreads of Chibcha, Guaraní, Mapudungun

Ñamandu Ru Ete tenondegua
...
Oámyvyma,
oyvárapy mba'ekuaágui,
okuaararávyma
ayvu rapytarã i
oikuaa ojeupe.
mboapy mba'ekuaágui,
okuaararávyma,
ayvu rapyta oguerojera,
ogueroyvára Ñande Ru.
Yvy oiko'eÿre,
pytû yma mbytére,
mba'e jekuaa'eÿre,
ayvu rapytarã i oguerojera,
ogueroyvára
Ñamandu Ru Ete tenondegua.

True Father Ñamandú, the First One...
Standing up straight
from the wisdom in his own godhead
and in virtue of his creating wisdom
conceived the origin of human language
and made it form part of his own godhead.
Before the earth existed
amidst the primordial darkness
before there was knowledge of things
he created what was to be the foundation of human language
and True First Father Ñamandú
made it form part of his own godhead.

Ayvu Rapyta, 'The Foundation of Human Language',
Mbyá-Guaraní creation myth[27]

Gradually we move away from the animals more and more. In the first times, the difference was tiny. All living beings had an Aché body, a person's body, and behaved as such. The main likeness was the possession of *javu*, language.

Aché Pyvé, 'The Beginnings of the Aché',
Aché-Guaraní creation myth[28]

Major Language Areas of South America, ca 1500 AD

IKA, KOGI

ATLANTIC
OCEAN

CHIBCHA
(MUISCA)

QUECHUA-
AYMARA

PACIFIC
OCEAN

MAPUDUNGUN

GUARANÍ

	Arawakan
	Cariban
	Chibchan
	Jê languages
	Quechumaran
	Tupí-Guaraní
	Other languages

—·— Modern international boundary

Far less is known about the careers of the other languages that had become widespread before the advent of the Spaniards.

The altiplano of Cundinamarca in the northern Andes was largely monolingual in the Chibcha (or *Muysca*) language when the Spanish arrived in 1536; the area was not politically unified at the time, however, and with at least three major centres at Tunja (*Hunza*) in the north, Bogotá (*Muykyta*) in the south, and Sogamoso (*Sugamuši*), a major religious centre in the north-east, there was also some difference in dialects. The conquistador Gonzalo Jiménez de Quesada (like Cortés, another lawyer at large) had brought interpreters with him from the coast, but, in view of the coastal languages as they are now (for example, Ika, Kogi), it is unlikely that they could have communicated in anything like their own language: more probably, they had some knowledge of Chibcha from traditional trade links between the mountains and the coast. Although there was already a clear social hierarchy among the Chibcha, and military organisation associated with formal campaigns among the different centres (as well as their non-Chibcha-speaking neighbours), there is no evidence that the language had been spread by any political, military or economic influence. More likely, the language had simply been established by the tribes who had settled there. And their ethnic group had clearly been there for some time: closely related languages had evolved a couple of hundred kilometres to the north-east, among the Duit (nowadays extinct), and the Tunebo (also known as *Uwa*), who still live, and speak their language, on the eastern slopes of the Andes.

Even less is known about the background of Tupí-Guaraní, but the language was spoken far more widely across lowland South America; forms of it have been found as far north as Suriname, north of the Amazon, and to the west in pockets on the Brazilian and Peruvian borders of Colombia. It was spoken (as Tupinambá) all over the centre and south-east of Brazil, in eastern Bolivia (known as Chiriguano), and in Paraguay (as Guaraní). Its spread may have been linked to the progress of Mesoamerican-style farming across the continent, of maize, beans and squash, supplemented with potatoes, manioc, peanuts and chili peppers.[29]

And of the Mapuche past, even less is known or can be inferred. They maintained their independence until the second half of the nineteenth century; and so Spanish contact with them came too late for any use of their language, Mapudungun, as a *lengua general*. The use of a single language across their extensive territory suggests that they were a single group who had taken possession of a not particularly fertile region, and were thinly spread across it.

We must now turn to the policies pursued by the Spanish to organise their colonies linguistically. But before we do so, it is worth pointing out that there is a clear correlation between the degree of political organisation of a group with a widespread language, and the development of a literature after Spanish contact (which took advantage of the transmission of a Romanised writing system). There are substantial literatures in Nahuatl and Quechua which date from the period immediately after the conquest, often written by immediate descendants of the elite who had ruled Mexico and Peru before.* Aymara, Chibcha and Guaraní, by contrast, did not develop an indigenous written literature, even though they had each been given a written standard by missionary linguists:[30] as far as we can see, literature in the languages remained confined to the productions of the Spaniards, and largely to support the process of Christianisation.

The Church's solution: The lenguas generales

Your Majesty has ordered that these Indians should learn the language of Castile. That can never be, unless it were something vaguely and badly learnt: we see a Portuguese, where the language of Castile and Portugal is almost all the same, spend thirty years in Castile, and never learn it. Then are these people to learn it, when their language is so foreign to ours, with exquisite manners of speaking? It seems to me that Your Majesty should order that all the Indians learn the Mexican language, for in every village today there are many Indians who know it and learn it easily, and a very great number who confess in that language. It is an extremely elegant language, as elegant as any in the world. A grammar and dictionary of it have been written, and many parts of the Holy Scriptures have been translated into it; and collections of sermons have been made, and some friars are very great linguists in it.

> Fray Rodrigo de la Cruz to Emperor Charles V
> Mexico, letter of 4 May [March?] 1550[31]

We are too few to teach the language of Castile to Indians. They do not want to speak it. It would be better to make universal the Mexican language, which is widely current, and they like it, and in it there are written doctrine and sermons and a grammar and a vocabulary.

> Fray Juan de Mansilla, Comisario General, to Emperor Charles V
> Guatemala, letter of 8 September 1551[32]

---

* Something of the same seems to have happened with the Mayan languages, but with less conscious collaboration with, or aping of, Spanish literary forms. The Mayans had not recently been united under indigenous leaders. Nevertheless, they did develop a literature, but it was one that largely followed the norms and content of their older traditions. It includes the heroic myths of the Popol Vuh, the elegiac and tragic dialogue with a doomed warrior (Rabinal Achi), and the Books of Chilam Balam, which are traditional almanacs. It was a form of underground resistance to Christian domination.

If the Spanish with very sharp intellects and knowledge of the sciences cannot, as they claim, learn the general language of Cuzco, how can it be achieved that the uncultivated and untaught Indians can learn Castilian?

Father Blas Valera
Peru, mid-sixteenth century[33]

In the papal bull of 1493 issued by Alexander VI, *Inter Caetera*, which formed the legal title of Spain to its colonies, and in the instructions issued to Columbus by King Ferdinand and Queen Isabella, the conversion of the natives was enjoined as the supreme objective in building the Spanish empire in the New World. Already in 1504, Father Boyl, who had been sent out with Columbus on his second voyage, was explaining to his royal masters that the spread of the gospel was being delayed by lack of interpreters.

Nevertheless, speedy progress was made with the Christianisation of the Caribbean, largely through Spanish. As we have seen, there was a babel of different languages in use in the Caribbean, and with no lingua franca the only alternative would have been to use each and every one of them. Cardinal Cisneros in 1516 required sacristans to teach the children of chieftains and important people to read and write, 'and to show them how to speak Castilian Romance, and to work with all the chiefs and Indians, as far as possible, to get them to speak Castilian'.[34] Twenty copies of Nebrija's *Arte de la lengua castellana* were delivered to Hispaniola in 1513, sent from the governmental Casa de Contratación de Indias. The process was effective in its intermediate goal of spreading Spanish. There are many reports of native chiefs who were masters of the language, and literate in it.[35] But in the slightly longer term, the real aim, a new community of Christian souls, was frustrated by the disconcerting tendency of the Indians to die off, under the extreme stress of Spanish exploitation, followed up by wholesale import of black slaves from Africa. At any rate, in a situation of catastrophic collapse of population, and no segregation of Spaniards from Indians, it is unsurprising that only the Spanish language survived.

The spread of Spanish power to the continent created a very different situation. Partly by virtue of the campaigning fury of Father de Las Casas, partly from the sheer fact of depopulation, there was already a guilty sense of what rampant exploitation had done to the largely innocent islanders of the Caribbean, and (at least in the Church and the royal court) a determination that this should not recur. The religious orders spread out across the new colonies, and immediately endeavoured to reach the inhabitants in their own languages.

Because of the prior activities of the Indians which we have just reviewed, they found that in many of the territories the linguistic situation was much more manageable than it had been in the Caribbean. Some languages were already widespread; and even if they were not known to the whole population, everyone knew of them, and usually found them easier to acquire than the wholly alien Spanish.

After a generation of work in the field, a direction was issued by the royal court on 7 June 1550, to the effect that the new citizens of Spain should as soon as possible be taught the Spanish language:

> As one of the main things that we desire for the good of this land is the salvation and instruction and conversion to our Holy Catholic Faith of its natives, and that also they should adopt our policy and good customs; and so, treating of the means which could be upheld to this end, it is apparent that one of them and the most principal would be to give the order how these peoples may be taught our Castilian language, for with this knowledge, they could be more easily taught the matters of the Holy Gospel and gain all the rest which is suitable for their manner of life.[36]

There was immediate resistance from the churchmen called to act on it. The nature of their arguments is clear from the quotations that head this section. Means for the propagation of the faith were already to hand, they said, and these used the languages widely spoken in the major centres of population. It seemed pointless to try to substitute Spanish. And even where there was not an appropriate and effective *lengua general*, they still felt that native languages were the best for their purposes. The Archbishop of Bogotá wrote to the king on 12 February 1577:

> And to take them by the hand and gather them by good means I have arrived at the best way for it, and none that I have found will compare with preaching and declaring the Holy Gospel in their own languages. I say 'in their own languages', because in this Kingdom every valley or province has its own language different from the others; it is not like Peru or New Spain, where although there are different languages, they have a *lengua general* in use throughout the land.[37]

There are those who say that the Church was not wholly disinterested in its promotion of the use of indigenous languages here. Maintenance of contact through the *lengua general* or other less accessible languages meant that the priests remained the sole effective channel between the pure-blood Indians (99 per cent of the population of Mexico at the turn of the sixteenth century, and still 55 per cent in 1810)[38] and the rest of the world. Besides holding them as some sort of power base, they could shelter them from the pernicious doctrines of the Reformation which were circulating in Europe, and to some extent protect the Indians from rapacious Spanish colonial interests. But there is no evidence that the Church deliberately restricted access to Spanish: rather, they made it part of the curriculum, along with Latin, in all their schools. It simply failed to catch on among Indians, largely isolated as they were in remote settlements, or in segregated communities (*reducciones*), with few non-bilingual Spaniards to talk to.

In any case, the reaction of the Spanish Crown was emollient. No immediate enforcement of the *Real Cédula* was attempted under Carlos V. Some of the clergy in America were convinced that efforts should be made to make Spanish compulsory 'within some adequate term', because there was no clear, standard terminology in which to preach.[39] In 1586 Felipe II commanded the viceroy of Peru to look into the matter, and take whatever measures seemed best; but in 1596 he rejected a draft *Cédula* which would have provided for the compulsory teaching of Spanish to Indians in New Spain, along with prohibition of any of their chiefs talking to his people in their own language, adding the personal note: 'Consult me on this and the whole issue here.' When on 3 July the *Cédula* was finally signed, it contained instead the instruction to 'put in place schoolmasters for those who would voluntarily wish to learn the Castilian language', but to ensure that 'the curates should know very well the language of the Indians whom they have to instruct'.

The result, maintained for the next two centuries, was very much the continuation of the status quo: Spanish in the cities, and increasingly in *mestizo* society; but elsewhere the *lenguas generales* were in use, and failing that other indigenous languages. The outcome in the long term seems to have depended on the prevalence of separate Indian settlements: for example, in New Granada, where these were few, the use of Chibcha gradually died out despite its recognition as an official *lengua general*, and Spanish replaced it. Nevertheless, even here Indian languages survived in remote areas. Meanwhile, in Mexico, Peru and Paraguay the *lenguas generales* flourished, in speech and in writing, even as small communities went on speaking their own languages.

What now occurred was a process whereby the content of the Spanish world-view was conveyed through the pre-existing languages of wider currency. The Spanish were spared the trouble of teaching their own language widely, or waiting a few generations for knowledge of it to spread; instead, they acquired, and turned to their advantage, the old languages, whether these had been spread by previous ruling powers—notably the Mexica, the Inca and (to a limited extent) the Chibcha—or were simply pre-existing languages of trade and intercourse—notably Aymara in southern Peru and Bolivia, and Guaraní in Paraguay.

The most flourishing of these in these first two centuries of Spanish rule was certainly Nahuatl. Since Spanish rule in Mexico created a 'republic of the Indians' separate from that of the Spaniards, and with separate courts, administrative use of the language was thriving. Moreover, there was not only a major effort by Spanish clergy to translate and publish liturgical material, supplemented as we have seen with linguistic analysis to aid in the training of Spanish learners; there was soon also a literature that recreated and retold the pre-Hispanic history of the country. This included above all the writing of history and of lyrical poetry. Besides the old genres, however, new ones were added: psalms, such as this one, composed by the Nahuatl encyclopedist, Fray Bernardo de Sahagún: 'The precious jades that I also shape with my lips, that I also have scattered, that I have uttered, are a fitting song. Not only are all these a gift for you, beloved son, you who are a son of the holy Church; even more are your due ... if you follow Christianity well as a way of life ... ',[40] and the *auto*, or religious play, which continued the Mexican dramatic tradition in the service of the Christian faith. Motolinía, one of the heroic group of twelve missionaries first sent to convert Mexico,* recounts with gusto a number of such plays performed in 1538 and 1539, including the Annunciation, the Fall of Adam and Eve, and the Crusaders' Capture of Jerusalem, presumably all scripted and directed by friars, but performed exclusively by Indians.[41] Seven generations later the tradition was still alive: in 1714 the Tlaxcalan writer Juan Ventura Zapata wrote a somewhat more imaginative work, the *Invention of the Holy Cross*, which contains a scene where the Aztec god of the dead, Mictlantecuhtli, confronts the Roman emperor Constantine.[42] To this day, in the town of Tepoztlán, a pageant of Christian conversion is presented every year on 8 September:

TLACAPAYAN: Mountain-dweller! Tlacapayan seeks you. Now I have come. I come to reduce you to earth and dust, and to earth and dust I will turn you. What do you now fear when you hear of my fame and my words? Where have you abandoned our revered gods? You have given yourself over to foreigners, those bad priests. Know what it is that Tlacapayan desires. He had never lost his vision. You will be destroyed and you will perish. And stout is my heart.

---

* *Motolinía* was a Nahuatl pseudonym, adopted by him because it meant 'poor'. The original name of this Franciscan friar had been Fray Toribio de Benavente.

TEPOZTECO: How is it that right at this time, why is it that right now you have come, when I am enjoying myself, resting, rejoicing, commemorating the eternal Virgin, the Mother of God, and our precious Mother?...Truly exalted is our precious Mother the lady Virgin as says the divine author in the book of the wise. There it is said in the holy songs that twelve stars circle her head and that with the luminous moon her feet are supported, thus over all earth and heaven it spreads forth.[43]

In Peru, attitudes to the *lengua general* were more complex. Quechua, like Nahuatl, was widely used to preach the gospel, and at the same time became the vehicle for a nostalgic literature harking back to life before the conquest. But it was also taken up by the *criollo* landowning class, not themselves descendants of Indians, as a symbol of local legitimacy: at once it distinguished them from the Spanish-speaking urban elite in Lima, but also denied the country people a linguistic means to keep their landlords at a distance. Nevertheless, over the two and a half centuries after the conquest, Quechua came increasingly to represent the dissatisfaction of the Peruvian peasants; this exploded into open uprisings in the last half-century, culminating in the general rebellion in 1780 under the self-styled Tupac Amaru II ('Royal Serpent'). It is said that, before the rebellion was crushed, the drama *Ollantay* had been staged before the leaders. This is known as the finest work of the Quechua theatre, and tells the tormented love story of an Inca princess and a warrior commoner, in the heyday of the great Incas Pachacutec and Tupac Yupanqui (mid-fifteenth century). Here is the section where the Inca, somewhat abruptly, shows the quality of his mercy.

INCA YUPANQUI: Choose your penalties. Speak, Willac Umu.
WILLAC UMU: To me the Sun gave a merciful heart.
INCA YUPANQUI: Rumi, then you must speak.
RUMI ÑAWI: The price of the misdeed must be a cruel death
                Inca, such is the desert of the man of the greatest sin...
INCA YUPANQUI: Have you heard the stakes being prepared?
                Take these rebels there! Kill these evil men!
                ...
                Release the prisoners: stand up before me.
                You are saved from death: escape now, mountain stag.
                You are fallen at my feet: today the world will know
                The goodness of my heart. I have to raise you up
                A hundred times, O banished enemy. You were
                The Governor of Anti-suyu: and you, I witness today,

> If it so please me, shall reach whatever level you desire:
> Be Governor of Anti-suyu, and my captain for ever ... *

Aymara, continuing to be spoken in the south of Peru and in what is now Bolivia (then the *Audiencia* of Charcas), underwent a kind of transfusion of vocabulary with Spanish: the many loans from Spanish were mostly for new Christian, or Western, ideas, but in some cases they were adapted to express traditional concepts: *Wirjina* (from Spanish *virgen*) and *Santa Tira* (from Spanish *Santa Tierra*, 'holy land') both came to stand for the Earth Mother (in Quechua *Pachamama*). In many other cases, Aymara words came to have Christian senses, as *jucha*, 'sin', in this short extract from an eighteenth-century sermon, where the Spanish borrowings are marked in bold:

> *Kamsta,* **cristiano**? *Janiti aka isapasina kharkatita? ...P'arxtama, machaña jucha jaytama,* **racional***jama, chuymanixama* **Dios***ana unañchapajama jakaskama : janiki* **animal** *kankañaru katuyasimti, janik sutiwisa kankañaru katuyasimti: tukuxpana machaña jucha, tukuxpana, munatanakay.*

> What do you say, Christian? Do you not tremble to hear this? ... Awake, put off the sin of drunkenness. As a rational being, be sensible, live in the path which God marks out. Do not make yourself an animal. Don't return to being something nameless. Make an end of the sin of drunkenness, make an end of it, beloved.[44]

Guaraní is the only indigenous American language that ultimately achieved permanent recognition as an official national language. Partly, the low pene-

* INKA YUPANKI: *Akllaychis k'iriykichista. Willaq-Umu, qan rimariy.*
WILLAQ UMU: *Nuqaman ancha khuyaqtan Inti sunqota qowarqan.*
INKA YUPANKI: *Rumi, qanñataq rimariy.*
RUMI ÑAWI: *Hatun huchaman chaninqa K'iri wañuypunin kanqa:*
  Chaymi runataqa hark'anqa Huchapakunanta, Inka...
INKA YUPANKI: *Ñachu uyarirqankichisña Takarpu kamarisqata.*
  Chayman pusay kaykunata! Awqataqa sipiychisña! ...
  Paskaychis chay watasqata: Hatarimuy kay ñawk'iyman!
  Qespinkin wañuyniykita: Kuman phaway, luychu k'ita.
  Ñan urmamunki chakiyman: Kunanmi teqsi yachanqa
  Sunqoypa llanp'u kasqanta. Huqariqaykin qanta,
  Pachak kuti awqa mink'a. Qanmi karqanki wanin'ka
  Anti-suyu kamachikoq: Qanllataqmi kunan rikoq,
  Nuqaq munayniy kaqtinqa, Chaymi maykamapas rinqa:
  Anti-suyuta kamachiy, Wamink'ay kapuy wiñaypaq...

tration of Spanish in the early years may be due to the extreme remoteness of the Guaraní-speaking areas in the Americas, and the resulting lack of Spanish-speaking women to found Spanish-speaking families there. But the language mostly owes its resilience to the exemplary settlement by Jesuit missions in Paraguay. Their *reducciones*, communities founded as a holy and philanthropic reaction to the oppressive system of *encomiendas** around Asunción, dominated relations between European and Indian in the period 1609–1767. The work was disrupted by raiding slavers (the dreaded '*mamelucos*') in 1628–40, and persistently by *encomenderos*. In the *reducciones*, all teaching was carried out in Guaraní, and the language thereby gained a very strong basis in Christianised culture. The utopian nature of the world so created by the Jesuits can be seen in the literal meaning of some of the new words that became current: *îbîrayararusú*, 'master of the big stick', i.e. chief constable; *kuarepotí*, 'excrement of the mines', i.e. money (something that had no use in the *reducciones*).[45]

An explicit motive in the Jesuits' language regime was to protect Indians from European vices. But cultivation of the decent obscurity of a classical language, specifically Latin, was a policy widely pursued by the learned friars in the Americas, not least because they were aiming to found a native priesthood there. Some of the friars became enchanted by the achievements of their pupils in classical learning. Fray Toribio Motolinía, one of the twelve original Franciscan missionaries to Mexico, preserves this anecdote of the collapse of a stout party from Castile:

A very fine thing happened to a priest recently arrived from Castile, who could not believe that the Indians knew Christian doctrine, nor the Lord's Prayer, nor the Creed; and when other Spaniards told him they did, he remained sceptical; just then two students had come out of class, and the priest thinking they were from the rest of the Indians, asked one of them if he knew the Lord's Prayer and he said he did, and he made him say it, and then he made him say the Creed, and the student said it perfectly well; and the priest challenged one word which the Indian had got right, and since the Indian asserted that he was right, and the priest denied it, the student had to ask what was the correct way, and asked him in Latin: *Reverende Pater, cujus casus est?*† Then since the priest

---

* The *encomienda* was an economic institution universal in the Spanish American colonies; it was a leasehold granted by the king, under which a designated *encomendero* was given full rights to exploit the labour of Indians on an estate, on condition only that the Indians received religious instruction.
† 'Reverend Father, what case is it in?'

did not know grammar, he was left quite at a loss, covered with confusion.[46]

In some places, the Spanish spread the *lenguas generales* beyond the range
of the pre-Columbian empires that had created them. Under the Spanish, and
with the aid of their Nahuatl-speaking allies, notably from Tlaxcallan, who
were only too happy to dispossess the Aztecs, Nahuatl spread down into Guatemala, which had hitherto been a preserve of Mayan speakers. This is why
so many Guatemalan place names are actually of Nahuatl origin: the name
of the beautiful Lake Atitlán means 'round the water', or as they put it in
the local Tz'utujil, *chi-nim-ya'*, 'by the great water'; Guatemala itself is
Quauhtemallan, 'place of many trees', translating the Mayan expression
k'i-chee' (still used to refer to the largest language group in the country, traditionally spelt Quiche). A common ending for town names, -tenango, is
from … *tenan-co*, 'in the citadel of …': Quetzaltenango, 'in the citadel of the
quetzal bird', Huehuetenango, 'in the old citadel', Momostenango, 'in the citadel of the chapel', Chichicastenango, 'in the citadel of the bitter nettle'.
These all have a decidedly foreign ring today, when Nahuatl is no longer spoken east or south of the isthmus of Tepehuantepec, 500 kilometres away. The
Tlaxcalans also took their Nahuatl northward, at least to Zacatecas; and in the
east Nahuatl was used by missionaries to preach to the Tarascans of Michua-
cán (Nahuatl 'place of those who have fish'), which had never been part of
the Aztec domains.[47]

In Peru, the evidence suggests that Quechua had already been spread,
whether through the fifteenth-century conquests of Tupac Yupanqui or the
travels of Chincha merchants, as far north as the borders of modern Colombia
well before the Spanish conquest.[48] The Incas had also established some level
of economic link with the Tucumán area to their south: there were roads, garrison stations and inns, and perhaps periodic labour corvées (*mit'a*) of the
type familiar in their empire. But the linguistic impact of this is unclear. At
any rate, under Spanish tutelage the language was to consolidate its spread
southward. There was net migration from Peru south into the Potosí area of
modern Bolivia, to support the vast development of silver mining there.
Later, Quechua also spread into the provinces of Tucumán, Santiago del Estero and Córdoba of modern Argentina. In all this area, Spanish inroads were
accompanied by larger numbers of attendant Peruvians and *mestizos*; and so
the linguistic advance of empire tended to be Quechua rather than Spanish.
Missionary activity too was a factor, after the Council of Lima in 1582–3,
which had set out a general plan for the conversion of the Americas: as everywhere, the friars found it more expeditious to preach in the *lengua gen-*

eral, and in this period Quechua must still have had some flavour of Inca prestige attached to it.* By the beginning of the eighteenth century, Tucumán had lost its previous languages, and was essentially a Quechua-speaking region.[49]

The state's solution: Hispanización

> The ministers of the church who do not attempt to advance and extend the Castilian language and take care that the Indians know how to read and write in it, leaving them shut up in their own language, are to my thinking the declared enemies of the natives, of their policy and rationality...
>
> Antonio de Lorenzana y Buitrón, archbishop of Mexico, 1769[50]

In the middle of the eighteenth century, when Spain had dominated the Americas for fully ten generations, many Spaniards were disappointed in the very much less than universal spread of their language. Rosenblat estimates that in the Spanish colonies in 1810 there were three mother-tongue speakers of an indigenous language for every one who had grown up with Spanish: 9 million rural Indians to 3 million whites, creoles and *mestizos*.[51] The archbishop of Mexico, Antonio de Lorenzana y Buitrón—himself a Spaniard, naturally—took the language question particularly to heart:

> This is a constant truth: the maintenance of the language of the Indians is a folly [*un capricho*] of men, whose fortune and learning is restricted to speaking that tongue learnt even as a child: it is a contagion, which separates the Indians from the conversation of the Spaniards; it is a plague, which infects the Dogmas of our Holy Faith; it is a prejudicial marker to separate the natives of some villages from others by diversity of their tongues; it is an increased cost for the parishes, which require ministers of different languages in their same domain; and it is an impossibility for the governance of the bishops.[52]

In 1769, in a pastoral letter to the archdiocese of Mexico, he proposed the abolition of all indigenous languages through the compulsory use of Spanish. He

---

* The echoes of this former majesty are widespread. Quechua was one of the eleven languages used by the Jesuits in their missions in Paraguay. It is also attested to this day, in small communities in the north of Chile, and Acre in the west of Brazil.

was a child of his time, the era of the Enlightenment, when the universal benefits to humanity of Reason were being ever more widely appreciated, and new, radical, policies were being proposed to give them effect. Almost as important, he had the ear of the king of Spain, Carlos III. As a result, even though his proposal was rejected by the then viceroy of Mexico, who felt that all that was needed was better enforcement of the existing (two-hundred-year-old) standards for teaching Spanish, and then by the full Council of the Indies, on the even more traditional grounds that the Council of Trent (1545) clearly required the teaching of the gospel in natives' languages, the king nevertheless ordered and signed the fatal royal *Cédula* of 16 April 1770, whose crucial phrase runs: 'in order that at once may be achieved the extinction of the different languages used in the said domains, and the sole use of Castilian...'*

The decree noted that previous royal commandments for schools in Castilian to be established in all villages had been to little avail. But in fact its only concrete requirement was for bishops to appoint curates henceforth without any concern for their competence in languages other than Spanish. This was directed not just to Mexico, but explicitly to every part of the Spanish empire, including the Philippines.

The decree was followed up in 1782 by a second, which required civil and religious authorities to provide for the funding of masters in Castilian. This did not lead to any wide-scale improvement in the teaching of Spanish in the empire. The gains for Spanish, though real, came about by default, almost as the first royal *Cédula* had imagined: Indians' use of their own languages was simply wished away, as the Spanish authorities increasingly addressed them in Spanish, willy-nilly. All official support for education in the indigenous languages came to be withdrawn; professorial chairs in the universities were discontinued; books written in them ceased to be published. Courts in Mexico ceased to entertain pleas written in Nahuatl. Furthermore, the same period was seeing a decline in the influence and the power of the Church within the empire, a process generally attributed to the spread of the Enlightenment in Europe, but evidenced most dramatically in the expulsion of the Jesuits from all their *reducciones* in South America in 1767.† The Indians were losing not only the institutional supports for their languages, but also their European protectors, the friars and priests. These trends turned out to be sufficient to bring on the decline of all the *lenguas generales*.

---

* '*para que de una vez se llegue a conseguir el que se extingan los diferentes idiomas de que se usa en los mismos Dominios, y sólo se hable el Castellano...*', quoted in Triana y Antorveza (1987: 511).
† The Portuguese Crown had expelled all Jesuits from Brazil in 1759. (See Chapter 11, 'Portuguese pioneers', p. 394.

But liberal enlightenment did not stop here, with the attempt to shed Spanish vernacular light into the corners of minds supposedly darkened by indigenous mother tongues, and a growing freedom of civil society from obligations to the Church. Its next step, enforced by revolutionary wars in the early nineteenth century, was to be towards political independence for the Spanish colonies. Unsurprisingly, the forces that found continued Spanish rule most irksome were the Europeanised elites, the *criollos*, closest in their manners and language to the ruling classes, but for ever subordinate to them through the accident of their birth in the Americas. Although they were happy to recruit *mestizos*, blacks and Indians to their cause, they were almost never prepared to see the indigenous languages as badges of authenticity for the new nations they wished to establish: rather, the *criollos* offered everyone an undifferentiated citizenship based on a common language, Spanish. The nationalist movements of Latin America found it hard to embrace local languages, seeing even the bigger languages as sources of division, rather than of a unity alien to Spain. Evidently, language outcomes have varied in the face of local conditions, too multiform even to review here; there are at least as many stories as there are Latin American nations. We must be content to look briefly at just two cases, where Spanish has competed with large surviving indigenous languages.

In Mexico, since independence in 1821, the existence of Indians has always constituted a kind of intellectual embarrassment, their separate identity acting as a standing refutation of Enlightenment egalitarianism: 'our political institutions do not distinguish between blacks, mestizos or Indians'.[53] In this respect, it is typical of most Latin American countries. In 1813, the revolutionary leader Morelos had appealed to the Mexica past to inspire his new Declaration of Independence: 'Spirits of Moctehuzoma, Cacamatzin, Cuauhtimotzin, Xicotencatl and Catzonzi, as once you celebrated the feat in which you were slaughtered by the treacherous sword of Alvarado, now celebrate the happy moment in which your sons have united to avenge the crimes and outrages committed against you ...'[54]

But by the Lerdo Law of 1856, communal rights of Indians to their lands were dissolved. In 1916 M. Gamío wrote in *Forjando Patria* ('Forging the Fatherland') that the solution to the 'Indian problem' lay in 'attracting these individuals toward the other social group which they have always considered the enemy, incorporating them, blending the two together, in short creating a coherent and homogeneous national race unified both in language and culture'.[55] Paradoxically, in Mexico this view is characterised as '*indigenismo*'; it values indigenous language and culture, but only the two major prestige groupings Nahuatl and Maya, and only as a kind of national credential of past cultural glory. Less surprisingly, it has been the intellectual background to precipitate growth in the use of Spanish since independence: if in 1810 there were 6.7 million inhabitants, 45 per cent of them Spaniards or *mestizos* presumably speaking Spanish,[56] by 1995 there were 95.8 million, with fully 88 per cent of them first-language speakers of that language.[57]

In Paraguay, by contrast, and uniquely, the bilingualism early established between Spanish and Guaraní has never begun to slip. It goes far back, to the earliest days of the colony, when Asunción was known as the 'Paradise of Mahomet' because of the highly favourable proportion of Spanish men to Guaraní-speaking women.[58] Uniquely in the Spanish empire, the country never had, even in its one city, Asunción, an urban elite who lived through contact with the rest of the Spanish-speaking world, rather than their own country. The isolation of the nation, cut off without a coastline or friendly neighbours, seems to have perpetuated this, even after independence. Every president of the country has been able to speak both languages. In fact, the two seem to have evolved a mutual dependency, like a stage double act, with Spanish cast as the smart, cultured brother (*culto, desarrollado*, or in Guaraní *iñarandu*) and Guaraní the lovable but unprincipled oik (*Guarango, que no tiene principios*, in Guaraní *tavi*). Guaraní did yeoman service, boosting morale and secrecy, in two wars against Paraguay's neighbours in 1864 and 1932; and it has long had an association in people's minds with nationalism and the Colorado party, as against the unsettling free-market philosophy of the Liberals.[59] Guaraní has been subject to official discouragement at times (when the Liberals have been in power); but at all levels of society it has gone on being a language learnt in the home, with Spanish the language acquired characteristically at school. In the 1967 Constitutional Congress, both were declared national languages, but Spanish was singled out as the official language. In 1996, of 5 million Paraguayans 95 per cent were said to be fluent in Guaraní, 52 per cent indeed monolingual in it; only 2 per cent were said to be monolingual in Spanish.[60]

The general verdict on the penetration of Spanish into the Americas must be that it has had a narrow escape. Despite over two centuries of residence, and elite dominance, in the continent, Spanish-speaking society—constantly refreshed as it was by immigration from the Iberian peninsula—did not put down deep roots in the colonies. Until the late eighteenth century, the Spanish maintained themselves as an alien elite, with the *mestizos* as a growing body. They had benefited from the linguistic unification of their domains that had been achieved by their predecessors, especially the Mexica and the Incas, and used it to accelerate the economic exploitation of their conquests, and the missionary duties that they felt justified their presence. But precisely where they had enjoyed these advantages, they had not provided a universal lingua franca of their own. The case is strangely reminiscent of the Byzantine Greek domination of the Middle East. Aramaic remained the language of the people from the Mediterranean to the Persian Gulf. And so the shock of Muslim conquest had been sufficient to blot out, within a couple of generations, all linguistic trace of a millennium of Greek rule. (See Chapter 6, 'Intimations of decline', p. 257.)

Coda: Across the Pacific

How superficial the linguistic hold of Spanish could be on Spain's colonies can be seen in the case of the Philippines, where a similar shock was delivered through defeat in the Spanish-American War (1898). We have already noted (see 'An unprecedented empire', p. 334) that this colony was in important ways unlike the Americas: it had not responded to Spanish conquest with a sudden epidemic-induced collapse of native population, and it had never attracted significant numbers of free-enterprise immigrants from Spain—or indeed any of the other Spanish colonies. As in the Americas, the local languages had been accepted as the medium for preaching the gospel; printing had started in the Philippines at much the same time as in the more advanced American colonies, Mexico and Peru: in 1593, a wood-block edition of *Doctrina Cristiana, en lengua española y tagala*, a parallel text in Spanish and Tagalog, was its first product.[61] Since there were few Spanish settlers, and little serious economic development, there was small inducement for the Spanish language to be used outside official circles.

Nevertheless, there was a significant belated effort to spread knowledge of it. Carlos III's royal *Cédula* of 1770 applied just as much to the Philippines as to the Americas, and on 20 September 1794 his successor, Carlos IV, issued a supplement to it, officially making instruction in Spanish free and compulsory for all. This never overcame the lack of resources needed to make it happen. The royal decrees kept coming, however. In March 1815 compulsory primary education in Spanish was imposed. In 1860, schools were instituted in the army: Spanish non-commissioned officers were to instruct their Philippine troops. In the nineteenth century, fairly respectable levels of school attendance were being achieved: in 1840, one child attended for every thirty-three inhabitants, a figure comparable with France in the same year: one child per thirty-eight inhabitants (and in Russia, one child per four thousand).[62]

But the American dispossession of the Spaniards and occupation of the

Philippines in 1898 revealed how fragile was the linguistic culture that the Spaniards had succeeded in planting. The census of 1903 showed that less than 800,000 (11 per cent) of the 7.5 million population spoke Spanish. Fifteen years later, the number who spoke English had already overtaken them: 896,258 for English, as against 757,463 for Spanish. Seventy years later, in 1988, the figures from the *Calendario Atlante de Agostini* put the Spanish speakers at 3 per cent;[63] this can be compared with the 51 per cent reported able to speak English in the 1975 census.

In the 1987 constitution, for the first time Spanish was no longer listed as an official language of the country. Tagalog (recast, and actively developed as 'Pilipino' or 'Filipino') now plays that role (available to some 62 per cent of the population, according to *World Almanac 1991*), with English 'until otherwise provided by the law'. Spanish is now, along with Arabic, 'promoted on a voluntary and optional basis'.*

The progress of English over the prone figure of Spanish here cannot be separated from the general worldwide advance of English in the twentieth century, which will be examined in Chapter 12 ('The world taken by storm', p. 505). Something too must have been due to the pre-existing network of schools available to the American incomers. Contrast the Spanish, labouring for centuries to build them up from a zero base. It is also true that much greater funds were available for US overseas activities than had ever been for those of Spain.

But the situation compares ironically with the contest of English and Spanish in North America in the same period, where if anything Spanish—in its version seeded to Mexico, Central America, Cuba and Puerto Rico—is growing at the expense of English, in many big cities and much of the south-west of the USA.† All these developments, however, tend to underline the true determinants of language spread: population growth and population movements. When an official language was an artificial thing, created by international elites, and spread as far as possible among local populations, it is understandable that the bigger budget should have created the bigger language. But when the population starts to grow, as the urban population of Metro Manila has, its language (Tagalog) has come to dominate the country just as its speakers have, English or no English.

* Quotes from the Philippine constitution of 1987 (cited in Quilis 1992: 83).
† The 2001 census figures place the Hispanic population of the USA at 37 million, 13 per cent of the total, and the largest minority in the country, having just now overtaken the African-Americans' 36.1 million. The Hispanics are the only US minority to retain routine usage of their heritage language, Spanish, with two TV channels, Univisión and Telemundo, and over two hundred publications with a joint circulation of over 12 million (*El País* newspaper, Madrid, 23 March 2003).

And when a population starts to move towards that irresistible attractor, the US economy, as the Mexican and central Caribbean populations now are, new speaker communities will begin to crowd in, even if this means encroaching on the heartland of the most dynamic, and widely spoken, language in the world, English.

11

In the Train of Empire:
Europe's Languages Abroad

Surveying the world's current top ten languages by population (the full top twenty are identified and discussed in Chapter 13), we note that no less than six of them have spread through the expansion of European global empires in the past five centuries: English, Spanish, Portuguese, Russian, German and French. The spread of Spanish, the earliest of these, distinguished by the leading—though somewhat spoiling—role of the Catholic Church, we have just reviewed. The spread of English, the most spectacular, where global market enthusiasm seems to have taken over just as national dominance left off, we reserve for the next chapter. Before that, we need to consider the careers of the others, so many classic cases of modern imperial expansion, driven by passions for wealth, exploration and national glory, often accompanied by the zeal of Christian missionaries.

The story of the languages is more ambiguous, and hence more interesting, than is often portrayed in the accounts, usually self-congratulatory, of modern European writers. The expansion of the home language in the train of a growing imperial power was by no means assured: we have to account for the curious fact, for example, that the lingua franca of modern Indonesia is a form of Malay, and not Dutch, the language of its overlords for over two centuries; and the linguistic effects of some imperial presences, for example of France in Indochina, of Russia in Muslim Central Asia, or of Japan in Manchuria and Korea, already seem far less durable than those of others. We need to ask what aspects of a conquest have made a linguistic spread apparently permanent, as that of Portuguese in Brazil, of French in the Congo, or of Russian in Siberia. Nebrija's glib dictum that 'language was the companion of empire, and followed it in such a way that jointly they began, grew, flourished; and afterwards joint was the fall of both' is in fact far too simple—in all its claims.

The attitudes to language of these imperial powers, and the degree of their belief in a link between language and culture, tended to be more self-regarding than that of the Spanish Catholic imperialists: that was a feature of their era. Catholic theology had been universal, and in no way a preserve or creation of the Spaniards whose privilege it had been to present it to the Americas. Marauding northern Europeans, by contrast, felt that they did have a particular national gift which accounted for their ability to dominate these previously 'benighted savages'. But inevitably, since the founders of empires were practical, often hard, men, their appreciation of the role of language too was practical, even superficial. A language would spread first as a kind of lingua franca, perhaps in a quite restricted form, a pidgin, that made all kinds of concessions to the first languages of those who picked it up. A language was seen as a tool for transacting business. European languages were, and often still are, used as second languages in commerce and government, while traditional languages persisted in familiar contexts. As such, the spread of such a language is hard to see as a spread of the linguistic community from which it came.

It makes sense, therefore, to look at the spreads of all these languages as a group, comparatively, rather than to go deeply into the stories of particular languages in particular countries. In this way, we can hope that the crucial features of this global phenomenon, European imperialism, will show through. But by the same token, it is harder to convey the individual flavour of a particular language's encounter with an alien environment.

Portuguese pioneers

Sustentava contra ele Vénus bela,
Afeiçoada à gente Lusitana,
Por quantas qualidades via nela
Da antiga tão amada sua Romana;
Nos fortes corações, na grande estrela,
Que mostraram na terra Tingitana,
E na língua, na qual quando imagina,
Com pouca corrupção crê que é a Latina.

Against him spoke up Venus fair
With affection for the race of Portugal
For all the qualities she saw in it
From Rome, that she so loved of old;
In their brave hearts, in the great star,
Which they showed in the land of Ceuta [their first conquest],

And in their tongue, which her imagination
Could take for a somewhat corrupted Latin.

Camões,* *Os Lusíadas*, i.33

The Portuguese were the first European power to project themselves, and their language, across the Atlantic and hence into the world at large. Their long coastline abuts on to little more than the open sea, and it seems to have been their fishing fleets and pirates, rather than merchants, who first took advantage of the great enabling maritime inventions which became available in the fourteenth century, the central rudder fitted to the keel, the magnetic compass, and the portolan chart, which gave pre-calculated directions from point to point. They were able to range widely in the Atlantic, and occasionally to raid infidel ports on the coasts of North Africa. Gradually this became a matter of import to the Portuguese Crown. It conquered the North African enclave of Ceuta in 1415; and it occupied the main uninhabited islands of the eastern Atlantic, Madeira ('wood', renamed in a Portuguese translation of its previous Spanish name *Legname*) in 1419, the Azores ('goshawks') in 1427. Thereafter, whether in pursuit of gold, fisheries, religious converts, slaves or other goods, the foreign-oriented Prince Henry (*infante Dom Henrique*), known as the Navigator, initiated a stream of exploratory expeditions southward along the African coast, planting settlements as far south as the Geba river (in modern Guinea-Bissau), some 4,000 kilometres (800 leagues) south of Lisbon, by the time he died in 1460.

The language that his soldiers and sailors (and merchants) spoke was the distinctive Romance spoken on the western flank of Iberia, originally one with Galician, which (probably since Roman times) had developed differently from the versions of the centre (Castilian) and the east (Catalan). It was, and is, distinguished by the palatalisation of sibilants (sh [š] and zh [ž], rather than s and z), the voicing of sibilants when they occur between vowels, and by the widespread nasalisation of vowels when they are followed by n and m (the latter two features also characteristic of French). It also reduces vowels when they are unstressed, and even deletes whole syllables.

An example that shows much of what makes Portuguese distinctive is the equivalent of 'will you give me hot eggs and bread': spelt *faz favor de darme*

---

* Camões is the doyen of Portuguese literature, and his great work celebrates the achievements of the Portuguese mariners. The name *Lusiadas*, although it recalls 'Iliad', is actually a learned equivalent for 'the Portuguese', meaning the progeny of Lusus, the mythical founder of the race who lived in (Roman) Lusitania. The work was actually written, for the most part, in Goa, so it is a product of Ultramar, as well as a celebration of it. It was published in 1572.

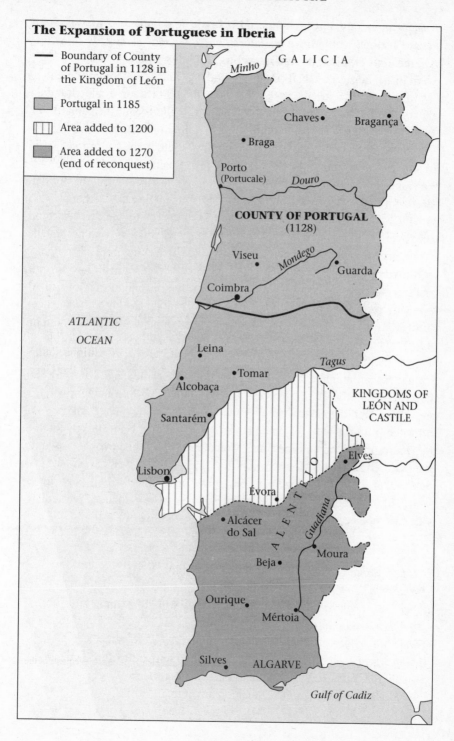

The Expansion of Portuguese in Iberia

—— Boundary of County of Portugal in 1128 in the Kingdom of León

Portugal in 1185

Area added to 1200

Area added to 1270 (end of reconquest)

GALICIA

Minho

Chaves •

• Bragança

• Braga

Porto (Portucale)

Douro

COUNTY OF PORTUGAL
(1128)

Viseu •

Mondego

• Guarda

Coimbra •

ATLANTIC

OCEAN

Leina •

Tagus

• Tomar

Alcobaça •

KINGDOMS OF LEÓN AND CASTILE

Santarém •

Elves •

Lisbon •

Évora •

A L E N T E J O

Guadiana

• Alcácer do Sal

• Moura

Beja •

Ourique •

Mértoia •

Silves •

ALGARVE

Gulf of Cadiz

ovos quentes e pão, it is pronounced **faž favor de darme ɔvəž kēntəš e pãw**, where Castilian would have *me haces el favor de darme huevos calientes y pan*, **me agas el faβor de darme weβos kalientes y pan**.

All in all, Portuguese had come to sound very different from its neighbour Castilian, with the strange result that nowadays Portuguese and Brazilians can still by and large follow spoken Spanish, while for most Spaniards and Spanish-speaking Americans Portuguese is quite impenetrable.

Its homeland was a wide band from north to south in the peninsula, including the area now known as Galicia in modern Spain. The whole region had been taken by (Arabic- and Berber-speaking) Moors in 713, but the northern part down to the Douro was retaken by Christians when the Berbers fell out with their Arab masters in the 740s. The rest of the region yielded very gradually over the next four centuries to the military advance of what became the Christian kingdom of León; but a division made by its king in 1128, assigning the provinces around Portucale (modern Porto) to his son-in-law for purposes of defence against a trying new threat, the onslaught of Moorish Almoravids from Africa, turned out to have very long-lasting consequences. Portugal, from the Minho to the Mondego, went on to establish its autonomy (1143), its dukes becoming kings (1179); but for the next century its expansion (at the expense of the Moors) was southward only. The Galicians and Portuguese, although still speaking essentially the same language, were sundered permanently. The capital was moved south in 1248 from Oporto to Lisbon (Roman *Olisippō*). The Portuguese dialects may have taken some influence from the old Lusitanian language, which had been spoken south of the Douro up to Roman times, and Mozarabic, which had evolved up under five hundred years of Moorish rule; but there is little written evidence for local features of the vernacular. Emerging on to the written page in the twelfth to fourteenth centuries, Portuguese came to be associated particularly with lyric poetry, used for this purpose even by a king of Castile.

E assi Santa Maria	Thus Saint Mary
ajudou a seus amigos,	helped her friends,
pero que d' outra lei eran,	although they were of another law,
a britar seus eemigos	to shatter their enemies,
que, macar que eran muitos,	for although they were many,
nonos preçaron dous figos,	they did not give two figs for them,
e assi foi ssa mercee	and thus was her mercy
de todos mui connoçuda.	made known to all.

Alfonso X of Castile (1221–84), *Cantiga de Santa Maria*, no. 181, last stanza

From the beginning of the sixteenth century this language began to be heard all round the coasts of Africa and southern Asia, and for the first time on the shores of Brazil.

An Asian empire

There had been a lull in exploration after the death of Henry the Navigator in 1460. But then in 1488 Bartolomeu Dias had ended the long years of Portuguese creep down the African coast, by demonstrating that its southward extent was finite: and who knew what lay beyond that last *Cabo da Boa Esperança* ('Cape of Good Hope')? There was then another short interlude, from 1488 to 1498, before the next step was taken; but exploration issues were not forgotten. In fact, it was then that Portugal attempted to challenge Castile's right to the lands newly discovered by Columbus in his first (1492) voyage to the west. The claim was not upheld, but it was ultimately highly beneficial, since when the dispute was resolved by the 1494 Treaty of Tordesillas (in Portuguese *Tardesilhas*), Portugal was granted all lands east of a meridian line drawn 370 leagues west of the Cape Verde Islands. This, ultimately, guaranteed its right to Brazil.

But this prospect was dimly appreciated, if at all, at the time. Far more striking, at first blush, was the achievement four years later of Vasco da Gama when he rounded that last cape, and sailed triumphantly, and arrogantly, into the ocean beyond: at long last, he had achieved the highest goal of a century of Portuguese navigation, and found the sea route to India. This achievement turned out to fulfil the most extravagant hopes of the previous century, for besides finding their way to India the Portuguese found that they also had enough strength to secure direct access to its fabulous merchandise, breaking the centuries-old monopoly of Muslim middlemen. And then, incredibly and immediately, another great prize fell into their laps. Acting swiftly to exploit their new Indian opportunity, they happened to take a roundabout course to the southern tip of Africa: the result was the discovery of Brazil, on 22 April 1500. Now they had the basis for an empire in the New World, as well as exclusive access to the most luxurious market of the Old. Fortune was really smiling on Portuguese enterprise.

It continued to smile for most of the rest of the new century. By the end of it, there were profitable Portuguese trading settlements, protected by fortresses and fleets, all along the coast of the Indian Ocean, and at strategic points beyond, in Malaya and the South China Seas. There were seven settlements in east Africa, six on the Gulf of Oman, fifteen on the western coast of India, four in Ceylon, and two on the eastern coast of India. Malacca, Macassar, Ternate, Tidore, Timor and Macao were all Portuguese possessions.

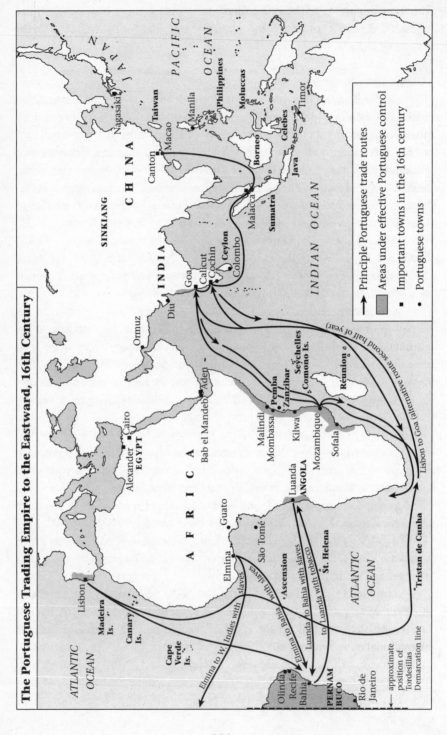

The Portuguese Trading Empire to the Eastward, 16th Century

Although they never achieved the full trade monopoly they were seeking, the Indian Ocean for a century or two was almost a Portuguese lake. Like the Phoenicians and Greeks of the first millennium BC, they did not attempt to control the hinterlands.

But unlike those Phoenicians and Greeks, they were interested in something beyond profit and adventure: after military and commercial expansion came a drive for religious conversion, and Catholic dioceses were set up in Mozambique in 1512, Goa in 1534, Cochin in 1558, Malacca in 1558, Macao in 1575, Meliapore (in eastern India) in 1606; there was even an attempt to spread the faith beyond the shelter of secure Portuguese trading posts, in Ethiopia in 1555, in Funay (i.e. Japan) in 1588, and Tonkin (i.e. Vietnam) in 1659. Like their Spanish cousins at that time in the far more vulnerable territories of the New World, the Portuguese were determined to vindicate the Pope's faith in them, and their own faith in the Christian God.

And besides deliberately attempting to spread the word of God, the Portuguese were inevitably also spreading their own. The linguistic effects of this commerce-led, and faith-reinforced, expansion were complex. But they give a foretaste of the kind of spread that this ship-borne imperialism would engender as different European nations followed in the Portuguese wake.

First of all, Portuguese was the language used in the fortresses and trading units that were set up as permanent agencies, small expatriate communities in port cities and their surrounds. This was not in itself very significant: inevitably, after all, emigrants go on using their own language to their own kind, and pass it on to at least some of their children and servants when they establish themselves in households in their new homes, especially if they are keeping in regular touch with their countrymen—and trade with Europe was the very *raison d'être* for all these Portuguese settlements, actively maintained against mounting competition until the middle of the seventeenth century. (This *carreira da Índia* averaged five ships a year from 1550 to the 1630s.[1]) The early shock value of their arrival and the attendant prestige may even have encouraged others for a time to associate with them, and learn from them; in the same way, Christianity proved most attractive in the first couple of generations after it was first preached in Asia, but its growth fell away once it became as well known as the Hindu, Buddhist and Muslim institutions it was bidding to replace.

From this native basis, however, Portuguese spread as a tool of trade and international communication, i.e. as a lingua franca. When Portuguese settlements were so widespread in the accessible spots of the coasts of Africa and Asia, it was inevitable that their business partners and other associates would begin to find that the language they had acquired to facilitate relations with the Portuguese had an extra utility in dealing with others of their partners and associates—who might indeed have no other language in common. In fact, this utility of Portuguese outlived its trading dominance by at least a hundred years, lasting until the eighteenth century, when a Frenchman opined: 'Merchants of the Hindus, Moors, Arabs, Persians, Parsees, Jews and Armenians who do business with the European factories, as well as black men who wish to work as interpreters, are obliged to speak this language; it serves also as a medium of communication among the European nations settled in India.'[2]

In 1551 the Englishman Thomas Wyndham, visiting the Gold Coast with a Portuguese companion, Antonio Pinteado, found that they could converse in Portuguese with the king of Benin, who had known it since his childhood.[3] In 1600, when Japan received its first ever English visitor, the pilot Will Adams, he was able to communicate only when his surprised host, the *shōgun* Tokugawa Ieyasu, managed to find a Portuguese-speaking interpreter.[4] In 1606 Brother Gaspar de San Bernardino, forced by lack of water to land in Persia, was amazed to be addressed by the local military commander: '*Padre, quem te trouxe a esta terra tam longe da Índia?*'* In 1638, another traveller wrote: 'Rare are the visitors to Gomron,† though they be for the most part Persians, Arabs and Indians, who do not speak or understand Portuguese, from the trade that they had in earlier years with the Portuguese, who long held the city of Hormuz.'[5] A little later, in the mid-seventeenth century, kings of Ceylon, and of Arakan on the other side of the Bay of Bengal (northern Burma), insisted on using Portuguese to correspond with the Dutch—even though the emperor of Kandy, Rajasinha II, was in fact in alliance with them against the Portuguese.

Portuguese soon transformed itself from a lingua franca of use to princes and elite travellers to a more generally understood language of the servant class and (often the same people) early converts to Christianity. In the early days, a few phrases in Portuguese might be all that converts gained. Fernão Mendes Pinto, on a visit to a city in southern China that he calls Sampitay in the late sixteenth century, encountered a woman dressed in red satin, who inveighed passionately against the evils of long sea voyages, and then pulled up a sleeve to reveal a cross elegantly branded on her arm.

---

* 'Father, what has brought you to this land so far from India?' Reported in his *Itinerario da Índia por terra*, quoted in Lopes (1936: 33–5).
† Now Bandar Khomeini, on the Straits of Hormuz.

…she gave a cry and lifting her hands to Heaven, said loudly:
Padre Nosso que estás nos Céus, santificado seja o teu nome…[i.e.
the Lord's Prayer in Portuguese]
This she said in Portuguese. And then returning to speaking in Chinese,
as she knew no more Portuguese than these words, she badgered us to
tell her if we were Christians…

She went on to reveal that she had inherited the faith from her father, who had
practised it for twenty-seven years, making over three hundred converts, and
that every Sunday they gathered for worship at her house.[6]

The Dutch, the principal successor power in the region, accepted the linguistic status quo; after 1692 they required arriving chaplains in Madras to
learn Portuguese within a year of their arrival as well as the local language of
their residence (usually Tamil) 'in order that they may be able to instruct in
Protestant religion the Pagans who are servants or slaves of the Company or
its agents'.[7] In 1704 the Dutch governor of Ceylon (now Śri Lanka), Cornelius Jan Simonsz, noted that someone speaking Portuguese could be understood anywhere on that island; and in 1807 the Reverend James Cordiner, in
his *A description of Ceylon*, wrote that 'A corruption of their original language is still spoken over all the sea coasts. It is very easily learned, and
proves of great utility to a traveller who has not time to study the more
difficult dialects of the natives.'*

Ironically, one of the strongest citadels of Portuguese was the Dutch
power's own capital in Batavia on the island of Java. To preach the gospel,
wrote Jean Brun in 1675, 'they will acquire Portuguese Bibles and various
devotional books in Portuguese and Indian languages and recite the catechism in these languages, because they are understood by most of the
Indians…'[8] In 1708 there was even an appeal by Protestant priests there to
the governor-general to maintain exclusive use of Portuguese in some
churches, claiming:

The Portuguese language is in everyday and familiar use by the slaves
of families who come from Ceylon and the [Coromandel] Coast; by all
the masters of slaves and by their children in daily dealings with the
slaves and Christian natives; by the persons who come from Siam, Ma-

---

* It became the default European language in the Indies, and apparently in western Java, in the region
of Preanger, even Dutch was known popularly as *basa Perteges*—an interesting conflation of language misnomers, with *basa*, through Malay *bahasa*, from Sanskrit *bhāṣā*, and *Perteges* a corruption
of *Portugues* (reported in Lopes 1936: viii).

lacca, Bengal, Coromandel Coast, the Isle of Ceylon, the Malabar Coast, Surat and even from Persia; and the leading pagans who inhabit this city and do business with the Christians or their slaves learn to speak Portuguese.[9]

But the language was changed by its expansion: it was widely pidginised, and while some Portuguese can still be heard over most of this area to this day, outside Portugal's most substantial long-term colonies (Angola and Mozambique in Africa, Goa in India) it is in the form of creoles heavily influenced by its local competitor languages. In Indo-Portuguese creoles, for example, still spoken in scattered communities along the Malabar coast of the subcontinent from Daman and Diu in Gujarat to Śri Lanka in the south, the diphthong spelt *ei*, absent in Indian languages, is reduced to a high [ẹ] vowel, very different from modern Portuguese, where it is pronounced more like [ai].* The complex inflexions of the language inherited from Latin have been replaced by less involved structures: in Diu, 'dog' may still be *cão* and 'son' *filho*, but in the plural, instead of *cães* and *filhos*, we have *cão-cão* and *fi-fi*; verbal tenses are likewise analytic, *eu tá vai*, 'I am going', *eu já comeu*, 'I ate', *eu had vai*, 'I shall go', instead of the standard (and irregular) *vou*, *comi*, *irei*. In Śri Lanka, they have even absorbed the local (Sinhala and Tamil) use of postpositions: *eu já vi terra por*, 'I came by land'.[10] Similar, transformed, varieties of Portuguese are still spoken in Malacca in Malaysia (where the language is known as Kristang, betraying its old religious overtones, from Portuguese *cristã*, 'Christian'), in Macao in southern China, and in Timor, on the southernmost edge of the East Indies.

The third, and now most significant, type of spread of Portuguese occurred when it was taken up, essentially unchanged, by a new population. This has happened, but only to a tiny extent, in the African colonies of Angola and Mozambique (where recent estimates[11] put the native-speaking 'Lusophone' populations at 57,600 and above 30,000—respectively 0.5 per cent and 0.2 per cent of their populations, even if the same source claims that 27 per cent of Mozambicans know Portuguese as a second language). There is also a small remnant of Portuguese in Goa.† But it has happened triumphantly in what was Portugal's largest colony, Brazil: the population is now 166 million, and 95 per cent of them, 158 million, have Portuguese as their first language. This means that speakers in Brazil now outnumber those in Portugal sixteen to one.

* To compare with English dialects, Indo-Portuguese makes it like the E in a refined Scots pronunciation of 'Edinburgh', standard Portuguese more like the a in Cockney 'mate'.
† Even so, in 2000 the state's official language was declared to be Konkani, an Aryan language related to Marathi and Hindi.

Portuguese in America

How, then, has the language come to be transplanted into Brazil so effectively, but nowhere else? The reasons are, of course, historical, but also political and above all economic. In brief, Brazil was the only one of its colonies where Portugal found both a significant source of wealth which was attractive to immigrants, and no pre-existing power strong enough to resist its domination.

India was certainly a source of wealth, from trade in a vast range of commodities; but the local powers that the Portuguese encountered there effectively resisted any Portuguese break-out from their coastal settlements. In Śri Lanka, known to them as *Ceilão*, the Portuguese at one time had effective control, and might well have established themselves, and perhaps their language, in the long term if they had not soon been expelled by the Dutch. Farther east, in the islands of the East Indies, the Portuguese looked for profit from the trade in spices; but the bottom fell out of the market for these commodities too soon. It is in any case arguable—not least from comparing the fate of other European empires in Asia—that the kind of wealth derivable from trade with these countries was never going to attract large numbers of immigrants, and so build a large Portuguese-language community. Trade requires capital, or at least a significant military force to impose terms; as a result, governments and large-scale organisations have an overwhelming advantage. Where trade, rather than production, is the source of wealth, the only way for large numbers of immigrants and small-scale outsiders to take part is if they become pirates.

In Africa, although Portugal had held small settlements all down the western coast since the fifteenth century, principally as staging ports for the *carreira da Índia*, no serious source of wealth besides the slave trade was ever discovered. They never attracted large numbers of Portuguese-speaking settlers. But this trade contributed mightily, at one remove, to the spread of Portuguese in South America. Of the 10 million African slaves shipped to the Americas between 1526 and 1870, 3.6 million went to Brazil alone,[12] at first to provide labour for sugar plantations, later for cotton and tobacco. As in the other slave economies of the Americas, the Africans could not bring their languages with them. They were in contact with too few of their ex-neighbours to speak those languages, for the slave markets distributed them without regard to origin all over the colonies, and they had perforce to learn the language of their new masters. Often too those very masters would become the fathers of their children; in a very few generations most of the population came to be of mixed blood, but nonetheless speakers just of Portuguese.

White immigration too was more substantial into Brazil than to anywhere else in the Portuguese possessions. Early on, neither Portugal's court nor its people had taken much interest in their American colony, since it had unaccountably not yielded anything like the copious gold and silver that the Spanish were extracting from their colonies in Mexico and Peru.

But the hostile attentions of other European powers, and the effort needed to repel them, then concentrated Portugal's sense that here was something worth having. The Spanish had respected the claims in accord with the 1494 Treaty of Tordesillas—indeed, from 1580 to 1640 Spain and Portugal were united under a single (Spanish) government—but other powers that were not party to it had been more dangerous. The French had posed the first challenge in 1555, with raids and attempted settlements that persisted until 1615, then the English (less seriously) from 1582 to 1595. Most aggressive were the Dutch. After some early inconsequential attacks in 1598–9, from the 1620s until 1641 they succeeded in taking possession of the whole of the Brazilian north-east from São Luis to Aracaju, and holding it until 1654. In 1624 they had even briefly taken the very heart of the Portuguese colony, its first capital at Baía (also called Salvador). The Portuguese seem to have found the determination, and hence the resources, to retake them only when they resigned themselves finally to the loss of most of their colonies in India and beyond. (Indeed, as we shall soon see, those became the next target of the Dutch.)

A series of resolute expeditions had mapped out most of the interior by the mid-seventeenth century. Known as *bandeiras*, 'flags', they were inspired by the (mostly unavailing) quest for gold, silver, jewels or natives to capture as slaves. Their main success had lain in pre-emptively defining borders with Spain's colonies that were being rather less actively explored from the opposite side of the continent. (The borders were actually agreed a hundred years later in the Treaties of Madrid, 1750, Pardo, 1761 and Ildefonso, 1777, which finally erased the notional Line of Tordesillas.)

Despite these explorations, until the second half of the seventeenth century the only Portuguese to settle more than 400 kilometres from the coast had been the missionaries, especially the Jesuits. And as in the Spanish colonies, they had found it easier to preach in a language other than their own. Most of the local languages they called *línguas travadas*, 'hobbled tongues', so there was evidently little enthusiasm for them. In a celebrated sermon preached to a departing mission in 1657, Father Antonio Vieira said he had heard someone call the Amazon the '*rio Babel*', for its eighty languages: 'What must it be to learn Nheengaíba, or Juruna, or Tapajó, or Teremembé, or Mamaianá, whose very names seem to strike terror? ... To the Apostles God gave tongues of fire, but to their successors a fire of tongues. The tongues of fire came to an end, but the fire of tongues did not, because this fire, this spirit, this love of God makes one learn, study and know those languages.'[13]

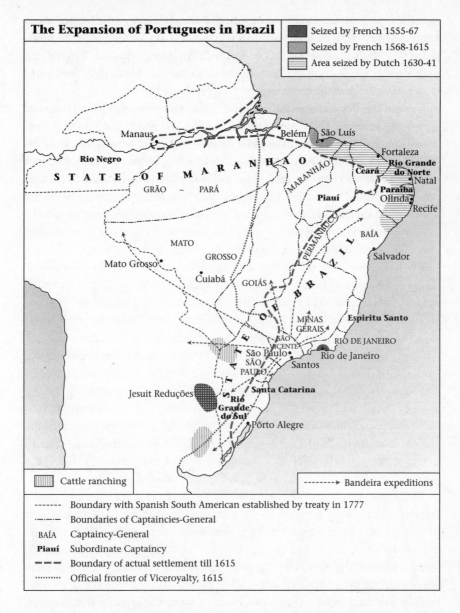

The Expansion of Portuguese in Brazil

Seized by French 1555-67
Seized by French 1568-1615
Area seized by Dutch 1630-41

Manaus • Belém • São Luís
Rio Negro   Fortaleza
                                             Rio Grande
S T A T E   O F   M A R A N H Ã O   do Norte
     GRÃO – PARÁ   Ceará   Natal
                                             Paraíba
                          Piauí   Olinda
                                             Recife
     MATO   BAÍA
        GROSSO
Mato Grosso •   Salvador
     • Cuiabá   GOIÁS

                              MINAS
                              GERAIS   Espiritu Santo
                          SÃO
                          VICENTE   RIO DE JANEIRO
                    São Paulo •   Rio de Janeiro
                    SÃO   • Santos
                    PAULO
Jesuit Reduções   Santa Catarina
                    Rio
                    Grande
                    do Sul • Pôrto Alegre

Cattle ranching   Bandeira expeditions

------- Boundary with Spanish South American established by treaty in 1777
-·-·-·- Boundaries of Captaincies-General
BAÍA   Captaincy-General
Piauí   Subordinate Captaincy
- - -   Boundary of actual settlement till 1615
········ Official frontier of Viceroyalty, 1615

For all this heady combination of language-learning and the love (or fear) of God, in Brazil it had turned out that Tupinambá (a language very closely related to the Guaraní of Paraguay) could be used everywhere (see Chapter 10, 'Past struggles: How American languages had spread', p. 348), and it came to be called the *língua geral* (the Portuguese equivalent of the Spanish *lengua general*). In the early days of the colony, it was the main

393

means of communication with the natives. One Jesuit witness wrote, about 1560: 'Almost all who come to the Kingdom and are settled and in communication with the Indians get to know it within a short time, and the sons and daughters of the Portuguese born here get to know it better than the Portuguese do, mainly in the captaincy of São Vicente.'[14]

Organising the Indians into *aldeias* (villages) and *reduções* (reserved areas), the Jesuits in fact resisted the inroads of other white settlers. This kind of resistance to a specifically colonial development of the interior was to last until the mid-eighteenth century. One effect was that the use of Portuguese remained confined to the coastal districts for the first two centuries of the colony's existence. Only in 1759 did the Jesuits lose their power to protect and organise the Indians in this way, when they were stripped of their powers and expelled from the country.* For good measure, the further use of the *língua geral* was banned at the same time.

But Brazil was now to become a more appealing prospect for settlers. After the reassertion of Portuguese power in 1654, a stream of economic developments at last provided a motive for large-scale immigration from Europe, and with it the spread of the Portuguese language. Ore beds with gold, emeralds, diamonds and other precious stones were found in the late seventeenth and early eighteenth centuries, principally in the southern central area henceforth called *Minas Gerais*, 'General Mines', but also inland in Baía, Goiás and Mato Grosso. The result was the world's first gold rush, coming mostly from Portugal, and thereafter an eighteenth-century economy with government revenues founded securely on gold. When the gold ran out towards the end of that century, its place was taken by the export profits from cattle ranching, especially in sales of leather, an industry that had taken advantage of the opening up of massive grasslands in these same south and central areas.

The result was a massive, and subsequently sustained, increase in Brazil's Portuguese-speaking population, both from immigration (including import of slaves), and from natural growth. This had comprised less than 150,000 around 1650; by 1770 they comprised over 1,500,000; and this in a period when the rest of the Americas (Spanish- and English-speaking alike) had just about doubled their numbers. In the same period, Brazil had come to provide the second and third most populous Portuguese-speaking cities in the world, Baía (Salvador) and Rio de Janeiro yielding only to Lisbon. This influx of rich and prolific immigrants from Europe, which reinforced the influx of up-

---

* This was part of the global impact of the Enlightenment on Catholic governments (see Chapter 10, 'The state's solution: Hispanización', p. 374).

rooted slaves from Africa, crowded out the previous *língua geral* of the interior, Tupinambá, to say nothing of the tiny languages spoken by individual tribes. It was estimated in 1985 that there were no more than 155,000 Brazilians who spoke indigenous languages, approximately one for every thousand speakers of Portuguese.[15]

Ultimately, then, the growth of Portuguese to its present status (176 million native speakers, ranking seventh in the world, ahead of German, French and Japanese) owes almost everything to the economic development, and consequent population growth, of Brazil over the past three hundred years, and very little to its spread from Portugal as a language for colonial administration, or as a lingua franca in Asia, both of which peaked over four hundred years ago.

Dutch interlopers

Saïdjah kwam te Batavia aan. Hy verzocht een heer hem in deenst te nemen, hetgeen die heer terstond deed omdat hy Saïdjah niet verstond. Want te Batavia heeft men gaarne bedienden die nog geen maleisch spreken en dus nog niet zo bedorven zyn als anderen die langer in aanraaking waren met europese beschaving. Saïdjah leerde spoedig maleisch, maar paste braaf op…

Saïdjah came to Batavia. He asked a gentleman to take him into service, which the gentleman at once did, because he did not understand Saïdjah['s language]. For in Batavia people liked servants who did not yet speak Malay and so were not so spoiled as the others who had been longer in contact with European civilization. Saïdjah learnt Malay quickly, but behaved well…

Multatuli, *Max Havelaar* (Amsterdam, 1860), ch. 17

Pelabur habis Palembang tak alah

Rations finished, Palembang not beaten

Malay proverb*

* Palembang in Sumatra was the principal city of Śrī Vijaya, the ancient state that was most likely responsible for the spread of Malay round the markets of the East Indies. This proverbial statement of wasted effort is said to refer to a failed Dutch attempt to take Palembang, in their day a prime source of pepper (Hamilton 1987: 60).

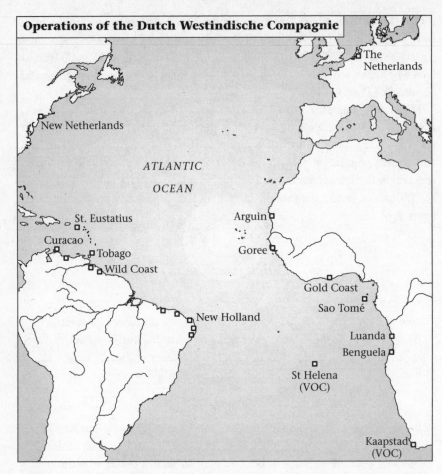

Operations of the Dutch Westindische Compagnie

The Netherlands

New Netherlands

ATLANTIC
OCEAN

St. Eustatius
Curacao
Tobago
Wild Coast

Arguin

Goree

New Holland

Gold Coast
Sao Tomé

Luanda
Benguela

St Helena
(VOC)

Kaapstad
(VOC)

After a century of stability, from the mid-sixteenth to the mid-seventeenth, the Portuguese trading empire in Asia was lost almost as rapidly as it was built up. This was overwhelmingly due to the efforts of another small European power, the Dutch.* The Dutch speedily divested Portugal of the sources of its Asian incomes, and became a fixture in the East Indies for three centuries. But in our history of world languages, they have only a negative part to play. The Dutch career demonstrates that a successful European imperial power may yet leave little or no linguistic trace in its domains—further evidence, in fact, that Nebrija was wrong.

The Dutch imperial career began against the odds, almost as a commercial

---

* Each country had between 1.25 and 1.5 million people in the seventeenth century (Boxer 1969: 114).

396

The Development of the Dutch East Indian Empire

Deshima

Chinsura

Formosa

Vengurla

Pulicat

Malabar

Nagapatam

Ceylon

Malacca

Moluccas

INDIAN

OCEAN

Batavia

Makassar

Kupang

Mauritius

□ Main settlement of VOC (Vereenigde Oostindische Compagnie) 1660s

sideline in their war of independence from Spain, a struggle that was to last intermittently from 1566 to 1648, but which in fact, from 1588, allowed the burghers of the new republic of the United Provinces considerable freedom of action. Despite the uncertain times, the supply of luxury goods to northern Europe (mostly from Asia, and often by re-export from Portugal) had become proverbially 'rich trades' for Dutch merchants in the 1590s. Then in 1598 Dutch ships, goods and merchants were embargoed from all ports in the Spanish/Portuguese empire. Minds were duly concentrated, and the immediate result was an explosion of East India trading enterprise—by 1601 fourteen Dutch fleets, with sixty-five vessels, had set sail on behalf of eight different companies.[16] Such a splurge of competition could only be adverse both at source in the Indies and in the customer markets of Europe, and so in 1602, with the collusion of all the companies involved, the United East India Company (*Vereenigde Oostindische Compagnie*—VOC) was founded as a state monopoly of such trade. Somewhat later, in 1624, a similar organisation, the West India Company (*Westindische Compagnie*—WIC) was established to control Dutch interests in the western hemisphere.

Of the two companies, WIC had far less long-term success as a procurer of Dutch real estate and colonial populations. It began well; from 1623 a tract of North America (covering most of what is now New Jersey, Delaware and Pennsylvania, and the southern half of New York State) was taken as 'Nieuw Nederland', and outright conquests from Portugal followed, of the Guinea coast in 1637–42, of northern Brazil (as 'Nieuw Holland') in 1631, of Angola in 1641, as well as the acquisition of less crucial holdings in the Antilles and Guyanas. Around 1640, WIC was in control of the Atlantic markets in sugar, slavery and furs. But by 1665 all but the Antilles and Guyanas had been lost. Besides the recaptures by Portugal, Nieuw Nederland was forcibly converted into New England (and New Amsterdam into New York) in 1664. WIC retrenched to being a simple trading company, making a good living where previously it had aspired to rule. There was still plenty of gold in Guinea, and a demand for African slaves in the Netherlands. Dutch remained, in the small colonies, as a language of administration. Nowadays there are a bare thousand native speakers of Dutch in the republic of Suriname (Dutch Guiana), while perhaps a quarter of the half-million population use it as a second language. The Antilles remain for the most part dependent on the Netherlands, but fewer than 10 per cent of the 185,000 people have Dutch as a first language.

The VOC, on the other hand, went on to real colonial greatness. In the East Indies, the source of the spice trade, they displaced the Portuguese permanently from Ambon, and later Ternate and Tidore, in the Moluccas (1605–62), Malacca in Malaya (1641), and Macassar (modern Ujung Pandang) in Sulawesi (1667). They also went beyond the scope of Portugal's holdings by seizing Jakarta in western Java (1619) as their centre of operations (comparable to Goa for the Portuguese), and renaming it Batavia.* Through intrigue rather than war, they displaced the Portuguese as monopolists in the Japan trade (1639), with a permanent base in Nagasaki.† In the Indian subcontinent, they established an early foothold at Pulicat (1613), and between 1638

---

* The Batavi were a Germanic tribe who had lived in the area of modern Holland, north of the Scheldt, around the turn of the first centuries BC–AD. They thus provided a useful classical pseudonym for historically minded Dutchmen, perhaps little appreciated by the Javanese among whom they settled.

† A major motive was the association of the Portuguese with Christianity, which the Japanese government of Tokugawa Iemitsu was determined to stamp out within their shores. The Dutch, prepared to restrict their concerns to secular matters of trade, were therefore the only foreign contact of the Japanese for the following two centuries.

This led to a famous linguistic incident in Japanese history (comparable to the use of Portuguese mentioned above, ['An Asian empire', p. 388]). In 1853, when the American Commodore Perry en-

and 1661 they took from the Portuguese Ceylon and their whole string of southern Indian possessions from Cannanore round to Nagappattinam. In Africa, they were unable for long to dislodge the Portuguese from Angola or Mozambique, but went on to found their own South African colony in between at Cape Town (*Kaapstad*) in 1652. Willem Bosman remarked in 1704 that the Portuguese had been 'as setting-dogs to spring the game, which as soon as they had done, was seized by others'.[17]

Curiously but significantly, it was only in Africa that their colonial intrusiveness bore any linguistic fruit. It was here that Dutch settlers were attracted, just as Brazil, in the end, attracted settlers from Portugal. The Dutch settlers were not merchants, nor miners, but farmers (i.e., in Dutch, *Boer*). Their language, a mildly simplified version of Dutch that came to be known as *Afrikaans* ('African'), developed and grew with their population, even after the British had gained control of the country.* Subsequently, in 1836, tiring of British rule, they spread out on the Great Trek, into the east of what is now South Africa, to found the Orange Free State and the Transvaal. Their influence was reduced temporarily after their defeat by the British in the Boer War of 1899–1902. But numbers prevailed in the white community—as they were later to do as between black and white—and in the following half-century Afrikaans came to be explicitly the language of the South African ruling majority. Afrikaans in 1991 had 6.2 million speakers in South Africa, centred in Pretoria and Bloemfontein, a million of them native bilinguals with English. Another 4 million there were using it as a second or third language. Taking all of them together, the 10 million who know the language compare significantly with the 20 million or so who now speak Dutch worldwide (13.4 million in the Netherlands, another 5 million in Belgium).[18]

Farther east, Dutch presence proved shorter lasting. Ceylon and southern India, like the Cape colony, passed into British hands at the turn of the eighteenth century as a side effect of political changes in Europe. The century and a half of Dutch influence that was then brought to an end is hard now to discern. But although there was some similar back-and-forth in the East Indies—during which a thirty-year-old Stamford Raffles became for five years lieutenant-governor of Java, and chanced on the lost Buddhist wonder

tered the port of Uraga with his 'black ships', determined to end Japan's isolation, one of the first Japanese to come alongside, Hori Tatsunosuke, said in very good English, 'I can speak Dutch.' Since one of the Americans, a Mr Portman, also knew the language, the first sustained exchange between an American and a Japanese actually took place in Dutch. (Hawks 1954, pp. 48–9)

* They originally stepped in to take pre-emptive control of Dutch possessions when revolutionary France occupied the Netherlands in 1795, but permanently annexed the Cape colony in 1806.

city of Borobodur—it ended with the British contenting themselves with the Malay peninsula and the northern coast of Borneo. Dutch control of the islands was ultimately maintained; in fact it lasted until the Second World War, a full three hundred years from their original dispossession of the Portuguese.

Why, then, is Dutch not now the official government language, or at least a lingua franca, in the state of Indonesia, the successor of the Dutch East Indies? Given that Dutch is another Germanic language, one is almost tempted to detect a 'curse of Germanic'. Remember that despite their awesome conquests in western Europe and North Africa in the fifth century AD, the Franks, Vandals and Goths, alone among the great conquerors of the era, had never spread their language across their domains. And now, in the modern age from the seventeenth to the twentieth centuries, their descendants the Dutch were no more capable of winning new speakers for their language, when around them the British were spreading English in Malaya, Portuguese was persisting in its enclave on Timor, the Spanish were trying to bring up the Philippines in Castilian, and indeed the French were attempting to seed Indo-China as an outpost of francophony.

The fundamental reason for the curious absence of the Dutch language is the pragmatism of its speakers in the Indies.* They were there, after all, with two motives: primarily to make money, and secondarily—a long way second—to spead Protestant Christianity in their own dear Calvinist form. In the event, both motives called for the use of a foreign contact language, rather than their own mother tongue. For trade, in the first instance, there was evidently a need to use whatever language came to hand; and it turned out that there was already a language that the trading community of the East Indies had had in common for at least two centuries, and perhaps much longer.

This was Malay, *Bahasa Mělayu* (or in Dutch spelling *Bahasa Melajoe*), best known as the jargon of merchants having dealings at the entrepôt of Malacca. Malacca had been founded only at the beginning of the fifteenth

---

* Anderson (1991: 110) suggests two other motives: the absence of nationalism as such in the early seventeenth century (the VOC was after all a corporation, not a nationality), and Dutch lack of self-confidence in their own language. Neither seems particularly convincing, especially in comparison with the Portuguese competitors whom the Dutch were quite consciously outdoing. On p. 133, he suggests further that the Netherlands, with only one substantial colony, could afford to adopt a non-European language for administration: it would have been unworkable, he says, for a multi-continental empire such as the British. But the Dutch empire too, for its first 150 years, had been just as multi-continental.

On the other hand, he may be right in pointing (p. 110) to the language policy as a means of keeping the native population underdeveloped: 'in 1940, when the indigenous population numbered well over 70 millions, there were only 637 "natives" in college, and only 37 graduated with BAs.'

century, but had grown very fast, through exploitation of its commanding position on the strait, and cultivation of the Chinese emperor. It is likely that the spread of the language had started earlier than this. Malacca had been founded by a wayward prince from Śrī Vijaya, a state that had cultivated wide trading interests from the seventh to thirteenth centuries AD. And Jambi, one of its principal cities, had also been called Malāyu. Whatever Malay's origins, with this one language in hand a Dutch merchant could do business all over the Indies,* an added advantage since the VOC was always interested in trade all over the area, not just simple exports from the sources of supply to the Netherlands.[19]

Likewise, in order to spread the faith and practice of the Dutch Reformed Church, it was easier, and quicker, to make converts when one was not restricted to those who already knew Dutch, or who might be willing to learn it. Early on, there had been an attempt to establish schools at Ambon in Dutch, with as many as sixteen of them running in 1627. But there were in fact few opportunities for children who learnt the language to use it after they graduated, and so they tended to forget it.[20] Probably this is a common feature of the early years of a language cohort, when they have not yet had time to be promoted up the system, and so are mostly dealing with adults who do not share the language. But the Dutch pragmatists were not prepared to wait, and the experiment was terminated. Malay became identified with Reformed religion too, designated as the language for 'a common indigenous Church'.[21]

We might briefly query why the Dutch pragmatism did not extend to making use of another pre-existing lingua franca in their domains, namely Portuguese, which we have already noted they were required to use in dealings in Ceylon, and had indeed spread, willy-nilly, into their own centre of operations at Batavia. Certainly, some Dutch pastors, notably François Valentijn in the 1680s, were inclined to favour it over Malay in the work of the Church.[22] It is notable that conversions, never very many, were found mostly in congregations that had previously been converted to Catholicism by the Portuguese; the Hindus, Buddhists and Muslims turned out to be largely impervious to the new creed. But the association between Portuguese and Catholicism remained strong in Dutch Calvinist hearts; and in business, there must also have been a residue of pride, resisting any place for the language

---

* The Italian Pigafetta, accompanying the Spanish circumnavigators in 1521, had been able to compile a list of 450 Malay words at Tidore in the Moluccas. Nevertheless, it was not yet well established there: 'even the scribes who had to write it for the infant Sultan of Tidore in 1521 and 1522 showed that they were "certainly very imperfectly acquainted with it"' (Hoffman 1979: 66–7, n. 9).

of their defeated enemies—indeed, until 1640 and the separation of Spain and Portugal, their resented overlords—in the mechanism of their own organisation.

And so Malay became the language of the Dutch Indies, first as a practical short-term measure, but by the eighteenth century by official policy.* In 1731–3 the Bible was issued in a Malay translation by Melchior Leydekker and Georg Henrik Werndly, and the latter brought out a grammar of the language in 1736. But despite the attempts to preach in it, knowledge of the language did not penetrate particularly deeply. Malay was a means of communication among administrators, managers, merchants and rulers, and so it stayed. Given the highly devolved nature of Dutch imperial administration, which largely kept the native power chiefdoms in place and was mediated through them, this at first worked well.

But the subsequent history of the language as used in the Dutch Indies was not a smooth one. In the mid-eighteenth century, as world markets came to value coffee from Java over spices from Ambon, the need grew to have direct dealings with the Javanese rulers, whose knowledge of Malay had never been good. The return of Dutch administration after the British interregnum under Stamford Raffles (1811–16) was on a new basis: the VOC had been abolished in 1795 after a collapse in its profitability, and there was a new concern for administrators to be in contact with the subject population. A decree of 1811 called for officials to know Javanese. Raffles himself, when he took over, was very much in favour, opining in 1813: 'Hitherto the communication with inhabitants of the country has been chiefly through illiterate Interpretors, or when direct, through the medium of a barbarous dialect of Malays, confounded and confused by the introduction of Portuguese and Dutch.'[23]

But when the Dutch were back in charge, there followed a controversy, which was to last throughout the nineteenth century, concerning the relative weight to be given to Javanese and Malay, with resolutions in 1827, 1837 and 1839 promoting Malay again. The practical value of knowing the actual language of a majority of the people was clear, but the embarrassing fact remained that Javanese, with elaborate inflexions and distinct sub-languages marking different levels of politeness, was far harder to learn tolerably than

---

* There was always speculation that the strange unwillingness of the Dutch to share their language with their colonial subjects was a sort of snobbery, to enhance their prestige among the Dutchless natives. This was roundly discouraged by the Dutch administration as a harmful attitude. Nevertheless, it was widely believed by foreign observers (e.g. Bousquet 1940: 88–9); and it did happen to fit in with a certain aspect of Javanese etiquette, whereby social status was marked by styles of language (*taalsoorten*).

Malay. Results were never good, and most officials reverted to their broken and undignified, but always serviceable, *dienst-Maleisch* ('service-Malay'), known less respectfully as *brabbel-Maleisch* or *klontong-Maleisch* ('jabber-' or 'clod-Malay').[24]

For all its faults (a standard system of Romanised spelling was specified only in 1901[25]) it is this Malay which has become the official language of the state of Indonesia, under the wishful title of *Bahasa Indonesia*. Even today, though, only 17–30 million people there actually have it as a first language, perhaps a tenth of those who can use it as a second language. Compare this with the 75 million whose first language is Javanese, and the 726 languages that are listed as spoken somewhere within Indonesia. The Dutch, through their fitful policy, had succeeded in giving a common language to their old colony, but not their own.

La francophonie

La langue française est une femme. Et cette femme est si belle, si fière, si modeste, si hardie, si touchante, si voluptueuse, si chaste, si noble, si familière, si folle, si sage, qu' on l' aime de toute son âme, et qu' on n' est jamais tenté de lui être infidèle.

The French language is a woman. And that woman is so beautiful, so proud, so modest, so bold, so touching, so voluptuous, so chaste, so noble, so familiar, so mad, so wise, that one loves her with all one's soul, and is never tempted to be unfaithful to her.

Anatole France, 1844–1924

This quotation, widely known to speakers and lovers of French, is eminently but characteristically self-conscious and self-regarding.* The French have taken enthusiastically to the notion that their language has particular virtues, even—and this is curious for such an emotional and ethnocentric idea—that it is more rational than other languages. Perhaps more honestly than others set on global conquests, they came to assert that they were fulfilling a *mission civilisatrice* which went beyond the making of foreign profits for themselves, and foreign converts for their God.

---

* It might even be seen, by an unsympathetic Anglo-Saxon, as an example of 'that tipsy, euphoristic prose-poetry which is one of the more tiresome manifestations of the French spirit', a phrase of Peter Medawar in a review of Teilhard de Chardin's *Le Phénomène humain* (accessible at <http://cscs.umich.edu/~crshalizi/Medawar/phenomenon-of-man.html>).

The outcome, in terms of actual expansion of the language community of native and second-language speakers, what they call *la francophonie,** has been modest, at least by the standards of its direct competitors (and neighbours): French can now count 77 million native speakers worldwide (two-thirds of them in France itself), and another 51 million second-language speakers.† This places it tenth in the list of language populations, effectively the smallest of the major European languages, and less populous even than German, which is hardly spoken at all outside its home continent.

French in Europe

French is by origin the species of Romance spoken in Gaul, which was broadly taken to be the realm of the Franks. Its modern name for itself, *français* [frãsé], comes from the Germanic adjective *frankisk*, through the Latinisation *franciscus*. For political and topographical reasons, it came to be typified and led by the dialect of the Île-de-France region in the north-east. The Île-de-France has many navigable rivers heading in different directions, hence is a natural crossroads. And so it was a place where speakers of many dialects met, and differences were levelled out. What is more, from the time of Clovis (late fifth century) it mostly had the royal court of the Franks somewhere within it. Different cities flourished and waned, but by the thirteenth century the city of Paris evidently enjoyed a particular cachet; a poet wrote:

Si m'escuse de mon langage	Excuse my language,
Rude, malostru et sauvage	rude, ungainly and wild,
Car nés ne sui pas de Paris.	for I am not a native of Paris.[26]

A milestone in the early history of French was the Ordinance of Villers-Cotterêts in 1539, by which King François I, among many other provisions, required that official documents, whether from courts or parish registers, should all be produced *en langage maternel françois et non autrement*—in French mother tongue, and not otherwise, specifically not in Latin.[27] But despite the homely-sounding phrase, the king was in fact referring to his own

---

* The term was invented by the geographer Onésime Reclus in 1880, to refer to the French-speaking community in the world. Nowadays, at least in the French-speaking world, it refers preferably to a voluntary association of states under a charter, not all of them ex-colonies of France, in spirit rather comparable with the British Commonwealth. (See <www.france.diplomatie.fr/francophonie>.)

† These figures are from Grimes (2000). The French Foreign Ministry's *francophonie* website claims that there are 160 million first-language and second-language speakers. Leclerc (2000) states that 145 million people have been to school in French. Either figure might lift its rank above German, but not to the level of Portuguese.

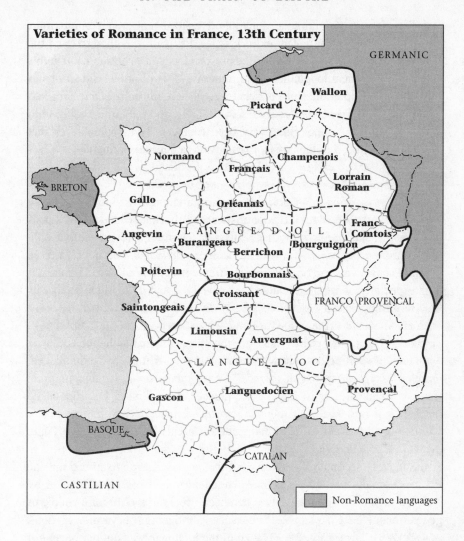

Varieties of Romance in France, 13th Century

GERMANIC

Wallon

Picard

Normand

Champenois

Lorrain
Roman

BRETON

Français

Gallo

Orléanais

Angevin

L A N G U E   D ' O I L

Franc-
Comtois

Burangeau

Berrichon

Bourguignon

Poitevin

Bourbonnais

Saintongeais

Croissant

FRANCO PROVENÇAL

Limousin

Auvergnat

L A N G U E   D ' O C

Gascon

Languedocien

Provençal

BASQUE

CATALAN

CASTILIAN

Non-Romance languages

mother tongue, not that of his subjects: the act was interpreted as requiring the use of Parisian French, and so provoked *merveilleuses complaintes* ('wondrous complaints') in the Provençal-speaking south.[28] The French political centre was henceforth to be language conscious, and to take action to enforce consistency at the official level, despite the persistence of different spoken languages in its realms.

What sort of language was French? To the ear, a major characteristic of French among its Romance cousins was the loss of almost all vowels in final syllables, and later of final consonants. (Final *a* usually survived, but was reduced to an indistinct [ə] 'uh' sound.) This slack pronunciation led to some major changes in the grammar, due to the breakdown of the Latin system of meaningful word endings (inflexion), at least in so far as they marked the function of nouns in sentences, and the person (I vs you vs he/she/it) of verbs. So French became a language with a rather rigid word order, and strings of short pronouns up at the front of sentences. Where Latin had *dico tibi illud*, 'I tell you that', French has *je te le dis* [žətələdi], and the Latin ending -o to mark the subject 'I' has effectively been replaced by a separable subject prefix *je* [žə].* But in other ways, French was rather like Portuguese, replacing n and m at the end of syllables with a nasalised twang, changing its y sound to [ž], and voicing s to [z] when it came between vowels. Common Romance *unum bonum vinum rubium*, 'a good wine red', became in France *un bon vin rouge* [œ̃ bõ vẽ ruž]. L after a vowel mostly changed to [w] (as it does in Cockney and Estuary English), and was written with *u*: *maledictum*, 'cursed', came out as *maudit*, *pellem*, 'skin', as *peau*, *collum*, 'neck', as *cou*.

And French was also prey to some extreme processes of vowel strangulation, especially of what are called mid vowels, *e* and *o*: so much so that its precise pronunciation has varied greatly down the centuries, and of course been given considerable scope for language snobbery, if people's diphthongs did not come out just right. These are the processes that have played havoc with French spelling, so that what was long ago written (and pronounced, more or less) *seniōres rēgālēs fāmōsī dēbent habēre unum bellum palātium*, 'famous royal lords must have a fine palace', came first to be pronounced much as it is now spelt, *les seigneurs royaux fameux doivent avoir un beau palais*, but then went on to sound quite different: [le seiñœr rwayo famœ dwavt avwar œ̃ bo palɛ].

In the early second millennium AD, this language began to spread outside France. Notably, in 1066 it was transplanted north of the English Channel, by Norman invaders, who themselves had been speaking it only for a couple of generations. (See Chapter 12, 'Endurance test: Seeing off Norman French', p. 458.) As it turned out, the advance of the language was not permanent. It flourished for over two centuries as a language for the elite in England, but gradually lost touch with the Île-de-France. As Chaucer wrote of his Prioress towards the end of the fourteenth century:

> And Frenssh she spak ful faire and fetisly
> After the scole of Stratford atte Bowe
> For Frenssh of Parys was to hire unknowe.[29]

---

* *Je* is a remnant of what was once a Latin pronoun of emphasis, *ego* (brutally reduced, after changing to something like *eieu*—cf. the Provençal equivalent, *eu*, *ieu*).

Then came the Black Death: a social revolution followed, and English-speaking commoners were able to move into more influential positions in the English cities. French died out in England.*

About the same time, the Crusades also spread French outside its native soil, but in the opposite direction. These military escapades derived most of their support from France, and they did succeed in setting up Frankish domains in Palestine which lasted out the twelfth century. Nevertheless, the language communities did not long survive the Muslim reconquests in the thirteenth. One long-term effect, though, was to create a special association of 'the Frank' with the idea of a European at large in the East—seen in the widespread Arab term for a European, *feringī*, and the still useful term *lingua franca*, denoting an unofficial language of wider communication, which was first used in the Levant.†

The Parisian standard for French spread to neighbouring countries before the French state started its serious efforts to spread its power and language abroad. Neither Belgium nor Switzerland, whose boundaries have always included Romance speakers as long as both the boundaries and the language have existed, ever attempted to set up a competing national standard. Geneva had its own distinct Romance dialect, Savoyard, but has used French for official business since the thirteenth century; it was the effective capital of the French Protestants during the wars of the Reformation. Farther south are Savoy, Nice and Monaco. They all had historic links across the Alps, and long resisted becoming part of metropolitan France. But they have largely accepted its language.

Why did French gain such an association with high culture in Europe, especially spreading eastward? The fundamental reason was the growth of France's population and agricultural wealth; the rich of France could afford the best, and their taste was influential.§ France was the most densely populated country in medieval and early modern Europe, and so tended to set the standard for the rest. French became the business language of European merchants. And the same principle of geographical centrality that had made Paris

---

* There will be more to say of this retreat of French, from the viewpoint of the language that benefited from it, in the next chapter.

† The term, and the institution, continued in the Mediterranean until the nineteenth century, but the actual language used was based not on French but Italian, probably because of the later influence of merchants from Venice.

§ Eleanor (Aliénor) of Aquitaine (1122–1204) played a cardinal role as a cultural sponsor. She could hardly have been better connected in society, being the wife of two kings, mother of two, and the mother-in-law of yet two more. But in the mid-twelfth century she made her court at Poitiers a centre for courtly love poetry and historical narrative.

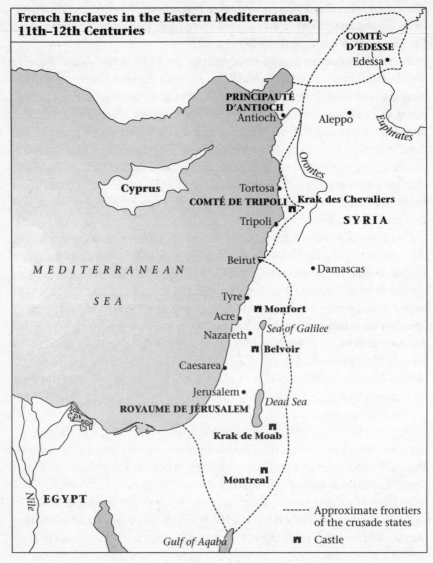

French Enclaves in the Eastern Mediterranean, 11th–12th Centuries

COMTÉ
D'EDESSE
Edessa •

PRINCIPAUTÉ
D'ANTIOCH
Antioch •

Aleppo •

Euphrates

Orontes

Cyprus

Tortosa •
COMTÉ DE TRIPOLI
Krak des Chevaliers

SYRIA

Tripoli •

MEDITERRANEAN

SEA

Beirut

• Damascas

Tyre •

Monfort

Acre •

Sea of Galilee

Nazareth •

Belvoir

Caesarea •

Jerusalem •

Dead Sea

ROYAUME DE JÉRUSALEM

Krak de Moab

Montreal

Nile

EGYPT

------ Approximate frontiers
of the crusade states

Gulf of Aqaba

Castle

the crossroads of France made France itself the crossroads of west European Christendom. In 1164 John of Salisbury wrote to Thomas à Becket: 'I took a detour by Paris. When I saw the abundance of foods, the happiness of the people, the consideration accorded to the clergy, the majesty and glory of the whole Church, the diverse activities of the philosophers, I thought I was seeing, filled with admiration, Jacob's ladder, its top touching the sky and angels passing up and down upon it.'[30]

This situation did not change until the nineteenth century. France remained the richest and most populous country in Europe; its geographical advantages simply could not be challenged until the power base of European politics spread beyond western Europe. Certainly, the cultural predominance of French was shaken by the rise of the Italian city-states in the fifteenth-century Renaissance, and by the sixteenth-century Reformation, since the French king chose to associate France resolutely with the Catholic Church. France itself ceased to be the centre of the action for a time, yet the Reformation prompted many influential French speakers to flee eastward: Huguenots, the French Protestants, took up residence in the Dutch- and German-speaking lands, and there was an explosion of French-language publishing, especially just over the border in the Netherlands. The Reformation added to the French language's eastward momentum as a language of culture.

In the seventeenth century, French power and influence in Europe reached their height, during the long reigns of Louis XIII, 1610–43, and of Louis XIV, the famed *Roi Soleil*, 'Sun King', 1643–1715. Increasingly complacent, France began to reflect on its own cultural attributes. As all nations do when they enjoy pre-eminence, the French began to look for some particular virtues that could explain their success. Increasingly, they saw evidence of excellence in their language itself. Cardinal Richelieu, Louis XIII's prime minister, founded the Académie Française in 1635, with a concern that transcended the practical: by its statutes its principal function was 'to give certain rules to our language and to render it pure, eloquent and capable of treating the arts and sciences'.

This was a new step in language consciousness, the world's first academy dedicated to the care of a language.* The particular concern of the French for accuracy and concision was crystallised at the time. In fact, the article of the Ordinances of Villers-Cotterêts in 1539 which enjoined the use of French had been immediately preceded by one that required clarity of expression in court judgments: they were to be 'done and written so clearly that there would not be, nor could be, any ambiguity or uncertainty, nor place to ask for interpretation'. Now in 1637 the already famous philosopher René Descartes published his *Discours de la méthode*. One notable feature of this work was that it was written in French, rather than Latin, acting perhaps in the radical spirit of the academy's statutes. Descartes was not willingly a revolutionary; indeed, one of his maxims in the *Discours* was to 'follow the most moderate

---

* It has continued to enjoy the sponsorship of the highest level in French government ever since, broken only during the Revolution in 1793–1803. Its first task was to compile a dictionary; the first edition took almost sixty years, coming out in 1694, but it has been updated periodically ever since, the latest edition, the eighth, appearing in 1992.

opinions and those most remote from excess as were commonly received in practice by the most sensible of those he lived with', and 'change his desires rather than the order of the world'.[31] But here, at the heart of the European intellectual debate, he proposed that knowledge must be founded exclusively on clear and distinct ideas.[32] Abolishing the need for divine revelation, this approach was new and radical, and came to be seen as quintessentially French.* It is often held to mark the beginning of modern philosophy and modern science, even if for Descartes, playing it safe as ever, it left all practical matters of faith and morals unchanged.

And the French belief in their linguistic advantages soon came to be shared by others not so fortunate. Descartes' great successor Leibniz (1646–1716), though a German from Leipzig, wrote all his major works in French. The intellectual superiority of French culture had become a self-fulfilling prophecy. To be read widely by the elite, one simply had in these days to write in French.

In the late seventeenth century, French culture, especially its classic dramatists Corneille, Racine and Molière, enjoyed a vogue throughout Europe, and Versailles set the standard everywhere for court style and etiquette. Novels in French were everywhere a favourite amusement for rich young ladies. It was especially in the areas of Europe with least cultural self-confidence that the elite set a high value on fluency in French: Sweden, Poland and above all Russia, where starting in the reign of Catherine the Great (1762–96) French became established as the language of polite society. Voltaire, the great wit of the age, rejoiced famously that there were French speakers in Astrakhan, and French language teachers in Moscow.[33] In Tolstoy's *War and Peace*, a novel whose action is set in the following generation, substantial parts of the dialogue, including the opening lines,† are written—presumably for realism—not in Russian but in French.

It was in this period that French also replaced Latin as the language of diplomacy, giving it another link with elegance and influence. By 1642 Richelieu's government had been corresponding in French with most of their northerly neighbours: but Spain, Italy and Switzerland had kept up resistance

---

* Hence the *bon mot* of Antoine de Rivarol, in his *Discours sur l'universalité de la langue française*, of 1784: '*Ce qui n'est pas clair n'est pas français!*' ('What is not clear is not French!').

† '*Eh bien, mon prince, Gênes et Lucques ne sont plus que des apanages, des поместья, de la famille Buonaparte. Non, je vous préviens, que si vous ne me dites pas, que nous avons la guerre, si vous vous permettez encore de pallier toutes les infamies, toutes les atrocités de cet Antichrist (ma parole, j'y crois)—je ne vous connais plus, vous n'êtes plus mon ami, vous n'êtes plus мой верный раб, comme vous dites.*'

to it, preferring their own languages. In the second half of that century, in negotiations with the Holy Roman Empire (whose domestic language was German), the French gradually presuaded them to shift the language of communication from Latin to French. In the next century, from the Treaty of Rastatt in 1712, the two sides switched to French exclusively. Treaties came to be written in French, even by powers with no direct French connections. The Danes used it for their *traité de commerce de Copenhague* in 1691, and the Russians and Ottoman Turks in the terms of their 1774 peace made at Küçük Kainarca (now Kaynarja in Bulgaria).[34] The general popularity of France itself evidently took a dive after Napoleon's attempts in the early nineteenth century to conquer the whole of Europe, but French ceased to play its general intermediary role only in the twentieth century, ironically at Versailles itself, when during the 1919 peace conference held after the First World War the Americans and the British insisted on working in their own language, and so ensured that the treaty was drafted and published in both French and English.

The first empire

What of *le français d'outre-mer*, French overseas? Developments here were very different from the steady, and sturdy, spread of French round Europe through which it became, almost by spontaneous acclaim, the prestige language for elites. The projection of French overseas was very much a result of royal policy.

The policy came in two fits of colonial expansion directed by the French king, punctuated by comprehensive defeat and deflation in the second half of the eighteenth century. These fits of expansion were both extremely ambitious—in 1714, and again in 1914, France held the second-largest colonial empire by land area in the world*—but, aside from the sugar barons' domain in the Caribbean, each of them produced only one territory that was to attract substantial French immigration: Canada in the seventeenth and eighteenth centuries, and Algeria in the nineteenth. In neither case was France, or its settlers, long able to retain political control; and so French imperialism has been more like Dutch in its linguistic effects than any of its other European competitors. That is to say, the French language has persisted only where its settlers have retained a solid identity and a large population, even under foreign (specifically British) domination: French has survived and grown in Canada, just as Dutch (of a kind) has remained strong in South Africa. The

---

* In the eighteenth century, it yielded only to Spain; in the twentieth, only to Britain.

situation in Algeria is clouded by politics.* But in the other colonies the French language has survived, if at all, as a lingua franca for the elite.

Although it was already a major power in the fifteenth century, France was not a player in the earliest voyages of exploration. Still, there was plenty of North America left to be claimed in the next few generations. Jacques Cartier, sent by the French king to discover a north-west passage to the East, discovered instead the St Lawrence river and explored it as far as Quebec and Montreal (then Stadacona and Hochelaga) in 1534–6.† Later, fur traders and missionaries enlarged the part of the new continent that could be claimed for France: in 1603–15 Samuel de Champlain entered the Great Lakes; in 1673 Père Marquette and Louis Jolliet broke out southward into the Mississippi; and in 1678–82 Robert Cavelier de la Salle charted its whole course down to the Gulf of Mexico. France had thereby outflanked and surrounded the English colonies, which were being strung out along the Atlantic coast.

It was an unstable situation, however, since the English colonists heavily outnumbered the French, perhaps by forty to one in the mid-seventeenth century: they would still be twenty times more numerous a century later, when the French settler population had multiplied by ten.[35] Arguably, the expulsion of French Protestants in the Reformation two centuries earlier was at the root of this imbalance between the two powers. As we have seen, their departure had seeded the spread of French, as the language of culture and high thinking, into central and eastern Europe. But by the same token, France had lost the mass of its population of willing emigrants, the kind of puritans, adventurers and utopians who formed the backbone of Britain's Thirteen Colonies. Nouvelle-France boasted a meteoric birth rate among those who came and stayed, but never became a magnet to immigrants equal to New England.

In the same period, largely with Richelieu in charge at home, French settlements were also being planted on the Caribbean islands of Martinique (1625) and Guadeloupe (1635), and at Cayenne on the mainland in Guyana (1637); on the other side of the Atlantic, the French claimed Senegal on the east African coast (1639) and Madagascar in the west (1643). Farthest of all,

---

* Estimates of the French-speaking population of Algeria vary from the *Ethnologue*'s almost absurdly low 110,000 (out of a population of 30 million) to 25 per cent of the population (i.e. 7.5 million). Many believe that it is still the second-largest francophone population in the world, ahead of Quebec with 6.7 million, and Belgium with 4 million. (These latter figures also come from the *Ethnologue*—Grimes 2000.) It is widely believed that the Algerian government's attempted 'arabisation' since 1962 has perversely increased use of other languages, notably Berber and French; but no survey data is available.

† One village he visited near Quebec City was known as *ganáda*, 'settlement' in the Huron language, which served as lingua franca along the river. This is the origin of the name *Canada*.

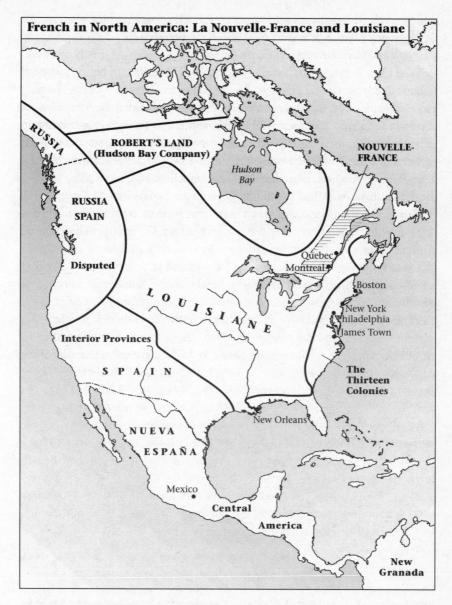

French in North America: La Nouvelle-France and Louisiane

RUSSIA

ROBERT'S LAND
(Hudson Bay Company)

Hudson Bay

**NOUVELLE-
FRANCE**

**RUSSIA
SPAIN**

Disputed

L O U I S I A N E

Québec
Montreal

Boston

New York
Philadelphia
James Town

Interior Provinces

S P A I N

**The
Thirteen
Colonies**

N U E V A

E S P A Ñ A

New Orleans

Mexico

Central

America

**New
Granada**

a French Jesuit missionary, Alexandre de Rhodes, made it in 1624 to south-eastern Indo-China, then known as Cochin-China.*

However, the only parts of the extensive territories claimed for France

---

* The mission flourished, although it did not lead to any French settlement at the time; indeed, de Rhodes was the only Frenchman in a Jesuit team consisting of six Europeans and a Japanese.

which received significant settlement by French-speaking colonists were the St Lawrence river area, known as *la Nouvelle-France* (New France), and the islands of modern Nova Scotia, then known as *l'Acadie* (originally *la Cadie*, derived from some Indian name).* Here the original French policy had been to hope that 'our sons will marry your daughters and we will become one people'. Unfortunately, this did not happen in a way that suited the French, since the early tendency was for arriving male settlers to go native, and bring up their children in their *sauvage* mothers' languages. In 1666, after three generations of French colonial presence, Louis XIV's minister for the colonies, Jean-Baptiste Colbert, complained that Frenchmen who wanted to trade—mostly for furs—*still* had to communicate in the natives' language.[36]

Part of the solution to this was to send out well-brought-up French girls, *filles à marier*, to marry the settlers and create French-speaking homes. Among them were the famous *filles du Roy*, 'king's daughters', mostly orphans from bourgeois families, whose travel and subsistence costs—and in some cases dowries—were borne by the Treasury. Some nine hundred of them were sent out between 1665 and 1673, to boost the population (3215 according to the census of 1665), and improve the sex ratio (2:1 male to female). Although the *intendant* of the colony, Jean Talon, told Colbert that he would have preferred village girls, ready to work like men, rather than these delicate young ladies, they seem to have been a good investment. The population of Nouvelle-France reached 20,000 in 1713 and 55,000 in 1755. The fertility rate averaged a whopping 7.8 children per woman. Although only some 40 per cent of the immigrants spoke *un bon français*, over half of the women did, and the variant dialects of the immigrant families seem to have been levelled out in the seventeenth century, in favour of standard French learnt at Mother's knee. In 1698 the Controller-General of the navy remarked: 'People speak here perfectly well without any bad accent. Although there is a mixture from almost all the provinces in France, none of their dialects can be distinguished in the Canadian provinces.'[37]

However, the need to protect the missions was later used to justify the massive French invasion of Indo-china which came in 1859. And de Rhodes himself is significant as the man who devised the script now known as *Quôc-ngu* (國語, 'National Language'), using Roman letters and accents. He had designed it as an aid to foreign missionaries learning Vietnamese. But in the late nineteenth century it was taken up, even by nationalists, as the key to mass literacy, and is now used universally in Vietnam.

* The poor Acadians were to fall victim to great power politics, their lands traded to England under the Treaty of Utrecht in 1713 in return for trading concessions in India. They were subsequently scattered along the coast, especially in Maine and the mouths of the Mississippi (where they became known as 'Cajuns'), some in the Antilles and many back to the maritime provinces. Wherever they went, French-speaking communities sprang up, at least for a time.

And the marquess of Montcalm, the French general who was to lose the city of Quebec to the British in 1759, had previously admitted: 'The Canadian peasants speak French very well.'[38]

The Treaty of Paris in 1763 spelt the end of France's empire in North America. American France yielded to the overpowering numbers in the British colonies, even if the *coup de grâce* had come from the dominance of the British navy in the Atlantic.* The French defeat did not, however, put paid to French-speaking in the north-east. Even though Canada soon became the destination for large numbers of English-speaking loyalists from the Thirteen Colonies, unwilling to live in an independent United States of America,† the French were still vastly preponderant, approximately by a factor of seven, in the settled areas of what was still a territory with a small European population. It is estimated that in 1791 there were 140,000 francophones and 20,000 anglophones in Canada.§ The French have since put up a redoubtable defence of their community's existence, polarised around the Catholic Church, French civil law and the continued use of their language.

They were, however, increasingly joined by immigrants who either spoke or adopted English, and certainly by the midpoint of the next century, when the European population was about 1.5 million, French speakers had ceased to be the majority. And the population movements had not yet peaked. Another 2.3 million were admitted between 1821 and 1910.[39] In 1998 the country's population had reached 30.5 million, of whom 6.7 million or 22 per cent spoke French natively, as against 60 per cent brought up to speak English.

Despite this disappointing finale, Canada is the main success story of French as transplanted overseas. But it is certainly not the only story. France had also had a major piece of the action in the sugar business, and throughout the seventeenth century the most populous francophone colony had in fact been the French Antilles, Guadeloupe and Martinique: by 1700 they were home to 25,000 French and 70,000 black slaves.[40] Their descendants are still there, with a population now of just over a million, all speaking French, or French creoles. Haiti too, becoming French in 1697 through the action of

---

* This can hardly have been a fundamental cause, since two decades later it was French naval power which crucially denied the British access to America when they were trying to hold on to their own colonies.

† The French had the satisfaction of providing Versailles as the site for the 1783 conference that divested Britain of its American colonies, just twenty years after the Paris conference when the British had taken Nouvelle-France from them.

§ These figures are drawn from a French source, Leclerc (2001, <HISTfrQC_s2_Britannique.htm>). There is amazing discrepancy with some English figures: e.g., Mackey (1998) says that 100,000 loyalists joined an existing population of 65,000 French and 9000 English.

pirates (*filibustiers*), became prosperous in the same business, although the French owners' term was ended violently by slave revolution in 1804. There too French and French creoles are spoken to this day, by some 7.5 million. The other colonies of the French Crown were either trading posts in highly populated regions (Chandernagore, Yanam, Pondicherry, Kāraikāl and Mahe along the coast of India), way-stations on naval routes to India (Senegal, the islands of Réunion and Mauritius, and (briefly) Madagascar) or the rumps of larger-scale conquests that never worked out (French Guiana).* None of them ever attracted major settlement from Europe, though almost all of them host small francophone communities to this day, notably 40,000 still in Pondicherry; and 160,500 can speak French in Réunion, amid half a million (90 per cent of the island's population) who speak a French creole.[41]

The French Revolution ushered in a new phase of imperial wars, but with the exception of Napoleon's somewhat romantic foray to Egypt in 1798–9, they were all waged within the continent of Europe; and they all amounted, in less than a generation, to nothing at all. Ironically, the great claims to fame of France in the early modern period, the Revolution and the reign of Napoleon, contributed little if anything to the spread of the French language, even if they sent French-speaking soldiers all over Europe.

But then, with the restoration of the monarchy in 1815, the French entered on a new bout of overseas imperialism.†

The second empire

Their motives were mixed. In one important case, France acted like ancient Rome, when in 1830 an attempt to rid the Mediterranean of pirates ended up with the full-scale invasion of Algeria, detaching what had been a province of the Ottoman empire. Still in accord with the Roman model, this was followed by an influx of settlers (*colōnī* for the Romans, *colons* for the French), in fairly large numbers: there were already 110,000 of them in 1847, and their numbers rose to just under a million in the next century.[42] But this was an exceptional case, even though it loomed largest in French conceptions of their new empire. In many other cases, French action was led by missionary compassion or zeal, as with the protectorates claimed in the Indian Ocean (*Comores*, 1840) and in the Pacific (in *les Îles de la Société*, 1843, Tahiti,

---

* Cayenne was founded in 1643 and with Caribbean sugar aplenty had been part of Colbert's plans for systematic colonisation. It was briefly used after the French Revolution as a place of exile for political prisoners (1794–1805). It never recovered economically from France's abolition of slavery in 1848, and thereafter was famous mainly for its prison camp, Devil's Island, in operation from 1852 to 1946.
† By a happy coincidence, during the reign of Napoleon III, 1852–70, the regime was even known as *le second Empire*.

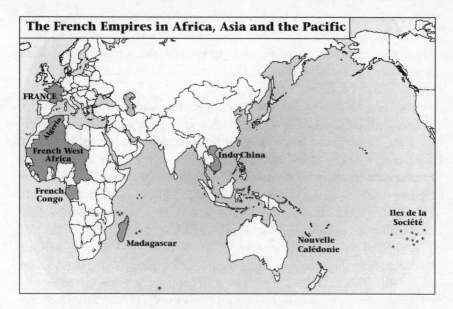

The French Empires in Africa, Asia and the Pacific

1846, *Nouvelle-Calédonie*, 1853). Similar motives, at some level, seem to have led to the expansion of French control from its ancient base in Senegal in the fifty years from 1817, training native infantry (*tirailleurs*) and priests and then taking action against malaria, and building schools and roads. It was persecution of Christian missions that gave France its justification for invading Cochin-China in 1859: by 1887 a French *Union indochinoise* controlled the whole of what is now Vietnam, Cambodia and Laos.

But these colonial acquisitions came at a time when Europeans were beginning to be highly impressed by their own technical superiority over people anywhere else in the world. Once again France began to look for explanations of its success: characteristically, it came to see itself as a power that could make a difference to the world for the better, spreading not just Catholic Christianity and respect for law, but also freemasonry, Saint-Simonian industrial policy, and in short *la civilisation française*. It was easy to combine this with an ambition to do well while doing good, and so there were few reservations felt when France, and Belgium too, joined in '*la course aux colonies*', what Britain knew as 'the scramble for Africa'.

The French and the British were the big winners in the sheer scale of territory acquired: both empires grew massively in the last decades of the nineteenth century. The French expanded from their existing possessions in Algeria and Senegal, but they also established new bridgeheads in Côte d'Ivoire (1842) and Gabon (1843). First, from 1876 to 1885, *Afrique-Équatoriale Française* (French Equatorial Africa) was carved out from the

Gabon shore, including what were to become Gabon, Congo, the Central African Republic and Chad; then from 1883 to 1894 *Afrique-Occidentale Française* (French West Africa) was taken from the west and south-west, comprising the modern Senegal, Mauritania, Mali, Guinea, Côte d'Ivoire, Burkina Faso, Niger and Benin.

And the French were not the only francophones in the race. In 1877–9, Belgium's King Léopold, adopting as his personal agent the British explorer Sir Henry Stanley, had brazenly claimed the area now known as the Congo, a claim accepted by the other European powers in 1885. Then, in 1896, the French went on to depose the queen of Madagascar, justifying their action by the immediate abolition of slavery in her old domains. And on top of it all, France was also claiming protectorates among Algeria's neighbours along the Mediterranean coast, Tunisia in 1881, and Morocco in 1912.

By 1913, French was the language of the rulers of a good third of Africa's land area, from the Atlas mountains on the north Atlantic to the Great Lakes of the Rift Valley. It was an expansion to compare with the adventures of Alexander, or the great Muslim jihad of the seventh century: fifty years earlier, the language had not been heard in Africa outside Algeria and Senegal.

In many ways, the French exerted themselves to be worthy of their sudden new domains, bringing roads, railways and the telegraph, scientific assaults on malaria and other tropical diseases, as well as the Christian faith, the French language, and—to a few privileged souls—an appreciation of Cartesian rationalism. They do seem to have succeeded in transmitting to their subjects a sense that the only practicable route to power and independence lay through mastery of their own skills: this kind of persuasion was one of their ideals, what they called *rayonnement*, 'beaming'. Far more than other European empires, they struggled with the question of what their true interest in these subjects was: exploitation, assimilation, evangelisation, education or simple political association. Was it *la gloire* that France was seeking, or *sa mission civilisatrice*? Taking their own culture so seriously, the French could not see these domains as anything other than parts of France: *la civilisation française* was indivisible. Everywhere French was used for administration, and instituted as the language of instruction in secondary and higher education, even where—as in Indo-China and North Africa—there was an ancient tradition of literacy in some other language.* Colonials could in most places aspire to full French citizenship.

---

* The Belgians, relying much more on foreign expertise to run their empire, also made less use of French as a pervasive language of administration. As in the British colonies, there was widespread use of any pre-existing lingua franca, notably Swahili and Lingala.

But, except in Algeria—where the native, Muslim, population were far less ready to see their Christian conquerors as role models—the French were always too thin on the ground truly to propagate their own society. There were few solid economic reasons to bring them out to these countries, or to keep them there, and rather soon it showed. In contrast to what happened in the other European empires, the typical Frenchman abroad remained a military man, a doctor, a missionary or a teacher. Napoleon, the pre-eminent French soldier, had famously slighted England as '*une nation de petits commerçants*'—a nation of shopkeepers—but it was precisely the lack of such people in the French colonies which demonstrated how unstable they were. Unlike Portuguese, Spanish, British or even Dutch possessions, there was no part of the French empire which attracted mass immigration. And the French government in the nineteenth and twentieth centuries was not able or willing, as it had been in the seventeenth, to finance any emigration. Consequently, French remained, everywhere but Algeria, a language of the governing elite, even while—at least in black Africa—the rest of the population might be heartily aspiring to its values.

The number of colonies under French-speaking administration grew after the end of the First World War, when the German and Ottoman possessions were parcelled out. Cameroon and Togo came to France, and Rwanda and Burundi to Belgium. Syria and Lebanon were also placed under a French mandate. But almost all were granted independence in the fifteen years after the end of the Second World War. The Near Eastern Arab countries were established as independent republics as part of the immediate post-war settlement. Indo-China and North Africa, as well as Madagascar and the Comoros, had to win their freedom by force of arms; in sub-Saharan Africa, by and large they were granted it at their earnest entreaty in 1960. The tiny nations of the Pacific, the Caribbean and South America are still, in effect, part of the empire: but they are now part of the French Union: according to the constitution adopted by the referendum of 27 October 1946,

la France forme avec les peuples d'outre-mer une Union fondée sur l'égalité des droits et des devoirs, sans distinction de race ni de religion.

France forms with the overseas peoples a Union founded on equality of rights and duties, without distinction of race nor religion.

And all its members as *ressortissants* (i.e. when they come to France) are French citizens. It is noticeable that language is not included as an aspect in

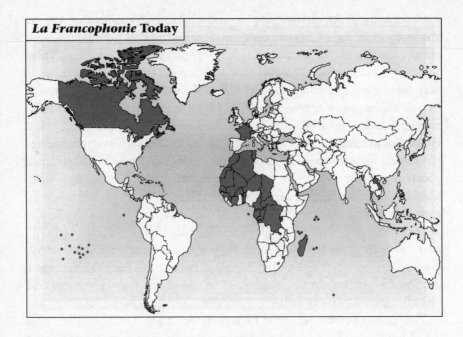

La Francophonie **Today**

which the Union is free from distinction: that is because in the Union, everyone's language is expected to be French.

In conformity with its explicit respect for clarity and reason, the French-language community seeks to order itself, and have an overall conception of itself, apparently far more than any other. So it is characteritic that it has given itself an international political, technical and cultural organisation, known as *la francophonie*. It is a matter of some satisfaction to the French government that the initiative for this came not from France but from a number of distinguished second-language speakers. Still, there may perhaps have been a certain political motivation: the founders were President Habib Bourguiba of Tunisia, Prince Norodom Sihanouk of Cambodia, President Léopold Senghor of Senegal, Charles Hélou of Lebanon, and—interestingly—Hamani Diori of Nigeria, which was never even a French colony. Nevertheless, France does provide up to two-thirds of the organisation's budget. It was founded on 20 March 1970 at Niamey in Niger, central Africa, and has held summit meetings regularly, with cabinet ministers in attendance, the ninth at Beirut in 2002. Membership is not restricted to former colonies of France; indeed, Egypt recently provided the secretary-general, Boutros Boutros Ghali: characteristically it chooses to emphasise some conceptual or moral, rather than historic, relatedness.

Its current emphasis, rather surprisingly, is on protecting and enabling cultural diversity, certainly a novelty as a francophone preoccupation, and not without a whiff of *l'esprit malin*, Gallic mischief, directed at the perennial rivals, *les anglo-saxons*. But it is well within the tradition of incisive, and sometimes disinterested, consideration of the rights of man. Political interests will out, however, and it has been difficult for the French state, in recent years, even to protect and foster such linguistic diversity as remains within its own domains. The action of the minister of education in 2002, for example, aimed at incorporating Breton-language schools into the state system, and so funding them nationally, fell foul of an article inserted into the French constitution as late as 1992—that the language of the French Republic is French.*

The Third Rome, and all the Russias

Но отъ окна въ Европу отвернуться трудно, тутъ фактумъ. А между тѣмъ, Азія—да вѣдь это и впрямь можетъ быть нашьисходъ в нашемъ будущемъ—опять восклицаю это! И если бъ совершилось у насъ хоть отчасти усвоеніе этой идеи—о, какой бы корень быль тогда оздоровленъ! Азія, Азіатская наша Россія,—вѣдь это тоже нашь больной корень, который не то что освѣжить. а совсѣм воскресить и пересоздать надо! Принципъ, новый принципъ на дѣло—вотъ что необходимо!

No ot okná v yEvrópu otv^{y}ernút^{y}s^{y}a trúdno, tut faktum. A, m^{y}éždu t^{y}em, Áziya—da v^{y}ed^y éto i vpr^{y}am^y možet bït^y naš isxód v nášem budúščem,—op^{y}át^y vosklit^{s}áyu éto! I yesli b sov^{y}eršílos^y u nas xot^y otčásti usvoyéniye étoi id^{y}éi—o, kakói bï kór^{y}en^y bïl togdá ozdoróvl^{y}en! Áziya, Aziátskaya náša Rossíya,—v^{y}ed^y éto tóže naš bol^{y}nói kór^{y}en^y, kotórïi n^{y}e to čto osvežít^y, a sovs^{y}ém voskresít^y i p^{y}er^{y}esozdát^y nádo! Prínt^{s}ip, nóvïi prínt^{s}ip, nóvïi vzgl^{y}ad na d^{y}élo—vot čto n^{y}eobxodímo!†

---

* Article 2 of the constitution: '*la langue de la République est le français*'. This is then given effect by the law of 4 August 1994, '*la langue de l'enseignement est le français*' (implemented in article L. 121–3 of the Code de l'Éducation).

† In our Romanisation of Russian, *y* has the value of English *y* in *yet* (often attached as a superscript to a consonant, showing that it is palatalised); *ï* represents a vowel not known in standard English: it is like the vowel i with the body of the tongue drawn back, which can be heard for instance in the Scottish pronunciation of the word *dirk*; ë, as in Cyrillic spelling, is pronounced *yo* as in 'yob'. The acute accent, ´, marks a heavy stress, and *o* when it is not stressed sounds more like *a*. In older Russian, the letter ѣ is transcribed ę, since it seems to have represented a more closed e sound, like *E* in the local pronunciation of 'Edinburgh', or *é* in French *été*.

But to turn away from the window on Europe is hard, that is a fact. But, that being said, Asia—this could really be our exodus in our future—again I exclaim it! And if we could accomplish the mastery of that idea, even in part, oh, what a root would then be revitalized! Asia, our Asiatic Russia,—this too is our sick root, which we need not just to refresh, but utterly to resurrect and reconstruct! A principle, a new principle, a new view on the affair, here is what is necessary!

Fyodor M. Dostoyevsky, Gök-Tepe: What Is Asia to Us?, 1881[43]

Russian, the last of the great European languages spread by an empire, is in many ways unlike the others.

Its domain was extended not by seaborne expeditions but overwhelmingly by military campaigns overland; hence it has come to occupy areas in a vast contiguous swath to the south and east from its homeland in the north European plain. Its bounds were expanded for the most part not by traders or missionaries, but by semi-nomadic Cossacks, explorers and military men: not out of enterprise, or a duty to win souls for Christ, but for reasons of rapine, and to buttress the global interests of its state. Russia began its conscious existence with no natural defences against the Turkic-speaking Tatars to its south, and it remained without natural defences against its Slavic-speaking cousins in Poland to the west. It was on the periphery of the cultural area with which it identified, Christian Europe; but it occupied a plain that was easily accessible to horse invaders, and also crossed by a network of navigable rivers. Ice denied it access to the open sea for most of the year. Its only natural defences lay in the severity of its winters, the sheer stickiness of its land in spring and autumn, and the vast distances that its enemies would need to cross in order to penetrate it. Conditions favoured the growth and consolidation of a single large power, with defence in depth: that power we call Russia.*

Nevertheless, there were points of similarity with the other successful empire-builders of Europe. There had been a commercial motive for the ex-

---

* The name is a Latinisation of *Rus*[y], first heard of in the ninth century. Its origins are obscure (and discussed in Franklin and Shepard 1996: 27–32). But the Finnish name for Swedes is *Ruotsi* (perhaps originally meaning 'oarsmen'); and the first recorded use of the term (as *Rhōs*, through Greek) is the Bertinian Annals' account of a visit to a Frankish court in 839, of 'certain men who said they were called Rhos, and that their king, known as *chacanus* [i.e. khagan - a Turkic title!] had despatched them ... The Emperor [Louis—he of the Strasburg Oaths; see Chapter 8] ... discovered that they were Swedes by origin.' But a contemporary source, the Arabic *Book of Routes and Kingdoms* (*c*.846), tells us: 'The Rūs are a tribe of Slavs. They bring furs of beavers and black foxes ...' (Milner-Gulland 1997: 53–5). There is also a small river called the Ros[y], which flows into the Dnieper just south of Kiev.

pansion eastward into Siberia, the drive of outdoorsmen to trap animals for their fur, just as the French, and later the British, were to do in the northern wilderness of Canada. The Russian Orthodox Church was for most of the last millennium a potent symbol of Russian identity,* which accompanied the advance of Russia's forces across south-eastern Europe and north and central Asia to the Pacific Ocean. Since its language was pointedly an antiquated form of Russia's own, this resembles above all the imperial practice of the Church of England. And just like the British and the French in the nineteenth century, the Russian government consciously planned the later stages of its global expansion. Central Asia, specifically the 'Silk Road' area of Turkestan south of the Aral Sea, was invaded in 1871–81 to protect the southern border, and as a prime source of cotton. Above all, the long-term spread of the Russian language within these vastly expanded borders was guaranteed by a flow of Russian-speaking immigrants out of the north-east into the newly Russian territories: after the 1861 abolition of the serfdom that had tied them to the land, half a million sought better fortunes eastward into Siberia in the rest of the nineteenth century.†

The origins of Russian

The eastern Slavs who founded Russia were among the descendants of the Veneti who, as we have seen (see Chapter 7, 'Einfall: Germanic and Slavic advances', p. 304), populated the shores of the Baltic in the early first millennium AD; a large number of them had not travelled southward to populate the Balkans and invade Greece (see Chapter 6, 'Intimations of decline', p. 257), but had rather settled towards the east, in uneasy rivalry with Baltic tribes to their north-west, and the Uralian tribes, among them the Finns, to the north-east. Indeed, the claim is made that the majority of the original population of Rus were of Finnish descent and hence language. The Slavs would have settled among them in the first centuries of the second millennium.

---

* The Russian for Orthodox, *pravoslavnii*, is a loan translation from the Greek. But tellingly, this word could as well be analysed to mean 'truly Slav' or indeed 'rightly glorious'.
† Barraclough (1978: 209, 230). In the early twentieth century there were substantial flows into Turkestan too, sometimes provoking large-scale departures of the locals eastward into China (Hosking 1997: 389–90). Later on, especially under Stalin, these flows were augmented by deliberate enforced deportations en masse, ostensibly for security, reminiscent of Tiglath Pileser and his successors in the Assyrian empire (see Chapter 3, 'Akkadian—world-beating technology: A model of literacy', p. 64). But the populations then deported into Kazakhstan and Siberia typically spoke languages other than Russian: 200,000 Turkic-speaking Tatars from the Crimea, 1.8 million Germans from the Volga. Some, like the Chechen-Ingush, Kabard-Balkar and Kalmyk, were later allowed to return. But there are even now 300,000 Koreans in modern Uzbekistan and Kazakhstan (Dalby 1998: 616, 223, 329; Comrie 1981: 30).

European Russia in the 13th Century

Russian principalities

Order of the Sword Brothers
(combined with Teutonic Knights 1237)

⚔ Battle

REPUBLIC OF NOVGOROD

Velikiy
Ustyug

Tallinn
to Denmark
Narva

to Rostov

Vyatka

Baltic Sea

Riga

CURONIANS

LITHUANIANS

Pskov

Novgorod
Sit river
4 March 1238

ROSTOV

Vologda

VLADIMIR
SUZDAL'

Torzhok

Yaroslavl'

Rostov

YURIEV

Nizhniy
Novgorod

Kazan'

Bulgar

TEUTONIC
KNIGHTS
PRUSSIANS

Pololsk

SMOLENSK

PEREYASLAVL' 1238

Suzdol'

Vladimir

MAZOVIA

POLOTSK

Moscow

Smolensk

Tula

Ryazan'

VOLGA
BULGARS

Minsk

CHERNIGOV

Kozelsk

MUROM
RYAZAN'

LITTLE
POLAND

TUROV-PINSK

Pinsk

NOVGOROD
SEVERSK

VOLYNIA

Kiev
Dec. 1240
taken by
Tartars

PEREYASLAVL'

Don

Volga

GALICH

KIEV

C U M A N S

HUNGARY

Kolka River
31 May 1223

to Kiev

Tunai

Serai

Astrakhan

Danube

to Kiev

Tmutorokan

ALANS

BULGARIA

Varna

Sudak

Kaffa

to Venice

Black Sea

Caspian Sea

SERBIA

LATIN
EMPIRE
(ROMANIA)

Constantinople

EMPIRE OF NICAEA

Trebizond

EMPIRE OF TREBIZOND

Tbilisi

GEORGIA

RUM
(ICONIUM)

LESSER
ARMENIA

AYYUBIDS

EMPIRE OF THE
KHWARAZM SHAH

These people spoke a language that was related to that of their German neighbours to the west, and that of their Baltic neighbours (Latvians, Lithuanians and Prussians) to the north, but noticeably softer in its tone, in that consonants were palatalised and often affricated before e and i:* as a result, the sounds š, č and ž are highly prevalent; compare the middle of the Lord's Prayer in the oldest forms of their languages: *[note * on next page]*

	Gothic (oldest Germanic)	Lithuanian (oldest Baltic)	Church Slavonic (forerunner of Russian)
Give us this day our daily bread,	*hlaif unsarana þana* *sinteinan gib uns* *himma daga,*	*Kasdienes usu duonos* *duok mums siandien*	**xlĕbŭ našĭ nas-** **toyĕštayego dĭne** **daždĭ namŭ dĭnĭ sĭ.**
And forgive us our trespasses,	*jah aflet uns þatei* *skulans sijaima,*	*ir atleisk mums musu* *kaltes,*	**i otŭpusti namŭ** **dlŭgi našĕ,**
as we forgive them that trespass against us;	*swaswe jah weis* *afletam þaim skulam* *unsaraim,*	*kaip ir mes atleid-* *ziame savo kal-* *tininkams.*	**yako i mĭ** **otŭpuštayemŭ** **dlŭžĭnikomŭ** **našimŭ**

The eastern Slavs, whose language would go on to form modern Russian, Ukrainian and Belorussian, almost close enough in form to be considered dialects, had been farmers rather than nomads, although the quest for furs was always a priority on their eastern frontier. By the end of the first millennium they were established in a vast forested area which ran from the Baltic coast near Novgorod due south to Kiev, and out to the east as far as Kazan. Although the people spoke Russian, their aristocracy was made up of Vikings (known as *varyági* or Varangians), seafarers who had invaded along the waterways from the Baltic, and who at first would have been Norse-speaking, but like so many Germanic conquerors had given up their own language. They organised the Russians on the basis of capitals ever farther south, in Novgorod, Smolensk and, in 882, in Kiev. The Dvina and Volkhov were linked by portages with the Dnieper, and so communications were established with the Black Sea, and thence the Byzantine empire. In 988 this link resulted in the conversion of Vladímir ('conquer the world') and his Kievan court to Orthodox Christianity. In the following four centuries, the religion spread to cover the full range of eastern Slavs.

To the south of the Kievan domain was grassy steppe, dominated in the second half of the first millennium by a series of largely Turkic-speaking nomadic peoples on horseback, who kept arriving from the east, conquering and settling down as the new masters: Avars, Khazars, Bulgars, Magyars, Pechenegs, Kipchak-Polovtsians, Alans, and finally Genghis Khan's Mongols. There was persistent warfare over the period, immortalised in the first

---

* Compare what happens to t and d in British English before long u: the words *tune* and *dune* are pronounced [t^{y}ūn] and [d^{y}ūn] in careful speech, but affricated to [tšūn] and [džūn] in everyday pronunciation.

surviving work of Russian literature, *Slovo o Polku Igoreve*, the Lay of Igor's Campaign, set in 1054 and apparently written in the twelfth century:

> *Uže, knyaže, tuga umĭ polonila;*
> *se bo dva sokola slętęsta sŭ otnya stola zlata*
> *poiskati grada Tĭmutorokanya,*
> *a lyubo ispiti šelomomĭ Donu.*
> *Uže sokoloma krilĭtsa pripęšali poganïxŭ sablyami,*
> *a samayu oputaša vŭ putinĭ želęznĭ…*

> O Prince, grief has now taken your mind captive;
> for two falcons have flown from their father's golden throne
> to gain the city of Tmutorokan,*
> or else to drink of the Don from their helmets.
> The falcons' wings have now been clipped by the sabres of infidels,
> and they themselves are fettered in fetters of iron…

At last the Mongols, constituted as the khanate of the Golden Horde, sacked Kiev and ended that city's hegemony of the Russians in 1240. Mongol suzerainty, entailing a heavy burden in tribute, came to be recognised all over the Russian territories, even in 1242 by Prince Alexander *Nʸevskiy* up north in Novgorod, despite his recent victories over the Swedes and the Teutonic knights. It has been reckoned that this early subjection, which lasted for almost three centuries, and was definitively ended only by the victories of Ivan IV *Groznïy* ('the Terrible'), planted a lasting pessimism in the Russian soul, establishing a deep-seated tradition of serfdom at the bottom of society, and absolutism at the top.

The new Russian polity, when it came, would be based not on Kiev but on Moscow, 800 kilometres (by Russian measure, 750 *vĕrst*) to the north-east. In 1328 the Orthodox Metropolitan moved his seat accordingly. Moscow had a good central position within Rus, and its triumph over the other city-states was partly due to the fact that it stayed unified, having the luck to produce a single male heir in each generation in the fourteenth century. The Grand Prince of Moscow, Dmitriy Donskoy, defeated the Mongols in 1380, and in 1480 Ivan III finally repudiated their suzerainty. The Moscow princes (*knyazi*) were going up in the world: about the same time, Ivan married Sophía Palaiológou, the niece of the last Byzantine emperor (deposed in

---

* A Varangian fortress on the strait between the Sea of Azov and the Black Sea: evidently the falcons were trying to beat a path far to the east of Kiev.

1453), and claimed to have inherited imperial status through a special donation of insignia from Constantinos Monómakhos (Byzantine emperor) to Vladimir Monomakh (Prince of Kiev) in the eleventh century. Moscow began to be represented as the Third Rome, and the monk Filofey of Pskov wrote to Ivan III at the end of the fifteenth century: 'Thou art the sole Emperor of all the Christians in the whole universe…For two Romes have fallen, the third stands, and there shall be no fourth.'[44]

In 1547, Ivan IV was the first ruler to be crowned not prince but T^sar^y, that is to say (in Russian pronunciation) Caesar.* He went on to prove he deserved it by conquering and incorporating both the major remnants of the Golden Horde, the Turkic khanates of Kazan (in 1552) and Astrakhan on the Caspian Sea (in 1556). The local nobility were absorbed into the Russian, and so a process of assimilation was begun. With these steps, Russians began their career of imposing themselves on other language communities, an imperial expansion of their language zone which would continue for the next three and a half centuries, and end up in the twentieth century with nominal coverage of the whole northern half of the land-mass of Asia.

Russian east then west

The greater part of this spread came about without the active initiative of the Tsar, his government or his armies. The immediate effect of the conquests of Kazan and Astrakhan was to remove the barrier to Russian penetration out towards the east; and this opportunity was soon taken up. The Stroganov family happened to hold the monopoly of fur-trading and salt-mining: they now engaged an army of Cossacks from the Don area, initially to protect against the khan of western Siberia, but then to attack the khan's capital on the lower Irtysh. The capital fell in 1582. Over the next fifty-seven years the Cossacks advanced rapidly and consistently, and in 1639 they reached the Pacific, founding the city of Okhotsk in 1648. They proceeded to move south down the coast to the Amur river, but were soon compelled by the Chinese to give up the area bordering Manchuria; the Sino-Russian border was defined, effectively for two centuries to come, at the Treaty of Nerchinsk in 1689.

Although their name is Turkic,† the Cossacks spoke Russian. They were a large but miscellaneous group of horsemen, militant Christians, disorderly

---

* The old title $knyaz^y$, 'prince', is likewise a borrowing of a Western term: it is the Russian reworking of the old Germanic title *kuningas*, literally 'man of birth', which is also the origin of English *king*.
† *Kozak* (in Crimean Tatar, Chagatay Turkic) means 'free man, wanderer, bandit'. In other Turkic languages (e.g. Kïrgïz, Azeri, Bashkir) the word *kazak, qazaq* has meanings such as 'independent man' or 'seeker of adventures'. All are derived from old the Turkic verb *kez-*, 'walk, wander, travel'.

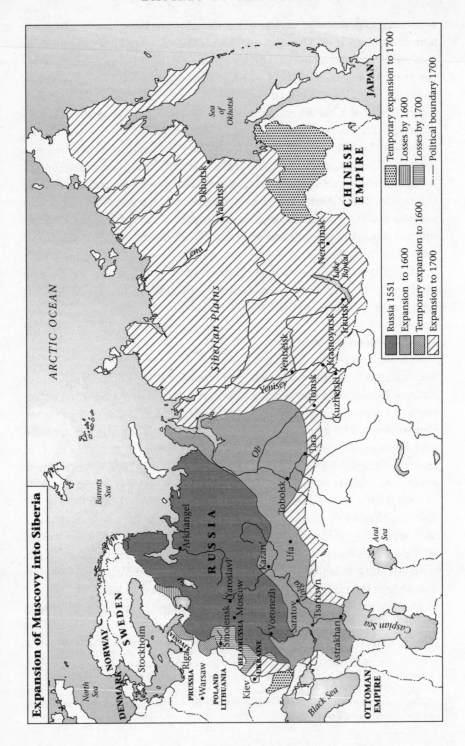

Expansion of Muscovy into Siberia

Map legend:

Temporary expansion to 1700
Losses by 1600
Losses by 1700
Political boundary 1700

Russia 1551
Expansion to 1600
Temporary expansion to 1600
Expansion to 1700

Labels on map:

JAPAN

CHINESE EMPIRE

Sea of Okhotsk

ARCTIC OCEAN

Okhotsk
Yakutsk
Lena
Siberian Plains
Nerchinsk
Lake Baykal
Irkutsk
Krasnoyarsk
Yenisejsk
Kuzhetski
Tomsk
Yenisey
Ob
Tara
Tobolsk
Ufa
Kazan
Saratov
Volga
Tsaritsyn
Astrakhan
Aral Sea
Caspian Sea
Barents Sea
Arkhangel
RUSSIA
Yaroslavl
Moscow
Smolensk
BELORUSSIA
UKRAINE
Kiev
Voronezh
LIVONIA
Riga
Warsaw
PRUSSIA
POLAND LITHUANIA
Stockholm
SWEDEN
NORWAY
DENMARK
North Sea
Black Sea
OTTOMAN EMPIRE

but proud, who had taken up nomadic ways in the long centuries of threat and domination by Turkic nomads, and were found all over the southern steppe country from Poland and Ukraine through to Kazakhstan. During their advance across Siberia, they built fortresses at the major river crossings, some of them now major cities (among them Tomsk in 1604, Krasnoyarsk in 1628, Yakutsk in 1632); but they only scantily settled the lands through which they advanced. They were followed by a dusting of soldiers, missionaries, tax-collectors (exacting the tribute, called by the Turkic name *yasak*, that was paid in fur pelts) and a very few Russian settlers, either peasants looking for land, or political exiles sent by the government; but the linguistic impact was at first thin. The Russians remained congregated along the major rivers, surrounded at first by a diversity of ancient Siberian peoples. Over the next three centuries, as extractive industries began to develop, they were joined by more settlers from the west.

This early expansion to occupy Siberia, taken together with the Russian heartland in the north European plain, accounts for most of the area that is now part of Russia. The non-Russian populations there were always too sparse, and too remote from any non-Russian source of civilisation, to organise independent states.

This was emphatically not true of Russia's other neighbours, most of whom found themselves succumbing to Russian conquest in the four centuries of Russia's expansion. They fall into four groups: the Slavic-language states to the west; the Baltic and Uralic-language states to the north-west; the Caucasian states to the south; and the central Asian states to the south-east. As it happens, at the time of writing in the early twenty-first century, most of them have regained their independence, and are seeking to rebuild links with their pre-Russian pasts; the few that have not, notably the Chechens and Ingush of the Caucasus, are seeking more or less bloodily to secede. It is a notable fact about Russia's old colonies that very few of them value highly the historic links symbolised by use of the Russian language, or indeed the potential for collaboration that Russian would give them if accepted as a lingua franca. It is worth enquiring why, alone of the European imperial languages, Russian has left this rather poisoned inheritance.

The Slavic-language states of the west include not just Ukraine (*Ukraína*, 'On the Border') and Belarus (*Byelarús*^y, 'White Rus'), but also Poland (*Pól*^y*ša*, 'Open Plains').* Early Russian expansion in this direction did not at

---

* These of course were not the only Slavic-language groups of central Europe. But the others, among them the Wends, Czechs, Slovaks, Slovenians, Serbs, Bosnians and Croats, were never available for

first expand the area of Russian speakers, since the kingdom of Lithuania had taken advantage of the destruction of Kiev in 1240 to take over most of the western Russian lands. Later, in 1385, Lithuania entered into a close alliance with Poland through a dynastic marriage, and the two countries were formally confederated in 1569, so in attempting to regain the western Russians, the new power centre in Moscow was actually facing a struggle with Poland. When Ivan the Terrible took up arms in the sixteenth century, he was significantly less successful in expanding against this Christian kingdom to his west than he had been against the Tatars to his east. Twenty-five years of Livonian wars from 1558 served only to lose Russia its foothold on the Baltic, and to destabilise its monarchy. In the *smútnoye vrémya*, the 'confused time', that followed, Poland invaded and briefly held Moscow from 1610 to 1612. Nevertheless, when order was restored in Russia under the new Romanov dynasty in 1613, the westward pressure was reasserted, and gradually Moscow's sway was increased: Smolensk, Kiev and the eastern Ukraine were gained by Tsar Aleksey in 1667; and the rest of the Ukraine and Belarus by Tsaritsa Yekaterina II (Catherine the Great) in 1772 and 1793.

At this point, most of the Russian speakers were back under a Russian government, arguably for the first time since 1240, but a rebellion by Poland against the settlement of 1793 led to war, which Russia won decisively; the result was that almost immediately, in 1795, Russia gained control of the whole east of Poland up to the Neman and Dniester rivers, a situation that prevailed until the remapping of Europe that followed the First World War in 1918. Linguistically, this control had little effect: although the Polish language is fairly closely related to Russian, it is less so than Ukrainian and Belorussian; above all, the Poles' political and religious history (as a Catholic nation) had been quite distinct, and in fact their literacy and general standard of living far exceeded those of the Russians. To start with, under Tsar Aleksandr I the country was accorded a separate constitution—but the Tsar found it hard to respect its terms; later, especially after 1863–4 (when Poland rebelled), attempts were made at 'Russification'. Among other measures, Russian was imposed as the language for official business; and not only the University of Warsaw but all Polish schools were required to operate exclusively in Russian. This proved unworkable, and Polish survived.

By contrast, about the same time, in 1863, a Ukrainian language law was introduced, far harsher, banning publication of all books in Ukrainian besides

incorporation into early modern Russia. Their languages, like Polish, were not mutually intelligible with Russian; and their peoples were firmly held within the bounds of other empires.

Expansion of Muscovy in Europe

— Boundary of Russia 1462
— Boundary of Lithuania 1462

The expansion of Muscovy

Muscovy territory end of 13th century

1451 Date of excession by Muscovy

Occupied by Muscovy 1462

Muscovy under Ivan III 1462-1505

Acquisitions during 16th century

Acquisitions during 17th century

Acquisitions during 18th century

Acquisitions 1801-15

Ceded te Sweden 1617 and Poland 1618

Recovered from Poland 1634

Recovered from Poland 1667

Pugachev uprising 1773-4

→ Route of Pugachev rebels

Orel 1564 Date of foundation of new towns

folklore, poetry and fiction, and was followed up in 1867 by a further ban on imports of such books from abroad; Ukrainian was prohibited on the stage too. This was more effective. Ukrainians were encouraged to see themselves as 'Little Russians'—conveniently for the Russians, since only if Ukrainians could be classed with them would Russians make up a majority of the population in the empire.* The Minister of the Interior wrote in 1863: 'there never has been a distinct Little Russian language, and there never will be. The dialect used by the common people is Russian contaminated by Polish influence.'[45] And in 1867 the rector of Moscow University could make the appeal: 'May one literary language alone cover all the lands from the Adriatic Sea and Prague to Arkhangelsk and the Pacific Ocean, and may every Slav nation irrespective of its religion adopt this language as a means of communication with the others.'[46]

The separate identity of Ukrainian as a language with its own culture, its own republic within the Soviet Union and indeed, as of 1990, its own state owed much to the fact that these writs did not run over the border into Galicia, a Ukrainian-speaking enclave (south of modern Lvov) that had somehow remained outside Russia, inside the Austro-Hungarian empire. It contained 20 per cent of all Ukrainians. There Ukrainian spelling and Ukrainian expressions could flourish, without hindrance, on the printed page, to remind all Ukrainians of what they might be. Stalin ended the region's independence in 1945, but to no long-term effect. Galicia went on to become the centre of the Ukrainian nationalist movement in the 1980s, the key to Ukraine's secession from the Soviet Union.[47]

Russian north then south

In the north-west, Russia also managed to gain control of the principal Baltic- and Uralic-language areas. The Uralic areas of the north-east, mainly Karelia, had been hunting grounds of the Russians at least since Moscow had conquered the northern empire of Novgorod in 1472. The people here were indigenous, and their contact with the Russians, though started a century earlier than the other Siberians', is essentially of the same type. Fundamentally they were ignored.

Estonia and Livonia came only much later, and brought with them a fair amount of European experience from the German colonists who had occupied them in the thirteenth and fourteenth centuries; they were wrested from Swedish control by the great Russian moderniser Tsar Pëtr I ('Peter the Great') in 1721 as part of his long-standing campaign to find Russia secure access to the Baltic. Farther south, Lithuania and Latvia were gained along

---

* In the census of 1897, the Ukrainians would constitute 18 per cent, the rest of the Russians 44 per cent.

with Poland in 1795; and farther north, Finland was incorporated in 1809 by Aleksandr I, on terms rather favourable to the Finns, after another successful war against Sweden.

Among these areas, the penetration of Russian immigrants, and of the Russian language, was only significant in the Baltic areas, especially Estonia and Latvia. But here, perversely, the German influence remained very strong; indeed, the traditional power structure of German-speaking *Ritterschaften*, 'knighthoods', persisted as an intermediate level of government until the revolution in 1917, so loyal were the German *Ritter* to the Tsar. But the toleration of this un-Russian hold-out did begin to wane in the late nineteenth century: Russian was introduced in administration and the courts in the 1880s, and Russian-language schools were encouraged, with an attempt to make the language compulsory at all but the introductory level. In 1893 Dorpat University, in Tartu, was converted into Yuriev, a strictly Russian-language institution. But when in 1899 the next Tsar, Nikolay II, tried similar language measures in Finland, there was a general boycott of Russian institutions, and in 1904 the Russian governor-general was assassinated. Since Russia was at war with Japan at the time, the Russians chose to play it safe, and restored the Finns' liberty to use their own language, as guaranteed in the constitution that the Russians themselves had given them.

The drive behind the Russians' takeover of the Baltic regions had been their need for access to trade. This motive also played a part in the beginnings of Russia's push south, but this could hardly be represented as naked Russian aggression, since raids into their territory from the last of the Turkic khanates, the Crimean Tatars, had been persistent since the sixteenth century. Russian strength grew in the seventeenth century, until they felt that something could be done; but it was only after a further century of attempts to put down the Tatars that in 1783 Catherine the Great at last defeated and destroyed their state. In 1792, she was then able to found Russia's principal warm-water port, Odessa on the Black Sea. This soon became a highly Russianised area, with continuing Russian immigration, and Tatar emigration, on a massive scale. Most of the Tatars went west and south into the Ottoman empire, which still surrounded most of the Black Sea coast.*

But in the spread of Russia's empire southward, this degree of Russian-language penetration was exceptional. The major reason for the extension of Russian in this direction was the rather curious one of an alliance with Georgia.

---

* Much later, in 1944, after Nazi atrocities in the region, Stalin deported the remaining 190,000 Crimean Tatars en masse to central Asia. In the 1990s about 50,000 of them returned (Dalby 1998: 616).

South of the Caucasus mountains, the two Christian peoples of Georgia and Armenia, each quite clearly marked out by their unique languages, confronted Muslim empires to their south: the Ottomans and the Persians. Catherine the Great, in the same year in which she overcame the Crimean Tatars, prevailed on King Irakli of the eastern Georgian principality of Kartalina-Kakhetia to enter into the Treaty of Georgievsk, whereby Russia would guarantee Georgia's integrity against its (Muslim) enemies, in return for control of its foreign policy. Georgia was seen as a useful buffer on the edge of the Muslim south. Catherine died in 1796, but she and her successors interpreted the treaty in an extremely one-sided way: they did not aid the Georgians against the Persian invasion in 1795, but from 1801 to 1806 they proceeded to annex first Kartalina-Kakhetia, and then all the other Georgian principalities, uniting and so strengthening them, but as a Russian province. They also made war on Persia itself, taking in the neighbouring (Turkic-speaking) territory of Azerbaijan in 1805. Armenians too for a time became enthusiastic members of the Russian empire, especially when Russia defeated both the Persians and the Ottomans, incorporating the Armenian province of Yerevan (1828) and briefly occupying the north-eastern quarter of Anatolia (1829). This guaranteed a massive influx of Armenians into all parts of the Caucasus, but especially the Nagorno-Karabagh area of Azerbaijan.

These interventions may seem to have been strategically ill advised, since the Caucasus range was one of the few natural borders that the Russian steppes possessed. Now Russia was gratuitously offering hostages to fortune beyond it. But Russian strategists, used to defending boundless plains, seem to have been happy only with a forward policy. General Rostislav Fadeyev commented in 1860: 'If Russia's horizons ended on the snowy summits of the Caucasus range, then the whole western half of the Asian continent would be outside our sphere of influence and, given the present impotence of Turkey and Persia, would not long wait for another master.'[48]

The price of these trans-Caucasian provinces was the 'sixty years of Caucasian wars', which was the title of General Fadeyev's book. What was required was nothing less than the Russian conquest of the whole mountain range, simply in order to assure their access to the Christian south. The fighting was particularly bitter for having a religious edge: almost the whole area was (and has remained) Muslim. The conquest was achieved, but only through immense brutality, and the current struggles in Chechnya show that many resentments are still unassuaged 150 years later.

Russian became the language of administration and education in all these provinces—not of course of the Church or of the mosque. But in general it did not supplant the native languages of the region, which is one of the most linguistically diverse in the world. This was as true of the mountain peoples of the north as of the hyper-educated and cultivated Georgians and Armenians of the south. In their society, the Azeris too developed a literary language of their own. The Russian government, especially in the late nineteenth century, won few friends with its sporadic attempts to make the population more Russian, for example closing Armenian parish schools and replacing them with Russian schools in 1885, but then rescinding the order. Now that Georgia, Armenia and Azerbaijan, after two centuries, have become independent nations, it can be seen that the penetration of Russian (measured by percentage of first-language speakers) remained very low: Armenia 2 per cent; Georgia 7 per cent; Azerbaijan 6 per cent.[49]

The story of Russia's expansion into Muslim central Asia can be briefly told, since by this time Russia had cast itself very much in the same mould as the other great powers of Europe, anxious to guarantee as high a degree of control as possible within their 'spheres of influence'. This vast area, which was always predominantly Muslim, seemed to have a different, more distant status than any other part of the empire: the Russians called its inhabitants *inoródt^sï*, 'aliens'. The conquest of the steppe-land of Kazakhstan,* begun under Catherine the Great in the late eighteenth century, was completed in 1848: it was thus opened up to settlers, rather on the same model as the American West that was being colonised at the same time.

In principle, linguistic (and religious) toleration was a feature of the Russians' approach to this part of the empire. Whether the Tatars accepted the Christian faith (the Bible and catechism were available in Tatar in 1803) or remained with Islam, Tatar (i.e. Chagatay Turkic) was authorised as the administrative language for the steppes. In dealing with Muslim nomads, the Russians had to keep in mind that they always had the option of decamping over the border, or, more worryingly, that they might become a fifth column for the Ottomans. In general, therefore, they endeavoured to offer them an attractive option if they accepted Russian rule. Catherine II's Holy Synod Act of 1773 established a religious directorate for Muslims in Russia, the *muftiyya*. She also decreed transit rights for Sunni Muslims who wanted to avoid Shia Iran on their pilgrimages to Mecca. And she even financed a Muslim religious school, a *madrasa*, in Bukhara. Muslims attended Russia's military academies, had their own (volunteer) regiments, and even served as

---

* The word *Kazakh* has the same Turkic etymology as Cossack; but here it refers to a real Turkic tribe of nomads, closely related to the Kyrgyz.

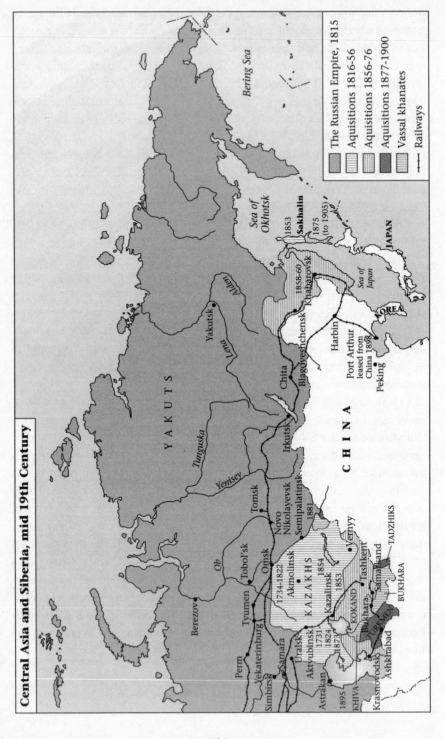

Central Asia and Siberia, mid 19th Century

The Russian Empire, 1815
Aquisitions 1816-56
Aquisitions 1856-76
Aquisitions 1877-1900
Vassal khanates
Railways

Bering Sea

Sea of Okhotsk

Sakhalin
1853
1875 (to 1905)

1858-60
Khabarovsk

Sea of Japan

JAPAN

KOREA

Harbin

Port Arthur leased from China 1898

Peking

Blagoveshchensk

Chita

Irkutsk

Yakutsk

Lena

Aldan

Y A K U T S

Tunguska

Yenisey

C H I N A

Tomsk

Ob

Novo Nikolayevsk
1881

Semipalatinsk

Tobol'sk

Omsk

Akmolinsk
1854

1734-1822

K A Z A K H S

Kazalinsk
1853

Vernyy

Tashkent

Samarkand

TADZHIKS

KOKAND

Bukhara

TURKMEN

BUKHARA

Berezov

Tyumen

Yekaterinburg

Perm

Simbirsk

Samara

Uralsk
1731
1824
1873

Aktyubinsk

Astrakan

KHIVA
1895

Krasnovodsk

Ashkhabad

officers in ordinary Russian regiments—something very different from the contemporary practice of the British or French empires.[50]

But for all this, the steppes did become effectively Russified. It was the incidence of European settlers which really changed the linguistic picture: 20 per cent in 1887, 40 per cent in 1911, 47 per cent in 1939.[51] Khrushchev's 'Virgin Lands' Policy of the 1950s added a further 1.5 million. (The number of native Russian speakers in Kazakhstan according to the 2000 *Ethnologue* is now 6.23 million, 38 per cent.)[52]

In 1854, Russia was defeated in the Crimea by its imperial peers, Britain, France and the Ottomans. Perhaps seeking some consolation, Russia immediately proceeded to the conquest of central Asia, due south of the Kazakh steppes. Colonial wars against natives without modern weapons were far easier to win, and somehow heartening for Europeans, as the opening quote from Dosteyevsky shows us.

The principal remaining powers in this area were the emirates of Khiva, Bukhara and Kokand. Despite the technical advantages of the incomers over the residents, the war took twenty-two years, and ended in 1876. Kokand, in the east, was annexed, but the other two emirates, Bukhara, which had contained the legendary Samarkand, and Khiva on the Caspian shore, were largely left as dependent powers. 'Turkestan' was created as a provincial envelope to hold these new acquisitions. Russia's main concern came to be the development of intensive cotton cultivation in the Ferghana valley, and this attracted large numbers of settlers into the area, which is part of modern Uzbekistan. Nevertheless, settlement in these areas never reached levels comparable to those of the steppes to the north: the four corresponding modern states are (from west to east) Turkmenistan, Uzbekistan, Tajikistan and Kyrgyzstan, and their population of 39 million embraces only 9 per cent native Russian speakers.[53]

The status of Russian

This completes our brief review of how Russian was spread by the Tsar's empire. It remains to consider why it never became a prestige language: why, unlike all the other imperial European languages that established themselves far from Europe, it did not come to symbolise the conquered peoples' aspirations to take part in a Westernised, globalised future. All the nineteenth-century European empires are now dissolved: but their languages are still used worldwide. Why is Russian, alone of the current top ten languages, set to lose speakers in the twenty-first century?

Four major institutions of the Russian empire had been crucial to the spread of Russian beyond its homeland in north-eastern Europe. They were the Orthodox Church, the army, the state bureaucracy and the educated elite—usually known in Russian as the *intelligentsi^ya*. All these still exist in some form, but none of them, in the early twenty-first century, seem likely to remain lively, either as dominant forces or as sources of inspiration worldwide.

The Church had early attached itself to its local language, now usually known as Old Church Slavonic, but always felt to be Russian in an appropriately reverent version. Even in the midst of major liturgical reforms, an advocate of the old ways could write to the Tsar: 'Say in good Russian "Lord have mercy on me". Leave all those *Kyrie Eleisons* to the Greeks: that's their language, spit on them! You are Russian, Alexey, not Greek. Speak your mother tongue and be not ashamed of it, either in church or at home!'[54] Its distinctive domes rising among the huts provided the most recognisable signs of Russia as its domain spread out across Siberia; as long as there were Tsars, it legitimated them. Church schools were the main source of Russian literacy well into the eighteenth century. But it never recovered from the 'Holy Synod' reforms of Peter the Great in 1721, when he made himself supreme protector of the Church, abolishing its internal democracy from the parishes up, and so effectively making it into an arm of the state. Thereby both Tsar and Church, although mutually supportive, became quite cut off from the grass roots of Russian society. They became increasingly unable to take the risks of any popular involvement. A telling example came in the linguistic sphere when, in the aftermath of Napoleon's 1812 invasion, the reforming Tsar Alexander I favoured the establishment of an Imperial Russian Bible Society, as a branch of the British and Foreign Bible Society: a multilingual publishing initiative was planned, but the project came unstuck on the proposal to distribute the Bible in *prostóye naryéčiye*, 'simple diction', i.e. plain Russian. The evangelicals were cast as agents of 'the Invisible Napoleon', undermining the respect due to the word of God, and in 1821 the Russian Bibles were burnt on the orders of the Holy Synod.*

Another institution which by its nature spread the use of Russian far and wide was the army. This was distinctive among its imperial competitors for its ethnic and linguistic unity. For the Military Commission of 1762–3, 'the strength of the Army consists in, most basic of all, the existence of common language, religion, customs and blood'; a century later, Russian military commentators on the wars of 1859 and 1866 stressed the pure Russianness of their

---

* The Bible was actually available in Kalmyk and Tatar (not to mention Finnish, Estonian, Latvian, Lithuanian, Polish, Armenian and Georgian) half a century before it came out in Russian. Publication of the Russian Bible could not be authorised until 1876, by chance just after the first Russian edition of Karl Marx's *Das Kapital* (Hosking 1997: 138–42, 233–4).

army in contrast with the Austrians' ragbag of races and languages: at the time, 90 per cent of the soldiers were from the homeland area of Russia, Belarus and the Ukraine, and most Muslims were exempt from military service.[55] In a way, though, the ethnic purity of the force diminished the effect of its single language: if more non-Russians had been obliged to join up, more of them would have had to learn Russian. In fact, though, there was little scope for Russian veterans, having served for twenty-five years or more, to return to civil life after their service. They would typically end up in towns, as coachmen, domestic servants or schoolteachers.[56] In this way, they were less able to seed the spread of their language than, say, the retired soldiers of ancient Rome.

The bureaucracy, the visible arm of the Tsar's government, was of course everywhere. But its influence in terms of spreading Russian discourse was less than might have been expected. Its higher levels were disproportionately (up to 20 per cent in the eighteenth and nineteenth centuries) full of German speakers from the Baltic, ever since Peter the Great had recognised their special potential to carry through his reforms.[57] And the minimal scope of its functions, mainly the gathering of poll tax and the recruitment of troops, must have limited its role and interaction in society.

Finally, there was the intelligentsia. In a sense, it was this group almost alone which put Russian on the global cultural map, with the literary efflorescence that they achieved in the eighteenth and nineteenth centuries. Peter the Great sparked it off, with his reforms aimed at creating a secular Russia, inspired by what he had encountered in his visits to Britain and above all Germany. Mikhail Lomonósov (1711–75), the greatest scholar of this era—who had somehow managed to promote himself out of an Archangel fisherman's family—combined expertise in chemistry and linguistics, and started the task of defining a Russian literary language, one that would incorporate foreign borrowings and colloquial speech into the rather ponderous style inherited from Church Slavonic. A Russian Academy, modelled on the Académie Française, was established in 1783; it compiled a major dictionary in 1789–94, and defined a Russian grammar that was published in 1802. Although, as we have seen in considering the history of French, foreign influence remained strong in the Russian elite's social life, the newly educated generations of Russian authors rose to the challenge of their new language, and included Pushkin, Gogol, Tolstoy, Dostoyevsky and Turgenev, to name only the most famous. They took seriously the task of defining what Russian literature could do for Russia and the world. Most famously, Turgenev and Dostoyevsky both projected their ideas back to Pushkin at the celebrations in his memory in 1880: Turgenev said that Pushkin spoke to the educated nát^{s}iya, the nation that had come about through Peter's reforms, but that the Russian *naród*, the people, would come to awareness through learning to read him; Dostoyevsky countered that Pushkin was intrinsically—and uniquely— universal in his appeal, something that gave Russia an immense advantage: 'To become a genuine Russian means to attempt to bring reconciliation to the contradictions of Europe and to offer relief for Europe's anguish in the all-human and all-embracing Russian soul.'[58]

Amazingly, Russian writers did succeed in reaching an audience all over Europe, though inevitably more among Turgenev's *nát*ⁱ*ii* than Dostoyevsky's *naródï*. But the realisation of their cosmic aspirations at home was limited by the very narrow base of the intelligentsia within Russia itself, almost cut off from the vast majority of their public. General literacy of the Russian population was still not above 10 per cent in the early 1880s, although it rose rapidly thereafter, approaching 30 per cent among the under-fifties by the end of the century.[59] And of course, those who could read did not all have a taste for the highest, preferring adventure stories, romances and horoscopes.[60]

But the Russian intelligentsia made no attempt at all to make a place within their ideals for the Asian multitudes that their armed forces had exerted themselves so long, and so bloodily, to bring within the Tsar's domains. From Ivan the Terrible's conquest of Kazan to the conquests of the early nineteenth century, foreign nobility had always been recognised, and accorded property rights within the Russian system, when their own territories had been subdued; no effort had ever been made actively to involve them culturally. Occasionally, intellectuals from their own traditions who managed to get a Western education would try to devise an accommodation. The best example of this is the Crimean Tatar educationist Ismail Bey Gaspirali (who adopted the name Gasprinsky). Educated first in a village *madrasa* (Islamic religious school), he went to St Petersburg to learn Russian, and Paris to learn French. Next spending four years in Istanbul (1871–5), he returned to Crimea with the conviction that Russia's Muslims must approach modernity through Russian, writing his first important book, *Russkoye Musulmanstvo* ('Russian Islam'), and long editing a journal, *Tercüman-Perevodčik* ('Interpreter' in Tatar and Russian). Gaspirali's peaceable views were not easily accepted in the Crimean Tatar community, but by 1905 his group had succeeded in founding over 350 schools, bilingual in Russian and Tatar. More revealing was the reaction from the Russians: rather than encourage this bridge-building from a potential ally, the authorities refused to allow Gaspirali to convene an all-Muslim congress; rather they worked to diminish the political participation of non-Russians (as well as workers and peasants), proposing an electoral law for the second Duma ('Parliament') in 1907 with the preamble: 'The State Duma, created to strengthen the Russian state, must be Russian also in spirit.' Gaspirali made no more progress.[61]

What Russia always lacked, above all, was a bourgeoisie, a class of merchants and professionals of independent status and means, which could serve as a link, both for social mobility and for flow of income, between the governing class and the workers on the land. Large-scale trade and industrial development was rarely undertaken by Russians in the pre-revolutionary era; and the small educated classes never built up significant guilds or professional associations. Russia remained a polity dominated by the arbitrary, and in principle unlimited, powers of the Tsar; and the linguistic effects of this were that the Russian language nowhere developed a strong base in a community with aspirations and influence.

In short, at least until the twentieth century, Russia, although unified politically and militarily by the Tsar's government, was not unified, nor even growing together, as a language community. In the Baltic provinces to the north-east, and the Muslim lands to the south, Russian was simply not penetrating beyond the ranks of settlers, and the small number of administrators.

The Soviet experiment

This account of the spread of Russian has concentrated on the Tsar's empire, because the Russian revolution of 1917, and the Soviet era that came after it, had little net effect on the language situation. Despite early expectations, and attempts at secession in all the non-Russian areas (including Belarus and the Ukraine), the new government proved able to reassert its control almost everywhere. Finland, by dint of arms, did manage to detach itself permanently; but the other Baltic states, which had a brief period of independence in the 1920s and 1930s, found themselves back under Russian control from 1940. Other parts of the empire were all back in the fold by 1922.

One thing that did change under the Soviets was language policy. Whereas, as we saw, the policy of the Tsars, even in their last decade, was 'to strengthen the Russian State, and keep it Russian in spirit', the Soviets' official policy for the Union was almost the polar opposite. In principle, all the peoples of the Union were to be equal; there would be no official language. Furthermore, everyone had rights, not only to the use of their own languages for all purposes, but also to education in them. Russian evidently remained the only choice for communication among different parts of the Union; one thing that did *not* change after the revolution was the centralised control of the country as a whole.

An immediate practical policy was to build mass literacy. This process had begun under the tsars, but the continuation was triumphantly successful, as the censuses showed. In 1897, 28.4 per cent of those aged between nine and forty-nine had been able to read; in 1920, the figure went up to 44.1 per cent; by 1926 it was already 56.6 per cent; in 1939, 87.4 per cent; in 1959, 98.5 per cent; and in 1970, 99.7 per cent.[62] Since this included literacy in languages other than Russian (even in 1970, only 77.5 per cent claimed to have Russian as a first or second language[63]), a necessary precondition of this was provision of effective writing systems for the country's languages. Russian orthography was simplified in 1918 to be more phonetic, mostly by replacing the letters i, ѳ and ѣ, which did not have a distinct pronunciation. (They can still be seen in the passage of Dostoyevsky that begins this section.) Other languages of the Union that had no writing tradition were given alphabets. In the 1920s, these were based mostly on Latin letters, since this alphabet had been most thoroughly developed by phoneticians. The systems often involved considerable skill by Soviet linguists in fixing a standard form among dialects, balancing considerations of majority usage with mutual intelligibility and ease of acquisition. By and large stability was achieved, creating dozens of new 'literary languages' (*lit^yeraturnïye yazïki*). Then the nature of the political power situation began to make itself felt.

The Soviet Union had remained, like imperial Russia before it, steadfastly governed from the centre, since 1918 more specifically from Moscow. The de facto dominance of Russians, therefore—admittedly leavened by much greater social and political mobility—began to take precedence over the theoretical equality of all, especially when it became clear in the 1930s that the Soviet Union was alone in having set up a stable Marxist-oriented regime, now surrounded on all sides by enemies. Now the primacy of Russian began to seem more important, even comforting; and in the 1930s, by choice or force, all the different nationalities (except for the Baltics, Georgian, Armenian and Yiddish) came to declare in favour of switching their orthographies to some variant of the Cyrillic alphabet used for Russian. The strange fact that the boundaries of the socialist world were coincident with those of the old Russian empire was now suffused in quite a different light. As a later apologist put it:

Because [Russian] is the language of the Union's most developed nation, which has guided the country through its revolutionary transformations and has won itself the love and respect of all other peoples, the Russian language is naturally being transformed into the language of communication and cooperation of all the peoples of the socialist state. This has been produced by ... a replacement of previous psychological barriers by bonds of brotherly friendship, mutual trust and mutual help.[64]

Russian was now in a position to make major strides. Universal education was a reality, and Russian was introduced as a compulsory subject in all schools. Far more than under the tsars, it should have been possible for it to become known and used by everyone throughout the country. Somehow, though, this did not happen. As we have already noted, in 1970 there were still 22.5 per cent who claimed not to have effective command of it. Whether through the survival of traditional communities—especially in central Asia—or the preservation of resentment at Russian dominance—especially in the Baltic—many continued to contrive to live their lives without Russian.

When the Soviet Union was dissolved on 1 January 1992, all its constituent republics, including Ukraine and Belarus, split off as independent states. The prospects for Russian in education, and hence as a long-term lingua franca among the old parts of the empire, were immediately diminished.

But although the use of Russian can no longer be enforced across the extent of the old Union, it has inevitably become an important political token, with different nuances dependent on local history. Among the Baltic states, Latvia and Estonia are setting linguistic exams to force their resident Russians to prove competence in their own languages; these are unnecessary in Lithuania, where the Russian-speaking minority is so much smaller.* The Belarusian government is maintaining Russian as its working language, after a radical shift in policy in 1995, and demeaning its own national language.† Republics with large Russian-speaking minorities inhabiting a single region, notably Moldova and Kazakhstan, have to be highly judicious in balancing the degree to which they can assert their majority language. In Kazakhstan Russian is recognised as a language of official communication, and it remains a standing joke how poor politicians' command of Kazakh tends to be. In central Asia, by contrast, there has been a discernible resurgence of national language use—and decline of Russian—among the political classes who were actually among the most prolific Russian speakers before independence.[65] Here, as in the Baltics, English is growing in use as a second language.§ Only in Siberia, Rus's oldest colony, can it be said that use

* In 1994, there were 436,600 Russians in Estonia, comprising 29.0 per cent of the total population; in Latvia, there were 849,000, 33.1 per cent. Meanwhile, in Lithuania, the Russian population stood at 316,000, just 8.5 per cent (*Europa World Yearbook*, 1995).
† A May 1995 referendum granted Russian the status of an official language, along with Belarusian. Russian is the language of instruction in virtually all university departments in Belarus. And whereas in 1994 220 schools in Minsk, the capital city, had taught in Belarusian, two years later under twenty did so.
§ At high cost, but with dubious symbolism, Turkmenistan, Uzbekistan and Azerbaijan, speaking Turkic languages, all converted their alphabets back from Cyrillic to Latin in the decade after independence. But each system is a little different, and none has adopted Turkey's own spelling conventions of 1928.

of Russian is secure, and probably still gaining speakers. Sadly, this is because most of Siberia's indigenous language communities are highly endangered, their traditional way of life shattered by the presence among them of
large numbers of European Russians. They are too small, too isolated, and
too weakened, to be able to envisage any future but collaboration with Russians.

Everywhere, use of Russian is more significant as a sign of feelings about
the Soviet past, and of aspirations for the future, than as a practical choice of
means of communication with the neighbours. Russian, even after the fall of
communism, remains a highly ideological language.

Conclusions

There are four main reasons why an imperial language lives on after the dissolution of the empire that spread it.

The first is because it remains the language of the people who dissolve the
empire. This can be called the *creole* reason. It was true of all the American
colonies that fought and obtained independence from their mother countries
in Europe: in every case, in the Thirteen Colonies of Great Britain, in Mexico,
in the republics of Central and South America, and the kingdom of Brazil, the
people who made the revolutions were not the indigenous people but the descendants of the European colonists, who were as attached to the metropolitan language as the mother country herself. Likewise it maintained Afrikaans
in South Africa, and French in Canada and Algeria. In some sense, the settlers' language communities have continued unbroken.

The second reason is because the newly independent countries want to retain a link, of trade or culture, perhaps even of defence, with the metropolitan
power. This can be called the *nostalgia* reason. It is part of the reason why
French has hung on in sub-Saharan Africa. It is also why there is still a trace
of Spanish in the Philippines, and also why East Timor, independent in 2002,
opted to continue—or rather resurrect—its use of Portuguese.

The second reason is often found in alliance with a third, which can be
called the *unity* reason. A colonial power inevitably imposes a single language on a domain, which ends up being essential to maintaining it as a coherent unit. When the power changes, the language may change too (as for
example it did when Spanish replaced both Nahuatl and Quechua in different
dominions of the Spanish empire). But quite likely it does not, especially
where there is no new conqueror but simply the culmination of a struggle for
independence. In that case, the colonial language may linger on: this is an-

other reason for the persistence of French in so many countries of sub-Saharan Africa: it just would not be practicable to administer Cameroon in any one of its 270-plus indigenous languages. And this is, perversely, why Malay was taken up as the unifying 'Bahasa Indonesia'—by the Dutch just as much as the Indonesian government that followed them.

There is a fourth reason, the *globality* reason. A country may persist with an imperial language, not because it gives a link to the old colonial power, but because it provides a means to transcend it. This is very widely true of countries that maintain or adopt English in the current era; but it is just as truly the motive for the Russian elite's adoption of French in the eighteenth and nineteenth centuries.

The apparent failure of the Russian language to survive strongly where its speakers' empire is no more can be viewed more clearly in the light of these four reasons.

The creole reason applies only in Siberia, since by and large it is only here that the Russian imperialists settled in large enough numbers to overwhelm the indigenous people. They are approaching this sort of concentration in Estonia and Latvia, and less so in Kazakhstan: but the power there—and hence the linguistic future—has ultimately remained with the previous inhabitants.

The need to retain nostalgic links with the Russians is not widespread in the old Soviet realms; sadly, their old subjects seem to remember little with affection from the long centuries of Russian power. But there is one exception: Belarus, whose government is actively seeking betterment through closer links with Russia, and whose enthusiasm for Russian is correspondingly strong.

By and large, the different republics can achieve substantial unity, each on its own territory, through use of its own language; there is no unity reason to persist with Russian, except in Russia itself, whose Siberian territories are by far the most multilingual in the old empire. And as we have seen, the tiny language communities there are too weak to put up substantial resistance to the unifying grip of organisation in Russian.

Finally, as to globality: sadly too for Russian, in the current age of world communications, it is very evident that the most profitable links are not to be had with the doyens of Russian culture; other lands appear to be freer, more stylish, more powerful and, above all, richer.

Ironically, though, it may be on just this ground that Russian may one day stage a comeback. As the nineteenth century showed, the Russian intelligentsia is capable of remarkable flights of human imagination; and as the twentieth century showed, their scientists, when given respectable financial support—even under tight, and blinkered, state control—are the equal of any in the world. Given a stable and more liberal government than it has hitherto known, Russian culture may yet grow into a form that will make Russia's former colonies glad to cultivate it, and its language.

Our quick review of the linguistic careers of most of the European imperial powers has revealed a bewildering variety of ways in which empire can be won, exercised and lost, with and without long-term transmission of the imperialist's language. The serious spread of Spain's language began some two centuries after it established its empire. The Portuguese language seemed to spread round the Indian Ocean almost independently of its speakers' progress; and ultimately, it grew strongest in Brazil, where the Portuguese had least scope for their great talent, commerce. The Dutch language, by contrast, hardly spread at all, though the Dutch themselves were far more effective, and more permanent, than the Portuguese as imperialists. French overseas conquests tended to vanish almost as quickly as they were built up; but sometimes French survived there, even under new overlords, and there was a pronounced tendency for those once exposed to the French language to want to keep in touch with it after they had expelled the conquerors. In another contrast, over five hundred years Russian spread itself in every direction from its central plain of north-east Europe, essentially until it encountered any power strong enough to resist it. Until 1992, its spread seemed irreversible. And yet, in the last decade, it has shown how few friends it made in all those centuries of stable advance.

But there is one simplistic prejudice that does seem to hold up: any foreign empire does tend to spread some language. It may not be a local language, not that of the dominant power, as Malay came to dominate the Dutch Indies; and it may not persist long after the departure of foreign control, as Russian is slipping away from Russia's ex-colonies. But a common language is a practical necessity in a territory brought under common, external, control, and this necessity tends to foster language spread if the domination persists over time, with recruitment of local people to represent, and interface with, the foreign power in later generations.

In this sense, Nebrija was right.

Curiously ineffective—German ambitions

Mit der Dummheit kämpfen Götter selbst vergebens.

With stupidity the gods themselves fight in vain

Friedrich von Schiller, Die Jungfrau von Orleans, 1801, iii.6

One major European language has been largely neglected in our pages, despite its major cultural status, and the sterling attempts to spread it round the world in the nineteenth century. This is German, none other than the language of Martin Luther, which led off the Reformation through a revolution in the printed word. (See Chapter 9, p. 326.) There is something almost accident-prone about German as a potential global language, many times disappointed.

In the opening years of the fifth century (see Chapter 7, 'Einfall: Germanic and Slavic advances', p. 304) its speakers overran the whole western Roman empire, from Britain to North Africa, permanently installing their leaders as hereditary monarchs in every country they took. Yet the only linguistic gain made was in England. Otherwise German remained largely restricted to its original territory in northern Europe, and in this early period even lost ground to Slavonic in the eastern parts down into the Balkans. (See Chapter 7, 'Slavonic dawn in the Balkans', p. 309.)* But in the tenth, and again in the twelfth and thirteenth centuries, there were large migrations of Germans eastward across the Elbe up to and beyond the modern Polish border on the Oder, turning them into predominantly German-speaking regions, and submerging and isolating many Slavic-speaking groups.

Meanwhile, farther north, something much more structured and warlike was afoot. In 1226, the Teutonic knights, called in to fight the heathen, were gifted East Prussia by the Holy Roman Emperor, Friedrich II. They made good their ownership with the sword and the plough, and were only stopped from pressing on into Russia by the famed Aleksandr N^{y}evskiy in 1242.† From 1280 to 1410, their followers founded 1400 villages and ninety-three towns along the Baltic shores,[66] and the German language was established from Prussia to Estonia. The German landowners succeeded in retaining their elite status for five centuries, through vicissitudes of Swedish and Russian overlordship, until the turmoil of 1917.

Meanwhile great events had shaken the German fatherland. It had sat out the Middle Ages under the alias of the 'Holy Roman Empire'—in combination often with much of Italy, though without any loss of its German language—but when the Reformation came and the old structures disinte-

---

* Another Germanic language, Norse, was also being taken far afield by its speakers in the latter centuries of this millennium: the Normans took it to Normandy, the Varangians to Rus, the Vikings to England, Scotland, Ireland and Iceland. In every case but one, they gave up their own language for that of the people with whom they settled: the only exception was in Iceland, where the Norse settlers found that they were the first human beings to arrive.

† The decisive battle on a frozen Lake Peipus, in Livonia, was memorably conceived on film by Sergei Eisenstein.

grated, Germany found itself vulnerable. In the seventeenth century the country was widely devastated by the Thirty Years War (1618–48), pitting Catholics against Protestants. But thereafter, although political stability and military security continued to elude them, German speakers were rewarded for their innovative seriousness—and later their Romanticism—with a golden age in science, the arts and all kinds of scholarship; and the German language and literature achieved world prominence, for the first time equalling French in international respect. The eighteenth century was the era of Lessing, Goethe and Schiller, Mozart and Beethoven, Herder and the brothers Humboldt, Kant and Hegel, ensuring that many of the key ideas of the Enlightenment (known to Germans as *die Aufklärung*) were first expressed in German.

Since the breakdown of the Holy Roman Empire, German speakers in the south had remained relatively united in the kingdom of Austria (*Österreich*—'the easterly kingdom'), ruled by the Habsburg dynasty. But in the nineteenth century, most of the Germans' territories to the north of this were forcibly united under the strong, avowedly militarist leadership of Prussia, billing its creation as a renewed *deutsches Reich*, 'German Empire'. As a nineteenth-century European power, this new Germany naturally felt that it needed colonies abroad: in short order, it took possession of four territories in Africa—Togoland, Cameroon, Southwest Africa (Namibia) and East Africa (Tanganyika)—in the 1880s, and north-east Papua and most of the Micronesian islands in the Pacific in the 1890s. All these new subjects of the Kaiser were just beginning to receive instruction in the German language when Germany emerged defeated from the First World War; at Versailles in 1919, the German language lost all its overseas territories, their administrations being switched to French, English and (in Micronesia) Japanese.

The expansive German spirit made a dramatic and desperate last throw in 1939, briefly imposing a new and greater *Reich* over most of the northern and central reaches of continental Europe from the Atlantic to the Urals; but the six years of *totalen Krieg*, 'total war', which made up the full period for which it was able to maintain its grip, were too short to show whether any linguistic gains for German were in train. Germany's style of conquest of its European neighbours was certainly not adapted to win friends or admirers; but there would probably have been post-war settlements of Germans to the east, aimed at sweeping aside speakers of Slavonic languages, and perhaps German-based creoles may have grown up among mixed populations in a vast network of forced labour camps. As it was, the politicians' demented push for military glory ended up almost erasing the language influence that German had achieved in the eighteenth and nineteenth centuries. In the 1930s, serious scientists, artists and intellectuals in every field, especially German-speaking Jews, left in droves for exile abroad—especially to the USA, where they became English speakers; and in the post-war era, the still-fresh Nazi associations of German discouraged much use of it outside its home countries.

Hitler's painfully direct *Drang nach Weltherrschaft*, 'drive for world domination', was mercifully soon defeated; but culturally, it had already proved self-defeating. It will be interesting to see whether the German language can begin to enhance its prestige in the changed conditions of the twenty-first century, with Germany and Austria now playing leading roles as well-established democracies, at the centre of a Europe which is, nominally at least, seeking 'ever closer union'.

Imperial epilogue: Kōminka

Kōminka: 公民化 The imperialization of subject peoples...Without this sense of profound gratitude for the limitless benevolence of the Emperor, provisional subjects cannot grasp the true meaning of what it is to be Japanese...While *Kōminka* as a concept may seem abstract and difficult to grasp, its fundamental principles are the same as those of the Imperial Rescript on Education; to understand one is to understand the other.

Washisu Atsuya, *Recollections of Government in Taiwan*, Taipei, 1943, p. 339

爾臣民　父母ニ孝ニ　兄弟ニ友ニ	*nanji shinmin, fubo ni kō ni, kētē ni yū ni;*
夫婦相和シ　朋友相信シ	*fūfu aiwashi, hōyū aishinji;*
恭儉己レヲ持シ　博愛衆ニ及ホシ	*kyō ken onore wo jishi; hakuai shū ni oyoboshi;*
學ヲ修メ業ヲ習イ以テ知能ヲ啓發シ	*gaku wo osame kyō wo narai, motte chinō wo kēhatsu shi*
徳器ヲ成就シ進テ公益ヲ廣メ	*tokki wo jōjushi; susunde kōeki wo hirome;*
世務ヲ開キ常ニ國憲ヲ重シ國法ニ尊ヒ	*sēmu wo hiraki tsune ni kokken wo omonji kokuhō ni shitagai;*
一旦緩急アレハ　義勇公ニ奉シ	*ittan kankyū areba, giyūkō ni hōji;*
以テ　天壤無窮ノ皇運ヲ　扶翼スヘシ	*motte tenjō mukyū no kōun wo fuyoku subeshi*

Ye subjects, be filial to your parents, affectionate to your brothers and sisters;
as husbands and wives be harmonious, as friends true;
bear yourselves in modesty and moderation; extend your benevolence to all;

pursue learning and cultivate arts, and thereby develop intellectual faculties
and perfect moral powers; voluntarily promote common interests;
embarking on public affairs always respect the Constitution and observe the
    laws;
in case emergency arises, serve courageously;
and thus aid the prosperity of the Imperial Throne eternal as heaven and earth.

From the *Kyōiku ni kansuru Chokugo*
(Imperial Rescript on Education) of 30 October 1890,
displayed in all Japanese schools, beside the portrait of the emperor

We have to establish a new, European-style empire on the edge of Asia.

Inoue Kaoru, Japanese foreign minister, 1887[67]

Japan is evidently no European power. But the motive with which it won for itself an overseas empire was of European inspiration. And viewed as a sequel to European empire-building, the brief story of this venture displays much of the causation, the methods and ultimate vanity of this type of language spread.

Japan had been a strictly isolationist state until visited in 1853 by the American Commodore Perry's 'Black Ships'; by 1858, it had been forced to conclude trade treaties with the major European powers. The traditional rule of the Tokugawa shogun was then unsettled in a number of violent incidents, which impressed some Japanese with the military power of the foreigners, especially the British navy. In 1868, shouting such slogans as 尊王攘夷 *son nō jō i*, 'honour emperor; expel barbarians', and 富國強兵 *fu koku kyō hei*, 'rich country; strong army',* these radicals overthrew the feudally based government that had lasted for the previous two and a half centuries, and established a new, radically Westernising, regime under the nominal supervision of the young Emperor Meiji, who had conveniently come to the throne in 1867. Expeditions were dispatched to Europe and the USA to find out how they were organised. By 1889 Japan had adopted a new constitution, with two houses of parliament (one hereditary and another elected by wealthy householders), centrally appointed prefectural governors, an army general staff directly responsible to the emperor (and hence immune from civilian control), and a national civil service, police force, banking and educational system. Within a single generation, Japan had put itself on a par with the leading Western powers, and proceeded to demonstrate its independence.

---

* These are not so much Japanese as strings of Chinese characters in Japanese pronunciation. This did not inhibit their effectiveness.

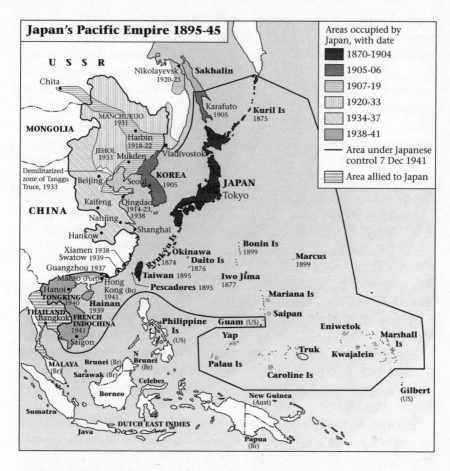

The main strategic motive for Japan's colonial wars was Korea. Japan was taking lessons in geopolitics from the West; and Major Meckel, the German adviser to the Imperial Army, had characterised Korea as 'a dagger thrust at the heart of Japan', thinking of its value to a hostile power. Dispossessed samurai, the ancient class of knights who were the main losers in Japan's modernisation, had almost drummed up an outright invasion of the country early in the 1870s. But in 1894 China was invited into Korea to help subdue a rebellion, and Japan—citing a treaty right to ensure Korea's neutrality—came too. The Japanese started throwing their weight about, kidnapping the Korean king and queen to make their point; and Chinese resistance proved not only futile but costly. In the settlement of the war in 1895, China was forced to cede the islands of Taiwan and the Pescadores to Japan: these became Japan's first colony.

Japan went on investing in Korea, and put increasing pressure on its government to provide for modernisation. In 1902 Japan struck an alliance with Great Britain, which was to last for twenty years. This emboldened it to resist Russian moves towards Korea, and start the Russo-Japanese War of 1904–5. Like China, Russia found that it had seriously underestimated Japan's military strength. The land battles (mostly in Manchuria) were bloody but inconclusive, but then Russia lost not just its Pacific, but also its Baltic, fleet. In the ensuing peace, Japan gained the Liaodong peninsula of Manchuria, with its two excellent harbours, Port Arthur and Dalian, and the southern half of Sakhalin island, called in Japanese *Karafuto*. Meanwhile the continuing Japanese pressure on Korea was now without competition from Russia or China: Korea buckled, becoming first a protectorate, and then, in 1910, a colony.

Japan's aggrandisement did not stop there. It joined the Allies in the First World War, and speedily grabbed the German possessions closest to it, the city of Qingdao in north-east China, and the islands of Micronesia. At Versailles in 1919—when French first yielded diplomatically to English—Japan was compelled to quit Qingdao, but its control of the islands, henceforth called *Nan'yō Guntō*, 'South Ocean Islands', was confirmed.

As a result of all this, during the inter-war years of the twentieth century Japan held a substantial overseas empire round the north-west Pacific: Taiwan, southern Manchuria, southern Sakhalin, all of Korea and the islands of Micronesia. Here it had between twenty-five and fifty years, one or two full generations, to impose itself and its language; and we shall now take a brief look at the results.*

The motives that had expanded the Japanese empire had some impact on the use of Japanese in the resulting territories. In these Pacific lands, the Japanese had not come to trade, nor for industrial exploitation. As a result, Japan sent few civilian settlers or residents: the newcomers were overwhelmingly soldiers and administrators. There would be relatively little interaction for daily business; most communication took the form of locals having to comply with Japanese instructions.

In the new colonies, the Japanese attitude to life was far from laissez-faire. Both Taiwan and Korea had in their different ways long been parts of China's

---

* Of course, Japanese imperialism was an extremely restless force, and did not stop here: for brief periods Japan also held parts of eastern Siberia as far as Irkutsk (1918–22), northern Sakhalin and the Lower Amur (1920–5), Manchuria (1931–45), north-eastern China (1934–45) and then, during the Second World War, the whole of South-East Asia, the East Indies, New Guinea, the Philippines and Burma (for various periods in 1941–5). But all these conquests were disputed, and so held on a temporary, military, basis. It was only in the older 'formal empire' that the Japanese had something of a chance to put down linguistic roots.

sphere of influence, and had their own systems of education in place; but the Japanese policy was gradually to undermine the locally run schools that had survived from the previous era, and to replace them—at local cost—with Japanese-language institutions. In Micronesia, where literacy and urban life were far more recent acquisitions, the aims were more modest, and years of schooling shorter: nevertheless, they remained aimed at basic literacy in Japanese. Although the attitudes of the Japanese to the colonial peoples increasingly emphasised their natural solidarity as fellow members of a potential 'Great East Asian Co-Prosperity Sphere' (*Dai-Tō-A Kyōeikan*), the effective pressure on them all to become members of the Japanese language community only heightened.

This was having its effect when the Second World War placed the whole empire in jeopardy. It is estimated that in 1942 62 per cent of the Taiwanese population could understand Japanese, and 20 per cent of the Korean.[68] But when it first took control of Taiwan in 1895, Japan had elected to follow characteristic French, rather than British, advice and aim at total integration of the territory into Japan.* This policy had then been followed, essentially without debate, as the other colonies were taken. Over the early twentieth century, this counsel proved disastrous in the large developed colonies, especially in Korea: the emperor's new subjects were never sufficiently trusted to allow them to contribute directly to policy-making in Tokyo, but they had no means to assert at least partial control of their fate locally. This became abundantly clear in the militant demonstrations by Koreans in 1919, bloodily put down by the Japanese; looking back in 1925, the Japanese analyst Aoyagi Tsunataro noted: 'nearly all educated Koreans, even those who were fluent in Japanese—even those who had studied in Japan—rejected Japanese rule'.[69]

It became wryly accepted among the rulers that for Koreans, 'to be educated was to be anti-Japanese'. A fresh rash of Korean student strikes, against Japanese assumed superiority, occurred in 1929–30. There was less trouble, and apparently less resentment, in Taiwan, even as their education became increasingly Japanese. Chinese studies were made optional there in 1922, and dropped in 1937; ironically, they continued on the curriculum—along with Korean—in the schools of Korea.

---

* The French advice came from Michel Lubon, suggesting that Taiwan should be 'a prefecture of Japan in future, if not now', immediately subject to the Imperial Consitution, a solution reminiscent of France's approach to Algeria. The British advice, from Montague Kirkwood, suggested viewing Taiwan as a colony with its own legislative council, and as many Taiwanese as possible as legislators, judges and administrators. Among other reasons, it was rejected on the grounds that the Japanese and Taiwanese belonged to the same race and used the same script (Chen 1984: 249–51).

Meanwhile Micronesia, with no tradition of developed literacy to be effaced by the Japanese, was far more receptive to the new education. Moreover, its 50,000 indigenous population were rapidly joined by an equal number of Japanese settlers, arriving to grow sugar. Plantations were established in the 1920s; by the early 1930s they accounted for over 60 per cent of government revenues there. If it had not been for the Pacific war, it is probable that Micronesia would have been overwhelmingly Japanese-speaking to this day.*

However, Japan's Imperial Plans for its Asian Co-Prosperity Sphere, and by implication for the spread of the Japanese language, were decisively disrupted by the political triumph of militarists, and the Pacific war into which they joyfully led Japan. Any hearts and minds that may have been won through fifty years of (relatively) peaceful colonialism were definitively lost in the terminal rampages of the Japanese army through East and South-East Asia. Although they briefly gained the whole western littoral of the Pacific Ocean, Japan ended 1945 confined to the islands it had controlled in 1868, even losing the outlying Kuriles in the north and the Ryukyus in the south. Taiwan was returned to Chinese rule, and Korea became independent. The more scarcely populated Sakhalin and Micronesia were placed under Russian and American control respectively. Nowhere in their hard-won colonies was a Japanese administration permitted to remain; and 6.5 million Japanese were repatriated to Japan. There was a forced intermission of all Japanese influence in Asia and the Pacific for a good fifteen years.

What, then, remains of the Japanese overseas language community, half a century after Japan's expulsion? Many who survive from the generations that attended Japanese schools can still converse in the language. But it seems that it is hardly used as a means of communication, even among this generation:[70] the opprobrium that the Japanese had stirred up lasted so long that it prevented any advantage being taken of this heritage when Japanese industrial interests began to spread again. The old Japanese empire has in no way served as a launch-pad for the global spread of Japanese products, and latterly of Japanese culture, in the last four decades of the twentieth century.

Japan's fifty years of language spread can be seen as a demonstration in miniature of the career of an imperial language. Like the other colonial empires, Japan took advantage of its technical and military superiority over

* As it was, the islands became part of the US Trust Territory of the Pacific Islands (gaining independence in 1986), and their own languages still predominate; in 1998, the UN put their total population at 114,000, with some 3500 English speakers (Grimes 2000).

other countries—in this case, its close neighbours—to increase its territory. It then faced the problem of what to do with the native populations there, people who did not think of themselves as Japanese. It attempted everywhere to convert them into members of its own community, certainly not trusting them to associate themselves voluntarily, but setting considerable store by education in the Japanese language. As everywhere else, this conversion process failed.

There was reasonable success in spreading the language, but once the political motive for using it was gone, the language turned out to have no independent staying power. The framework suggested to explain the decline of Russian can be applied here too. The creole motive was absent, since essentially the whole overseas population had been repatriated. There was no nostalgia for life under the flag of the Rising Sun, nor any wish to preserve unity with its speakers. Indeed, the bitter memories that the few years of Japan's control had caused were such that even when there were globalisation reasons to renew economic links through the language, they were disregarded. Permanent language spread, it turns out, is not to be achieved through planning, or naked force.

12

Microcosm or Distorting Mirror?
The Career of English

> We shall not cease from exploration
> And the end of all our exploring
> Will be to arrive where we started
> And know the place for the first time.
>
> T. S. Eliot, 'Little Gidding'[1]

The career of the English language, like that of most of the world's major languages, is often retold to its own speakers, and seldom without some element of triumph. The glories of any language community are hard for a speaker-patriot to resist, and few have any true conception of ages other than their own.

But even from the perspective of this book, there is still a sense in which the story of English deserves a special position among world languages. True, it happens to be the language with the widest spread in the era when these words are written. And in this era the world has become a single community linked by instant communications, making English uniquely prevalent, and leaving us wondering whether there could still be anywhere for a successor language to spring from. But the material fact for us is that English is a language with a remarkably varied history. This history is short: English as an identifiable language is no more than 1.5 millennia old, and its substance changed radically about halfway through its short life. But it has packed into this short span such a variety of crises and unpredictable outcomes that it can almost be seen as a personal summary of the adventures of its predecessors, all the way back to Memphis, Patna, Chang-an and Babylon.

One advantage of viewing English in the light of so many parallels is to reveal the essential strangeness of many developments that are usually taken for granted. We have already noted the success of Germanic Anglo-Saxons and Frisians in implanting their language, a striking feat when set against the achievement of other Germanic invaders, above all their contemporaries the

456

Franks and the Goths settling in other parts of the western Roman empire. More than a thousand years later, the early English settlers in North America were spontaneously to establish a populous English-language community, while the French Crown was having to send out *filles à marier* to prevent the young settlers from going native and bringing up families without French. And a century after that, the activities of the English East India Company led to the spread of its own language, English, while the Dutch East India Company, over the same period, succeeded only in spreading a pre-existing lingua franca, Malay. These are just three of the cases where a certain kind of situation has contributed to the expansion of English, but has had no similar effect on other languages. The historic spread of a language is a hard thing to account for fully; but keeping a range of languages in mind may at least help us to escape some half-truths.

The history of English, at least as viewed from the beginning of the twenty-first century, falls into two very unequal periods: one of *formation*, from the fifth to the end of the sixteenth centuries, during which the language took shape, growing up in the island of Britain; and one of *propagation*, from the seventeenth century to the present, in which it took ship, spreading to every continent of the world.

We have already considered the beginning of the formation period, when, as part of the turmoil at the end of Rome's empire, it coalesced from a group of Germanic dialects (see Chapter 7, 'Against the odds: The advent of English', p. 310). Despite political disunity and military threat, it had developed by the ninth century into a major literary language. Nevertheless, two centuries later, French-speaking conquerors were to stifle its written expression. Somehow, in the course of the next two centuries, it succeeded in assimilating the language community that was dominating it, to re-emerge as the foremost language of the realm. In the same period, it also spread geographically, establishing bridgeheads in every kingdom in the British Isles, among the Welsh, the Scots and the Irish. There was a further period of turmoil, in the fourteenth to sixteenth centuries, when the population was halved by the plague, the royal succession repeatedly disrupted by war, the Church shaken by protest and schism, and the currency racked by inflation. During all this time, English was spoken and written, but with no national standard uniting the various dialects. Linguistic stability came at much the same time as political stability, both focused on London, and mass readership of the Bible.

In the propagation period, when English speakers begin to travel and settle abroad, the temper of the English, and so by association their language too, becomes much more worldly, in both literal and figurative senses; the world is opened up to the English, but above all to their business and trading enterprise, with government and Church concerns very much in the rear. This idea of 'English—the Businessman's Friend' may be what is really distinctive about the spread of this language, though equally distinctively reinforced by English-speaking science and technology. Certainly, this commercial and scientific character sets it apart from such major rivals as Spanish, French and Russian. It has become even more dominant in the very recent history of the twentieth century, when a single English-speaking ex-colony has become the world's greatest power, competence in the language itself has become a major industry, and the spread of the language has accelerated well beyond the influence of the states that speak it natively. It is estimated that those who use English for convenience as a lingua franca now outnumber—by perhaps three to one—the total population of all native English speakers. Language prestige does not go much higher than this.

This apparent autonomy acquired by English means that, unlike most of the languages considered in this book, it is not yet possible to trace the beginnings of a downward trend in use of the language, even if the political and economic forces that put English up there have largely peaked. But we shall not be deterred. The life-histories of the many languages we have considered have shown various factors that can end the reign of a world language. It will be instructive to finish our account of English by using them to conjecture various paths downward from its present heights, unassailable as they appear.

Endurance test: Seeing off Norman French

Quant la bataille dut joster,	When the battle was to be engaged
la noit avant, ço oï conter	the night before, I heard tell
furent Engleis forment haitié,	the English were very happy
mult riant e mult enveisié;	with much laughter and merriment.
tote noit maingierent e burent,	They ate and drank all night long,
onques la noit el lit ne jurent,	and that night they never went to bed.
mult les veïssiez demener,	You should have seen them carry on,
treper e saillir e chanter.	dancing, jumping and singing.
Bublie *crient e* **weisseil**	'*Beo bliðe*' they cry and '*wes hæl*
e **laticome** *e* **drincheheil,**	and '*læt hit cuman*' and '*drenċa hæl*'
drinc hindrewart *e* **drintome,**	'*drinc hinderweard*' and '*drinc to me*'
drinc helf *e* **drinc tome.**	'*drinc healf*' and '*drinc tome*'.*

---

* Old English 'Be happy'; 'stay healthy'; 'let it come' (i.e. the loving-cup passed around); 'drink lustily'; 'drink backwards'; 'drink to me'; 'drink half'; 'drink to the dregs'. These are all English

Issi se contindrent Engleis;	This is how the English behaved;
e li Normant e li Franceis	and the Normans and the French
tote noit firent oreisons	spent the night in prayer
e furent en afflictions;	and in acts of contrition;
de lor pechiez confés se firent,	they made confession of their sins
as proveires les regehirent,	and avowed them to the priests;
e qui nen out proveires pres	and those who had no priests nearby
a son veisin se fist confés…	made confession to their neighbour…
Li proveires par lor chapeles	The priests in their chapels
qui esteient par l'ost noveles,	which had been newly established
	throughout the army
ont cele noit tote veillié,	watched throughout that night,
Deu reclamé e Deu preié;	called on God and prayed to God;
junes font et afflictions	they fast and do penance
e lo privees oreisons,	and say their private prayers,
salmes dient et misereles,	recite psalms and *Misereres*,
letanies e kirieles,	litanies and *Kyrie Eleisons*,
Deu requerent e merci crient,	they beseech God and cry for mercy,
paternostres e messes dient,	say *Pater Nosters* and masses,
*li uns **Spiritus domini**,*	some *Spiritus Domini*,
*li altre **Salus populi**,*	others *Salus populi*,
*plusors **Salve sancta parens**,*	many more *Salve sancta parens*,*
qui aparteneit a cel tens;	which was fitting for that time.
a cel jor bien aparteneit	It was very fitting for that day
ker samedi cel jor esteit.	As that day was Saturday.

Wace, *Roman de Rou*,† III, ll. 7323–42; 7365–80

toasts and drinking boasts to be heard as the English caroused the night away before the crucial battle of Hastings. Geoffrey of Monmouth, writing *c*.1140, says '… to this day the tradition has endured in Britain that at a banquet the one who drinks to another says "*waesseil*", and he who receives the cup after him replies "*drincheil*"' (*Historia Regum Britannie* §100, ms 568, f. 46v.).

* Latin titles of prayers, 'Spirit of the Lord', 'Salvation of the people', 'Hail Holy Mother', following naturalised French forms of 'Take pity', (Greek) 'Lord, have mercy', 'Our Father'.

† Robert Wace, a Norman from Jersey, was commissioned in the 1160s by King Henry II to write a celebration of Norman history, named for its patriarch Rollo (i.e. *Rou*). This was to parallel his earlier *Roman de Brut*, on Britain before the Normans (likewise supposedly founded by Brutus). This section tells of the different demeanours of the English and Normans on the night before Hastings, 1066; but it also neatly illustrates the different roles of English, Norman French and Latin in Norman England.

In a sense, the Norman conquest of England in the mid-eleventh century was an anachronism, the last of the Germanic invasions to convulse a European country, a couple of centuries too late.*

The Normans, after all, were only five or six generations away from their Norwegian ancestry as Vikings, and *Normanni* is just a Latinisation of *Norð-menn*, 'north men', which is still the word for Norwegians in Icelandic Norse. At the end of the ninth century, under their leader Rollo, they had been living by their swords, but they sailed south, and settled in what became Normandy, having coerced the Frankish king Charles III (the Simple) into granting them title, by the Treaty of St-Clair-sur-Epte, *c.*911. There they proceeded to put away their roving and marauding ways, including the Norse language; as typical Germanic invaders, in a couple of generations they had given up using their own language, and adopted the local Romance tongue, which on their lips is known as Norman French. When Rollo's descendant, William the Bastard, led his successful invasion of England in 1066, he brought this language into England with him.

English overlaid

But the Norman invasion of England was quite unlike the previous Germanic conquests of England in both scale and political consequence.

In scale, it was small, at least by comparison with the then population of England: William came with some five thousand knights, and the total numbers who 'came over with the Conqueror', all told, will have amounted to at most four times this number, twenty thousand to set against an English population of 1.5 million.[2] So in the first generation of Norman rule, perhaps one person in a hundred spoke Norman French.

In political consequence, it was not a raid, nor a mass migration, but a discrete invasion, grounded on a serious *casus belli*: William claimed that the king of England owed him allegiance, and went on to prove God's support for his right through battle. The result was almost instant conversion of England from a Saxon to a Norman kingdom. The Normans, though few, effectively decapitated the English regime.

The linguistic effect of this looks devastating, especially to us reading the written record a millennium later. Now that the king and the nobility are

---

* In this section, 'Norman' will include the governing classes of England and its dependencies from 1066 to 1399. Their vernacular was initially Norman French, also known as Anglo-Norman; but after 1154, the varieties of French spoken at court would have been more broadly based, since Henry II and his barons were based in Anjou, in south-western France. Thereafter the dynasty is known as Angevin.

French speakers, there is a new audience for the literary production of England; English vernacular literature—which with Irish had been the earliest to flower in the whole of Europe—ceases, and in its place comes Anglo-Norman courtly romance. From now on, laws, court judgments and legal depositions are almost all in French, a switch that shows up blatantly in the records; for increasingly it is legal documents which set the rules for Norman society and become the main objects of political struggle. The new order had less concrete effect among monks and clerics, since Latin remained the basic language of their intellectual work; but beside liturgy and theology, Latin also took over the functions of record-keeping and the writing of history. The Anglo-Saxon Chronicle, which had been kept continuously since the reign of Alfred in the ninth century, dies out in 1155. By the mid-twelfth century, this division of functions between the languages had become rigid. There was little apparent role left for English, at least in written form. But this does not mean that the language was endangered in use: despite its low profile in the records, there is no reason to believe that it was spoken any the less among the vast majority of the people.

Partly, the spread of Norman French would have been limited by the very rigidity in the social hierarchy over which the Normans presided. Within the feudal system, the status of every English man and woman was largely determined by birth, with the Church providing the only paths for advancement through merit, and that severely limited through constraints of celibacy. As a result, the French-speaking nobility remained almost a closed society—though fresh blood, and hence no doubt some English in childhood, came in through marriages to Saxon maidens—and there was little or no scope for people to better their prospects through aping their masters. In feudal England, people knew their place, one usually defined within a village, and had little opportunity even to meet people with wider horizons.

Spreading the Anglo-Norman package

Such social dynamics as did occur in these centuries were more horizontal than vertical, and due to the unmatched prowess of the Normans in fighting wars against their neighbours. Normans were fine cavalrymen, in fact the first invaders to bring their mounts with them across the Channel.* Once won on

---

* These were an asset to their literary culture as much as to their politics. Although Arthur comes out of Celtic legend, it was Anglo-Norman literature which created the ideal of the gallant knight in shining armour, the *chevaler*, a word that originally meant 'horseman'. In Old English *knight* (usually spelt *cniht*) had just meant 'lad', hence someone young enough to fight, without overtones of cavalry, let alone chivalry.

The Expansion of the Anglo-Norman Package, 11th-14th Centuries

(Norwegian to 1266, then Scottish) **Kingdom of Man**

INVERNESS

SCOTLAND

ABERDEEN

● Aberdeen

ATLANTIC

PERTH

Perth

Stirling

OCEAN

Bannockburn

1314 Edinburgh

LOTHIAN

Roxburgh

AYR

DUMFRIES

St Andrews

Firth of Forth

Berwick

Bamburgh

NORTHUMBERLAND

Hexham

NORTH

SEA

ULSTER

Armagh ●

CONNAUGHT

IRELAND

Dublin

LEINSTER

Limerick

MUNSTER Waterford

Cork ●

Irish **Man**
Sea

Isle of

Carlisle

CUMBRIA

DURHAM

YORKSHIRE

ENGLAND

GWYNEDD

CHESTER

FLINT STAFFORD-

CAERNARVON SHIRE

MERIONETH

WALES

Cardigan

CARDIGAN

St David's

Llandaff

Severn

MARCHER LORDSHIPS SHROP-
SHIRE

The Wash

NORFOLK

SUFFOLK

ESSEX

Bristol Channel

SOMERSET

DEVON DORSET

CORNWALL

SUSSEX

English Channel

**Channel
Islands**

NORMANDY

FRANCE

BRITTANY

—— Boundary of England
and Scotland 1157

Land claimed by
Scotland 1139–57

Pura Wallia

Territory conquered by
Normans, c. 1200

the battlefield, however, their power was cemented by the building of castles, fortified strongholds so permanent that many of them stand to this day. These were their main innovation. The Normans rapidly unified the somewhat loosely coordinated state of the Saxons, and proceeded to push back its borders. Beyond them lay Celtic-speaking regions, the north and west of the

British Isles. Cornwall had already been part of the Anglo-Saxon weal, but in each of Cumbria, Wales, Scotland and Ireland, the Normans now made serious inroads.

Cumbria was the scene of a struggle that lasted from 1092 to 1157. Wales took longer; Gwent in the south-east was taken by 1087, but although 'Marcher Lordships', dependent on the Norman king, were soon established across the whole of southern Wales, resistance did not die away. In the twelfth century, most of the country aside from the southern coast and western borders had reasserted its independence, and there was a period of de facto acceptance of an indigenous *Pura Wallia*, surrounded by a Norman *Marchia Wallie*. Only in 1283 did the Angevin king Edward I complete the conquest. Even then, there were two more Welsh rebellions, a decade and then a century later.*

The penetration of Scotland, hitherto largely Gaelic-speaking, was less warlike. Lothian, in the south-east, had already been English-speaking since the Angles had taken Edinburgh in 638. King Malcolm III,† on the throne at the time of the Norman conquest of England, had been exceptionally Anglophile; he had spent some of his youth in England, 'knew the English language quite as well as his own', and had married an English princess, Margaret, who opened the Scottish court (then still at Perth) as a market for luxury goods from England. No natural ally for the advancing Norman power, then, Malcolm actually spent much of his reign on aggressive raids into Northumbria. Nevertheless, his successors, particularly David I (1124–53), were highly partial to Norman influence: Anglo-Norman became the language of the court, so that in the thirteenth century the Englishman Walter of Coventry remarked: 'The more recent kings of Scots profess themselves to be rather Frenchmen, both in race and in manners, language and culture; and after reducing the Scots [i.e. Gaels] to utter servitude, they admit only Frenchmen to their friendship and service.'[3]

But French-speaking nobles brought English-speaking attendants. And to sustain their way of life, they were joined by communities of burgesses, English-speaking, who profited from cross-border trade. Cross-border influence swelled, and people began to refer to their language as 'Inglis', and later (equivalently—for this was a very distinctive kind of English) as 'Scot-

---

* After the first of these, Edward, in 1301, is supposed to have offered to give the Welsh a prince 'born in Wales, and without a word of English'—then presented his own son, just recently born at campaign headquarters in Caerfyrddin. The story, however, goes back only to the sixteenth century, and would be more credible if Edward himself had been a speaker of English rather than French.

† *Calum Ceann Mór*, 'Big Head', who reigned from 1059 to 1093. This was the famed Malcolm who had deposed and killed Macbeth.

tis'. It hardly mattered that the Scottish and English crowns remained intermittently at war through the late thirteenth century and into the fourteenth.

In Ireland, the Normans had accepted an invitation around 1166 from Diarmait Mac Murchada, newly deposed king of Leinster, to intervene on his behalf against the Irish High King. It was an act of opportunism on the part of the English king Henry II—neatly backed by a papal bull, *Laudabiliter*— but enabled him to channel some of the animal spirits of Marcher Lords looking for new conquests beyond Wales. The result was a settlement of Normans around Dublin, soon spreading out northward and westward, which became a permanent feature of the Irish landscape, and ultimately expanded to give the English Crown fitful control of the whole island.

In all these extensions to its domain, Norman influence brought the same rather complex linguistic regime: French for the rulers, English for their retinue, and Latin for technical support. In the long run, the English apex of the triangle proved the most influential, although functionally it was the most gratuitous: in all these lands, after all, it had to be superimposed on a subject population who spoke yet another language, Cumbrian, Welsh or (as in Scotland and Ireland) Gaelic, and which in the Gaelic case had as strong a literary tradition as English.

Language was not an explicit issue in the early days, before foreign domination had had a chance to spell out its effects over the generations; but when it did, it was English, and only English, which received the benefit of formal reinforcement. So when in 1366 the Norman authorities felt threatened by a resurgence of Gaelic influence in Ireland, causing that language to be used even in the English Pale around Dublin, their response was to issue (in French) the Statute of Kilkenny, which, after expressing a concern about the freedom of the Church and requiring strict apartheid in *marriage compaternitie nurtur de enfantz concubinance ou de caise*, 'marriage, godparenting, fostering of children, concubinage or by amour', curiously brackets a concern for language with proper saddle etiquette:

> iii. Also it is ordained and established, that every Englishman do use the English language, and be named by an English name, leaving off entirely the manner of naming used by the Irish; and that every Englishman use the English custom, fashion, mode of riding and apparel, according to his estate; and if any English, or Irish living among the English, use the Irish language among themselves, contrary to this ordinance, and thereof be attainted, his lands and tenements, if he have any, shall be seized and placed in the hands of his immediate lord, until he shall come to one of the places of our Lord the King, and find sufficient

surety to adopt and use the English language … and also that beneficed persons of holy Church, living amongst the English, shall use the English language; and if they do not, that their ordinaries shall have issues of their benefices until they use the English language in the manner aforesaid; and they shall have respite in order to learn the English language, and to provide saddles, between this time and the feast of St Michael next coming.[4]

Later, continued use of one of these Celtic languages was considered not so much a threat to the survival of English abroad as a token of dubious loyalty. So Henry VIII, though himself the son of a king who had taken power with Welsh and Cornish support, included the following in the Act of Union of 1536 (now delivered in English):

Also be it enacted that all justices, Commissioners, sheriffs, coroners, escheators, stewards and their lieutenants, and all other officers and ministers of the law, shall proclaim and keep the sessions, courts, hundreds, leets, sheriff's courts and all other courts in the English tongue; and all oaths of juries and inquests, and all other affidavits, verdicts and wagers of law to be given and done in the English tongue; and also that from henceforth no person or persons that use the Welsh speech or language shall have or enjoy any manner of office or fees within this realm of England, Wales or other the King's dominion upon pain of forfeiting the same offices or fees, unless he or they use the English speech or tongue.[5]

In the same year, King Henry was writing to the citizens of Galway in the west of Ireland, urging: 'every inhabitante within the saide towne indever theym selfe to speke Englyshe, and to use theym selffe after the English facion; and specially that you, and every one of you, do put forth your childe to scole, to lerne to speke Englyshe'.[6]

But five years later, the bill declaring Henry VIII king of Ireland still had to be presented in Irish both to the Irish Commons and Lords.[7] Although the Norman invasions had caused use of English to spread into all parts of the British Isles, it had not thereby eliminated the use of other languages.

The waning of Norman French

Had the Norman and Angevin kings retained their twin domains on both sides of the Channel, it is possible that at some point there would have been enough flexibility in the social system to allow the prestige language, French, to trickle down, and become widespread all over their realm. But it was not to be. The French realm had never been able to abide the independence of the Norman kings, originally its vassals, and in 1204 King Philip II seized the opportunity to defeat one of them (King John) in battle, and so end their control of Normandy. Within the rigours of the feudal system, it was impossible for barons to maintain a divided loyalty: henceforth they must declare fealty either to the king of England or the king of France, and give up any lands they might hold in the other kingdom. In the sequel, English barons became determinedly English. Soon, as the Provisions of Oxford showed in 1258—a measure for the first time promulgated in English as well as French—they would no longer tolerate excess influence from France, even if coming from the king's remaining fiefs in Anjou.

> ...we hoaten all ure treowe, in þe treowþe þæt heo us oʒen, þæt heo stedefæstliche healden and swerien to healden and to werien þo i-setnesses þæt beon i-makede þurʒ þan toforen i-seide rædesmen oþer þurʒ þe moare dæl of heom, also alse it is beforen i-seide...

> ...comandons et enjoinons a tuz nos feaus et leaus, en la fei k'il nus deivent, k'il fermement teignent, et jurgent a tenir et a maintenir les establissemenz ke sunt fet, u sunt a fere, par l'avant dit cunseil, u la greignure partie de eus, en la maniere k'il est dit desuz...

> ...we command all our subjects, in the fealty which they owe us, that they steadfastly keep and swear to keep and to protect the ordinances that are made and are to be made by the aforesaid counsellors or by a majority of them, as is said above...[8]

In England, from lack of day-to-day practice, French began to be a subject learnt at school, rather than the living language of the elite.

Earlier, when trying to explain the remarkable linguistic impact of the Anglo-Saxons, we conjectured that English originally established itself in Britain in the wake of a major epidemic, in the fifth century AD (see Chapter 7, 'Einfall: Germanic and Slavic advances', p. 313). But when it comes to the effects of the Black Death, no conjecture is necessary. This plague first reached England in 1348, and returned twice more before the century was out. No sector of society was safe, but by its nature—borne by fleas on people or rats—it was most virulent in highly populated areas, among them cities, courts and monasteries. England's population was halved, and as an economic consequence net personal worth doubled. Even those who had no assets but their own health—or survival—benefited, since labour had become a scarce resource in relation to the still-constant amount of land. The result was massive disruption of the feudal system, including a rise in income at the lower end, and an increase in personal mobility, especially from country to town, as men became in effect free to seek their fortunes away from home. Linguistically, the position of the French-speaking nobility was undercut: professions throughout society were increasingly open to merit, but increasingly all that anyone really needed to make a career was literacy in Latin and English. A sign of the times was the Statute of Pleading of 1362: court proceedings would henceforth take place in English, though 'enrolled in Latin'.

John de Trevisa, a curate and former fellow of Oxford, commented on the situation in 1385, taking issue with a text he was translating. Ranulph Higden had written, in his *Polychronicon* (Universal History) of the mid-fourteenth century, that there were two reasons for the corruption he saw in many people's language, namely that children were taught to construe (i.e. translate Latin) into French, not their own language, and that country people laboured to pass themselves off as gentlemen by affecting French. After translating this, Trevisa adds:

> This maner was moche used to fore the Grete Deth [i.e. the Black Death]. But syth it is somdele chaunged. For Sir John Cornouayl, a master of gramer, chayngede the lore in gramer scole and construction of Frenssh in to Englysshe. And other scoolmasters use the same way... and leve all Frenssh in scoles and use al construction in Englissh. Wherin they have avauntage one way, that is they lerne the sonner theyr gramer, and in another disavauntage, for now they lerne no Frenssh ne can none, which is hurte for them that shal pass the see, and also gentilmen have moche left to teche theyr children to speke Frenssh.[9]

By the late fourteenth century, then, French had been dropped as a medium of education in England as a needless barrier to vernacular understanding; there was no more presumption that any children would grow up with French. It was now a language that was only of use in overseas travel, if at all; but there was still a feeling that a proper gentleman should make sure that his sons had a decent grounding in it.*

---

* It is all very reminiscent of the emotional, nostalgic and somewhat desperate tone of the defence for learning Latin itself, offered in the grammar schools of England in the middle of the twentieth century.

In the century after the Black Death, even royalty stopped using French. Richard II, with his deft handling of the Peasants' Revolt in 1381, showed that he was quite able to appeal to a common crowd in English. After deposing him, Henry IV made his coronation speech of 1399 in English—the first of its kind, as were his son Henry V's dispatches from the Agincourt campaign of 1415.* So ultimately, the Normans lost their French too, just as four hundred years earlier they had lost their Norse. The language vanished like a last ghostly reminder of their former identity, for by the fifteenth century there were no more Normans anywhere.

Stabilising the language

Also Englischmen, þeyȝ hy hadde fram þe bygynnyng þre maner speche, Souþeron, Norþeron, and Myddel speche (in þe myddel of þe lond), as hy com of þre people of Germania, noþeles, by commyxstion and mellyng furst wiþ Danes and afterward wiþ Normans, in menye þe contray longage ys apeyred, som useþ strange wlaffyng, chyteryng, harryng and garryng grisbittyng.

Also englysshmen though they had fro the begynnyng thre maner speches Southern northern and myddel speche in the middel of the londe as they come of thre maner of people of Germania. Netheless by commyxtion and medlyng first with dans and afterward with normans In many thynges the countreye langage is appayred // for somme use straunge wlaffyng // chyteryng harryng garryng and grisbytyng.†

John de Trevisa, *Polychronicon Ranulphi Higden*, i, 59
Original text, Cornwall, 1385; William Caxton's transcription, London, 1482

This book has deliberately avoided much talk of distinct dialects. No language is totally homogeneous, and all widespread languages have their regional variants. But by their nature dialects have a much vaguer identity than full languages: they do not define the boundaries of language communities as wholes, but rather regional identities within them. Lacking a clear group

---

* Characteristically conservative, the law held out longest: Law French did not finally disappear from the English courts until eliminated by an act of Parliament in 1733. By the same standard of retrospection, the law's fondness for eighteenth-century wigs and gowns has still a century to run.
† '…in many the country language is impaired; some use a strange babbling, twittering, snarling, growling and gnashing.'

identity, they tend to overlap, even to merge at the edges; and linguists often find it easier to speak of distinct features, such as an unrounded pronunciation of u, a verb plural ending in -en, a tendency to delay verbs to the end of the clause, or a particular choice of words, such as *eyren* instead of *eggs*, and map these across the whole language area, than to try to characterise each regional variant as a discrete whole sub-language with its own separate phonology, grammar and vocabulary. It is far easier to count languages than to count the dialects within a language.

The preferred 'standard' form of a language is, from a formal point of view, just one of the dialects, a preferred selection of features from among all the alternatives that are in use somewhere in the language community's territories. Nevertheless, it is not always easy to reach agreement on which dialect should be taken as the standard. Early Modern Irish, for example, had a distinct code for courtly and literary use, which was lost when Gaelic lordship was overthrown at the end of the sixteenth century, and which it has been very hard to rebuild out of the three main varieties of the language current in twentieth-century Irish. In the history of English, it is still debated how close the language had come to having a national standard in the tenth and eleventh centuries before the Normans took over; but clearly, in the period of its re-emergence in the fourteenth and fifteenth centuries it was very difficult for anyone to decide what sort of language should be dignified with the title of 'the best English'. And at first, no decision was made. The literature that has survived tends to show the speech style and vocabulary of the writer in idiosyncratic combinations that nonetheless usually identify him as a Midlander, a Londoner, a Kentishman, a Southerner, a Northerner or a Scot. When writing was all in manuscript, and important writing was all in Latin anyway, perhaps it mattered little that books in the vernacular were hard to read outside their local region. If a good book needed to be read more widely, someone could always convert its dialect, as the author of the *Cursor Mundi* did the story of the Assumption of Mary.

In sotherin englis was it draun,	In southern English it was drawn
And turnd it haue i till our aun	And I have turned it to our own
Langage o northrin lede,	Language of northern folk
þat can nan oiþer englis rede.	That can read no other English.[10]

But the absence of a standard came to be a problem in two major areas of language use, the official and the literary. Once the sovereign and his courts again spoke English, it would have to be the pre-eminent English: but how should they express themselves in official laws and proclamations, so that they could be published, understood and acted upon, all over the land? And England was not just a government. It was a nation, increasingly felt to have a distinctive character, and a part to play in the world, and hence needing a distinctive, and distinct, voice. It was all very well to blandly name this 'the English tongue'. But when an author got down to writing, which variety of all the English words and inflexions on offer should prevail, in the books that would more and more be known as English literature? This question became much more urgent when the printing presses began mass production of books in the late fifteenth century. Henceforth, identical copies of a single book might expect to go to all parts of the kingdom: what form of the language should appear in them to take full advantage of the new economies of scale?

This is not an artificial question of historians, put to dramatise a predicament confronting society as a whole, to which an answer emerged as if blindly. For some people it presented itself quite explicitly. Geoffrey Chaucer, in the final *envoi* of his poem *Troilus and Criseide*, written in London English in the 1380s, adds a verse:

And for ther is so gret diversite	And because there is such great diversity
In Englissh and in writyng of oure tonge,	In English and in writing of our tongue,
So prey I God that non myswrite the,	So pray I God that none mis-write you,
ne the mysmetre for defaute of tonge.	Nor mis-scan you for ignorance of language.
And red wherso thou be, or elles songe	And wherever you are read, or else sung,
That thou be understonde, God I biseche!	I beseech God that you be understood,
But yet to purpos of my rather speche.	and in the sense meant by my earlier words.[11]

Here he is apparently as much worried about the corruption of the text that may come from copying from one dialect to another as he is for the poor reader or listener trying to make sense of the text.*

One possible solution that never seems to have suggested itself in England was for different dialects to become standard for different types of writing, although we have seen that this is what had happened in the early days of Greek literature, and to some extent also in Iberia, when Portuguese devel-

---

* From another point of view, the dialects of English were a boon to a naturalistic author like Chaucer, who was the first to use them to give realism to dialogue. In *The Canterbury Tales*, the Reeve, himself scripted as a Norfolk man, tells a story of Cambridge students John and Aleyn, who are clearly lads from the North. And the Summoner and the Friar both keep breaking into broad Northern English (Robinson 1957: 686, 688, 704–5).

oped a role as the vehicle of love poetry, even in Spain. It would have been conceivable, for example, that the success of 'The Owl and the Nightingale', and 'The Fox and the Wolf', two beast dialogues in verse of the thirteenth century, might have made Southern English the preferred language for this type of conceit. But nothing like this ever happened. Instead, a single dialect came to be preferred for all.

William Caxton, the first English printer and publisher, faced the problem in the most extreme form, and was highly influential in solving it. We can predict what the answer would be: overwhelmingly (as we shall note in Chapter 13, p. 529) the dialect spoken in a capital city has become the standard for its national language. Before declaring his policy, Caxton did point out the predicament:

> Certaynly it is harde to playse every man by cause of dyversite & chaunge of langage. For in these dayes every man that is in ony reputacyon in his countre, wyll utter his commynycacyon and maters in suche maners & termes that fewe men shall understonde theym. And som honest and grete clerkes have ben wyth me, and desired me to wryte the moste curyous termes that I coude fynde. And thus bytwene playn, rude & curyous, I stande abasshed. But in my judgemente the comyn terms that be dayli used ben lyghter to be understonde than the olde and auncyent englysshe. And for as moche as the present booke is not for a rude uplondyssh man to laboure therin, ne rede it, but onely for a clerk & a noble gentylman that feleth and understondeth in faytes of armes, in love, & in noble chyvalrye, therfor in a meane bytwene bothe I have reduced & translated this sayd booke in to our englysshe, not ouer rude ne curyous, but in suche termes as shall be understanden, by goddys grace, accordynge to my copye.[12]

Caxton, then, claimed to be following a classic English policy of reasonable compromise. But what he was actually doing was converting texts into London English. This is clear, for example, in the passage that begins this section, where the text that John de Trevisa had originally written is set out above the version published a century later by Caxton. Examined closely, it is a fairly slight set of changes—here using *they* for *hy*, eliminating the verbal ending *-eþ* in the plural, and replacing þ and ȝ throughout with th and gh—but it is still amazing what a difference it makes in bringing a text into the ambit of readability for a speaker of modern English, even now, some five hundred years on. Standard English, as we now know it, still bears the mark of those decisions taken by Caxton and his contemporaries.

Once this decision was taken, the growing availability of printed literature, in concert with growing powers of literacy among the public, strongly reinforced use of the particular dialect that was being printed. It helped that the main sources of book-writing in English, Oxford and Cambridge, were also located in the same broad dialect area, often known as southern West Midlands.* Printing, once enough people could read and did read, became the first of the mass media, with the polarising, 'winner takes all' effects now familiar from TV culture. People inevitably learnt from the books they read how English should be written, and the King's English thereby became the people's English too, at least on the page. 'The English tongue', for the first time, was being defined.

This process was not confined to English. Almost precisely comparable processes of language definition were under way at the same time for other languages of western Europe, notably French, Spanish and German, which in speech had been at least as dialectally riven as English. French typographers in the first half of the sixteenth century begin to give rules for spelling and use of accents, beginning the task—one never completed—of pruning the vast numbers of consonants traditionally written by purists but never pronounce in that language. Spanish, whose pronunciation had changed less since it had been Latin, could afford to be more rigorously phonetic; but the existence of Nebrija's 1492 grammar of Castilian meant that there was a basis for excluding forms characteristic of other dialects, particularly the closely related Aragonese.

The comparison shows that political unification was in no way essential to the definition of a national language in this natal age for print literature. The lands where German was spoken had no single government. Nevertheless, in 1522 Martin Luther, a native of Lower Saxony and Thuringia, brought out his translation of the New Testament into his own German, aspiring all the while 'to be understood by the inhabitants of Germany High and Low'. He added

---

* The basic linguistic features of this area were: using ō not ā in words like *woe, stone, go*—north of the Humber they kept the Old English ā; using y (i.e. ü, French u) and later i, in words like *hill, sin, fire, mice*—in Kent and East Anglia they said ē—and this explains most instances of the apparently gratuitous y in Caxton's spelling; using the modal verb *shall*, as against Northumbrian *sal*; using pronouns, *she, they, them, theyr*, as against West and South Country *heo, hy, hem, here*. In verbs, the present participle and gerund generalised Southern and Midland *-ynge*, as against Northern *-ande*; the plural ends in *-en* or nothing: *we speken, they use*, as against the South Country *we speketh, hy useth*. In fact, the present tense of verbs became subject to a lot of confusion, since this *-eth* ending was also used as a third singular ending in the South, and is widely used as such in Shakespeare and the King James Bible: *the wind bloweth, he goeth*. Ultimately, this too was replaced, but by the *-es* ending, which had been used for every person but first singular in the North: *I here*, but *thou/ he/ we/ ye/ they heres*. (These details are gathered from Mossé 1962, who gives many more.)

the Old Testament in 1534. Through the popularity (and excellence) of his work, he succeeded in establishing standard German in the image of his local dialects. Local editions of the Bible were made in farther parts of German-speaking territory, in Basel, Strasburg, Augsburg and Nuremberg, but localised only to the extent of adding glossaries of Luther's more distinctively westerly terms; and for the first time, whole grammars of the German language began to be written, explicitly based on Luther's usage.[13] Thus was *Hochdeutsch* defined.

The Bible was cardinal also in the definition of English. Evidently, the explosion of print literacy in the early sixteenth century was a major support to Protestant ideas, which were rocking western Christianity at exactly this time. Luther was, after all, only defining the German language as a by-product of his passionate concern that the word of God be available directly to everyone, not just the learned. Readers of English were just as avid for this boon; indeed, such enthusiasm went back to 1382, when John Wyclif's translation had been put into circulation through handwritten volumes, only to be rigorously suppressed in 1407–9: there is always a party who believes that great blessings must be distributed only under rigorous supervision, and this view largely prevailed until the end of the fifteenth century.

A series of English-language Bibles came out in print in the sixteenth century, led off by William Tyndale's 1525 New Testament.[14] They were at first seditious documents, of course; but none the less popular for that. By the reign of Elizabeth, 1558–1603, the right to read the Bible in English* was firmly established; and with it, perhaps even more important as a text that everyone was reading, the Book of Common Prayer. Then in 1611 the King James Bible, produced by a royal committee, established the definitive text of the Bible, as it would be read in English for the next three centuries, a single work common to ten generations of English-language Christians.

With such a text justifying and fulfilling their increasingly widespread literacy,[15] speakers more and more had a clear and distinct idea, indeed a single concrete model, of the English language in use. This model was soon to be transported to the uttermost parts of the earth.†

---

* And indeed in Welsh: Elizabeth I also authorised the publication of *Y Beibl Cyssegr-lan*, which was printed in London in 1588, and joined the Welsh translation of the Prayer Book (*Y Llyfr Gweddi Gyffredin*) in Welsh churches.

† A corpus of texts that is usually mentioned in the same breath as the King James Bible, and accorded almost equal status in the textual definition of English, is the poetry of William Shakespeare. The two are almost exact contemporaries, this 'Authorised Version' of the Bible being compiled from 1604 to 1611, and Shakespeare writing from 1590 to 1611. But unlike the Bible, Shakespeare (first fully published in 1623) did not immediately become an iconic text of the English language, his reputation

What sort of a language?

What kind of a language had English become? This was to become a question fraught with global implications. But it is a particularly hard one for an ordinary native speaker of the language to appreciate. The architecture of a language is invisible for the same reason that a conjuring trick deceives: by force of habit, everyone's attention is on the apparent business in hand, not its means of execution. Even when the means is singled out, and a poet describes his craft, or a critic draws attention to the composition of a text, there is still a tendency to take the links between sounds and word, phrase and object, utterance and thought as either too obvious to mention, or totally mysterious. If language head has its reasons, the literary heart knows little of them, and cares less. Speakers and writers, listeners and readers deal deftly, and often intuitively, with outcomes they all accept and recognise, in a medium that is largely unanalysed—much as they breathe, digest and regulate their body temperatures.*

Nevertheless, there are properties of English that make it the language it is, and no other. Most of these were already present in the sixteenth century. From the perspective of the world's plenty, it is a language with a very wide range of distinctly different vowels and diphthongs (e.g., in the British standard, *mat, met, mitt, motte, mutt, put, mart, mate, meet, might, moat, moot,*

---

growing through the seventeenth century until it was fully canonised by Samuel Johnson in the eighteenth.

The Shakespeare phenomenon recalls the place of Homer in the history of Greek. Each was a poet of encyclopedic range and unchallenged quality but obscure identity, at or near the very foundation of the language's main tradition of literary classics. Each seems to have acquired this status at least a century after he actually lived and composed. Each went on to have an overwhelming role in the heritage of his language, endlessly praised by critics and schoolteachers, and also to inform traditional ideas of the language community's history. Perhaps this is best explained by emphasising that each of them is indebted more than most to a rich ancient tradition, Homer to that of the travelling bard or *aoidós*, Shakespeare to that of the strolling player. This was less remarkable to their contemporaries, who saw them in context, but somehow, as time went on, their works were felt to sum up the tradition, and so replaced it in memory.

* Too many remarks proffered as comments on the nature of English, especially by writers, are thinly disguised praise of the traditions and aspirations of its speakers. Consider Sir Arthur Quiller-Couch's words introducing the *Oxford Book of English Verse*: 'Our fathers have, in the process of centuries, provided this realm, its colonies and wide dependencies, with a speech as malleable and pliant as Attic, dignified as Latin, masculine, yet free of Teutonic guttural, capable of being as precise as French, dulcet as Italian, sonorous as Spanish, and captaining all these excellences to its service.' Or Walt Whitman: 'Viewed freely, the English language is the accretion and growth of every dialect, race and range of time, and is the culling and composition of all. From this point of view, it stands for Language in the largest sense, and is really the greatest of studies' ('Slang in America', *North American Review*, 41, 1885). Such confidence may of course be useful in using the language eloquently. Any language carries a vast network of associations with the past, which grow in power as that past is remembered.

mute, mouth, moist, as well as *mere, mire, flower, more, moor* and *immure*)
and relatively more restricted range of consonant sounds (*bun, pun, spun,
dun, ton, stun, con, gone, scone, chin, gin, Hun, train, drain, son, shin, led,
red, bum, bun* and *bung,* with *zoom* and *leisure* added later), although these
have become more challenging when account is taken of the combinations
allowed: consider *scrounged, widths, strengths, fifths, sixths, sevenths,
eighths, shrinks, mostly, thrust, scripture, contemptibly, constraints, spindly,
adze* and *stupid.* Some of the rules of its sound system come as a surprise to
native speakers, since they have no role in the spelling, and so are seldom
mentioned at school: for example, that the length of the vowels has everything to do with the last consonant in a syllable, and nothing to do with the
vowel itself: *mat, mace, mitt, right, rot, lout, motes, route, kilt, health* and *Alf*
all have short vowels, while *mad, maze, mid, ride, rod, loud, modes, rude,
killed, delve* and *pals* all have long ones; or that the crucial puff of air that
distinguishes, say, *pin* from *bin,* and *tab* from *dab,* is actually missing in *spin*
and *stab*—so from a phonetic point of view, they might with more justice be
written '*sbin*' and '*sdab*'. The stress rules of English are complex (e.g. swéet
sixtéen, but síxteen swéet lámbs), but are essential for the understanding of
fluent speech; and intonation patterns for whole sentences are also highly various.

The structure of English words is fairly straightforward: the inflexion system of Old English, reminiscent of Latin or Greek, has long been lost, and
most words are either simple, or clearly composed of stem with a few prefixes
and suffixes.* Irregularity in English grammar mostly concerns the details of
how suffixes are applied to particular words (not man+s but *men,* not
strike+d but *struck*). Main verbs may appear with sequences of smaller verbs
called auxiliaries and modals (*be, have, do, shall, will, can, may, must*),
which may be mirrored under rather complex conditions (e.g., *He **has*** *been
taken for a ride, **hasn't he**? **They have** too, **haven't they**?* but *Everybody **seems**
to have, don't they?*) Word order is crucial. In the simple sentence it is fairly
rigidly Subject–Verb–Object (*You saw a tiger*), but a plethora of variations
and nuances arise in questions and more complex sentences. *Who saw a
tiger?* is still S–V–O, but then the fun begins: *Such a tiger I saw!* (O–S–V),
Never have I seen such a tiger (Aux–S–V–O), *Did you see a tiger?* (Aux–S–
V–O), *What did you see?* (O–Aux–S–V), *What do you think you saw?* (O–
Aux–S–V–S–V), *What do you think saw you?* (S–Aux–S–V–V–O). This
juggling with word order, though common in Germanic languages, was

---

* I should reassure linguists reading this that I am consciously ignoring the structure latent in the vast
amount of vocabulary borrowed from, or constructed out of, Latin, French and Greek.

beyond the ken of grammar as developed by the Greeks and Romans, and hence as taught in medieval and early modern Europe. In fact, it was only in the 1950s that theoretical linguists found a fitting means to analyse it. Not surprisingly, it was only then that English became the prime subject for theoretical linguistics.

If we compare English to the other languages that have achieved world status, the most similar—as languages—are Chinese and Malay. Of course, we need to discount the main sources of its vocabulary: English has been in close touch all its short life with French and Latin; and since 1500 the education of very many of its elite speakers has involved Greek too. As a result these three languages have provided the vast majority of the words that have come into the language, whether borrowed or invented. But when the origins of its words—and hence their written look on the page—is set to one side, the amazing fact emerges that the closest parallels to English come not from Europe but from the far east of Asia.

Like English, Chinese and Malay have Subject–Verb–Object word order, and very little in the way of verb or noun inflexion. Words are simple, and complex senses result from stringing them together. By contrast, all the other languages we have considered have a high degree of inflexion, although Portuguese, in the form in which it established itself in Asia, has most of this stripped away.

The peculiarly conservative, and hence increasingly anti-phonetic, system is another facet of English that bears a resemblance to Chinese (though not to Malay—in any of the writing systems that have been used to represent it). As has happened with Chinese (and of course Egyptian), the life of English as it is spoken has become only loosely attached to the written traditions of the language. True, words are still written in the order in which they are spoken.* But spelling has not been revised to keep up with changes in pronunciation: hence the remains of *gh*, a combination of letters still found in many words, but nowhere keeping anything like its original pronunciation as [x], the *ch* in Scots *loch*; hence the bizarre spelling of the English tense vowels, seen in the words spelt *mate*, *meet*, *mite*, *mote*, *mouth* and *mute*, but which would be written *meit*, *miit*, *mait*, *mout*, *mauth* and *miuwt* if the letters were still being used vaguely with the values they had until the fifteenth century, values that they have largely retained in every other language that uses the Roman alphabet. As a result of the complexity of relation between spelling and sound, a large proportion of the primary teaching profession, in England at least, was

---

* To my knowledge, only the Japanese '*kanbun*' tradition of marking up classical Chinese text to be read out just as if it were in Japanese has had the chutzpah to dispense with that basic convention.

until recently of the opinion that phonics are more confusing than helpful when teaching children to read and write: hence the notorious 'Look and Say' method, which essentially treated each word as if it were a Chinese character.

As with Chinese, one can say that, for learners, the English language has been literate too long.

Westward Ho!

The language I have learned these forty years,
My native English, now I must forego:
And now my tongue's use is to me no more
Than an unstring'd viol or a harp;
Or like a cunning instrument cas'd up,
Or, being open, put into his hands
That knows no touch to tune the harmony:
Within my mouth you have engaol'd my tongue,
Doubly portcullis'd with my teeth and lips;
And dull, unfeeling, barren ignorance
Is made my gaoler to attend on me.
I am too old to fawn upon a nurse,
Too far in years to be a pupil now:
What is thy sentence, then, but speechless death,
Which robs my tongue from breathing native breath?

(The Duke of Norfolk, on being exiled)
Shakespeare, Richard II, act I, scene iii

Norfolk's words stand as the first example of an Englishman's despair, now almost traditional, at the prospect of having to learn another language: could exile hold any greater terror? English was then a language spoken exclusively within the confines of the British Isles. When the words were written, most likely in 1595, there had been only a single English-speaking colony outside the British Isles, Ralegh's 1586 colony at Roanoke, 'Virginia', and no one in England then knew if it was still in existence.*

---

* It, and the island of Croatoan, to which it famously but mysteriously decamped, were actually on the coast of modern North Carolina. The few survivors, merging with local Algonquian speakers, were to drop their English in the seventeenth century. But English did survive in the follow-up colony at Jamestown, later moved to Williamsburg.

Little by little, it was going to become more and more unnecessary for travellers from Britain to learn other languages, because English speakers were now to spread new settlements around the world, and many of those settlements were going to expand, to become—with Britain—among the largest, richest and most powerful nations on earth. The motives for British settlements over three centuries were various: the glory of the realm, gains from piracy, founding new utopias, wealth from agriculture or mining, trade, personal glory, a stirring of duty to spread the gospel, global strategy, windfall spoils from military victories, even in the end some sense of obligation to educate the native inhabitants. In this, they were unlike their greatest predecessors, the Portuguese, the Spanish, the Dutch and the French, who were each moved by just one or a few of these. The British were in this sense the universal exponents of European imperialism.* And the sheer variety of the motives could almost be parleyed into a claim of no motive at all. In 1883, the publicist Sir John Seeley was famously to claim: 'We seem, as it were, to have conquered and peopled half the world in a fit of absence of mind.'[16] This has well suited British conceits of their own virtuous innocence.

Pirates and planters

The first extensions of the English language across the Atlantic recall the stirrings of Sanskrit across the Bay of Bengal a millennium and a half before, when glamorous *sāhasikāḥ* pirates could scarce be distinguished from *sādhavaḥ* merchants (see Chapter 5, 'The spread of Sanskrit', p. 199). Britain was the last of the Atlantic-fronting powers to seek new fortune in the west, and it was not, at first, an easy game to break into. In the sixteenth century, when Spain was drawing vast profits from its mines in Mexico and Peru, and Portugal stitching up the trade of the Indian Ocean, when even France was exploring the extent of the St Lawrence river, England's Henry VIII and Elizabeth I had supported a very few exploratory voyages across the North Atlantic which yielded nothing, hardly even a landfall. But Francis Drake had discovered a line that could be profitable, euphemistically known as the 'taking of prizes'. In fifteen years from 1573 he alone had brought back, from a mixture of raids on Spanish ports, high-sea robberies of Spanish and Portuguese ships, and trading in the East Indies, booty to the value of three quarters of a million pounds, twice the annual tax revenues at the time; Elizabeth's share was enough to clear the national debt in 1581, and provide another

---

* It is interesting to note that one major motive for Rome and Russia, the drive to secure borders by conquering neighbours, was largely absent.

£42,000 to found the Levant Company (which went on to become the financial basis of the East India Company itself).[17] And he was not alone. From 1585 to 1604, at least a hundred ships set off every year to plunder the Caribbean, netting at least £200,000 a year.[18]

But one thing that the Elizabethan voyages had shown was that lines of supply were the point of greatest weakness in any long expedition. Even piracy, in the long term, calls for a secure base, defensible and self-sustaining, but close to the action. And this was prominent in the rationale offered in the prospectus to investors for Ralegh's newly planted colony in Virginia, written by Richard Hakluyt in 1584. In the executive summary,* after pieties about 'the inlargement of the gospell of Christe', and the Spanish threat to decent 'englishe Trades…grown beggerly or daungerous', he promises that 'this westerne voyadge will yelde unto us all the commodities of Europe, Affrica, and Asia'; most especially, '5. That this voyage will be a great bridle to the Indies of the kinge of Spaine and a means that wee may arreste at our pleasure for the space of tenne weekes or three monethes every yere, one or twoo hundred saile of his subjectes shippes at the fysshinge in Newfounde lande.'

In the way of business plans, it did not turn out quite like that. The colony was at first hard put to it even to grow its own food, and survive the attentions of the Indians; it had no energy, indeed no ships, to harry the Spanish. But Hakluyt's term *planting*, originally just an elegant metaphor for 'colony', became in the event very appropriate: the Virginia colony, once re-established at Jamestown, was to find its sustenance through the commercial plantation of tobacco. And although English royal sponsorship of piracy ended when James I came to the throne, this was not the only pirate base that came good in the end through commercial agriculture. British naval strength grew through the seventeenth century, and Britain was able to take possession of some of the islands of the Caribbean, until then really a Spanish lake: most importantly, Jamaica was captured in 1655. At first, piracy targeted on the Spanish remained the major British activity in the region. But increasingly, Britons were noticing the potential in producing sugar, an Asian crop that the

---

* The term is an anachronism, but the concept is not. Hakluyt organises the document, *Discourse of Western Planting*, with all the striking content on the second page, chapter headings that tell it all:

A particuler discourse concerninge the greate necessitie and manifolde comodyties that are like to growe to this Realme of Englande by the Westerne discoveries lately attempted,
Written In the yere 1584 by Richarde Hackluyt of Oxforde at the requeste and direction of the righte worshipfull Mr. Walter Raghly [Ralegh] nowe Knight, before the comynge home of his Twoo Barkes: and is devided into xxi chapters, the Titles whereof followe in the nexte leafe.

Portuguese had pioneered in Brazil. Henry Morgan, the most famous pirate of them all, invested the proceeds of his freebootery in Nicaragua, Cuba and Venezuela to buy land in Jamaica; Morgan ended up a sugar baron, with a knighthood to boot.[19]

The possession of land, taken for whatever reason, made possible commercial cultivation of exotic crops for the European market. There was no gold or silver in the British possessions, but supplying consumers rather than bankers turned out to be much better business. Cultivating crops also meant that a workforce was needed: if these were indentured workers from Britain (as most were at first, especially in North America), they would of course go on speaking English; if they were purchased slaves from the western coast of Africa, they would learn it when they arrived, since all links with their home communities were lost. The revenues from sugar, and later cocoa, in the Caribbean islands, and from tobacco, and later indigo and cotton, in the North American continent, became the firmest foundations of sustainable English-speaking communities across the Atlantic.

Someone else's land

They call Old England **Acawmenoakit**, which is as much as from *the land on t'other side*. Hardly are they brought to believe that water is three thousand English miles over.

...

Chauquock; a knife. Whence they call Englishmen **Chauquaquock**, that is *Knive-men*; stone formerly being to them instead of knives, awl-blades, hatchets, and hoes.

...

Wunnaumwayean; if he says true. Canounicus, the old Sachim of the Narroganset bay, a wise and peaceable prince, once in a solemn oration to myself, in a solemn assembly, using this word, said, 'I have never suffered any wrong to be offered to the English, since they landed, nor never will.' He often repeated this word, '**Wunnaumwayean English-man**, *if the Englishman speak true*, if he mean truly then shall I go to my grave in peace, and hope that the English and my posterity will live in love and peace together.' I replied, that he had no cause, I hoped, to question Englishman's **Wunnaumwauonck**, that is, *faithfulness*, he having had long experience of their friendliness and trustiness. He took a stick, and broke it in ten pieces, and related ten instances, laying down a stick to every instance, which gave him cause thus to fear and say.

...

This question they often put to me: 'Why come the Englishmen hither?' and measuring others by themselves, they say, 'It is because you want firing.' For they, having burnt up the wood in one place, wanting draughts to bring wood to them, are fain to follow the wood, and so re-move to a fresh place for the wood's sake.

Roger Williams, A Key into the Language of America, 1643[20]

The growth of English in the Caribbean had been achieved with little friction. Very few of the Arawak or Carib population had survived the Spanish take-over of the sixteenth century, and so the English pirates and planters, and the slaves that they imported, were entering an emptied domain. The situation on the North American mainland was very different.

In Virginia and Massachusetts, the first bridgeheads for English settlers, there was still a substantial indigenous population. What with visiting cod fishermen and other scouting voyagers, they were already to some extent fa-miliar with Europeans.* This was lucky for the settlers, since in both places it was only through the active help of these knowledgeable neighbours that they survived those first years. In Virginia, John Rolfe, who founded the cultivation of tobacco in Virginia, married in 1612 none other than Poca-hontas, the spirited daughter of the Powhatan chief Wahunsonacock.† This kept relations with the Powhatan sweet until 1622; in 1616 the couple had even led a party of Virginians to London, where they were presented to King James I. In Massachusetts, the colonists were helped crucially in the first few years by two bilingual natives, Samoset, who had learnt some En-glish from cod fishermen, and Tisquantum. Tisquantum was quite fluent in English, having crossed the Atlantic already six times, spending nine years in England, four in Spain and a further year mapping the New England coast, returning home just a year before the arrival of the English settlers in November 1620.

The task facing the English colonists was quite comparable to the chal-lenge to Cortés and the Spaniards who had invaded Mexico just a century

---

* Chesapeake Bay, the site of the Virginia colony, had in fact been the northern boundary of Spanish Jesuit activities in 'la Flórida'. From 1565 this had included small settlements in the modern Georgia, Carolinas and Virginia, but the whole area was abandoned in 1572 after eight missionaries were killed at Chesapeake.

† Pocahontas was in many ways an exceptional woman. Seven years earlier, when still a girl, she had intervened with her father to save the life of another English pioneer, Captain John Smith, who went on to become the Jamestown colony's first governor. When John Rolfe won her hand, she had still been confined against her will on an English ship on the Potomac river. She later became an early convert to Protestant Christianity.

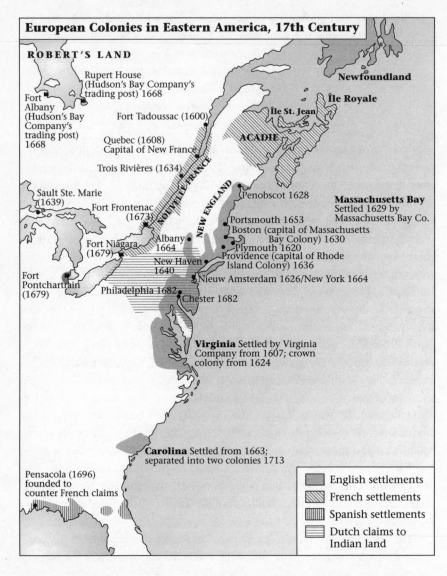

European Colonies in Eastern America, 17th Century

ROBERT'S LAND

Rupert House
(Hudson's Bay Company's
trading post) 1668

Newfoundland

Fort
Albany
(Hudson's Bay
Company's
trading post)
1668

Fort Tadoussac (1600)

Île Royale

Île St. Jean

Quebec (1608)
Capital of New France

ACADIE

Trois Rivières (1634)

NOUVELLE-FRANCE

Sault Ste. Marie
(1639)

Fort Frontenac
(1673)

NEW ENGLAND

Penobscot 1628

Massachusetts Bay
Settled 1629 by
Massachusetts Bay Co.

Portsmouth 1653

Boston (capital of Massachusetts
Bay Colony) 1630

Fort Niágara
(1679)

Albany
1664

Plymouth 1620

Providence (capital of Rhode
Island Colony) 1636

New Haven
1640

Fort
Pontchartrain
(1679)

Nieuw Amsterdam 1626/New York 1664

Philadelphia 1682

Chester 1682

Virginia Settled by Virginia
Company from 1607; crown
colony from 1624

Carolina Settled from 1663;
separated into two colonies 1713

Pensacola (1696)
founded to
counter French claims

	English settlements
	French settlements
	Spanish settlements
	Dutch claims to Indian land

before, to establish themselves, as masters, in the midst of someone else's country. But English motives for being in America were rather different. They were not looking for gold, converts or even dominion. Rather, they were looking for land. This prospect had been the chief inducement for volunteers, ever since Humphrey Gilbert's prospectus for the first failed expedition of 1583. For Englishmen, the intent to create a 'New England' was quite literal, and many showed their earnest by bringing wives and small children out with them.

Since they had no interest in the inhabitants, except as intrusted and expendable helpmeets, it was of little concern to them that there was no major overlord fit for conquest in the part of America into which they had projected themselves, nor that—as it happened—the language spoken by the first inhabitants they met was actually very widespread there and far beyond: they were more struck by the fact that the language as they encountered it was highly riven dialectally, which meant that even those few who made the effort to learn to speak it could scarcely be understood when they wandered farther afield:

I once travelled to an island of the wildest in our parts...I was alone having travelled from my bark, the wind being contrary; and little could I speak to them to their understanding, especially because of the change of their dialect and manner of speech; yet much, through the help of God, did I speak...that at my parting, many burst forth, 'Oh, when will you come again, to bring us some more news of this God?'
...
Anum; *a dog*...the variety of their dialects and proper speech, within thirty or forty miles of each other, is very great, as appears in that word: **Anum**, the Cowweset dialect; **Ayim**, the Narroganset; **Arum** the Quunnipicuck; **Alum**, the Neepmuck.[21]

Unknown to anyone at the time, members of the linguistic family in fact extended in two almost unbroken strips for 2500 kilometres, across the central and northern reaches of the continent as far as the foothills of the Rocky Mountains, from Powhatan to Shawnee to Miami to Illinois to Arapaho to Cheyenne, and from Massachusett to Abenaki to Algonquin* to Ojibwa to Menominee to Cree to Blackfoot. In between Powhatan and Massachusett lay speakers of another related language, Lenape. These languages were very different from English, highly polysyllabic in their words, and with profusions of prefixes and suffixes. But they were fairly similar to each other, as a few animal names show: 'moose' is Abenaki *mos*, Miami *moswa*, Ojibwa *mōns*, Menominee *mōs*; 'seal' is Abenaki *àhkik*^{w}, Ojibwa *āskik*, Cree *āhkik*; 'bison' is Abenaki *pəsihkó* or *wásihko*, Menominee *pesɛhkiw*, Ojibwa *pišikki*, Cree *pisihkiw*; and 'bobwhite', a species of small bird (*Colinus virginianus*), is Lenape *pōhpōhkəs*, and Miami *pohposisia*. In the Massachusett translation of

* The French had, as it happened, already studied the Algonquin language, when exploring the Ottawa river valley in 1541.

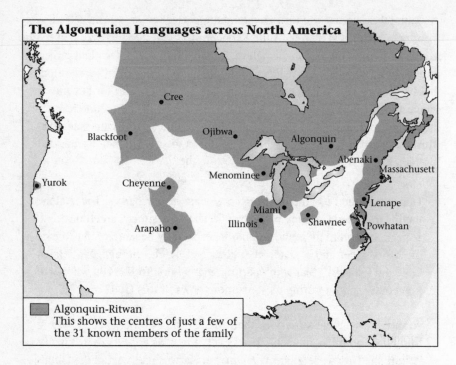

The Algonquian Languages across North America

Cree

Blackfoot

Ojibwa

Algonquin

Abenaki

Massachusett

Yurok

Cheyenne

Menominee

Lenape

Miami

Arapaho

Illinois

Shawnee

Powhatan

Algonquin-Ritwan
This shows the centres of just a few of
the 31 known members of the family

the Bible, the word for 'quails' is *poohpoohqu-tteh*.[22] It is revealing that only
in one of these four examples was the Indian word actually borrowed into English: the settlers had never seen a *pəsihkó* before, but they still preferred to
stick with their own linguistic world, and name it for something similar that
they did know.

The settlers' attitude to the Indians was to attempt to coexist peacefully until they needed to dispossess them to provide more land for their expanding
community. There was little or no cohabitation, but hostilities followed
sooner or later; and the natives of New England in the end died out far more
thoroughly and rapidly than those of Mexico or Peru. Nevertheless, the English never undertook to subjugate the whole country militarily, as the Spanish did immediately in any new territory that they explored. As a result, the
British authorities never felt responsible for the Indians in the way that the
Spanish did; and there was far less effort to convert them. It was only an exceptional Englishman who endeavoured to reach the natives spiritually, or
was concerned to try to build solidarity with them. Two such were the Cambridge graduates Roger Williams (1603?–83) and John Eliot (1604–90), who
learnt their local language, and published books about it: Williams 'A Key
into the Language of America', and Eliot 'The Indian Grammar Begun, or an
Essay to bring the Indian Language into Rules, for the help of such as desire

484

to learn the same, for the furtherance of the Gospel among them'.[23] Williams was more a political activist, expelled from Massachusetts for his views, and also acting as negotiator for the Narragansetts during hostilities; his 'Key' is full of observations on how the natural behaviour of the natives is often at least as good as that of declared Christians. Eliot was more a missionary. Since 1646 he had preached in Massachusett, and translated the whole Bible into it by 1663.[24] Within thirty years there was a ring of towns round about Boston, inhabited by 'Praying Indians'. But in the next generation, when the London-based Corporation for Propagating the Gospel suggested printing a new edition, it was effectively resisted by the colonial authorities. A Puritan divine wrote back:

The Indians themselves are Divided in their Desires upon this matter. Though some of their aged men are tenacious enough of Indianisme (which is not at all to be wondred at) Others of them as earnestly wish that their people may be made English as fast as they can. The reasons they assign for it are very weighty ones; and this among the rest, That their Indian Tongue is a very penurious one (though the Words are long enough!) and the great things of our Holy Religion brought unto them in it, unavoidably arrive in Terms that are scarcely more intelligible to them than if they were entirely English. But the English tongue would presently give them a Key to all our Treasures and make them the Masters of another sort of Library than any that ever will be seen in their Barbarous Linguo ...[25]

By then, Massachusett speakers would already have been few: their principal tribes had been all but destroyed in 'King Philip's War' (1675–6), the last act of resistance by the Massachusett Indians to white expansion, and the Praying Indians were particularly hard hit, having gained no reward from their loyalty to the whites but a two-year deportation to Deer Island, barren and cold, in Boston harbour.

The Virginia and Massachusetts colonies were joined in 1670 by a third, the Carolina colony, set up by eight English lords under a charter from King Charles II. It had originally had the exotic purpose to subsist on silk farming, but eventually reconciled itself to cultivation of rice and indigo.

Manifest destiny

Texas is now ours. Already, before these words are written, her Convention has undoubtedly ratified the acceptance, by her Congress, of our proffered invitation into the Union;...other nations have undertaken to intrude themselves into it, between us and the proper parties to the case, in a spirit of hostile interference against us, for the avowed object of thwarting our policy and hampering our power, limiting our greatness and checking the fulfillment of our manifest destiny to overspread the continent allotted by Providence for the free development of our yearly multiplying millions...It is wholly untrue, and unjust to ourselves, the pretence that the Annexation has been a measure of spoliation, unrightful and unrighteous—military conquest under forms of peace and law—territorial aggrandizement at the expense of justice, and justice due by a double sanctity to the weak. This view of the question is wholly unfounded...

John L. Sullivan, United States Magazine and Democratic Review,
vol. 17, July/August 1845

So the English settlers established themselves in farming communities on the eastern coast of North America. The next challenge came less from the indigenous peoples than from fellow Europeans. In the seventeenth century, the English did not have the eastern seaboard to themselves, but had to share it with colonists from France to the north, and Spain in Florida to the south (see map on p. 413). Even the centre was not uncontested, since there were Dutch and even Swedish territories intervening between Britain's Massachusetts and Virginia plantations. In all these cases, the field was cleared by wars in the mother country's strategic interests. The Dutch were expelled fairly briskly from Nieuw Nederland (Pennsylvania, New Jersey, Delaware and the southern half of New York State*) in 1664, and the French, after a century of wars, from Nouvelle-France (eastern Canada), and Louisiane east of the Mississippi, in 1763. Britain also briefly acquired title to Florida from Spain, in exchange for Havana, which it had captured in 1762; it lost it again after the war of 1812. These were the proceeds of global struggles between the European powers, but nonetheless they opened the territories up to settlement by speakers of English.

The next major event was the war from 1775 to 1783 in which the English-speaking colonies made themselves independent of their home government in London, the 'American Revolution' which created the USA. This was highly significant politically, in that it formed an autonomous source of expansion for the English colonies in the continent; henceforth the chief

---

* Swedish presence on the Atlantic seaboard was of fairly short duration (1638–55); their settlement in Delaware had been summarily evicted by the Dutch.

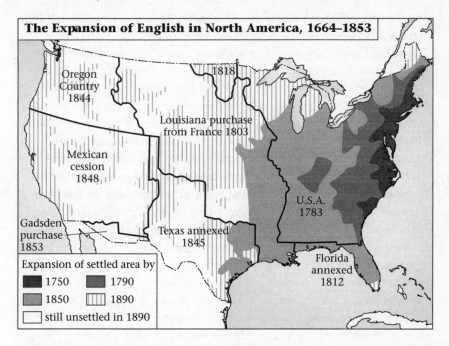

The Expansion of English in North America, 1664–1853

Oregon
Country
1844

1818

Louisiana purchase
from France 1803

Mexican
cession
1848

U.S.A.
1783

Gadsden
purchase
1853

Texas annexed
1845

Florida
annexed
1812

Expansion of settled area by

■ 1750   ■ 1790
■ 1850   ▦ 1890
□ still unsettled in 1890

English-speaking power in North America was a state 'with a built-in em-pire',[26] and, as it transpired, a western frontier that constantly receded until it reached the Pacific coastline. The federal form of government that was de-vised in 1777 turned out to be well suited to this new empire with dynamic borders, as new acquisitions progressed from territorial status to statehood. But it also had immediate linguistic effects outside the USA. Many who could not accept the new dispensation decamped northward to Canada, and so created a significant English-speaking community in Ontario. In the fol-lowing century, this was to attract one of the main streams of immigration into North America, thereby boosting its English-speaking population quite independently of the USA.

By 1783, less than two centuries after the first English colony at Roanoke, English was the official language of every settlement in the east of North America. At that point, three-quarters of what is now the continental USA ('the lower 48') was still under the nominal control of foreign powers, France, Spain and—north-west in the Oregon territory—Great Britain. But in the lapse of two generations, by 1853, the whole area was taken by the USA.* Furthermore, by 1890 settlers had set up cities and farms in every part of the

---

* In 1867, Alaska too was acquired, by purchase from Russia.

area. North of the Rio Grande and Gila rivers there was nowhere left for a significant, independent, language community to flourish.

It had all happened so easily, in just a few major constitutional gulps. President Thomas Jefferson took advantage of the brief supremacy of Napoleon in France to purchase the remaining extent of the French Americas, *la Louisiane*, in 1803; this alone doubled the area of the USA. The next two presidents, James Madison and James Monroe, annexed Florida from Spain, ratifying the deed in 1821; it turned out to be harder to detach Seminole Indians than the Spanish, and the wars with them, begun in 1817, lasted until 1842. Most of the rest of the country was taken during the administration of a single president, James Knox Polk. In 1845 he accepted the accession of Texas, which had detached itself from Mexico—itself newly independent of Spain. In 1846 he split the difference with Britain to end a long wrangle over ownership of the Oregon country, and so created the present western border between the USA and Canada at the 49th parallel. The annexation of Texas, and imposition of war reparations, led to war with Mexico: the USA promptly won it, taking Mexico City in the process, but in 1848 declared itself content to absorb California and the rest of the west.[27] It might have held out for the whole of the rest of Mexico, but eventually decided it was too heavily populated with foreigners. As Senator John J. Calhoun opined—in amazing defiance of two centuries of American history: 'To incorporate Mexico, would be the very first instance of...incorporating an Indian race; for more than half of the Mexicans are Indians, and the other is composed chiefly of mixed tribes. I protest against such a union as that! Ours...is the Government of a white race.'[28]

All the lands that had been gained in this rapid onset had of course long been populated, though hardly at all by the European powers from whom they were acquired. The people who had been there—some two hundred separate language communities in English-language America, and over fifty in California alone—found that contact with the settlers followed a fairly predictable course. In the first instance, before they even appeared, mysterious and deadly diseases would beset the tribe. Then, when the white man came to meet them in person, there would be an attempt at conciliation, which might lead to a treaty as between independent nations, the United States (or His Majesty's) Government and the tribe, which would designate boundaries, and mutual obligations. There might be as much as a generation of peaceful coexistence; but later, as more and more white people arrived, and began to encroach on tribal land, the tribes would find that the white men's willingness to enforce the agreement against their own people was highly limited; the tribes would find their territories violated, and their livelihoods destroyed.

This might mean war, but ultimately the tribes would always lose it. There were just too many whites, and they were far better armed. All too often, the final stage was a unilateral action by the white men to confine or deport the tribes to a reservation, which might be thousands of miles away. This was the English way with the natives of America, and it was repeated over and over again.

It was essentially an exercise in distancing and exclusion. Although US law recognised the tribes as distinct nations, there was no plan to accommodate them or to integrate them as such within the constitution of the republic. Rather, if there was a plan, it was for their members, individually or as families, to become citizens and householders of the republic. Thomas L. McKenney, in charge of Indian affairs from 1816, claimed: 'We want to make citizens out of them'; and part of the process lay in changing their language to English, 'the lever by which they are to elevate themselves into intellectual and moral distinction'.[29] On 3 March 1819 the US Congress passed an act to give education to provide 'against further decline and final extinction of the Indian tribes ... to instruct them in the mode of agriculture suited to their situation, and for teaching their children in reading, writing and arithmetic'. Expenditure increased from $10,000 in 1819 to $214,000 in 1842, when there were thirty-seven schools and eighty-five teachers. Rule 41 of the Reservation Boarding Schools (1881) read: 'All instruction must be in the English language. Pupils must be compelled to speak with each other in English, and should be properly rebuked or punished for persistent violation of this rule. Every effort should be made to encourage them to abandon their tribal language.'[30]

The official intent to eliminate the ancestral peoples of North America as separate entities has not, ultimately, been fulfilled. Indeed, the population pendulum is at last swinging back. In 1999 the indigenous population of the USA (American Indian, Eskimo and Aleut) was estimated as 2.4 million, up from 1.4 million in 1980. As a percentage of the total population, this represents a recovery from 0.6 per cent to just under 1 per cent.[31] But viewed as a means for spreading English, the official policies must be seen as having been effective, and far harder to reverse than a sheer loss of numbers. By now, passive knowledge of English is almost universal. Furthermore, census figures show that by 1990 fewer than a quarter of American Indians were speaking any language but English at home. Even where native language use was holding up best, on the Navajo reservation in the south-west, the number of those among the school-age population speaking only English went up, in this same period of growing Indian numbers, from 11.8 per cent in 1980 to 28.4 per cent in 1990.[32] Now it is reported that fewer than half of Navajo children still speak the language.[33] In the present situation, the prospect for long-term survival of any of North America's own languages, even in coexistence with English, seems very bleak.

Winning ways

Ask these Pilgrims what they can expect when they git to Kentuckey the Answer is Land. have you any. No, but I expect I can git it. have you anything to pay for land, No. Did you Ever see the Country. No but Every Body says its good land…

Moses Austin, 1796[34]

'Land is the only thing in the world that amounts to anything,' he shouted, his thick, short arms making wide gestures of indignation, 'for 'tis the only thing in this world that lasts, and don't you be forgetting it! 'Tis the only thing worth working for, worth fighting for—worth dying for.'
'Oh, Pa,' she said disgustedly, 'you talk like an Irishman!'

Margaret Mitchell, *Gone with the Wind*, 1936

At this point, with English having completed its spread across North America, it is worth pausing a moment to contemplate this awesome development. By 1890, English had become the presumed common language over 9,303,000 square kilometres of territory, thirty times the area of the British Isles. It was far more than a convenient lingua franca or trade jargon, since for most speakers it was their first language; and for the rest, it was rapidly coming to replace any other language they knew, whether in indigenous tribes or among recently arrived parties of immigrants. Within a single century, a linguistic monoculture had grown to overwhelm a sparsely scattered cornucopia of over two hundred different languages. The only expansion comparable to this in its suddenness and its radical penetration is the Muslims' spread of Arabic across the Middle East and North Africa. Others that come to mind—the spread of Greek across the Persian empire by Alexander, or that of French across north and central Africa in the nineteenth century—were as sudden, but far less penetrating; and the deep-set and permanent advance of Latin through western Europe, or of Chinese across the plains and mountains of eastern Asia, took many centuries to bring about. How was this first explosion of the English speech community possible?

In order to give a satisfactory answer, the question is best broken into two. How could a single European language take over the whole of North Amer-

490

ica? And why of all the contenders was it English which expanded, and not other European languages that were already in place?

The first English colonists' own motives for coming to America were largely the product of delusion. Backers of early voyages of discovery and settlement were courted with prospects of a North-West Passage to enable trade with China and India, of landed estates, and of secure bases to derive wealth from fishing and piracy. The actual returns on capital invested, which came from the fur trade, and from cultivation of crops such as tobacco and indigo, were not foreseen. But from the language point of view, the important thing is not capital, but labour. And after the colonies had become established, there were yet other reasons for people to go out to live there. Most often they were economically desperate, and went under contracts of indentured labour, serving out terms of four or five years before they were free to settle. Others came out to found a new society on ideal principles: such were the famed Pilgrim separatists who came to Massachusetts in 1620, and were followed by so many Puritans in the decades that followed, when the home country was racked by civil war, Commonwealth and Restoration. But what many found, when they arrived, was a string of English settlements where good arable land was available, and as yet largely unfarmed. Crops, when planted, flourished, and there were good markets for the harvests. Gradually, the colonies acquired a reputation for plenty, and emigration began to seem ever more attractive to those facing an uncertain future in Britain. They embarked for the west, often bringing wives and children with them. Governments were never oppressive in the colonies; but after the war for independence which prevailed in 1783, the new beacon of political liberty could be added to the attractions of ready wealth on offer.

It is this introduction of wide-scale agriculture, from hundreds of thousands of new farms, which accounts for the spread of the white settlers at the expense of the natives. It gave them the wherewithal to raise large families, far bigger than what was needed to replace their strength in the next generation: instead, the surplus would head off farther west. The population of New England quadrupled in the two generations between 1650 and 1700. And so it continued, unrelenting for more than three centuries from 1600: startling fertility coupled with an unceasing flow of new recruits from Europe.

For choice of language, it turned out to be crucial that the immigration for the first half of this period had been predominantly from the British Isles. Some 220,000 had immigrated during the seventeenth century, and perhaps twice as many in the eighteenth. Small numbers, compared with the 40 million who would come in the next two centuries. But the first immigrants' language influence was decisive: the vast majority of them had come from

Britain and Ireland, and spoke English. Not exclusively so: at the beginning of the eighteenth century, already perhaps 8 per cent of the population were of German origin. Nevertheless, in 1794 German-speaking farmers in Augusta County, Virginia, were dismissed when they asked the US House of Representatives for a German translation of the laws. The Speaker of the House at the time, F. A. C. Mühlenberg, happened to be a German himself, but still refused to support the request.*

Since 1820, English speakers have in fact been a minority among immigrants, at 43 per cent.† But although immigrants have here and there established communities where many can understand a given foreign language, the USA as a country—perhaps taking its lead from the traditional British stance—has remained resolutely monolingual in English. Despite the vast opportunity to found new towns and cities right up until the end of the nineteenth century as the settlers moved west, English was everywhere accepted as the public language in these new communities as they arose.

Why, then, was it predominantly from Britain that North America was colonised in those first two centuries? Britain, after all, had hardly been the first to establish a foothold on the eastern American shores: Quebec was founded as the capital of Nouvelle-France in 1608 almost simultaneously with Jamestown in Virginia; and Nieuw Nederland had been begun at Fort Nassau up the Hudson river in 1617, three years before the Pilgrims settled in Massachusetts. For seventeen years, 1638–55, even the Swedes had maintained a settlement, *Ny Sverige*, at Delaware Bay, in the area claimed by the Dutch.

What distinguished the British was their desire to settle. From the very beginning, they looked for individual holdings of land, on which they could make a living, and bring up a family. However far they may have travelled, they aspired to do this on much the same terms, and with the same religious beliefs, that they had accepted in their original homes. The resulting large

---

* This has been transmuted into the legend that at one point German was almost to be declared the official language of the USA.

German remained the second-largest language of immigrants (at 25 per cent) during the nineteenth and twentieth centuries. There was a surge of German-speaking immigrants in the early nineteenth century, and a tendency early on for them to congregate in Pennsylvania. It peaked in the 1870s, when 600,000, among a state population of 4 million, are said to have had German ('Pennsylvania Dutch') as their everyday language, with another 150,000 outside the state. The popular use of German in public was very severely damaged by the First World War. It survives today only in small sectarian communities such as the Mennonites and Amish (Adams 1990: ch. 7).

† This is made up of 14 per cent from the UK, 13 per cent from Ireland, 12 per cent from Canada, 4 per cent from the Philippines and 1 per cent from Jamaica. After German with 25 per cent, the next languages are Russian (10 per cent), Hungarian (4 per cent) and Chinese (3 per cent) (US Dept of Justice, 1998 Statistical Yearbook, quoted in Wright 2000: 291).

families would then grow up to repeat the cycle. It was the drive and then the proven ability to do this which meant that, after the first couple of generations, when competition arose with other European powers, the British were always present in larger numbers; this translated into winning armies, but it also meant that they soon occupied any territorial gains that they made.

The crunch came with the Dutch after fifty years. In that time, the Dutch West India Company (see Chapter 11, 'Dutch interlopers', p. 395) had gone on from a culture of trading posts for beaver furs, through a supporting infrastructure of farms (*bouwerijen*),* to offering wealthy businessmen quasi-feudal tenancies called *patroon*ships, a system designed to ensure the delivery of colonists in packages of fifty. It was only when this preferential treatment for the wealthy was shelved, and the company began to offer mechanics and farmers free passage for themselves and their families in 1656, with as much land as they were able to cultivate, that settlement took off, from an estimated two thousand in 1648 to ten thousand in 1660. But it was too late. Settlers were slow to follow the company's urgings to fortify their holdings, and the British neighbours still outnumbered the Dutch four to one.[35] In 1664, when Colonel Nicolls arrived with four men-of-war, as one operation in the then global Anglo-Dutch war, Nieuw Nederland surrendered without a fight. It changed hands once more nine years later, but in 1674 was finally awarded to Britain. In the strictly business negotiations that ended the wars, a North American colony famous chiefly for its beaver pelts counted for less than the sugar cane of Suriname, and the nutmeg of Rūn Island in the East Indies.

The French connection with North America was a decidedly harder nut to crack. French policy had begun quite differently from British, with a strong lead from the king and his court in establishing settlements, yet a decidedly laissez-faire approach to life once there, as long as the furs continued to flow back to France. The result was a marked variance in social profile, with young single males going out alone to Nouvelle-France to become *coureurs de bois*, wild frontiersmen, and settling down—if they ever did—*à la façon du pays*, to found bilingual ménages with local women, producing *métis* children who would hardly consider themselves French at all, and might well not speak the language. This approach made them much more popular with the American Indians, who for the most part sided with them in wars with the Dutch and British. But this turned out not to be the support they needed. The economic focus on the proceeds of hunting—furs—did not make for widespread settle-

---

* New York's 'Bowery' perpetuates the name of the farm of Pieter Stuyvesant, the last Dutch governor.

ment or domestication of the land, and the reliance on local brides—thereby of course denying issue to as many indigenous men—meant that their population did not increase. The French government attempted to intervene in the process in the 1670s by providing a supply of *filles à marier*, with some success (see Chapter 11, 'La francophonie', p. 414). But even this could not compete with the natural growth of the land-hungry British.

In the event it was the terms of peace after almost a century of global war, the Treaty of Paris in 1763, which were to end direct French involvement in America. But if North America alone had been the battlefield and the prize, it had long been clear who would prevail. There were over twenty Britons for every Frenchman in the continent at the time.* And if proof were needed of the importance of men on the ground, it was provided by the English rebels of the Thirteen Colonies twenty years later, who defeated the British army as the French never could. As a final insult, the infusion of British loyalists into Canada which the war caused, together with subsequent immigration that excluded France, meant that British subjects, and English speakers, quite directly minoritised the French in what had been their own colony.

The final serious obstacle to English-speaking dominance of North America was provided by the first entrant to the colonial competition, the empire of Spain. Although Spain and England had been at royal loggerheads during the sixteenth century, and English pirates had pursued the quarrel unofficially in the Caribbean during the seventeenth, the British and Spanish governments had largely given each other a wide berth during the seventeenth and eighteenth centuries. Then they had come to blows briefly and inconclusively, and exchanged control of Florida back and forth between 1763 and 1783. The real reckoning was to come between their two successor states, the United States of America and the Republic of Mexico, over Texas.

Once again it was the propensity of English immigrants to settle which led to trouble. Moses Austin, discovering deposits of lead, had acquired from Spain—in 1820, just before it granted independence to Mexico—a permit to bring three hundred American families into this territory, hitherto seen as a very barren area. By 1832 his colonies amounted to about eight thousand souls, and others had brought the Anglo population up to twenty thousand. In 1833 a coup in Mexico city installed Antonio López de Santa Anna, and reversed Mexican policy on Texas: the Anglos' response was to declare independence and—while staving off Mexican attempts to reclaim the territory—appeal to Uncle Sam. They had to wait out two unsympathetic admin-

---

* Over 1.2 million Britons for 55,000 French.

istrations, but in 1845 President Polk agreed to annexation. Polk got the war he wanted, and was then able to get by force of arms what he had been denied as a purchase, namely the Pacific stretch of Mexico north of the Gila river, including California. In one mighty throw, the USA's bounds had been extended 'from sea to shining sea'. Then a new surge of Anglo-Saxon mass settlement sealed the acquisition, though the motive this time was one that the Spanish could very much appreciate: the settlers this time were not farmers but Forty-Niners, prospectors on the track of gold.

The fact that such a vast area—essentially what is now the whole American West—could change hands so lightly demonstrates how superficial the Spanish presence had been in the three centuries of their control. As the French had reached a non-intrusive accommodation with the natives through the fur trade in Canada and Louisiane, so the Spanish, at last planting a string of Catholic missions along the coast from 1769 to 1823, had established only the lightest contact with the Californian subjects of *Su Majestad el Rey*. Nevertheless, agriculture and stock ranches, with a significant export trade in hide, horns and tallow, had briefly flourished under the auspices of the *padres*. In the very last years, after Mexican independence in 1821, there had been a movement for more radical settlement, and from 1834 a flurry of land grants were made to Mexicans who came to be known as *los Californios*, nonclerical settlers who quickly achieved a brutal reputation. But politically, the transition to Anglo control was almost instant.

Linguistically, the situation has turned out to be far more ambivalent. It seems that those *padres* and even *Californios* had quite an influence. Today, one and a half centuries after the appropriation of Florida, Texas and northern Mexico, 20 million US citizens, 7.3 per cent of the population, still consider Spanish to be, not their second, but their *first* language.[36] Since almost all of these will live in one of the nine states* that used to be, at least in part, Spanish territory (total population 83 million), the language situation there is actually one where one person in four is still happiest to speak Spanish. The incoming Anglo settlers, resident for five or six generations, have clearly established English as dominant: but the Spanish-language community is not dying out. Indeed, it is still growing.

---

* Arizona, California, Colorado, Florida, Nevada, New Mexico, Texas, Utah, Wyoming.

Changing perspective—English in India

The tongue, which is the key to the treasures of the heart and mind, and which serves as a medium to strengthen the bands of society, as well as an organ to unlock the secrets of the heart, happens to be deprived of its office between the Hindostanies and the English. Most of the English Gentlemen do not understand the language of their subjects, and none of these last understand a word of English. It follows, of course, that a company of Hindians, having business with their English rulers, looks very much like a number of pictures set up against the wall...

Sied Gholam Hossein Khan, 1789[37]

I have no knowledge of either Sanscrit or Arabic. But I have done what I could to form a correct estimate of their value. I have read translations of the most celebrated Arabic and Sanscrit works. I have conversed both here and at home with men distinguished by their proficiency in the Eastern tongues. I am quite ready to take the Oriental learning at the valuation of the Orientalists themselves. I have never found one of them who could deny that a single shelf of a good European library was worth the whole native literature of India and Arabia. The intrinsic superiority of the Western literature is, indeed, fully admitted by those members of the Committee who support the Oriental plan of education.

Thomas Babington Macaulay (aged thirty-five), 1835[38]

A merchant venture

An interesting and profound coincidence unites English with Portuguese. Each of the two enjoyed a wide and permanent spread as an everyday language of colonists in the Americas. But around southern Asia each language also expanded, ultimately used more among the local population than by the relatively few sailors, merchants and soldiers who came there from Europe. We have just seen that the property essential for language spread in the Americas had been the propensity for speakers to settle and raise large families, so displacing local peoples, who were thinly spread and technically less developed. Something else must have proved telling in southern Asia, which is home to massive populations long used to foreign traders, and where few of the incomers would ever settle permanently. Especially to the British, India and their other Asian colonies were always places for careers, not lives—for postings, not family homes. More than other conquerors, they remained reserved and distant in their control. Yet paradoxically, the British left their mark on these parts of Asia in their language, far more indelibly, as it now appears, than any known previous invader.

The parallel with Portuguese breaks down when the role of the languages in trade is considered. When the English East India Company acquired its crucial bases in India—Madras (1654), Bombay (1668) and Calcutta (1690)*—the effective lingua franca was still very much Portuguese, 'the language that most Europeans learn first to qualify them for general converse with one another, as well as with different inhabitants of India'.[39] The company stocked two hundred Portuguese dictionaries, and every branch office, or 'factory', had a Portuguese linguist, even if the directors in London wrote to Bombay requiring local translation of paperwork because 'the Portuguese spoken in India differed so much from that spoken in Portugal'.[40] More informally, much business was done in what the Indians called Feringhee, an informal pidgin of European languages: by the end of the seventeenth century, Portuguese, Danish, French, Dutch and English all had factories within a radius of 10 miles in Bengal. English was at this time usable only among the company's own agents, and never became a lingua franca for trade. In practice, business was usually done through the mediation of a bilingual Indian trader, known as *banyan* in Calcutta and Bombay, *dubash* in Madras.†

It is also clear that until the nineteenth century higher-level dealings with Indian authorities, above all the Mughal government, were conducted in Persian.§ Company agents could become fluent in it, although they retained the services of a *munshi*,¶ a combined interpreter, translator, secretary and language tutor. A paragon of such expertise was Antoine-Louis Henri Polier, a Frenchman in the English company's service and a friend of Warren Hastings, who published his Persian correspondence in the late eighteenth century. This shows him highly accomplished, too, in the courtly style that went with the language.[41]

On this basis the real question is: how did English ever spread in India at

---

* By interesting coincidence, the cities that grew up around them, which went on to become the first centres of government for British India, have all been renamed in the 1990s: as Chennai, Mumbai and Kolkata.

† Gujarati *vāṇiyān*, 'merchants', Hindi *dubhāṣiya*, 'bilingual' (Yule and Burnell 1986 [1903], s.vv.).

§ The Mughals had brought Persian to India in the sixteenth century as their language of culture, although their ordinary *sipāhi* ('sepoy') spoke Turkic. There is something strangely analogous to the Norman conquest of England here, with Persian in the role of French, and Delhi's vernacular, developing into '*Urdū*' under Persian influence, in the role of English. In this sense Urdu, literally 'language of the camp', was the distinctive linguistic creation of the Mughals in India. And it was this, not English, which was to become the major language of the British Indian Army. (See Chapter 5, 'Sanskrit no longer alone', p. 222.)

¶ Arabic 'educator, composer' (Yule and Burnell 1986 [1903], s.v.).

all, beyond the transplanted society of the 'writers' (i.e. clerks) of the East India Company, and British regiments serving in the country? The situation, after all, was almost identical with that of the contemporary Dutch in the East Indies, with Persian cast in the role of Malay, Urdu as Javanese, and Portuguese as its very own self. And as we have seen, after a first half-hearted attempt to teach their own language, the Dutch had contented themselves with the linguistic status quo: Dutch never became the language of any but the colonial rulers in the Dutch East Indies (see Chapter 11, 'Dutch interlopers', p. 395). If this pattern had been followed, Persian would have remained the preferred common language of India to the present day.

And there was an extra motive in the back of British minds which drained any enthusiasm for wider use of their native language in India. As a member of the British Parliament put it in 1793: 'We have lost our colonies in America by imparting our education there; we need not do so in India too.'[42] This loss was very fresh in memories in the late eighteenth century: Lord Cornwallis, the very general who had delivered the British surrender to George Washington in 1781, went on to become governor-general of Bengal from 1786 to 1793. Settler communities of Europeans, if they became well established, might follow the American example, and look for independence on their own terms. On this reasoning, India must remain a foreign country, albeit one kept open reliably for British business; it should not be a new British home. Richard Wellesley, governor-general from 1797, wrote to the chairman of the Board of Control in 1799:

> … with relation to powers of banishing Europeans from the British possessions in India … those powers appear to me still to be too limited.
>
> The number of persons [not in the company's service] resident in these provinces, as well as in all parts of the British empire in India, increases daily. Among these are to be found many characters, desperate from distress, or from the infamy of their conduct in Europe. Their occupations are principally … at Calcutta, the lowest branches of the law, the establishment of shops and taverns, or of the places of public entertainment, or the superintendence of newspapers … Amongst all these persons, but particularly the tribe of editors of newspapers, the strongest and boldest spirit of Jacobinism prevailed …
>
> In Madras, the evil resulting from Europeans not in the Company's service is still greater. The advisers of the nabob of the Carnatic, as well as the principal instruments of his opposition to the British government, and of his oppressions over his own subjects, are almost exclusively to be found among that class of Europeans.[43]

British settlement in India, then, apart from activities directly sponsored by the company, was not even seen as desirable by the British authorities. From 1757 to 1856, *Kampanī Sahib*, as it was known, proceeded to expand its financial, political and military control first across Bengal to Delhi, then across the Deccan, and finally to most of what is now India, Pakistan, Śri Lanka and Burma. The one thing the company hardly spread at all was a body of speakers of its own directors' language.

Protestantism, profit and progress

In the end, the wider spread of English was begun not by the East India Company, but by British Protestant missionaries.* The company was in general suspicious of missionary involvement in its domains, on much the same grounds—and with better evidence—as those on which they shunned other Europeans. The bloody mutiny of their Indian troops in Vellore, near Madras, in 1806 was associated with rants by one Claudius Buchanan on Hindu indifference to Christianity, demanding 'every means of coercing this contemptuous spirit of our native subjects'; in 1808 the company had speedily to suppress a tract put out by the Baptist Mission Press in Serampore (Śrirampur), near Calcutta, 'Addressed to Hindus and Mahomedans'.[44] India has long been a dangerous place for pressing a religious point, and the company was sensitive to this hazard, which could be highly damaging to trade.

Nevertheless, there had been churchmen at the company's settlements from the earliest days. Early on, they had had to work in Portuguese, like everyone else, a requirement made explicit in the company's renewed charter of 1698.[45] But soon they began to found English-language schools, primarily for children—often orphans—of company employees and servants: at Madras in 1715, Bombay in 1719, and Calcutta in 1731. The schools grew in attendance, then multiplied, and became centres of access to English, with attached printing presses and libraries. It was clear to anyone that English influence and power were growing massively throughout the eighteenth century: not surprisingly, ambitious Indian parents increasingly tried to obtain for their children a knowledge of English, to share in this growth. Around 1780 the raja of Ramnad (Ramanathapuram) sent his own son to Schwartz's missionary school at Tanjore (Thanjavur), south of Madras. Schwartz's

---

* Comparing this with the role of missions in the spread of Spanish points up another irony. For as noted in Chapter 10 ('The Church's solution: The lenguas generales', p. 364), the Spanish missions had served to retard the spread of Spanish, while the state was inclined to encourage it. In Brazil, something similar had occurred (see Chapter 11, 'Portuguese pioneers', p. 392). But in British India, the effects of Church and state—or state monopoly—were the reverse of this.

schools were being supported by all the main powers in the region: the English Company, the Muslim Haidar Ali and nawab of Arcot, and the Hindu raja of Tanjore.[46]

The market soon responded. By the turn of the century, 'mushroom' schools were growing up in all the centres of English power, but especially round Calcutta. The teachers, 'the broken down soldier, the bankrupt merchant and the ruined spendthrift',[47] were in it mostly for the money, but they included respectable British ladies, such as one Mrs Middleton of Dinapur, outside Patna, and even the celebrated Baptist missionary William Carey of Serampore. They were aimed at prosperous Indians, and the fees charged were high. Nevertheless, the attitudes of the teachers were increasingly patronising. Writing to a military officer on the first day of 1801, the Reverend D. MacKinnon revealed his motives:

> ...I could not discover one particle of classical taste, of the knowledge of mathematical truth, or of genuine moral or religious principle in any class nor in any individual of the human species born and educated in Hindostan or even in all Asia. The dark race appeared and do appear to me, buried in darkness, moving like mere mechanism and utterly void of those sentiments which dignify and ennoble our species and entitle us to claim kindred with the Gods.
>
> All my speculations were at last reduced to two simple propositions.
> 1. That the natives of India cannot be illuminated by their own languages, nor by the Books now existing in those languages.
> 2. That therefore they must be enlightned by the acquisition of other languages & by reading Books capable of forming their taste & of teaching them useful & solid knowlege as well as genuine moral and religious principles.
>
> So long ago as the year 1787 after preaching a Sermon on Christmas Day on the field of battle of Kudjuah...I seriously resolved to try the effect of my own feeble efforts. I compiled a Grammar of the English language of which the rules & instructions were written in the Persian language & character. This Book was published in 1791 at the expence and risk of the Proprietors of the Calcutta Gazette Messrs Harington & Morris. I also was at the trouble & expence of causing a Version of the Grammar to be made into the Bengal-language, but that version was not printed.
>
> You will smile when I mention, that when I resolved to make this effort, I formally applied to Government for permission to let in day-light on the Natives of this country. But I mention it, to observe & testify with

gratitude, that in all my applications public and private to Government and respectable Individuals, I met with decided encouragement & approbation.

It is but too true that these efforts have not as yet produced any visible effect; altho I can produce instances of Individual natives who have acquired a competent knowlege of the English language by the help of my Grammar...[48]

As the actions of the East India Company were more and more subjected to scrutiny and control in London, these attitudes—often shared by such influential reformers as Charles Grant, William Wilberforce and James Mill—were becoming the motive force of policy. In 1813 the House of Commons resolved that 'it is the duty of this Country to promote the interests and happiness of the native inhabitants of the British dominions in India, and that measures ought to be introduced as may tend to the introduction among them of useful knowledge, and of religious and moral improvement'.[49]

In the nineteenth century, as British political control expanded and hardened in India, the old laissez-faire business ethic in dealing with the natives, which had entailed a robust mutual respect, was increasingly replaced by an unashamed belief in European superiority, coupled with a duteous endeavour to bring up 'the dark race' to the moral and intellectual level of the God-fearing Briton.

The company's Charter Act of 1813 included the provision that 'a sum of not less than a lac [100,000] of rupees in each year shall be set apart and applied to the revival and improvement of literature and the encouragement of learned natives of India, and for the introduction and promotion of a knowledge of the sciences among the inhabitants of the British territories in India...' But at this stage the company's traditional distrust of missionary priorities was still effective: the funding was explicitly aimed at 'fostering both Oriental and Occidental science...a reliable counterpoise, a protecting backwater against the threatened deluge of missionary enterprises'.[50] The decision on how this small sum was to be applied turned out to be crucial for the language history of the subcontinent.

The missionaries' wish to give priority to the English language was all the time gathering support from the home government, and at last from the Indians themselves. In the late eighteenth century the company, following popular urging, had founded a number of prestige colleges for the acquisition of Indian learning: for Muslims the Calcutta Madrassa in 1781, for Hindus the Benares Sanskrit College in 1791, and for incoming civil administrators from Britain the Fort William College in Calcutta in 1800. All of these had some classes conducted in English; and Fort William had little else. In the early nineteenth century spontaneous foundations were also made by eminent citizens, notably in 1817 the Hindu College of Calcutta, for 'the cultivation of the Bengalee and English languages in particular; next, the Hindustanee tongue...; and then the Persian, if desired, as ornamental general duty to God'.[51] Ram Mohan Roy, who is considered its presiding genius, was a scholar of Sanskrit and Arabic, but vociferous in his appeals for greater access to English.

> ... we understand that the Government in England had ordered a considerable sum of money to be annually devoted to the instruction of its Indian subjects. We were filled with sanguine hopes that this sum would be laid out in employing European gentlemen of talents and education to instruct the natives of India in mathematics, natural philosophy, chemistry, anatomy, and other useful sciences, which the natives of Europe have carried to a degree of perfection that has raised them above the inhabitants of other parts of the world... We now find that the Government are establishing a Sanskrit school under Hindoo pundits to impart such knowledge as is clearly current in India...[52]

Several new government colleges were also founded, often in oriental disciplines, but under pressure from London the oriental ones were offered various inducements to improve their English-language instruction. Then in the early 1830s came catastrophic falls in the enrolments for all non-English subjects, and corresponding surges for English. A public meeting in 1834 protested against patronage of the classical languages, and in favour of English and the vernaculars.[53]

In this context, the General Committee of Public Instruction made its long-delayed decision on how to spend the company's annual lakh of rupees to promote literature and knowledge. Reversing their previous preference, which had followed the hints in the charter, for native learning (and the translation of European scientific texts into Sanskrit, Arabic and Persian), they decided on 7 March 1835 that 'the great object of the British Government ought to be the promotion of European literature and science among the natives of India; and that all the funds appropriated for the purposes of education, would be best employed on English education alone'.[54]

This decision, although still controversial at the time, proved fateful.* The

---

* This was the very period when British academic studies of India's history were making giant strides: between 1835 and 1837 James Prinsep, Assay Master at the mint, and secretary of the Asiatic

number of the government's English-language schools more than doubled within three years of the English Education Act.[55] This was just the beginning. When in 1857 universities were founded in the classic three British cities, Bombay, Calcutta and Madras, English would be their language of instruction. And this educational preference was simultaneously reinforced in 1835 by a regulation that English was to replace Persian as the official state language and the medium of the higher courts of law, with lower courts using the local vernacular.[56] Sanskrit, Arabic and Persian had hitherto kept a half-practical value, comparable to the survival of Latin into early modern Europe: henceforth, like Latin after the Enlightenment, they would be consigned to purely classic status, symbols of heritage rather than vehicles of learning and research. And English, which had been little more than the mark of a foreign ruling caste, was now going to serve as the means for opening the whole subcontinent to foreign traditions of culture.

The basic language balance had been struck, and it persisted in India through to independence in 1947. And in practice, although English is now classed as an Associate Official language of India, theoretically inferior to the eighteen official vernaculars, it has persisted right up to the present day. English is universal in South Asia as the lingua franca of the educated: how many actually know it is harder to say, with estimates over the past twenty years rising from 3 per cent to 30 per cent of Indians, but fewer in the other states of the region.[57]

Another long-term influence that favoured English, especially in the south, was the absence of any other useful lingua franca: Britain's domain had always included the south of the country, and went on to encompass the whole subcontinent; but Persian or Hindi-Urdu were never acceptable south of the old Mughal boundary. If India, especially a democratic India, is to stay united, it needs a common language that seems neutral, or at least equally oppressive to all.

Society of Bengal, succeeded in deciphering the Brahmi writing of the emperor Aśoka's third-century BC inscriptions, and so unlocked the central story of the Maurya dynasty. (See Chapter 5, 'The character of Sanskrit', p. 188.) James's brother Henry Thoby, then Chief Secretary to the government, had spoken out eloquently against Macaulay's minute, possibly even leaking it and so providing the basis for a petition from eight thousand Muslims and another from Hindus. James, in an editorial in the Asiatic Society's *Journal*, condemned 'a measure which has in the face of all India withdrawn the countenance of the Government from the learned natives of the country, and pronounced a verdict of condemnation and abandonment on its literature' (Allen 2002: 166–7).

Success, despite the best intentions

Although Britain had certainly not conquered South Asia in Seeley's 'fit of absence of mind', the spread of Britain's language which followed on from the conquest was almost fortuitous.

The success of English here came about by processes totally different from those that worked themselves out in North America; and these processes were different even from those that had put Britons and Indians in contact in the first place. In North America, English spread while remaining quite detached from local populations, simply displacing them over time by overcrowding numbers and overwhelming settlements. In South Asia, English spread by recruiting the local elites. Despite the company's early fears, English-language immigrants never became very numerous, never stayed for long, and by and large have all now left.

One essential force driving the recruitment was cultural prestige, definitely a British characteristic by the nineteenth century; and the attractions of this prestige went beyond the early motives of gaining preferment in the government or business. Yet it was not cultural prestige which had made India British, but rather the animal spirits of the men in the East India Company. The one point at which these romantic chancers* drew the line was any thought of meddling with local religions, or the roles of the languages that seemed so closely associated with them. Protestant missionaries, for all their many scruples, did not have this one, and it was precisely on this point that they gradually won the argument back in the home country. The company men at last were forced to take the risk of a prescriptive line on native education: imagine their surprise when it not only did not cause riots, but even proved popular with the (thinking) public. Indian scholars found that English did indeed give them access to a world of thought beyond Indian tradition, in law, physical and social sciences, politics, literature—even, here and there, religion.

In fact, the only disappointment was felt by the Protestant missionaries, who, having won the linguistic and cultural argument, and accepted the gratifying popularity of English-language education, still failed to find many converts among the new English speakers. By and large, the worldly content of modern European culture proved much more attractive to Indians under British rule than any new and readier access to Protestantism. In that sense, the missionaries, who had confidently predicted that 'a thorough English education would be entirely subversive of Hinduism',[58] were deceived.

English has remained all over the region, long after the conquest that made

---

* Motto: 'A lass and a lakh a day' (Dalrymple 2002: 33).

its presence possible has been undone. English will probably continue to spread here, or rather to thicken, with the growth of higher education (and other cultural influences, as we shall see). For this reason, the growth of English in India and the rest of southern Asia provides a far better model for any likely future spread of the language than does the history of English in North America.

The world taken by storm

'North America speaks English.'

> Answer attributed to German chancellor Bismarck,
> when asked by a journalist in 1898 to identify the defining event of his times

An empire completed

These two means to the spread of English—what we may call American sweep-aside and Indian re-education—were to be applied, one or the other, across the whole British empire as it expanded to cover a quarter of the earth. Revealingly, the choice was correlated as much with climate as population: the typical—and ultimately most influential—settler is a farmer, and European farmers only really know temperate-zone crops. In temperate colonies, above all Australia and New Zealand, British long-term settlers became a majority of the population, and so English became the principal language. But in the tropics, where British activities were restricted to government, trade and commercial exploitation, the spread of English was more superficial, affecting local elites, and those in contact with British power centres, through school education and gradual recruitment of the locals into British government and enterprise: this was the pattern in most of the Asian colonies—Burma, Hong Kong, Malaya, Singapore, Sarawak, Brunei and Sabah.

In the sweep-aside countries,* the action was concentrated in the nineteenth century. Australia is estimated to have accommodated 300,000 people (speaking two hundred languages) when the British began arriving in the 1790s; by 1890 they were down to 50,000 (with 150 languages left). Their population had always been concentrated in the south-east, just as the English speakers are today: that is where there is water. In the same period, English speakers went from nil to 400,000 by 1850, and nearly 4 million by 1900.[59] As in the Americas, after the first few years no serious effort was

---

* English law, especially as applied in Australia, has a revealing quasi-synonym for this: *terra nullius*, literally 'land belonging to nobody'.

made to accommodate the Aboriginals, let alone learn any of their languages; even the missionaries were rather unsuccessful in making non-destructive contact.

In New Zealand, although the British found it in 1770 held by a single people speaking a single language, Maori, a similar story ultimately played out. After the 1840 Treaty of Waitangi was struck between the Maori and Britain, British immigration took off, growing twelvefold in the following decade, from 2000 to 25,000 by 1850. In the next half-century, their population grew thirtyfold again, now boosted by big families, as well as an unceasing flood of hopeful new settlers: by 1900 it had reached 750,000. In the same nineteenth century, Maori numbers sank from well over 100,000 to 42,000. They may have had the advantage of knowing the country for a millennium before the British arrived; but they could not contend with European diseases, and above all the productivity of European farm animals, cattle and sheep, evolved to thrive on temperate grasslands. They put up a bitter fight, but like the Australian Aboriginals, they were swept aside.[60]

Both Australian Aboriginal and Maori populations have rebounded in the late twentieth century, but their proportions in their own countries remain tiny: 170,000—a little less than 1 per cent—Australians are now reckoned to be of Aboriginal descent (47,000—0.03 per cent—with some knowledge of an Aboriginal language), and there are now over 310,000 Maori—8 per cent of New Zealanders—of whom some 70,000 speak the language, 1.8 per cent. They are simply engulfed by the modern English-speaking nations of Australia (18.5 million) and New Zealand (3.8 million) in which they still struggle to survive.[61]

Farther north, English speakers came in earnest to South-East Asia only in 1786, when the English East India Company acquired Penang, a small island just off Kedah, largely as a base for naval refitting.* Lord Cornwallis was still governor-general at the time, as keen as ever to avoid settlement, and above all any political involvement. But one thing led to another; the British kindly stewarded the Dutch empire from 1795 to 1814, while its metropolis was occupied by the French, and in the meantime Penang gained a mercantile life of its own, eclipsing the ancient entrepôt of Malacca. The British lieutenant-governor, Sir Stamford Raffles, who had opposed return of the Dutch colonies, felt that Penang, lying outside the Straits, was not quite right to protect the burgeoning trade (largely in opium) between India and China. Through

---

* The company had attempted early on (1612–22) to set up agencies for spice trading at Patani (in Halmahera, the far east of Indonesia) and Ayutthaya, then capital of Siam, and in 1669 for tin at Kedah in the Malay peninsula, but they had always been expelled by the Dutch.

an act of diplomatic legerdemain, installing there a Malay sultan who had been slighted by the Dutch, he was able to acquire Singapore for Britain in 1819. It was then a fairly small settlement, but the population instantly went up to five thousand, and began to develop as the new major entrepôt.

Subsequent intrigues and wars, always undertaken by the British with an eye to the commercial main chance, resulted in British political control being extended to the whole of Burma (1853–86), Malaya (1883–95) and the northern region of Borneo (1888). As icing on the cake, Britain also acquired its own base in China, Hong Kong (1848, enlarged in 1860 and 1898). The linguistic effect was extension of English for law and administration, all over these parts of South-East and East Asia. Others soon saw which way the language wind was blowing: the *Straits Times* of Singapore began publication in 1845 (current circulation 386,000, for a national population of 3 million), and the *South China Morning Post* of Hong Kong in 1903 (circulation 200,000, for a population of 6 million).

Nowadays, knowledge of English is still a mark of the elite in all the successor states of the British colonies. It is often difficult to know what proportion of the people speak it. Its status has become politically controversial in Malaysia since independence in 1957; there is an active policy to 'standardise' on Malay in education, but as in India, English is popular with the large minorities, here Chinese- and Tamil-speaking, who feel threatened by this. In Burma (or, to use its more ancient name, Myanmar) use of English is nowadays not readily admitted by government sources. Its future in Hong Kong, since 1997 returned to mainland China, is obscure, but a survey in 1992 suggested that over 25 per cent had some competence in it. In Singapore, a 1975 survey put competence among the over-forties at 27 per cent, but among fifteen-to-twenty-year-olds at over 87 per cent.[62]

In Africa, there were no major European settlements until the nineteenth century, except for those of the Portuguese and Dutch. But when the scramble for colonies had exhausted the available territory, the spread of English in British possessions followed the re-education pattern as against sweep-aside. The temperate parts of South Africa did attract large numbers of white settlers, but they tailed off as British territory extended northward; the Bantu population, who were fairly recent arrivals themselves, held their ground well. As a result we find 3.5 million English speakers in South Africa, 9.1 per cent of the population, but even grouping together the English and Afrikaans speakers, a million of them mutually bilingual, they amount only to 22 per cent. Farther north, the percentage of native English speakers—essentially white citizens—is far less, 3 per cent in Zimbabwe, 0.5 per cent in Zambia. English is a more significant secondary language in East Africa; there are few native speakers, but 5 per cent of Tanzanians, Kenyans and Ugandans use it, despite the availability of Swahili as an alternative lingua franca. This, of course, is a figure very comparable to countries of Asia that accepted re-education; and in all these countries, as in so many Asian ones, English remains as an official language.

The other major area of old British colonies in Africa is the west, from Cameroon out out along the coast to Nigeria, Ghana, Sierra Leone and the Gambia. In this area also is Liberia, another country with English-speaking links, but in this case through its foundation as a preserve for freed slaves from the United States of America. They all have different histories; but they share the fact that their climate has always discouraged white settlement. All define English as an official language, but it appears that only a smallish minority of their populations, again in the region of 5 per cent, are actually speakers. Since all the countries are highly multilingual, another widespread means for communication is the use of English-based creoles, such as Nigerian Pidgin in Nigeria, Krio in Ghana, Liberian English in Liberia.[63]

The last major area for expansion of English was into the islands dotted across the Pacific. British colonisation of this area came rather later than the French (see Chapter 11, 'La francophonie', p. 417): Fiji in 1874, the Gilbert and Ellice Islands in 1892, the Solomons in 1893, Tonga in 1900. New Guinea's western half was reserved by the Dutch, but Germany and Australia claimed the rest in 1884. Like many German colonies in Africa, this one fell into British hands after the German defeat in the First World War, but in this case the hands were specifically Australian. At the same time, the German (western) half of Samoa was assigned to New Zealand. In the New Hebrides, British missionaries and French planters shared control from 1887.

None of these territories was of great interest to British imperial strategists, except in some notional competition with French influence; the islanders in general were left to the shifting mercies of whale and sea-slug hunters, sandalwood cutters, the cultivators of sugar cane, cotton and coconut, and of course missionaries. One result was the temporary recruitment of large gangs of South Sea Islanders to work on plantations in Queensland, Fiji and Samoa, where they learnt to communicate in pidgin English. Another was a vast infusion of Indians into Fiji to engage in sugar planting and processing, so that now close to half its population speak a form of Hindi. But as a long-term result of all those indentured workers, the South Pacific has become a prime area for English-based creoles, and two of them are now accepted as official languages: Tok Pisin is the language of Papua New Guinea, independent since 1975, and Bislama of Vanuatu (once the New Hebrides), independent since 1980. These creoles are very different from the English spread by missionaries. Anyway, the communities that speak this English are all very small minorities in their countries, as one would expect where the language has been spread by re-education.

English was also coming to the Pacific islands from the opposite direction. Since the early nineteenth century Hawaii had been a winter harbour for whalers, and from 1820 it became the focus of interest for fifteen companies of missionaries from New England. US businessmen were also increasingly active, perhaps looking for a new frontier after the fulfilment of their country's 'Manifest Destiny'; they were the main beneficiaries of a land division organised in 1848–50. For a short time, Hawaiian independence survived, balanced among the contending interests of Britain, France and the USA. But American pressure was unabating: a special treaty of reciprocity was struck in 1875, the Hawaiian monarchy was deposed in 1893, and in 1898 the whole archipelago was annexed to the USA.

In 1896 one of the first acts of the Hawaiian republic, formed briefly after the fall of the monarchy, was to require English as medium of instruction for no less than half the school day; but in practice no Hawaiian at all was allowed. In that generation, the transmission of the language from parent to child stopped dead. One grandmother told her granddaughter before her first day of school:

E pa'a pono ka 'ōlelo a ka haole. Mai kālele i kā kākou 'ōlelo, 'a'ohe he pono i laila. A ia ke ola o ka noho 'ana ma kēia mua aku i ka 'ike pono i ka 'ōlelo a ka po'e haole.

Learn well the language of the whites. Do not rely on our language, there's no value there. One's future well-being is dependent upon mastering the language of the foreign people.[64]

This sounds like particularly harsh re-education, but in fact Hawaii conforms at least as well to the sweep-aside model: by 1996, with the population now standing at 1.2 million, only 18.8 per cent were ethnic Hawaiians, and half of these had less than 50 per cent Hawaiian ancestry. Outside the one small island of Niihau, everyone on the islands is now at least bilingual in English, and the vast majority know no other language.

In the same year of 1898, the USA took the Philippines and Guam forcibly from Spain in a flush of imperialist glee (see Chapter 10, 'Coda: Across the Pacific', p. 377); and a year later they also enforced their own solution to a long-standing dispute over Samoa, taking the eastern half of the archipelago. There was then a respite for forty years, as these new territories got used to the sound of English; but on 7 December 1941 an attack on Pearl Harbor, in American Hawaii, unleashed the Pacific war with Japan. At the war's end, having got to know a decidedly unbalmy side of the islands as battlefields, the USA found itself in possession of all the Japanese colonies in Micronesia. Though no longer colonies after the 1970s, they have all kept close ties to the USA. English has become the lingua franca of the Pacific, but outside Hawaii, Australia and New Zealand it is nowhere a majority language.

Wonder upon wonder

This chapter, like all those before it, has mainly focused so far on the political developments that have spread a language. But something else has been acting in favour of English, at least for the last two centuries, and increasingly so as decade follows decade. A glimmer of it was seen in the 1823 remark of Ram Mohan Roy, pleading for access to English education: '...useful sciences, which the natives of Europe have carried to a degree of perfection that has raised them above the inhabitants of other parts of the world...'

It has not only been self-assured aggression, superiority in fire-power or unrivalled access to capital which has carried British enterprise—and so, directly or indirectly, its language—around the world. All these things have played a role, but they had flowed from, and been reinforced by, the amazing status of Britain as centre and source of the Industrial Revolution. In the nineteenth century, when, as we have seen, people all over the world avidly accepted re-education in English, Britain was evidently the richest, and the most dynamic, country in the world. To quote a historian's pithy and overwhelming summary:

> Between 1760 and 1830, the United Kingdom was responsible for around 'two-thirds of Europe's industrial growth of output' (– *P. Bairoch 1982*), and its share of world manufacturing production leapt from 1.9% to 9.5%; in the next thirty years, British industrial expansion pushed that figure to 19.9%, despite the spread of the new technology to other countries in the West... 'With 2% of the world's population and 10% of Europe's, the United Kingdom would seem to have had a capacity in modern industries equal to 40–45% of the world's potential, and 55–60% of that in Europe' (– *F. Crouset 1982*). Its energy consumption from modern sources (coal, lignite, oil) in 1860 was 5 times that of either the United States or Prussia/Germany, 6 times that of France, and 155 times that of Russia! It alone was responsible for one-fifth of the world's commerce, but for two-fifths of the trade in manufactured goods.[65]

Bathed in the aura of such a stunning reality—even if the full statistics were not then available—it is hardly surprising that Indian students had usually been more impressed by the material benefits of British methods than the imperishable rewards promised by the Protestant missionaries. The prestige of English in the nineteenth century was elevated to the skies through the same process that had made French the leading language of European culture throughout the Middle Ages and the early modern period. At root, the thought was: 'if you're so rich, how can you *not* be smart?'

France had had a good natural endowment of fertile farmland and abundant labour on which to found this, but Britain had had quite a modest starting capital. In the early seventeenth century, when the British had first turned up in the East Indies, and tried to get involved in the spice trade, their main problem had been the lack of goods for which there was any local demand. But now, after over two centuries of trading, finagling, shipbuilding and warring, their capital and influence gave them access to pretty much anything they might desire: as the economist Stanley Jevons crowed in 1865:

> The plains of North America and Russia are our corn fields; Chicago and Odessa our granaries; Canada and the Baltic our timber-forests; Australasia contains our sheepfarms, and in Argentina and on the western prairies of North America are our herds of oxen; Peru sends her silver, and the gold of South Africa and Australia flows to London; the Hindus and the Chinese grow tea for us, and our coffee, sugar and spice plantations are in all the Indies...[66]

Britain, as a power, was going to find that some of these other powers, especially one in North America, would have a tendency to shift the terms of trade against it; but this was no loss to the English-language community; if anything it was a net gain when the English-speaking inhabitants of America began to look beyond their own domain, and use their resources, in fertile fields, in productive mines, and in a highly educated and massive population, for schemes of their own devising.

Amid the general splurge of galloping wealth creation, there was a particular surge in the power and speed of communications. The nineteenth and twentieth centuries witnessed progress that was unheard of, first in inventing, and then in speedily applying, all over the world, systems for transport of people and merchandise. Perhaps even more impressive is the parallel progress made, largely using electronics, in systems to transmit and store all sorts of information. A hundred and fifty years from 1830 takes us from the first railway engine through the steamboat to mass-market air transport, and from telegraph through the telephone to global broadcasts of radio and television, as well as the first approaches to effective computer networks. In the same period, means were found to store, and to access at will, all kinds of sounds, including speech and music, visual scenes and pictures, and views of events and actions as they took place. Any one of these would have had the potential to transform the world in an earlier age; but in this age, when humanity's dreams of magical powers came true, they all came together.

Almost every one of these new technologies was invented by a speaker of English—Stephenson, Fulton, Wright, Bell, Baird, Edison—or by a speaker perhaps of another language who had to work in the English-speaking world, as Marconi and Reuter had. And even when they were not—think of Benz's German internal combustion engine, or the French photograph and motion picture, due to pioneers such as Daguerre and Lumière—it was English-speaking developers, such as Henry Ford or the film-makers of Hollywood, who first demonstrated what could be done with the new media on a truly vast scale. This inevitably meant that the key talk about these achievements, how to replicate them and what was to be done with them, took place above all in English. For scientists and engineers, but crucially for businessmen, English has been the language in which the world's know-how is set out. Never since cuneiform writing set up Akkadian as the diplomatic language of the Near and Middle East has technology been so effective in spreading a language. (See Chapter 3, 'Akkadian—world-beating technology: A model of literacy', p. 58.)

These triumphs in what is called 'communications' all tend to reduce the time-taking and effort-costing effects of distances in the world. But they also tend to reduce the differences between the world as it is presented to distant people. Quite literally, they make certain descriptions of experience 'common' to more and more people. They make regional and international business routine, allow international contacts to involve the highest level of personnel, turn far-distant destinations into sites for brief visits, even holidays. But they also standardise the images and phrases that people carry in their memories, from advertising through entertainment to education; nowadays there are not only classic texts and works of art that we are taught to appreciate, but classic jingles, classic ads, classic kitsch, which we can't get out of our heads from one end of the country or one end of the world to another: and quite likely the words we remember will be in English, even if we are Hungarian, Balinese, South African or Mongolian.

The new technologies of communication have made possible new institutions too, institutions that exist above all to spin words, to decorate them and transmit them. Newspapers, magazines, film studios, cinemas, song-sheet publishers and recording companies, radio stations, television production companies, website designers: the list will no doubt continue long into the future. And within every medium, advertising—the supreme meta-product of the language media, acting as a kind of fertiliser or growth hormone, promoting distribution and sales of all these language-based products through its explicit content, even as its payments for space on the channels enable the communications media to cut their prices and reach farther; and at the same time, a major producer of language material in its own right. None of these new institutions of the nineteenth and twentieth centuries is restricted to English—but they all became available first in English, and English has remained the biggest producer.

As the Portuguese found when they first gained a reputation for trade in the Indian Ocean, a national language need not remain restricted to its own nationals. Portuguese became the lingua franca of international trade—and indeed the Christian Church—in South and South-East Asia for ten generations and more, long after Portugal itself had yielded in influence to the Dutch and British. The same thing has happened to English, but on a global, rather than an oceanic, scale. So many people in different parts of the world were finding that they needed to deal with English speakers that their dealings began to overlap: non-natives, and even those without any direct connection to the English-speaking world, started using English among themselves, purely for their own convenience. In the words of the English proverb, 'nothing succeeds like success', and the spread of a language is no exception. In the twentieth century English replaced French as the usual language for international conferences. The language of air traffic has always been (a restricted form of) English—unsurprising, perhaps, since aviation is a US invention; but English has anyway become the world's *interlingua* of choice. For 1996 it was estimated that 85 per cent of international associations made official use of English, and 33 per cent used nothing else. In Asia and the Pacific, 90 per cent of international organisations work only in English.[67]

And the English-speaking world, with its characteristic eye for a business opportunity, has converted this too into a paying proposition: English Language Teaching (ELT) has become not only a field of education, but—as in those early days in Bengal—a commercial service industry in its own right. Now it flourishes in almost every country of the world: if the ambient language is English, it must be a good place for the students to get plenty of practice; and if it is not, English must be an eminently desirable skill to learn. The influential philosopher James Mill (1773–1836) had once remarked that the imperial civil service was little more than 'a vast system of outdoor relief for the upper classes' of Great Britain: ELT could be seen as a new answer to the same problem, though now the qualifications in background and nationality are a little less demanding than they were then.

This spread of English is harder to map geographically than the expansion of British colonies. In spirit, it follows in direct descent from the re-education policy that the British introduced in India. But the mechanism is almost pure diffusion, since—unlike in India—the language has travelled with very little presence of its native speakers. It is probably the best example of a language spread by the sheer prestige of the culture associated with it. Our previous examples have shown the possibility in principle, as when the Egyptian and Hittite courts of the fourteenth century BC corresponded in Akkadian, when the Cambodians and Javanese of the fifth century AD chose to inscribe their temples with literary Sanskrit, or when the Mughals, sweeping down into India from Afghanistan in the sixteenth century, preferred Persian to their native Turkic as their court language. The seventeenth- and eighteenth-century vogue for French in eastern Europe, too, should be seen in this light. But the spread of English was the first time that a language and culture had simultaneously made themselves desirable to peoples all over the world, truly a unique event.

In one way, our account of this process has differed from the usual one. This is in our lack of emphasis on the role of the USA.

The worldwide take-up of English in the twentieth century, and particularly in its latter half after the Second World War, is mostly set down to the influence of the USA, its globally stationed armies and fleets, its outreaching commercial enterprises, and above all its ubiquitous films, pop music, TV shows, news media and computer software. Certainly, all these things have been significant, and mass enthusiasm for English-language culture is now focused on the products of the USA. Among the native speakers of English, the USA's 231 million are clearly the largest single group, four times the size of the UK's 60 million, and alone make up two-thirds of the global total.[68] And arguably, the preferred brand of English now—to judge from accents fashionable outside their own regions—is General American, verging to African American Vernacular English; by contrast, the UK's current broadcast favourite of 'Estuary English', a London-oriented alternative to the traditional Oxbridge 'Received Pronunciation', is very much a local taste.*

---

* Even today, location in the UK provides the best medial point from which to understand speakers of English from all over the world: US, South African, Caribbean, Indian, Singaporean and Australian varieties are all frequently heard on the British media, together with a range of UK regional dialects (notably Scots, Ulster, Newcastle, Liverpool, Yorkshire, Birmingham and cockney); all are assumed to be intelligible to a British audience. The USA, by contrast, has for over thirty years already applied dubbing or subtitles to films in the English of Australia.

But our concern in this book has always been the spread of language communities, bodies of people who can understand one another through a given language. In this sense, distinctions of accent are irrelevant until they threaten mutual understanding. And looked at historically, it is quite evident that the springboard from which English made its jump to global status was built far less on the recent exploits of Uncle Sam than on the adventures over the previous 350 years of John Bull.

We have to consider the growth of second-language speakers, since it is they who have dominated expansion of English use in the twentieth century: by the 1950s, all sizeable countries whose first language was English had already slowed the growth in their populations. For second-language speakers, a good estimate, or range of estimates, is provided by David Graddol's 1999 essay 'The decline of the native speaker'. He identifies recent growth in Latin America, sub-Saharan Africa and South Asia, growth that will almost certainly lead on to second-language speakers outnumbering native speakers within the next fifty years, if they don't already.

The levels persisting in ex-British colonies range between 2 per cent and 5 per cent, but are usually estimated to amount in total to around 200 million speakers. Other recent estimates put the rate much higher, as much as 20 per cent in India and Pakistan, 10 per cent in Bangladesh.[69] If these are correct, the total should already stand at 395 million. Contrast Latin America and sub-Saharan Africa, where knowledge of English is clearly growing, but where Graddol estimates current percentages as no more than 1 per cent of the population (73 million, 43 million). In the very few parts of the world with significant use of English directly due to US influence, the proportions of people knowing it are 50 per cent in the Philippines (36 million), and 85 per cent in Liberia (2 million—although this last represents speakers of English creole). All in all, these English-speaking regions of non-British origin may represent a total of 152 million.

Already in this second-language-speaking part of the English world, then, it seems that the growth of British-origin English remains more significant than the radical effects of the US influence. But this leaves out of account what may currently be the fastest-growing area of second-language English, namely Europe.* It is purely a matter of definition whether European English should be considered as part of the foreign-language or the second-language domain, but it is clear that it has become the major working language of the

---

* It is difficult to attribute this directly either to British or US influence; English was already widely used as a (then neutral) working language of the European Community before UK accession in 1971. But British English remains the majority option when English is taught in Europe.

European Union, as well as being widely used in commerce, industry and academia in northern European countries, particularly Scandinavia. Graddol's analysis of the European Union's *Eurobarometer* surveys from 1990 to 1998 suggests that English competence in Europe was high, but fairly static, until 1980, at under 20 per cent; it then perked up and since 1990 has begun to take off meteorically. It now stands at over 100 million, approaching a third of the European Union's population.*

English among its peers

O wad some Pow'r the giftie gie us
To see oursels as others see us.
It wad frae monie a blunder free us
An' foolish notion.
What airs in dress an' gait wad lea'e us
An' ev'n Devotion.

Robert Burns, 'To a Louse', 1798

A language that links together a speech community, even a vast one like the global multitude who think and speak in English, is given its character not so much by its phonetics and phrasings as by the patterns of associations that have piled up on its words as they are transmitted down the generations. A language bespeaks a history—the history, of course, of those who have spoken it—and this is the main creator of its reputation abroad, as it is of its attractions to those who may want to learn the language, and so join its community. This is one reason why study of a language has long emphasised its literature, 'the best that has been said and thought'† using that language, as selected by its own tradition. But not all the experiences in a language's long memory may have been hallowed by good writing.

Looking back on the history of English as formative of its present character and reputation, memory can afford to be quite selective: the past before

---

* The 42 million Continentals capable of taking part in an English conversation in 1950 grew to 60 million (18 per cent) over the thirty years to 1980; the figure had reached 80 million (21 per cent) by 1990 and 105 million (31 per cent) by 2000. Taking account of differing competence at different ages—in 1994, 10 per cent of the over-fifty-fives knew some English, but 55 per cent of those between fifteen and twenty-four—Graddol expects the numbers of English-speaking Continentals to peak around 190 million in 2030.

† An allusion to Matthew Arnold's memorable remark, in the preface to *Literature and Dogma*, that 'Culture is to know the best that has been said and thought in the world.' But we are now less committed than Arnold (or Macaulay) to the view that one language can offer privileged access to the whole sweep of human culture.

the sixteenth century of the Reformation and the beginnings of colonial expansion seems to have left only the very faintest of traces. But from that era
on, the kinds of adventures that spread English, and which were prized most
highly by many of its speakers, do have a certain consistency. English is associated with the quest to get rich, the deliberate acquisition of wealth, often
by quite unprecedented and imaginative schemes. This quest has sometimes
had to struggle with religious and civic conscience, and the glories of patrio-
tism, but has largely been able to enlist them on its side. In general, it has been
the ally, rather than the rival, of freedom of the individual. English has been,
above all, a worldly language.[70]

There is little left in English from the epoch before the arrival of the Germanic dialects that were destined to fuse into Anglo-Saxon: perhaps only the
name Britain itself, from a presumably Gaulish term to describe the ancient
Britons, 'the figured ones' (*Pretanoi*—Welsh *pryd*, Old Irish *cruth*, 'form'),
for their custom of body painting. Even older might be the name Albion, used
in Greek *c*.300 BC, and still used in Gaelic to refer to Scotland, *Alba*: for this
the only suggested etymology is pre-Indo-European, making it cognate with
the *Alps*, and two ancient Roman cities called *Alba*: a truly ancient word for
'highlands'.[71] It is also just possible that some features seen in Irish English,
such as 'I'm after finishing my work' and 'I saw Thomas and he sitting by the
fire', imported from typical phraseology in Irish, are features that happen to
go back to the language spoken here before the Celts even got here. Similar
phraseology is after all found in Egyptian and the Semitic languages respectively, and one hypothesis to explain this, and much else, is that there was
prehistoric trade among these regions.[72]

We can briefly recapitulate English's first millennium of existence. The
language, once established in Britain in the fifth century, found itself surrounded by Celtic to the west and the north. Celts could not stand against its
advance at spear-point, but gradually forces bent on converting its speakers
to Christianity converged from the north-west and south-east, finally meeting
and ending the competition at the Synod of Whitby in 664, when King Oswy
ruled in favour of the Roman tradition. English reacted well to the sophisticated missionaries of Roman Christianity, becoming actively literate, with
translations from Latin but also its own poetry and prose set down in books.
Overlaid by French in the eleventh century, it suffered a setback to its literary
life, but benefited from the invaders' military prestige in that it began to expand into all the remaining Celtic areas of both Britain and Ireland. Its life
under French domination could perhaps be compared to the early years of Aramaic, submerged militarily by speakers of Akkadian from Assyria, but gradually replacing it as the empire's elite faced crises that shook its power

structure (see Chapter 3, 'Akkadian—world-beating technology: A model of literacy', p. 64). For the chivalrous romance of Norman French, the disrupting crises came as bubonic plague, which struck repeatedly in the fourteenth century, especially in towns and monasteries, and military severance of England and Wales from southern France. In the new dispensation, where feudal ties were dissolved and politics was firmly focused north of the Channel, English came into its own as the unifying language of the kingdom.

This long period, a full millennium, created the substance of English as we know it, but socially it was so different from the bourgeois life that followed that it has contributed little to the language's modern character. In the sixteenth century England's rulers began to conceive the country as an agency independent of, and in principle equal to, any power in Europe, secular or spiritual. In this period the foundation was also laid for the formal union with the outlying parts of the British Isles, Scotland and Ireland. The governance of the whole region was firmly in London's hands. At the same time, with the advent of printed books, the spelling and grammar of English became standardised. England, and English, was positioned for growth.

This growth, when it came, was based on sea power and commercial credit. Over the course of the seventeenth and eighteenth centuries the strength of the Royal Navy and the City of London became unassailable, and both enabled English to be projected around the world. As the language that settlers brought to North America, English simply persisted and spread: the colonies were self-sufficient, and grew at the expense of their neighbours. Not surprisingly, as they became richer they also became more self-confident and overbearing: they never had serious cause to revise their early, self-regarding, attitudes, especially since they could hardly fail to notice that whenever they came up against opposition, whether indigenous or from another colonial power, they came off best. A belief in 'manifest destiny' could almost be seen as the lesson of experience.

In the other great overseas enterprise that spread English, the English East India Company—founded like Virginia at the beginning of the seventeenth century—business acumen was more to the fore. This enterprise was driven not by desperate or hopeful people committing their lives, but by rich people committing part of their capital. But as in the American colonies, the venturesome spirit of those engaged made it a success. Nonetheless, it did not begin seriously to spread English for the first two centuries. It was only when a more earnest spirit began to prevail at home, and the colonies taken for profit came to be seen as conferring a responsibility to uplift the less fortunate, that schools were founded actively to spread the intangible benefits of Britishness, starting with the language.

By this time a third stream of English-based enterprise was beginning to flourish, the host of ventures in ways to profit from fossil fuels and the sheer ingenuity that go under the name of the Industrial Revolution. This same revolution began the shrinking of the world, with news ever more available of achievements far away. English was from now on identified not only with self-regarding settlers and self-righteous governors but self-inventing and self-aggrandising entrepreneurs too: and so it became seen as a passport to self-improvement for ambitious people all over the world.

This progress of English contrasts in many ways with the careers of other world languages.

Compared with its contemporaries, the fellow European imperial languages, the advance of English is remarkably informal. With the exception of the state's first charter of a trading monopoly for the East India Company, and until the British parliament began to concern itself with policy in the nineteenth century, there is a sense of do-it-yourself. Maintenance of the Royal Navy became a state responsibility, after the glory days of profitable Caribbean piracy were over; but the actual activity of spreading English settlement, British business and indeed the Anglican word of God around the world was left up to private initiative.

This contrasts starkly with the mode of operation of Spain and Portugal, where individual *conquistadores* might open the way, but state involvement of viceroys, and the whole apparatus of state and Church, immediately followed; until the revolutions of the nineteenth century, all Spain's and Portugal's colonies were ruled by governors sent out directly from Europe. This made for strained relations, and a lack of solidarity, between the home governments and the *criollos* who had succeeded in establishing themselves abroad. The Romance-speaking settlers were not really trusted as representatives of their Catholic Majesties. In the early days, the allocation of land through *encomienda* meant that they were at best leaseholders from the king; and as we have seen, many settlers' descendants in Peru adopted Quechua to emphasise their separateness from the European establishment. (See Chapter 10, 'The Church's solution: The lenguas generales', p. 364.) In these circumstances, it is hard to say what the Spanish and Portuguese languages came to represent overseas: perhaps more than anything else, the continuing link with the Catholic Church—ironic, when we remember how the policies of the religious orders had delayed the spread of these languages in Latin America for hundreds of years.

And for France, too, overseas expansion was under government control, ever since King François I had sent Jacques Cartier out to seek a North-West Passage in 1534. In the seventeenth century, Colbert had fretted over the non-expansion of the French language; but a century later, the French colonists on the ground had taken so little interest in de la Salle's explorations along the Mississippi, let alone effective occupation of them, that Napoleon volunteered to sell them, sight unseen, to the USA. All the colonies that the French acquired in the nineteenth century, from Algeria to Indochina, were taken by French arms for the glory of France: *la gloire* remained an active motive. At the same time France was clearly still a major force in the scientific civilisation that it promoted, so that use of French could be presented as a channel to modernity. Settlers did move into Algeria, but elsewhere the force that made the French colonies a reality—and so spread the use of French—was the central government. Apart from in Algeria and Indo-China, this centralised approach meant that withdrawal of French control, when it came in the 1960s, was surprisingly speedy and painless. What often remained was an affection for the French language, a symbol of *la civilisation française*, rational in aspiration, national in sentiment.

Given that Russian was spread over three centuries rather nakedly as a mark of the power of the Tsar's empire—of limited appeal to those not accepted as Russian—and that the twentieth-century attempt to convert it, after the fact, into a vernacular for 'Scientific Socialism' collapsed with the Soviet Union in 1991, the Russian language has something of an image problem. The heavy-handedness with which its materialism was asserted contrasted with the lighter touch of French rationalism, and the even-handedness of British pragmatism, and the open-handedness of American consumerism. Russian's associations with group effort and economic austerity are almost the converse of English's conjuring up of initiative and ingenuity by individuals, leading to wealth through enterprise.

English, as a quintessentially 'worldly' tongue, can also be set against the atmospheres of world languages from a more distant past. Chinese and Egyptian, and indeed Greek and Latin in the ancient world, were all vehicles of civilisations that emphasised the value of the here and now, and at their best were able to provide a high standard of living to their citizens, as well as a degree of peace and security. Arabic and Sanskrit, by contrast, like Latin and Greek in the Christian era, were and are promoted by much more otherworldly cultures, focusing their speakers' aspirations on spiritual aims, and seeing their degree of visible success or gratification in daily life as only a small part of what is really important.*

This difference of language culture is in our age very evident. In the early

---

* Phoenician and Hebrew, though neither achieved great expansion, and both were as languages highly alike, are classic cases of language communities on opposite sides of this divide. As for languages such

twenty-first century, the aspiration to learn English or Arabic has become distinctive for many young people all over the world. In the countries of western Asia and North Africa, Arabic Language Teaching has become a service industry seeking foreign customers, just like ELT in so many other parts of the world. English and Arabic are in some ways remarkably similar: both have a written history of about one and a half thousand years, have been spread around the world by speakers who often knew no other language, and have bodies of literature that freight them with associations many centuries old. But rare is the young person who strives to learn Arabic for Avicenna's philosophy, the stories of the *Thousand and One Nights* or the novels of Naguib Mahfouz; even rarer is one who struggles with English hoping to read the King James Bible, or the Book of Common Prayer. In our age, Arabic is for foreign learners the language of the Koran, English the language of modern business and global popular culture.

as Akkadian or Aramaic, Nahuatl or Quechua, we know too little about their contemporary societies to place them in this framework.

PART IV
LANGUAGES
TODAY AND TOMORROW

Ohē, iam satis est, ohē, libelle,
iam peruēnimus usque ad umbilēcos.
Tu procedere adhuc et ire quaeris,
nec summā potes in schidā tenēri,
sic tamquam tibi rēs peracta non sit,
quae prīmā quoque pāginā peracta est.
Iam lector queriturque dēficitque,
iam librārius hoc et ipse dīcit
« Ohē, iam satis est, ohē, libelle. »

Whoa there, that's enough, whoa there, my book.
Now we've the reached the endpapers.
You want to keep going on and on,
And can't be stopped on the last page,
As if your subject was not exhausted
As it actually was on the first.
The reader is complaining and flagging,
even the publisher is saying:
'Whoa there, that's enough, whoa there, my book.'

Martial, *Epigrams*, iv.89 (December AD 88)[1]

13

The Current Top Twenty

The simplest, biological, criterion for success in a language community is the number of users the language has. In setting the boundaries for such a community the linguist's main guideline is 'mutual intelligibility': the community is, after all, the set of people who can understand one another using the language.

There are many difficulties with this definition. There are practical difficulties, having to do with the impossibility of actually testing whether populations can understand one another, one to one. How much understanding counts as knowing the language? And what if people typically know the language of their neighbours, and so can understand them even when they are speaking a different language? This is a common situation in Aboriginal Australia, but also in many other multilingual parts of the world. Then there are political difficulties, having to do with people's desired or imagined membership of one community rather than another, and the tendency of census data to confuse members of an ethnic group with speakers of its traditional language. And there are, of course, many theoretical difficulties. Importantly, how many languages should be counted when they fade off at the edges into the next language, something they often do. Sometimes speakers of A can talk to B, and B to C, but A can't talk to C. This is a common situation in the northern plain of Pakistan and India, extending up into Nepal, Panjabi gradually merging into Hindi and then Nepali. Sometimes speakers of A can understand B, but not vice versa, as in the notorious case of Portuguese and Spanish: intelligibility is not always mutual.

A further difficulty comes when the languages are considered historically. Mutual intelligibility has no doubt always been assured in each generation as between parent and child, but this is not enough to guarantee that the language has stayed the same down the centuries. We can't easily understand what was written in English before the sixteenth century, and if we could hear their speech, we should probably have difficulty with our ancestors in the eighteenth. In fact, languages, even those spoken in the most standardised

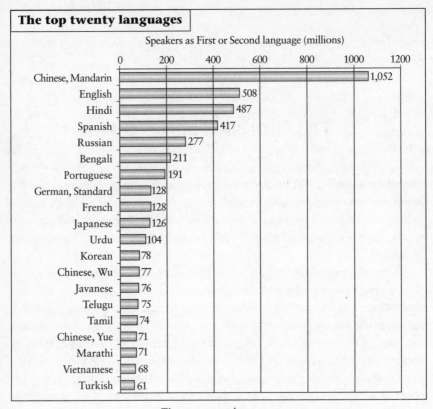

The top twenty languages

Speakers as First or Second language (millions)

Language	Speakers (millions)
Chinese, Mandarin	1,052
English	508
Hindi	487
Spanish	417
Russian	277
Bengali	211
Portuguese	191
German, Standard	128
French	128
Japanese	126
Urdu	104
Korean	78
Chinese, Wu	77
Javanese	76
Telugu	75
Tamil	74
Chinese, Yue	71
Marathi	71
Vietnamese	68
Turkish	61

The top twenty languages

and widespread communities, almost always change. Should this have an impact on our assessment of language identity, and so of the success of a language over time?

Consider, for example, the case of Latin. Should this language be considered dead, a noble tradition sadly ended, because it has no native speakers whose words are close to what we find in the texts of the Roman empire? Or should it rather be considered to have gone to language heaven? Its texts from every period are still read, and its modern forms, collectively called the Romance languages—Spanish, Portuguese, French, Italian, Romanian, Catalan, Occitan and many more—are spoken worldwide, with a total speaker population of over 660 million, making it up to the present the second-most successful language in the world (after Mandarin Chinese). *O death, where is thy sting?*

Still, it is possible to construct the league table of the world's most widespread languages as they are spoken today, even if it is necessary to make a few arbitrary decisions to do so. The table, once revealed, gives useful hints on the factors behind a large body of people coming to speak the same language. It is also a useful corrective to the linguistic bias that tends to be created by our usual reliance on Eurocentric media.

These figures[2] are based on use of the languages as first and second languages, i.e. not just native speakers but also people who have acquired the language for some other purpose and use it actively. Such 'secondary' speakers are clearly part of the language's community. But we must be cautious about the numbers and hence the detailed ranking. The figures here are based ultimately on census returns, which may be subject to distortions with political intent. And English particularly has a large tail of 'foreign language' learners who are quite competent in it and use it frequently, even if it plays no official role in their countries, and may be unrecorded in census figures.[3] However, the identity of the mega-languages is in practice uncontroversial.

The size distribution of the world's languages is a lesson in itself. Adding together the native-speaker communities of these top twenty languages, we already have 57 per cent of the world's population. Indeed, the top twelve alone account for 50 per cent of the world, hinting at how tiny the populations of most of the other six and a half thousand languages still spoken must be.

In the world's top twenty, all the languages have their origins in the south or east of Asia, or in Europe. There is not one from the Americas, from Oceania or (most surprisingly) from Africa.* But quite naturally, and conversely, these absent areas are precisely where the world's remaining linguistic diversity is concentrated.

The languages can be divided into two sets: those that have grown 'organically' and those that have been put together through processes of 'merger and acquisition'. Organic growth is principally through population increase in the area of origin, but it can also include encroachment on neighbouring areas. Merger and acquisition spreads a language to discontinuous areas of

---

* The first language of African origin is in fact Egyptian Arabic, with 46 million speakers, which ranks it no higher than twenty-third. The different 'dialects' of Arabic, of which there are over twenty-five, offer quite solid barriers to mutual intelligibility, so they are well cast in this list as distinct languages. If they are consolidated as a single hyper-language community, united by the elite's use of classical Arabic as a lingua franca, they would amount to something over 205 million, placing them between Bengali and Portuguese. Those who know classical Arabic number about 100 million. (The distant ancestry of Arabic, like all the Semitic languages, lies in Africa. See Chapter 3, 'Akkadian—world-beating technology: A model of literacy', p. 58. The next major African language is Hausa, with 39 million native and secondary speakers.)

the world, principally through seaborne invasion and settlement. All the languages that have spread in this latter way, English, Spanish, Portuguese and French, had their origins in western Europe, and indeed are daughter languages of Latin, or profoundly influenced by it. Although the other three European languages in the list, Russian, German and Italian, are not known in recent history for their associated governments' attachment to peaceful methods of expanding their domains, their linguistic growth has been in practice predominantly organic. It is worth noting, as an early antidote to any militaristic presumptions about the causes of language growth, that outside the activities of the European colonists in the second half of the second millennium AD, very little of the growth of these giant languages in the top twenty can be set down to imperial aggression.*

What does account for their growth, then? It is noticeable that a great many of the languages (nine out of twenty) are spoken in civilisations sustained by rice as a staple crop (Bengali, Japanese, Korean, Wu and Yue Chinese,† Javanese, Tamil, Marathi, Vietnamese). Evidently, rice is capable of supporting dense and extensive populations, and its cultivation, through controlled flooding, requires a high level of organisation. Other languages which are not predominantly in the rice area are spoken in neighbouring areas that have assumed political control of the rice areas (Mandarin Chinese, and Hindi and Urdu, which are linguistically in a dialect continuum if they are distinct at all). It is also inescapable that, outside the European languages, the list is predominantly made up of languages of the two cultural giants of Asia, China and India.

Looking farther down the list (to the top fifty), many of the same patterns obtain: more variants of Chinese (Jinyu, Xiang, Hakka, Min, Gan), more Indian minority languages (Gujarati, Kannada, Malayalam, Oriya, Panjabi, Bhojpuri, Awadhi, Sindhi), more rice economies (Burmese, Sundanese (of western Java), Thai), more large European languages, grown organically (Polish, Serbo-Croat), despite (in one case) a colonial past (Dutch).

Politically, it is noteworthy that almost all these languages have been under a centralised authority for at least a millennium: large-scale languages do

---

* Another exception is the campaigning advances of the Arabs and Turks, moving in opposed directions from the seventh to the twelfth centuries, and replacing the languages of the Middle East and Anatolia with their own. By a quirk of these statistics, Arabic does not make it into the top twenty, and Turkish only just. Turkish, however, has 61 million speakers, and when all the (mutually intelligible) Turkic languages are included, the community has 147 million, making it a clear member of the top ten.

† They are better known in the West as Shanghainese and Cantonese.

not flourish in areas of small-scale political units, although curiously the languages that have grown organically in western Europe, Italian and German, are exceptions to this. Evidently, the longer-term history of Italy gives something of an explanation: there had been political unity until the breakdown of the western Roman empire in the fifth century AD; the political union achieved in the last two centuries, the basis for its apparent linguistic unity today, harks back to that golden era. German is likewise an artefact of the politics of the last two centuries; but the fact that the speakers of the various German dialects have stayed close enough over the last two millennia to accept a common literary standard is surprising and impressive, for there is little overall political unity at earlier stages of the language community's history. (See Chapter 11, 'Curiously ineffective—German ambitions', p. 446.)

Another question concerns the choice of the language that spreads out in these favourable environments. Is there a criterion that predicts which language in a group will spread out to eclipse its neighbours? In a centralised kingdom, this is often a matter of policy, conscious or unconscious: unsurprisingly, the standard chosen for promotion is usually the variety used in the national capital. Hence Mandarin Chinese is historically the form of the language closely associated with the city of Beijing,[4] as Japanese is with Tokyo.[5] In Middle English, the dialect that came to predominate and so set the standard was that of London.[6] Among the various middle Indian dialects, Hindi/Urdu was characteristic of the Delhi region.[7] Russian is by origin the Moscow variant of eastern Slavonic;[8] Vietnamese is based on the region of Hanoi;[9] and French is the Romance speech of Paris.[10] Sometimes, the national capital has moved: so standard Spanish derives from the speech of Toledo, capital of the kingdom of Castile in the mid-thirteenth century;[11] and Korean is believed to have originated in the region of Silla in the south of the Korean peninsula, which was dominant in the seventh to tenth centuries.[12]

Grossly, then, one could claim that, in the political economy of languages, it pays to be the dialect of a city that becomes a national capital; it pays to be in a tropical plain, especially if it grows rice; and above all it pays to be in East or South Asia. But all these criteria have exceptions: indeed, English started out with none of these advantages. As in business, it is evident that merger and acquisition can outpace organic growth.

A disadvantage in basing our observations on the properties of the most widespread languages in the world, as they happen to be today, is that the top twenty list gives no intrinsic sense of the dynamics of language growth: which, for example, are the new entrants, and which languages are moving up, which down? How would the list have looked a century ago, and how will it look a hundred years hence?

To answer these questions we need to combine demographics with some sense of language prestige as it waxes and wanes.

The demographics are a matter of common knowledge: the Asian languages in the list, whose growth has been organic, will continue to grow, with the exceptions of China (by policy) and Japan (through falling natural fertility). The Asian languages are in the list because of their countries' huge populations, which by their very nature did not develop overnight. Therefore, they must be permanent members of the list, until and unless these populations show some tendency to change their language (for example, to adopt the local national language in place of their own regional speech), or are hit by some immense catastrophe, so frighteningly huge that it would have to be comparable to the epidemics that devastated the Americas after the advent of the Europeans from the sixteenth century.[13]

Some jockeying and rebalancing among languages in China and the Indian subcontinent is likely in the next fifty years: the fertility rate per woman in China in the period 1995–2000 has been 1.8, in Japan 1.4, whereas in India and Bangladesh it has been 3.1, in Pakistan 5.0. On these trends, India's overall population is projected to overtake China's by 2050; in the same period, Pakistan (majority language Panjabi, spoken by perhaps a third of the population) is set to become the third most populous country in the world (overtaking the USA), but Bangladesh (speaking Bengali) will just hold its position (as eighth most populous). Applying the population growth percentages to these languages, the main effect should be a jump in the speaker numbers for Urdu and Panjabi, while the Indian regional languages Telugu, Marathi and Tamil may overtake the regional forms of Chinese, Wu and Yue. Mandarin Chinese is so far ahead (with three speakers for every one of English, Hindi-Urdu or Spanish today) that it will still be by far the most widespread language in the world, though perhaps in fifty years only double the size of its nearest rival.

Birth rates are high across the Arabic-speaking countries, so their population may more than double in the next half-century. This should be enough to maintain Arabic's position as the fifth-biggest language; but it will still be necessary to add together what are in effect twenty-five separate spoken languages—there is no trend towards a unified standard outside elite usage. Most of the more southerly parts of Africa are also growing far beyond the global average, so we can expect its languages to move up the league table: if they keep pace with Nigeria's population as a whole, the two largest, Hausa and Yoruba, will treble their native-speaker populations by 2050, rising from thirty-eighth and forty-ninth positions to twenty-first and twenty-third. Even with such growth, however, the languages of sub-Saharan Africa will remain outside the top twenty for the next fifty years.

Unsurprisingly, the European languages on the list are in a much more fragile position. German and Italian have owed their large numbers to organic growth of their home populations; in terms of current fertility rates, though, these are set to fall, perhaps by as much as 10 per cent in the next fifty years. This would be enough to demote German towards the bottom of the top twenty, and relegate Italian altogether. But any decrease in either of these countries is in present conditions likely to be made up by increased immigration, effectively maintaining speaker communities through foreign recruitment.

Russian too is in decline. Augmenting its organic growth in eastern Europe, it has had a role as the lingua franca of a vast empire, which at its height took in the whole of north Asia in a gigantic crescent from the Caucasus to the Sea of Japan. At the moment, however, populations are shrinking all across the remaining parts of greater Russia; and where they are not, in the newly independent states of central Asia, people are reawakening to the fact they have a pre-existing lingua franca to use with the neighbours in their own, closely related and mutually intelligible, Turkic languages. If these do not suffice, the people are also increasingly coming to believe that their global links may be better served by adopting English rather than Russian as their language of wider communication. For all these reasons, the future does not look rosy for Russian.

The other major European languages, English, Spanish, Portuguese and French, all owe their status to the colonial empires that came to dominate the earth in the second half of the second millennium AD. They are the languages of colonial populations that were able to grow massively in their new, transplanted, homes, adding the strength of immigrants to their natural increase; they were also able to spread at the expense of languages previously local to the colonised lands: in this way, languages of wider communication often ended up monopolising all the communication.

For all of them except French, their most populous ex-colony now vastly outnumbers their motherland: the USA has over four times the population of the UK, Mexico almost three times that of Spain, Brazil seventeen times that of Portugal. It is extremely difficult to predict their positions among the most widespread languages of the world fifty years from now. Spanish and Portuguese should maintain their share in countries that are still growing strongly: Mexico and Brazil, for example, are expected to add some 50 per cent to their populations in this period, and the other colonies in the Americas and Africa will not be that different. Meanwhile, the USA may add a quarter to its population, although this may not benefit the English-language community—significantly, the growth is mainly among Spanish speakers.

In fact, it is for French and English that the future is hardest to predict. These are the languages that might be seen as vehicles of globalisation, each in its way a lingua franca for contact with a wider world. Their native-speaker populations tend to be in countries where the population has stabilised and may even be decreasing. This would imply that their prospects for future growth are limited. However, those same countries are the most influential in the world, economically, culturally and militarily. As a result, English and French are widely acquired as second languages by people all over the world, for business and cultural reasons that have everything to do with the prestige of the languages. In the case of French especially, the language's status is locked in politically, since so many of France's ex-colonies, especially in central Africa, have adopted it as their official language. (See Chapter 11, 'La francophonie', p. 419.) As for English, the prestige has sometimes very little to do with historic links: witness the current surge of interest in learning English around the Baltic Sea, a zone that has never had dealings with Britain or America. More generally, US-centred mass culture enjoys global popularity at the moment. But the long-term linguistic effect of this, as we have seen, may be surprisingly transient. (See also Chapter 14, 'Way to go', p. 541.)

The future balance among languages worldwide is now very much in contention. Demographically, the role of the European languages, and especially English, could have been expected to decline, as the rest of the world grows both absolutely, and in terms of relative wealth. (One key milestone was passed recently, when English traffic on the Internet was exceeded by the total in other languages.) But as that wealth grows, there appears to be an increasing demand to learn and use these languages, for they are now seen less as symbols of colonial domination and more as crucial keys for access to the global system. In some sense, the languages' importance in the role of lingua franca, and as symbols of commitment to a way of life that goes beyond local interests, counteracts the decline of their dominance as first languages.

This tension between inward and outward growth, between the increasing importance of a mother tongue as its speaker population grows and the concurrent popularity of a lingua franca seen as developing links to a wider world, is felt not only at this, global, level. In principle, it is nothing new: the same tension has a long history in the struggles to transcend tribal and communal frictions in order to build federated nations.

It is notable that the two largest languages in Indonesia, Javanese (75 mil-

532

lion) and Sundanese (27 million), both spoken on the highly populated island of Java, are growing fast, and are far larger than what is promoted as the national language of the country, Bahasa Indonesia (17 million)—which is linguistically none other than Malay, the lingua franca of the East Indies, and as such spoken not only in Indonesia but also in Malaysia, Brunei and Singapore, with 47 million speakers in all.* For most people in Indonesia, as in the world, local life and its contacts still loom far larger than national or global aspirations.

Likewise, in East Africa the lingua franca is Swahili. This language, of Bantu origin but transformed through trade contact with Arabic (see Chapter 3, 'Arabic—eloquence and equality: The triumph of 'submission'', p. 103), has some 30 million speakers in all, but only 5 million of them acquired it naturally as their first language. Nevertheless, it is the official language of Tanzania, and the most widely spoken language in neighbouring Kenya and many other countries in the area. Everywhere, it has fewer speakers than the countries' largest languages.

For many purposes, it is less important how many there are in a linguistic community than who those people are—and how well distributed.

---

* Nevertheless, its association with Indonesia was strong enough for it to be pointedly discarded as an official language in the new state of East Timor, which has nostalgically opted instead for a return to the language of the earlier colonial power, Portuguese.

14

Looking Ahead

What is old

The most evident judgement to emerge from our global survey is that migration of peoples, the first force in history to spread languages, dominates to this day. A farmers' migration brought Chinese south to the banks of the Yangtze Kiang and beyond; nomads' and refugees' migrations brought Aramaic east from Syria and down the Euphrates to Babylon; a merchants' migration brought Punic across the Mediterranean sea from Tyre to Carthage and North Africa. Migrations organised politically as state colonies, but still attracting volunteers, seeded Latin among the Gauls of northern Italy and southern France in the second and first centuries BC, as they seeded English along the eastern shores of North America in the seventeenth AD, and along the shores of Australia in the nineteenth. Even now the quasi-spontaneous migration dynamic of Spanish speakers moving north across the Rio Grande is the greatest challenge to the complete dominance of English in the USA.

It appears that, until the interesting developments with English in India in the nineteenth century, foreign conquests led to language shift only if the conquest was followed up with substantial immigration of people who already spoke the conquerors' language. In this sense, it is migration rather than conquest which is really at root when a military conqueror apparently spreads his language into new territories.

The importance of attracting immigrants may account for a major difference that we noted between the Greek and Roman empires. Greek-speaking only superficially followed Alexander's conquests in the far-flung provinces of the Persian empire, even though Greek control was politically secure. In Persia itself, Greek was eliminated after five or six generations when Parthians reasserted indigenous control; and even in Syria, Palestine and Egypt, where Greek administration was taken up under the Romans and so continued for a millennium, the popular language for all that time remained Aramaic (with Egyptian in Egypt). When the Arabs took over administration in the seventh century, Greek was eliminated altogether within a couple of generations, even after a thousand years. By contrast, the Roman conquests on the continent of western Europe have proved permanent in their linguistic effects. Even where there were no explicit colonies (and we have noted how these led the way for Latin in northern Italy—see Chapter 7, 'Rún: The impulsive pre-eminence of the Celts', p. 293), all over the empire the Roman army provided a continuing source of settlers, veterans often settling down and working the land where they had served.[1]

Likewise, the cracking early pace of English-speaking immigration into North America was influential in promoting English over all the other colonial languages in the seventeenth and eighteenth centuries. (See Chapter 12, 'Westward Ho!', p. 481.) And as the exception that proves the rule, Canadian French established itself, and throve, through a deliberate policy of assisted emigration for French-speaking women. (See Chapter 11, 'La francophonie', p. 414.) The later massive immigration to North America was an exception in a different sense: it did not diminish the now settled English-speaking tendency of the continent because immigrants did not, in general, move or settle in with others of the same language; as a result these later immigrants tended mostly to acquire English, rather than passing their own languages on to their new neighbours.

Immigration is the basic seed of language spread, but very often the propensity of newcomers to settle, and so displace older populations with different languages, is compounded and reinforced by the greater fertility of the newcomers. Finding themselves at some sort of advantage over the natives, they turn out to have larger families, and hence in a few generations are more numerous than the indigenous population. This has very likely always been a concomitant of large-scale immigration—without some sort of advantage, whether in health, wealth or even acceptance of lower wages, it is difficult to see how any immigrant population can become established over residents— but it has been particularly clear in the early history of the USA, Australia and New Zealand, where the growth was meteoric and documented by census. In all these cases, the immigrants were introducing temperate-zone crops and livestock. One can conjecture, however, that similar factors must have played out very often in the past—for example, in favour of the first Semitic speakers in many parts of western Asia, when they first introduced arable crops into new territories that had previously known only hunters, gatherers and pastoralists. Larger families mean heightened demand for land, but also larger armies to take and defend it, and all this benefits the languages the farming immigrants speak. This is in fact nothing other than the 'natural growth' that we found responsible for so many large language communities in Chapter 13.

One factor that is often credited for language spread we have found of very little long-term effect. This is trade. Formal trade relations are of course of great antiquity, at least as old as written language. (We saw that the origin of written language in Mesopotamia seems to have been due to a reinterpretation of trading tokens (Chapter 3, 'Sumerian—the first classical language: Life after death', p. 51).) But no community famous for specialisation in trade has passed its language on permanently as a vernacular, or even as a lingua franca, to its customers. At most such activity tends to infiltration of the language, or even diffusion, since the instances where merchants have set up permanently as immigrants into the customer community are rather rare. Carthage, which carried the merchants' language Phoenician, or Punic, into a substantial part of North Africa would be one such rare example. In general, these merchants' languages—other examples are Sogdian along the Silk Road, Arabic and later Portuguese in the Indian Ocean—do not make the jump from a restricted business use. When the market disappears, or others muscle in, the language too is dropped. So suggestions that English nowadays is benefiting from its position as the language of global business need to be received with some scepticism: English may well be today's pragmatic preference, but trade patterns change over time, and a trade connection alone will not guarantee a language community.

However, merchants do not always just bring goods on their visits to exotic locations. Sometimes they bring with them a new faith, and either act as missionaries for it themselves, or bring vocational missionaries with them. These missions can be important vehicles of a new language, if the faith has such an association. The Sanskrit and Pali that reached South-East Asia in the first millennium AD came with Hindu and Buddhist traders or buccaneers; a thousand years later, other traders from India were bringing in Islam, while the first European merchants, mostly Portuguese, were offering them Catholic Christianity. Of these four religions, each with an attendant language, only Christianity—the least language-conscious—seems to have projected its language as a vernacular; while Sanskrit, Pali and Arabic have remained languages confined to worship, Portuguese actually became the first language of many converts, and survives to this day in popular creolised forms from India to Malaya. And the English East India Company, which had come to India merely in search of profit, stayed long enough for missionaries to build up their strength and end up teaching the population English too.

But missionaries are not always traders with an ulterior motive. Missions may themselves offer a major motive for travel to distant parts: and such pilgrim missionaries have spread many languages, especially in Asia. In the first century AD Buddhist monks rounded the Himalayas, through Afghanistan and the Pamirs, to take the Four Noble Truths to the Chinese, and with them sacred Sanskrit. In the eighth century Nestorians, coming all the way from Syria via Persia, reached the entrance of the same Silk Road, and through it brought Christianity—and at least briefly Aramaic—into the heart of China. They had already taken it to the southern tip of India. (See Chapter 3, 'Second interlude: The shield of faith', p. 88.) Muslims too had come along the same trans-Asiatic route to spread their faith, which survives, especially on the coasts of China, to this day; and Islam is unthinkable without Arabic. Just recently, in the nineteenth century, Protestant Christian missions brought the first words in English into central Africa, and to most of the Pacific Islands. (See Chapter 12, 'The world taken by storm', pp. 507ff.)

Sadly, missionary motives are not always so peaceable. Put another way, dominant peoples sometimes feel an urge, usually conceived as a duty, to impose their faith on foreigners they have defeated, to 'enlighten' them. In extreme cases—not rare in the second millennium AD—the duty is sharpened into a righteous aggression: the believers must attempt to defeat their neighbours simply to impose their faith on them.

This 'crusading' motive seems particularly characteristic of the faiths derived from Hebrew revelation, Judaism, Christianity and Islam. It has been mitigated for the Jews by the fact that they have almost always been in much smaller force than their enemies or neighbours, and hence can only endorse the doctrine nostalgically, recalling biblical tales of their early conquests. For Muslims, there was always the doctrine that *ahl al-kitāb*, Peoples of the Book—Jews, Christians and Zoroastrians along with Muslims themselves— were owed a special tolerance, and so a certain moderation was shown to most of those they defeated. It fell to Christians to try out the full rigours of waging aggressive and imperialistic wars in the name of religion.

The doctrine was forged in the crusades against Islam of the twelfth and thirteenth centuries, when the Christians had insufficient advantage to create long-term dominance. But in the expulsion of the Moors from Spain in the fourteenth and fifteenth centuries, and even more in the Americas, forces were far less even. The kings of Spain and Portugal received formal authorisation to dispossess other kings, and establish their own empires, explicitly in order to extend the domains of the Catholic faith.[2] But it was one of the greater ironies of this global review to discover that all over Latin America it was the religious communities which tended to sustain use of America's indigenous languages: Europe's languages began to wipe the others out only when the special concern with and for natives lapsed. (See Chapter 10, 'The state's solution: Hispanización', p. 373.) Whatever the Christians' original intent, it was settlers, rather than missionaries or their crusading Faith, who spread languages.

What is new

Human nature may not change much, but in the last half-millennium—the period we have represented as Languages by Sea—some new factors have come into play which affected radically the capacity of languages to spread.

The first of these is global navigation. The motive for developing this was mercantile, a fifteenth-century European ambition to acquire Asian commodities, especially spices, more cheaply. The ambition was very soon fulfilled, but an immediate side effect was to operate in the reverse direction—the gradual establishment of speech communities of Europeans far away in Asia and the Americas, communities that very soon gained new members locally. It was no longer necessary for speech communities to be contiguous, or linked by brief cruises across familiar seas.

It is possible to quote forerunners for this breakthrough—the Chinese commerce with South-East Asia that briefly expanded to take in the whole Indian Ocean in the early fifteenth century (see Chapter 4, 'Language from Huang-he to Yangtze', p. 147); the Arab, Persian and Indian traders who had taken the Indian Ocean for their domain in the early first millennium AD; the much earlier Polynesian mariners of the Pacific in their outrigger canoes, who island by island reached every habitable landmass there; indeed, the primeval navigators who many thousands of years ago made their way through the East Indies and across the Torres Straits to Australia. But none of these forerunners succeeded in mapping the whole world once and for all, providing the complete inventory of what lands there were to be discovered, and where they lay. In the sixteenth century, the world shrank from an open system to a closed and definite sphere, still dangerous but now for the first time manageable. Now it became conceivable that fellow-speakers could set up home on the other side of an ocean, indeed many oceans away: they might be hard to reach, but their address would be known. Though they were scattered across the world, contact could be maintained.

Once this network of discontinuous communities had been established, maintainable through regular sea traffic, the scope of inter-communal relations changed too. In the Americas, the onset of epidemic disease very quickly readjusted the relative size of resident and incomer communities, and in Latin America extensive interbreeding soon blurred the borders, linguistic and cultural, between them. As a result, the settler communities largely replaced, by incorporation or by simple displacement, the previous resident populations.* Nothing new there, except for the continental scale of what was

---

* Everywhere the situation was complicated by the simultaneous surge in the use of third parties, mostly black Africans, as slaves; to an extent they, or a mix of them and the indigenous pop-

happening; something analogous must have happened, for example, when the Romans invaded Gaul, or the Saxons took over England. But in India and the East Indies, the indigenous community was not vulnerable to disease brought by the immigrants: on the contrary, the diseases endemic there kept the immigrant population small. The result was a persistently small minority community of outsiders, the Europeans, living on the edge of the resident population, but increasingly influential within it. This was a new situation and the response to it, the spread of a language by re-education, was new too.

Effectively, the outsider minority passed its prestige language on to the elite of the majority, not as a lingua franca, but as a symbol of a kind of cultural recruitment. The novelty of this development is underlined by the fact that it happened in British India, but not in the highly similar Dutch East Indies. Both the Dutch Vereenigde Oostindische Compagnie and the English East India Company had brought a Germanic language to a long-standing commercial market in South Asia; both had succeeded in displacing European competitors, the Portuguese or the French; both had attracted Protestant missionary camp-followers who were keen to spread their spiritual world-view to the local population. But the Dutch were content always to use the local lingua franca, Malay, as the language for their religion, and their administration. The *mijnheer*s' own world was separate from that of their local suppliers, employees and (ultimately) subjects, and so it would remain. (See Chapter 11, 'Dutch interlopers', p. 395.) Only the British provided the means to switch to their own language, English. When they did this, they were yielding certainly to pressure from their own missionaries, but also from their home population and many elite Indians. The emerging new attitude to the colony demanded nothing less, seeing it not just as a place in which to make a profit, but as British India, to be developed as a part of Greater Britain.

This step turned out to open the way to English as a world language, available to any who wanted to take part in the Industrial Revolution, wherever they might live. The motives at the time may recall those of Archbishop Lorenzana, calling in the eighteenth century for the use of Spanish throughout Spain's empire, not least as a duty to the education of the Indians. (See Chapter 10, 'The state's solution: Hispanización', p. 373.) But he was really calling for the use of Spanish to be imposed, not conceded; and so it ultimately was, largely through neglect of education in other languages. The case

---

ulation, became the representatives of a new minority community, with the immigrants now the majority. But this slave-associated minority was never divided by language from the majority community, since they had become a community themselves only by adopting some version of the slave-owners' language.

of English in India did involve some symbolic withdrawal of government support for Sanskrit and Arabic; and the generalised use of English which followed has contributed to the closing of English-speaking minds, where foreign languages are concerned. ('After all, they all speak English, don't they?') But this spread of the language, ultimately worldwide, through what we have called re-education, was never an imposition; English remained the language of a small minority, and even among Indian nationalists its acquisition felt more like the development of an opportunity. It was a new and significant development in the history of language spread, and was later taken up as a deliberate policy by at least one other power, the French, in their empire's conceived *mission civilisatrice*. (See Chapter 11, 'The second empire', p. 416.)

Another important innovation in language spread over the past five hundred years, and especially the last two hundred, was the growing role of technology. Civilisations are, by their nature, technology-driven; indeed, by one definition a civilisation is just a distinctive accumulation of technical innovations. And the spread of language had been advanced by technology before: recall how Akkadian's availability in cuneiform writing on clay made it the diplomatic lingua franca of ancient West Asia (see Chapter 3, 'Akkadian—world-beating technology: A model of literacy', p. 58), and how the alphabetic system invented by Phoenicians had provided the basis not just for a new elite role for Aramaic speakers as scribes in Assyria and Babylon, but in the end for administration and education throughout the world from Iceland to the East Indies.

But in the modern era language spread has been effected above all by mass production of language texts, and later the means to disseminate them instantly over any distance. First came printing, already starting up in Europe in the fifteenth century. It played a cardinal role in western Europe's encounter with many unknown languages, as well as in spreading its own.* Then, four hundred years later, came electronic links, first point-to-point and then broadcast. The effects on language spread have been profound. Language communities have become sustainable despite physical separation.† This may have an effect—as yet unknown—on the development of the languages themselves: electronic technology, if it becomes totally pervasive, might

---

* A little-noted spin-off of this was the first use of printed books as language tutors, initially of Latin. This in turn led to the development of missionary linguistics, originally as an aid to preaching in exotic places (Ostler: 2004).

† This can be expected soon to benefit small language communities, as well as the great languages that have been the subject of this book.

even bring about not only the widely announced 'death of distance' but even 'the death of dialect'. But it has had indirect effects already. The withdrawal of the European imperial powers in the quarter-century after the Second World War, especially from Africa, was above all a policy response to a new globally sensed politics, the 'Wind of Change' famously detected by the British prime minister Harold Macmillan in 1960: 'The wind of change is blowing through the continent. Whether we like it or not, this growth of national consciousness is a political fact.'[3]

The foreign elites were departing, in deference to the voices of the world's many, among them the people they governed. Those voices had become audible through those same elites' own mass media, indeed now speaking in their own languages.

Way to go

We must be doing something right to last two hundred years.

Henry Gibson, song entitled '200 Years'[4]

We have yet to consider what future may await English.

The past four hundred years have been almost absurdly affirming for the English-speaking peoples, as political, military and cultural victories have succeeded one another. The language community has expanded overseas from England, first by stealth in tiny crevices, then by imperial assertion over ever vaster domains, and finally, after the demise of arrant colonialism, to apparent acclaim in a single world marketplace. It is a creature first of the human social faculty for creating a language among disparate groups who share a single territory, then the ability discovered by that one island community to use its naval strength to spread its citizens and its political influence wherever it found points of weakness all over the world, and most recently of being the language most readily to hand when Europe, North America and then the world discovered how to profit from fossil fuels, science and mass markets. This tremendous run of luck has created an enormous reserve of prestige, reflected in the global enthusiasm for English-language popular culture. As the French language showed five hundred years ago, association with wealth and power is highly attractive.

But English can hardly expect that its linguistic vogue will continue for ever. The presence of a single language for communication worldwide is stabilising, giving it the appearance almost of being a neutral part of the world order, as much beyond the control of great powers as it is of any one society.

541

Likewise the Latin language, lasting almost a millennium after the demise of the Roman empire in the west, gave western Europe at least, in its long separate development, good reason to believe that it had become the permanent and pure language of thought and reality. But the printing press, long-distance navigation and the rise of global empires changed all that. The world remains a highly dynamic place. For languages, as for any human institution, when you are on top, sooner or later there is only one way to go.

The current status of English has three main pillars that support it: population, position and prestige.

First of all, English has as many speakers as any other language. When its 375 million native speakers are added to the equal number of second-language speakers and the three-quarters of a billion people who have learnt it at school or in other classes, it is reasonable to claim that a quarter of mankind is familiar with English. The only comparable language is Chinese, when all those educated in Mandarin are added together; but the average income, status and global location of the English speakers give English very much the edge. Learning English is a majority school subject in the People's Republic of China; Chinese, by contrast, remains off the syllabus in all English-speaking countries' schools.

Second, there is now no language to match English for global coverage. English has a special status in countries on every continent, a status it shares only with French. But there are four first- or second-language speakers of English for every one of French. The complacency of English speakers speaks for itself: while English speakers still predominate in all measures of commercial and scientific achievement, it remains the norm in every English-speaking country for those completing compulsory education to be monolingual in English. Effective competence in any foreign language continues to elude the vast majority of those who are made competent in the technical basis of modern civilisation. And this is how they stay throughout their lives. But it is not just that the majority of English speakers are complacent. It is more that the world has as yet exacted no price for this; if anything, it has rewarded English speakers for not swerving from their own traditions and sources of wisdom.

Finally, English is consciously associated with technical progress and popular culture in every part of the world. This kind of high prestige associated with the language seems particularly well founded because it is based not on a spiritual revelation—revelations are always local, even if they claim universal validity—nor on yearning for a particular regime, which would guarantee freedom or social justice. It is based on the perception of wealth, as it may be made to flow from scientific advance, and its rational application.

Since this has been the recent experience of all the richest countries in the world today, in some sense it has objective truth on its side.

Practical human beings are notoriously short sighted, so the 'smart money' (itself a very English concept) is naturally backing the belief that the recent course of English, and hence its present status, will continue indefinitely. Just as the *bien pensants* of the 1990s could be brought to believe briefly in 'The End of History', the ultimate victory of liberalism and markets,[5] so many to-day argue that the progress of English may have passed some key global point in the development of world communications, permanently outdistancing any possible competitor, and providing all language-learners with a one-way bet. David Crystal is a highly knowledgeable and perceptive commentator on languages in the modern world; and at the end of his book *English as a Global Language* he has reviewed the factors that might endanger its position, notably foreign negative reactions, the changing balance of populations, and the prospects of dialect fission. But even he can only speculate in the end that 'it may be that English, in some shape or form, will find itself in the service of the world community for ever'.[6]

Our background study of five millennia of world language makes the eternity of this prospect seem unlikely. The modern global language situation is unprecedented, but the constituents of modern language communities are still people. And, above all, people use language to socialise. Human societies have always had a way of multiplying languages.

First of all, most people in the world are still bilingual; this points to the fact that global languages have seldom established themselves as anything more than second languages, useful as a lingua franca where long-distance communication is important, but not particularly commanding as vehicles for everyone's daily life. The major exceptions to this have been the grass-roots spread of Latin over Gaulish and the Iberian languages in western Europe, and Chinese over East Asia, where literate language communities have spread over contiguous areas, without necessarily filling them up with native-speaker settlers. English, starting on an island and without a European bridgehead, never enjoyed this kind of contiguous spread; and its main mode of spread today, via education, the electronic media and literate contact, does not lead to it replacing home community languages.*

Second, English is not seen everywhere as a neutral medium of access to

---

* However, the nature of the home community is changing, partly under the influence of English. Rising levels of female education, more and more including English, and the prevalence of domestic media such as radio and television, mean that the 'mother-tongue' situation for learning a first language in the home will increasingly include English.

wealth and global culture. Some policy-makers, typically in ex-British or ex-American colonies, have 'seen too much of it', and resist it, often combining historic associations with domestic power politics. In 1948, Ceylon (now Śri Lanka) excluded English as an official language, partly because it was believed that its continued use would benefit the (predominantly middle-class) Tamil minority; the sequel, including the establishment of Sinhala as the only official language in 1956, has not been happy, and much use of English continues. In 1967, English was stripped of its status as an official language in Tanzania and Malaysia, and in 1974 in Kenya; in 1987, the Philippines promoted Tagalog to equal status with it, 'until otherwise provided by the law'. This resistance may fade in later generations, along with memories of colonial history;[7] but global interventions by the USA, sometimes in alliance with other English-speaking powers, show no sign of diminishing in the twenty-first century. They will do much to preserve an easy depiction of English in some quarters as the global bully's language of choice.

Lastly, even if English persists worldwide, there is no guarantee that it will stay united as a language. Although the world in the early third millennium AD is a very different place from western Europe in the early first, English could well follow the example of Latin, and reshape itself in different ways in different dialect areas, ultimately—say within a few centuries—becoming a language family. This is particularly likely wherever the language has established itself as a vernacular, as in Jamaica or Singapore, or where most of a population becomes bilingual, so that code-switching is an attractive mode of conversation, as for example it is today among educated Indians. Evidently this is less likely to happen, or will at least be slowed, if the communities that speak English stay in regular two-way touch, by phone and correspondence, and receiving each other's media. English probably still holds the best position among large languages worldwide for preserving its unity by mutual contact. As one indication, international telephone traffic is overwhelmingly dominated by conversations in English.* But not all English-speaking communities may play a full part in the global conversation; and long-term rifts and rivalries may come to dominate—as Spain and France contested for influence in Renaissance Italy, a mere millennium after they had all been provinces of a single empire.

It is possible to outline a variety of scenarios for a turn in the fortunes of

* Of the forty-eight most heavily used intercontinental flows of telephone calls in 1994, 46.9 per cent (53 billion minutes) were between English speakers. Another 50.4 per cent (57 billion) were between English speakers and countries of other languages (figures from TeleGeography Inc., as cited in Graddol 1997: 37).

English, drawing inspiration from the later years of many dominant languages of the past. Both as a first language of large populations, and as a world lingua franca, English may find that the seeds of its decline have already been planted.

As a first language, English has already peaked demographically.* In this it is no different from most of the other imperial languages from Europe. Its native speakers are still growing in numbers, but at a far slower rate than those of some other major languages. As a result, according to one intelligent estimate,[8] English, Hindi-Urdu, Spanish and Arabic should just about be on a par in the year 2050, with Chinese still exceeding each of them by a factor of 2.5. This is a time when world population is predicted to level off, but the heritage of the different past growth rates will be a massive difference among the average ages of the speakers of the various languages. English and Chinese will then be predominantly languages of older people, Arabic of the young, with Spanish and Hindi-Urdu somewhere in between. This is not to predict the average wealth of the different communities, which may be an important determinant of the evolving power relations among them, and also— as we have seen in the careers of French and English—of the attractiveness of their languages to outsiders. English may still have the greatest global spread of a language, and its speakers even the highest average income; but it will no longer have its current positional advantage, at least as to numbers of native speakers. If the English-speaking economies come to seem less dynamic, it is entirely possible that linguistic leadership too will shift away.

And even in the big native-speaker countries, the language may increasingly have to accommodate the presence of other large language communities—in the USA Spanish, in the UK perhaps some of the major southern Asian languages, and in Canada, as ever, French, but perhaps also Inuktitut. The different varieties of English will be under very different local pressures; bilingualism with different languages may become significant, and the dialects may progressively move apart. Like the Aryan language of India in the first millennium BC, diversifying into Prakrits and then separate languages, even while Sanskrit was preserved as an interlingua, or like the fate of Latin in Europe in the first millennium AD, English could find itself splitting into a variety of local versions among native speakers, while the world goes on using a common version as a lingua franca.

But as a lingua franca too, English could still face difficulties. Witness the fate of Sogdian, from the eighth to the fifteenth centuries AD the merchant and

---

* See Chapter 13, p. 532.

missionary language of the Silk Road from China to Samarkand; or the fate of Phoenician, the mercantile jargon of the whole Mediterranean throughout the first millennium BC, and eminent spreader of literacy. Both are today non-existent. A language associated with business is soon abandoned when the basis of trade, or the sources of wealth, move on; businessmen are notoriously unsentimental. And it is hardly rational to expect that the extreme imbalance in the world's distribution of wealth is going to continue in the anglophone favour indefinitely into the future. One day, the terms of trade will be very different, and soon after that day comes, the position of English will seem a highly archaic anomaly.

Likewise the association of English with world science may fail to save it. Dispassionate enquiry has never been an activity that appeals to a majority, however widely education is made available. Serious research remains a minority activity, which because it is disinterested will always need patronage from others who have accumulated power or wealth. But those political, military, business or religious elites cannot be trusted, especially if it seems that the results of enquiry are telling against their own power, or failing to buttress it: they will then often adjudicate in favour of tradition, or popular ignorance. It is easy to forget how much the ongoing popularity of science depends on its continuing to offer new golden eggs, or new golden bombs. When the flow of goodies slackens, as one day it may, the pursuit of science will be widely seen as an expensive indulgence by its paymasters, in industry and government.

In the same way, when the many themselves enjoy market power, as they did to some extent in the print revolution of the Reformation, and as they often do now in the anglophone world, they will use their money to demand what they can understand, and think they need. That is the way of markets. But their judgement will be heavily coloured by tradition. We can already see creationism, and an oracular approach to some of Christianity's ancient texts, flourishing at the heart of the richest, and most technically developed, country in the English-speaking world. If powers within the USA, now the provider of the world's greatest sources of information and learning, were to start to bear down on its freer thinkers, one could imagine other parts of the world beginning to guard their own learning behind the cloak of their own languages.

In fact, academic traditions too have a fairly poor record, even on their own account, for sustaining interest in genuine open-mindedness; there is always the temptation to appeal to authority, and the accepted canon of 'normal science': recall how the *sképsis* and *theōría* of third- and fourth-century Greece hardened into later linguistic conservatism and scholasticism, how

the lively disputations underlying Sanskrit grammar and Buddhist logic congealed and ceased to develop in medieval India, and how the Abbasid golden
age of research in Arabic petered out with Averroës in the twelfth century.
There is plenty of scope for the worldwide scientific community to go into at
least a temporary eclipse; and if global scientific exchange falters, English
too will lose out. The second death of Latin shows vividly how such a thing
can, and did, happen on an international scale.

There are already new potential centres of world civilisation growing, with
different language backgrounds. In East and South-East Asia, Chinese-
language communities are increasingly apparent as masters of investment,
and look likely at last to work in concert with their fellow Chinese in the
rapidly developing People's Republic. (See Chapter 4, 'Foreign relations',
p. 161.) In the Middle East, Arabic-speaking peoples are growing in numbers
with some sense of solidarity, part of the global *ummah* bound together by
acceptance of Islam. The militant actions of radical Islamists, and the inequi-
ties of income and power caused by the dominance of oil revenues in their
economies, may slow their real integration. But ultimately it is hard to doubt
that this very large and self-conscious group, sharing a faith and a language,
and increasingly able to communicate at all levels through modern media,
will make common cause, even without political leadership from one of the
main states of the region.

Less prominently, too, we can note that two-thirds of the world's 147 million Turkish-speaking peoples, notably Turks, Uzbeks, Turkmens, Kazakhs
and Kyrgyz, are now organised independently of foreigners for the first time
since the Russian advance into central Asia.* As a total community, there are
more of them than there are speakers of any of German, French or Japanese.
With better communications, they will begin to consider themselves a unit,
for most of their languages are mutually intelligible.

Such reorganisations will not immediately threaten, or even at first
significantly diminish, the global use of English. But they may offer early
signs that the equilibrium of languages used in global communication is beginning to shift in a different direction.

To foresee Chinese or Arabic as major international languages requires no
imagination: it follows from extrapolation of current population trends, in
combination with well-known economic and political facts. But in reality, the
future language history of the world will quite likely involve surprising new

---

* Seventeen per cent (mostly Azeris) are in Iran; 7 per cent are in China (mostly Uyghurs); and 7 per
cent (made up of Tatars, Chuvash and Bashkirs, and a variety of tiny groups) are in Russia.

developments that alter population balances. Who could have foreseen that discovery of gold in Brazil in the 1790s would suddenly spur that place to fill up with Portuguese speakers, when Portugal had already held the land for three centuries without any great linguistic effect? Sometimes a single event is enough to trigger a potential that has long been possible, but remained unrealised.

And who, even in the eleventh century, could have foreseen that the import into Europe of paper-making (twelfth century), gunpowder (fourteenth century) and printing (fifteenth century) would have first revolutionised its religious life in the Reformation, and then sent its adventurers out to settle, and to dominate others all over the non-Christian world? These three were all imports of techniques that had been known in China since the early first millennium, without any noted effect in their homeland. So even in a closed system, new interactions can have revolutionary consequences.

Major events and interactions, now unforeseen, will disrupt and reroute the future too; there seems little doubt of this. Most easily predictable—but not, I hope, certain—is some kind of military holocaust, something that is nowadays technically all too easy. This could profoundly alter the balance of populations in the world, as the Anglo-Saxon advance through North America led rapidly to the extinction or endangerment of all its indigenous languages. An epidemic too could have a massive balance-tipping effect—as everywhere in the Americas when Europeans came, but as perhaps also twice in Britain, during the twilight years of Celtic British and Norman French—especially in situations where there is pre-existing bilingualism. A truly horrific epidemic, even if localised, could well permanently alter the linguistic situation in Malaysia, or in Canada.

Not every unforeseen event need change the status quo to the detriment of English, of course. Remember the Persian emperor Darius, who decreed the use of Aramaic throughout his realm, although it was then a foreign language with nothing to recommend it but a very strong background as a vehicle of administration. It is quite possible, on that analogy, that some pragmatic government might hasten the spread of English to a part of the world hitherto without it—in the Baltic, perhaps, or central Asia. Indeed, something like this happened when Lee Kwan Yew decreed English for the largely Chinese-speaking colony of Singapore in the 1960s.

Whatever happens, any changes that do occur may have a surprisingly disturbing effect on the English speakers who remain. For three centuries now, the bounds of the language have continually expanded. Typical speakers may pride themselves on their pragmatism, and welcome the breaking down of language barriers, in the interests of wider understanding and easy communication. But when the language whose use is to be reduced is their own, expect discomfort to be registered. In 1984, some 8 per cent of the US population professed a first language other than English. This was enough for a programme of legislation to get under way in the early 1990s, to 'recognize English in law as the language of the official business of the Government'.[9] There is now a continuing hubbub of proposal and appeal on the topic in many states' assemblies, which remains inconclusive. We have yet to see how other English-speaking countries will react when they too can no longer easily assume that the option of communication in English is always open.

But no law and no decree anywhere has ever yet stemmed the ebbing of a language tide.

Three threads: Freedom, prestige and learnability

Wovon man nicht sprechen kann, darüber muss man schweigen.

What one cannot speak of, one must pass over in silence.
Ludwig Wittgenstein, Tractatus Logico-philosophicus

Freedom
At various points in this narrative, there has been a temptation, almost a duty, to speak of freedom. Many language traditions make a particular claim to speak with it, or for it. Freedom of speech is one of the cardinal ideals, upheld in the great modern statements of human rights, and endlessly controversial in practice. For many civilisations, freedom is the virtue that gives speaking its main purpose. Yet in the end, we have said next to nothing about it. Why?

Freedom is a particular concern of some kinds of states, particularly republics. Some peoples that have particularly exhibited freedom as an ideal are the Greeks, the Romans, the Venetians, the French after their Revolution in 1789, the British (though discreetly) after their 'Glorious Revolution' in 1688 which asserted the supremacy of Parliament over monarch, and the United States of America. But although it is generally agreed that *eleuthería*, *libertās*, *libertá*, *liberté* and *freedom* are translation equivalents, there has never been widespread agreement on what makes a person, a people or a state free—even in these polities, which are in a continuous, and very self-conscious, tradition of European political philosophy.* Is it independence from foreign overlordship, civic self-governance, non-recognition of heredi-

---

* *Thai*, too, means 'free': so the ideal can also be found outside the European tradition.

tary rights, or the right of personal choice over religion, location and means of support? All these ideals suggest different ways in which the right of choosing what to say should be exempt from restriction.

From our perspective, the avocation of all these ideals, dear as they are to so many, has made little concrete difference to the survival and spread of any language community. Greek-language culture, as ostentatiously propagated round the Levant, Egypt and Persia by Alexander and his successors, and taken up by the Roman elite, involved little or no democracy, and mostly allegiance to absolute rulers—*basíleis*—who declared themselves the legitimate successors of the kings of Macedon and Persia and the pharaohs of Egypt. Rome went on purveying Latin round its empire when the free, civic, institutions of the republic had been placed in thrall to a single family with army backing. French had become the preferred international language of European culture under the auspices of the Bourbons' absolutist monarchy; the French Revolution projected the slogan '*Liberté! Égalité! Fraternité!*' and made France much more aggressive militarily, but it had little or no effect on the attractions of its language; its popularity began to falter only in the early twentieth century, long after the Restoration and the second fall of the French monarchy. The political freedoms so prized by Englishmen and Americans, which had brought the former to behead one monarch and depose his son, and then the latter to declare independence from the British state altogether, turned out to be quite compatible with a ruthless disregard for American First Nations' rights as specifically granted by treaty, and the use of military force to build a global empire out of other peoples' territories. Even 'free trade' turned out to be no bar to imperial preference within the British empire, or in our day to continuing massive subsidies to domestic producers. None of this in any way diminished the spread of the English language, whether by sweep-aside or re-education, all round the world.

Freedom of speech may now be a reality, not just an unfulfilled ideal, in all these languages' current territories. But over the centuries and millennia of their development, freedom, under any definition, has never for very long been more than a hollow boast, or at best an aspiration. Our review of their histories has chosen to dwell rather on what life in these languages really meant.

Prestige

Prestige is about positive associations: in the case of languages, the roots of prestige are associations with wealth (in Europe, this above all), but also practical wisdom, enjoyment, and spiritual enlightenment.

The attractions of French in early modern Europe stemmed from the abundance delivered by the French economy, and much the same is true of English today. Somehow, speakers feel that they can share in the wealth by accepting the language. But the prestige of Latin, in the years of the Renaissance and after, and of Greek, in the heyday of the Roman empire, came not so much from abundance of wealth as from wisdom—perhaps itself a result of positive associations, since it is only when wealth is in good supply that that luxury product, education, can also be afforded. This underlay the attraction of Chinese and Akkadian: the sheer inaccessibility of written competence in these languages, paid for through a decade or more of study, added greatly to their prestige, and hence curiously their attractiveness.

And certain sorts of knowledge also offer greater access to wealth: the Greek sophists of the fifth century BC showed this, making the power of persuasive speech available at a fee; modern governments are buying into the same motive when they see competence in English as the road to economic development.

> *kaì toûto pleîn è̄ muríōn est' áxion statérōn*
> *hairoúmenon toùs héttonas lógous épeita nikân*

> And this is worth more than 10,000 staters
> to take the weaker argument and then win
>
> Aristophanes, *Clouds*, ll. 1041–2 (Athens, 423 BC)

All prestige languages give access to a special enjoyment, because they all have extensive literatures, and the first purpose of literature is to give enjoyment to the people who can appreciate it. Usually, knowing that not many others can share the appreciation has been part of the pleasure. This has been a charm of classical languages down the ages, from the Akkadian epics recited in the Hittite tablet-house of the thirteenth century BC to the Persian poetry quoted in seventeenth-century India and the French novels read in nineteenth-century Russia. But in the present age the charm of the prestige language, English, is somewhat reversed—perhaps as a side effect of the first globalised market in culture. English, especially as the American entertainment industry promotes it, is meant to convey that its culture is universally accessible, that it gives a release from other languages' traditions and restraints. The purported special link with freedom is part of this, but as we have just argued, this is hard to sustain as serious politics. All the same, if you are rich, it's much easier to be free and irresponsible.

Despite the current vogue for English as the language of the young and free—as well as the learned and the rich—ultimately the association of a language with profound religious truth gains the most loyal adherents, creating a reputation that may last for thousands of years. This is the only basis for a language to claim a value above simple association with some historic success. Hebrew, Sanskrit and Arabic all claim a mystic force which goes beyond the mere expression of meaning, or exchange of information among speakers.* As such, they may vanish from everyday discourse, but can never be demeaned as old fashioned or irrelevant, as long as there are believers to revere and treasure them.

Languages sometimes spread without any of these forms of prestige, of course. Brute military force can be powerful too, and it is difficult to see any charisma arising from the spread of Turkish to Anatolia, Spanish to Peru, Russian to Siberia, Japanese to Korea, or indeed English to Massachusetts. This is not to say that the conquerors will not have found their own behaviour impressive; especially in pre-literate societies, they may celebrate their conquests in word and song. Such heroic poetry is good for an indigenous literature, but it is unlikely to appeal to outsiders, let alone the conquered.

A prestige language, in general, is any foreign language that is learned for cultural advantage. Sumerian, Akkadian, Chinese, Sanskrit, Greek, Latin, Arabic, Turkish, Persian, Italian, French, German and English have all been such languages in their time. But the time will not last for ever. To be a prestige language, its native speakers—or the written records they have left— must somehow impress, and so attract imitators. This impact will depend on the cultural development of the recipients, as well as the merits of the originals. As potential recipients grow in wealth, knowledge and self-confidence, and begin to distinguish themselves, the attraction of a foreign model will shrink. It is unsurprising, therefore, that the charms of what was available in Latin and Greek diminished in the nineteenth century while the speakers of English were taking the world by storm with their own technical innovations and a global empire that left the achievements of the classics in the shade. Likewise, the charms of French and even the recently developing German faded before the self-confident speakers of English.

What makes a language learnable
There are three different ways in which languages are learnt.

Every native language is learnt by small children almost without effort, from their families and older siblings. For this to happen, there has to be a rea-

---

* There is some irony in that this claim is also made by many small indigenous communities for their own languages, which never spread at all.

sonably stable environment, where most of the community around the child speaks the given language.

If this is absent, so that the surrounding people do not share a common language, a language may still be learnt, but it will be a new formation, distinct from all the languages that the adults knew, a mixture of them reconstructed on first principles. When a group of children learn such a language, a creole comes into being. If the learners are older, adults looking for some common means of de facto communication, the result is a pidgin.

The third possibility is that the language is consciously studied and learnt, either through daily exposure to it, or through formal instruction, perhaps at a school. This process does not depend on the native capacity for language-forming that is active in the minds of small children; in fact, it can be put into effect whatever the age of the learner. In this case, the learner must already speak another language, and use it—explicitly and implicitly—in acquiring the new one.

The first two ways are not in any way dependent on the structure of the languages being learnt. It is generally accepted by linguists that any natural language, of whatever structure, can be learnt by any normal child—regardless of the child's ancestry or its parents' own linguistic background. Some sounds, and some linguistic structures, may take longer to get implanted than others, but everything will come in time. This fact is almost the definition of what it is to be a natural language. As for the genesis of creoles, the matter is controversial, but it appears that they all tend to have a common structure, which emerges naturally as the language is formed. The structures of the contributing languages, from whose parts the learners are constructing the creole, have no effect on the structure of the new language as it comes together.

The third case, which is common when a language is spreading in a territory new to it, may, however, have some interesting consequences for the possible succession of languages. In this case, learners of a language will retain in their minds some background formed by the language or languages they knew before, what is called the *substrate*. This substrate may impose a constraint on the kind of language that can then be successfully learnt.

Such a constraint may be of two kinds. It may cause the learners to come up with a new version of the language, influenced by their old speech. English spoken in India has lost its characteristic diphthongs: the words *gate* and *boat*, [geyt] and [bəwt] in England, are pronounced [gēt] and [bōt] in India. Likewise, the stress-timed tempo of English has been replaced by a more even, syllable-timed, pace. But more radically, the constraint may act as a major block on the learners ever gaining effective command of the new language. An example of this might be seen in the widespread failure of English

Language Teaching (ELT) in Japan for several decades after the Second World War, despite Herculean efforts on all sides to give the next generation competence in this new skill.

The idea that there might be this kind of structural constraint on the adoption of a language is highly controversial; it will be difficult to demonstrate in a particular case because there will always be a multitude of non-linguistic reasons which might be inhibiting take-up of the language. But the perspective of this book, where language dynamics have been surveyed over centuries, gives some new arguments to show that it may be a real factor limiting the spread of certain languages into certain territories, or rather among certain populations.

Consider, then, the curious retrenchment in the domain of Arabic, which seemed to roll back from its farthest limits in the east and the west, about three centuries after its first spread following the death of Muḥammad. (See Chapter 3, 'Arabic—eloquence and equality: The triumph of 'submission'', p. 93.) It settled permanently only in the territories that had previously spoken an Afro-Asiatic language, i.e. one that was structurally close to Arabic itself. First of all, Arabic took over the whole of the Aramaic-speaking world, modern Syria and Iraq. Here Arabic could have replaced Aramaic almost word for word. It then overran quickly, and subsequently pervaded, the countries in North Africa, whose vernacular was Egyptian (now known as Coptic) and Berber, although in these cases the spread was far slower, and—at least in the case of Berber—is by no means complete. But in al-Fārs (Persia) and in el-Andalūs (southern Spain), despite their early reputation as centres of Arabic scholarship, the language was expelled, except in the liturgy of Islam. These are precisely the countries where the substrate language was Indo-European, respectively Persian and Spanish; perhaps it is not so easy for a population speaking an Indo-European language to pick up an Afro-Asiatic one.* Certainly, the next major language spreaders to come through, the Turks, did not pick up Arabic, although they did accept, and even spread into Europe, the religion of Islam. The Turks' language is even less similar structurally to Arabic than Indo-European is. Islam continued to spread in the second millennium, into the Far East; but never again did it carry Arabic with it outside the mosques.

Consider the varying success of Greek in western Asia and Egypt, after Al-

---

* And on the other side of the coin, when such a language is successfully picked up, but then effaced by another Indo-European language, the evidence may still be seen in deeply alien features surviving three millennia later. This is what was suggested to account for quirks of British Celtic (see Chapter 7, 'Rún: The impulsive pre-eminence of the Celts', p. 292).

exander's epochal conquests in 332–323 BC. In principle the administration
was everywhere converted from Aramaic to Greek, and there were Greek settlements all over, at least within bigger cities; but Greek only became pervasive in Asia Minor, the great peninsula of Anatolia. (See Chapter 6, 'Kings
of Asia: Greek spread through war', pp. 247ff.) In other words, Greek was
most successful in the old domain of the Phrygian language in the centre
(known from inscriptions to have been closely related to it), and of the
Lydian and other Anatolian languages, Indo-European tongues whose structure was also fairly similar to Greek. Greek was unsuccessful, except in
planted communities of native speakers, in Syria, Palestine and Mesopotamia
(where people spoke Aramaic), in Egypt (where people spoke Aramaic and
Egyptian), and in Persia (where people spoke Aramaic and Persian). It is
most surprising structurally that Greek did not take root in Persia, since Persian is a fairly similar Indo-European language (and was famously learnt in
a year by an ageing Greek Themistocles—see the Plutarch quote on p. 5); but
perhaps there are non-linguistic reasons why an alien language should be particularly resented and so resisted in the heartland of what had been an independent and mighty empire for over two centuries.

A third example where language structure seems to have been crucial in the
life prospects of a language is almost total absence of Mongolian from central
and western Asia and from Europe, since the far-reaching conquests of the
Mongols under Tamerlane across Iran in the fourteenth century, and previously under Genghis Khan and his successors in the thirteenth. The Golden
Horde which sacked Kiev in 1240 was a Mongol army; and even Babur's dynasty, which dominated India from the sixteenth century, rejoiced in the name
'Mughal', that is to say Mogul or Mongol, although his language, as we have
seen, was Turkic. (See Chapter 3, 'Third interlude: Turkic and Persian, out-
riders of Islam', p. 106.) None of the Mongol invasions was soon undone or
rolled back: what had happened to all these successful Mongolians?

A crucial feature of the Mongol-led invasions was the fact that they largely
recapitulated earlier conquests of Turks (such as Huns and Khazars). Furthermore, they were conducted perdominantly with contingents of Turkic-
speaking warriors. Now Turkic and Mongolian, even if they are not geneti-
cally related, have become highly similar to each other structurally. (See
Chapter 4, 'Northern influences', p. 145.) It was very easy, therefore, for a
Mongol speaker to pick up Turkic, so to speak—and no doubt often quite
literally—on the trot. Outside Mongolia, Mongols tended to be in a minority,
and so their language was submerged in the language of their Turkic allies.

A fourth example has been suggested by a student of the Roman takeover
of Gaul. We have seen that this led to a rapid, and surprisingly thorough,

spread of Latin in place of Gaulish. Brigitte Bauer presents evidence that Latin and Gaulish were in many respects highly similar languages.[10] This similarity would have allowed the kind of word-for-word language replacement that we have just posited in the spread of Arabic over Aramaic. By contrast, the structure of British—still perhaps bearing the influence of a pre-Celtic substrate—was rather different, above all being a verb-initial language: verbs come first in the sentence. It would have been harder for Britons to learn to express themselves in Latin than it was for Gauls, and this stubborn fact may be at the root of why France today speaks a Romance language, but Great Britain does not.

Overall, it seems that—despite the received wisdom of linguists over two centuries and more—there may be circumstances in which the very essence of a language, its structure, can play a role in its viability. Languages, we suggest, are more easily learnt by a new population, and hence spread more easily, when they are structurally similar to the old language of that population. No particular structure is preferred in this process, just similarity of new with old. Otherwise learning a new language is an uphill struggle, perhaps too difficult for many who are already grown.

Vaster than empires

If this book has shown one thing, it is that world languages are not exclusively the creatures of world powers. A language does not grow through the assertion of power, but through the creation of a larger human community.

Clearly, military or economic might can act as strong inducements to community growth. Rome's irresistible armies, Spain's *adelantados* and Britain's Royal Navy have all played essential roles in the wider projection of Latin, Spanish and English in their eras. But failures of naked conquest or commercial development to cause linguistic spread have been too frequent to ignore: the political success of Turkic, Mongol and Manchu in mastering northern China did not extend their languages, nor did the Germanic invasions of the Roman empire dislodge or even reduce Latin. The Netherlands' commercial success for two centuries in South-East Asia did nothing for Dutch. Those universal traders, the Phoenicians in the Mediterranean and the Sogdians up and down the Silk Road, may have spread literacy skills along with their merchandise; but they did not convert their customers to wider use of their languages.

It appears that military conquest or economic domination will usually spread a language only if the conquerors come in overwhelming numbers, either through long-term immigration or a collapse of the native population.

A less brutal alternative is for the conquerors to enlist the conquered into what is clearly a more technically developed, and potentially enriching, civilisation, as the Romans did in Gaul, and the British in India.

But this is just another aspect of the fundamental point about language spread, namely that it depends on community growth. This is how Sanskrit was able to spread in South-East Asia for a millennium without a conquest, how Quechua took over the domains held by the Inca, and how French was taken up at the eastern end of Europe by the elite of foreign powers who simply wanted to imitate the highest culture they knew. Aramaic too was first spread through a widely scattered community of bilingual scribes capable of originating and interpreting messages written in it, even as communities that spoke it were being uprooted and resettled over the entire Assyrian empire. There are more ways, and indeed more effective ways, than violence by which to enlarge a community. A common language is what enables ever more members to participate in it. As Anderson puts it: 'Much the most important thing about language is its capacity for generating imagined communities, building in effect *particular solidarities*. After all, imperial languages are still *vernaculars*, and thus particular vernaculars among many.'[11]

Each community is differentiated with its own particular approach. Each is given its character by the traditions of its past, and many or most of them are conveyed by narratives and rituals shared in its own language. Contrary to the assumption of most twentieth-century Western philosophy, a language is never simply 'language'. Each language has its own colour and flavour. In this book, we have glimpsed some of the distinctive traits of the various traditions: Arabic's austere grandeur and egalitarianism; Chinese and Egyptian's unshakeable self-regard; Sanskrit's luxuriating classifications and hierarchies; Greek's self-confident innovation leading to self-obsession and pedantry; Latin's civic sense; Spanish rigidity, cupidity and fidelity; French admiration for rationality; and English admiration for business acumen. These manifold qualities can sometimes be seen in the languages' literatures. But they leap out when the languages' histories are told.

It is a paradox that this book, which has told the stories of languages that have so vastly extended their reach, often at the expense of others, is above all a tale of diversity. After all, the kinds of developments recounted here are what have led to the modern crisis of language endangerment, a situation so serious that it is reasonable to believe that, for half the world's languages, their last speakers may already be alive today.[12] But there are still over six thousand languages in the world, even if the dozen or so whose tales have been told in this book now account for about two-fifths of the world's speakers.

It is worth asking whether the diversity of consciousness and identity that each language represents can or should survive in the modern world. Past industrial and scientific revolutions argue that there is a single, unified path to valid knowledge and industrial organisation, and boast a display of seemingly magical achievements to prove it. Nevertheless, at least until the mid-nineteenth century it was the interplay of research in half a dozen different languages which kept up the pace of intellectual advance. And even today, a penetrating observer of the role of English in the modern world can remark: 'in 500 years' time … if [English] is by then the only language left … it will have been the greatest intellectual disaster that the planet has ever known'.[13]

But we should not be too overwhelmed by forecasts of impending unity. Half a dozen spiritual revelations have offered themselves as universal truths in the past 2500 years, and most of them are still in contention. Likewise the languages whose histories this book has reviewed have been spreading in increasing circles for twice that period of time. Despite all this rampant competition, almost all of them—or their successors—are still in existence at the beginning of the twenty-first century.

A lingua franca is a convenience: for speakers to convey a message across the world, certainly, but also for listeners when one language community appears to have more than its fair share of useful knowledge. But despite the myth of the Tower of Babel, and its vulgar interpretation as a cautionary tale, language diversity is not a liability for the human race. Most people in the world are multilingual, and everyone could be; no one is rigorously excluded from another's language community except through lack of time or effort. Different languages protect and nourish the growth of different cultures, where different pathways of human knowledge can be discovered. They certainly make life richer for those who know more than one of them.

In writing this book, I have consciously been embarking on a new approach within the general field of linguistics. Instead of looking at the current status of the world's major languages, I have taken a historical view. But instead of comparing words in different languages systematically, with a view to reconstructing their past, as a historical linguist usually does, or comparing the overall structures of different languages, like a language typologist, I have considered the evolving status of each language over the centuries of its career. Where any comparison has been attempted, it is the comparison of those careers. This kind of work might be called the study of *language dynamics*.* It is an approach, previously little explored, to understanding hu-

---

* Or, more explicitly and technically, diachronic sociolinguistics. Another recent example, largely focused on Africa, is Mufwene (2001).

man societies: how language, in all its evolving variety, organises not just the human mind but also the large groups of human minds that constitute themselves into societies, which communicate and interact, as well as think and act.

From this point of view, our focus on large languages has been above all a convenience. All languages have their own histories, but few are well enough documented to reveal very much about them. It is the large and famous languages that typically have the most adequate documentation. This is where we needed to start, to lay down the outlines of this new field. And this we have done. But ultimately language dynamics must encompass the history of human language in all its diversity.

kva sūryabhavo vaṃśaṃ kva cālpaviṣayā matiḥ
titīrṣur dustaraṃ mohād uḍupenāsmi sāgaram

here the lineage born of the Sun, and here my weakly endowed mind:
would I in folly cross the impassable ocean in my canoe?

Kālidāsa, The Line of Raghu, i.2

NOTES

Prologue: A Clash of Languages

1 As such, it was recorded in many near-contemporary chronicles. For Motecuhzoma's words in Nahuatl, I here quote from the contemporary encyclopedia of Aztec civilisation, *General History of the Affairs of New Spain* (xii.16), compiled by Fray Bernardino de Sahagún, and for Cortés's in Spanish from the eyewitness account of his serving soldier, Bernal Díaz del Castillo, *True History of the Conquest of New Spain* (ch. lxxxix).

1 Themistocles' Carpet

1 Sykes (2001, chs 7, 10); Weale et al. (2002). See Chapter 7, 'Against the odds: The advent of English', p. 310.
2 Anderson (1991) is a good guide to the short but fraught history of the concept of the nation, and its transplantation for use all over the world.
3 Sahagún, vi.13.
4 Karttunen (1990: 291–4).
5 Quotations from three Nahuatl speakers, cited in King (1994: 136–7).
6 Aulus Gellius, *Noctes Atticae*, xvii.17: *Quintus Ennius tria corda habere sese dicebat, quod loqui Graece et Osce et Latine sciret.*

2 What It Takes to Be a World Language; or, You Never Can Tell

1 e.g. in Lipiński (1997: 46).
2 Firth (1964: 70–1). This is a reissue of works originally published in 1937 and 1930.
3 Whitfield (1999: 36).

3 The Desert Blooms: Language Innovation in the Middle East

1 Tablet II, ll. 36–48; text from Lambert (1960: 40); trans. W. G. Lambert in Pritchard (1969: 596–600), slightly modified.
2 ll. 70–8; text from Lambert (1960: 148); trans. W. G. Lambert in Pritchard (1969: 601).
3 Lipiński (1997: 42–4).
4 The Words of Ahiqar, col. xiv, 208–23; text from Lindenberger (1983: 209), with vowels supplied by Peter T. Daniels; trans. from Pritchard (1969: 430).
5 The evidence is in the Elamite pronoun system, and some features of noun and verb morphology; Diakonoff (1985: 3); McAlpin (1981). But the attribution is still controversial.
6 Lancel (1997: 437).
7 Such colonies included Seleuceia on the Tigris, Seleuceia on the Eulaeus—none other than Susa, formerly the Elamite and Persian capital—and modern Aï Khanum in the Bactrian far east, i.e. modern Afghanistan (Wiesehöfer 2001: 111–12).
8 Pritchard (1969: 56): Inanna's Descent to the Nether World (trans. S. N. Kramer).
9 Tsereteli (1959 [1912]).
10 Expounded in Schmandt-Besserat (1997).
11 Hallo (1974: 185–6); the Hymn to Inanna is translated in Pritchard (1969: 579–82).
12 Pritchard (1969: 496): Love Song to a King (trans. S. N. Kramer), slightly adapted.
13 Pritchard (1969: 652): Ua-aua, a Sumerian lullaby (trans. S. N. Kramer), slightly

adapted; <www.etcsl.orient.ox.ac.uk:/section2/c24214.htm>.

14 Thomsen (1984: 293–4), quoting from *Proceedings of the American Philosophical Society*, 107(4), pp. 1–12; (trans. S. N. Kramer), slightly adapted.

15 Pritchard (1969: 651): The Curse of Agade, vv. 279–81 (trans S. N. Kramer); <www.etcsl.orient.ox.ac.uk:/section2/tr215.htm>.

16 McAlpin (1981: 60).

17 Malbran-Labat (1996: 56).

18 Wiesehöfer (2001: 10).

19 Diakonoff (1985: 24).

20 Hallo (1974: 184).

21 Kramer (1979: 39).

22 This is the analysis of Malbran-Labat (1996).

23 Roux (1992: 276).

24 Sawyer (1999: 14).

25 Oded (1979); Oded, quoted in Garelli (1982: 438); and Roux (1992: 308).

26 Pritchard (1969: 284): from a display inscription in Sargon II's show capital of Khorsabad (Dûr Sharrukîn).

27 Tadmor (1982: 451).

28 Parpola (1999) claims it was quite deliberate: 'The Aramaization of Assyria was a calculated policy aimed at creating national unity and identity of a kind that could never have been achieved, had the Empire remained a loose conglomeration of a plethora of different nations and languages.'

29 Garelli (1982: 442).

30 Kaufman (1997: 114–15).

31 Dietrich (1967: 87–90).

32 ibid.: 90, citing Dietrich (1979: item 10).

33 Kaufman (1974: 165–70). And Parpola (1999) notes a slip of the stylus in Ashurbanipal's library copy of Gilgamesh (mid-seventh century), which could only have been made by an Aramaic speaker: the glyph for 'lord' (*mara* in Aramaic) in place of that for 'son' (*mara* in Akkadian).

34 Pritchard (1969: 317): Historical documents, 5. Antiochus Soter (trans. F. H. Weissbach).

35 ibid.: 136: Poems about Baal and Anath, f.C (trans. H. L. Ginsberg).

36 Genesis xxvii.28 and 39. See also Gordon (1971: 122).

37 Ezekiel xxvii.3–11, 25–6, 32.

38 Lancel (1997: 357); Cribb et al. (1999: 225, 227).

39 Augustine, *Letters*, xvii.2 (Letter to Maximus Madaurus).

40 Pliny, *Naturalis Historia*, xviii.22.

41 Hanno, *Periplus* (Codex Palatinus Graecus 398, fols 55r–56r).

42 Augustine, *Sermones*, clxvii.4.

43 Plautus, *Poenulus*, 930–1028.

44 ibid., 1002–12: the translations of the Punic follow Sznycer (1967: 141–3).

45 Livy, xxviii.46.16.

46 Kaufman (1997: 115).

47 Greenfield (1985: 708); Polotsky (1971).

48 Thucydides, iv.50.

49 Daniel i.4.

50 Lemaire and Lozachmeur (1996: passim).

51 Greenfield (1985: 701, n. 2).

52 Pritchard (1969: 428): The Words of Ahiqar (trans. H. L. Ginsberg).

53 ibid.: 491: Letters of the Jews in Elephantine (trans. H. L. Ginsberg).

54 Schlumberger et al. (1958).

55 Henning (1949).

56 There is one curse-tablet of the fourth century BC, recently discovered at the Macedonian capital, Pella, which suggests that it was a variant Greek dialect, of the north-western type (Voutyras 1994).

57 Brock (1989: 19).

58 Saeki (1937).

59 Their paradoxical use of English to protect the use of German is described in Johnson-Weiner (1999).

60 Described from a Welsh learner's viewpoint by Pam Petro (Petro 1997: 259–319).

61 Hadith of disputed authenticity. Al-Tabrizi (1985: 6006).

62 Attempted in Miquel (1968) and Planhol (1968).

63 Qur'ān, xcvi.1–2. Tantalisingly, the last word here is also often translated as 'blood clot'. The semantic root of *'alaqin* seems to be the idea of clinging.

64 Braudel (1993: 72), quoting the Arab historian Baladhori.

65 Lewis (1995: 184–6).

66 Frye (1993: 99).

67 ibid.: 123.

68 ibid.: 169.

69 ibid.: 113.

70 ibid.: 169.

71 Guichard (2000: 143), quoting Jean-Pierre Molénat.

72 Corriente (1992: 34).

73 Haddadou (1993: 87).

74 Ibn Khaldūn, quoted in Ellingham et al. (2001: 552); this thirteenth-century author also wrote a history of the Berbers.

75 Ibn Khaldūn, *Muqaddimat*, quoted in Armstrong (2000: 90).

76 Shaw (1976: 5).

77 Schoff (1912).

78 Hourani (1995: 92–7).

79 Dalby (1998: 591–5).

80 Clauson (2002: 50, 183).

81 'Abd al-Ghanī (1929).

82 Mango (1999: 496).

83 Khaulavi (1979, vol. ii : 37).

84 Braudel (1993: 45).

85 ibid.: 112.

86 ibid.: 41–2.

4   Triumphs of Fertility: Egyptian and Chinese

1   trans. Lichtheim (1973: 52).

2   trans. Soothill (1910: 73–4).

3   Pritchard (1969: 415).

4   Erman (1894: 544).

5   ibid.: 106.

6   ibid.: 244.

7   Noted by Loprieno (1995: 71).

8   Moran (1992: xx–xxi).

9   Bacchylides (1961: 14–16), frag. 20B; also Oxyrhynchus Papyrus 1361.

10 Greenfield (1985: 701, n. 2).

11 See Loprieno (1995).

12 Johnson (1999: 177); Dodson (2001: 90, 92).

13 According to the Cairene Arab Maqrizi (1365–1442), reported in Lipiński (1997: 29).

14 By the Translators' Bureau in late imperial times: Ramsey (1987: 32).

15 Bazin (1948).

16 Ramsey (1987: 102–3, 139–40, 236–7). Strictly speaking Cantonese has nine tones, having added one more split.

17 Hashimoto (1986) argues a little too desperately that Chinese was effectively 'Altaicised' in the north, but his evidence is confined to transitory pidginised states of the language in Beijing, and a deviant contemporary dialect in Qinghai, where speakers are probably bilingual in Tibetan.

18 Norman (1988: 20).

19 Wang (1992: 11).

20 Hall (1981: 212).

21 Coedès (1968: 37). See Chapter 5, 'Sanskrit in South-East Asia', p. 204.

22 Wang (1992: 16).

23 Grousset (1970: 66).

24 Mote (1999: 25, 980).

25 The figures for Egypt are derived from Dollinger (2002), and for China from Barraclough (1978: 80, 127). McEvedy and Jones (1978) suggest a rather lower figure for Egypt in Roman times, 5 million. They simply dismiss the estimate in Diodorus (i.31) of 7 million for Egypt in 300 BC as 'too high'. For China, they point out that the AD 2 census figures are actually for 11.8 million households. They estimate that China's population then stayed close to 50 million until the beginning of the second millennium AD, when it began to rise with the greater cultivation of rice in the Yangtze valley, reaching 115 million in 1200, but then falling back in the Mongol era and not recovering until 1500. None of the above affects the general point about the exceptionally high population density of Egypt and China in the pre-modern world.

26 Figures derived from Russell (1958).

27 Pritchard (1969: 415).

28 Arnett (1982: 45–7).

29 Sallier 2,9,1 = Anastasi Papyri 7,4,6, quoted in Erman (1894: 328).

30 Anastasi Papyri 5,10,8ff., quoted in Erman (1894: 328).

31 Ramsey (1987: 121–3). See Chapter 5, p. 209.

32 Norman (1988: 257–63).

33 Wilkinson (2000: 735).

34 *The Economist*, 9 March 1996, p. 4, cited in Graddol (1997: 37).

35 Karlgren (1954). Its principles are set out succinctly in Norman (1988: 34–42).

36 Pritchard (1969: 440).

37 Wilkinson (2000: 723).

38 Translated by Mote (1999: 156), from Lin Tianwei (1977): *Bei Song jiruo de sanzhong xin fenxi. Song shi yanjiu ji* 9, 147–98.

39 Gao (1991: 145).

40 Ramsey (1987: 224).

5 Charming Like a Creeper: The Cultured Career of Sanskrit

1 Rig Veda, vii.103.

2 ibid., x.34.

3 *Mahābhāṣya*, i.1.

4 Ojha, *Bhāratīya Prācīna Lipi Mālā*,14, no. 6, attributed to *Cānakya-nīti*.

5 Caesar, *De Bello Gallico*, vi.14.

6 Martin Prechtel, personal communication.

7 Plato, *Phaedrus* 275A.

8 *Mahābhārata*, quoted by Kesavan (1992: 3).

9 Brough (1968: 31).

10 Deshpande (1993: 24), quoting *Mahābhāṣya*, i, p. 2.

11 Patanjali, *Mahābhāṣya* on Panini, vi.3.109, trans. Deshpande (1993: 62).

12 Manu, ii.18–22.

13 Deshpande (1993: 86).

14 ibid.: 16; *Rājaśekhara, Kāvyamimāṃsa,* iv.

15 Strabo, xv.1.21.

16 ibid., xv.1.64.

17 *Milindapañha*, i.9.

18 Fo-Kwo-Ki, xxxvi (in Beal 1884: lxxi).

19 ibid., xl (in Beal 1884: part 1, p. lxxix).

20 ibid., xl (in Beal 1884: part 1, p. lxxxiii).

21 Coedès (1968 : 81–2).

22 Si-Yu-Ki, ii.9 (in Beal 1884: part 1, pp. 77–8).

23 Gidwani (1994).

24 Rig Veda, ii.20.7.

25 Chatterji (1966: 78).

26 Si-Yu-Ki, x.9–11 (in Beal 1884: part 2, pp. 204–8).

27 *Pañcatantra*, v. 31.

28 Keith Taylor, in Tarling (1999: 195).

29 *Kamara, Pōdoukē* and *Sōpatma*, 'lying in a row', are quoted in the first century AD *Periplous of the Erythraean Sea* (ch. 60). Of these, the first two are presumably on the delta of the Kaveri river and at Puducherry (better known as Pondicherry).

30 Yule and Burnell (1986: 456): 'It is a saying in Goozerat,—"Who goes to Java Never returns. If by chance he return, Then for two generations to live upon, Money enough he brings back …"' Râs Mâlâ, ii.82 (1878 edn: 418).

31 Majumdar (1975: 21).

32 Coedès (1968: 26–7, 36, 275).

33 ibid.: 37, 276.

34 Majumdar (1975: 13).

35 ibid.: 19–20.

36 ibid.: 48.

37 *Mahābhārata, Āraṇyakaparva,* 173; Majumdar (1975: 25–7).

38 Coedès (1968: 369).

39 Fo-Kwo-Ki, xl (in Beal 1884: part 1, p. lxxxi).

40 Coedès (1968: 17); Bechert and Gombrich (1984: 147).

41 Ramsay (1987: 121–4).

42 For the details of the Tibetan script and its origin, I have been dependent on Beyer (1992: 40–50).

43 There is some evidence that Tibetans could write earlier than this. There are extant contemporary annals of the period 650 to 747, and for the year 655 we find:

The King stayed at *Mer-khe*, and the prime minister *Stoñ-tsan* wrote the text of his commands to *Ngor-ti*.

In fact the introduction of the script is traditionally (i.e. in a history from the fourteenth century) credited to a Tibetan scholar and government minister, Thon-mi Anui-bu, said to have been sent on a mission to India in the mid-seventh century. But Thon-mi may have been an invented figure, since he is omitted from genuinely ancient records of Tibet found in central Asia, while the earliest grammatical works on Tibetan are also attributed to him.

44 Beyer (1992: 36–7).

45 As conjectured in van Leur (1955: 113) and discussed in Hall (1981: 231–3).

46 Basham (1967: 491).

47 Rangarajan (1992: 18–21).

48 Si-Yu-Ki, ix (in Beal 1884: part 2, pp. 171–2).

6 Three Thousand Years of Solipsism: The Adventures of Greek

1 Old Oligarch, Athenian Constitution, ii.8: *kaì hoi mèn Héllēnes idíāi mãllon kaì phốnēi kaì diaítēi kai skhḗmati khrõntai, Athēnaîoi dè kekraménēi ex hapántōn tõn Hellḗnōn kaì barbárōn.*

2 Herodotus, viii.144 (quoted in the epigraph to this chapter).

3 ibid., iv.183.4. They lived along the Red Sea coast, according to Strabo, xvii.1.2.

4 Aeschylus, *Agamemnon*, 1050–1.

5 Thucydides, ii.35–46.

6 *tền pólin pãsan tễs Helládos paídeusin eînai*: Thucydides, ii.41.

7 Menander, fragment 72, ed. Kock.

8 Heraclitus, fragment 119.

9 Aristophanes, *Knights*, 1169.

10 Hesiod, *Catalogues of Women* (Loeb edn, fr. 4).

11 Thucydides, iii.38.4.

12 Buck (1955: 10–14).

13 Strabo, vi.1.2.

14 Segs 30.1664 and 20.326 (Greek–Aramaic Buddhist text), Schlumberger et al. (1958). See Chapter 5, 'The character of Sanskrit', p. 187, and Chapter 3, 'Aramaic—the desert song: Interlingua of western Asia', p. 84.

15 Salomon (1998: 265–7). *Hēliodōros* comes out as *Heliodora-*, but *Antialkidas* as *Aṃtalikita-*. Very much in the Aśoka tradition, it contains gratuitous urgings to Buddhist virtue. See Chapter 5, 'Outsiders' views', p. 192.

16 Ghirshman (1954: 229–30).

17 Mango (1980: ch. 1).

18 Plutarch, *Mark Antony*, xxvii.

19 *Cambridge Ancient History*, vol. vii.1², p. 180.

20 Drew-Bear et al. (1999).

21 Strabo, iv.1.5.

22 Plautus, *Epidicus*, iii.3.29.

23 Polybius, *Histories*, iii.59.

24 Vergil, *Aeneid*, vi.847–53.

25 *pergraecari est epulis et potationibus inservire*: in the dictionary of Sextus Pomponius Festus of the late second century AD. The word is common in Plautus, the great adapter of Greek plays for Roman audiences in the second century BC.

26 Sawyer (1999: 37).

27 ibid.: 35.

28 The source is an Athenian sophist, Philostratus, whose *Life of Apollonius of Tyana* was commissioned at the end of the second century AD by the wife of the Roman emperor Septimius Severus. This is a work of devotional literature, and so its accuracy has been questioned; but Woodcock (1966: 130) argues that archaeology shows the author was in fact well informed about details of this land so remote from contemporary Rome and the Mediterranean.

29 Wiesehöfer (2001: 122).

30 ibid.: 155.

31 *Itinerarium Aetheriae* (ed. H. Pétré, Paris, 1948), xlvii.3–4 (quoted in Mango 1980: 19).

32 Mango (1980: 25).

33 *De Thematibus*, Introduction, Pertusi

edn, 1952, quoted in Horrocks (1997: 150).

34 Procopius, *Secret History*, xviii.20–21.

35 *Third Part of the Ecclesiastical History of John Bishop of Ephesus*, trans. R. Payne Smith. Oxford, 1860, pp. 423–4 (quoted in Mango 1980: 24).

36 P. Lemerle, *La Chronique impropre-ment dite de Monemvasie*, in *Revue des études byzantines*, xxi (1963), pp. 9–10 (quoted in Mango 1980: 24). The Kafirs were perhaps Muslim converts; the Thracē-sians were not Thracians, but from the Thracēsian theme, in the west of Anatolia.

37 Leo VI, *Tactica*, in *Patrologia Graeca*, ed. J. P. Migne, cvii, 969A (quoted in Mango 1980: 28).

7 Contesting Europe: Celt, Roman, German and Slav

1 Herodotus, ii.33, iv.49. The Cynetes, aka Cynesians, may have been correctly placed just beyond the Pillars of Hercules, since Strabo, iii.1.4, calls this area, the modern Algarve, Cuneus—though he thought that it was named in Latin after its wedge-like shape.

2 Jacoby (1923: no. 70, fr. 30).

3 Strabo, vii.3.8; Arrian, i.4.6–8.

4 *Táin Bó Cúailnge* (Book of Leinster, 2nd Recension), ll. 4733–6, trans. Cecile O' Rahilly: *mono tháeth in fhirmimintni cona frossaib rétland for dunignúis in tal-man nó mani thí in fharrgi eithrech ochar-gorm for tulmóing in bethad nó mani máe in talam…*

5 Caesar, *De Bello Gallico*, i.1.

6 Diodorus Siculus, v.29–31.

7 Strabo, vii.1.2.

8 Aristotle, fr. 610; *Politics*, vii.10.

9 Pliny, iii.57, quoting Clitarchus, who was there. Arrian, vii.15.5–6, is inclined to discount it, 'given that no other people [than the Romans] was so possessed by ha-tred of despotism and its very name'.

10 Polybius, *Histories*, i.1.5.

11 ibid., vi.52.

12 ibid., vi.56.

13 Strabo, vi.1.2.

14 Pliny, *Natural History*, 29.1.7.§14.

15 Juvenal, vi.455.

16 Aulus Gellius, *Noctes Atticae*, xvii.17.

17 Strabo, v.3.6.

18 Tacitus was right to classify the Veneti and Fenni as neither Germans nor Sarma-tians (who were Iranian nomads, related to the Scythians). But he goes on to identify the Peucini with the Bastarnae, known to have been Germanic (Strabo, vii.3.17).

19 Tacitus, *Germania*, xlvi.

20 Ptolemy, *Geography*, iii.5: '*katékhei dè tền Sarmatían éthnē mégista hoí te Ouené-dai par' hólon tòn Ouenedikòn kólpon*'.

21 Strabo, vii.3.2, vii.5.2.

22 Lambert (1997: 123). These two were found in the regions of Nièvre and Autun in France. The ordinal numbers from the pot-ter's kiln in La Graufenesque are on p. 131.

23 Polybius, *Histories*, ii.17; Livy, v.34. Cf. Cunliffe (1997: 71).

24 Martial, *Epigrams*, iv.60.8.

25 Lehmann (1987: 76ff.).

26 Isidore, *Etymologiae*, xiv.6.6: '*Scotia idem et Hibernia proxima Britanniae in-sula, spatio terrarum angustior, sed situ fecundior. Haec ab Africa in BoExplream por-rigitur. Cuius partes priores Hiberiam et Cantabricum Oceanum intendunt, unde et Hibernia dicta…*'

27 Avienus, *Ora Maritima*, ll. 108–16: '*Ast hinc duobus in sacram, sic insulam | Dix-ere prisci, solibus cursi rati est. | Haec in-ter undas multa[m] caespitem iacet, | Eamque late gens Hiernorum colit. | Pro-pinqua rursus insula Albionum patet. | Tar-tesiisque in terminos Oestrumnidum | negotiandi mos erat. Carthaginis | Etiam coloni[s] et vulgus inter Herculis | Agitans columnas haec ad[h]ibant aequora.*'

28 ibid., ll. 98–9: '*…metallo divites | stanni atque plumbi …*'

29 Cunliffe (1997, ch. 8); Cunliffe (2001, esp. ch. 7).

30 They are detailed meticulously, and compared globally, in Gensler (1993).

31 Polybius, *Histories*, ii.17.

32 Reported in Cary (1954: 180).

33 Gildas, *De Excidio Britonum*, 6: '... *ita ut in proverbium et derisum longe lateque efferretur quod Britanni nec in bello fortes nec in pace fideles*'.

34 Tacitus, *Dialogus de Oratoribus*, x.1–2.

35 Irenaeus, *Adversus Haereses*, i, preface.

36 Domitius Ulpianus, *Digest*, xxxi.1.11.

37 Sidonius Apollinaris, *Epistulae*, iii.3.

38 Plutarch, *Marius*, fin.

39 Tacitus, *Agricola*, xxi.

40 Juvenal, *Satires*, xv.110–12.

41 Jackson (1994 [1953]: 107–10); Smith (1983).

42 Tomlin (1987).

43 Menéndez Pidal (1968: 19).

44 Harris (1989: 315–16).

45 Augustine, *De Doctrina Christiana*, prologue 4.

46 Caesarius Arelatensis, *Sermones*, vi.1–2; viii.1.

47 Eutropius had written in the fourth century: 'Trajan, having conquered Dacia, had transferred there boundless numbers of people from all over the Roman world to tend the fields and the cities.' *Breviarium ab urbe condita*, viii.6.

48 Bourciez (1967: 30, 135–7).

49 The evidence is marshalled in Keys (1999, chs 13–16).

50 Weale et al. (2002).

51 Terrence Kaufman's calculation, using the standard Swadesh list of two hundred basic word meanings. Thomason and Kaufman (1988: 365).

8 The First Death of Latin

1 *Monumenta Germaniae Historica, Scriptorum*, i, l.31.14.

2 This is quoted in Wright (1982: 109), as at Vienna Nationalbibliothek 795. I have followed Migne (also quoted by Wright) in correcting *sene* to *sine*.

3 I am stating here as simple fact the thesis established with great documentary effort by Roger Wright since 1982. The alternative would be to suppose that the pronunciation of Latin had been kept constant for the preceding four centuries, without any special pleading or teaching. The experience in England since the Great Vowel Shift (fifteenth to sixteenth centuries) shows that scholars even of a written language that is quite distinct from their own do not, without copious urging and dispute, exert themselves to keep its sound system separate from that used in their daily speech.

4 *De dissensionibus filiorum Ludovici pii*, iii, ch. 5, dated by Studer and Waters (1924: 24) to 841–3. The text is there quoted in full.

5 Wright (1982: 124).

6 '... *Et ut easdem omelias quisque aperte transferre studeat in rusticam Romanam linguam aut Thiotiscam, quo facilius cuncti possint intellegere quae dicuntur.*' As quoted in ibid.: 120, 122, from *Monumenta Germaniae Historica, Legum*, iii, 2.1.

7 Menéndez Pidal (1972: 24–5); also quoted in Wright (1982: 173).

8 Dante, *De vulgari eloquentia*, i.9.8–11: '*nec aliter mirum videatur quod dicimus, quam percipere iuvenem exoletum, quem exolescere non videmus: nam quae paulatim moventur, minime perpenduntur a nobis, et quanto longiora tempora variatio rei ad perpendi requirit, tanto rem illam stabiliorem putamus. non etenim admiramur, si extimationes hominum, qui parum distant a brutis, putant eandem civitatem sub invariabili semper civicasse sermone, cum sermonis variatio civitatis eiusdem non sine longissima temporum successione paulatim contingat, et hominum vita sit etiam, ipsa sua natura, brevissima. si ergo per eandem gentem sermo variatur, ut dictum est, successive per tempora, nec stare ullo modo potest, necesse est, ut disiunctim abmotimque morantibus varie varietur, ceu varie variantur mores et habitus, qui nec natura nec consortio confirmantur, sed humanis beneplacitis localique congruitate nascuntur. hinc moti sunt inventores grammaticae facultatis: quae quidem grammat-*

ica nihil aliud est quam quaedam inalterabilis locutionis identitas diversibus temporibus atque locis.'

9 Dante, *Convivio*, i.2.9: *'Movemi timore d'infamia, e movemi desiderio di dottrina dare la quale altri veramente dare non può.'*

III Languages by Sea

1 *Dialogues in the English and Malaiane Languages: or, Certaine Common Formes of Speech, first written in Latin, Malaian, and Madasgascar tongues, by the diligence and painfull endeuour of Master Gotardus Arthusius, a Dantisker, and now faithfully translated into the English tongue by Augustine Spalding Merchant, for their sakes, who happily shall hereafter undertake a voyage to the East-Indies.* At London, Imprinted by Felix Kyngston for William Welby, and are to bee sold at his shop in Pauls Church-yard, at the signe of the Swan, 1614.

9 The Second Death of Latin

2 Reynolds and Wilson (1968: 120).
3 Febvre and Martin (1976: 248–9).
4 ibid.: 289–95.
5 Anderson (1991: 39–41).

10 Usurpers of Greatness: Spanish in the New World

1 Herodotus, iv.106; Strabo, iv.5.4.
2 *'E certifico a vuestra alteza que yo conté desde una mezquita cuatrocientos treinta y tantas torres en la dicha ciudad, y todas son de mezquitas.'* Cortés, *Cartas de Relación de la Conquista de México, Carta Segunda* (1982, Madrid: Espasa Calpe, 7th edn, p. 50).
3 Joseph de Acosta, *The Natural and Moral History of the Indies*, i, p. 160 (quoted in Crosby 1972: 38).
4 *'...pareció al Almirante que debía llevar a Castilla...algunos indios paraque aprendiesen la lengua de Castilla y saber dellos los secretos de la tierra, y para in-*

struillos en las cosas de la fe ...' De las Casas (1957 [c.1530], i.46: 163). De las Casas, describing the events fifty years later, found this act unpardonable, since it amounted to kidnapping.
5 e.g. in Rosenblat (1964: 192–3).
6 Inca Garcilaso, according to Gómez (1995: 82).
7 Inca Garcilaso, according to Abbott (1996: 685).
8 *Instrucción Real*, 20 and 29 March 1503, to Nicolás Ovando, in *Collección de documentos inéditos del Archivo de Indias*, xxxi, pp. 163–4.
9 This is described in, for example, Alvar (2000).
10 There is a list of noted *mestizo* generals and writers, especially historians, in Rosenblat (1964: 211).
11 Father Blas Valera's words, quoted by Inca Garcilaso, *Commentarios Reales*, part I, vii.3: *'... La cual opinión ninguno que la oye deja de entender que nació antes de flaqueza de ánimo que torpeza de entendimiento.'*
12 By Abbott (1996: 91).
13 Father Blas Valera's words, quoted by Inca Garcilaso, *Commentarios Reales*, part I, vii.3: *'...porqué la semejanza y conformidad de las palabras casi siempre suelen reconciliar y traer a verdadera unión y amistad a los hombres.'*
14 Ricard (1933 [1966]: 23) says that in Mexico in 1559 there were 380 Franciscans, 210 Dominicans and 212 Augustinians. They were thinly spread: the average convent had five religious staff. Rosenblat (1964: 210) gives the then population of Mexico as 4.5 million, with the number of Spanish *vecinos* (heads of households) as 6,464.
15 La Paz (Bolivia) followed in 1610, Guatemala in 1660. Other major capitals in the Americas did not, however, begin to produce printed books until the eighteenth century, e.g. Bogotá in 1737, Buenos Aires in 1780 (Quilis 1992: 46–7). So for the Chibcha language, although it was

officially constituted as the *lengua general* in New Granada, the first extant grammar had to be printed in Madrid in 1619. This was a serious problem for such technical publications in foreign languages, because the author, an ocean away from the printing house, would be unable to correct errors in the proofs, and the learners of course might well be misled by them.

16 Viñaza (1892). These could be compared with the Summer Institute for Linguistics' estimate of the number of distinct languages in the Americas: 888, with 408 of them in South America (Harmon 1995: 26–7).

17 Rosenblat (1964: 191).

18 Sherzer (1993: 251).

19 Lara (1989: 99).

20 Lara (1971: 14) mentions a manuscript codex by Pedro Aparicio of 1540 (*Arte, vocabulario, sermones etc…en quichua*), and notes that in the *Relación del consilio Limense*, published in 1551, the language is referred to as *Quichua o general del Perú*.

21 Cerrón-Palomino (1987: 35). He finds support for this in the words of the chroniclers Pedro Cieza de León (*El señorío de los Incas*, 1550), xxiv.119, and Bernabé Cobo (*Historia del Nuevo Mundo*, 1653), xiv.1.235.

22 In this account, I follow Hardman (1985), an author whose lifetime of experience in the area makes her a better guide than most to this murky and complex area of pre-Hispanic history. It is reassuring that Cerrón-Palomino also comes down (1987: 348) in favour of a coastal origin for Quechua. Their major inspiration is Alfredo Torero (e.g. 1974).

23 Father Blas Valera's words, quoted by Inca Garcilaso, *Commentarios Reales*, part I, vii.3.

24 ibid., part I, vii.2.

25 Triana y Antorveza (1987: 157).

26 Cieza de León, p. 296, cited in Triana y Antorveza (1987: 157).

27 From Cadogan (1959), quoted in Vanaya (1986: 42).

28 From Godoy (1982), quoted in Vanaya (1986: 51).

29 Vanaya (1986: 6–7).

30 *Arte y Grammatica muy copiosa de la lengua Aymara*, Father Ludovico Bertonio, Jesuit (Rome, 1603); *Gramatica de la Lengua general del Nuevo Reino, llamada Mosca*, Father Fray Bernardo de Lugo, Dominican (Madrid, 1619); *Arte, y Bocabulario de la lengua guarani*, Father Antonio Ruiz, Jesuit (Madrid, 1640).

31 Cuevas (1914: 159).

32 Colleción Muñoz, vol. 86, fol. 54v.: '*Somos muy pocos para enseñar la lengua de Castilla a indios. Ellos no quieren hablalla. Mejor sería hacer general la mexicana, que es harto general y le tienen afición, y en ella hay escrito doctrina y sermones y arte y vocabulario.*'

33 Father Blas Valera's words, quoted by Inca Garcilaso, *Commentarios Reales*, part I, vii.3: 'Si *los españoles que son de ingenio muy agudo y muy sabios en ciencias, no pueden como ellos dicen, aprender la lengua general del Cuzco, ¿cómo se podrá hacer, que los indios no cultivados ni enseñados en letras aprendan la lengua castellana?*'

34 Quilis (1992: 64); Rosenblat (1964: 194).

35 Rosenblat (1964: 193–5); Quilis (1992: 55).

36 Carlos V, *Real Cédula* of Valladolid, to the viceroy of New Spain, 7 June 1550, copied with some variants to all the Dominican, Augustinian and Franciscan provincials of Mexico, and to the viceroy of Peru and the *Audiencia* of Lima (Rosenblat 1964: 206).

37 Quoted in Triana y Antorveza (1987: 300). 'This Kingdom', the New Kingdom of Granada, was supposed have Chibcha as its *lengua general*, but evidently the archbishop found it inadequate for his mission. Probably it was never used beyond the original area of Chibcha dominance, a rather small part of the whole.

38 Figures derived from Rosenblat (1964:

210–12). In 1810, according to him, *mesti-zos* would have made up 27 per cent of the Mexican population.

39 Rosenblat (1964) quotes a letter on these lines from Domingo de Almeida, writing in the name of the bishopric of Charcas (in Peru). It explicitly did not ask for priests to stop learning the natives' languages.

40 Arthur J. O. Anderson, *Psalmodia Christiana* (Salt Lake City: University of Utah Press, 1993), p. 33.

41 Motolinía (1990 [1541]: i.15).

42 León-Portilla (1992: 301).

43 Trans. Frances Karttunen and Gilka Wara Céspedes, *Tlalocan*, vol. ix (1982), pp. 119–27.

44 Father Francisco Mercier y Guzmán, *Sermon for Friday of Lent*, July 1765. Quoted in Albó and Layme (1992: 40–1).

45 Dietrich (1995: 289); Tovar (1964: 249). Tovar offers a different etymology for the money word, as *cua repotí*, 'piece of dross'.

46 '*Una muy buena cosa aconteció a un clérigo recién venido de Castilla, que no podía creer que los indios sabían la doctrina cristiana, ni Pater Noster, ni Credo bien dicho; y como otros españoles le dijesen que sí, él todavía incrédulo; y a esta sazón habían salido dos estudiantes del colegio, y el clérigo pensando que eran de los otros indios, preguntó a uno si sabía el Pater Noster y dijo que sí, e hízosele decir, y después hízole decir el Credo, y díjole bien; y el clérigo acusóle una palabra que el indio bien decía, y como el indio se afirmase en que decía bien, y el clérigo que no, tuvo el estudiante necesidad de probar cómo decía bien, y preguntóle hablando en latín: Reverende Pater, cujus casus est? Entonces como el clérigo no supiera gramática, quedó confuso y atajado*' (Motolinía 1990 [1541]: iii.12.389).

47 Lastra and Horcasitas (1983: 267); Quilis (1992: 44).

48 Cerrón-Palomino (1987: 343–4).

49 ibid.: 346, 67–75.

50 '*Los ministros eclesiásticos que no procuran adelantar y extender el idioma castellano y cuidar que los indios sepan leer y escriber en él, dejándolos cerrados en su nativo idioma, son en mi concepto, enemigos declarados del bien de los naturales, de su policía y racionalidad…*' *Cartas pastorales y edictos*, Mexico, 1770, p. 47.

51 Rosenblat (1964: 210).

52 Lorenzana, *Cartas pastorales y edictos*, Mexico, 1770, quoted in Triana y Antorveza (1987: 504).

53 Deputy Mateos in 1910, quoted in King (1994: 58).

54 José María Morelos, *Sentiments of the Nation*, quoted in English translation in King (1994: 57).

55 King (1994: 59).

56 Rosenblat (1964: 212).

57 Grimes (2000: 100).

58 Rosenblat (1964: 214).

59 Rubin (1985: 111–12).

60 Grimes (1996: 115).

61 Quilis (1992: 46).

62 ibid.: 79–80.

63 ibid.: 82.

11 In the Train of Empire: Europe's Languages Abroad

1 Oliveira Marques (1972: 343).

2 Anquetil du Perron (first translator of the Iranian Zend Avesta), in *Recherches historiques et géographiques sur l'Inde*, vol. ii, pp. xii–xiii, quoted in Lopes (1936: 60).

3 Santarém (1958 [1841]), and *Dictionary of National Biography*, s.v. Wyndham, Thomas (compact edn, p. 2343).

4 Samuel Purchas, *Purchas His Pilgrimes*, ii, p. 345 (Glasgow 1905 [1625]), quoted in Lopes (1936: 32).

5 Mandelslo, *Voyages célèbres et remarquables faits de Perse aux Indes Orientales*, p. 33 (Amsterdam, 1727), quoted in Lopes (1936: 38).

6 *Peregrinação*, xci (Lisbon, 1614), quoted in Tarracha Ferreira (1992: 432–3).

7 This is from the Charter of the VOC (the Dutch United East India Company) of 1698, quoted by Revd Frank Penny, *The Church in Madras*, vol. i, pp. 190–2 (London, 1904), and thence by Lopes (1936: 47).

8 Jean Brun, *La véritable Religion des Hollandais* (Amsterdam, 1675), p. 267, quoted in Lopes (1936: 48).

9 François Valentijn, *Oud en nieuw Oost-Indien* (Amsterdam, 1724–6), quoted in Lopes (1936: 48).

10 Vásquez Cuesta and Mendes da Luz (1971: 151).

11 Grimes (2000).

12 Barraclough (1978: 166).

13 Father Antonio Vieira, *Sermon of the Holy Spirit* (Oporto, 1683), quoted in Tarracha Ferreira (1992: 480–4).

14 Fernão Cardim, *Tratados da terra e gente do Brasil*, p. 121, quoted in Johnson and Nizza da Silva (1992: 481). São Vicente is on the southern coast of Brazil, near São Paulo.

15 Grimes (2000). The estimate for current speakers of Tupinambá (now known as Nhengatu), the old *língua geral*, is just five thousand.

16 Israel (1995: 321).

17 *Nauwkeurige beschryving van de Guinese Goud-, Tand- en Slave-Kust* (Amsterdam, 1704), quoted in Boxer (1969: 106).

18 Grimes (2000).

19 Israel (1995: 941).

20 François Valentijn, *Oud en nieuw Oost-Indien*, iii, 1, pp. 35–44 (Amsterdam, 1724–6), quoted in Hoffman (1979: 66).

21 Hoffman (1979: 66–8).

22 ibid.: 70.

23 Discourse delivered at a Meeting of the Society of Arts and Sciences in Batavia, on 24th day of April 1813...*Verhandelingen van het [Koninklijk] Bataviaasch Genootschap van Kunsten en Wetenschappen*, 7, Batavia, 1814, p. 13. Quoted in Hoffman (1979: 73).

24 Hoffman (1979: 74–5).

25 *Bijblad op het Staatsblad van Nederlandsch-Indië*, 1904, no. 5821, pp. 78–9; Charles Adriaan van Ophuijsen, *Maleische Spraakkunst*, Leiden, 1910. The context is described in Hoffman (1979: 87–92). It was reformed in 1947 and 1972, ironing out most differences with the spelling used in Malaysia.

26 Jean, in his translation of Boethius. He was in fact a native of Meun-sur-Loire, near Orléans.

27 Ordonnance de Villers-Cotterêts, Art. 111: '*Et pour ce que telles choses sont souventes fois advenues sur l'intelligence des mots latins contenuz esd. arrestz, nous voulons que doresnavant tout arrestz, ensemble toutes autres procedures, soient de noz courtz souveraines ou autres subalternes et inférieurs, soient des registres, enquestes, contractz, commissions, sentences, testamens et autres qielzconques actes et exploictz de justice ou qui en deppenden, soient prononcez, enregistrez et delivrez aux parties en langage maternel françois et non autrement.*'

28 Picoche and Marchello-Nizia (1989: 29).

29 Chaucer, *Canterbury Tales*, Prologue, ll. 124–6.

30 Quoted in Picoche and Marchello-Nizia (1989: 143).

31 Descartes, *Discours de la méthode*, troisième partie: '*suivant les opinions les plus modérées et les plus éloignées de l'excès qui fussent communément reçues en pratique par les mieux sensés de ceux avec lesquels j'aurais à vivre...tâcher toujours plutôt à me vaincre que la fortune, et changer mes désirs que l'ordre du monde...*'

32 ibid., quatrième partie: '*je jugeai que je pouvais prendre pour règle générale que les choses que nous concevons fort clairement et fort distinctement sont toutes vraies...*'

33 Picoche and Marchello-Nizia (1989: 154).

34 ibid.: 150.

35 Leclerc (2001: *La Nouvelle-France (1534–1760)*, pp. 2, 4) gives an estimate of about 2500 French in 1663, as against 80,000 English and 10,000 Dutch even in 1627. In 1754, his figures are 69,000 French (55,000 in Nouvelle-France, 10,000 in Acadie, and 4000 in Louisiane) against 1 million English colonists with their 300,000 slaves.

36 *'Colbert qui rêvait de voir ces indigènes et ces Français de la Nouvelle-France ne former «qu'un mesme peuple et un mesme sang», se plaint à Talon en 1666 qu'on n'ait pas obligé les sauvages à «s'instruire dans notre langue, au lieu que pour avoir quelque commerce avec eux nos français ont été nécessités d'apprendre la leur»'* Dorion and Morissonneau (1992).

37 He was Le Sieur de Bacqueville et de La Potherie, and he actually wrote: *'On y parle ici parfaitement bien sans mauvais accent. Quoiqu'il y ait un mélange de presque toutes les provinces de France, on ne saurait distinguer le parler d'aucune dans les canadiennes'* (Leclerc 2001: *La Nouvelle-France (1534–1760)*, pp. 4, 5).

38 *'Les paysans canadiens parlent très bien le français'* (Leclerc 2001: *La Nouvelle-France (1534–1760)*, p. 9).

39 Barraclough (1978: 208).

40 Picoche and Marchello-Nizia (1989: 64).

41 Grimes (2000). The figure for Pondicherry comes from Leclerc (2001, *Les États où le français est langue officielle ou co-officielle*, <www.tlfq.ulaval.ca/axl/Langues/2vital_inter_francaisTABLO.htm>).

42 Unfortunately for them, the Muslim majority was also growing at a comparable rate, from 2 to 8.7 million in the same period (Picoche and Marchello-Nizia 1989: 86, 104).

43 F. M. Dostoyevsky, *Collected Works*, vol. 21, in *Writer's Diary for 1880–81*, iii, pp. 517–18. The Cyrillic spelling has not been modernised. These words were written in reaction to a celebrated Russian victory over the Turkmens at Gök Tepe ('Blue Hill'), on which Lord Curzon also commented: 'The terrifying effect of such a massacre as Geok Tepe survives for generations' (*Russia in Central Asia in 1889 and the Anglo-Russian Question*, London: Frank Cass, 1967, p. 386).

44 Hosking (1997: 5–6).

45 ibid.: 379.

46 ibid.: 369.

47 Lieven (2000: 334).

48 Hosking (1997: 18): Gen. Rostislav Fadeyev, *60 лет кавказской войны*, Tbilisi 1860, p. 9.

49 These figures are calculated from those in Grimes (2000). Evidently, Russian is very widely known and used as a second language in these countries (e.g. Grimes quotes 30 per cent for Armenia).

50 Roy (2000: 30–31).

51 ibid.: 32.

52 This figure is calculated from those in Grimes (2000).

53 This figure is calculated from those in ibid.

54 Archpriest Avvakum, quoted in Hosking (1997: 69).

55 Lieven (2000: 255, 435, 278 and 437); he relies strongly on Gudrun Persson's 1999 London University PhD thesis: *The Russian Army and Foreign Wars 1859–1871*.

56 Hosking (1997: 187).

57 ibid.: 36, quoting Erik Amburger, *Geschichte der Behördenorganisation Russlands von Peter dem Grossen bis 1917*, 1966, pp. 502–19, and Walter Laqueur, *Russia and Germany*, 1965, pp. 40–1.

58 Hosking (1997: 309–10).

59 ibid.: 402; Comrie (1981: 28).

60 Hosking (1997: 311), quoting Jeffrey Brooks, *When Russia learnt to read: literary and popular culture*, 1985.

61 Fisher (1978: 100–4).

62 Comrie (1981: 28).

63 ibid.: 1.

64 M. I. Isayev, *National Languages in the USSR: Problems and solutions*, 1977, pp. 300–1, quoted in Comrie (1981: 36–7).

65 Roy (2000: 169).

66 Barraclough (1978: 140).

67 Tsurumi (1984: 277).

68 Chen (1984: 242), quoting Ken'ichi Kondō (ed.), *Taiheiyō senka no Chōsen oyobi Taiwan*, 'Korea and Taiwan during the Pacific War', Tokyo, 1961.

69 Tsurumi (1984: 303), paraphrasing Aoyagi Tsunatarō Keijō (Seoul), *Shin Chōsen*, 'New Korea', 1925.

70 See Miyawaki (2002): he notes a married couple in Micronesia, still using Japanese as a convenient means of communication that their children will not understand.

12 Microcosm or Distorting Mirror? The Career of English

1 T. S. Eliot, *Four Quartets* (1942), 'Little Gidding', part 2.

2 Brandt (1969: 374).

3 Smith (2000: 164).

4 Crowley (2000: 15). The original Norman French reads:

'III. Item ordine est et establie que chescun Engleys use la lang Engleis et soit nome par nom Engleys enterlessant oulterment la manere de nomere use par Irroies et que chescun Engleys use la manere guise monture et appareill Engleys solonc son estat et si nul Engleys ou Irroies [conversant entre Engleys use la lang Irroies] entre eux-mesmes encontre cest ordinance et de ceo soit atteint soint sez terrez et tentz sil eit seisiz en les maines son Seinours immediate tanque qil veigne a un des places nostre Seignour le Roy et trove sufficient seurtee de prendre et user la lang Engleis…et auxiant que les beneficers de seint Esglise conversantz entre Anglois use la langue Engleis et sils ne facent eint leur ordinaries les issues de leur benefices tanque ils usent la langue Angloise en le maniere susdit et eient respit de la langue Engloise apprendre et de celles purvier entre cy et le feste seint Michael prochin avent.'

5 Act of Union 1536, section xvii, as quoted in Evans (1992: 298).

6 S.P.Hen. VIII to the Town of Galway, 1536, as quoted in Evans (1992: 296).

7 Crowley (2000: 19).

8 Proclamation of Henry III, 18 October 1258; Patent Rolls, 42 Henry III m. 1, n. 1, Public Record Office, London; as reproduced in Mossé (1962: 234).

9 Trevisa re. *Polychronicon Ranulphi Higden*, i, 59. The text is given in the (London) form published by William Caxton in 1482, since this is substantially easier to read than Trevisa's own Cornish dialect. The punctuation and capitalisation are also adjusted for ease of modern reading. The relevant words of Higden are: *'Haec quidem nativae linguae corruptio provenit hodie multum ex duobus; quod videlicet pueri in scholis contra morem caeterarum nationum a primo Normannorum adventu, derelicto proprio vulgari construere Gallice compelluntur; item quod filii nobilium ab ipsis cunabulorum crepundiis ad Gallicum idioma informantur. Quibus profecto rurales homines assimilari volentes, ut per hoc spectabiliores videantur, francigenare satagunt omni nisu.'*

10 *Cursor Mundi*, Assumption of Our Lady, ll. 51–4.

11 Chaucer, *Troilus and Criseide*, v, ll. 1793–9.

12 From William Caxton, Prologue to *Eneydos*, 1490.

13 The most celebrated was Johann Clajus, *Grammatica Germanicae linguae…ex Bibliis Lutheri Germanicis et aliis ejus libris collecta*, Leipzig, 1578. These last two paragraphs are heavily dependent on Febvre and Martin (1958: 481–91).

14 They are listed in Nicolson (2003: 247–50), along with many of their Continental contemporaries, starting with the first printed Bible in Czech in 1488.

15 By the 1620s, all the gentry could read. By the 1640s, so could 45 per cent of the yeomanry, and perhaps 5 per cent of labourers. Literacy was higher among men

than women, and in London than in the provinces (Nicolson 2003: 122).

16 Sir John Seeley, *The Expansion of England*, Lecture I.

17 Keynes (1930: 156–7).

18 Ferguson (2003: 11).

19 ibid.: 13.

20 Williams (1643: chs i, vi, viii). The full title is: 'A Key into the Language of America, or An help to the *Language* of the *Natives* in that part of America called New England. Together with brief *Observations* of the Customes, Manners and Worships, &c of the aforesaid *Natives*, in Peace and Warre, in Life and Death. On all of which are added Spirituall Observations, Generall and Particular, of the *Authour*, of chiefe and speciall use (upon all occasions,) to all the *English* Inhabiting those parts; yet pleasant and profitable to the view of all men.' The author was expelled from Massachusetts for his liberal opinions, but went on to found Providence, Rhode Island.

21 Williams (1643: chs iii and xvii).

22 Examples derived from Silver and Miller (1997: 319). Penobscot, referred to there, is a variety of Abenaki.

23 Eliot (1666). Although a formal grammar, it does not pass up the odd opportunity for improving comments, e.g. p. 7: 'And hence is that wise Saying, *That a Christian must be adorned with as many Adverbs as Adjectives*: He must as well *do good*, as *be good*. When a man's virtuous Actions are well adorned with Adverbs, every one will conclude that the man is well adorned with *virtuous Adjectives*.'

24 Eliot (1663): this has the distinction of being the first translation of the Bible in the Americas, although the Spanish, with their Catholic approach to Christianity, had been publishing prayers and confessionals in American languages since 1539. See Chapter 10, 'First chinks in the language barrier: Interpreters, bilinguals, grammarians', p. 341.

25 Cotton Mather (1663–1728), quoted in (indirectly) Bailey (1992: 73).

26 Barraclough (1978: 221).

27 The border with Mexico was finalised a little later, by the Gadsden Purchase of 1853, which added a southern sliver to the modern states of Arizona and New Mexico to field a new route for the Southern Pacific Railroad.

28 Quoted in Milner et al. (1994: 168). The acquisition of the west was immediately cemented by the discovery of gold at Sutter's Mill in northern California in January 1848, and the world's most famous gold rush. The resulting jump in population accelerated California's acquisition of statehood to a period of two years, a new record.

29 Quoted in ibid.: 146.

30 Quoted in Sharon Gangitano, *Indian Language* (<www.sonoma.edu/depts/amcs/upstream/Indian.html>).

31 US Census Bureau, quoted in Wright (2000: 266).

32 US Census Bureau 1989, 1994, quoted in Crawford (1998).

33 Slate (2001: 391).

34 *Memorandum of M. Austin's Journey, 1796–1797, Amer. Hist. Rev.*, v, pp. 518–42.

35 Welling (2001).

36 US Census Bureau, quoted in Wright (2000: 490); state populations likewise, pp. 169–201.

37 Gholam Hossein Khan (1902 [1789]: iii, 191–2).

38 Thomas Babington Macaulay, *Minute of 2 February 1835 on Indian Education*, 1835 (reprinted in Young 1957: 721–4). Although this a particularly pernicious example of cultural chauvinism on behalf of English, and played a major role in the withdrawal of support for Sanskrit education in India, Macaulay was thinking not of English's own culture exclusively but rather of his belief that English could provide access (where necessary, through texts already translated) to every aspect of world culture. But his easy assurance that Indians could afford to neglect their own

traditions is a monument to the kind of cultural overconfidence bred by successful imperialism.

39 J. J. Campos, *The History of the Portuguese in Bengal*, 1919, p. 173, cited in Sinha (1978: 3).

40 Holden Furber, *Bombay Presidency in the Mid-Eighteenth Century*, 1965, p. 2, cited in Sinha (1978: 6).

41 Polier (2001). Characteristically, the work is called *I'jāz-i Arsalānī*, the 'wonderment of Arsalān', alluding to the author's own Persianate title, *Arsalān-i-Jang*, 'lion of battle', bestowed by the Mughal emperor Shah Alam himself (p. 9). In their Introduction, p. 70, the modern translators point out Polier's classic approach to a dispute between his two Indian wives, threatening one mother-in-law while appealing to her sense of shame for her daughter. Polier went on to marry a third wife after his return to France in 1788.

42 S. N. Mukherjee, *History of Education in India*, 1961, p. 30, cited in Sinha (1978: 27).

43 Ingram (1969: 235–6).

44 Sinha (1978: 28).

45 'All Ministers shall be obliged to learn within one year after their arrival the Portuguese language and shall apply themselves to learn the native language of the country where they shall reside, the better to enable them to instruct the Gentoos that shall be the servants or the slaves of the company, or of their agents, in the Protestant Religion' (J. W. Kaye, *The Administration of the East India Company*, 1853, p. 626, cited in Sinha (1978: 10).

46 Sinha (1978: 13); Kachru (1983: 21).

47 W. H. Carey, *The Good Old Days of Honourable John Company*, 1906, p. 397, cited in Sinha (1978: 10).

48 British Library, Additional Manuscripts, 13828, pp. 306v–308r; McKinnon goes on to propose setting up a seminary, teaching English and classical Greek, in Lucknow, on the basis of an existing library of classical books.

49 Parliament Debate (1813), 26: 562–3.

50 *Selections from Educational Records* I (H. Sharp, 1920), p. 22, and II (J. A. Richey), p. 152, cited in Sinha (1978: 32).

51 Sir Hyde East's letter to J. Harrington, 18 May 1816, cited in Sinha (1978: 36).

52 Ram Mohan Roy's letter to Lord Amherst, 11 Dec. 1823, cited in Kachru (1983: 60).

53 *Samachar Darpan*, 23 April 1834, cited in Sinha (1978: 41).

54 Duff (1837: 3). The member of the committee representing the law interest, Thomas Babington Macaulay, made a particular impression. Damning quotations from his *Minute on Indian Education*, which was accepted by the committee, appear in the epigraph to this section and in a footnote in Chapter 2.

55 Duff (1837: App., p. 2).

56 Spear (1965: 127).

57 Crystal (2003: 46). In his summary of world English-speaking populations, Crystal plumps for about 19 per cent of Indians in 2001 (200 million), but 12 per cent of Pakistanis (17 million), 10 per cent of Śri Lankans (1.9 million), and barely 3 per cent of Bangladeshis (3.5 million).

58 Alexander Duff's words, in another 1837 pamphlet, *Vindication of the Church of Scotland's India Missions*, p. 27.

59 Flannery (1994: 326); Dixon (1980: 1); Crystal (2003: 41).

60 Flannery (1994: 338); Crystal (2003: 41).

61 Grimes (2000).

62 Crystal (2003: 57).

63 ibid.: 62–5 offers some surprising estimates for some of these countries, suggesting that 45 per cent of Nigerians, and 84 per cent of Liberians, speak English. These may well reflect the number who have received some English-language education, since the literacy levels in these countries are rather high. But Crystal's explicit reason is the prevalence of English-based pidgins and creoles.

64 Sarah Nākoa, *Lei Momi O 'Ewa* ('Gar-

land of Pearls Awry'), 1979, p. 19, cited in Warner (1999: 71).

65 Kennedy (1988: 151); P. Bairoch 1982 is 'International Industrialization Levels from 1750 to 1980', *Journal of European Economic History*, 11, and F. Crouzet 1982 is *The Victorian Economy*, London.

66 W. S. J. Jevons, *The Coal Question*, London: Macmillan, 1865.

67 Crystal (2003: 88). French was the runner-up in official use with 49 per cent; otherwise, only Arabic, Spanish and German achieved over 10 per cent.

68 ibid.: 65.

69 *India Today*, 18 August 1997: 'Contrary to the census myth that English is the language of a microscopic minority, the poll indicates that almost one in three Indians claims to understand English, although less than 20 per cent are confident of speaking it.' Cited in Graddol (1999: 64).

70 This 'worldliness' of English is a major theme of Pennycook (1994), considered especially as it shows up in Malaysia and Singapore: its overtones are seen as political, as well as economic. And Phillipson (1992) develops a view of ELT as malign, characterising it as Linguistic Imperialism.

71 Guilarte (1998: 22–3).

72 Joyce (1977 [1910]: 33, 85); Gensler (1993: 235–42); and see Chapter 7, 'Rún: The impulsive pre-eminence of the Celts', p. 290.

IV Languages Today and Tomorrow

1 Following the date given by Mario Citroni, in Hornblower and Spawforth (1999). Martial is referring, of course, not to the parts of a modern book, but to *umbilici*, 'navels', the rods around which the scroll was wound up; *librarius* means copyist or bookseller rather than a publisher.

13 The Current Top Twenty

2 The principal source of these figures is the fourteenth edition of *Ethnologue* (Grimes 2000), itself a compilation of figures from a variety of sources. The population sizes for native and secondary speakers of major languages are derived from Funk & Wagnall's *World Almanac*.

3 Some consideration of how radically the true figures for English may differ from these can be found in Crystal (2003), Graddol (1997) and Graddol (1999).

4 Wilkinson (2000: 27); Norman (1988: 48–9, 187).

5 Miller (1967: 144).

6 Baugh and Cable (2002: 194).

7 Masica (1991: 27–8).

8 Entwistle and Morison (1949: 288).

9 Dalby (1998: 668).

10 Bourciez (1967: 287).

11 ibid.: 397.

12 Dalby (1998: 328); for Korean, it is impossible in practice to trace any dialectal variation earlier than the establishment of a phonetic writing system in the fifteenth century.

13 The source of population statistics is United Nations Population Fund (UNFPA), *The State of World Population 2000*, and United Nations Department for Social Information and Policy Analysis, Population Division, *World Population 1996*, as reported in Wright (2000: 468–72).

14 Looking Ahead

1 Bauer (1996: 27).

2 Papal Bull of Alexander VI, *Inter Caetera* (3 May 1493): '...We, then, commending greatly to the Lord your holy and praiseworthy purpose, and desiring that the same attain the due end, and that in those regions the name of our Saviour be introduced, we exhort you with all our power in the Lord and by the reception of holy baptism by which we are obliged to obey the Apostolic commands and with the entrails of mercy of our Lord Jesus Christ we require you intently that you pursue in this manner this expedition and that with spirit

imbued with zeal for the orthodox faith you will and must persuade the people who inhabit the said islands to embrace the Christian faith without ever quailing at the labours or the dangers, with the firm hope and confidence that Almighty God will happily accompany your endeavour ...'

3 Harold Macmillan, speech to South African parliament, 3 February 1960.

4 Composed for, and sung in, Robert Altman's 1975 film *Nashville* (music by Richard Baskin).

5 Fukuyama (1992).

6 Crystal (2003: 191).

7 As Salman Rushdie, admittedly a major exponent of English himself, believed already in 1981: 'The debate about the appropriateness of English in post-British India has been raging ever since 1947; but today, I find, it's a debate which has meaning only for the older generation. The children of independent India seem not to think of English as being irredeemably tainted by its colonial provenance. They use it as an Indian language, as one of the tools they have to hand.' 'Commonwealth literature does not exist', in *Imaginary Homelands* (London: Granta, 1991).

8 The 'engco' model, expounded in Graddol (1997: 26).

9 First-language English speakers in the USA were estimated at 210 million in 1984 (Grimes 2000). Between 1980 and 1990, the US population grew from 226,542,203 to 248,709,873 (US Census Bureau, 1980 figure revised in 1987; cited in Wright 2000: 264). The quote is from a summary of Bill Emerson's English Language Empowerment Bill, presented to the US House of Representatives on 4 January 1995, as cited by Crystal (2003: 130). No such provision has yet (as of September 2004) been adopted as law.

10 Bauer (1996: 33-40).

11 Anderson (1991: 133-4).

12 Krauss (2001: 19).

13 Crystal (2003: 191).

BIBLIOGRAPHY

Abbott, Don Paul (1996), *Rhetoric in the New World*, Columbia: University of Southern Carolina Press.

'Abd al-Ghani, Muhammad (1929), *A History of Persian Language & Literature at the Mughal Court. With a brief survey of the growth of Urdu language, etc.*, Allahabad: Indian Press.

Adams, Willi Paul (1990), *The German Americans: an Ethnic Experience* (US ed., trans. Lavern J. Rippley and Eberhard Reichmann from *Die Deutschen im Schmelztiegel der USA*), Indianapolis: Max Kade German Center, <www.ulib.iupui.edu/kade>.

Ainger, A. C. and H.G. Wintle (1891), *An English–Latin Gradus or Verse Dictionary*, London: John Murray.

Albó, Xavier and Félix Layme (eds) (1992), *Literatura Aymara, I. Prosa*, La Paz: CIPCA (Centro de Investigación y Promoción del Campesinado).

Allen, Charles (2002), *The Buddha and the Sahibs*, London: John Murray.

Al-Tabrizi (1985), *Mishkat al-Masābih*, Beirut and Damascus: Al-Maktab al-Islami.

Alvar, Manuel (2000), *América la lengua*, Universidad de Valladolid.

Anderson, Benedict (1991), *Imagined Communities*, London and New York: Verso.

Armstrong, Karen (2000), *Islam: a Short History*, London: Phoenix Press.

Arnett, William S. (1982), *The Predynastic Origin of Egyptian Hieroglyphs*, Washington, DC: University Press of America.

Bacchylides (1961), *Carmina cum fragmentis* (ed. Bruno Snell), Leipzig: B. G. Teubner.

Bailey, Richard W. (1992), *Images of English*, Cambridge University Press.

Barraclough, Geoffrey (ed.) (1978), *The Times Atlas of World History*, London: Times Books.

Basham, A. L. (1967), *The Wonder that was India*, London: Sidgwick and Jackson.

Bauer, Brigitte L. M. (1996), 'Language Loss in Gaul : Socio-Historical and Linguistic Factors in Language Conflict', *Southwest Journal of Linguistics* xv(1–2): 23–44.

Baugh, Albert C. and Thomas Cable (2002), *A History of the English Language* (5th edn), London: Routledge.

Bazin, Louis (1948), 'Un texte proto-turc du IVe siècle: le distique hiong-nou du Tsin-chou', *Oriens* I, pp. 208–19.

Beal, Samuel (1884) (reprinted 1995), *Si-Yu-Ki: Buddhist Records of the Western World*, Delhi: D. K. Publishers.

Bechert, Heinz and Richard Gombrich (eds) (1984), *The World of Buddhism*, London: Thames and Hudson.

Beyer, Stephan V. (1992), *The Classical Tibetan Language*, Albany, NY: SUNY.

Black, Jeremy, Andrew George and Nicholas Postgate (2000), *Concise Dictionary of Akkadian*, Wiesbaden: Harassowitz.

BIBLIOGRAPHY

Blake, Robert and Christine Stephanie Nicholls (eds) (1990), *Dictionary of National Biography*, Oxford University Press.

Bourciez, Édouard (1967), *Éléments de linguistique romane*, Paris: Klincksieck.

Bousquet, G. H. (1940), *A French View of the Netherlands Indies* (trans. Philip E. Lilienthal), Oxford University Press.

Boxer, Charles Ralph (1969), *The Portuguese Seaborne Empire*, London: Hutchinson.

Brandt, Rolf (1969), 'The Linguistic Situation in England from the Norman Conquest to the Loss of Normandy', in Roger Lass (ed.), *Approaches to English Historical Linguistics*, New York: Holt, Rinehart and Winston, pp. 369–91.

Braudel, Fernand (1993), *A History of Civilizations* (*Grammaire de civilisations*, trans. Richard Mayne), New York and London: Penguin.

Braudel, Fernand (2001), *The Mediterranean in the Ancient World* (trans. of *Les Mémoires de la Méditerranée*), London: Allen Lane.

Braun, T. F. R. G. (1982), 'The Greeks in the Near East', Article 36a, in *Cambridge Ancient History* (2nd edn), vol. III. pt 3.

Briquel-Chatonnet, Françoise (ed.) (1996), *Mosaïque de langues mosaïque culturelle: le bilingüisme dans le Proche-Orient ancien*, Paris: Jean Maisonneuve.

Brock, S. P. (1989), *Spirituality in the Syriac Tradition*, Kerala: Mōrān 'Ethō Series no. 2.

Brooks, E. Bruce, and Taeko Brooks (2002), 'The Nature and Historical Context of the Mencius', in Alan Ko Lo Chan (ed.), *Contexts and Interpretations*, Hawaii.

Brough, John (1968), *Poems from the Sanskrit*, Harmondsworth: Penguin.

Buck, Carl Darling (1955), *The Greek Dialects*, University of Chicago Press.

Cadogan, León (1959), *Ayvu Rapyta. Textos míticos de los Mbyá-Guaraní del Guairá*, University of São Paulo, Faculty of Philosophy, Sciences and Letters, Bulletin 27, Anthropology no. 5.

Caplice, Richard (1988), *Introduction to Akkadian*, Rome: Biblical Institute Press.

Cary, M. (1954), *A History of Rome down to the Reign of Constantine*, London: Macmillan.

Cavalli-Sforza, Luigi Luca (2001), *Genes, Peoples and Languages*, London: Penguin.

Cerrón-Palomino, Rodolfo (1987), *Lingüística Quechua*, Cuzco: Centro de estudios rurales andinos Bartolomé de Las Casas.

Chatterji, S. K. (1966), *The People, Language, and Culture of Orissa*, Bhubaneshwar: Oriya Sahitya Akademi.

Chen, Edward I-Te (1984), 'The Attempt to Integrate the Empire: Legal Perspectives', in Myers and Peattie (1984: 240–74).

Clauson, Gerard (2002 [1962]), *Studies in Turkic and Mongol Linguistics* (2nd edn), London: RoutledgeCurzon.

Coedès, Georges (1968), *The Indianized States of Southeast Asia* (ed. Walter F. Vella, trans. Sue Brown Cowing), Honolulu: University of Hawaii and East–West Center Press.

Comrie, Bernard (1981), *The Languages of the Soviet Union*, Cambridge University Press.

Cook, B. F. (1987), *Greek Inscriptions*, London: British Museum.

Corriente, Federico (1992), *Arabe andalusí y lenguas romances*, Madrid: Mapfre.

Crawford, James (1998), 'Endangered Native American Languages: What Is to Be Done, and Why?', in Ricento and Burnaby (eds), *Language and Politics in the US and Canada*, Mahwah, NJ: Lawrence Erlbaum Associates.

Cribb, Joe, Barrie Cook and Ian Carradice (1999), *The Coin Atlas*, London: Little, Brown.

Crosby, Alfred W. (1972), *The Columbian Exchange*, Westport, CT: Greenwood Press.

Crowley, Tony (2000), *The Politics of Language in Ireland 1366–1922: a Sourcebook*, London: Routledge.

Crystal, David (2003), *English as a Global Language* (2nd edn), Cambridge University Press.

Cuevas, Mariano (1914), *Documentos inéditos del siglo XVI para la historia de México*, Mexico City: Porrua.

Cunliffe, Barry (1997), *The Ancient Celts*, Oxford University Press.

Cunliffe, Barry (2001), *Facing the Ocean: the Atlantic and Its Peoples*, Oxford University Press.

Dalby, Andrew (1998), *A Dictionary of Languages*, London: Bloomsbury.

Dalrymple, William (2002), *White Mughals*, London: HarperCollins.

De Las Casas, Fray Bartolomé (1957 [c.1530], *Historia de las Indias* (vols. 95–6 of Biblioteca de Autores Españoles), Madrid: Ediciones Atlas.

Deshpande, Madhav (1993), *Sanskrit and Prakrit: Sociolinguistic Issues*, Delhi: Motilal Banarsidass.

Diakonoff, Igor M. (1968), *Predistoriya Armyanskogo Naroda*, Yerevan, trans. (1984) Lori Jennings as *Pre-history of the Armenian People*, Delmar, NY: Caravan Books.

Diakonoff, Igor M. (1985), 'Elam.', in Gershevitch (1985: 1–24).

Dietrich, Manfried (1967), *Neue Quellen zur Geschichte Babyloniens. (I), Die Welt des Orients*, iv, pp. 61–103.

Dietrich, Manfried (ed.) (1979), *Cuneiform Texts from Babylonian Tablets in the British Museum*, part 54 ('Neo-Babylonian letters from the Kuyunjik Collection'), London: British Museum Publications.

Dietrich, Wolfgang (1995), *La importancia de los diccionarios guaraníes de Montoya para el estudio comparativo del las lenguas tupí-guaraníes de hoy*, Paris: Association d'Ethnolinguistique Amérindienne, Amerindia, 19/20, pp. 287–99.

Dixon, R. M. W. (1980), *The Languages of Australia*, Cambridge University Press.

Dodson, Aidan (2001), *The Hieroglyphs of Ancient Egypt*, London: New Holland.

Dollinger, André (2002), *The People of Ancient Egypt*, <http://nefertiti.iwebland.com/people>.

Dorion, Henri and Christian Morissonneau (1992), 'Autour du 500e anniversaire de Christophe Colomb: l'Amérique francophone, une Amérique retrouvée', *L'Année francophone internationale* 36: 24–35.

Drew-Bear, Thomas, Christine M. Thomas and Melek Yildizturan (1999), *Phrygian Votive Steles*, Ankara: Museum of Anatolian Civilisations.

Duff, Alexander (1837), *New Era of the English Language and Literature in India*, Edinburgh: John Johnstone.

Electronic Text Corpus of Sumerian Literature, Oxford University, <www-etcsl.orient.ox.ac.uk>.

Elimam, Abdeljlil (1977), *Le maghribi, langue trois fois millénaire*, Algiers: ANEP.

Eliot, John (1663), *Mamusse Wunneetupanatamwe Up-Biblum God naneeswe Nukkone Testament kah wonk Wusku Testament* [The Bible in Massachusett], Cambridge, MA: Samuel Green and Marmaduke Johnson.

Eliot, John (1666), *The Indian Grammar Begun*, Cambridge, MA: Marmaduke Johnson.

Ellingham, Mark, Don Grisbrook and Shaun McVeigh (2001), *Rough Guide to Morocco*, London: Rough Guides.

Entwistle, W. J. and W. A. Morison (1949), *Russian and the Slavonic Languages*, London: Faber.

Erman, Adolf (1894), *Life in Ancient Egypt* (*Aegypten*, trans. H. M. Tirard), London: Macmillan.

Evans, Gwynfor (1992), *Land of My Fathers*, Talybont, Ceredigion: Y Lolfa.

Febvre, Lucien and Henri-Jean Martin (1958), *L'apparition du livre*, Paris: Albin Michel.

Febvre, Lucien and Henri-Jean Martin (1976), *The Coming of the Book* (trans. of Febvre and Martin 1958), London: New Left Books.

Feng, Shengli (1998), 'Prosodic structure and compound words in Classical Chinese', in Packard (1998: 197–260).

Ferguson, Niall (2003), *Empire: How Britain made the modern world*, London: Allen Lane.

Firth, J. R. (1964), *The Tongues of Men & Speech*, Oxford University Press.

Fisher, Alan (1978), *The Crimean Tartars*, Stanford, CA: Hoover Institution Press.

Fitzgerald, C. P. (1986), *China: a Short Cultural History*, London: Century Hutchinson.

Flannery, Tim (1994), *The Future Eaters*, Sydney: Reed Books Australia.

Franklin, Simon and Jonathan Shepard (eds) (1996), *The Emergence of Rus 750–1200*, London: Longman.

Frye, Richard N. (1993), *The Golden Age of Persia*, London: Weidenfeld and Nicolson.

Fukuyama, Francis (1992), *The End of History and the Last Man*, Harmondsworth: Penguin.

Gao, Yuan (1991), *Luring the Tiger out of the Mountains*, London: Piatkus.

Gardiner, Sir Alan (1957), *Egyptian Grammar*, Oxford University Press.

Garelli, Paul (1982), 'Importance et Rôle des Araméens dans l'Administration de l'Empire Assyrien', in Nissen and Renger (1982: 437–47).

Gensler, Orin David (1993), *A typological evaluation of Celtic/Hamito-Semitic syntactic parallels*, PhD dissertation, University of California, Berkeley.

Gershevitch, Ilya (ed.) (1985), *The Cambridge History of Iran*. Volume 2: *Median and Achaemenian periods*, Cambridge University Press.

Ghirshman, Roman (1954), *Iran. From the Earliest Times to the Islamic Conquest*, Harmondsworth: Penguin.

Gholam Hossein Khan, Sied (1902 [1789]), *The Seir Mutaqherin: or Review of Modern Times: Being an History of India, From the Year 1118 to 1194*, Calcutta.

Gidwani, Bhagwan S. (1994), *Return of the Aryans*, New Delhi: Penguin, India.

Godoy, Lucio (1982), 'Textos Aché. Ciclo Mberendy', Asunción: *Suplemento Antropológico* xvii, June.

Gómez Mango de Carriquiry, Lidice (1995), *El encuentro de lenguas en el « Nuevo Mundo »*, Córdoba: Cajasur.

Gordon, Cyrus H. (1971), *Forgotten Scripts: the Story of Their Decipherment*, Harmondsworth: Penguin.

Gordon, Cyrus H. (1997), 'Amorite and Eblaite', in Hetzron (1997: 100–13).

Gordon, E. V. (1957), *Introduction to Old Norse* (2nd edn, rev. A. R. Taylor), Oxford University Press.

Gorrochategui, Joaquín (1995), 'The Basque Language and Its Neighbours in Antiquity', in Hualde, Lakarra and Trask (eds), *Towards a History of the Basque Language*, Amsterdam: John Benjamins, pp. 31–64.

Graddol, David (1997), *The Future of English?*, London: British Council.

Graddol, David (1999), 'The decline of the native speaker', in Graddol and Meinhof (1999: 57–68).

Graddol, David and Ulrike H. Meinhof (eds) (1999), *English in a Changing World*, Milton Keynes: Catchline, and *AILA Review* 13.

Greenfield, J. C. (1985), 'Aramaic in the Achaemenian Empire', ch. 15 in Gershevitch (1985: 698–713).

Grimes, Barbara (ed.) (2000), *Ethnologue: Languages of the World* (14th edn), Dallas, TX: Summer Institute of Linguistics.

Grimm, Jakob (1876), *Deutsche Mythologie* (4th edn), Berlin: Dümmler.

Grousset, René (1970), *The Empire of the Steppes*, Paris: Payot; New Brunswick: Rutgers.

Guichard, Pierre (2000), *Al-Andalus 711–1492*, Paris: Hachette.

Guilarte, Alex (1998), 'Alba? What do you mean?', in Celtic League: *Carn* 101 (spring): 22–3.

Haddadou, M. A. (1993), *Guide de la Culture et de la Langue Berbères*, Paris: ENAL-ENAP.

Hall, D. G. E. (1981), *A History of South-East Asia*, London: Macmillan.

Hallo, William W. (1974), 'Toward a History of Sumerian Literature', in Lieberman (1974).

Hamilton, A. W. (1987), *Malay Proverbs*, Singapore: Times Books International.

Hardman de Bautista, Martha (1985), 'The Imperial Languages of the Andes', in Wolfson and Manes (1985: 182–93).

Harmon, David (1995), 'The Status of the World's Languages as Reported in Ethnologue', *Southwest Journal of Linguistics* 14(1–2): 1–28.

Harris, William V. (1989), *Ancient Literacy*, Cambridge, MA: Harvard University Press.

Hashimoto, Mantaro (1986), 'The Altaicization of Northern Chinese', *Contributions to Sino-Tibetan Studies*, Brill, pp. 76–97.

Hawks, Francis L. (1954), *Narrative of the Expedition of an American Squadron to the China Seas and Japan* (ed. M. Wallach), London: Macdonald.

Henning, W. B. (1949), 'The Aramaic Inscription of Asoka found at Lampaka', *Bulletin of School of Oriental and African Studies* xiii: 82.

Hetzron, Robert (ed.) (1997), *The Semitic Languages*, New York and London: Routledge.

Hoffman, John (1979), 'A foreign investment: Indies Malay to 1901', Cornell Modern Indonesia Project: *Indonesia* 27 (April): 65–92.

Hornblower, Simon and Antony Spawforth (eds) (1999), *The Oxford Classical Dictionary*, Oxford University Press.

Horrocks, Geoffrey (1997), *Greek: a History of the Language and its Speakers*, Harlow: Longman.

Hosking, Geoffrey (1997), *Russia: People and Empire*, London: HarperCollins.

Hourani, George F. (1995), *Arab Seafaring*, Princeton University Press.

Ingram, Edward (ed.) (1969), *Two Views of British India: the private correspondence of Mr Dundas and Lord Wellesley: 1798–1801*, Bath: Adams & Dart.

Israel, Jonathan I. (1995), *The Dutch Republic: its Rise, Greatness, and Fall 1477–1806*, Oxford University Press.

Jackson, Kenneth (1994 [1953]), *Language and History in Early Britain*, Dublin: Four Courts Press [Edinburgh University Press].

Jacoby, Felix (1923), *Fragmente der griechischen Historiker*, Berlin.

Johnson, Harold and Maria Beatriz Nizza da Silva (eds) (1992), *O Império Luso-Brasileiro 1500–1620*, Lisbon: Editorial Estampa.

Johnson, Paul (1999), *The Civilization of Ancient Egypt*, London: Weidenfeld and Nicolson.

Johnson-Weiner, Karen (1999), 'Educating in English to Maintain Pennsylvania German: the Old Order Parochial School in the Service of Cultural Survival', in Ostler (1999: 31–7).

Joyce, P. W. (1977 [1910]), *English as We Speak It in Ireland*, Tokyo: Shinkosha [Dublin].

Kachru, Braj B. (1983), *The Indianization of English: the English language in India*, Delhi: Oxford University Press.

Karlgren, Bernhard (1954), 'Compendium of Phonetics in Ancient and Archaic Chinese', *Bulletin of the Museum of Far Eastern Antiquities* 12: 1–471.

Karttunen, Frances (1990), 'Conventions of Polite Speech in Nahuatl', *Estudios de Cultura Nahuatl* 20: 281–96.

Kaufman, Stephen A. (1974), 'The Akkadian Influences on Aramaic', University of Chicago: *Assyriological Studies* 19.

Kaufman, Stephen A. (1997), 'Aramaic', ch. 7 in Hetzron (1997).

Kennedy, Paul (1988), *The Rise and Fall of the Great Powers*, London: Unwin Hyman.

Kesavan, B. S. (1992), *The Book in India*, Delhi: National Book Trust.

Keynes, John Maynard (1930), *A Treatise on Money*, London: Macmillan.

Keys, David (1999), *Catastrophe: an Investigation into the Origins of the Modern World*, London: Century.

Khaulavi, P. N. (1979), *History of the Persian Language* (trans. N. H. Ansari), New Delhi: Mohammad Arhad for Idarah-i-Adabiyat-i Delli.

King, Linda (1994), *Roots of Identity: Language and Literacy in Mexico*, Stanford University Press.

Kramer, Samuel Noah (1979), *From the Poetry of Sumer: Creation, Glorification, Adoration*, Berkeley/Los Angeles: University of California.

Krauss, Michael (2001), 'Mass Language Extinction, and Documentation: the Race against Time', in Osamu Sakiyama (ed.), *Lectures on Endangered Languages*, 2, Kyoto: ELPR, pp. 19–40.

Lambert, Pierre-Yves (1997), *La langue gauloise*, Paris: Éditions Errance.

Lambert, W. G. (1960), *Babylonian Wisdom Literature*, Oxford: Clarendon Press.

Lancel, Serge (1997), *Carthage: a history*, Oxford: Blackwell.

Lara, Jesús (ed.) (1971), *Diccionario Qhëshwa–Castellano Castellano–Qhëshwa*, La Paz and Cochabamba, Bolivia: Los Amigos del Libro.

Lara, Jesús (ed.) (1989), *Tragedia del fin de Atawallpa*, Buenos Aires: Ediciones del Sol; Cochabamba, Bolivia: Los Amigos del Libro.

Lastra de Suárez, Yolanda and Fernando Horcasitas (1983), 'La lengua nahuatl de México', in Bernard Pottier (ed.), *América Latina en sus lenguas indígenas*, Caracas: UNESCO and Monte Avilá, pp. 263–81.

Leclerc, Jacques (2000), *Langues du monde*, <www.tlfq.ulaval.ca/axl/Languages/acces languesmonde.htm>.

Leclerc, Jacques (2001), 'Histoire du français au Québec', in Quebec: TLFQ, Université Laval, *L'aménagement linguistique dans le monde*, <www.tlfq.ulaval.ca/axl/franco phonie/histfrnqc.htm>.

Lehmann, Winfred P. (1987), 'Linguistic and archaeological data for handbooks of proto-languages', in Festschrift for Maria Gimbutas, Washington, DC.

Lejeune, Michel (1974), *Manuel de la langue vénète*, Heidelberg: Carl Winter.

Lemaire, André and Hélène Lozachmeur (1996), 'Remarques sur le plurilinguisme en Asie Mineure à l'époque perse', in Briquel-Chatonnet (1996: 91–124).

León-Portilla, Miguel (1992), *Literaturas indígenas de México*, Mexico: Editorial Mapfre.

Lewis, Bernard (1995), *The Middle East*, London: Phoenix Press.

Lichtheim, Miriam (1973), *Ancient Egyptian Literature*. Vol. I: *The Old and Middle Kingdoms*, Berkeley and Los Angeles: University of California Press.

Lieberman, Stephen J. (ed.) (1974), 'Sumerological Studies in Honour of Thorkild Jacobsen', University of Chicago: *Assyrological Studies* 20.

Lieven, Dominic (2000), *Empire: the Russian Empire and Its Rivals*, London: John Murray.

Lindenberger, James M. (1983), *The Aramaic Proverbs of Ahiqar*, Baltimore, MD: Johns Hopkins University Press.

Lipiński, Edward (1997), *Semitic Languages: Outline of a Comparative Grammar*, Leuven: Uitgeverij Peeters.

Lopes, David (1936), *A Expansão da Língua Portuguesa no Oriente durante os séculos XVI, XVII e XVIII*, Barcelos: Portucalense Editora.

Loprieno, Antonio (1995), *Ancient Egyptian*, Cambridge University Press.

Luft, Ulrich (1992), 'Νεῖλος. Eine Anmerkung zur kulturellen Begegnung der Griechen mit den Ägyptern', in *The Intellectual Heritage of Egypt*, Budapest: Studies Kákosy, pp. 403–10.

Mackey, William F. (1998), 'The foundations', ch. 1 in John Edwards (ed.), *Language in Canada*, Cambridge University Press.

Majumdar, Ramesh Chandra (1975), *Study of Sanskrit in South-East Asia*, Calcutta: Sanskrit College.

Malbran-Labat, Florence (1996), 'Akkadien, bilingues et bilinguisme en Élam et à Ougarit', in Briquel-Chatonnet (1996: 33–62).

Mango, Andrew (1999), *Atatürk*, London: John Murray.

Mango, Cyril (1980 [1994]), *Byzantium: the Empire of the New Rome*, London: Weidenfeld and Nicolson. References are to the 1994 edn reissued by Phoenix.

Markoe, Glenn E. (2000), *Phoenicians*, London: British Museum Press.

Masica, Colin P. (1991), *The Indo-Aryan Languages*, Cambridge University Press.

McAlpin, David (1981), 'Proto-Elamo-Dravidian: the evidence and its implications', Philadelphia: *Transactions of the American Philosophical Society* 71(3).

McClure, Erica (2001), 'The role of language in the construction of ethnic identity on the Internet: the case of Assyrian activists in diaspora', in Moseley et al. (2001: 68–75).

McCrum, Robert, William Cran and Robert MacNeil (1987), *The Story of English*, London: Faber and BBC.

McEvedy, Colin and Richard Jones (1978), *Atlas of World Population History*, Harmondsworth: Penguin.

Menéndez Pidal, R. (1968), *Manual de Gramática Histórica Española* (13th edn), Madrid: Espasa Calpe.

Menéndez Pidal, R. (1972), *Origenes del español* (7th edn), Madrid: Espasa Calpe.

Miller, Roy (1967), *The Japanese Language*, University of Chicago Press.

Milner, Clyde A., Carol A. O'Connor and Martha A. Sandweiss (eds) (1994), *The Oxford History of the American West*, New York: Oxford University Press.

Milner-Gulland, Robin (1997), *The Russians*, Oxford: Blackwell.

Miquel, André (1968), *L'islam et sa civilisation (VIIe–XXe)*, Paris: Armand Colin.

Miyawaki, Hiroyuki (2002), *Colonial Language Policies and Their Effects*, Barcelona: World Congress on Language Policies, <www.linguapax.org/congres/taller/taller1/miyawaki.html>.

Moran, William L. (ed.) (1992), *The Amarna Letters* (trans. of *Les lettres d'el-Amarna*, 1987), Baltimore: Johns Hopkins University Press.

Moseley, Christopher, Nicholas Ostler and Hassan Ouzzate (eds) (2001), *Endangered Languages and the Media*, Bath: Foundation for Endangered Languages.

Mossé, Fernand (ed.) (1962), *Manuel de l'anglais du Moyen Age: II Moyen-anglais*, Paris: Aubier Montaigne.

Mote, F. W. (1999), *Imperial China 900–1800*, Cambridge, MA: Harvard University Press.

Motolinía (Fray Toribio de Benavente) (1990 [1541]), *Historia de los Indios de la Nueva España* (5th edn), Mexico: Editorial Porrua.

Moule, C. F. D. (1959), *An Idiom-book of New Testament Greek*, Cambridge University Press.

Mufwene, Salikoko S. (2001), *The Ecology of Language Evolution*, Cambridge University Press.

Muhly, J. D., R. Maddin and V. Karageorghis (eds) (1982), *Early metallurgy in Cyprus, 4000–500 BC*, Nicosia: Pierides Foundation.

Myers, Ramon H. and Mark R. Peattie (eds) (1984), *The Japanese Colonial Empire 1895–1945*, Princeton University Press.

Nicolson, Adam (2003), *Power and Glory: Jacobean England and the Making of the King James Bible*, London: HarperCollins.

Nissen, Hans-Jörg and Johannes Renger (eds) (1982), *Mesopotamien und seine Nachbarn*, Berlin: D. Reimer.

Norman, Jerry (1988), *Chinese*, Cambridge University Press.

Oded, Bustenay (1979), *Mass Deportation and Deportees in the Neo-Assyrian Empire*, Wiesbaden: Dr Ludwig Reichert Verlag.

Oliveira Marques, A. H. de (1972), *History of Portugal — volume I : from Lusitania to Empire*, New York: Columbia University Press.

Ostler, Nicholas (ed.) (1999), *Endangered Languages and Education*, Bath: Foundation for Endangered Languages.

Ostler, Nicholas (2004), 'The Social Roots of Missionary Linguistics', in Hovdhaugen and Zwartjes (eds), *Proceedings of the First International Conference on Missionary Linguistics*, Oslo, 13–16 March 2003, pp. 33–46.

Packard, Jerome L. (ed.) (1998), *New Approaches to Chinese Word Formation*, Berlin: De Gruyter.

Parpola, Simo (1999), 'Assyrians after Assyria', *Journal of Assyrian Academic Studies* xiii(2).

Pedersen, Holger (1972), *The Discovery of Language* (5th edn), Bloomington: Indiana University Press.

Pennycook, A. (1994), *The Cultural Politics of English as an International Language*, Harlow: Longman.

Peremans, Willy (1964), 'Über die Zweisprachigkeit im Ptolemäischen Ägypten', in *Studien zur Papyrologie und antiken Wirtschaftsgeschichte. Friedrich Oertel zum achtigsten Geburtstag gewidmet*, Bonn, pp. 49–60.

Pertusi, A. (1952), *Constantine Porphyrogenitus: de thematibus*, Vatican.

Petro, Pamela (1997), *Travels in an Old Tongue*, London: HarperCollins Flamingo.

Phillipson, Robert (1992), *Linguistic Imperialism*, Oxford University Press.

Picoche, Jacqueline and Christiane Marchello-Nizia (1989), *Histoire de la langue française*, Paris: Nathan.

Planhol, Xavier de (1968), *Les fondements géographiques de l'histoire de l'Islam*, Paris: Flammarion.

Polier, Antoine-Louis Henri (2001), *A European Experience of the Mughal Orient: the I'jāzi Arsalānī (Persian Letters, 1773–1779)* (trans. Muzaffar Alam and Seema Alavi), New Delhi: Oxford University Press.

Polotsky, Hans Jacob (1971), 'Aramäisch *prš* und das „Huzvaresch"', in E. Y. Kutscher (ed.), *Collected Papers*, Jerusalem: Magna Press, Hebrew University, pp. 631–43.

Price, Glanville (ed.) (2000), *Languages in Britain and Ireland*, Oxford: Blackwell.

Pritchard, James B. (ed.) (1969), *Ancient Near Eastern Texts Relating to the Old Testament* (3rd edn with supplement), Princeton University Press.

Prokosch, E. (1938), *A Comparative Germanic Grammar*, Baltimore, MD: Linguistic Society of America.

Pym, Dora and Nancy Silver (1952), *Alive on Men's Lips*, Slough: Centaur.

Quilis, Antonio (1992), *La lengua española en cuatro mundos*, Madrid : Editorial Mapfre.

Ramsey, S. Robert (1987), *The Languages of China*, Princeton University Press.

Rangarajan, L. N. (ed. and trans.) (1992), *Kautilya: the Arthashastra*, New Delhi: Penguin, India.

Reynolds, L. D. and N. G. Wilson (1968), *Scribes and Scholars*, Oxford University Press.

Ricard, Robert (1933), *The Spiritual Conquest of Mexico* (trans. Lesley Bird Simpson, 1966), Berkeley: University of California Press.

Robinson, F. N. (ed.) (1957), *The Complete Works of Geoffrey Chaucer*, Boston, MA: Houghton Mifflin.

Rosenblat, Angel (1964), 'La Hispanización de América: el castellano y las lenguas indígenas desde 1492', in *Presente y futuro de la lengua española : Actas de la Asamblea de Filología del I Congreso de Instituciones Hispánicas*, Madrid, pp. 189–216.

Roux, Georges (1992), *Ancient Iraq* (3rd edn), Harmondsworth: Penguin.

Roy, Olivier (2000), *The New Central Asia: the Creation of Nations*, London and New York: I. B. Tauris.

Rubin, Joan (1985), 'The Special Relation of Guarani and Spanish in Paraguay', in Wolfson and Manes (1985: 111–20).

Russell, J. C. (1958), 'Late Ancient and Medieval Population', Philadelphia, PA: *Transactions of the American Philosophical Society*, New Series 48(3).

Saeki, P. Y. (1937), *The Nestorian Documents and Relics in China*, Tokyo: Maruzen.

Sale, Kirkpatrick (1990), *The Conquest of Paradise*, New York: Knopf .

Salomon, Richard (1998), *Indian Epigraphy*, New York: Oxford University Press.

Santarém, Visconde de (1958 [1841]), *Memória sobre a prioridade dos descobrimentos portugueses na Costa da África Ocidental*, Paris; reissued Lisbon: Comissão Executiva das Comemoracões do Quinto Centenário da Morte do Infante D. Henrique, 1958.

Sawyer, John F. A. (1999), *Sacred Languages and Sacred Texts*, London: Routledge.

Schlumberger, Daniel, Louis Robert and André Dupont-Sommer (1958), 'Une bilingue gréco-araméenne d'Asoka', *Journal asiatique* ccxlvi.

Schoff, W. H. (1912), *The Periplus of the Erythraean Sea: Travel and Trade in the Indian Ocean by a Merchant of the First Century*, London, Bombay and Calcutta.

Schmandt-Besserat, Denise (1997), *How Writing Came About*, Austin: University of Texas.

Shaw, Stanford J. (1976), *History of the Ottoman Empire and Modern Turkey*, vol. 1, Cambridge University Press.

Sherzer, Joel (1993), 'A Richness of Voices', in Alvin M. Josephy (ed.), *America in 1492*, New York: Random House, pp. 251–75.

Silver, Shirley and Wick R. Miller (1997), *American Indian Languages: Cultural and Social Contexts*, Tucson: University of Arizona Press.

Sinha, Surendra Prasad (1978), *English in India*, Patna: Janaki Prakashan.

Sinor, Denis (ed.) (1990), *The Cambridge History of Early Inner Asia*, Cambridge University Press.

Sircar, D. C. (1971), *Studies in the Geography of Ancient and Medieval India*, Delhi: Motilal Banarsidass.

Slate, Clay (2001), 'Promoting Advanced Navajo Language Scholarship', in Hinton and Hale (eds), *The Green Book of Language Revitalization in Practice*, San Diego, CA: Academic Press, pp. 389–410.

Smith, Colin (1983), 'Vulgar Latin in Roman Britain: epigraphic and other evidence', in Temporini and Haase (1983: 893–948).

Smith, Jeremy J. (2000), 'Scots', in Price (2000: 159–70).

Soothill, William Edward (1910), *Confucius: the Analects*, Edinburgh: Oliphant, Anderson & Ferrier (reissued: Dover, 1995).

Spear, Percival (1965), *A History of India*, vol. 2, Harmondsworth: Penguin.

Stephens, Susan A. and John J. Winkler (1995), *Ancient Greek Novels: The Fragments*, Princeton University Press.

Strange, John (1980), 'Caphtor/Keftiu; a new investigation', *Acta Theologica Danica* 14, Leiden: E. J. Brill.

Studer, Paul and E. G. R. Waters (1924), *Historical French Reader: Medieval period*, Oxford University Press.

Sykes, Bryan (2001), *The Seven Daughters of Eve*, London: Bantam.

Sznycer, Maurice (1967), *Les passages puniques en transcription latine dans le 'Poenulus' de Plaute*, Paris: C. Klincksieck.

Sznycer, Maurice (1996), 'Le bilinguisme en Afrique du Nord à l'époque romaine', in Briquel-Chatonnet (1996).

Tadmor, Hayyim (1982), 'The Aramaization of Assyria: Aspects of the Western Impact', in Nissen and Renger (1982: 449–70).

Tarling, Nicholas (ed.) (1999), *Cambridge History of Southeast Asia, volume 1, part 1. From early times to c.1500*, Cambridge University Press.

Tarracha Ferreira, Maria Ema (1992), *Literatura dos Descobrimentos e da expansão portuguesa*, Lisbon : Biblioteca Ulisseia.

Temporini, H. and W. Haase (eds) (1983), *Aufstieg und Niedergang der Römischen Welt*, 2, Berlin and New York: Principat.

Thomason, Sarah and Terrence Kaufman (1988), *Language Contact, Creolization, and Genetic Linguistics*, University of California Press.

Thomsen, Marie-Louise (1984), *The Sumerian Language: an Introduction to its History and Grammatical Structure*, Copenhagen: Akademisk Forlag.

Tomlin, R. S. O. (1987), 'Was ancient British Celtic ever a written language? Two texts from Roman Bath', Cardiff: *Bulletin of the Board of Celtic Studies* 34: 18–25.

Torero, Alfredo (1974), *El quechua y la historia social andina*, Lima: Universidad Ricardo Palmá.

Tovar, Antonio (1964), 'Español y lenguas indígenas. Algunos ejemplos', in *Presente y futuro de la lengua española: Actas de la Asamblea de Filología del I Congreso de Instituciones Hispánicas*, Madrid, pp. 245–57.

Triana y Antorveza, H. (1987), *Las lenguas indígenas en la historia social del Nuevo Reino de Granada*, Bogotá: Instituto Caro y Cuervo.

Tsereteli, Mikheil (1959 [1912]), 'Das Sumerische und das Georgische', Paris: *Revue de Kartvelologie*, nos. 32–33. Original in Georgian ('Sumerian and Georgian') in *Tbilisi Collection* 'Gvirgvini' ('Crown').

Tsurumi, E. Patricia (1984), 'Colonial Education in Korea and Taiwan', in Myers and Peattie (1984: 275–311).

Van Leur, Jacob Cornelis (1955), *Indonesian Trade and Society*, The Hague: W. van Hoeve.

Vanaya, Marta (1986), *Mitos y Leyendas Guaraníes*, Buenos Aires: Jamkana Libros.

Vásquez Cuesta, Pilar and Maria Albertina Mendes da Luz (1971), *Grámatica da Língua Portuguesa*, Lisbon: Edições 70.

Viñaza, Conde de la (1892), *Bibliografía de Lenguas Indígenas de América*, Madrid : Ediciones Atlas.

Voutyras, E. (1994), 'Bulletin épigraphique', in *Revue d' Études Grecques* 413.

Wang Gungwu (1992), *Community and Nation: China, Southeast Asia and Australia* (2nd edn), ch. 2, 'A Short History of the Nanyang Chinese, St Leonards', Kensington, NSW: Asian Studies Association of Australia in association with Allen and Unwin.

Warner, Sam L. No'eau (1999), '*Kuleana*: The Right, Responsibility, and Authority of Indigenous People to Speak and Make Decisions for Themselves in Language and Cultural Revitalization', *Anthropology and Education Quarterly* 30(1): 68–93.

Weale, Michael E., Deborah A. Weiss, Rolf F. Jager, Neil Bradman and Mark G. Thomas (2002), 'Y chromosome evidence for Anglo-Saxon mass migration', *Molecular Biology & Evolution* 19(7): 1008–21.

Welling, George M. (2001), *The United States of America and the Netherlands*, University of Groningen: Dept Alfa-informatica, <http://grid.let.rug.nl/~usa/E/newnetherlands/nlxx.htm>.

Whitelock, Dorothy (1967), *Sweet's Anglo-Saxon Reader*, Oxford University Press.

Whitfield, Susan (1999), *Life along the Silk Road*, London: John Murray.

Wiesehöfer, Josef (2001), *Ancient Persia*, London: I. B. Tauris.

Wilkinson, Endymion (2000), *Chinese History: a Manual Revised and Enlarged*, Cambridge, MA: Harvard University Asia Center.

Williams, Roger (1643), *A Key into the Language of America*, London: Gregory Dexter.

Woodcock, George (1966), *The Greeks in India*, London: Faber.

Wolfson, Nessa and Joan Manes (1985), *Language of Inequality*, Berlin: Walter de Gruyter.

World Almanac and Book of Facts (1995), Mahwah, NJ: Funk & Wagnalls.

Wright, John W. (ed.) (2000, 2001), *New York Times Almanac*, Harmondsworth: Penguin.

Wright, Roger (1982), *Late Latin and Early Romance in Spain and Carolingian France*, Liverpool: Francis Cairns.

Young, G. M. (ed.) (1957), *Macaulay, Prose and Poetry*, Cambridge, MA: Harvard University Press.

Yule, Henry and Arthur Burnell (1986 [1903]), *Hobson-Jobson: a glossary of colloquial Anglo-Indian words and phrases*, New Delhi: Rupa & Co.

INDEX

Language, family and dialect names are marked in bold. Literary titles are marked with italics, with the author's name in parentheses.

PICTURE CREDITS